Google SketchUp

THE MISSING MANUAL

*The book that
should have been
in the box*®

Google SketchUp

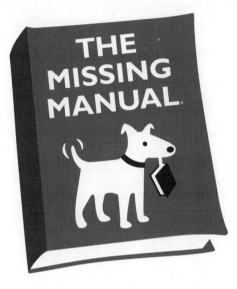

Chris Grover

POGUE PRESS™
O'REILLY®

Beijing · Cambridge · Farnham · Köln · Sebastopol · Taipei · Tokyo

Google SketchUp: The Missing Manual

by Chris Grover

Copyright © 2009 O'Reilly Media, Inc. All rights reserved.
Printed in the United States of America.

Published by O'Reilly Media, Inc., 1005 Gravenstein Highway North, Sebastopol, CA 95472.

O'Reilly books may be purchased for educational, business, or sales promotional use. Online editions are also available for most titles (*safari.oreilly.com*). For more information, contact our corporate/institutional sales department: (800) 998-9938 or *corporate@oreilly.com*.

Printing History:

May 2009:   First Edition.

 This book uses RepKover,™ a durable and flexible lay-flat binding.

ISBN: 978-0-596-52146-2

[M]

Table of Contents

Part Two: Building a House

Part Four: Adding Realism and Movement

Part Five: Saving, Printing, and Sharing Projects

The Missing Credits

About the Author

 Chris Grover is a veteran of the San Francisco Bay Area advertising and design community, having worked for over 25 years in print, video, and electronic media. During that stint, he's had freelance articles published in a variety of magazines from *Fine Homebuilding* to *CD-ROM World*. Throughout his career, he's worked with clients involved in construction, building materials, and architectural design. Chris is owner of Bolinas Road Creative (*http://BolinasRoad.com*), an agency that helps small businesses promote their products and services. He's also the author of *Word 2007: The Missing Manual* and *Flash CS4: The Missing Manual*.

About the Creative Team

Nan Barber (editor) is associate editor for the Missing Manual series. She lives in Massachusetts with her husband and G4 Macintosh. Email: *nanbarber@oreilly.com*.

Nellie McKesson (production editor) lives in Brighton, Mass., where she makes t-shirts for her friends (*http://mattsaundersbynellie.etsy.com*) and plays music with her band Dr. & Mrs. Van Der Trampp (*http://myspace.com/drmrsvandertrampp*). Email: *nellie@oreilly.com*.

Jan Jue (copyeditor) enjoys freelance copyediting, a good mystery, and the search for the perfect pot sticker.

Ron Strauss (indexer) is a full-time freelance indexer specializing in IT. When not working, he moonlights as a concert violist and alternative medicine health consultant. Email: *rstrauss@mchsi.com*.

Jason Arnold (technical reviewer) lives in Santa Rosa, CA with his wife and two daughters. He spends his free time practicing Japanese, martial arts, and photography.

Lewis Wadsworth (technical reviewer) is an artist, illustrator, and designer with degrees from Dartmouth College and Yale School of Architecture. He teaches at the Boston Architectural College, and his own architectural designs (illustrated using SketchUp) have been published in AIArchitect and elsewhere. He currently lives in Boston, Massachusetts with his wife Karen, a cellular biologist, and his two young daughters Sofia and Athena.

Acknowledgments

It takes a team to move a Missing Manual from concept to publication, and I want to thank all the pros who helped with *Google SketchUp: The Missing Manual*. Thanks go out again to my editor Nan Barber for her skillful editing and long hours spent keeping us all on track. Thanks also to Jan Jue for the copyediting and Ron Straus for the index, and to Dawn Frausto for coordinating their work. A special thanks to Lewis Wadsworth for letting us reproduce his spectacular SketchUp models and for the sharp-eyed technical review. His experience as an architect and SketchUp master was much appreciated. My sincere appreciation to Jason Arnold, also a technical reviewer, who brought great enthusiasm to the SketchUp exercises and asked the all the right questions. Thanks to the Go-2-School guys, Mike Tadros and Alex Oliver, for letting us base many of the exercises on their excellent video series (*www.go-2-school.com*), and to Bryce Stout of Google's SketchUp team for generously contributing his time and assistance. And once again, thanks to Peter Meyers for first signing me up to the Missing Manuals team. Thanks, as always, to my beautiful wife Joyce, and my wonderful daughters Mary and Amy.

—*Chris Grover*

The Missing Manual Series

Missing Manuals are witty, superbly written guides to computer products that don't come with printed manuals (which is just about all of them). Each book features a handcrafted index; cross-references to specific pages (not just chapters); and RepKover, a detached-spine binding that lets the book lie perfectly flat without the assistance of weights or cinder blocks.

Recent and upcoming titles include:

Access 2007: The Missing Manual by Matthew MacDonald

AppleScript: The Missing Manual by Adam Goldstein

AppleWorks 6: The Missing Manual by Jim Elferdink and David Reynolds

CSS: The Missing Manual, Second Edition by David Sawyer McFarland

Creating a Web Site: The Missing Manual by Matthew MacDonald

David Pogue's Digital Photography: The Missing Manual by David Pogue

Dreamweaver 8: The Missing Manual by David Sawyer McFarland

Dreamweaver CS3: The Missing Manual by David Sawyer McFarland

Dreamweaver CS4: The Missing Manual by David Sawyer McFarland

eBay: The Missing Manual by Nancy Conner

Excel 2003: The Missing Manual by Matthew MacDonald

Excel 2007: The Missing Manual by Matthew MacDonald

Facebook: The Missing Manual by E.A. Vander Veer

FileMaker Pro 9: The Missing Manual by Geoff Coffey and Susan Prosser

FileMaker Pro 10: The Missing Manual by Susan Prosser and Geoff Coffey

Flash 8: The Missing Manual by E.A. Vander Veer

Flash CS3: The Missing Manual by E.A. Vander Veer and Chris Grover

Flash CS4: The Missing Manual by Chris Grover with E.A. Vander Veer

FrontPage 2003: The Missing Manual by Jessica Mantaro

Google Apps: The Missing Manual by Nancy Conner

The Internet: The Missing Manual by David Pogue and J.D. Biersdorfer

iMovie 6 & iDVD: The Missing Manual by David Pogue

iMovie '08 & iDVD: The Missing Manual by David Pogue

iMovie '09 & iDVD: The Missing Manual by David Pogue and Aaron Miller

iPhone: The Missing Manual, Second Edition by David Pogue

iPhoto '08: The Missing Manual by David Pogue

iPhoto '09: The Missing Manual by David Pogue and J.D. Biersdorfer

iPod: The Missing Manual, Seventh Edition by J.D. Biersdorfer and David Pogue

JavaScript: The Missing Manual by David Sawyer McFarland

Mac OS X: The Missing Manual, Tiger Edition by David Pogue

Mac OS X: The Missing Manual, Leopard Edition by David Pogue

Microsoft Project 2007: The Missing Manual by Bonnie Biafore

Netbooks: The Missing Manual by J.D. Biersdorfer

Office 2004 for Macintosh: The Missing Manual by Mark H. Walker and Franklin Tessler

Office 2007: The Missing Manual by Chris Grover, Matthew MacDonald, and E.A. Vander Veer

Office 2008 for Macintosh: The Missing Manual by Jim Elferdink

PCs: The Missing Manual by Andy Rathbone

Photoshop Elements 7: The Missing Manual by Barbara Brundage

Photoshop Elements 6 for Mac: The Missing Manual by Barbara Brundage

PowerPoint 2007: The Missing Manual by E.A. Vander Veer

QuickBase: The Missing Manual by Nancy Conner

QuickBooks 2009: The Missing Manual by Bonnie Biafore

QuickBooks 2010: The Missing Manual by Bonnie Biafore

Quicken 2008: The Missing Manual by Bonnie Biafore

Quicken 2009: The Missing Manual by Bonnie Biafore

Switching to the Mac: The Missing Manual, Tiger Edition by David Pogue and Adam Goldstein

Switching to the Mac: The Missing Manual, Leopard Edition by David Pogue

Wikipedia: The Missing Manual by John Broughton

Windows XP Home Edition: The Missing Manual, Second Edition by David Pogue

Windows XP Pro: The Missing Manual, Second Edition by David Pogue, Craig Zacker, and Linda Zacker

Windows Vista: The Missing Manual by David Pogue

Windows Vista for Starters: The Missing Manual by David Pogue

Word 2007: The Missing Manual by Chris Grover

Your Body: The Missing Manual by Matthew MacDonald

Your Brain: The Missing Manual by Matthew MacDonald

Introduction

When it first came out, SketchUp caused quite a stir in the three-dimensional (3-D) art world for a couple of reasons. First, it's the easiest program you can use to create three-dimensional models of buildings, furniture, and everyday objects. And second, you can get your hands on a fully useful copy for free.

People haven't always found it easy to draw three-dimensional images on two-dimensional surfaces. Just ask the Lascaux cave artists or anyone who sat in art class studying 2-point and 3-point perspective. Even with computers helping out, you can still run into problems. Most 3-D graphics programs have learning curves like the Eiffel Tower and they cost a fortune. In 2000, SketchUp came along and changed the rules by making 3-D drawing almost as easy as drawing on the back of a napkin. Three years later, Google acquired the company that developed SketchUp (@Last Software), since the program works so well with their online program Google Earth.

With SketchUp, you start off with simple tools that are familiar if you've ever used a computer to draw rectangles or circles. Then, to create 3-D objects, you use specially designed tools to push and pull your objects into the desired Ferraris or hot-air balloons (Figure I-1). Pushing and pulling may sound like a haphazard way to build models, but that's far from the case. SketchUp lets you create models that are accurate down to a fraction of an inch. Also, using SketchUp's component tools, you can minimize repetitive tasks and build complex models quickly. When you're done, go ahead and place your model on a map of the world using Google Earth.

So, what's the catch? There isn't one. All you have to do is download the program from *http://sketchup.google.com*. Then follow along in this book, and you'll become a SketchUp master artist in no time.

Note: SketchUp Pro, the pay-to-play version, costs $495. It's meant primarily for architects and builders who need to share their 3-D work with programs like AutoCAD. If you're not one of them, relax. You can use the free version of SketchUp forever, and the program won't even nag you to upgrade to Pro.

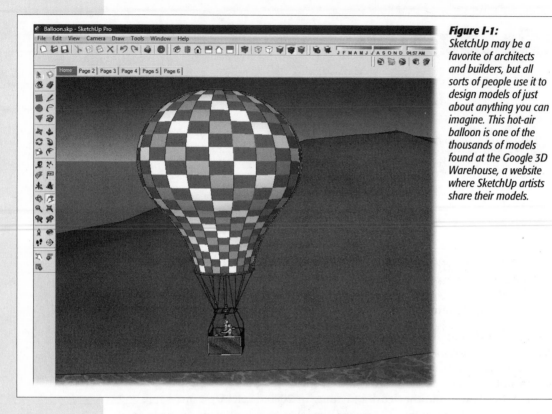

Figure I-1:
SketchUp may be a favorite of architects and builders, but all sorts of people use it to design models of just about anything you can imagine. This hot-air balloon is one of the thousands of models found at the Google 3D Warehouse, a website where SketchUp artists share their models.

What You Can Do with SketchUp

As the name implies, SketchUp lets you create 3-D artwork quickly. SketchUp does a few things, and it does them very well. Here's a short list of the jobs SketchUp does well:

- Create models of buildings, furniture, and other everyday objects.

- Design models with interior and exterior details, like houses with individual rooms.

- Quickly design special architectural elements, like pitched or complex roofs.

- Create reusable parts that you can use in other models.

- Easily add colors and textures.

- Create landscaping around buildings.

- Add accurate shadow effects based on geographic location, time, and date.

- Place models in a specific location on the Google Earth map.

- Develop 3-D models from 2-D photographs or drawings.

- Produce walk-through animations.

By contrast, here's a short list of jobs other—that is, more expensive—3-D programs perform better than SketchUp:

- Character animation with moveable joints.

- Organic elements such as realistic hair or fur.

- Complex lighting using multiple light sources.

- Kinetic effects in animation such as bouncing balls or flying bullets.

- Elemental effects such as flames, smoke, and explosions.

- Animations where characters move about a scene.

- Complex architectural designs detailing every electrical wire and pipe in a building.

So, you won't use SketchUp to create a 3-D feature film that competes with *Shrek* or to design a computer game. But once you get the hang of it, you can create great-looking 3-D drawings very quickly. Most people use SketchUp to model buildings, but you can just as easily create other 3-D objects like furniture and appliances. Because SketchUp can export artwork in Google Earth's .kmz format, you can place your SketchUp models on the map as shown in Figure I-2.

SketchUp vs. SketchUp Pro

SketchUp is available in two flavors: the free version and the $495 SketchUp Pro version. Let your wallet and your 3-D needs be your guide.

SketchUp (free)

With the free version, you can design complex 3-D models and print pictures and export 2-D art to use in websites or other programs. You can save your model as a JPEG or PNG file and edit it in Photoshop. You can also save your models in the .kmz file format that lets you place models in Google Earth. Here's the lowdown on the file formats you can create with SketchUp:

- **Standard 3-D file format: .skp.** You can also save to formats used by earlier versions of SketchUp.

- **Google Earth: .kmz.** Place your models anywhere on the planet!

- **2-D image files:** JPEG (.jpg), **Portable Network Graphics (.png), Tagged Image File (.tif), Windows Bitmap (.bmp).** You can both import and export images in all of these formats, and also import Targa files (.tga).

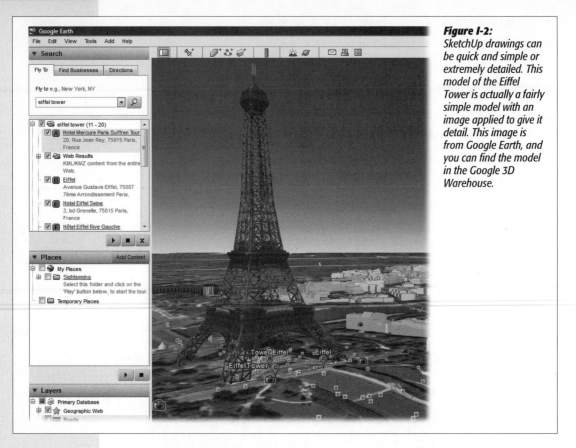

Figure I-2:
SketchUp drawings can be quick and simple or extremely detailed. This model of the Eiffel Tower is actually a fairly simple model with an image applied to give it detail. This image is from Google Earth, and you can find the model in the Google 3D Warehouse.

- **3-D models: SketchUp (.skp); Google Earth terrain, 3DS (.3ds); AutoCAD (.dwg, .dxf); DEM (.dem, .ddf).** You can import models created in all of these formats, and export your own models as SketchUp (.skp) or Google Earth (.kmz).

- **Animations and walk-throughs.** Video for Windows (.avi); QuickTime (.mov) files on Mac.

Tip: You'll learn all about importing and exporting with SketchUp in Chapter 13.

SketchUp Pro ($495)

The SketchUp Pro version gives you many more ways to share your 3-D models with other programs, like AutoCAD, or 3d Studio Max. It lets you use all of the same file formats as the free version, plus more:

- **2-D image files.** You can import and export all of the same file formats as the free version, plus *export* in the following additional formats: Portable Document Format (.pdf), Encapsulated PostScript Format (.eps), Epix (.epx), and AutoCAD (.dwg, .dxf).

- **3-D models.** You can import and export all of the same file formats as the free version, plus *export* in the following additional formats: 3DS (.3ds), AutoCAD DWG (.dwg), AutoCAD DFX (.dfx), FBX (.fbx), OBJ (.obj), XSI (.xsi), and VRML (.vrml).

The Pro version includes two additional programs:

- **LayOut** gives you a set of tools that let you place, arrange, title, and annotate SketchUp models for computer and print presentations.

- **Style Builder** helps you customize the look of your SketchUp drawings. Want to produce a 3-D drawing of a client's new home that looks as if it were laboriously hand-drawn? It's a snap with Style Builder.

In short, the Pro version gives you better ways to work with other pros and the ability to communicate more complex 3-D details to clients and colleagues.

Entering the Third Dimension

In most graphics programs like Adobe Illustrator or Photoshop you move only in two dimensions: up/down and left/right. It's like looking at a flat sheet of paper through a window. You move the window up/down or left/right to see other parts of the paper. Even if you zoom in or zoom out, the details on the paper merely get larger or smaller, while the relative positions of drawings on the paper remain the same. In 3-D programs like SketchUp, you have another dimension, which you can think of as *depth*. Imagine you're walking forward into the scene, or backing away, expanding your field of vision. SketchUp refers to your view as the *Camera*, and that's a great way to understand the difference between 2-D and 3-D. Instead of looking through a window at a flat piece of paper, you're looking through a camera at a three-dimensional world. You can look at any of the objects in this world from any angle including front, back, top, or bottom. As you move the camera in the 3-D world, the positions and relationships of the other objects appear to change. They aren't really moving, but because you've changed position everything looks different, as shown in Figure I-3.

Drawing in 3-D Without Getting Lost

If you're new to the world of 3-D design, sooner or later you're bound to get lost. It happens to everyone, and it's just part of the learning process. For example, you may have zoomed in so closely to a part of your model that nothing looks familiar. Or maybe you've maneuvered the view so you don't see your model at all; you think you're looking off into blank space.

Don't panic. This book provides tips throughout for finding your bearings and moving around your SketchUp world. Here's your first tip for returning to a familiar view of your project: Choose Camera → Zoom Extents to get a view of every object in your SketchUp world. Then choose Camera → Standard Views → Front to see those objects in a familiar orientation. This camera two-step returns your view to a recognizable perspective.

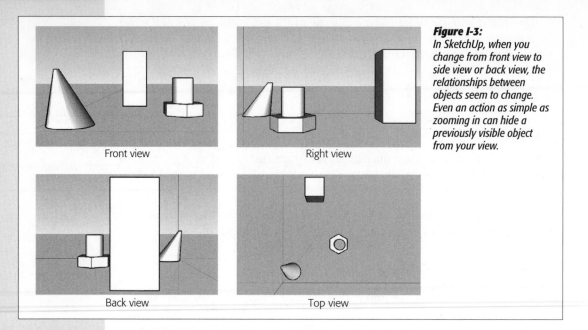

Front view

Right view

Figure I-3:
In SketchUp, when you change from front view to side view or back view, the relationships between objects seem to change. Even an action as simple as zooming in can hide a previously visible object from your view.

Back view

Top view

About This Book

Not surprisingly, Google doesn't provide a printed manual for a program it offers for free over the Internet. Instead, Google provides an online help system. It's at *http://sketchup.google.com/support*, and you can read all about it in Appendix A. But with this book, you'll get a full course in creating models in SketchUp, and you won't need to jump back and forth between Google's online help and your project.

This book serves as the kind of manual that should come with every program. You'll find step-by-step instructions for using every feature in SketchUp, including those you may not even have understood, let alone mastered, such as the intricacies of, say, components or the Photo Match tools.

About the Outline

Google SketchUp: The Missing Manual is divided into six parts, each containing several chapters.

Part One: Basic SketchUp Skills introduces the SketchUp workspace and then lets you jump in and create your first model: a simple bench. With these new skills under your belt, you're ready to explore in detail some of the differences between working in two dimensions and working in three dimensions. Step-by-step tutorials show you how to draw 2-D lines and shapes in SketchUp. By the end of Part 1, you're drawing in three dimensions and using a wide variety of SketchUp tools to build increasingly detailed models.

Part Two: Building a House is where you become a journeyman builder. You start by building simple 3-D shapes and learn how to save them as reusable components. Along the way, you become an expert at adjusting the SketchUp view, so you can easily see and work with your model. At the end of this part, you use SketchUp's Outliner to keep track of your components and to show and hide parts of your model as you work.

Part Three: Advanced Construction Techniques tackles more complicated construction projects like buildings with hipped roofs. You learn even more about the power of components and how to save tons of time by using them. You're introduced to another timesaving tool, the Follow Me tool, which can build a complicated edge as fast as you can click.

Part Four: Adding Realism and Movement explores the ways you can place your models into the virtual world provided by scenes and Google Earth. What better way to show the beauty of your finely constructed 3-D building than with a walk-through? You'll also learn how to dress up your models with realistic material shading and shadows. Most likely, your building has a place in the real world. You can find that spot in Google Earth and plop your model down where it belongs.

Part Five: Saving, Printing, and Sharing Projects is where you learn how to show off all your hard work and, if you wish, use the advanced tools in SketchUp Pro. You'll find out about importing and exporting to a variety of file formats. You'll learn about the Style Builder program that lets you customize the line styles used by SketchUp. This section also introduces SketchUp Pro's LayOut tool, used to place your SketchUp models into documents for presentation to clients.

Part Six: Appendixes. Appendix A, *Installing SketchUp and Getting Help*, explains how to download and install SketchUp. You also learn where to look for additional help from sources such as Google and SketchUp user groups and forums. Appendix B, *SketchUp Menu by Menu*, provides a menu-by-menu description of the commands you find in SketchUp.

The Very Basics

You'll find very little jargon or nerd terminology in this book. You will, however, see a few terms and concepts that you'll encounter frequently in your computing life:

• **Clicking.** This book gives you several kinds of instructions that require you to use your computer's mouse or trackpad. To *click* means to point the arrow cursor at something on the screen and then—without moving the cursor at all—to press and release the clicker button on the mouse (or laptop trackpad). To *double-click*, of course, means to click twice in rapid succession, again without moving the cursor at all. To *drag* means to move the cursor while pressing the button continuously. To *right-click* or *right-drag*, do the same as above, but press the mouse button on the right.

When you see an instruction like *Shift-click* or *Ctrl-click*, simply press the key as you click.

Tip: For Macintosh computers with a one-button mouse, to do the same thing as a right-click or right-drag, press the Mac's Control key as you click or drag. (Or buy a multi-button mouse.) See the next section for more Windows/Mac differences.

- **Keyboard shortcuts.** Sometimes, when you're flush with design enthusiasm, you want to work as efficiently as possible. Many experienced SketchUp artists work with one hand on the mouse for drawing and the other hand on the keyboard, where they type shortcut keys to change views and swap tools. You'll see your fair share of keyboard shortcuts in this book, usually in parentheses next to a tool's name or command. Ctrl+C (⌘-C on the Mac), for example, is a keyboard shortcut for Copy in SketchUp and most other programs.

  When you see a shortcut like Ctrl+S (⌘-S on the Mac), which saves changes to the current document, it's telling you to hold down the Ctrl or ⌘ key, and, while it's down, type the letter S, and then release both keys.

- **Choice is good.** SketchUp frequently gives you several ways to trigger a particular command—by choosing a menu command, or by clicking a toolbar button, or by pressing a key combination, for example. Some people prefer the speed of keyboard shortcuts; others like the satisfaction of a visual command array available in menus or toolbars. This book lists all of the alternatives, but by no means are you expected to memorize all of them.

Macintosh and Windows

SketchUp works much the same way in its Mac and Windows incarnations, except for a few interface differences. This book's illustrations give Mac and Windows equal time, alternating by chapter, so you get to see how all of SketchUp's features look, no matter what kind of computer you're running.

One small difference between Mac and Windows software that you need to be aware of is keystrokes. The Ctrl key in Windows is the equivalent of the Macintosh ⌘ key, and the key labeled Alt on a PC (and on non-U.S. Macs) is the equivalent of the Option key on American Mac keyboards.

Whenever this book refers to a key combination, therefore, you'll see the Windows keystroke listed first (with + symbols, as is customary in Windows documentation); the Macintosh keystroke follows (with - symbols, in time-honored Mac tradition). In other words, you might read, "The keyboard shortcut for saving a file is Ctrl+S (⌘-S)." This book mentions any other significant differences between the Mac and Windows versions of SketchUp as they come up.

In SketchUp there are lots of single-letter shortcuts like R for the Rectangle tool and P for the Push/Pull tool. Most of the time these commands are the same on Windows and Mac. Often this book uses the common, single-letter command even when there's an alternative command on the Mac.

About These Arrows

Throughout this book, you'll find instructions like, "Open your Program Files → Google SketchUp → Templates folder." That's Missing Manual shorthand for much longer sentences like "Double-click your Program Files folder to open it. Inside, you'll find a folder called Google SketchUp; double-click that folder to open it. Inside that folder is a folder called Templates; open it, too." This arrow shorthand also simplifies the business of choosing menu commands, as you can see in Figure I-4.

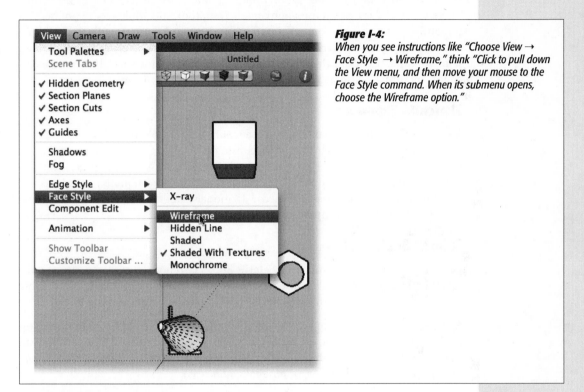

Figure I-4:
When you see instructions like "Choose View → Face Style → Wireframe," think "Click to pull down the View menu, and then move your mouse to the Face Style command. When its submenu opens, choose the Wireframe option."

About MissingManuals.com

At *http://missingmanuals.com*, you'll find articles, tips, and updates to *Google SketchUp: The Missing Manual*. In fact, we invite and encourage you to submit such corrections and updates yourself. In an effort to keep the book as up to date and accurate as possible, each time we print more copies of this book, we'll make any confirmed corrections you've suggested. We'll also note such changes on the website, so that you can mark important corrections into your own copy of the book, if you like. (Go to *http://missingmanuals.com/feedback*, choose the book's name from the pop-up menu, and then click Go to see the changes.)

Also on our Feedback page, you can get expert answers to questions that come to you while reading this book, write a book review, and find groups for folks who share your interest in SketchUp.

While you're there, sign up for our free monthly email newsletter. Click the "Sign Up for Our Newsletter" link in the left column. You'll find out what's happening in Missing Manual land, meet the authors and editors, see bonus video and book excerpts, and so on.

We'd love to hear your suggestions for new books in the Missing Manual line. There's a place for that on missingmanuals.com, too. And while you're online, you can also register this book at *www.oreilly.com* (you can jump directly to the registration page by going here: *http://tinyurl.com/yo82k3*). Registering means we can send you updates about this book, and you'll be eligible for special offers like discounts on future editions of *Google SketchUp: The Missing Manual*.

SketchUp Examples

As you read the book's chapters, you'll encounter a number of step-by-step tutorials. You can work through the tutorials using your own SketchUp documents, or you can use the examples provided on this book's Missing CD page. You can download them using any Web browser at *http://.missingmanuals.com/cds*. You'll find raw materials (like half-finished 3-D models) and in some cases, completed models with which to compare your work.

Safari® Books Online

 When you see a Safari® Books Online icon on the cover of your favorite technology book, that means the book is available online through the O'Reilly Network Safari Bookshelf.

Safari offers a solution that's better than eBooks. It's a virtual library that lets you easily search thousands of top tech books, cut and paste code samples, download chapters, and find quick answers when you need the most accurate, current information. Try it free at *http://my.safaribooksonline.com*.

Part One:
Basic SketchUp Skills

1

Building a Bench: Your First SketchUp Model

At first glance SketchUp doesn't look much different from other programs you use to work with photographs, drawings, or even words. You have menus, toolbars, and a large work area. The difference, of course, is that SketchUp's work area is a window into a three-dimensional world where you can build just about anything. It can be as big as the Empire State building or as small as an iPod. By using SketchUp you can design your new beach house inside and out, and build all the furniture for each room. It's your world, and this chapter is your first-class introductory tour.

In the first part of this chapter, you'll learn about SketchUp's menus, tools, and the drawing window. You'll see how to customize your workspace to make it easier to follow along with the exercises in this book. The rest of this chapter describes how to build a simple bench made from just four pieces of wood, as shown in Figure 1-1.

Tip: If you'd like to see how the finished bench looks in SketchUp, you can find the document file *bench_finished.skp* at *http://missingmanuals.com/cds*.

Even though the bench is simple, the step-by-step exercises introduce many of SketchUp's drawing and navigation tools. You'll get a taste of how much fun it is to push and pull your 3-D drawings into shape. You'll also learn some valuable techniques for navigating a 3-D workspace and for moving and aligning 3-D objects. Don't worry if it seems that the exercise moves quickly. In later chapters, you'll see the concepts introduced here explained in much greater detail. In fact you'll see references along the way that point to more detailed explanations. So if you're ready for a fast-paced tour of SketchUp, grab your virtual sculptor's chisel and follow along.

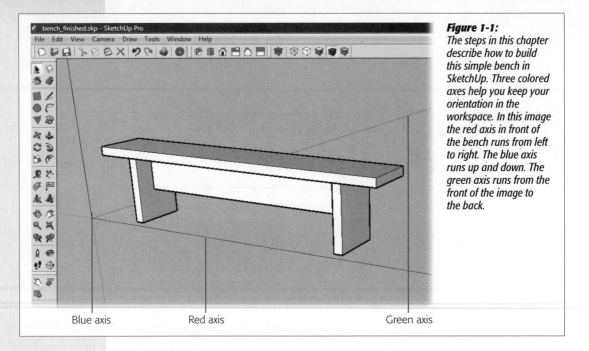

Figure 1-1:
The steps in this chapter describe how to build this simple bench in SketchUp. Three colored axes help you keep your orientation in the workspace. In this image the red axis in front of the bench runs from left to right. The blue axis runs up and down. The green axis runs from the front of the image to the back.

Firing Up SketchUp for the First Time

After you first install SketchUp (page 529), you start it just like you would any program. For Windows computers:

- Go to Program Files → Google → Google SketchUp 7, and then double-click the program's icon.

- Click Start → All Programs → Google SketchUp 7.

- Click Windows → Recent Items, and then click a SketchUp (.skp) document.

If you're of the Mac persuasion:

- Go to the Applications → Google SketchUp 7 folder, and then double-click the program's icon.

- Drag the SketchUp icon from the Applications → Google SketchUp 7 file to the Dock. Once that's done you can always start the program from there.

- Choose → Recent Items → Google SketchUp 7.

You can always double-click any SketchUp document to start up SketchUp and open that document. That's probably the easiest way to start SketchUp on any platform.

At first, every time you start the program, SketchUp greets you with a "welcome" window. This window includes a few subpanels, which vary depending on whether you're running SketchUp 7 or SketchUp Pro. Both versions, though, display Learn and Template subpanels. SketchUp Pro also shows a License subpanel. The purpose of the Learn panel is to introduce some basic SketchUp concepts. After a quick introductory animation, you can click links to "Watch more videos" or "Read the documentation". The Template subpanel holds several preformatted documents that you can use to get a head start on your project. For example, if you're beginning a furniture or woodworking project (as shown later in this chapter), click the "Product Design and Woodworking – Inches" template. If you grow tired of the welcome window popping up every time you run SketchUp, turn off the "Always show on startup" box in the lower-left corner.

The other window that appears when you first start SketchUp is the Instructor window (Figure 1-2). This clever feature provides quick visual and written tips on how to use whatever tool you've selected. When you're first starting out, the Instructor tips can be pretty helpful. If you've had enough, you can close the window by clicking its close button. (You can always bring it back with Window → Instructor. Use Help → Welcome to SketchUp to show the welcome window.)

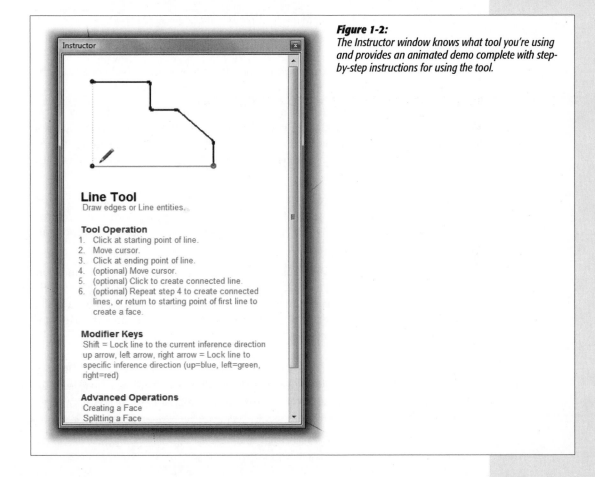

Figure 1-2:
The Instructor window knows what tool you're using and provides an animated demo complete with step-by-step instructions for using the tool.

A Tour of SketchUp's Main Window

Once you're past the Learning Center, you see the main window. You use its five main areas when you're building in SketchUp (Figure 1-3):

- **Menus.** Just as in your word processor, you get menus and submenus that give you access to SketchUp's tools and commands.

- **Toolbars.** Click an icon in a SketchUp toolbar, and you've got a new tool in hand. SketchUp has several different toolbars that you can show, hide, or drag around the workspace. In Windows, you can reach toolbar central by going to View → Toolbars, where you see over a dozen toolbars that you can show or hide with a mouse click. On a Mac, choose View → Tool Palettes. You have as many toolbars to choose from, but Macs have their own nifty toolbars. Control-click on the top of the SketchUp document window and choose Customize Toolbar. A window opens with all of SketchUp's tool buttons. Drag buttons on and off the toolbar to customize your workspace.

Note: Toolbars are one of the areas where the Windows and Mac versions of SketchUp appear slightly different. Most of the differences, though, are in the program's appearance rather than function.

- **Drawing area.** The main portion of the SketchUp window is devoted to your drawing area. Think of it as your camera's view of a 3-D world.

- **Status bar.** In the lower-left corner is the status bar. Like a friend of few words, the status bar's Hint tool gives you facts related to the tool and job at hand. If you need a hint about what to do next, look to this corner. For more verbose instructions, click the question-mark button to open the Instructor window (Figure 1-2).

  The latest version of SketchUp added three new buttons to the status bar. From left to right they display geographic references (in Google-speak, it's called *geo-referencing;* see page 389 for details), credits (the model or component's designer), and the Google account login.

- **Measurements toolbar.** Previously known by SketchUp fans as the Value Control box (VCB), this humble-looking box is magic. You use it to enter the dimensions of objects or the distance you want to move something, but that only scratches the surface. Once you learn how smart and versatile the Measurements toolbar is, you'll be a fan, too.

Note: Traditionally, the Measurements toolbar appears in the lower-right corner of SketchUp. But it can also be displayed some other ways. In Windows, choose View → Toolbars → Measurements, and SketchUp produces a toolbar that can float anywhere on your screen and that you can dock at any edge of the window. On Mac, when you customize your toolbars (page 20), you can place the Measurements toolbar at the top of the Document window.

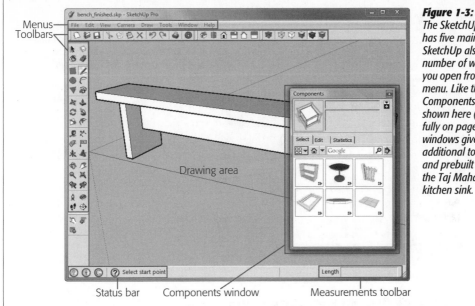

Figure 1-3:
The SketchUp workspace has five main areas. SketchUp also has a number of windows that you open from the Window menu. Like the Components window shown here (and described fully on page 332), these windows give you access to additional tools, settings, and prebuilt models from the Taj Mahal to a kitchen sink.

In addition to the five main workspace parts, SketchUp uses several different windows, such as the Components window that's open in Figure 1-3. You can open and close them as needed by using the Window menu. With the tools in these windows, you'll apply color and shading to your models, select prebuilt components, add shadows and lighting effects, and organize your project.

Don't Be Afraid to Play

Before you get started, here's the most valuable SketchUp tip of all. *Don't be afraid to play.* This book is full of exercises that carefully show you how to build models step-by-step, but that doesn't mean you shouldn't head off the beaten path from time to time. The more you experiment and say "what happens if I try this…" the faster you'll learn. It's true with all computer programs, but it's especially true with a graphics program like SketchUp.

So, download some of the models from this book from *http://missingmanuals.com/cds.* Open them in SketchUp, and then disassemble them. Twist them into funny shapes. Add new parts. If you ruin them beyond all recognition, don't worry. You can always download the original version again.

SketchUp's menu bar is stocked with the usual suspects, such as File, Edit, Window, and Help. SketchUp's View menu is a little different from the ones in most programs (Figure 1-4). The View menu lists items in the SketchUp window that you can show or hide, including things like drawing guides, axis lines, measurement marks, and even different toolbars. If you're looking for tools that change your view of the drawing window, such as a Zoom or Pan tool, look under the Camera menu.

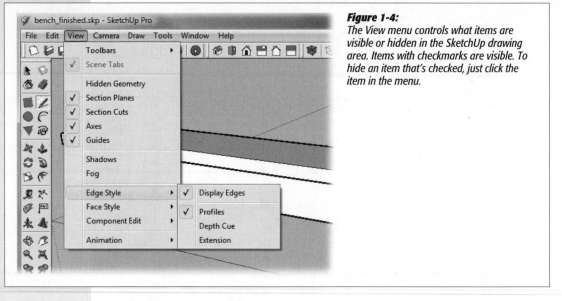

Figure 1-4:
The View menu controls what items are visible or hidden in the SketchUp drawing area. Items with checkmarks are visible. To hide an item that's checked, just click the item in the menu.

Looking Around with the Camera

The concept behind SketchUp's camera is that the drawing area is your view of a 3-D world. Imagine you're a movie director, you've set up your camera, and the drawing area is your view through the camera. Want to see a different view? Move the camera. For example, in Figure 1-1, you have a front view of the bench. To view the bench from above, you use the command Camera → Standard Views → Top. For a side view, you can use Camera → Standard Views → Right (or Left).

When you make these changes, you're moving the *camera view*. You're not moving the *bench*. It's remaining in the same place. When you use some of the tools from the toolbar such as the Orbit or Pan tools, there's a tendency to think that you're moving objects in the 3-D world when actually it's just your viewpoint of the world that's changing.

Tip: In SketchUp, the mouse is your primary building tool, so it helps to have a mouse that plays well with SketchUp. Whether you're working in Windows or Mac, it's more convenient to have a three-button mouse, where the middle button is a scroll wheel. You can use that middle button to easily move around the drawing window without disrupting your work in progress. For Mac users, the standard Mac mouse with the roller button doesn't work quite as well with SketchUp as it should. You may want to invest in a cheapo three-button mouse to use with SketchUp.

Customizing Your Workspace

The folks at Google don't want to overwhelm you with too many tools and options when you're just starting out. In both the Mac and Windows versions of SketchUp, your first view shows a minimum number of tools. This tool set is officially dubbed the Getting Started tool set. However, to work along with the exercises in this book, you may as well make a few changes so your SketchUp workspace matches the pictures in this book. The suggestions in this section display, with a minimum of onscreen clutter, the tools you'll use most often and will save you from digging into a lot of menus to find commands. You can always change them later as you adjust to working in SketchUp. When you add or remove toolbars, SketchUp remembers those changes even after you close the program.

For Windows

Follow these steps, and your Windows version of SketchUp will look like Figure 1-3. If you're a Mac fan, skip to the next section and set up your workspace to match Figure 1-5.

1. **Choose View → Toolbars → Large Tool Set.**

   A new toolbar appears with buttons running vertically down the left side of the window. This new toolbar includes all the tools that are in the Getting Started toolbar, so in the next step, you'll hide the Getting Started toolbar. Initially, the large toolbar is attached to the drawing area, but by clicking the bar at the top, you can drag it away from the drawing area to create a floating toolbar.

2. **Choose View → Toolbars → Getting Started.**

   Before you click, checkmarks are next to both the Large Tool Set and the Getting Started options. In the View menu a checkmark indicates that an option is visible in your workspace. Clicking a checked item hides it from view and removes the checkmark.

3. **Choose View → Toolbars → Standard.**

   The Standard toolbar provides the tools that you find in almost every program, though the buttons look a little different. These buttons let you create, open, and save SketchUp files. You also see Cut, Copy, Paste, and Erase buttons. In the next group, you see Undo and Redo arrows. Bringing up the rear is a Print button. Last but certainly not least is a button that's unique to SketchUp. The blue circle with the letter *i* is the Model Info button, which provides juicy tidbits about the model you're building.

4. **Choose View → Toolbars → Views.**

   When you work in 3-D, you change views frequently; or from the "SketchUp think" perspective, you *move the camera*. For example, suppose you want to make sure your model is fitting together properly. Sometimes the only way to see whether a gap exists between two objects is to view them from a different angle. The six view buttons get a lot of use. The Camera Standard Views buttons are Iso (short for *isometric* or angled view), Top, Front, Right, Back, and Left.

Note: The Bottom view option is missing from the View toolbar buttons. You don't need it as much as the other views, but when you do, you find it in the menu: Camera → Standard Views → Bottom.

---

5. **To add one final toolbar, choose View → Toolbars → Face Style.**

The six buttons on the Face Style toolbar change the way SketchUp objects appear in the drawing area. For example, the X-ray button makes object surfaces semitransparent—helpful for working with complex models. The other face styles are wireframe, hidden line, shaded, shaded with textures, and monochrome. (Face Styles are covered in detail on page 193.)

For Mac

The Mac toolbars have some of the tools embedded above the drawing area (Figure 1-5). Here's how to set up your Mac version of SketchUp to match the examples in this book.

The suggestions in this section display, with a minimum of onscreen clutter, the tools you'll use most often and save you from digging into a lot of menus to find commands. You can always change them later as you adjust to working in SketchUp.

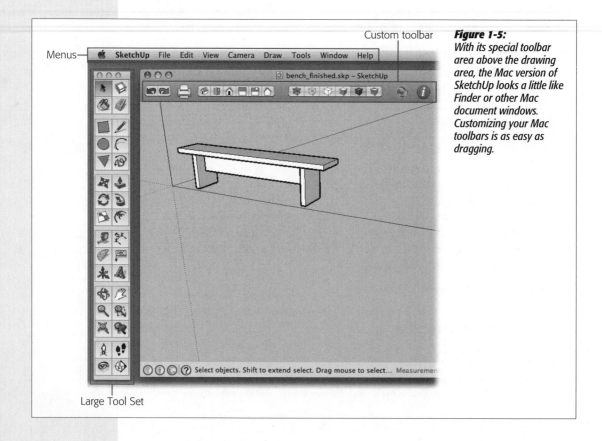

Figure 1-5:
With its special toolbar area above the drawing area, the Mac version of SketchUp looks a little like Finder or other Mac document windows. Customizing your Mac toolbars is as easy as dragging.

1. **Choose View → Tool Palettes → Large Tool Set to display the Large Tool Set.**

   The Large Tool Set shows two columns of buttons. The position of the individual tools and the appearance of the icons are identical on Mac and Windows. In Mac tradition, this toolbar is always floating.

   Initially, SketchUp displays a few basic tools in the custom toolbar. Once you've displayed the Large Tool Set, you don't need these duplicate tools, so in the next steps you'll replace them with some more helpful tools.

2. **Choose View → Customize Toolbar to open the "Customize toolbar" window (Figure 1-6).**

   At the top of the window, you see the tools that appear on the custom toolbar. Below, you see a palette with dozens of tools you can add. It's simply a matter of dragging tools on and off the toolbar as shown in the next few steps.

3. **Drag all the tools on the toolbar away from the toolbar.**

   To remove tools from the toolbar, just drag them off the silver bar area. As you do, they disappear in a poof of smoke. (Don't worry, you still have a copy in the palette below if you need it later.)

4. **Drag the Undo and Redo buttons to the toolbar.**

   These handy buttons let you step forward and backward through actions that you've taken in SketchUp.

5. **Drag the Print button to the toolbar.**

   With a click of the Print button, you can send your SketchUp image to the printer.

6. **Drag the Views tool set to the toolbar.**

   When you work in 3-D, you change views frequently; in SketchUp-speak, you *move the camera.* For example, you can do so to make sure your model is fitting together properly—sometimes the only way to see whether there's a gap between two objects is to view them from a different angle. Put these six view buttons on the main toolbar, because you'll be clicking them a lot. The Camera Standard Views buttons are Iso (short for *isometric* or angled view), Top, Front, Right, Back, and Left.

7. **Drag the Face Styles tool set to the toolbar.**

   These buttons change the way SketchUp objects appear in the drawing area. For example, the X-ray buttons make object surfaces semitransparent, which helps when working with complex models (page 194). The other face styles are wireframe, hidden line, shaded, shaded with textures, and monochrome. (Face Styles are covered in detail in the section on materials, page 193.)

8. **Drag the Get Current View tool to the toolbar.**

   This tool copies a view from Google Earth so you can use it in your document. You must have the Google Earth application running to get a snapshot.

9. **Drag the Model Info button to the toolbar.**

   The blue circle with the letter *i* is the Model Info button, which provides juicy tidbits about the model you're building.

10. **Click Done to save your changes.**

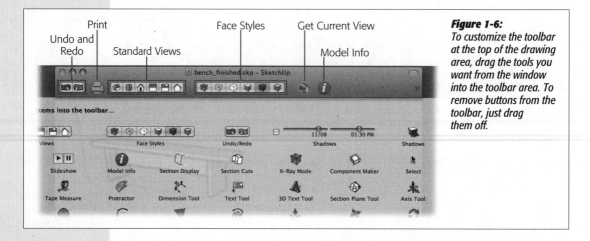

Figure 1-6:
To customize the toolbar at the top of the drawing area, drag the tools you want from the window into the toolbar area. To remove buttons from the toolbar, just drag them off.

Note: You're free to move your toolbars around as much as you like, but don't move them constantly. Leave them in one place for a while, and see how your new setup works. If it works well, you'll soon find yourself automatically clicking tools and zipping right along. If not, you'll be able to see what's not working and change it.

Creating Your First SketchUp Document

Just as in Microsoft Word or Adobe Photoshop, before you start working in SketchUp, you have to create a new document to work in. Unlike some other programs, SketchUp always creates documents from a template that defines the units of measure and sets up the background colors for the drawing area. Some templates may even include prebuilt models or other objects. For example, the Architectural Design templates include a human model as a visual reference. The Product Design and Woodworking templates include a carpenter's square for the same purpose. This section shows you how to choose the right template for your project.

Choosing a Drawing Template

SketchUp comes with a bunch of templates that give you a head start depending on the type of model you're building. When you choose the right template, you don't have to begin your project by setting all the preferences—like units of measure, the way objects snap to each other, the way the ground is represented, and the geographic location.

Here are the questions to ask when deciding which template to choose:

- Are you working in feet and inches, or metric?

- What size is your project? For example, is your basic scale inches or feet?

- Are you working in 3-D or 2-D? (Yes, once you get used to SketchUp's tools, you'll find yourself firing it up for quick 2-D projects.)

After you answer those questions, it's easy to make your choice from SketchUp's standard templates. Just look over the helpful template names and the description of typical projects for each template. For each template style, you can choose either feet and inches, or metric measurements. Here are the templates that come with SketchUp:

- **Simple Template.** This general-use 3-D modeling template offers basic styling and simple background colors—green for earth, blue for sky. The line styles are simple, with the sketchy, hand-drawn look used in the other templates. As the name implies, it's great for quick sketching and a variety of projects large and small.

- **Architectural Design.** Another 3-D template, with a large measurement scale for designing buildings and their interiors. The line styles in this template match the hand-drawn effects used by architects.

- **Google Earth Modeling.** Use this template if you are designing a building and want to place it on the map in Google Earth (Chapter 14).

- **Engineering.** If you're a mechanical or design engineer, this template is for you. For example, the Feet and Inches version of the engineering template displays decimal units of feet. Use this when you're designing an electric car or the innards of a blender.

- **Product Design and Woodworking.** Use this template for smaller-scale projects like furniture design or building a birdhouse.

You can't create a SketchUp document without using a template. For this example, choose a 3-D template that's suitable for furniture building: "Product Design and Woodworking – Feet and Inches". To change from one template to another, you change SketchUp template preferences and then start a new document. SketchUp doesn't give you a way to change a template in an open document nor, oddly, a way to choose a template when you use a File → New command.

1. **Choose Window → Preferences (Windows) or SketchUp → Preferences (Mac).**

   The System Preferences window opens, as shown in Figure 1-7. Along the left side of the box, you see the all the types of preferences you can set.

2. **From the list on the left, choose Template.**

   You see a list of templates with the heading Default Drawing Template.

3. **Choose "Product Design and Woodworking – Feet and Inches" and then click OK.**

   With this setting, SketchUp starts with a 3-D woodworking template when you open a new document. It doesn't change the document that's already open.

4. **To open a new document using the template you just chose, go to File → New.**

   A new document opens. You may see changes in the drawing area from the last time you opened a document—like a different background color. More importantly, the units of measure and other settings are preset for a woodworking project.

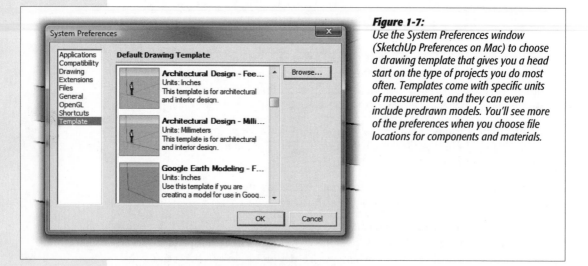

Figure 1-7:
Use the System Preferences window (SketchUp Preferences on Mac) to choose a drawing template that gives you a head start on the type of projects you do most often. Templates come with specific units of measurement, and they can even include predrawn models. You'll see more of the preferences when you choose file locations for components and materials.

Creating Your Own Templates

Once you're a SketchUp pro, you'll probably want to create templates that are set up for specific projects. For example, imagine you're designing houses for a development; you could save the structure of a basic home in your template. From the template, you could design a neighborhood full of fancier custom homes by adding extra rooms, five-car garages, or balcony decks.

Here are the basic steps to create and save a new template:

1. **Open a new file by choosing File → New.**

   A new empty document opens.

FREQUENTLY ASKED QUESTION

Double Document Dilemma

Can I work with two SketchUp documents at the same time?

Sometimes you'll want to have two SketchUp documents open at the same time. Perhaps you're building cars and you want to copy the wheels from one model to another. It's easy on a Mac to open a second document. Just choose File → Open and select a SketchUp document. In Windows, it's different. If you use the same File → Open command, SketchUp closes the current document before it opens the new one. Fortunately, SketchUp asks whether you want to save the current document before closing it.

Windows also closes the current document if you try to start a second SketchUp document from a file. You can work around SketchUp's single-minded behavior—start up two copies of the SketchUp program. For example, in Vista, while you have a SketchUp document open, press the Windows key. Your cursor is automatically placed in the Start Search box as shown in Figure 1-8. Type *SketchUp* and you see a list of SketchUp-related files. At the top of the Programs list is Google SketchUp. If it's highlighted, just press Enter; if it's not highlighted, click it. Either action starts a second copy of the SketchUp program. You can open different models in each copy, and cut and paste between them.

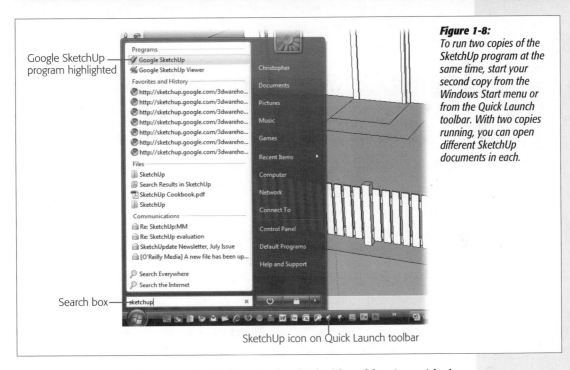

Google SketchUp program highlighted

Search box

SketchUp icon on Quick Launch toolbar

Figure 1-8:
To run two copies of the SketchUp program at the same time, start your second copy from the Windows Start menu or from the Quick Launch toolbar. With two copies running, you can open different SketchUp documents in each.

2. **Open the Model Info box with the button that looks like a blue *i* or with the menu Window → Model Info.**

   The Model Info box shows details about your project and gives you a way to change settings for Units, Text Size and Font, Animation settings, and more. You'll learn more about all these features later in this book.

---

3. **Adjust the settings in the Model Info box.**

As you go through this book, you'll learn about all of these options and which ones you need for various kinds of projects. In most cases, you change settings by typing directly into text boxes or choosing from lists. When you're done, close the box by clicking the close button in the upper-right corner.

4. **Choose Window → Preferences (Windows) or SketchUp → Preferences (Mac) to open the System Preferences window (Figure 1-9).**

Change the settings to create the SketchUp environment you need. For example, you can change the locations where SketchUp saves files, components, and materials. You can create your own shortcut keys for features you use frequently. You'll find more details about creating shortcut keys in the box on page 31.

Note: Mac preferences are always in the same spot under the first menu that bears the name of the program. In Windows, the Preferences command (sometimes called Options) may appear in different menus. In many programs, it's under the Edit or the Tools menu. The Windows version of SketchUp stashes Preferences in an unusual spot under the Window menu. There's some logic to this choice, in that the command opens a *window* where you set your preferences.

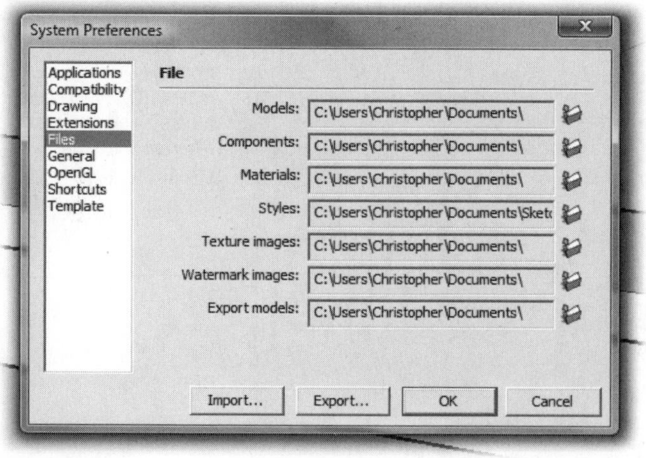

Figure 1-9:
Use the System Preferences window to set up preferences for your custom template. Click the topic on the left, and then fine-tune your preferences with the settings that appear in the large panel on the right.

5. **In the drawing area, add to your SketchUp template any drawings, models, or components that you want.**

Here's where you can add the geometry for that basic house for your development.

6. **Choose File → Save As Template (Figure 1-10).**

The Save As Template dialog box opens, where you provide a Name and File Name for the template. It's also helpful if you provide some more details about the purpose of the template in the Description box.

SketchUp automatically saves the template in the proper directory. In Windows, it's usually *C:\Program Files\Google\Google SketchUp 7\Resources\en-US\Templates.* On a Mac, the location is *Macintosh HD/Users/username/Library/Application Support/Google SketchUp 7/SketchUp/Templates.*

After you've saved your file in the SketchUp Templates directory, it appears in the list along with the other templates. In fact, any .skp file that's in your Templates folder appears on the list, so if you've already got a SketchUp document that has everything you want in your template, just copy it to your Templates folder.

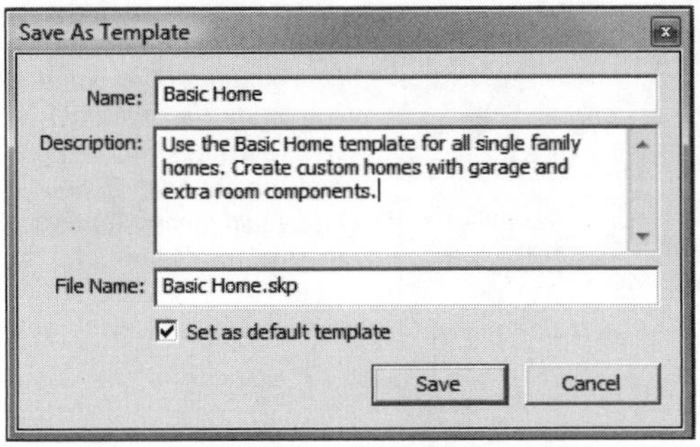

Figure 1-10:
When you create a template, give it a name that will appear in the Preference → Templates view and give it a file name. A description is optional, but it's usually helpful for you and anyone else who uses the template. Turn on the "Set as default template" option if you want SketchUp to automatically use this template when you create new documents.

Changing Your Camera View

When you work in 3-D, you constantly change views, so it's important to learn where the view tools are and how to use them. It's one of the most important skills you can develop for 3-D work. View tools fall into two categories: tools that jump to the Camera Standard Views, like the Front, Back, Left, and Right commands, and tools that let you gradually move from one view to another, like the Zoom tool or the Pan (hand) tool.

The factory settings for the Standard Views are buried under the Camera menu (Camera → Standard Views) as shown in Figure 1-11. If you followed the setup steps earlier in this chapter (page 18), then you added the View toolbar to your SketchUp window for easier access. In the View toolbar (Figure 1-12), you find these handy buttons to jump to a new view, in the following order:

- **Iso.** A slightly angled front view, as you can tell by the icon. It's great when you need to get a feeling for perspective and the relationship of objects.

- **Top.** Viewing your model from the top sometimes makes it seem flat and two-dimensional, even unrecognizable (here, you're looking down on the roof and chimney). On the other hand, if something feels odd about the relationship of objects, it can help to change to a top view and to Zoom out or to use Zoom Extents (Shift-Z). You may find that the objects are farther from each other than you think.

- **Front.** A straight-on front view, usually a good place to start when you're building a model.

- **Right.** It's common practice to jump back and forth between Front, Right, and Left views as you build.

- **Back.** Depending on the object, the back may get less attention, or it may be just as important as the other views. This house apparently has no back door, which helps distinguish it from the front.

- **Left.** It's anybody's guess why the button for Left view is at the right end of the toolbar. You can glance at the Front view button to remind yourself that the left side is the one with no chimney.

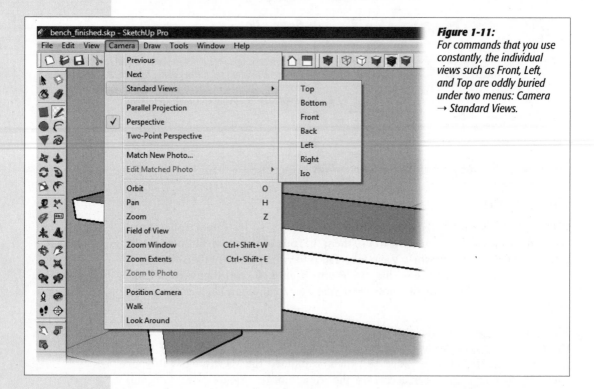

Figure 1-11:
For commands that you use constantly, the individual views such as Front, Left, and Top are oddly buried under two menus: Camera → Standard Views.

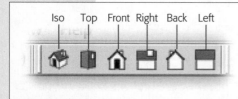

Figure 1-12:
The View toolbar is a handier way to jump to a new standard view. Think of changing view as positioning your camera in a new location. If you have trouble remembering which is which—how does a house with no door signify "Back"?—just hover your mouse over the button.

Often, instead of jumping to a completely new view, you want to gradually move the camera from one spot to another, so you can inspect your model at different angles along the way. The tools you use to move to a new view are in the Camera toolbar (Figure 1-13). It's also the best way to change your angle of view in small increments. If you followed the setup steps earlier in this chapter (page 18), you added these tools to your workspace when you selected the Large Tool Set. Here's a rundown of the tools, with keyboard shortcuts (when available) in parentheses:

- **Orbit (Windows shortcut O; Mac shortcut ⌘-B).** You can move in any direction with the Orbit tool. Just drag your drawing in the direction you want to turn it. It may take a little practice to get used to the Orbit tool, but once you've mastered it, you'll love it. If you have a three-button mouse or a mouse with a scroll wheel, you can use the Orbit tool by pressing the center mouse button and dragging.

UP TO SPEED

Four Ways to Do Just About Everything

As you may have noticed, you have four ways to do just about everything in SketchUp: click a toolbar; use a keyboard shortcut; right-click to display a shortcut menu; or choose a command from a menu.

Which method is easiest depends on what you're doing at the time and your preferences. If you've already got a mouse in hand, it may be easiest to click a toolbar button. If you've got a hand on the keyboard, a shortcut key might be just the thing. The biggest problem with shortcuts is that you have to remember them; however, after using them a few times, they become second nature. Here are a few shortcuts to learn early. (As explained in the tip on page 30, the single-letter shortcuts work on both Windows and Mac; Mac-only keystrokes are included, too, if you can't keep your finger off that ⌘ key.)

View shortcuts:

- Orbit – O (Mac only: ⌘-B)
- Pan – H (Mac only: ⌘-R)
- Zoom – Z (Mac only: ⌘-\)

Tool shortcuts:

- Select – space bar (Mac only: ⌘-/)
- Erase – E
- Move – M (Mac only: ⌘-0)
- Push/Pull – P (Mac only: ⌘-=)

That's enough to get started. You'll learn your own faves as you go along.

Menus are seldom the handiest route to a command, but menus have a few good points. First of all, some commands are available *only* in the menus. Also, the way menus are organized can help you find the command you need. It's worth checking out the menus when you're first learning SketchUp, since the menus helpfully list the shortcut keys (even the ones you create, as described in the box on page 31). Keep an eye out for those shortcut keys, and maybe you won't have to go digging through the menus next time.

If you're of the Mac persuasion, you may notice different keyboard shortcuts listed in the menus. In most cases the Windows shortcut keys such as those listed here work, too. You can use whichever key suits you best, but you may find the Windows keys a little more intuitive.

- **Pan (Windows shortcut H; Mac shortcut ⌘-R).** Using the Pan tool with its hand icon (hence the H in the Windows shortcut) feels like you're grabbing the image and dragging it to a new spot. If you have a three-button mouse, an even easier way to pan is to press Shift, and then drag with the middle button. (But you know you're really just changing the camera position, right?)

- **Zoom (Windows shortcut Z; Mac shortcut ⌘-\).** The grander your model, the more you'll be zooming in to see details and then zooming out to view the big picture. If your mouse has a scroll wheel, you can spin it to zoom. (Whee!)

- **Zoom Extents (Windows shortcut Shift-Z or Ctrl+Shift+E; Mac shortcut ⌘-[).** A very handy button, Zoom Extents zooms out just far enough so that all the objects in your drawing are in view. If you accidentally lose an object by moving it far away from everything else, you can use Zoom Extents to find it. Another time Zoom Extents comes in handy is when *you're* lost. Perhaps you're staring at an empty drawing area and wondering why your model disappeared. The problem may be that the camera is pointed at nothing. Click Zoom Extents and the camera shows all the objects in your drawing, so you can get your bearings.

Tip: If you like using these keyboard shortcuts and want more, see the box on page 29 for a list of popular shortcut keys you should memorize. SketchUp even lets you make your own! See the box on page 31 for instructions.

Bonus Tip for Mac Users: Almost all of the Windows single-letter shortcuts work on Macs. So, if you'd rather use "O" for orbit than use ⌘-B, go ahead. In general, the single-letter shortcuts are easier to use because they're mnemonic and they're single letters as opposed to key combinations. To keep things simple, this book uses the single-key shortcuts when they work on both Windows and Mac. If you need to look up a shortcut, check out Appendix B. It includes all the shortcuts for every command.

- **Previous.** Jumps to your previous view. Points of view are automatically saved as you work in SketchUp.

- **Next.** Works just like the Next button on a web browser. For example, if you used the Previous button, click the Next button to move back to your original view.

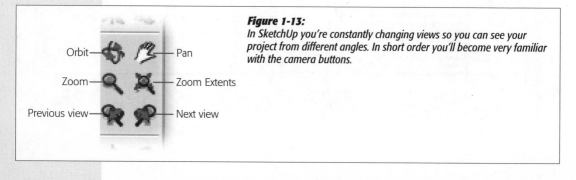

Figure 1-13:
In SketchUp you're constantly changing views so you can see your project from different angles. In short order you'll become very familiar with the camera buttons.

Orbit — Pan
Zoom — Zoom Extents
Previous view — Next view

Setting Up View Shortcut Keys

Lots of SketchUp artists work with one hand on the mouse and another on the keyboard. You'll find shortcut keys for the view tools as described in the list on page 29. You may want to make some shortcuts for the standard views, too. That way you can jump to a particular view quickly.

One method is to use the Alt key (Option on a Mac) along with nearby keys to create a logical pattern of views. To add new shortcut keys go to Windows → Preferences → Short-cuts (Windows) or SketchUp → Preferences → Shortcuts (Mac) as shown in Figure 1-14. In the Function list, click the command that needs a shortcut.

For Windows: In the Add Shortcut box, type the keys for the shortcut you want to use, and then click the + button. If your shortcut key is already being used, you see a warning that lists the command currently using that shortcut, and you have a chance to change your mind. When you're done with all your shortcuts, click OK to save them.

For Mac: Click in the box at the bottom, and then type the shortcut you want to use. If the shortcut is available, you see the keys listed next to the command. If the shortcut is already being used, you hear the Mac warning noise (bonk!).

Here's a layout that some folks find easy to use with their left hand on the keyboard. For Macs, use Option or Control in place of Alt. The keyboard layout hints at the keys' functions:

Alt+A: Left

Alt+D: Right

Alt+W: Back

Alt+S: Top

Alt+X: Front

Alt+Z: Previous

Alt+C: Next

Alt+Q: Iso

You can use the same method to create or change the shortcut keys for just about any command in SketchUp. For example, if you frequently use Adobe programs, you may want to change SketchUp's shortcuts to match the Adobe shortcuts that are embedded in your brain.

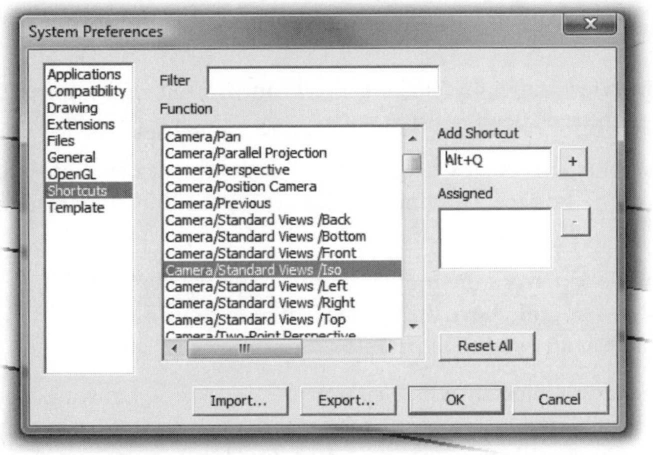

Figure 1-14:
If you're a fan of shortcut keys, you can set up some shortcuts for the standard views. In the System Preferences window choose a command, and type the shortcut in the Add Shortcut box. Click the + button to save the command. Here Alt+Q is being assigned to the Iso view.

Bench: Starting Your First Model

If you're building a bench in the real world, you need to go to the lumberyard and buy some lumber. For this project, building a bench in SketchUp, you're going to mill up your own lumber. You'll create the four boards you need for your bench, making sure that their dimensions are just right. No sawdust or wasted short ends in SketchUp! Then you'll fit the pieces together.

Note: The exercises in the remainder of this chapter focus on building a simple bench. If you'd like to jump ahead to see the finished bench, you can download the file *bench_finished.skp* from the Missing CD for this book found at *http://missingmanuals.com/cds*.

Building a Board

The board that makes the seat for this bench is a 2×12 that's 72 inches long. These boards are kind of expensive at Home Depot, but with SketchUp, you've got your own lumber mill. All SketchUp objects start as 2-D drawings, which you'll learn all about in the next chapter (page 59). They get their third dimension when you use the Push/Pull tool to give them shape. Follow these steps to get a feel for the full procedure:

1. **Open a new SketchUp document with File → New.**

   A new SketchUp document opens in Iso view. You see colored lines that are guides for the three axes in your SketchUp world. In this view, the blue line runs somewhat vertically, representing up and down directions. The red line runs somewhat horizontally, representing left and right. The green line represents near (closer to the camera) and far (away from the camera).

Note: If your view is different from the one described in step 1, make sure you've chosen Inches ("Product Design and Woodworking – Feet and Inches")-3D as your Template preference as described in step 3 on page 24.

---

2. **Change to a Front view either by clicking the Front button or by using the menu Camera → Standard Views → Front.**

   In Front view, the blue axis runs straight up and down the drawing area, and the red axis sits on the horizon running straight across the drawing area from left to right.

3. **Choose the Rectangle tool from the toolbar or click Draw → Rectangle; then, to the right of the blue axis and above the red axis, drag to draw a small rectangle of any size and shape as shown in Figure 1-15.**

   When you're done, don't click anywhere else or press any keys. Drawing a precise rectangle in SketchUp is a two-step process. First you draw a basic shape, and then you enter the specific dimensions as described in the next step.

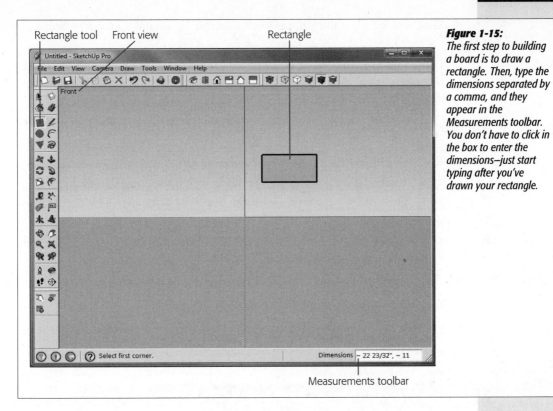

Rectangle tool   Front view   Rectangle

Measurements toolbar

Figure 1-15:
*The first step to building
a board is to draw a
rectangle. Then, type the
dimensions separated by
a comma, and they
appear in the
Measurements toolbar.
You don't have to click in
the box to enter the
dimensions—just start
typing after you've
drawn your rectangle.*

4. **Using your keyboard, type the numbers separated by a comma: *72, 2*. Don't
   worry about clicking anywhere; just press the keys.**

   As you type, the numbers appear in the Measurements toolbar in the lower-
   right corner. You never have to click the Measurements toolbar to enter
   dimensions—it knows what you're doing! When you type *72*, the Measurements toolbar knows you're saying you want the rectangle you just drew to be
   72 inches long—the width of your bench. The comma is a separator, telling
   SketchUp that the next number will be another dimension measurement. When
   you enter the *2*, you're saying you want the rectangle to be 2 inches tall—the
   thickness of your bench seat. If you make a mistake while typing, press Esc and
   enter new dimensions. You can keep changing the dimensions until you choose
   another tool or menu command. To save the dimensions, press Enter.

   Chances are your rectangle doesn't fit in your drawing area or it's not centered.
   You'll resolve that problem in the next step.

5. **Click the Zoom Extents (Camera → Zoom Extents) button to get a complete
   view of your rectangle.**

   The Zoom Extents button zooms the drawing window so every object in your
   drawing is in the view. It's a handy button that you'll use frequently, so early on,
   it's worth noting its location in the toolbar and memorizing the shortcut key
   (Shift+Z for Windows and ⌘-[for Mac).

6. Click the Iso view button, or use the menu command Camera → Standard Views → Iso.

   The Iso button looks like a small house viewed at an angle. The Iso view gives you a better 3-D view of your rectangle as you turn it into a board in the next couple steps.

7. Choose the amazingly handy Push/Pull tool by clicking its toolbar button or by choosing Tools → Push/Pull (Figure 1-16).

   The Push/Pull button looks like a box with an arrow sprouting from the top.

8. Click once on the rectangle's face (avoid clicking on one of the black edge lines). Then move your mouse around, but don't click anywhere else or press any keys.

   As you move the mouse, your bench seat starts to change shape. In the next step, you specify the width of your bench seat.

9. Type *12* and the numbers appear in the Measurements toolbar.

   Your bench seat becomes 12 inches wide.

Congratulations! You just finished your first model and created a bench seat that's $2 \times 12 \times 72$ inches.

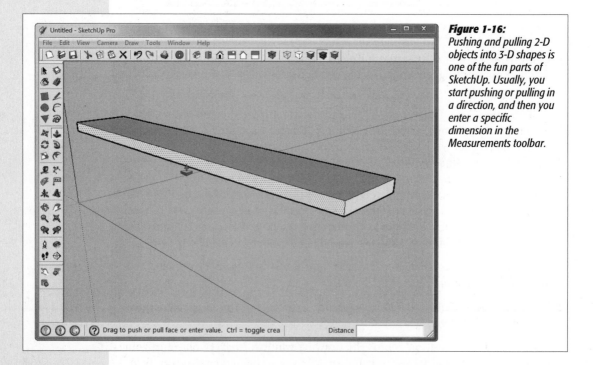

Figure 1-16:
Pushing and pulling 2-D objects into 3-D shapes is one of the fun parts of SketchUp. Usually, you start pushing or pulling in a direction, and then you enter a specific dimension in the Measurements toolbar.

Tip: The Measurements toolbar makes SketchUp so easy to use. This magic box always seems to know what you want to do. You never have to click in the Measurements toolbar to enter numbers. Simply type numbers right after you use a tool. The Measurements toolbar knows what to expect based on your most recent action. If you change your mind or make a mistake entering numbers, you can press Esc to start over.

Selecting Objects

Before you can move an object you create in SketchUp, you have to select it. Similarly, if you want to change the shape of an object, you need to select the edge or face of the object that you want to change. In fact, before you can do pretty much anything in SketchUp, you need to make a selection. If you've used drawing or animation programs, you're probably pretty confident about your selection skills. That's great—but SketchUp has a few quirks that you need to know about:

- All SketchUp objects are made up of edges and faces. Those are the two basic elements of the SketchUp universe. No matter how complicated a SketchUp model is, it's simply a collection of edges and faces.

- All SketchUp objects are hollow inside. That board you created in the previous section? It's not solid wood; think of it instead as a cardboard box. You'll learn some of the implications of this hollowness in later chapters.

- When you select an edge, a highlight shows the selection as a blue line.

- When you select a face, it's highlighted with a pattern of dots as shown in Figure 1-17.

- A single click selects the edge or face that you click, nothing else. So if you click an edge and then use the Move (M) tool, you change the shape of your object because you're moving a single edge. The faces adjacent to the edge you're moving change shape, and your object shrinks or grows accordingly. Go ahead and try it on your board now—you know you can't wait. Use Esc or Ctrl+Z (⌘-Z) to undo any weirdness and to return your 2×12×72-inch seat to its former shape.

- Double-clicking a face selects the face *and* all adjacent edges.

- Double-clicking an edge selects the edge *and* the faces that it bisects.

- Triple-clicking selects an entire object—all the edges and all the faces. This move is an important one, because you'll often want to select an entire object.

- Ctrl-click (Option-click) to add objects to your selection. (The cursor shows a + symbol.)

- Shift+Ctrl-click (Shift-Option-click) to remove objects from a selection. (The cursor shows a – symbol.)

- Shift-click to add objects to *or* remove objects from your selection. (The cursor shows both a + and – symbol.)

• Deselecting (making sure that nothing is selected) is just as important as selecting. To deselect, click in an empty part of the drawing area, or Edit → Select None (Ctrl+T or Shift-⌘-A).

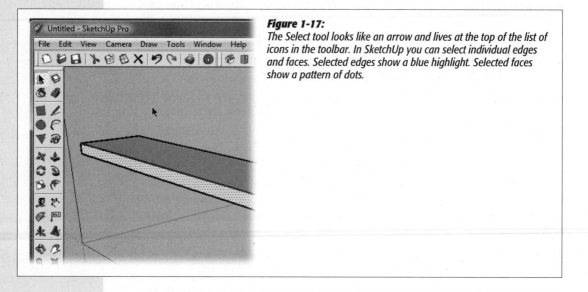

Figure 1-17:
The Select tool looks like an arrow and lives at the top of the list of icons in the toolbar. In SketchUp you can select individual edges and faces. Selected edges show a blue highlight. Selected faces show a pattern of dots.

Tip: Remember, if you find yourself dragging a finely designed object into a hideous shape because you didn't completely select it, you can use a couple of standard emergency measures. If you haven't completed your distortion with a final click, you can always press Esc; the object returns to its original shape. If you've made that final click, press Ctrl+Z (⌘-Z) to undo your last action.

Turning Your Bench Seat into a Component

When you place one SketchUp object against another, they tend to glue themselves together. Sometimes this behavior is helpful, but other times it's annoying. (For complete details see page 313.) Suppose you place a 2×4 on top of the bench seat. Later, if you move the 2×4 with an edge or surface glued to the bench seat, one of two things happens. Either both the seat and the 2×4 move, or moving the 2×4 distorts the lovely shape of your bench seat. The way to keep this from happening is to turn the bench seat into a *component*. Components have many advantages and you'll read all about them in Chapter 5. The immediate advantage for your bench seat is that a component keeps its shape; you can place it against another object without gluing its edges and surfaces to that object. Here are the steps to turn your bench seat into a component:

1. **With the Select tool (space bar), triple-click the 2×12×72-inch bench seat to select all of its faces and edges.**

   The selected edges turn blue, and the selected faces are highlighted with dots.

2. **Press G to open the Create Component box.**

   You could also click the Create Component button (it's next to the selection arrow) or choose Edit → Create Component.

3. **In the Name box, type** *Bench Seat,* **as shown in Figure 1-18.**

   Use a descriptive name that will mean something to you (and others) 12 months from now.

4. **In the Description box, type** *2x12x72 inch piece of lumber.*

   This description may come in handy later if you're looking through your components for a piece of lumber.

5. **Leave the rest of the options as they are and click the Create button.**

   Your bench seat is still selected, and it's highlighted as a component with an envelope of blue lines.

6. **Open the Components window (Window → Components) and click the Select tab.**

   The Components window has three tabs: Select, Edit, and Statistics. It shows different details for each.

7. **Under the tabs, click the button that looks like a house.**

   The house button is named "In Model" because it's used to display the components that are in your model. You see this button in the Materials and Styles windows, too. At this point, Bench Seat should be the only component showing.

8. **In the Components window, click the Bench Seat component to select it, and then click the Statistics tab.**

   Notice that the Statistics tab provides details about the selected component. In the case of your Bench Seat, it shows that there are 12 edges and 6 faces. How rectangular!

9. **Click the close button to close the Create Component window.**

   If there's a bench seat attached to your mouse cursor, that's because SketchUp thought you wanted to add a component to your drawing. Press Esc to make it go away.

10. **Use File → Save to save your project.**

    A standard file box appears, where you can navigate to a directory and type in a file name. Even though you're not finished with your bench, it never hurts to save early and save often.

So, you turned your bench seat into a component. Now it won't get confused when it comes up against other objects. If you want another, identical bench seat or a 2×12×72-inch board for any other purpose, all you have to do is drag it out of the Components window. Make sure you're on the Select tab and drag. In the

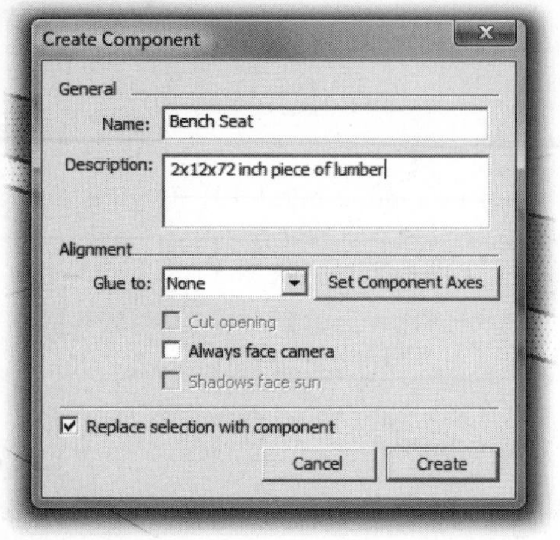

Figure 1-18:
The Create Component box gives you a way to name and describe components, which is helpful when you reuse them later. The gluing options determine the way your component behaves when attached to other objects. Here it's set to None, because you don't want to glue it to anything.

drawing window you can select an entire component with a single click—no triple-clicking is needed for components. Notice that components are highlighted with extra blue lines like an envelope when you select them. That's a visual reminder that they're components and that you can't modify them like other objects. You'll learn some more details about components when you make the bench legs. The complete story on editing components is in Chapter 5. For now, if you've got an extra bench seat in your drawing, click it and press Delete. You'll only need one from here on out.

Building a Bench Leg

The legs for this bench are also 2×12 pieces of lumber. The legs are 15 inches tall, which puts the top of the bench seat a comfortable 17 inches off the ground.

Here are the steps to create the first leg:

1. **Click the Front view button or choose Camera → Standard Views → Front.**

   It's usually easier to draw your initial 2-D shape in Front view or Top view. That way it's easier to keep all the edges of your shape on a single axis.

2. **Press R to choose the Rectangle tool.**

   The SketchUp cursor changes to a pencil, indicating that you're ready to draw something. A hint that says "Select first corner" appears in the status bar.

3. **Below the bench seat, draw a small rectangle of any size and shape, but don't click anywhere or press any keys.**

   You don't need to worry about the exact placement of the leg in the drawing—you'll position it later.

4. **Type the following: *2, 15*.**

   Remember, you don't have to click first; the numbers automatically appear in the Measurements toolbar. These dimensions create a rectangle that's taller than it is wide—just the thing for your bench leg.

5. **Click the Iso view button or choose Camera → Standard Views → Iso.**

   You see a 3-D view of the drawing area, which makes it easier to turn your rectangle into a board in the next few steps (Figure 1-19). If necessary, use the Zoom (Z) and Pan (H) tools to get a good view of your bench leg.

6. **With the Push/Pull (P) tool, click and push the face toward the upper-left corner of the drawing area.**

   Stop as soon as you begin to see it change shape, and don't click anywhere or press any keys. You want to accurately enter a dimension for the bench leg.

7. **Type *12* for the width of the bench leg.**

   As you type, the numbers appear in the Measurements toolbar. (It's not necessary to click in the Measurements toolbar before you type the dimension.) If you make a mistake, press Esc and enter the number again. When you're done, the bench leg is fully formed as a 2×12 that stands 15 inches tall.

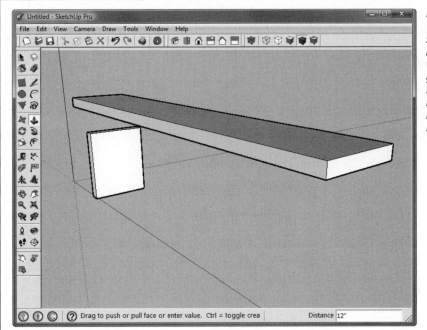

Figure 1-19:
Your bench starts to take shape as you create more parts. Using the Iso view, the perspective gives you a better feeling for the dimensions of the bench seat ($2 \times 12 \times 72$ inches) and the bench leg ($2 \times 12 \times 15$ inches).

8. **Triple-click the leg and then press G to open the Create Component box.**

Triple-clicking selects all the edges and faces of the bench leg. When you press G, the Create Component box appears.

9. **In the Name box type** *Bench Leg,* **and in the Description box type** *2x12x15 inch piece of lumber.*

10. **Click Create.**

SketchUp saves the Bench Leg component. You now have two components in your model: Bench Seat and Bench Leg.

Unless you enjoy sitting at an angle, your bench needs two legs. You have two ways to create an identical second leg component. You can select the leg with the Selection arrow (space bar), and then copy (Ctrl+C) and paste (Ctrl+V) a new leg component into your document. Because your leg is a component, you can also open the Components window (Windows → Components), set the drop-down menu under the tabs to In Model, and then *drag* a second instance of the Bench Leg component into your document as shown in Figure 1-20. Either way, you have two instances of the Bench Leg component in your document. If you edit the component—add color to it, make the leg longer, and so on—the changes take place in both bench legs in your document.

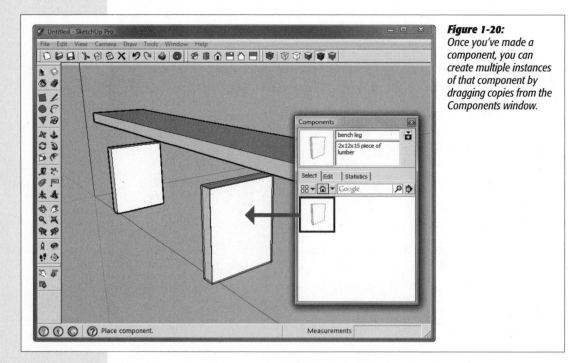

Figure 1-20:
Once you've made a component, you can create multiple instances of that component by dragging copies from the Components window.

Building the Bench Support

At this point, you've milled three pieces of lumber: a bench seat and two legs. You have only one more piece to go. To make sure that your bench is sturdy, you need a support piece of lumber that connects and stabilizes the other three pieces. That'll cure the wobbles. The bench support is $2 \times 8 \times 52$ inches. You're probably a pro at milling up lumber by now, but in any case, here's a short version of the steps again:

1. **Click the Front view button or choose Camera → Standard Views → Front.**

   Front view makes it easier to draw a rectangle on the red axis.

2. **Choose the Rectangle (R) tool, and then draw a small rectangle of any size and shape.**

   Don't worry about the size; you'll enter the dimensions in the Measurements toolbar.

3. **Type *2, 8* for your dimensions, and then press Enter.**

   The numbers appear in the Measurements toolbar, creating a rectangle that's 2 inches wide and 8 inches tall.

4. **Click the Iso view button or choose Camera → Standard Views → Iso.**

   Iso view provides a better angle for pushing the 2×8 rectangle into a three-dimensional piece of lumber.

5. **Press P to select the Push/Pull tool, and then begin to push the face of the rectangle into a 3-D shape.**

   You don't have to be accurate as you're pushing, just get the motion started, and you can enter a precise dimension in the next step.

6. **Type *52* and press Enter.**

   The numbers appear in the Measurements toolbar. The board becomes a 2×8 that is 52 inches long.

7. **Triple-click the support board to select all its edges and faces.**

   All the edges and faces of the support board are highlighted.

8. **Press G to open the Create Component box. Name the component *Support*, and for a description, type *2x8x52 inch piece of lumber*.**

   SketchUp adds the Support board to your component library. You've created all the lumber you need to build your bench.

Okay, you've milled all the pieces of lumber you need for this bench (Figure 1-21). Grab your virtual nails. It's time to put this baby together. Along the way, you'll learn how to move and rotate objects and how to show and hide components in the drawing area.

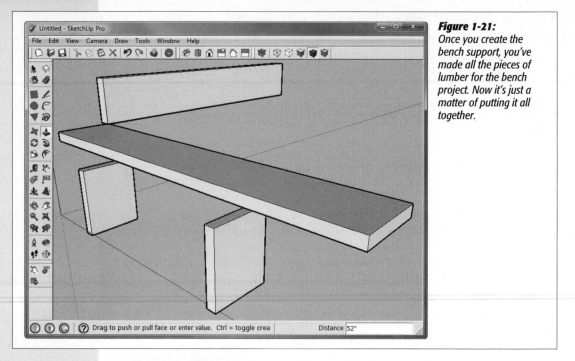

Rotating an Object

You've got lumber scattered all over the SketchUp drawing window. You may have noticed that they're all kind of oriented in the proper direction to piece together into a bench except for that last piece, the support. You could have designed it to be properly oriented by simply changing the order of the numbers as you entered them into the Measurements toolbar (but then you wouldn't have had an opportunity to practice rotating objects).

1. **Click the Top view button or choose Camera → Standard Views → Top.**

   You see one of the narrow faces of the 2 × 8, as well as your other bench parts.

2. **If necessary, use the Zoom (Z) and Pan (H) tools to drag the support into view.**

   It's good to get used to positioning your work so you have just the right view of your model.

3. **Press Q or choose Tools → Rotate.**

   The cursor changes to a protractor, and you're ready to apply the Rotate tool to objects in the drawing area.

4. **Move the Protractor tool over the support component.**

   The protractor flips around depending on which face it hovers over. The dot in the middle, between the two curved arrows, snaps to endpoints, midpoints, and edges. This behavior is typical for SketchUp—it tries to anticipate what you want to do.

5. **Position the center of the protractor over the midpoint of the left edge of the bench support, as shown in Figure 1-22.**

Moving the cursor over the left edge of the support, you notice a snapping action when you reach the midpoint. Pause there, and a tooltip appears that reads "Midpoint in Component".

6. **Click to select the midpoint, and then move the cursor a few inches off to the right.**

A guideline appears between the midpoint and the cursor. The line snaps to a position that is perpendicular to the support.

7. **Click to set this first reference guideline, and then begin to move the cursor in an arc.**

When you click, the reference guideline appears on the screen. The support rotates as you move the cursor. A new guideline follows the cursor. Using this line, you can accurately select an angle with the protractor. The Measurements toolbar shows the value of the angle in degrees.

8. **Move the cursor so the support board rotates 90 degrees.**

There's a snapping action when you reach 90 degrees. The value of the angle appears in the Measurements toolbar.

9. **Click to complete the rotation and 90 degrees.**

When you complete the rotation, the Rotate tool's guidelines disappear.

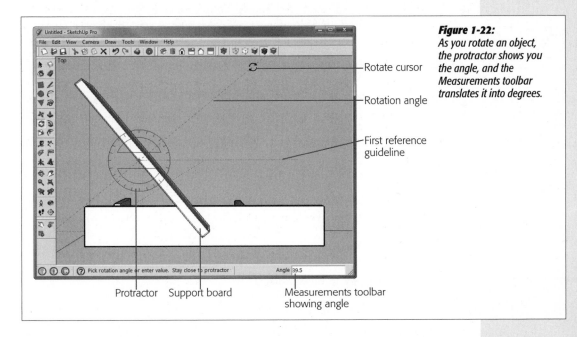

Figure 1-22:
As you rotate an object, the protractor shows you the angle, and the Measurements toolbar translates it into degrees.

Tip: Two tools change your cursor into a protractor—the Rotate tool and the Protractor tool (page 283). If you ever find that the Rotate tool is behaving oddly, double-check to make sure you haven't chosen the Protractor tool instead, or vice versa if you intended to protract.

Moving, Copying, and Deleting Components

Up to this point you created individual components. Now it's time to build your bench by putting those components together. When you've done that, you can select everything and create a Bench component that's made up of the other components. The fact that you can have components inside of components comes in very handy as you build complex models. Assembling your bench requires some patience, because you have to successfully navigate SketchUp's 3-D space. The first few times you try to move your camera view around or to move objects in the drawing area can be a little disorienting. Here are some tips to help you build and navigate:

- **Save your work early and often.** Don't wait until you're done and everything is perfect to save your document. Save frequently when you're at a comfortable spot. If you save your SketchUp drawing under different names, like Bench-1.skp, Bench-2.skp, Bench-3.skp, and so on, you can go back to a previous stage if something goes wrong.

- **Use the Esc key to undo when you're in the midst of an action.** When you type numbers, they automatically appear in the Measurements toolbar, but they don't become permanent until you click a new tool or click in the drawing area. Up until that point you can start over by typing a new number or by pressing Esc.

- **Use Ctrl+Z (⌘-Z) to undo after you've completed an action.** As with most programs, Ctrl+Z (⌘-Z) is SketchUp's undo keystroke. It undoes the last complete command. If you need to go back several steps, just keep pressing Ctrl+Z (⌘-Z).

- **Use Camera → Previous and Camera → Next to jump back and forth between camera views.** It's often helpful to view your model from different angles as you position and tweak its elements. You'll find the Previous and Next views such valuable tools that you may want to assign them keyboard shortcuts as described in the box on page 31.

Moving components

In most programs from word processors to basic paint programs, you move objects by clicking anywhere on the object and dragging it to a new spot. You can do that in SketchUp, but you'll make your life easier if you retrain yourself to use SketchUp's best practices:

- **Don't** drag to move objects.

- **Do** click-move-*click* to move objects.

In SketchUp you often want to place objects with precision, because you're trying to align components like the parts of your bench perfectly. You don't want sloppy, overlapping, or misaligned edges. Chapter 2 gives a lot more detail about the intricacies of moving objects. For now, remember these basic steps when you move an object in SketchUp with the click-move-click method:

• Click a specific point on the object you want to move. Often that's a corner or a midpoint.

• In your drawing, click the specific point where you want to place *that point* of your object. By using specific reference points, you place objects with precision.

To practice, change to Iso view and then zoom in on one of the bench legs in your drawing. To start off, you can move it from place to place without worrying about lining it up with any other object.

1. **Zoom in so one of the bench legs looms large in the drawing window.**

    Leave enough room so you can move the leg to a new location a couple inches away.

Tip: Use the Select None command (Ctrl+T or ⌘-A) to make sure nothing is selected before you use the Move command.

---

2. **Press M to select the Move tool, or choose Tools → Move from the menu.**

    Your cursor changes to a cross with arrowheads.

3. **Move the cursor over one of the broad faces of the Bench Leg component.**

    Highlights appear on the leg. Blue envelope lines highlight the object, indicating that it's a component. Red crosses appear on the face, indicating points you can use to rotate the component. These marks can also help you to find midpoints of the component. You'll have a chance to test these in later steps.

4. **Hold the cursor over one of the corners of the bench leg.**

    A tooltip appears saying "Endpoint in Component". The tooltip lets you know that if you click now, you'll select the Endpoint as your reference point for the move. Don't click now though; you're not done yet.

5. **Move the cursor along one of the edges.**

    The tooltip changes to "On Edge in Component", as shown in Figure 1-23.

6. **Keep moving the cursor down the edge until you find the midpoint.**

    When you near the midpoint, the cursor snaps slightly and the tooltip reads "Midpoint in Component".

---

7. **Move the cursor over one of the red crosses on the face of the bench leg.**

The cursor changes to the protractor, indicating that you can use this point to rotate the bench leg if necessary. For this model, the bench leg is probably already correctly oriented. If you spin the leg and realize you didn't need to, just press the undo keystroke when you're done (Ctrl+Z for Windows; ⌘-Z for Mac).

8. **Click the lower corner of the Bench Leg closest to you.**

Move the cursor over the corner. When the tooltip reads "Endpoint in Component", click.

9. **Move the mouse to a new location in your drawing and click again.**

As you move the cursor around the drawing window, the bench leg follows. When you click a spot, SketchUp places that lower corner of the bench leg exactly where you click.

Note: When working with components, one click with the Move tool selects the entire component, making it a cinch to move. Not so with non-component objects. If you click a non-component object with the Move tool, you select only the clicked edge or face. When you make the move, only that edge or face moves, changing the object's shape. To move a non-component, triple-click the object with the Select tool. When you see highlights on all the edges and faces of the object, you can use the Move tool to reposition it without changing its shape.

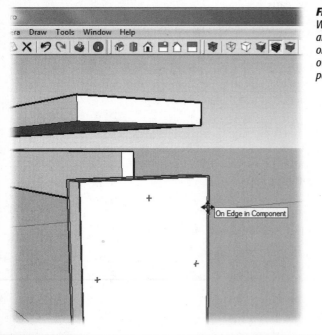

Figure 1-23:
When you hover (that is, pause the cursor) over an object, a tooltip appears that names the type of object. Here the tooltip shows that the Move tool is over one of the component's edges—a perfect point to grab to move the bench leg precisely.

You may want to experiment some more with the Move tool before you begin to assemble your bench pieces. Get used to finding and selecting endpoints and mid-points on your bench leg. Notice how you can drag the bench leg completely through the other objects on the screen. (Can't do that with real lumber!) You can even place and leave a component so that it runs right through another component.

While you're in move mode, drag the bench leg all over the screen. Notice how sometimes it gets really big as if it's close to you, and other times it's really small as if it's far away. In fact it sort of jumps and changes size as you move it. That's because SketchUp is constantly guessing what type of a move you're trying to make. Are you trying to push the bench leg far into the distance? Or are you trying to move it up and down over the same spot? In Chapter 2 you'll learn how to tell SketchUp exactly which direction you intend to move an object.

Copying and deleting components

Copying and deleting components in SketchUp is similar to just about any other program you've ever used. Press the space bar to choose the Select tool; the cursor looks like an arrow. Then click a component, like one of the bench legs. Choose Edit → Copy to copy the object. To paste it back into the drawing, choose Edit → Paste. At that point, you find that your cursor changes to the Move tool with the new bench leg attached. Click in your drawing to place the bench leg at that spot. Copying and pasting a component like this bench leg does the same thing as drag-ging a new Bench Leg out of the Components window. All of the Bench Leg com-ponents are identical, and in SketchUp-speak, they're considered *instances* of the Bench Leg component. If you edit the Bench Leg component, those changes appear in every bench leg instance in your model.

Deleting an object is even easier. You can practice on that third bench leg you just created: you only need two for this project. Again, use the Select tool (space bar, or Tools → Select). Click the doomed bench leg and then press Delete. Poof! It's gone.

SketchUp uses the standard shortcut keys for Copy (Ctrl+C for Windows; ⌘-C for Mac), Cut (Ctrl+X for Windows; ⌘-X for Mac), Paste (Ctrl+V for Windows, ⌘-V for Mac), and Delete (Delete).

Component Hide and Seek with the Outliner

In the not too distant future, when you're a SketchUp wizard, you'll be building very complex models made up of dozens of components. At times you'll want to zero-in on one specific component amidst a vast confusion of others. That's when you'll turn to the Outliner. To open the Outliner, choose Window → Outliner. The Out-liner window opens showing a list of the components in your drawing. Your bench is a simple four-component model, so you should see a list that looks like Figure 1-24.

Clicking a component in the Outliner is the same as selecting a component in the drawing area. Click the Bench Seat in the Outliner and you see highlights sur-rounding the seat in the drawing window. In the next section, you'll assemble the two legs and the bench support into a single component. Even though your bench

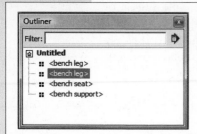

Figure 1-24:
The Outliner window provides a list of the components in your drawing. When you select a component in the Outliner window, it's also selected in the drawing area, and vice versa. Even though they form one bench, the four parts are actually individual components. You'll combine them in the next section.

is relatively simple, suppose you want to hide the bench seat while you work with the other three components. To hide the bench seat, right-click (or ⌘-click) its name in the Outliner, and then choose Hide from the shortcut menu. The name in the Outliner fades to gray. When you want to see the bench seat again, just right-click its name in the Outliner and then choose Unhide.

Assembling the Bench Components

Okay, now you're an expert at selecting points on components and moving them. It's time to piece this thing together. The first step is to connect one of the bench legs to the bench support.

1. **Move (M) one bench leg and the support so that they're relatively close to each other, but not touching.**

   Remember to use the click-move-click technique (page 44) instead of dragging.

2. **Zoom (Z), Pan (H), and Orbit (O) so you can see the objects from the top with a little bit of perspective to help you judge depth.**

   You may want to jump to a different view: Front, Left, or Top. Just make sure the objects are relatively close to each other. If necessary, use the Move (M) tool to readjust.

3. **Press the space bar, and then click an empty portion of the drawing area.**

   This is a quick way to make sure nothing is selected. You can also use the shortcut keystroke (Ctrl+T for Windows or Shift-⌘-A for Mac).

4. **Choose the Move (M) tool, and then hover over the top edge of the bench support closest to the leg.**

   When the center of the Move tool is over the edge, you see a tooltip message, like "On Edge in Component".

5. **Move the cursor toward the middle of the edge until the tooltip says "Midpoint in Component".**

   When you're at the right spot, you see a message like the one in Figure 1-25.

6. **Click to select the midpoint as a reference point for the move.**

Once the bench leg is selected, it becomes attached to the cursor. Move the cursor and the leg follows. If your bench leg is spinning instead of moving, you've clicked the rotation point that's close to the midpoint. Use Esc or Undo to put your components back in place and try again.

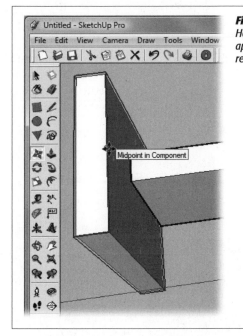

Figure 1-25:
Hold the Move tool over an edge, a midpoint, or a face, and a tooltip appears that identifies the object. Click to select that point as the reference point for moving the object.

7. **Move the cursor (and the bench leg) to the bench support, and then find the midpoint of the support.**

When you reach the midpoint, there's a small snapping action as SketchUp anticipates that you want to move your component to the midpoint.

8. **Click the midpoint to complete the move.**

Your bench leg is properly positioned next to the bench support as shown in Figure 1-26.

9. **Use the Orbit tool (O) to view your bench parts from a couple of different angles.**

It's always good practice to check your work to make sure objects are connected as you expect. Sometimes the perspective can fool you.

10. **Repeat these steps to attach the second leg to your partially assembled bench.**

When you're done, the three pieces of the leg assembly look like Figure 1-27. Now that the legs and the support that joins them are positioned just right, they'll be easier to work with as a single component.

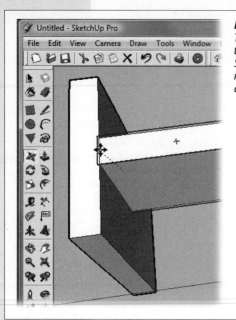

Figure 1-26:
To center the bench leg on the bench support, select the midpoint on the bench leg, and then move it to the midpoint on the bench support. SketchUp's snapping action signals when you have the cursor near a midpoint. When you pause with the cursor over a midpoint, a tooltip appears that reads "Midpoint in Component".

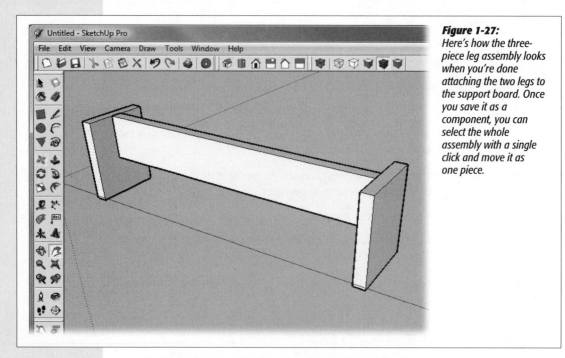

Figure 1-27:
Here's how the three-piece leg assembly looks when you're done attaching the two legs to the support board. Once you save it as a component, you can select the whole assembly with a single click and move it as one piece.

11. **Ctrl-click (Option-click) both legs and the support.**

    Each component shows a highlight envelope when it's selected.

12. Press G to open the Create Component box, name the component *Leg Assembly*, and for a description, type *2 legs and support piece for bench*.

    This new component is made up of three other components.

13. Click Create.

    By combining the three parts into a single leg assembly, you've made it easier to move and position the entire assembly as a single unit.

Placing Components with Precision

Fitting the bench seat on top of the leg assembly takes a couple of steps to get everything positioned precisely. The width of the bench legs and the seat is the same, 12 inches, so the components fit snugly front and back without any over-hang. The first step is to place the bench seat on top of the leg assembly and to make sure the 12-inch bench seat is centered properly over the 12-inch legs.

The bench seat is longer than the leg assembly, so the sides of the bench seat hang can-tilevered over the leg assembly. So the second step is to center the bench seat over the leg assembly lengthwise. To do this, you use one of SketchUp's handiest tricks, known as an *inference*. An inference is SketchUp's way of helping you find a particular point. It may show up as a dotted line or a colored point on an edge. The following steps also illustrate why it's best to use the click-move-click method instead of dragging.

Note: If you hid the bench seat while working through the previous section, reveal it again now. Open the Outliner (Window → Outliner), right-click Bench Seat, and then choose Unhide from the shortcut menu.

---

1. **Use the Move (M) tool to position the bench seat so it's close to the leg assembly.**

    To accurately position objects, it's sometimes necessary to move the objects, change your camera position, and then move the objects again.

2. **Use the Orbit (O), Pan (H), and Zoom (Z) tools to get a good view of the bench seat and the top of one of the legs.**

    Be patient and find the camera view that makes the job easier.

3. **Use the Move (M) tool to move the lower-right corner of the bench seat to the upper-right corner of the leg, as shown in Figure 1-28.**

    When the two endpoints (corners) are close, the bench seat snaps into position.

4. **Change to the Front view (Camera → Standard Views → Front).**

    Using the Front view makes it easier to move the bench seat along the red axis (left to right) without inadvertently changing its position on the green axis (front to back).

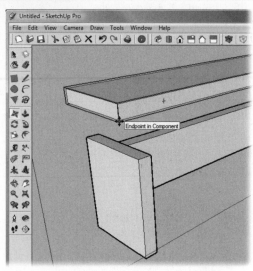

Figure 1-28:
Move the corner (or "endpoint" in SketchUp-speak) of the bench seat to the corner of one the legs, and you line up the seat along two axes: the height (blue axis) and the depth (green axis).

The last step (not shown here) is to center the bench seat over the legs by moving it in the direction of the red axis.

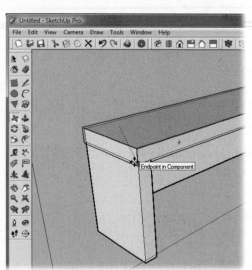

5. **Use the Move (M) tool and select the bench seat's midpoint.**

   It doesn't matter if you choose the midpoint on the top edge or the bottom edge of the seat, because in the next step, you'll restrict the movement of the seat to movement along the red axis.

6. **Slowly start to drag the bench seat to the left and then pause.**

   When you pause, a tooltip appears reading, "On Red Axis". If you don't see this tooltip, you may be moving the bench seat off the red axis. Press Esc (or Undo if you've completed the move), and try again with a steady hand.

Tip: If you don't see the message "On Red Axis", or if the bench seat starts to slip off in the wrong direction, press Esc and start over, dragging the seat at a slightly different angle. It may help to use the Orbit (O) tool to view the bench at a slightly different angle.

7. **When you see the "On Red Axis" tooltip, as shown in Figure 1-29, press Shift.**

Pressing Shift restricts the movement to the red axis, keeping it aligned properly over the bench legs. You see a red dotted line that signals the movement is restricted to the red axis. As long as you press Shift, you restrict the bench seat's movement, and you can't move the bench seat up or down (blue axis) or back into your drawing area (green axis).

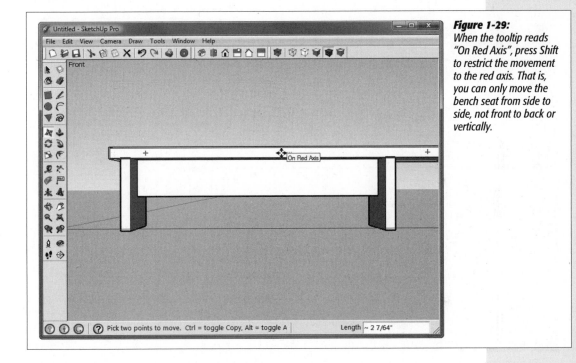

Figure 1-29:
When the tooltip reads "On Red Axis", press Shift to restrict the movement to the red axis. That is, you can only move the bench seat from side to side, not front to back or vertically.

Tip: There's another way to restrict movement to a particular axis by using the arrow keys. For example, to move up and down on the blue axis, press the up arrow. Use the right arrow for the red axis and the left arrow for the green.

8. **Move the cursor down to find the support's midpoint.**

With the bench seat's movement restricted, you can move your cursor away from the bench seat without dragging the seat off track. The bench seat moves in a level trajectory as you move the mouse cursor to find the midpoint of the support. All you need to do now is line up the center of the bench seat with the center of the leg assembly. You'll feel that familiar "snap to" action and see a tooltip that reads "Constrained on Line from Point", as shown in Figure 1-30.

9. **When you find the support's midpoint, click to place the seat.**

    At this point the bench seat is perfectly centered over the Leg Assembly.

10. **Use the Orbit (O) tool to check the bench from different angles.**

    Check to make sure it fits and is centered properly. If necessary, make adjustments by realigning the midpoints.

11. **Ctrl-click (Option-click) to select both the bench seat and the leg assembly, and then press G to create a new component named Bench.**

    As always, give your Bench component a name and description. You can create new instances of your bench by dragging them from the Components window.

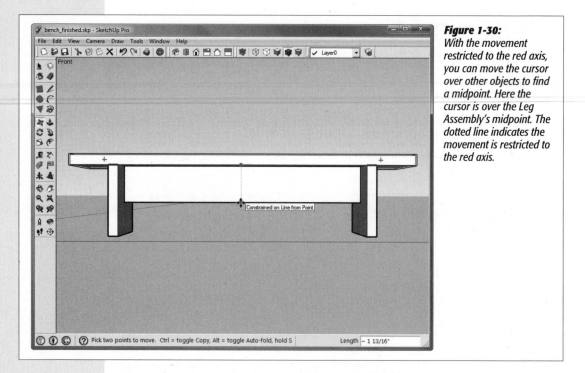

Figure 1-30:
With the movement restricted to the red axis, you can move the cursor over other objects to find a midpoint. Here the cursor is over the Leg Assembly's midpoint. The dotted line indicates the movement is restricted to the red axis.

Painting Your Bench with Materials

In SketchUp world, you can apply color or materials to the faces of your 3-D objects. SketchUp *materials* are patterns that simulate the look of real-world materials such as concrete or wood, giving your models a more realistic appearance. Since none of the faces in your bench component have been painted with a color or material, you can paint the entire bench at once by dragging a color or material from the Materials window (Window → Materials) onto the component. However, in this exercise, you paint the different components individually to get a feeling for the way nested components work. You'll see how you can open components for *editing* by double-clicking them or by using the Outliner window.

Here are the steps to apply a cherry wood material to the bench leg components.

1. **With the Select tool (space bar), double-click the bench.**

   A marquee box appears around the bench to show that you are editing a component. With one click you can select either the bench seat or the leg assembly. Remember, the bench legs and support are part of a component called the Leg Assembly.

2. **Right-click (Control-click) the Leg Assembly and choose Edit Component.**

   The Edit Component command opens the Leg Assembly for editing. That means you can select the individual parts inside the component—in this case the bench legs and support. These parts are also components that group their individual edges and faces. A dotted *bounding box* appears around the component that's open for editing. Objects that are outside of the component appear faded out.

3. **Double-click one of the legs.**

   Double-clicking a component is the same as choosing the Edit Component command above; it opens the Bench Leg component, so you can edit the individual edges and faces. At this level, clicking selects a single edge or face.

4. **Triple-click the leg to select all of its edges and faces.**

   You want to apply the cherry wood material to all the visible faces of the Bench Leg.

5. **Open the Materials window (Figure 1-31) by choosing Window → Materials.**

   The Materials window opens, showing a square of material in the upper-left corner. Below are two tabs: Select, where you choose materials to apply, and Edit, where you can create your own custom materials.

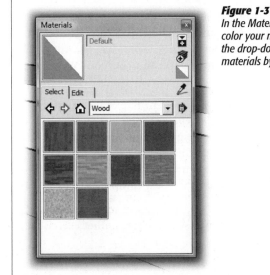

Figure 1-31:
In the Materials window, you can apply and create materials to shade and color your models. Use the Select tab to choose and apply a material using the drop-down menu and sample palettes. Use the Edit tab to create new materials by adjusting existing materials.

6. **Click the Select tab, and then choose Wood from the drop-down menu.**

   You see a palette of wood samples. Hold your cursor over a sample, and a tool-tip appears showing the sample's name.

7. **Click a sample you want to use for your bench.**

   The Wood_Cherry_Original material is a good choice for outdoor furniture. After you select a material, your cursor becomes a paint bucket when it's in the drawing area.

8. **Click the selected bench leg.**

   SketchUp "paints" your bench leg with the material. Best of all, you have no messy brushes to clean up. In fact SketchUp paints *both* legs with the material, since the legs are both instances of the Bench Leg component. When you edit the component, it automatically changes every instance of the component.

9. **Press Esc three times.**

   The first time you press Esc, you close the Bench Leg component. Press it one more time, and you close the Leg Assembly component. With a third Esc, you close the Bench component and you're back where you started. Both your bench legs have the material you applied.

Tip: As an alternative to pressing Esc, you can choose Edit → Close Group/Component.

Using the Outliner to Select Nested Components

There's another way to select components and apply materials. You can use the Outliner—the same tool you used to hide and show components. Choose Windows → Outliner to open the Outliner window (Figure 1-32). Just like the outline you write for a thesis, the Outliner shows which parts and components belong to larger components.

From the Outliner window, you can select a component like Support by clicking its name. Triple-click Support and you drill-down through the Bench and Leg Assembly components and open the Support component, selecting all the edges and faces, ready for editing. That's a lot of action for a single click. You simply click your material in the Materials window and then click the support. To finish, also use the Outliner to apply a material to the Bench Seat component.

Now that your bench is complete (Figure 1-33), it's a good idea to save it (File → Save). If you want to keep your finished bench separate from other exercise files, use File → Save As and give it a unique name.

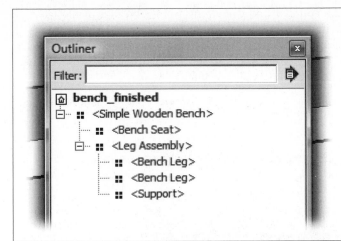

Figure 1-32:
When you have components inside of components, the Outliner indents them to show you what's going on. Here the Outliner shows that the Support component is inside the Leg Assembly component, which in turn is inside the Bench component.

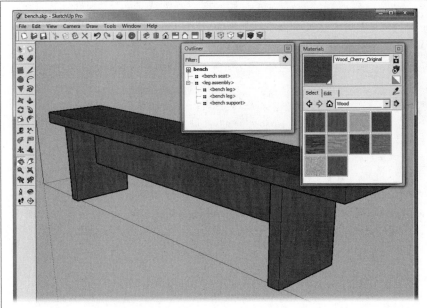

Figure 1-33:
Here's the finished bench with the Wood_Cherry_ Original material applied. Keeping the Outliner and Materials windows open makes it easy to add colors and textures to individual components.

Adding to Your Scene

If you've followed the steps up to this point, you have one snazzy-looking bench in your SketchUp world, but things around it look a little dull. You can fix that in a hurry by borrowing some components from the Components window (Windows → Components). Choose the Select tab, and then choose Landscape from the drop-down menu. Inside you find folders with names like Built Constructions or Exterior Furniture. Browse through the folders and drag out some additions to go along with your bench. You can find everything from arbors to picnic tables to water fountains. Experiment to see the wild variety SketchUp gives you, as in Figure 1-34. If you change your mind and want to remove a component, just select it and press Delete. If you're really adventurous, you can double-click your way into some of the other components to see how they're built.

Congratulations on building your first SketchUp model. Happy landscaping and exploring!

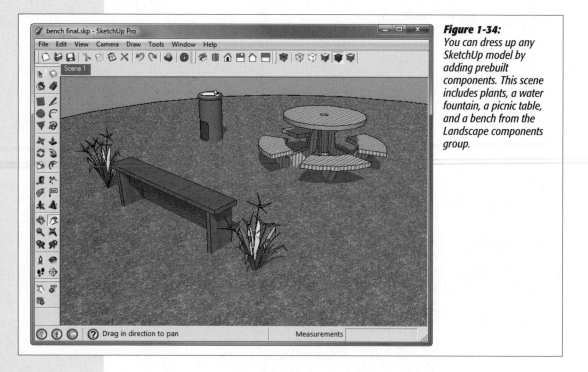

Figure 1-34:
You can dress up any SketchUp model by adding prebuilt components. This scene includes plants, a water fountain, a picnic table, and a bench from the Landscape components group.

Starting Off in Two Dimensions

Every SketchUp model begins with drawing lines and shapes in two dimensions—and that's the focus of this chapter. After you create 2-D shapes, you use the Push/Pull tool to turn them into 3-D objects, as you'll see in the next chapter. The better you understand all the nuances of drawing lines and creating surfaces in two dimensions, the more success you'll have creating 3-D models.

If you've used other 2-D graphics programs like Adobe Illustrator or CorelDraw, you may be tempted to skip this chapter and jump right into the juicy 3-D stuff, but at least give this chapter a quick review. SketchUp breaks some of the rules when it comes to drawing—that's part of the reason the program can create accurate 3-D objects so quickly. In the first part of this chapter, you'll learn about the behavior of SketchUp's edges (lines) and faces. Also important, you'll learn to take advantage of the unique Measurements toolbar to set precise dimensions quickly.

Drawing Lines with the Line Tool

For any artist, the line is one of the most basic tools, and that's true for SketchUp masters, too. In SketchUp, lines are called *edges* because they define the edges of 2-D shapes and 3-D objects. When you use a shape tool like the Rectangle, you create four edges and a single face in one stroke. SketchUp has so many great tools for creating standard shapes such as rectangles, circles, and polygons that you'll probably use the Line tool mostly to modify other shapes and to make complex or irregularly shaped objects.

Think back to geometry class, and you'll remember that a line connects two points. That's a good way to remember that in SketchUp you should draw lines by clicking a start point, moving your mouse, and then clicking the endpoint. As is almost always the case in SketchUp, the click-move-click method works better than the click-and-drag method you may use in other programs.

For this exercise use the Architectural Design – Feet and Inches template. If that's not the template that appears when you create a new document, go to Help → Welcome to SketchUp. When the welcome window opens, click the Template button, and then choose the "Architectural Design – Feet and Inches" template. When you create a new document, "Architectural Design – Feet and Inches" template displays a plane for the ground, a slightly blue sky, and the 2-D SketchUp model, Sang. If you don't need Sang's supervision while you work, you can delete him from the scene.

Note: Sang is one of the many two-dimensional people models that you find in the Components window (Window → Components). You use these models to dress up architectural or outdoor scenes and to provide a sense of scale. SketchUp has a tradition of using people from the SketchUp programming team as models. Sang—as well as Bryce in earlier versions of SketchUp—are so honored.

1. **Choose Camera → Standard Views → Top.**

    Your view changes so you're looking down at the drawing area. When you're drawing 2-D objects in SketchUp, it's easiest if you're in one of the standard views: Front, Back, Top, Left, or Right. Because these views are aligned with one of the basic axes, you're less likely to create off-axis lines or shapes that straddle a plane in 3-D space.

2. **From the toolbar, choose the Line tool (pencil icon).**

    The cursor changes to a pencil, and right away the status bar (lower-left corner) suggests what to do next: "Select a start point."

3. **In the drawing area, click where you want the line to begin.**

    The status bar hint changes to "Select endpoint or enter value."

Tip: You can use the keyboard here to type a precise length value for your line in lieu of eyeballing and clicking. You'll see an example of that in step 6 on page 62.

4. **Move the mouse.**

    A rubber band line follows the pencil cursor around the screen, showing you where your line will be when you click. In the lower-right corner the Measurements toolbar tells you what length the line will be when you click.

5. **Click to finish your line.**

Your line is drawn. There's still a rubber band action from the tip of the pencil cursor: SketchUp's all ready for you to draw another line. Your drawing area looks something like Figure 2-1.

6. **Draw another line from the endpoint or press Esc to stop.**

SketchUp can't imagine that you'd want to draw just one line, so you're ready to keep on drawing lines. Just keep clicking to draw more lines. If you don't want to draw a line from the last endpoint, press Esc or choose another tool.

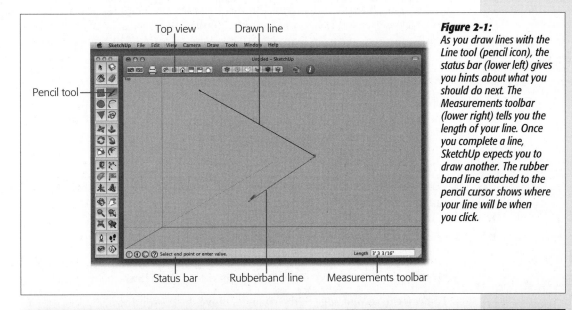

Figure 2-1:
As you draw lines with the Line tool (pencil icon), the status bar (lower left) gives you hints about what you should do next. The Measurements toolbar (lower right) tells you the length of your line. Once you complete a line, SketchUp expects you to draw another. The rubber band line attached to the pencil cursor shows where your line will be when you click.

Top view   Drawn line

Pencil tool

Status bar   Rubberband line   Measurements toolbar

UP TO SPEED

Esc vs. Undo

Remember (page 44) that the Esc key cancels a current action, so if you're in the midst of drawing a line with the rubber band on the tip of the Line tool, pressing Esc stops that action. The Undo command (Ctrl+Z on a PC; ⌘-Z on a Mac) undoes the last action that you completed. So suppose you just drew a rectangle and then chose the Line tool.

You clicked to create your starting point for your line and now choose the Undo command. SketchUp deletes your rectangle, because that was the last *completed* action. On the other hand, if you press Esc in the same situation, SketchUp removes the line's starting point, and the rubber band line disappears.

Drawing a Triangle with the Line Tool

You can draw shapes using the Line tool, or you can use one of the specific shape tools—Rectangle, Circle, or Polygon. If your shape is irregular, though, the Line tool is the only way to go. One of the reasons you can draw so quickly in SketchUp is that it always anticipates what you want to do and gives you hints to make the job easier. Drawing shapes with the Line tool is a perfect example. Follow these steps to draw a triangle:

1. **With the Line tool, click to create a start point.**

   Make sure you're in the Top view, as you were in the previous exercise. You're creating one of the top points of your triangle, so be sure to start near the top of the drawing window, and leave room to draw your triangle below.

2. **In the drawing area, move the pencil cursor vertically from the start point.**

   The rubber band line follows your cursor around the drawing area. When the rubber band line is nearly parallel to the green axis (which indicates vertical in Top view), it snaps into position and a tooltip appears that says "On Green Axis", as shown at top in Figure 2-2. To create the top line of the triangle, you have to draw a horizontal line, so…

3. **Move the pencil cursor horizontally away from the start point.**

   When the rubber band line is nearly parallel to the red axis, it snaps into position and temporarily turns red; a tooltip appears that says "On Red Axis". When your line isn't aligned with any of the axes, no tooltip appears, as shown at the bottom of Figure 2-2.

Tip: Once your line is "on axis," holding down the Shift key constrains it to the axis. In other words, even if your mouse drifts a bit, the line is still drawn on the axis.

---

4. **Click a point on the red axis to draw one edge of the triangle.**

   Your first line (known as an *edge* in SketchUp-speak) is complete. The rubber band line is still attached to your pencil cursor, ready to draw the next line.

5. **To draw the second edge of the triangle, move the cursor down.**

   When the rubber band line is parallel with the green axis, you see the tooltip message "On Green Axis". The Measurements toolbar tells you how long your second line will be if you click now.

6. **Type *12* and the foot mark ('), and then press Enter.**

   Your second line is completed using the exact length you entered: 12'. To draw a line that's a precise length, it's easiest to enter a number in the Measurements toolbar. Remember, you never have to click in the Measurements toolbar to enter a number; just start drawing your line and then type the number. It automatically appears in the Measurements toolbar as you type.

Tip: Use the standard ' symbol for feet to tell SketchUp you're entering a dimension in feet; otherwise SketchUp assumes you're entering a dimension in inches. To enter a dimension that includes both feet and inches, just type it as you normally would. For example: *12'6"*.

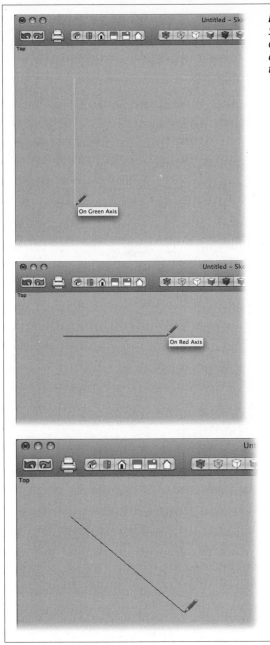

Figure 2-2:
*SketchUp knows that many of your lines will be parallel to one
of the three axes, so as you draw lines, they snap to the axes,
and a tooltip appears telling you when you're drawing along
the red, green, or blue axis.*

7. Move the pencil cursor horizontally back in the direction of the very first starting point as if you were drawing a rectangle.

   If your cursor is parallel to the red axis, you'll see the tooltip confirmation.

Note: When your cursor approaches a point perpendicular to the starting point of the first line, it snaps to that point—and you see a green dotted line from the starting point of the first line to the cursor. That's the *inference line*. It's SketchUp's way of saying "click now and you'll be aligned with this point."

8. **Move the pencil cursor to the midpoint of the first (horizontal) line.**

   When you get close to the midpoint, the cursor snaps into place and a tooltip appears that reads "*Midpoint*", as shown in Figure 2-3.

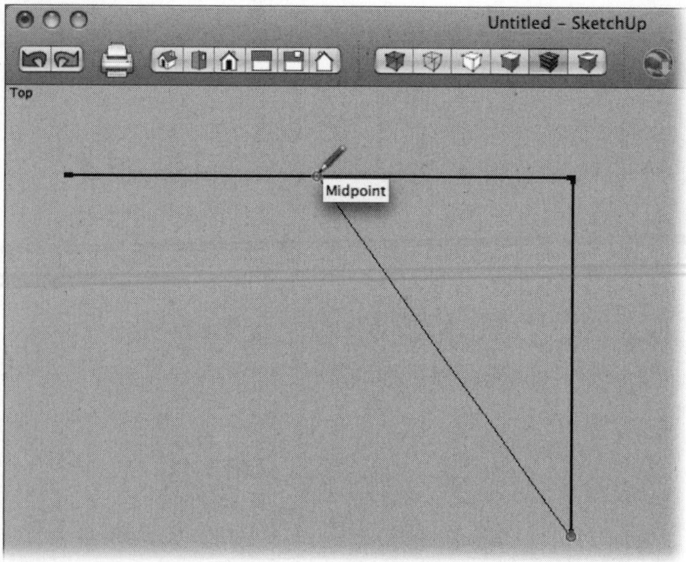

Figure 2-3:
Move most tools along a line, and they snap to the midpoint. As confirmation, you see a tooltip with the message "Midpoint". As you practice with SketchUp, get used to finding midpoints and endpoints in edges (lines), since you'll be using them a lot.

9. **Move the Line tool straight down in the drawing window to create an inference line.**

   As long as you move parallel to the green axis, you see a dotted, green inference line. Don't click the inference point yet; you'll learn what to do with inference points in later exercises. (You can find more details on inferences in the box on page 66.)

10. **Move the Line tool to the midpoint in the second (vertical) line, and create an inference line from that midpoint by moving the cursor horizontally.**

   SketchUp displays tooltips and displays inference lines whenever you near the midpoint for any edge (line) in your drawing area. This feature comes in handy when you're drawing more complex shapes.

11. **Complete the triangle by clicking the starting point of your first line.**

   When your cursor gets near the endpoint of the first line, it snaps to that point. SketchUp is guessing where you're headed. When you're done drawing the last line, all the lines turn into thick lines, and the face formed by the lines fills in with a color.

SketchUp fills in the face between edges under two conditions:

- First, all the edges must be connected in a closed loop.

- Second, the endpoints for those edges must be on the same plane. Figure 2-4 shows what happens when one of the endpoints isn't on the same plane.

In other words, when three or more edges form a closed loop, and they're all on the same plane, SketchUp fills in the interior face formed by the edges. If there's a break in the loop, there's no face to fill in.

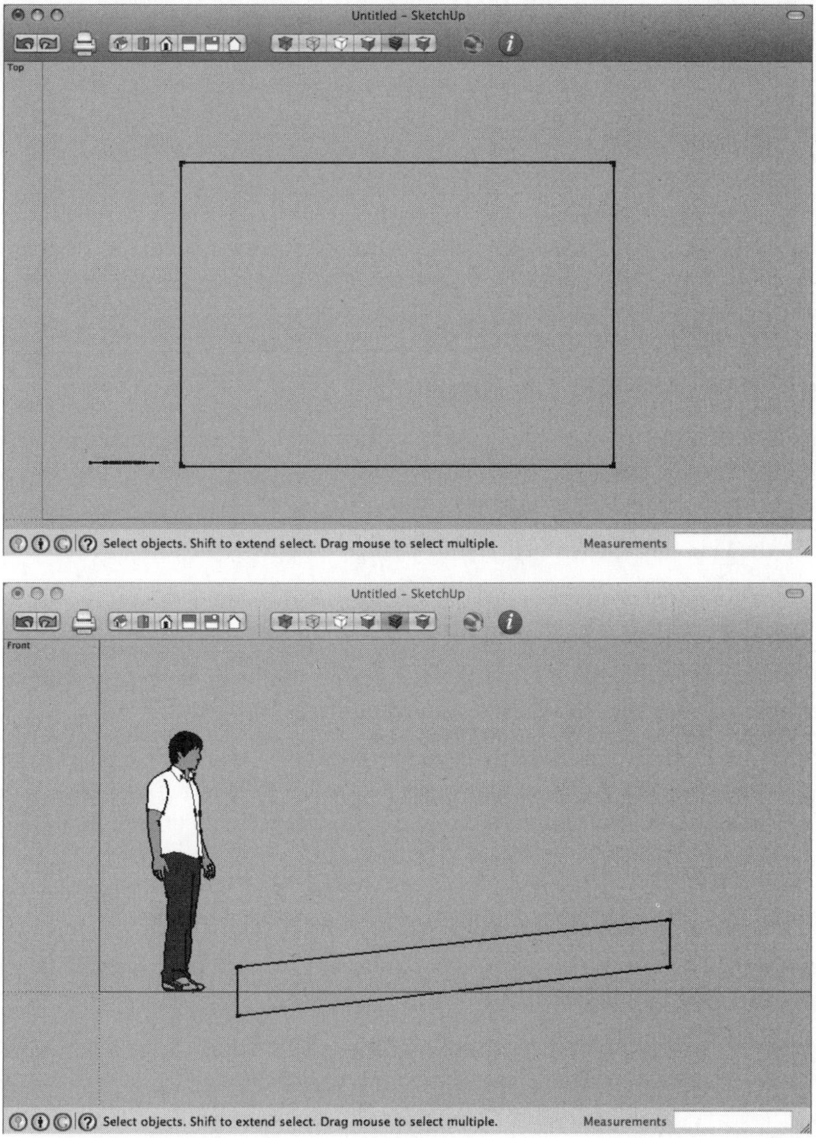

Figure 2-4:
Top: When you view this object from the top, it may look like a trapezoid, with all the endpoints on the same plane.

Bottom: Viewed from the front it's clear that one of the endpoints is not on the same plane, so there's actually no complete trapezoid.

Your Friend, the Inference

One of the concepts that makes SketchUp such a quick and easy drawing tool is the inference. Want to find the mid-point on a line? Slowly move your cursor down that line; it snaps to an inference point and sprouts a tooltip that reads "Midpoint". Want to align the endpoints of several parallel lines? It's easy if you let inference lines guide you. SketchUp is pretty good at guessing where to draw temporary inference guidelines. If it's not showing you a line you need, let the program know by showing interest in a particular point. Just hover your cursor over a point long enough to coax a tooltip from the point. Then return to drawing your line.

Because you've shown recent interest in that particular point, SketchUp shows inference lines when you reach related points in the drawing area.

If an inference line is showing and your mouse moves away from the inference line, the line disappears. SketchUp assumes that you're not interested in that particular inference. Sometimes it takes a steady hand and a little practice to move the cursor and keep an inference line displayed. Just move slowly and steadily. If necessary, try zooming in on the drawing area a little more.

Tip: If you can't see the status bar or the Measurements toolbar at the bottom of your SketchUp window, the bottom of the window may be extending below the bottom edge of your screen. Use the maximize button to make your window fill the available screen space. On a PC, the maximize button is the rectangle button in the upper right; on a Mac, it's the green dot in the upper left.

Turning a Triangle into a Rectangle

As mentioned earlier in this chapter, you can use the Line tool (pencil) to modify existing shapes. For example, with the help of inference lines, you can use the Line tool to turn your triangle into a perfect rectangle.

1. **With the Line tool (pencil), click your triangle's upper-left endpoint.**

    A green dot appears on the endpoint, signaling that it's an endpoint for the new line you're drawing.

2. **Move the cursor along the green axis (vertically) until you see the red inference line coming from the triangle's lowest endpoint.**

    When you reach a point level with the lowest point of your triangle, a dotted red inference line appears, as shown in Figure 2-5. It's dotted to indicate that it's an inference line; it's red to indicate that it's aligned with the red axis.

3. **Click to finish the line.**

    You still need to connect one more line to complete the rectangle.

4. **Draw a final line over to the lowest endpoint of your triangle to complete your rectangle, as shown in Figure 2-6.**

    The second triangular face you created fills in, completing a rectangular face. Your rectangle now has four heavy lines around the perimeter.

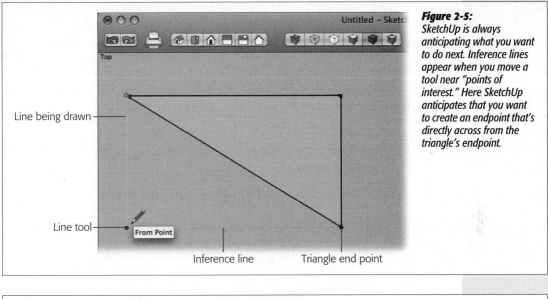

Figure 2-5:
SketchUp is always anticipating what you want to do next. Inference lines appear when you move a tool near "points of interest." Here SketchUp anticipates that you want to create an endpoint that's directly across from the triangle's endpoint.

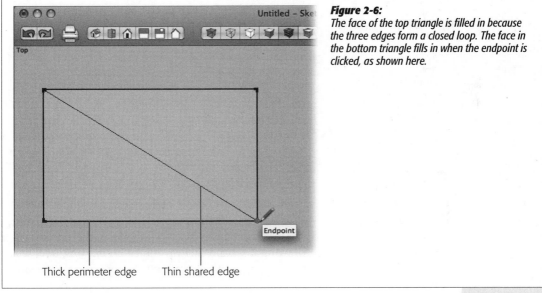

Figure 2-6:
The face of the top triangle is filled in because the three edges form a closed loop. The face in the bottom triangle fills in when the endpoint is clicked, as shown here.

Erasing Lines and Surfaces

Often when you modify existing shapes to create more complex shapes, you end up with extra, interior lines, like the diagonal running across the rectangle in Figure 2-6. A little cleanup with the Eraser tool (Tools → Eraser or E) takes care of the problem; just click the line you want to remove and it disappears.

You can erase a shape's face, too, but you can't do it with one click of the Eraser tool. If you could, it would be too easy to accidentally erase faces when you're trying to click edges! To erase a face, you need to choose a command from a shortcut menu, as shown in Figure 2-7. You can bring up the shortcut menu simply by right-clicking the face. (If you're on a Mac and don't have a three-button mouse, press Control as you click.) Shortcut menus, by the way, show commands related to the selected object or to the object immediately below the cursor. So, for example, you can access a command like Erase even when you're using a drawing tool.

Note: Shortcut menus are also called pop-up menus or context menus, because their commands are related to the item beneath the cursor.

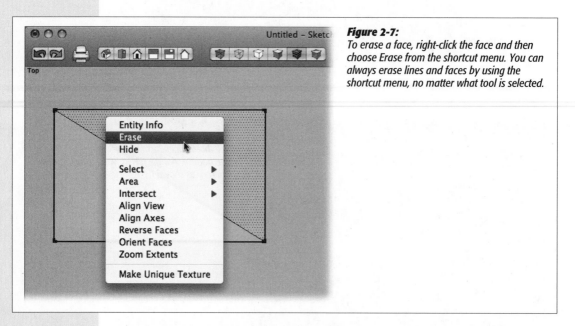

Figure 2-7:
To erase a face, right-click the face and then choose Erase from the shortcut menu. You can always erase lines and faces by using the shortcut menu, no matter what tool is selected.

To renew a surface that you've erased or that's disappeared while you were editing an object, use the Line tool to trace back over the edges that form the surface. Even though you appear to be drawing a second line on top of an existing line, when you're done, SketchUp just sees a single line. Technically, the process of renewing a surface is called *healing* the surface.

You can practice by erasing the edges in your rectangle. Use the Undo command (Ctrl+Z or ⌘-Z) to restore the lines you want to keep. When you erase the diagonal edge that's shared by the two triangles, only the line disappears and the rectangle has a single face.

Note: The thin lines are known as *shared* edges because they're shared by two surfaces. See the box on page 76.

If you erase one of the four edges that form your rectangle, a face disappears because the edges no longer form a closed loop. If you close the loop by drawing a line between the two open endpoints, the face fills in again.

When you're finished experimenting, save your SketchUp document so it has a simple rectangle without the diagonal edge.

Adding a Face to Create a New Shape

On page 66 you modified a triangle by adding lines and surfaces to create a rectangle. You can also modify shapes by divvying them up and *removing* lines. The following steps remove part of your rectangle to create a triangle. Start with a simple rectangle with no interior lines, like the one from the previous exercise. Or create a new one for good practice.

1. **Draw a diagonal line across the rectangle to divide it into two triangles.**

    Make sure your line is connected to the endpoints in the corners of the rectangle. It's not difficult, since SketchUp's snap-to action takes over when you click near an endpoint.

2. **With the Eraser tool, erase the left and bottom edges.**

    When you erase the first line, you break the loop that creates the face, so the face disappears, as shown in Figure 2-8.

As the previous exercises show, the Line tool is great for modifying existing shapes (whether you draw them with the pencil or with the shape tools described later in this chapter). You can modify shapes either by adding new lines outside the shape to create larger shapes, or, with the help of the Eraser tool, you can draw interior lines to slice and dice a shape.

Drawing Polygons and Circles

Drawing polygons and circles is easier than drawing shapes with the Line tool. For perfect shapes like the ones in this section, the *radius*—the distance from the center to an endpoint on the perimeter—is the key dimension that determines its size. The other defining element is the number of sides. Begin with a new document (File → New), and then follow these steps to create the simplest of polygons—the triangle.

1. **Click on the Polygon tool in the toolbar, or choose Draw → Polygon from the menu.**

    The cursor for polygons is the pencil, just like the one for drawing lines.

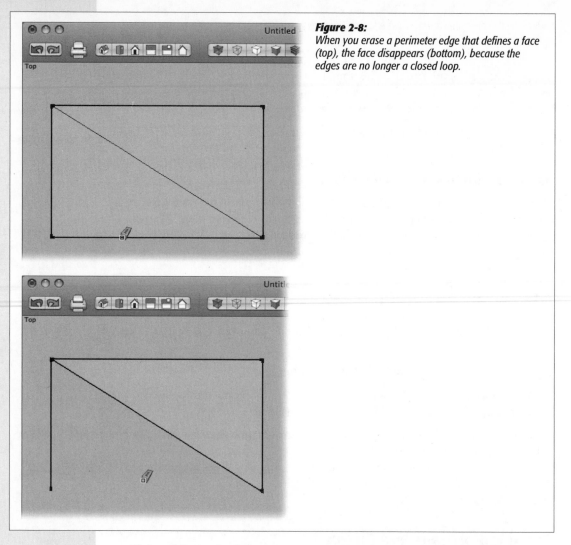

Figure 2-8:
When you erase a perimeter edge that defines a face (top), the face disappears (bottom), because the edges are no longer a closed loop.

2. **Click a point in the drawing area, and then release the mouse button.**

   Remember to click-move-click—don't click and drag. Your first click defines the center point for the polygon.

3. **Move the cursor to define the radius of the polygon (but don't click yet).**

   As shown in Figure 2-9, SketchUp initially uses a six-sided polygon, but it's easy enough to change the number of sides, as shown in the next step.

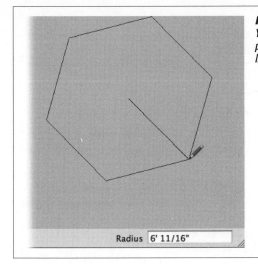

Figure 2-9:
*You draw polygons by clicking a center point and then clicking a
perimeter point to set the radius. As you move the cursor, the VCB
lists the radius.*

Radius 6' 11/16"

4. **Type *3s* for three sides and then press Enter.**

The polygon changes to a triangle (Figure 2-10). As always, there's no need to
click in the Measurements toolbar to enter a number; just start typing. But you
do need to set the number of sides before you click anywhere. In fact, you can
set the number of sides as soon as you click the Polygon tool. Just remember to
type the number of sides, the letter *s* (so SketchUp knows you're talking sides,
not dimensions), and press Enter.

5. **In another part of the drawing area, create a second polygon.**

SketchUp creates a triangle because it remembers the last type of polygon you
created. If you want, you can change the number of sides by typing a new value.

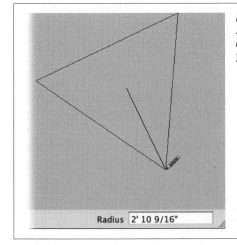

Figure 2-10:
*Set the number of sides for your polygon by entering the number and the
letter s. Set the radius by entering a number and the unit of measure. (If
you don't enter a unit of measure, SketchUp uses inches.)*

Radius 2' 10 9/16"

Tip: If you ever need to break a polygon or a circle into parts so that you can work with the pieces, right-click its edge and then choose Explode Curve from the shortcut menu. This maneuver breaks the shape into a face and individual lines—all selectable and movable.

Changing the Radius of a Polygon

After you've clicked to mark your polygon's center point, you can set a precise dimension for the radius. Just type a number along with the appropriate unit of measure, such as feet (') or inches ("). Table 2-1 shows the different symbols you can use for units of measure.

Table 2-1. *The Measurements toolbar is very obliging when it comes to units of measure. It uses whatever you throw at it, as long as you include the correct symbol. You can mix symbols, as in 6'5". You can even mix English and metric in the same document.*

Unit of Measure	Measurements Toolbar Symbol
Inches	"
Feet	'
Millimeters	mm
Centimeters	cm
Meters	m

Changing a Polygon Using the Entity Info Window

Suppose you've created an octagon and a few steps later decided that what you really need is a hexagon. How do you edit a polygon after you've moved on and done other things in SketchUp? Easy—turn to the Entity Info window (Windows → Entity Info), as shown in Figure 2-11.

Before the Entity Info window can give you details, it needs to know which of the many items in your SketchUp drawing you want to examine. So the first step is to select an object. When you click one of your polygon's edges, you select all edges defining your polygon, and the Entity Info window provides details like the radius and the number of segments (sides). The Length entry gives a rough estimate of the distance around the polygon's perimeter.

If you select the polygon's face, the Entity Info window provides information about the face rather than the edges. So instead of Length, for example, you'll see a number defining the face's surface area. That's handy if you're calculating how much flooring or siding you need for your new beach cottage.

To make changes to your polygon, you edit the same numbers you used to create it. Make sure you've selected the edges, not the surface. Then type a new number of segments (sides) and a new radius. In fact you can use the Entity Info window to examine and modify anything in the drawing area.

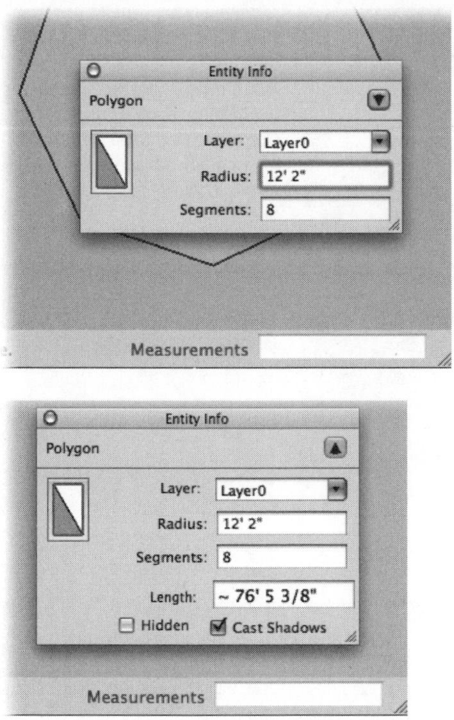

Figure 2-11:
The Entity Info window not only provides info, it also gives you a quick way to edit selected objects. A simple version of the Entity Info window (top) shows the options you most often want to change. Click the triangle button to see more entity info (bottom).

Note: You can't change a polygon when its surface is selected, and you can't directly change the length or area settings. Instead click the edges of the polygon and make changes to the radius.

Drawing Circles

Once you've mastered polygons, creating circles is a cinch, since they work almost exactly the same way. Click to set the center point; release the mouse button; move to a new point to determine the radius; and click again. The face of your circle fills in because it's automatically a closed loop in one plane.

If you want to create a precise circle, you can enter a specific dimension for the radius. In that case, click to set the center point, and then type the dimension and measurement symbol—like *6'*—and then press Enter. SketchUp automatically draws your circle using 6 feet as the radius. You can change the dimension in the Measurements toolbar as many times as you want by typing a new number and pressing Enter. (After you go on to a new tool or command, you'll need to use the Entity Info window to make changes.)

When you open the Entity Info window, you learn one of SketchUp's little secrets—a circle is not a circle. It's actually a 24-sided polygon, as shown in Figure 2-12.

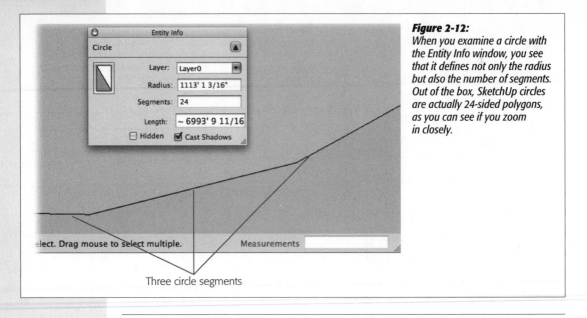

Figure 2-12:
When you examine a circle with the Entity Info window, you see that it defines not only the radius but also the number of segments. Out of the box, SketchUp circles are actually 24-sided polygons, as you can see if you zoom in closely.

Three circle segments

Tip: If you're doing more complicated work with circles, you may find it easier to change the segments from 24 to 36 segments. That not only smoothes your circle slightly, it makes it easier to perform circle math in 360 degrees.

Creating Complex Shapes

Whether you're designing a new luxury home, an Adirondack chair, or a new hi-tech device, chances are you're going to use some irregular shapes. You can create complex shapes from scratch with the Line tool, or you can use circles and polygons as a starting point. Then you can use the Line and Eraser tools to make modifications. That process is sometimes called *editing an object's geometry,* and it involves adding or subtracting edges and surface area from the original object. The next few examples focus on drawing a two-dimensional, cartoonish character—you can call him Skeeter. If you want to add some of your own touches, feel free. This section is all about drawing complex and irregular shapes.

1. **Using the Line tool (pencil), draw Skeeter's face—a four-sided polygon like the one in Figure 2-13.**

   Make your polygon in the top half of the drawing area, and leave some room at the top to add to it. (The polygon doesn't have to align with the axis.)

2. **Click the Select tool, and then select the polygon's top line.**

   The entire line changes to a highlight color when it's selected showing that it's a single line segment.

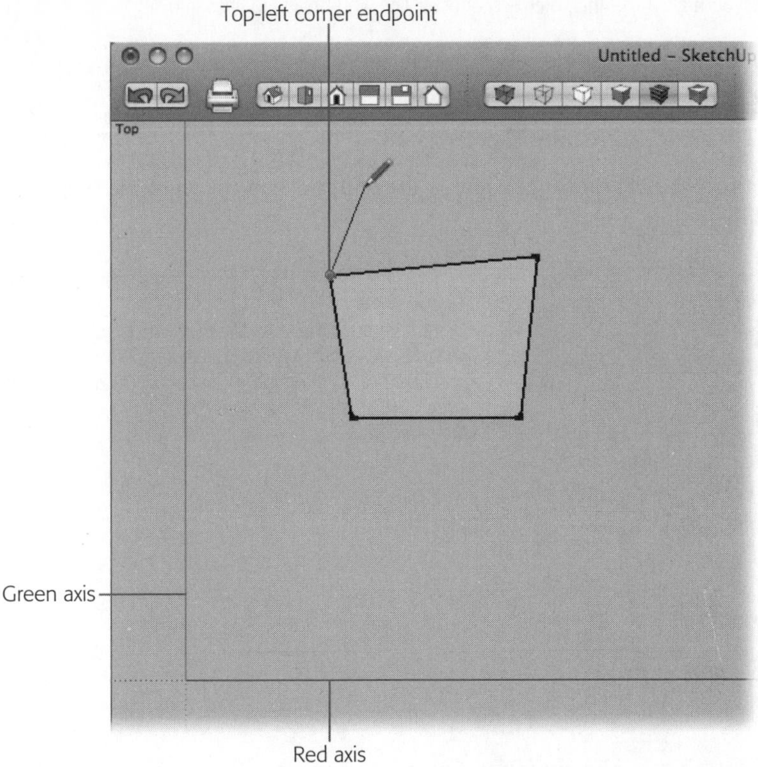

Top-left corner endpoint

Figure 2-13:
Your polygon doesn't have to align with any of the axes for this exercise. In Top view, you see lines representing the green and red axes.

Green axis

Red axis

3. **With the Line tool (pencil) hover over different parts of the polygon, and note how the point of the pencil changes color and shape.**

   When you're over the face of the polygon, the pencil point is a blue square and a tooltip says "On Face". Hover over an endpoint, and the point turns into a green circle and the tooltip says "Endpoint". For midpoints, the circle changes to cyan (light blue), and, you guessed it, the tooltip says "Midpoint". When you're on the edge but not over an endpoint or midpoint, the color is red, and the tooltip reads "On Edge". (Please note, when it says "On Edge", SketchUp isn't reporting on its emotional well-being.)

4. **With the Line tool, click the top-left endpoint to begin drawing a line, as shown in Figure 2-13.**

   When it's near the endpoint, the Line tool snaps to the point. After you click, a rubber band line extends from the endpoint to the tip of the pencil cursor.

5. **Draw a triangle that projects from the top of the polygon with both of the bottom points attached to its top line, as shown in Figure 2-14.**

   By drawing the lines for the triangle, you split that top line of the polygon into two segments. You can double-check this by moving the Line tool along the top line. You now have two midpoints, one for each line segment.

Tip: Anytime you draw a line that intersects another line, you break the lines into segments at the intersection point.

6. **Still using the pencil, continue to draw a series of jagged lines like the ones in Figure 2-14. You're creating Skeeter's hair.**

   When you complete the jagged line at the endpoint on the right, the face fills in with a solid color.

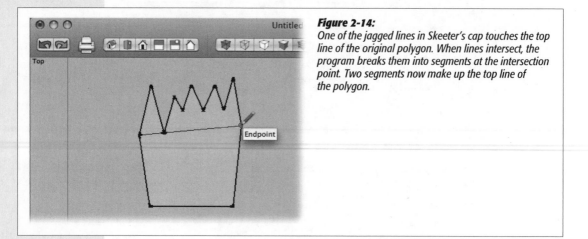

Figure 2-14:
One of the jagged lines in Skeeter's cap touches the top line of the original polygon. When lines intersect, the program breaks them into segments at the intersection point. Two segments now make up the top line of the polygon.

7. **Use the Eraser to remove the thin interior lines in the drawing.**

   The thin lines are known as *shared* edges because they're shared by two surfaces. See the box on this page.

8. **Choose the Arc tool, and then click the polygon's lower-left endpoint.**

   As shown in Figure 2-15, creating an arc is a three-point affair. First you draw a straight line between two points, and then you set a third point to bend your arc into the desired shape.

UP TO SPEED

Edges Bold and Thin

The Architectural Design template uses a feature called Profiles, which gives you visual cues about the edges in your drawings. Edges with bold lines are profiles or perimeter edges. Erase a profile edge, and the face disappears because you broke the closed loop that forms the face. Edges with thin lines are called *shared* edges, meaning that the edge is shared by two surfaces. Erasing a shared edge joins the two surfaces, creating a larger, single face. Sometimes as you create complex or irregular shapes, you end up with unneeded shared edges as a natural result of the drawing process. The shared edges are unneeded because they no longer define the shape. In that case, you're best off erasing the shared edges. Always keep your model as simple as possible, and you'll be able to work faster with fewer headaches.

---

9. Click the rectangle's lower-right point to complete Skeeter's chin.

You're creating a straight line that's identical to the rectangle's lower line.

10. Move the Arc tool below the rectangle, and then click to set the arc's radius.

As you move the cursor, the arc changes shape. There's a snapping point that creates a half circle. For the chin, you want an arc that's a little shallower than a half circle.

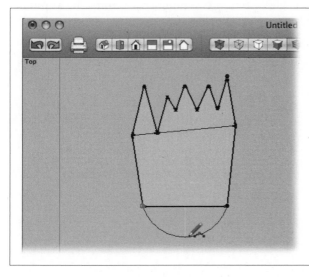

Figure 2-15:
To draw an arc, set two endpoints of a line, and then set the radius of the arc with a third point. When it's complete, this chin arc joins with the existing face polygon to create a closed loop, so the face fills in.

Drawing Rectangles and Arcs

If you're like most SketchUp artists, you'll be drawing lots of rectangles. Some may stay rectangles, while you might slice and dice others into more complex shapes. It's easy enough to create a rectangle. You can simply click-move-click to set two points in the drawing area, or you can click to set a corner and then type in specific dimensions. Drawing arcs is a three-click process in SketchUp. You click twice to set the endpoints of a line, and your third click sets the curve of the arc. The Arc tool even snaps to a point to create perfect half circles.

You'll see rectangles and arcs in action as you create Skeeter's shirt and mouth.

1. Choose the Rectangle tool, and then draw a rectangle in the lower portion of the drawing area.

As you size your rectangle, you may notice that the Rectangle tool snaps to either of two shapes—the square or the *golden section*—usually known as the golden rectangle.

Architect's Glossary: Architects and artists have called the *golden rectangle* the "divine proportion" for centuries. The proportion is roughly 1:1.618. This proportion is the "golden ratio" symbolized in math by the Greek letter phi. If you remove a square from a golden rectangle, the remainder forms another golden rectangle.

The Parthenon in Ancient Greece is an early example of the golden section used in architecture. Centuries later, Leonardo da Vinci was another big fan.

2. **Adjust the size of the rectangle by typing two numbers separated by a comma, as in *28', 16'*. Press Enter to complete the change.**

    You enter two dimensions to form a rectangle: the width and the height, using a comma to separate the numbers. As always, you don't need to click in the Measurements toolbar to enter a number. You can always change your rectangle's dimensions by entering new numbers (Figure 2-16).

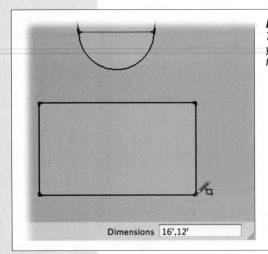

Figure 2-16:
The Rectangle tool's cursor is a pencil with a square. You size your rectangle by typing dimensions. Be sure to use the ' symbol for feet. Otherwise SketchUp assumes your dimension is in inches.

Dimensions 16',12'

3. **With the Arc tool, click the rectangle's left edge.**

    You can choose any spot near the middle of the edge.

4. **Move the Arc tool to the top edge of the rectangle, and click to set a point that creates a 45-degree angle.**

    As you move the cursor over the top line, the tool snaps to a point that creates a 45-degree angle. The line formed by the Arc tool turns magenta.

5. **Set the third point to form an arc that's tangent to both edges.**

    As you move the Arc tool, the curve formed by the arc is black, unless it's snapping to a specific form. When the arc is tangent to the edge, the arc line turns magenta and a tooltip says "Tangent to Edge".

Architect's Glossary: A *tangent line* is a line that touches a curve at a single point where it's closer to the curve than at any other point.

6. **Create an arc on the other side of the rectangle so that it's also tangent to both edges.**

    When you set your first two points, make sure they create a 45-degree angle. Otherwise the arc can only be tangent to one of the two edges. (Sorry, nothing you can do about it; that's just geometry.)

7. **Erase the line segments to create curved corners on the top of the rectangle, as shown in Figure 2-17.**

    If the surface disappears after you erase the edges, you can heal the surface (page 68) by tracing over one of the existing edges.

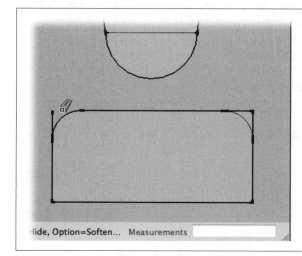

Figure 2-17:
When you first draw the arcs in the rectangle, they each create a shared edge and an additional face. When you erase the line segments at the corner, the face disappears and the arc becomes the perimeter edge, as shown by the bold line on the left.

8. **On Skeeter's head, erase the shared edge (straight line) that connects the top of the arc.**

    When the shared edge is erased, Skeeter's head and hair consist of a single face defined by many different perimeter edges.

9. **Using the Arc tool, draw a mouth on Skeeter's face surface.**

    Initially, the arc is simply an arc. As far as SketchUp is concerned, the arc does not define any surfaces.

10. **Use the Line tool to draw a straight line that closes the arc.**

    Once you create a closed shape, you have two separate surfaces (inside the mouth and outside the mouth), so the edges become shared edges.

    Now Skeeter needs some eyes, which you can create with simple circles.

11. **Use the Circle tool to draw two eyes.**

    The complete circles also create shared edges.

12. **Right-click (⌘-click on a Mac with a single-button mouse) each eye and the
    mouth, and choose Erase from the shortcut menus.**

    The interior faces for the eyes and mouth disappear. You don't have to choose
    the Eraser tool to erase the surfaces; just right-click them and choose Erase from
    the shortcut menu.

Using the Freehand Tool

In the toolbar you find the Freehand tool under the Line and Arc tools, or choose
Tools → Freehand. There's an exception to almost every rule, and for SketchUp,
it's the Freehand tool. This tool is the one drawing tool that you use by dragging,
not click-move-clicking. This flexibility gives you the ability to draw a line that follows any shape you create. Freehand lines have a starting point, where you first
click, and an ending point, where you release the mouse button. In between the
two points, the line follows everywhere you go with your mouse. SketchUp considers
a freehand line to be a single object and keeps that shape unless you bisect the line,
in which case it turns into separate line segments.

In these steps, you'll use the Freehand tool to draw two ears for Skeeter SketchUp:

1. **Using the Freehand tool, find a good point for the top of the ear. Click and
   hold the mouse button.**

   When the mouse is over the line that qdefines the head, you see a tooltip message
   "On Edge", meaning that's where you'll connect the ear to the head.

2. **Drag to trace the shape of the ear, and then click another point on the head's
   edge to complete the ear.**

   As you trace, a line forms in the trail of your Freehand cursor.

3. **When you're back over the edge of the face, release the mouse button to set the
   ear's endpoint.**

   The face defined by the ear shape fills in when you close the shape. The line
   dividing the surface of the ear and the surface of the face is a shared edge, as
   shown in Figure 2-18. If your results are different, consult the box on page 81.

4. **Repeat the steps to create a second ear for Skeeter.**

   When you finish the second ear, Skeeter has two eyes, two ears, and a mouth. If
   you think he also deserves a nose, you're on your own.

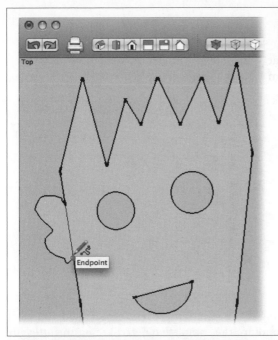

Figure 2-18:
If your freehand line is connected properly to two points on the edge of the face, the line between the ear and the face is a thin line, indicating that it's a shared edge.

GEM IN THE ROUGH

Freehand Line Gotchas

One of the benefits of the Freehand tool is that you can create an irregular line that moves as a single object. It doesn't lose its shape, even if you connect it to other parts of your drawing, as with Skeeter's ears. For it to work properly, the freehand line's endpoints have to be connected to single points of the edge defining the head. You can't connect the freehand endpoint to the face's surface; that won't create a closed loop. Also, the endpoints of your freehand line can touch only on a single point. For example, if at the end of the line you trace over part of the edge, the ear breaks up into several line segments instead of remaining a single, fixed shape.

Moving Objects

It's highly unlikely that you'll draw everything exactly where you want it. Instead, you'll probably move objects around all the time. The Move tool looks like a cross with arrowheads on each tip. You use the click-move-click method to move SketchUp objects, and more often than not, you want to move them with precision. For example, suppose you want to place a door at a specific location in a wall. First you click the corner of the door; then you move the mouse to the wall and find exactly where you want to place that corner of the door. Click that spot and voilà! Door installed, as shown in Figure 2-19.

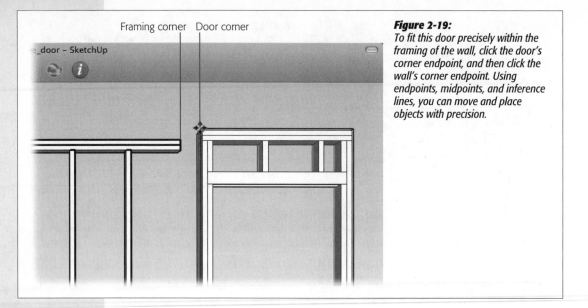

Framing corner   Door corner

_door – SketchUp

Figure 2-19:
To fit this door precisely within the framing of the wall, click the door's corner endpoint, and then click the wall's corner endpoint. Using endpoints, midpoints, and inference lines, you can move and place objects with precision.

A major part of moving something is the selection process, especially if you want to move just an edge or a point and not the complete object. Skeeter, the little guy you drew earlier in this chapter, makes a good testing ground for different selection and moving techniques.

Moving a Face

To move a face (surface), choose the Select tool, and then click anywhere on the face, as shown in Figure 2-20. Move the cursor to a new spot, and then click to place the face there. You can think of this action as clicking to pick up an object and then clicking again to place it down. When you move an object by selecting the face, the face and the edges that define it all move together. If you're in the midst of a move and change your mind, pressing Esc undoes the move, putting you back at the beginning. If you've completed the move with the second click, use Edit → Undo (Ctrl+Z or ⌘-Z).

If you want to move a precise distance, begin the move, type a number for the distance, and then press Enter. The number appears in the Measurements toolbar, and the object moves that distance. You can make an object move in the opposite direction that you started moving by typing a negative number. The object goes back to the original spot and then moves in the opposite direction by the distance entered in the Measurements toolbar.

You can select an object with the Select tool and then use the Move tool. In this case you don't have to click the object to move it. Click anywhere in the drawing area to set a start point; then as you begin to move, the selected object moves the same distance and the same direction. This scheme is helpful when you want to make a move measured by other existing objects. Suppose you want to place a series of windows in a wall. With the select-and-move method, you can use the distance between the first two windows to create the distance between all of the rest.

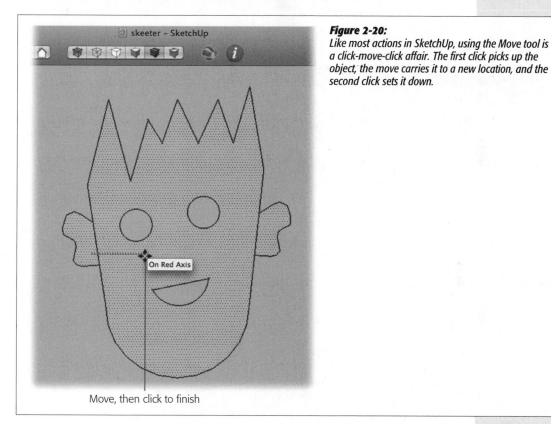

Figure 2-20:
Like most actions in SketchUp, using the Move tool is a click-move-click affair. The first click picks up the object, the move carries it to a new location, and the second click sets it down.

Move, then click to finish

You can move more than one object by selecting multiple objects first and then moving them. Using the Select tool, choose the first object. Then press Shift and choose the second object. You can keep choosing as many as you like. If you want to remove an object from the selection, just click it again while pressing Shift. When you press Shift while using the Select tool, you see + and − characters on the cursor—a handy reminder that whatever you click will be added to or removed from the selection.

Tip: When using the Selection tool, the Shift key lets you both add and remove entities from a selection. There are other modifier keys that perform similar functions. Hold down Ctrl (⌘) to add to the selection, or use Shift+Ctrl (Shift-⌘) to remove objects from the selection.

Moving a Point

Moving a single point is a special case. You can't preselect a point with the Select tool. If you try, you end up selecting an entire edge. You can select it only with the Move tool. Click the center of the Move tool on the point you want to select, move it, and then click again to set the new point. Because you can use just the Move tool to select a point, you can move only a single point at a time (see Figure 2-21).

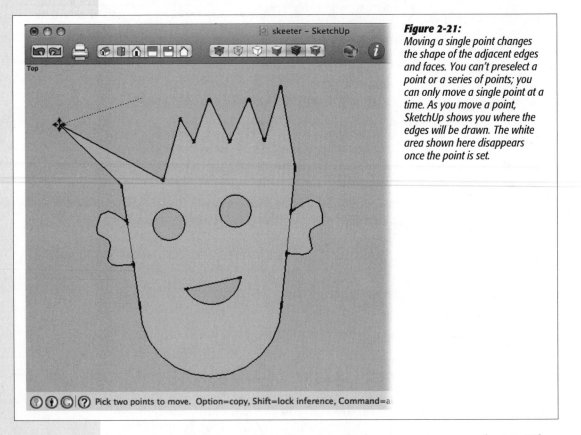

Figure 2-21:
Moving a single point changes the shape of the adjacent edges and faces. You can't preselect a point or a series of points; you can only move a single point at a time. As you move a point, SketchUp shows you where the edges will be drawn. The white area shown here disappears once the point is set.

Also, you can't have anything else selected when you move an endpoint. When you're using the Select tool, the quickest way to make sure nothing is selected is to click an empty spot in the drawing window. You can also use the command Edit → Select None (Ctrl+T or Shift-⌘-A).

The Effects of Moving

When you're moving things, what you grab hold of makes a big difference. For example, if you grab an edge (line) in the middle, the whole edge moves. If you grab it by one of the endpoints, that point moves, making the edge longer, or shorter, or angled in a different direction. Practice your moves on Skeeter.

(Don't worry if he yelps a little bit in the process.) The following steps give you some things to try, but don't be afraid to perform your own nefarious experiments:

1. **Use the Move tool to move the line that forms the ear.**

   The freehand line that makes the ear moves as one piece. The other edges connected to the ear change shape to stay attached to the ear (Figure 2-22).

Figure 2-22:
The freehand line that forms the ear moves as a single piece if you grab it in the middle; but if you grab an endpoint, you can resize and rotate the line.

2. **Move the ear again, but choose one of the endpoints of the freehand line.**

   The point you selected moves, and the freehand line scales larger or smaller depending on where you move. The endpoint that's not selected remains in place.

3. **Use the Move tool to select the arc of the mouth, and then move the mouth.**

   The arc of the mouth changes to a highlight color when you hover over it with the Move tool. When you select and move, the entire mouth moves as one piece.

4. **Use the Move tool to move the endpoint that's at the corner of the mouth.**

   A tooltip says "Endpoint" when you hover over the endpoint with the Move tool. When you move the endpoint, the mouth changes shape, scaling larger or smaller as the endpoint moves (Figure 2-23).

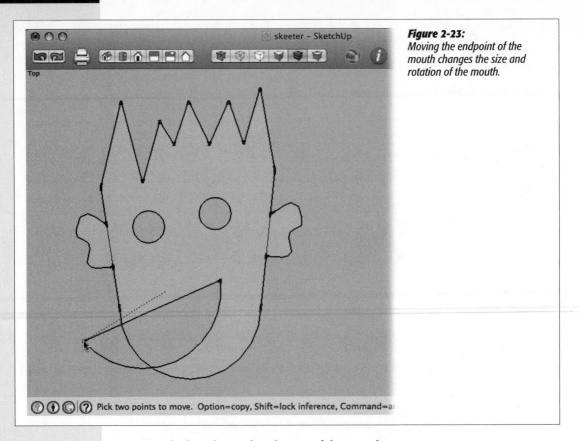

Figure 2-23:
Moving the endpoint of the mouth changes the size and rotation of the mouth.

5. **Move the line that makes the top of the mouth.**

   When you move the line that forms the top of the mouth, the mouth moves as one piece, unless you select one of the endpoints.

6. **Click the endpoint of the arc that's in the middle of the curve, and then move the cursor.**

   Every arc has one endpoint that changes the shape of the arc when it's moved (Figure 2-24). As you move your cursor along the curve, every so often it snaps to a point and displays a tooltip that says "Endpoint". When you move the middle endpoint, you set a new radius and the arc changes accordingly. Move any of the other interior endpoints and you move the entire arc. Move either of the endpoints at the very ends of the arc and you reshape the arc.

7. **Click the edge of one of the eyes and move the eye.**

   The circle forming the eye shows the highlight color when you hover over it with the Move tool. When you make the move, the entire eye moves as one piece.

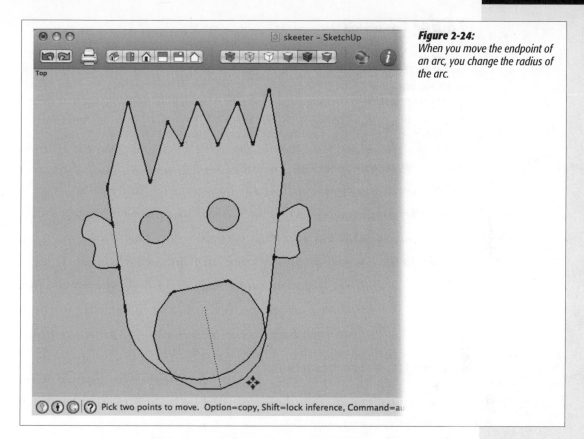

Figure 2-24:
When you move the endpoint of an arc, you change the radius of the arc.

8. **Click one of the controlling endpoints of the eye circle and move the endpoint.**

Every circle has four controlling endpoints spaced 90 degrees apart. When you move a controlling endpoint of a circle, you're setting a new radius for the circle, making the eye larger or smaller. To learn how to make it easier to find the endpoints of your circles, see the box on this page.

GEM IN THE ROUGH

Making Circles Easier to Edit

Every circle has four endpoints 90 degrees apart. You can find the endpoints by moving the cursor around the circle until it snaps to the endpoint. The edge of the circle loses its highlight, since you're no longer selecting the entire edge; you're just selecting a single point. You can make it easier to find the endpoints if you use one of the three axes when you create your circle. Remember, you create a circle by setting two points. Click the center point and then, when

you move to set the radius, make the temporary guideline run parallel to one of the axes. When you're moving along an axis, you see the tooltip that says "On Red Axis" or something similar. When you set the endpoint on the perimeter of the circle, SketchUp creates the other three endpoints in 90-degree increments from that point. Create your circles this way and you'll find the endpoints are always at the 3, 6, 9, and 12 o'clock positions.

Editing Geometry

When you're building complex models, the difference between perimeter edges and shared edges (page 76) becomes more important. In SketchUp 7, when you draw shapes that overlap, they create intersections where the lines meet. In earlier versions of SketchUp this wasn't the case. In a two-dimensional image that difference may not be important, but when you start working in 3-D, the relationships of edges and the way shapes intersect become important (see page 112). This section shows some tricks of the trade to turn perimeter lines into shared edges that you can then erase, simplifying your model.

In the following steps, you'll use this technique to lengthen Skeeter's shirt:

1. **Draw a rectangle that crosses over the bottom of the rectangle of Skeeter's shirt.**

   When you've created the rectangle, it should look like Figure 2-25.

2. **With the Select tool, select some of the different lines in the rectangle.**

   The longer lines were broken up into shorter line segments wherever the lines intersected.

Note: SketchUp 7 behaves differently than previous versions. In SketchUp 7, two lines or edges crossing in a single plane split into four segments at the point of intersection. In previous versions, crossing lines had to be explicitly split by tracing over the lines.

---

3. **Use the Eraser tool to erase the shared edges so that Skeeter's shirt becomes a single face.**

   You can delete each shared edge using the Eraser tool. If you lose a face that you intended to keep, like the shirt itself, you can heal the surface by tracing over the edges that form that face.

Tools Tour

This chapter covered several tools from the Large Tool Set (Figure 2-26). Here's a quick review of the tools, their keyboard shortcuts, and some related tips:

- **Select (space bar).** The cursor changes to an arrow, and you click objects to select them. Shift-click to select more than one object or to deselect an object.

- **Eraser (E).** The cursor changes to an eraser. Click directly on objects you want to erase. If you're already using another tool, you can always erase an object by right-clicking and choosing Erase from the shortcut menu. You can also select a line and then press Delete.

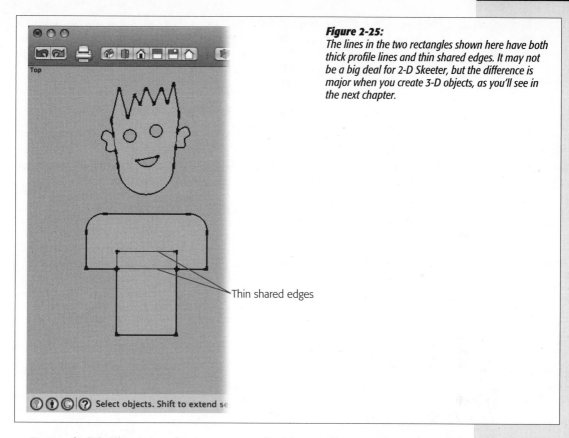

- **Rectangle (R).** The cursor changes to a pencil with a small square. You can create a rectangle by clicking two points, or you can click once and enter dimensions in the Measurements toolbar.

- **Line (L).** The cursor changes to a pencil. You set the two endpoints for a line by clicking, moving the cursor, and clicking again. You can create lines of a specific length by entering a distance in the Measurements toolbar.

- **Circle (C).** The cursor changes to a pencil and a circle. Click once to set the center of the circle, and click again to set the radius. You can also set the radius using the Measurements toolbar.

- **Arc (A).** The cursor changes to a pencil with an arc. Click to set each endpoint for the arc, and then click a third time to set the radius. You can set the radius using the Measurements toolbar.

- **Polygon.** The cursor changes to a pencil and a polygon. Click to set the center point; click again to set the radius. Enter a number and the letter *s* to set the number of sides for the polygon. For example, *6s* creates a hexagon. You can also set the radius using the Measurements toolbar.

- **Freehand.** The cursor changes to a pencil. Drag to create freehand lines. Freehand lines move as a single shape as long as they aren't bisected by other lines.

- **Move (M).** The cursor changes to a cross with four arrowheads. Click an object to pick it up. Move the object to a new position, and click again to set it down. You can preselect one or more objects with the Select tool and then move them together. The only object that you can't preselect is a point.

- **Pan (H; think *hand*).** Changes the camera view as if the camera were pivoting on a tripod. With a three-button mouse, hold down the Shift key, and then drag with the middle mouse button.

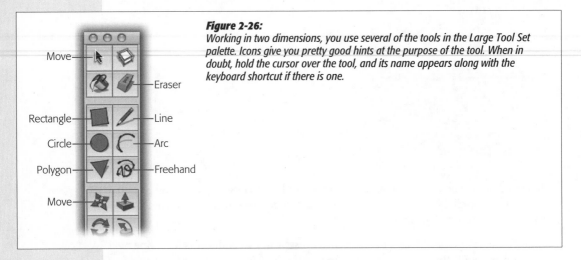

Figure 2-26:
Working in two dimensions, you use several of the tools in the Large Tool Set palette. Icons give you pretty good hints at the purpose of the tool. When in doubt, hold the cursor over the tool, and its name appears along with the keyboard shortcut if there is one.

The Large Tool Set (Figure 2-27) has several handy view tools:

- **Orbit (O).** Moves the camera view as if it were moving about in 3-D space to view the scene from different angles. On a three-button mouse, you can press the middle button or scroll wheel to use the Orbit tool.

- **Zoom (Z).** Shows you more or less of a scene, like the zoom lens on a camera. On a mouse with a scroll wheel, you can use the wheel to zoom in and zoom out.

- **Zoom Extents (Shift+Z).** Great tool if you're lost. Zoom Extents brings every object in your model back into view.

- **Zoom Window.** Drag to create a marquee in the drawing area, and SketchUp zooms to show the area within the marquee.

- **Previous.** Use this button to toggle back and forth between the most recent views.

Tip: The Undo key doesn't affect the view. If you want to go back to a recent view, you have to use the View Previous tool.

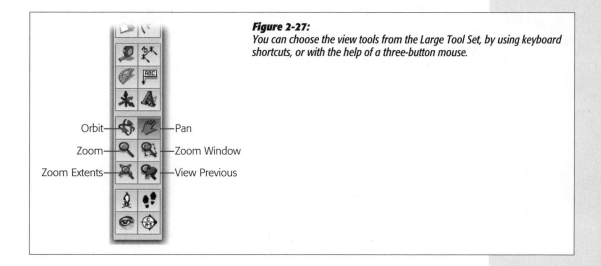

Orbit

Zoom

Zoom Extents

Pan

Zoom Window

View Previous

Figure 2-27:
You can choose the view tools from the Large Tool Set, by using keyboard shortcuts, or with the help of a three-button mouse.

Drawing in Three Dimensions

When you work with SketchUp in three dimensions, it feels less like drawing and more like model building. It's exciting building an object piece by piece and being able to look at it from different angles. You almost feel like you're holding the model in your hands. Above all, a 3-D model is a much more powerful communication tool than a 2-D drawing. Whether you're an architect showing ideas to a client or the owner of a beach house trying to entice renters, SketchUp lets you show a building inside and out. Unlike with many more complicated 3-D programs, with SketchUp you can opt for instant gratification, and pull something together quickly. And when it's worthwhile, you still can spend more time and create models with elaborate details.

If you followed the steps in Chapter 1, you got a taste for building 3-D models. This chapter expands on the concepts introduced in those exercises. You'll be formally introduced to the blue axis, and learn some survival skills for navigating 3-D space. You'll also learn even more about SketchUp's amazing Push/Pull tool, which you can use to stretch your 2-D shapes into 3-D masterpieces. Also, you already saw how the Move tool changes 2-D shapes (page 82). In this chapter, you'll see how it works when you add another dimension.

Navigating 3-D Drawings

Navigation is an important skill when you're working with 3-D graphics. For some folks, it's a cinch; for others, it doesn't come naturally. If you're good at looking at blueprints and then visualizing the building in three dimensions, you may be one of the lucky ones. If not, this section has tips that will help.

In the SketchUp world, you can view objects from absolutely any angle—and that includes from the inside looking out. You can even view and or build objects upside down. After all, there's no gravity in the SketchUp universe! On the other hand, things are a little easier if you follow the formula SketchUp suggests in its Front view, where the blue axis represents up and down, the red axis represents left and right, and the green axis represents near and far. If you stick with this orientation, it's easier to find your way around your 3-D world.

Sometimes as you're working, you may get completely lost. All the walls are in the wrong place, and the stairs that you laboriously constructed are nowhere to be found. Don't panic. You may just be viewing your model from an unfamiliar viewpoint. Before you do anything drastic, perform the take-me-home two-step:

Note: You need some objects in your document to see how this works. You can use the bench from Chapter 1, or just draw a few random shapes in the window.

1. **Click the Front view button, or choose Camera → Standard Views → Front.**

   SketchUp changes to a Front view of your drawing area, as shown in Figure 3-1. No matter where your camera view may have been, you return to the Origin (where the three axes meet), and you're positioned right side up.

2. **Click the Zoom Extents button (Shift+Z).**

   Zoom Extents zooms your viewing area so you see all the objects in the drawing area. It zooms out or in to accommodate everything. Why is this helpful? Sometimes bits of your model may get pushed off to the side. It's like losing your car keys; you know they have to be *somewhere*. When you know your carefully sculpted garden trellis is somewhere, use the Zoom Extents command to find it.

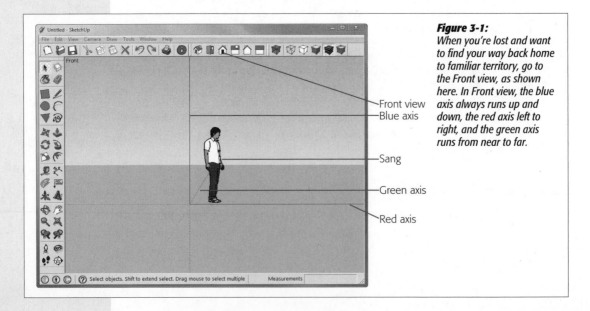

Figure 3-1:
When you're lost and want to find your way back home to familiar territory, go to the Front view, as shown here. In Front view, the blue axis always runs up and down, the red axis left to right, and the green axis runs from near to far.

Introducing the Blue Axis

When you open a new SketchUp document using the "Architectural Design – Feet and Inches" template, you see Sang, the faceless SketchUp model standing next to a blue line that rises up into infinity. Meet the blue axis, as shown in Figure 3-1. When you create 2-D works of art, like those in Chapter 2, the blue axis is there, but it's irrelevant. You have the green axis, which appears to run up and down the drawing area, and the red axis, which runs left to right. The blue axis runs perpendicular to that plane, but you never draw lines or move objects along that axis. When SketchUp opens a new document with the "Architectural Design – Feet and Inches" template, you start off in an angled view that gives you a better feeling for the three axes and the three-dimensional world. As you work in SketchUp, you'll find it helpful to use one of the head-on views—Top or Front—when you want to draw on a particular plane. Then use the Orbit tool to see an angled view, where it's easier to visualize all three dimensions and inspect your project, as shown in Figure 3-2.

Note: If you need a refresher course on setting up templates, see page 23.

Front view is a head-on view, similar to Top view. In Front view, the blue and red axes rule, and the green axis isn't really available. The thing to remember is that if you want to make sure a line runs along a particular axis, use one of the head-on views that presents the axis you need.

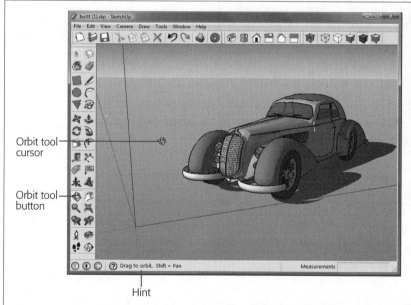

Orbit tool
cursor

Orbit tool
button

Hint

Figure 3-2:
Select the Orbit tool, and then drag to change your view of the model. With a three-button mouse, drag the middle button to orbit. Probably the most entertaining view tool, the Orbit tool makes your model come alive in three dimensions.

The model for this classic 1938 Alfa Romeo 8C 2900B came from the Google 3D Warehouse.

As you've seen in the earlier chapters, SketchUp helps you draw with its snapping action, making it easy to draw lines along a particular axis. To get a feel for drawing lines in 3-D, follow these quick steps.

---

1. Go to Top view Camera → Standard Views → Top.

   Your drawing area changes to look like Figure 3-3.

2. **With the Line (L) tool, draw a line parallel to the green axis, and then press Esc.**

   When you click the first point, a rubber band line stretches from that point to the Line cursor. When you're on the green axis, the rubber band line turns green and a tooltip says "On Green Axis". When you click a second time, you set the endpoint for the line. The rubber band line is replaced by your newly drawn line, and a new rubber band line connects your cursor to the last clicked point. When you press Esc, the rubber band line disappears.

3. **Draw a second line (not connected to the first) parallel to the red axis, and then press Esc.**

   Your two lines are on the same plane. In Top view, you can't position objects up and down the blue axis, but you can see a diagonal blue line that represents the blue axis.

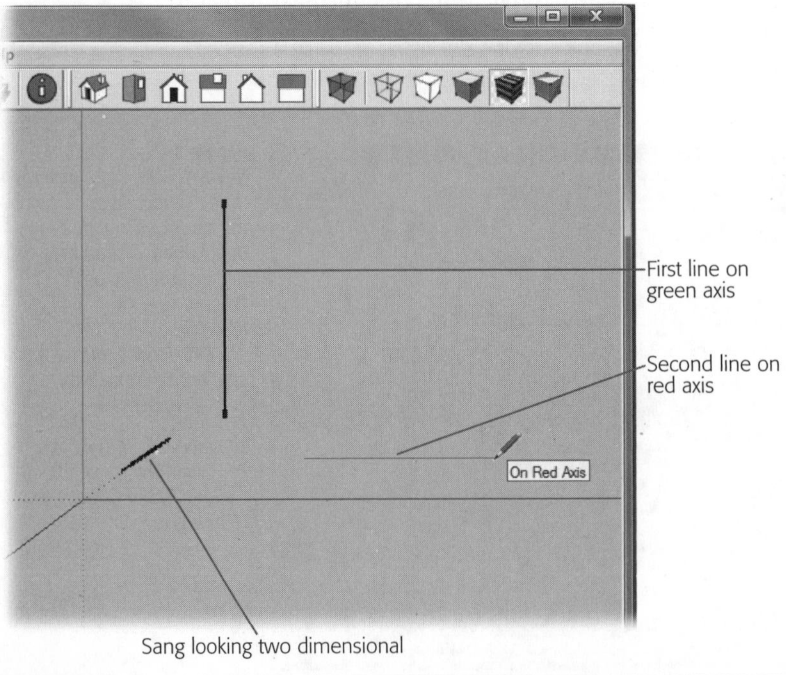

Figure 3-3:
When you're in Top view, it's easy to draw lines or move objects along the red and green axes. Because the Top view is one of the head-on views, everything feels very two-dimensional. The blue axis isn't available until you change views.

First line on green axis

Second line on red axis

On Red Axis

Sang looking two dimensional

4. **Change to the Front view Camera → Standard Views → Front, and use the Line (L) tool to draw two more unconnected lines parallel to the blue and red axes.**

   In Front view it's easy to snap your lines to the blue and red axes, but you can't draw on the green axis.

5. **Change to the Iso view (Camera → Standard Views → Iso).**

   In this view you have a better 3-D view of the drawing area. The line you drew in the blue axis is obviously in a different plane from the first two lines you drew. In Iso view you can draw along all three axes, but it takes a little more patience to get the right angle to show the "on axis" tooltip.

Architect's Glossary: Isometric projection is a drawing method that provides an accurate scale for measurements. It's a useful design tool, but it doesn't simulate the way we see objects in perspective. SketchUp's Iso view is simply an angled view, not an isometric projection. You can get an approximate sense of an isometric projection by clicking Iso and then choosing Camera → Parallel Projection. To switch back from Parallel projection, choose Camera → Perspective.

---

6. **With the Line tool, draw a line parallel to the blue axis, and then (without pressing Esc) draw a connected line parallel to the green axis.**

   The two lines create an L shape. If you find it difficult to draw a line on the blue axis, press the up arrow key. This key forces the line to be drawn on the blue axis. (Use the right arrow for the red axis and the left arrow for green.)

7. **Draw a third connected line parallel to the red axis, and then press Esc.**

   Remember, when the lines are on axis, they change to the color of the axis. This three-part line clearly lives in 3-D space.

8. **Use the Orbit (O or middle mouse button) tool to examine your creation,** *Sticks in Space* **(Figure 3-4).**

   Move around so you can see this abstract masterpiece from top, bottom, front, back, left, and right. As you move, you get a sense of the spatial relationship between the lines.

As you work in 3-D, remember that if you want to draw on a single plane, you can use one of the head-on views: Front, Back, Top, Bottom, Left, or Right. These views make it easy to draw on two axes and prevent you from accidentally spilling over into another plane. If you want to understand the 3-D relationship of objects, the Iso view and the Orbit tool are your friends.

Finding 3-D Inferences

In the 2-D drawings in Chapter 2, you saw how inference points and lines help you align and scale the objects you draw. When you add a third dimension to your drawings, inference lines are even more helpful. You might even say they're critical when it comes to drawing accurately and quickly. Suppose you want to scale a group of Ionic columns so they're exactly the height of a certain wall—SketchUp inferences provide a quick and easy solution (Figure 3-5).

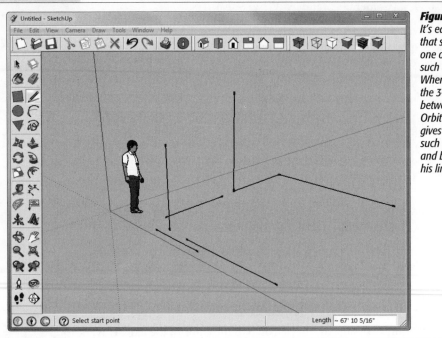

Figure 3-4:
It's easy to draw lines that snap to an axis in one of the head-on views such as Top or Front. When you want to see the 3-D relationships between objects, use the Orbit (O) tool, which gives you a perspective such as this that's below and behind Sang and his lines.

Figure 3-5:
The height of these columns is set to match the height of the wall. After you select the columns and click the Scale tool, the cursor moves to a point at the top of the wall. An inference line appears when the columns are scaled to the same height as the wall.

In this exercise, you begin to create 3-D objects, starting with a simple box, and then you learn how to use inferences to speed up the process.

1. **Open a new document, and then change the camera view to Top.**

   In the Top view, the red appears to run horizontally in the drawing area while the green axis runs vertically. The blue axis appears as a diagonal line if you're in Perspective view (Camera → Perspective). If you're in Parallel projection (Camera → Parallel Projection), you won't see any indication of the blue axis. Whether they're all visible or not, the three axes meet near the middle of the drawing area at a point called the *Origin point*.

Tip: If your friend Sang, the faceless SketchUp model, is in your drawing area, you may want to remove or hide him. You can right-click → Erase or right-click → Hide him. As an alternate method for hiding him, open the Outliner (Window → Outliner). Right-click (Control-click) the word <Sang>, and then choose Hide from the shortcut menu. You may be wondering how to unhide something. After all, it's difficult to click an object you can't see. Hidden groups and components appear grayed out in the Outliner list. Right-click a hidden item and choose Unhide.

---

2. **With the Rectangle tool, draw a rectangle over the Origin point.**

   The Origin point is where the colored axis lines meet, as shown in Figure 3-6.

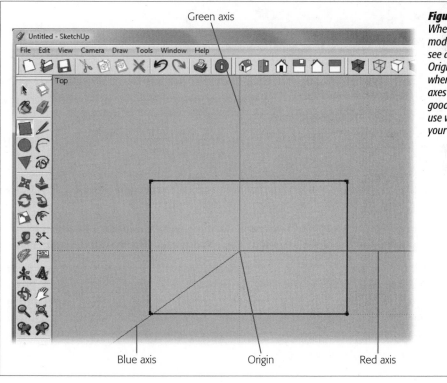

Green axis

Top

Figure 3-6:
When you first begin a model in SketchUp, you see a point known as the Origin. This point is where the three colored axes meet, and it's a good reference point to use when navigating your model.

Blue axis   Origin   Red axis

---

3. Use the Orbit tool to move to a three-dimensional view of the rectangle with the blue axis pointing up and down in the drawing area, and the red and green axes pointing to the right, as shown in Figure 3-7.

This angle makes it easier to work in three dimensions and to draw lines along the blue axis. Your flat rectangle takes on a different shape when you begin to view it from different 3-D angles.

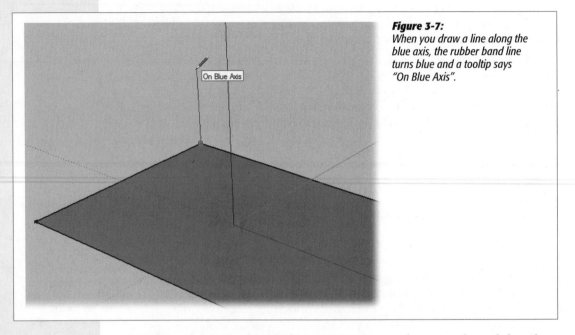

Figure 3-7:
When you draw a line along the blue axis, the rubber band line turns blue and a tooltip says "On Blue Axis".

4. With the Line (L) tool, click the topmost point in the rectangle, and then draw a new line along the blue axis.

As you draw with the Line (L) tool, from the endpoint adjust the angle until your line turns blue and you see a tooltip that says "On Blue Axis", as shown in Figure 3-7. Hold down the Shift key to lock the line to the blue axis. When your line is on the blue axis, it's perpendicular to the rectangle's surface. Don't press Esc, because the next line is drawn from this endpoint.

5. Draw a line along the red axis, and click to set the endpoint directly above the right-rear corner of the rectangle. Use an inference line to find the exact point.

If you merely try to eyeball the exact point that's above the corner, you're unlikely to get it right. You need the help of an inference line to find the precise point to end the line. When you're in the right location, SketchUp shows an inference line from the corner to your Line cursor. If the inference line doesn't show up, you can coax it out of hiding by hovering over the corner until you see a tooltip that says "Endpoint" (Figure 3-8). Then slowly move up from the corner. As you move the cursor, you see a dotted inference line from the corner to the tip of the Line tool. When you're in just the right spot, you still see the inference line, and the line that you're drawing turns red, because it's aligned with the red axis.

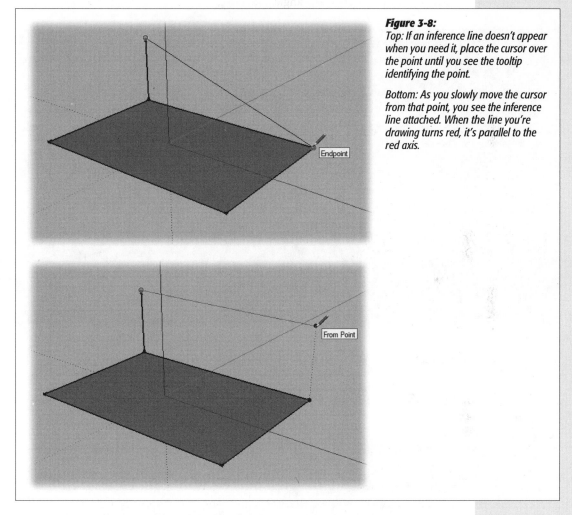

Figure 3-8:
Top: If an inference line doesn't appear when you need it, place the cursor over the point until you see the tooltip identifying the point.

Bottom: As you slowly move the cursor from that point, you see the inference line attached. When the line you're drawing turns red, it's parallel to the red axis.

6. **Complete the back surface of the box by drawing a line down, to the rear-right corner.**

   When you click to set the point, the back face of your box-to-be fills in, and you have two rectangles at a right angle to each other. One rectangle is on the red/green plane, and the other is on the red/blue plane.

7. **Use Orbit (O) to admire the shape of your two rectangles.**

Every so often, use the Orbit tool to view the model you're building from different angles. It gives you a feeling for the three-dimensional shape you're creating, and you can catch any problems sooner rather than later. What kind of problems, you ask? Problems can arise when lines and points aren't actually on the axis you intended. See the box on this page.

TROUBLESHOOTING MOMENT

Checking for Off-Axis Edges

Sometimes when you're drawing in 3-D, things aren't exactly lined up as you think. For an example, check Figure 3-9, where the box has the requisite number of edges, but one face isn't filled in. (If you'd like to see this example in a SketchUp file, go to *http://missingmanuals.com/cds* and download this book's file called *off_axis.skp*.) The most common cause for a missing face is that one of the endpoints isn't on the same plane as the others, which means a couple of the edges are off axis. They're straddling a plane, instead of being truly coplanar.

Here's a way to identify which lines are off axis. Open the Styles window: Window → Styles. At the top of the Select tab, choose In Model from the drop-down menu. Then click the Edit tab. At the bottom, use the Color drop-down menu

to select "By axis". This option changes the color of the edges (lines) in your model. For example, if an edge is aligned with the red axis, it's red. Lines not aligned to an axis are black.

So what's the solution to endpoints that are off axis? Erase the black lines and redraw the edges. Make sure that you see both the "on axis" tooltip and the inference line when you click to set the endpoints. If you think the Line tool is snapping to an unintended point, try using the Orbit tool (page 28) to slightly change the 3-D view.

Sometimes with really complex models the edge Styles colors stop being reliable. Hopefully, this is something the SketchUp programming wizards can resolve.

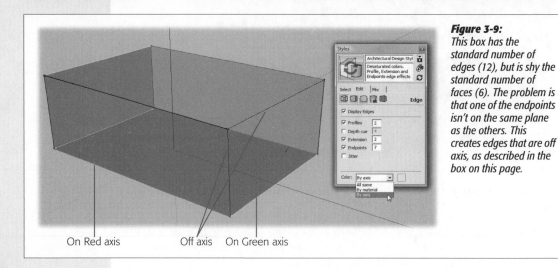

Figure 3-9:
This box has the standard number of edges (12), but is shy the standard number of faces (6). The problem is that one of the endpoints isn't on the same plane as the others. This creates edges that are off axis, as described in the box on this page.

On Red axis   Off axis   On Green axis

8. **Draw two more lines to create the left face of your box.**

   Align the top edge to the green axis and the left edge to the blue axis. The faces of your box fill in when the edges form a closed loop on a single plane.

   Remember, if you need to coax the inference line from an endpoint, hover over the endpoint until you see a tooltip, and then slowly move the line cursor along the axis on which you want your line.

9. **Create the front panel of the box with two more lines.**

   Align the top edge to the red axis and the right edge to the blue axis.

10. **Connect the two upper-right corners.**

   When you draw the last edge, the last two faces of the box fill in as shown in Figure 3-10. If some of the faces didn't fill in the way you expected, see the box on the previous page.

11. **Use the Orbit tool to check your box from different angles.**

   All six faces of the box should be filled in with a surface. If you can't seem to find your way back to the original view, use the take-me-home two-step described on page 94 (click Front and then click Zoom Extents).

12. **Save your model as *box_finished.skp.***

   You'll use this model again in the next exercise.

When you think about how your box was created, it's worth noting that SketchUp objects are hollow like cardboard boxes, rather than solid like blocks of wood. This feature makes it easy to create buildings that have interior spaces.

Using the Push/Pull Tool

If you've ever seen those camping tents that spring from flat to fully formed, you have an idea how SketchUp's Push/Pull tool works. You start with a flat 2-D drawing, and you stretch it to whatever length you want. Push/Pull works its magic on any shape that forms a face.

In these steps, you use the Push/Pull tool to alter the simple box created earlier in this chapter. If you need a box model to start with, as shown in Figure 3-10, go to *http://missingmanuals.com/cds* and download the file *box_finished.skp.*

1. **Open the file *box_finished.skp,* and then click the Iso button or Camera → Standard Views → Iso.**

   You may even want to use the Orbit tool to get a good view of three faces of the box.

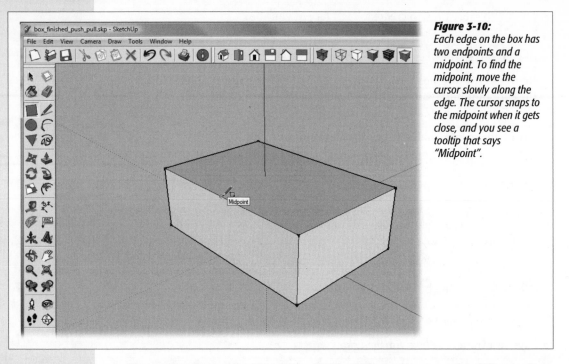

Figure 3-10:
Each edge on the box has two endpoints and a midpoint. To find the midpoint, move the cursor slowly along the edge. The cursor snaps to the midpoint when it gets close, and you see a tooltip that says "Midpoint".

2. **Choose the Rectangle (R) tool, and move the cursor over the different faces and points of the box.**

   When the cursor is over a face, a tooltip says "On Face". When the cursor is over an endpoint or midpoint, the marker at the tip of the pencil changes color, and you see appropriate tooltip messages. In the next step, you'll use an endpoint and a midpoint to draw a rectangle on the box's top surface.

3. **With the Rectangle tool, click the front upper-right corner, and then click the upper midpoint on the back of the box, as shown in Figure 3-11.**

   After you create the rectangle, your box has an edge down the middle that divides it in half. The top of the box has two separate faces.

4. **With the Push/Pull (P) tool, click the top-left face, and move the mouse up and down.**

   As you move the mouse, the model changes shape. When you pull up with the Push/Pull tool, you're *adding geometry* (in more familiar terms, *adding volume*) to your simple box. When you push it down, you're *subtracting geometry*.

5. **Pull the face up a bit, and then click when you're done.**

   This leaves the face pulled up, creating a new vertical face in the model.

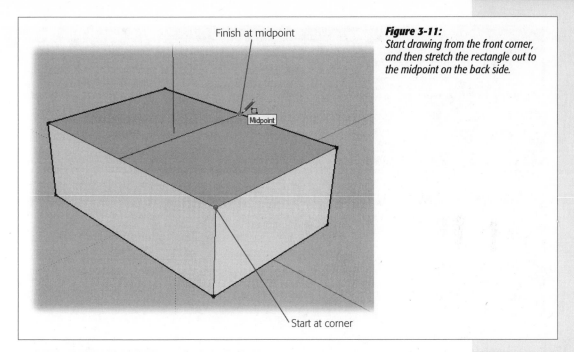

Finish at midpoint

Midpoint

Figure 3-11:
*Start drawing from the front corner,
and then stretch the rectangle out to
the midpoint on the back side.*

Start at corner

6. **With Push/Pull, push the vertical face back.**

   As you push the face as shown in Figure 3-12, you subtract volume from the model, making it smaller.

7. **Continue to push the face until you reach the back edge of the box; then click.**

   The face snaps to the back edge, and then when you click, the face disappears. Your box looks as it did when you started.

As you'll see in the next sections, the ease of Push/Pull, combined with the accuracy of the Measurements toolbar and inferences, gives you a rapid way to build 3-D models.

Aligning Surfaces and Finding References

In addition to letting you pull shapes from existing shapes, the Push/Pull tool helps you to accurately align different faces. Remember the tiresome insistence that you use the click-move-click technique when drawing and moving? Now your well-learned habit pays off. In the next few steps, you'll use Push/Pull to create 3-D shapes and align their surfaces with other objects in the model. No need for elaborate measurements—you do it all with Push/Pull and inferences.

1. **With the Rectangle tool, draw a square in the middle of the box's top surface.**

   You see a diagonal line and a tooltip that says "Square" when the Rectangle tool forms a square shape.

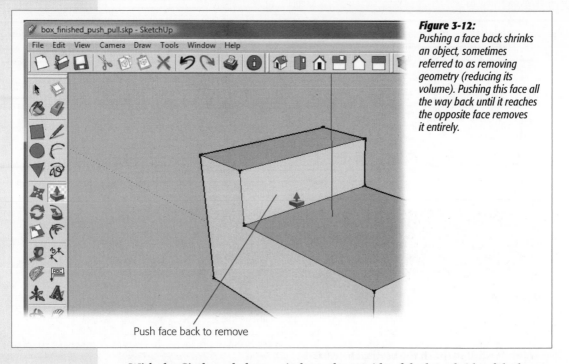

Figure 3-12:
Pushing a face back shrinks an object, sometimes referred to as removing geometry (reducing its volume). Pushing this face all the way back until it reaches the opposite face removes it entirely.

Push face back to remove

2. **With the Circle tool, draw a circle on the outside of the broad side of the box to the left.**

   The snap-to action is even more evident with the Circle tool's cursor. You see the initial circle shape change angle as it affixes itself to the different surfaces.

3. **With the Polygon tool, draw a polygon on the right side of the box.**

   Initially the polygon is a hexagon, but you can change it to any number of sides by simply typing the number and the letter *s*, like this: *8s*.

4. **Use the Push/Pull tool to pull out the square, circle, and polygon surfaces so they extend from the box, as shown in Figure 3-13.**

   Many SketchUp models begin with simple shapes. The surfaces are then sliced and diced using either the pencil cursor or the shape tools such as the Rectangle, Circle, and Polygon tools.

5. **Use the Rectangle tool to draw a rectangle in front of the box, and then pull it up to a height roughly equal to the first box.**

   Now you have lots of different surfaces in the drawing area, but what if you want to align the flat surface of the cylinder with the front surface of the new box?

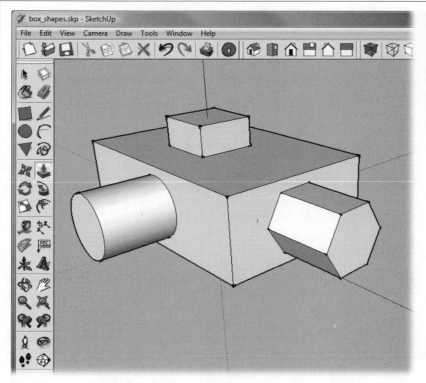

Figure 3-13:
You can use any of the drawing tools to create shapes that can be push/pulled into 3-D objects. Those shapes can be standalone or drawn on the face of other objects, as shown here.

6. **With the Push/Pull tool, click the flat face of the cylinder and release the mouse button.**

   As you move the cursor back and forth, the cylinder shrinks and grows. Now that you've released the mouse button, you can move the cursor all over the drawing area, and the cylinder just keeps shrinking or growing depending on the position of the cursor.

7. **Hold the cursor over the front face of the new box, and then click to align the two faces, as shown in Figure 3-14.**

   When the cursor is over the face, a tooltip appears saying "On Face", and you see a dotted inference line from the face of the box to the face of the cylinder. When you click, the faces of the cylinder and the box are aligned.

8. **Use the Orbit tool to confirm that the two surfaces are actually aligned.**

   You can also use the Top view to confirm that the two faces are aligned.

You can align any of the surfaces using the Push/Pull tool and the On Face inference points. Try aligning the top surface of the new box with one of the top surfaces on the original box or on the box you pulled out the top. Try to align the

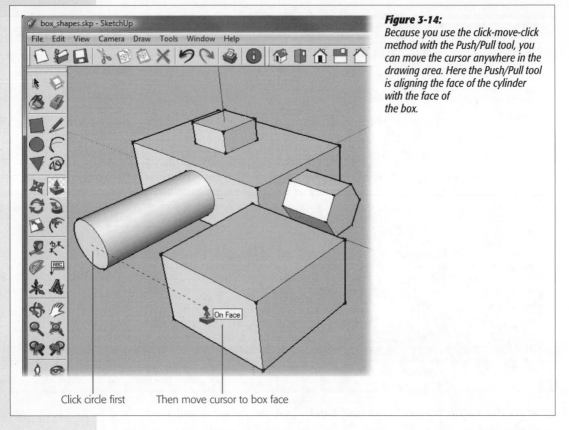

Figure 3-14:
Because you use the click-move-click method with the Push/Pull tool, you can move the cursor anywhere in the drawing area. Here the Push/Pull tool is aligning the face of the cylinder with the face of the box.

Click circle first   Then move cursor to box face

face of the polygon with the face of the new box. You can also use a point such as a midpoint as a reference. Try aligning the surface of the cylinder with the midpoint of the box.

Pop Quiz: Put the Circle Back

Here's a chance to practice your new push/pull and alignment skills without seeing each step written out.

1. Draw a circle on the face of your new box, pull it out from the box, and then click to set the distance.

2. Realign the face of the circle with the face of the box again.

So how did you do? Here's a quick and easy way to align one face with another that always works. Click the face of the circle, and then click the face of the box. You get perfect alignment every time. If you laboriously try to align, pushing and pulling by sight, chances are you'll get it wrong.

Bonus Question: Bore a Round Hole Through the Box

How do you push the circle through the box so that it aligns perfectly with the back side? Click the surface of the circle, and then click any point on the back edge of the box, as shown in Figure 3-15. The circle aligns perfectly with the back face, which means it disappears. Go ahead, orbit around and check it. You should have a clean hole.

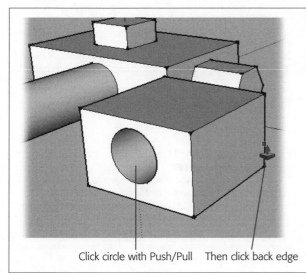

Figure 3-15:
Whenever you want to align a Push/Pull move with a particular face or point, click the surface you're moving, and then click the point or surface you want to align to. Here the surface of the circle is aligned with the back edge, boring a hole through the box.

Click circle with Push/Pull   Then click back edge

Click and Rotate to Find a Reference

If you have a three-button mouse, you can use another trick to align to a concealed surface. For example, after you've clicked the circle's surface to start the Push/Pull procedure, you can hold down the middle mouse button or scroll wheel. The cursor temporarily changes to the Orbit tool, and you can maneuver around to the back side of the box. Release the middle mouse button, and you're still in Push/Pull mode. Now just click the back face, which is now visible, and you have yourself a hole.

Surface Orientation and Surface Colors

You may have noticed in your Push/Pull adventures that SketchUp faces have two colors. One side is white (if you want to be technical, it's actually off-white). The other side is blue. But these shades aren't just eye candy. SketchUp uses this color system to designate the inside and the outside of objects.

This section continues from the earlier exercises. If you'd prefer, you can download the SketchUp file *surface_orientation.skp* from the Missing CD page (*www. missingmanuals.com/cds*).

To get a better view of this topic, you'll lift the lid off that box with the circle on the front. Then you'll use the Push/Pull tool to see how SketchUp determines the inside and outside colors for models. Sometimes SketchUp's view of your model may not coincide with your plans. In those instances you can use a few tricks to change the surface orientation.

Other times when you use the Push/Pull tool, the surface colors can get a little confused. Follow these steps and you'll see how that happens:

1. **Start with a box with a circle drawn on its face.**

   Make your own box and circle or use *surface_orientation.skp.*

2. **With the Select tool, right-click the top, and then choose Erase from the pop-up menu.**

   After popping the top, you see the outside of the box is white and the inside is blue, as shown in Figure 3-16.

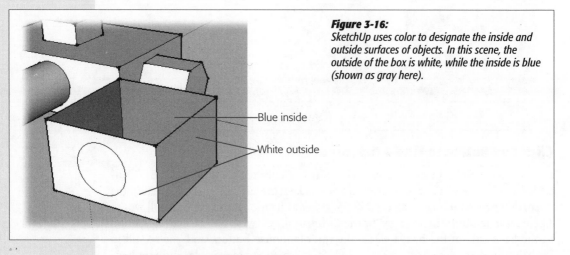

Figure 3-16:
SketchUp uses color to designate the inside and outside surfaces of objects. In this scene, the outside of the box is white, while the inside is blue (shown as gray here).

Blue inside

White outside

3. **Pull the circle out from the box.**

   The outside of the cylinder is white because it's on the outside.

4. **Push the circle inside the box.**

   Inside, the surface of the cylinder is blue. So far, so good.

5. **Push the circle all the way through the box.**

   Where the cylinder extends beyond the back face of the box, it's still blue, even though it's an outside surface, as you can see in Figure 3-17.

At first you might think this isn't such a big deal. But as you work in SketchUp, you'll find situations where inside and outside faces behave differently. In those cases it's more than a cosmetic issue. Fortunately SketchUp gives you a way to remind it where the interior and exterior surfaces are supposed to be. Read on.

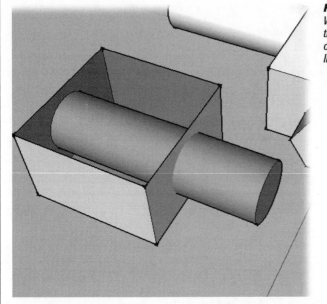

Figure 3-17:
When you push the cylinder through two faces of the box, SketchUp gets a little confused. The face of the cylinder outside of the box should be white, like all the other exterior faces.

Changing Surface Orientation: Reversing Faces

SketchUp has a command called Reverse Faces that lets you turn a face inside-out (see Figure 3-18). It comes in handy when you Push/Pull shapes from the inside to the outside of a model and SketchUp's interior/exterior facing colors get confused, as described in the previous section (Figure 3-17). To use Reverse Faces, right-click (Control-click) the object that you want to turn inside-out, like the cylinder in this example, and choose Reverse Faces.

However, when you try this command on the cylinder sticking out of the box, it changes the face of the entire cylinder. Now the part of the cylinder that's *inside* the box has turned white. You now have the opposite problem: an inside surface has the white coloring of an outside surface. If this image leads you to believe the cylinder and the box are 3-D shapes passing through each other like a ghost walking through a wall, you're exactly right. The two shapes don't intersect where they meet, so there's no shared edge. Click the curved surface of the cylinder, and you see that the selection includes surfaces inside and outside of the box, as shown in Figure 3-18. If there's no shared edge, there's no way to divide the cylinder and to color each section appropriately.

The solution is to create an intersection or a shared edge, much like the 2-D shared edges in Chapter 2 (page 9, for example). In the next section, you'll see how to create a 3-D shared edge for the box and cylinder.

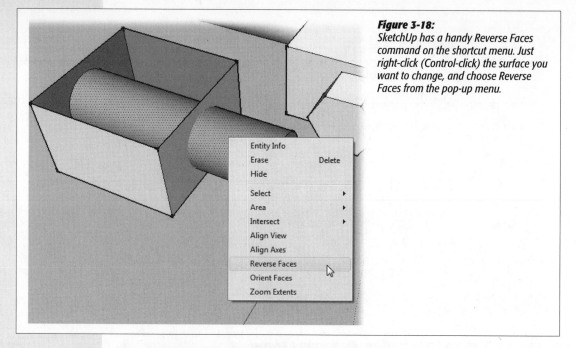

Figure 3-18:
SketchUp has a handy Reverse Faces command on the shortcut menu. Just right-click (Control-click) the surface you want to change, and choose Reverse Faces from the pop-up menu.

Intersections in 3-D Objects

When two objects share no edges, they aren't joined—they merely pass through each other. One way to join objects is to trace from intersection point to intersection point until you create a shared edge. Remember that circles are made up of 24 segments, as shown in Figure 3-19. So you could create a shared edge by tracing from intersection point to intersection point all around your cylinder—24 segments' worth. Fortunately, there's an easier way, using the Intersect with Model command. First, choose the Select tool, and then right-click (Control-click) → Intersect → Intersect with Model. This single command does all the tracing for you. To confirm that it did a thorough job, select the cylinder surface inside the box and then outside the box. Notice how each surface shows independent selection highlights.

Now you can use Reverse Faces (right-click → Reverse Faces) on the faces so that all outside faces are white and inside faces are blue, as shown in Figure 3-20.

Because the cylinder is now divided into two parts, you can perform other operations on the individual parts. For example, you can use the Eraser (E) or right-click → Erase to delete the part of the cylinder that extends beyond the box and the face of the circle, leaving you with a box that has a hole bored through the middle. And that's exactly what you need to begin the next section.

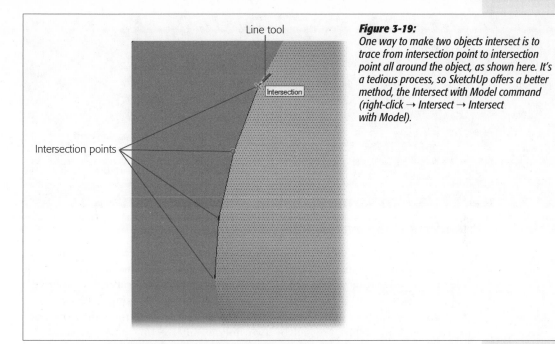

Figure 3-19:
One way to make two objects intersect is to trace from intersection point to intersection point all around the object, as shown here. It's a tedious process, so SketchUp offers a better method, the Intersect with Model command (right-click → Intersect → Intersect with Model).

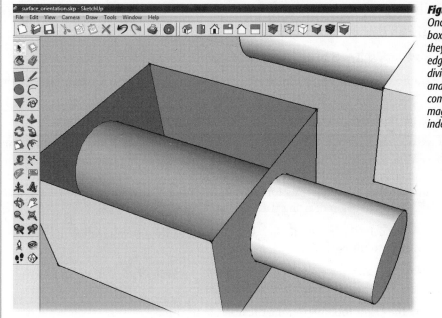

Figure 3-20:
Once the cylinder and the box have a shared edge, they're joined at that edge. The cylinder is divided into two parts, and the Reverse Faces command can do its magic on each part independently.

NEW IN SKETCHUP 7

Changes in Joined Edge Behavior

In previous versions of SketchUp, the whole issue of joined edges was a little more complicated. When you were working in two dimensions, shapes almost always overlapped each other, rather than creating shared edges. If you wanted to create a shared edge, you had to laboriously trace from point to point. In SketchUp 7 that's no longer the case. Now, instead of overlapping, two lines crossing a single plane automatically break into four segments, creating shared edges. Old SketchUp pros may have to get used to this change in behavior. For SketchUp newbies it's likely to make life easier.

Still, sometimes 3-D objects don't divide the way you'd like, as is the case with the cylinder in the square. When that happens, as explained on page 112, you need to use the Intersect with Model command and Reverse Faces.

Working with Complex Intersections

As your SketchUp models become more complex, their connections and intersections naturally become more complicated. As an example, consider the box with the hole bored through the center, at the end of the previous section. (If you don't have that, you can download *two_holes_begin.skp* from the Missing CD page.) Suppose you want to bore another hole through the other sides of the model? In other words you want a box crossed by two hollow, intersecting holes, as shown in Figure 3-21.

1. **Open *two_holes_begin.skp*, or use your project from the previous exercise.**

   The file holds two models from earlier exercises in this chapter.

2. **Use the Orbit tool to get a good view of one solid face of the box.**

   In the drawing area, you have a box with the top removed. There's a large hole bored through the box from one side to another.

3. **With the Circle tool, draw a circle on one of the solid sides of the box.**

   After you click the Circle tool, move the cursor over one of the edges until you find a midpoint. Then slowly move to the middle of the face until you see the inference line from the midpoint on an adjacent edge. When you see inference lines from both midpoints forming an L, you're in the center of the face. Click the center to begin drawing your circle.

4. **With the Push/Pull tool, click the circle, and then create a hole all the way through to the back side.**

   After you click the circle's face, click the box's back edge. This move pushes the circle all the way through to the back edge.

5. **Use the Orbit tool to examine the holes in the box.**

   You may be surprised to see that your hole intersection is somewhat obstructed. That's because the two holes are passing through each other. They aren't joined by shared edges.

6. **Through the top of the box, with the Select (space) tool, right-click (Control-click) one of the cylinders and choose Intersect → Intersect with Model.**

The Intersect with Model command creates shared edges where the two holes intersect with each other. You still have pipe obstructions, but you'll fix those in the next step.

7. **One by one, select each of the obstructions and then press Delete.**

You may need to use the Orbit tool to get a good view of the obstructions before you select and delete them. When you're done, you should be able to see all the way through the holes, as shown in Figure 3-21.

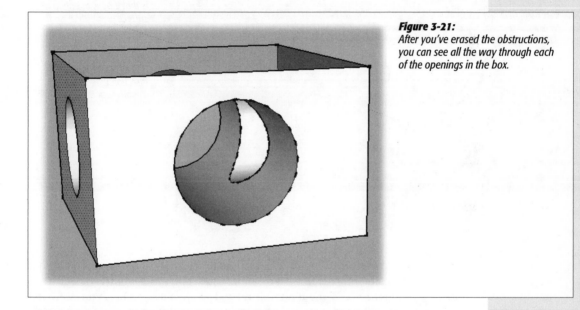

Figure 3-21:
After you've erased the obstructions, you can see all the way through each of the openings in the box.

Note: For a finished copy of this model, go to *http://missingmanuals.com/cds* and download *two_holes_finished.skp*.

Double-Clicking with Push/Pull

The Push/Pull tool has another timesaving trick that lets you repeat your last Push/Pull action by double-clicking a new surface. Here's how it works:

1. **In a new document, draw two rectangles next to each other.**

Make sure they're both on the red/green plane.

2. **Use the Push/Pull tool to pull one of the rectangles up into the shape of a box. Then double-click the second rectangle.**

The second rectangle springs up to exactly the same height as the first. That's because the Push/Pull tool remembers the last action, and you can repeat that action with a double-click.

3. **Draw a rectangle in the top of one of the boxes, and then double-click the rectangle.**

   Instead of pulling up, the rectangle you double-clicked moves down, creating a rectangular hole through your box, as shown in Figure 3-22.

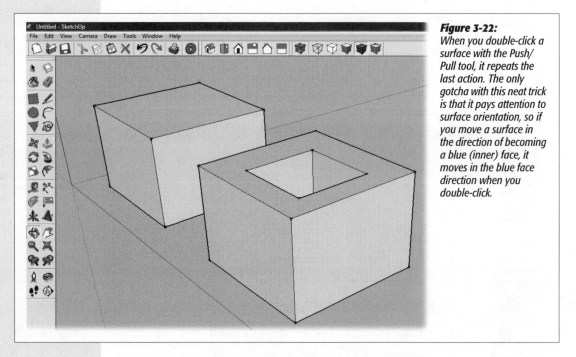

Figure 3-22:
When you double-click a surface with the Push/ Pull tool, it repeats the last action. The only gotcha with this neat trick is that it pays attention to surface orientation, so if you move a surface in the direction of becoming a blue (inner) face, it moves in the blue face direction when you double-click.

So why the reverse action when you double-clicked? It has to do with that white/blue, inside/outside face orientation issue. The Push/Pull tool keeps track of face orientation and the direction related to the faces. When you drew the rectangles, the white surfaces faced down, and you pulled them up toward the blue face. When you double-clicked the rectangle on the top of your box, it also moved in the blue direction—that is, toward the inside of the box. It moved exactly the same distance, aligning with the face on the bottom and creating a rectangular hole in the box.

You may not encounter this behavior frequently, but if double-clicking with Push/Pull does the opposite of what you expect, check the face orientation of your objects.

Using the Move Tool in 3-D

When you build 3-D models in SketchUp, you're always moving something. Perhaps you're moving model furniture around the inside of your model beach house. Or maybe your hot tub needs to be bigger, so you're moving one of the endpoints on a circle. In any case, you're moving, tinkering, and fiddling. It's all part of the 3-D design process.

When you use the Move tool with 2-D objects, you click a point, release the mouse button, and then move the cursor. The shape seems to be attached to the cursor until you click a new spot to set the shape down. It's the same drill when you move 3-D objects in 3-D space. One obvious challenge is that you can move the objects in three dimensions instead of just two. Also, remember how moving surfaces, edges, and endpoints of 2-D shapes had different effects? That's true with 3-D objects, too.

SketchUp tries to make movement easier by initially restricting the motion along axis lines. It's pretty good at guessing which direction you want to move a face or an edge most of the time. What about the other times? If you want to overcome movement restrictions, you use a keyboard toggle dubbed Auto-fold (for the origin of that name, see page 118). On a PC, you press and release the Alt key. On a Mac, the toggle is the ⌘ key. The Auto-fold toggle turns off movement restrictions until you press the key again.

In the following steps, you'll learn how to move objects along the three axis lines, and how to overcome movement restrictions:

1. **In Top view, draw a triangle with the Line tool.**

    Any type of triangle will do. Remember to click-move-click.

2. **Orbit to a 3-D angle, and then pull the triangle up with the Push/Pull tool.**

    The triangle becomes a 3-D object.

3. **With the Move tool, click one of the points and move it up and down.**

    The endpoint moves along the blue axis, as shown in Figure 3-23.

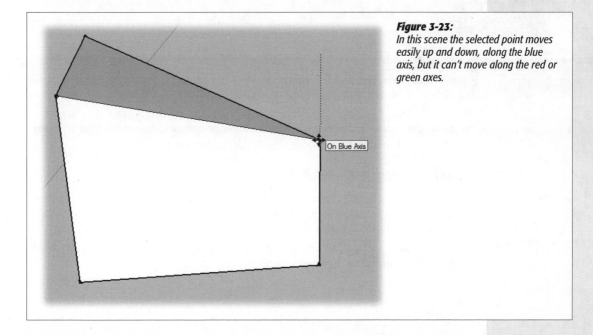

Figure 3-23:
In this scene the selected point moves easily up and down, along the blue axis, but it can't move along the red or green axes.

On Blue Axis

4. **Click and move the top surface up and down.**

The entire face moves up and down, along the blue axis. A blue dotted line signals the direction of the movement. The object increases or decreases in volume with the motion.

5. **Try to move the surface in either the red or green direction.**

You can't move in red or green directions. SketchUp figures that most of the time you want to move along a particular axis, but it gives you an escape hatch for the occasions when you want to do something different. In the status bar in the lower-left corner a message says "Alt = toggle Auto-fold" on a PC and "⌘ = toggle Auto-fold" on a Mac.

6. **Press and release Alt (⌘ on a Mac), and then try to move the face off the blue axis.**

Two diamond shapes appear on the Move cursor to show that Auto-fold is on, as shown in Figure 3-24. With Auto-fold on, you can move the face, edge, and endpoints and edges in any direction. To turn the move restrictions back on, just press the Alt (or ⌘) toggle key again.

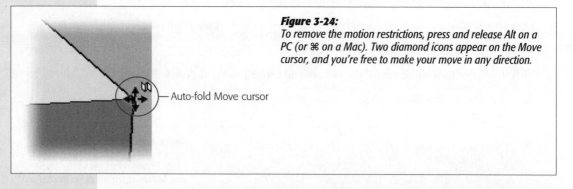

Figure 3-24:
To remove the motion restrictions, press and release Alt on a PC (or ⌘ on a Mac). Two diamond icons appear on the Move cursor, and you're free to make your move in any direction.

— Auto-fold Move cursor

Notice that when you move a single point of the triangle, the shape changes—new edges and faces are added to the object as shown in Figure 3-25. These new edges are called *folds*. SketchUp adds them automatically to accommodate the movement of the endpoint. When you move a point off axis, SketchUp has to create new faces for the object. For more details see the box on the next page.

Understanding Auto-Fold

SketchUp creates faces (surfaces) when coplanar edges (lines) form a closed loop. If any point on the edges isn't on the same plane, SketchUp can't create a face. So when you move an endpoint or an edge off of that plane, SketchUp has to create additional faces and edges. The process is called *Auto-fold* because the new edges look like folds added to the original object.

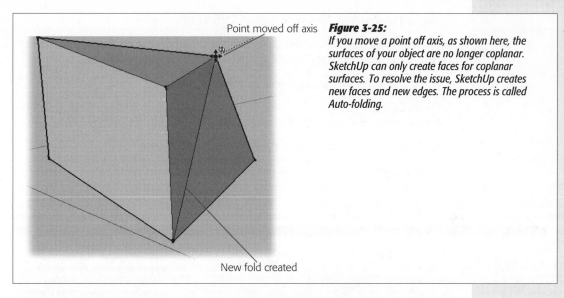

Point moved off axis

Figure 3-25:
If you move a point off axis, as shown here, the surfaces of your object are no longer coplanar. SketchUp can only create faces for coplanar surfaces. To resolve the issue, SketchUp creates new faces and new edges. The process is called Auto-folding.

New fold created

In general, if a movement has to create multiple fold lines, SketchUp restricts that movement, just to make sure you really want to do it. Toggle the Auto-fold with the Alt key (⌘ key on a Mac), and you can do as you please.

Moving the faces, edges, and endpoints on rectangles and polygons works much like the triangle example in the previous section. If you'd like a little practice moving faces, edges, and points, draw some polygons and rectangles. Push/Pull (P) them into 3-D objects. Then, use the Move (M) tool to select and move the objects' different parts. Try moving the faces, edges, and points with Auto-fold toggled off, and then try it with Auto-fold toggled on.

GEM IN THE ROUGH

Motion Restrictions and Auto-Fold

In many ways, SketchUp's behavior when you move a face, an edge, or a point is the same in 3-D as it is in 2-D. The main difference is that moving any part of a 3-D object changes the shape and volume of that object.

- **Moving a face.** Faces retain their shape. The face and all the edges move together, with or without Auto-fold on. With Auto-fold off, faces of 3-D objects can only move perpendicular to the surface.

- **Moving an edge.** You select an edge by clicking anywhere *except* an endpoint or midpoint. The entire edge moves as one piece. With Auto-fold off, edges of 3-D objects only move perpendicular to the edge.

- **Moving a point.** Click the endpoint or midpoint of an edge, and you can move that single point, which can have a dramatic effect on the shape of an object. Moving a point changes the shape of the connected edges and adjacent faces.

Using Auto-Fold with Circles and Cylinders

Circles and cylinders behave a little differently than polygons. Follow these steps to see how you can use the Move tool and Auto-fold to create a cone:

1. **Open a new SketchUp document and draw a circle.**

   Use the Origin point as the center of your circle, and click the red axis to set the radius. Now you can easily find one of the four endpoints with the Move tool.

2. **Use the Push/Pull tool to pull the circle up to a cylinder.**

   Your cylinder takes shape. If you zoom in close, you can begin to see the 24 segments that make up the circular shape, as shown in Figure 3-26.

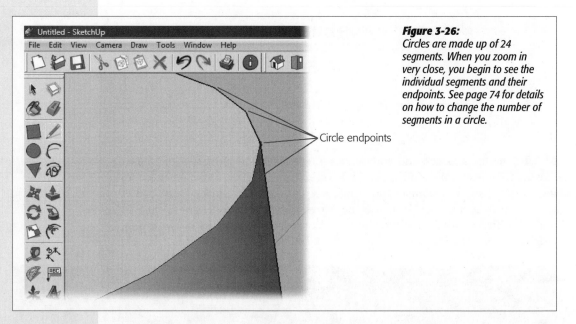

Figure 3-26:
Circles are made up of 24 segments. When you zoom in very close, you begin to see the individual segments and their endpoints. See page 74 for details on how to change the number of segments in a circle.

3. **With the Move tool, click the curved surface of the cylinder, and then move a little to another position and click again.**

   The entire cylinder moves.

4. **Click and move the top surface of the cylinder.**

   The circular face moves up and down the blue axis, and the cylinder shrinks and grows.

5. **Place the Move cursor over the edge of the top circle. Find a spot where the circle is highlighted, and then click and move the edge.**

   When you click and move the highlighted edge, the cylinder shrinks and grows as it did when you selected the top face. If the entire edge isn't highlighted, that means you found one of the four *controlling endpoints,* and the result of the move is different.

6. **Find and then move one of the four controlling endpoints at the top of the cylinder.**

   The controlling endpoints are along the red axis and the green axis. Move a controlling endpoint, and you change the radius of the circle. You can change the bottom and top radii independently.

Tip: Having trouble finding a controlling endpoint? When you hover over a controlling endpoint, the circular edge of the cylinder changes from a thick blue line to a thin black line, as shown in Figure 3-27. If this sounds confusing, see the box on this page.

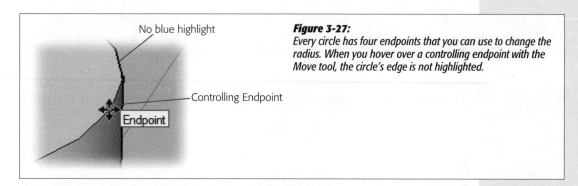

No blue highlight

Controlling Endpoint

Endpoint

Figure 3-27:
Every circle has four endpoints that you can use to change the radius. When you hover over a controlling endpoint with the Move tool, the circle's edge is not highlighted.

7. **Move the endpoint all the way to the center to create a cone, as shown in Figure 3-28.**

   Your cylinder becomes a cone. The bottom is still made up of 24 separate segments and endpoints, but at the top, everything is smushed together. What if you want to turn it back into a cylinder? You'll do that in the next steps.

TROUBLESHOOTING MOMENT

Clearing Up Circular Endpoint Confusion

The endpoints on circles and cylinders can be a little confusing because circles have two types of endpoints. SketchUp makes circles by creating 24 line segments. Endpoints are everywhere these segments meet. Four of these endpoints are special, because when you move them, you change the radius of the circle. You could call them *controlling endpoints.* Unfortunately SketchUp tooltips simply call them endpoints, so it can be tough to distinguish one endpoint from the other.

One easy way to see if an endpoint is a plain old endpoint or if it's a controlling endpoint is to hover over it with the Move tool. When you're over a plain old endpoint, the entire circular edge is highlighted with a thick blue line. When you hover over a controlling endpoint, the circle changes to a thin black line. If you're working with a cylinder, you can find a dotted highlight line that bisects the curved surface running from controlling endpoint to controlling endpoint. Move this line (technically, it's an edge) to simultaneously change the radius of both circles that define the cylinder.

---

8. Use the Move tool along the curved surface of the cone until you find the dashed line that marks the controlling edge of the cylinder.

When the cursor is over the controlling edge, you see a thick, dotted highlight line as shown in Figure 3-28.

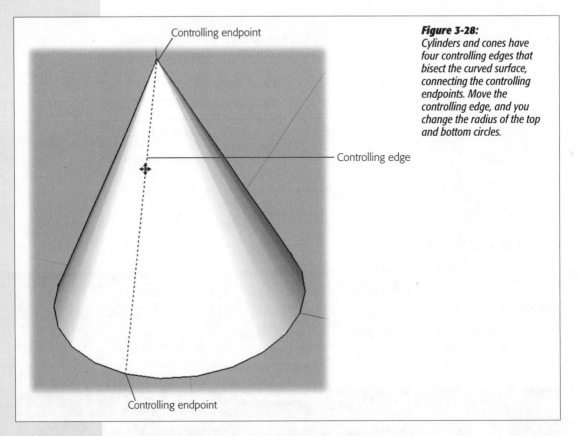

Controlling endpoint

Controlling edge

Controlling endpoint

Figure 3-28:
Cylinders and cones have four controlling edges that bisect the curved surface, connecting the controlling endpoints. Move the controlling edge, and you change the radius of the top and bottom circles.

9. Move the edge away from the center of the cone.

The radii of both the top and bottom circles increase. You can now change the radius of either the top or bottom circle independently, by using one of the controlling endpoints.

Using Info Entity to Edit 3-D Objects

If you mangled your cylinder as described in the previous section, you may have ended up with a shape similar to the one in Figure 3-29.

What's a precise yet easy way to return it to its former cylindrical glory? The Entity Info window is the right tool for the job (Figure 3-30). Use the Select (space bar) tool to select the top circle, and then open the Entity Info window (Windows → Entity Info), as shown in Figure 3-30. Set the radius to a specific dimension, such as *12'*. Repeat the process with the bottom circle, and you have a perfect cylinder.

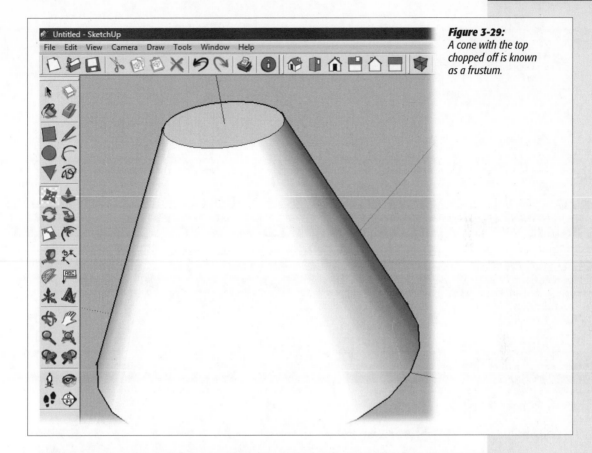

Figure 3-29:
A cone with the top chopped off is known as a frustum.

Figure 3-30:
You can modify 3-D objects using the Entity Info window. Here, the Entity Info window is being used to change the radius of a circle.

Another way to change a cone or frustrum back into a cylinder is to click one of the controlling edges and then push the edge all the way to the center and pull it back out.

Tip: The status bar in the lower-left corner is always working hard to provide helpful, pertinent information. You saw how it provided a timely hint about the Auto-fold toggle. If you get in the habit of glancing at the status bar when you're using other tools, you'll learn about other handy modifier keys. For example, if you're using the Orbit tool, the hint says "Shift = Pan." That's SketchUp's shorthand way of saying: "Wanna use the Pan tool? Hold the Shift key down now."

Part Two:
Building a House

2

Drawing a Basic House

It's time to apply the drawing techniques you've learned to a practical project. In this chapter, you'll build a house with an overhanging roof and a garage. You'll model the doors and windows and trim them out in realistic detail. To complete the project, you'll add a driveway and a front path.

Along the way, you'll add some new skills and techniques to your SketchUp toolkit. To start with, you'll learn new techniques for coaxing inferences from the points, edges, and faces of your model. Equally important, you'll learn how to lock your drawing tools so they move only along specific inferences and axes. After you've mastered these techniques, you'll use them time and again. They're one of the main reasons SketchUp artists are able to draw so quickly and accurately. You'll also learn how to use the Offset tool to quickly model new elements—like trim details—based on the outlines of existing objects like doors and windows. So hop in your pickup truck, and drive out to the construction site. It's time to start building.

Locking an Inference

Chapter 3 introduced inferences (page 97)—handy lines that pop up from time to time to show you what SketchUp thinks you want to do. Inferences appear as temporary, dotted lines. They help you align your work to SketchUp's main axes or find an edge's midpoint or endpoint (Figure 4-1). You use these inferences as guides when you draw new lines and shapes. Letting SketchUp do the aligning and measuring for you makes your work go a lot faster.

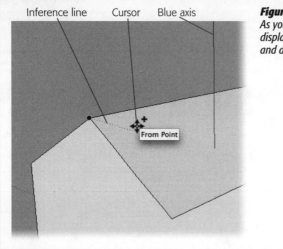

Inference line   Cursor   Blue axis

From Point

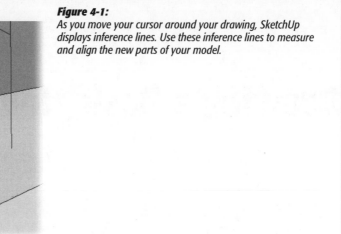

Figure 4-1:
As you move your cursor around your drawing, SketchUp displays inference lines. Use these inference lines to measure and align the new parts of your model.

As you move a drawing tool (like the Line tool) around in 3-D space, SketchUp works behind the scenes to figure out which inference you need. When it sees a likely candidate, the program displays an inference line or highlights a particular point. Inference lines usually run from your cursor back to a point that you might find helpful. When specific points are highlighted, you see a large colorful dot under the cursor. For example, when your cursor is over an edge, a green dot indicates an endpoint, and a blue dot indicates a midpoint. Usually, accompanying tooltip messages explain the inference.

In earlier exercises when you saw an inference that you needed, you moved your cursor slowly and carefully, so you didn't lose the inferences as you drew new shapes and lines. In this exercise, you learn how to *lock* an inference, so you can work more quickly instead of making your mouse tightrope walk to use the inference.

1. **With the rectangle tool, draw a 20 × 10-foot rectangle.**

   Draw the rectangle on the plane formed by the red and green axes. The blue axis is perpendicular to the rectangle.

2. **With the Push/Pull tool, pull the rectangle up into a box.**

   Pull the box up so it's a good height for a one-story house—about 8 feet works well.

3. **Click the Iso view button or choose Camera → Standard Views → Iso.**

   You see an angled view of the box.

4. **Click the box's lower-left corner to start a line, and then move along the green axis, as shown in Figure 4-2.**

   When you move your cursor along the green axis, you see a thin green line. If you happen to move off the green axis, your cursor changes to a black line.

5. **While the line is still green, press and hold Shift to lock the inference in place.**

   When you press Shift, the thin green line changes to a thick green line, as shown in Figure 4-2. Once you lock in the green inference, you can move your cursor all over the drawing, and no matter where you move the cursor, the line you're drawing is locked to the green axis.

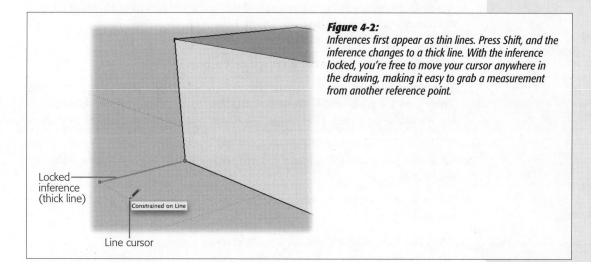

Figure 4-2:
Inferences first appear as thin lines. Press Shift, and the inference changes to a thick line. With the inference locked, you're free to move your cursor anywhere in the drawing, making it easy to grab a measurement from another reference point.

Locked inference (thick line)

Constrained on Line

Line cursor

6. **With the Shift key still down, click to finish the line.**

   The line is drawn parallel to the green axis. SketchUp assumes you want to continue drawing lines, so there's a rubber band line between your cursor and the recently clicked point.

7. **Position the cursor so that the rubber band line is aligned with the red axis.**

   When your line is parallel to the red axis, the rubber band line changes to a thin red line.

8. **Press and hold Shift to lock the red inference line.**

   The thin red line changes to a thick red line. You can move the line cursor around your drawing to reference other points, edges, or faces.

9. **Move the line cursor to the box's lower-right corner to reference that point.**

   When you move the cursor to the corner of the box, the line that you're drawing extends along the red axis. SketchUp displays three signals when you move the cursor to the corner of the box—kind of like a basketball coach waving wildly from the sidelines:

   • A green dot appears at the box's corner.

   • A new dotted inference line runs from the corner to the tip of the line you're drawing.

- A tooltip appears that reads, "Constrained on Line from Point." This is SketchUp's cryptic way of saying that you're using the corner point as a reference for the new line.

10. **With your cursor still referencing the corner point, click to complete the line along the red axis.**

   A new line appears along the red axis. This line is parallel to the bottom edge of the box, and it's exactly the same length. Best of all, you didn't need a carpenter's square or a tape measure to draw it.

11. **Draw the next line to the corner point on the box.**

   This line's a cinch, and it completes a rectangle that's attached to the box. There's no longer a rubber band line attached to the cursor, because SketchUp knows you've completed the shape. Now that you've built out, in the next steps you'll build up.

12. **Click the new rectangle's lower-left corner, and then begin to draw a line up the blue axis.**

   When your line is on the blue axis, the rubber band line changes to a thin blue line (see Figure 4-3).

13. **Press and hold Shift to lock the blue inference.**

   The rubber band line changes to a thick blue line, and the line is locked to the blue axis.

14. **Move the line cursor to the top edge of the box, and then click to complete the line.**

   You can reference any point on the top edge or face of the box to set the height of your line.

15. **Continue by drawing a new line along the green axis back to the box.**

   This should only take one click, because SketchUp's all ready for you to draw another line. When you're done, a new face fills in.

16. **Draw a new line along the blue axis from the right corner of your rectangle.**

   Use the same techniques (steps 12–14) to lock the inference and reference a point on the top of the box to set the height for your line.

17. **Draw a horizontal line to the corner of the first box to complete the face of this new box.**

   After you've drawn the line, the face fills in.

18. **Complete your new box by drawing a line from top corner to top corner, as shown in Figure 4-4.**

   Once this last line is drawn, the faces on top and to the right fill in. You've drawn a perfect, new box by using inferences from the first box.

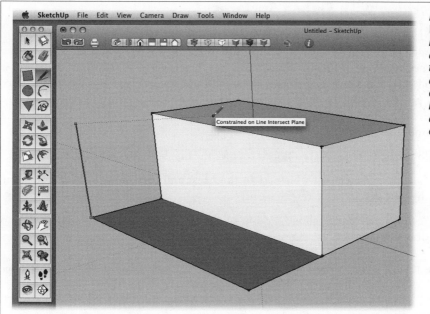

Figure 4-3:
When you're drawing a new line along the blue axis. pressing Shift locks the inference to the blue axis. To make the line exactly the height of the box, you can reference any point along the top edge of the box.

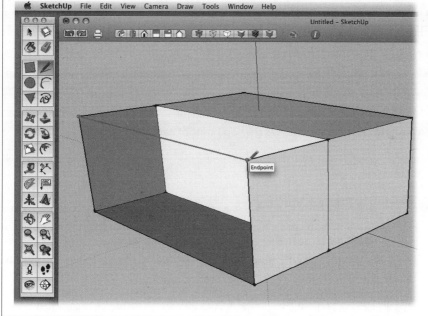

Figure 4-4:
Drawing this last line from corner to corner will complete the new box. With a click of the mouse, the last two faces fill in.

Working with Sloped Surfaces

Up to now, most of the exercises have concentrated on edges and faces that are parallel and perpendicular to each other. Most of the edges and faces have been aligned with one of the three main axes: red, green, or blue. However, the world is filled with odd angles and sloped surfaces. And for good reason—a sloped surface is a great way to keep rainwater off your roof. In this section, you learn how to create sloped surfaces and how to reference an existing sloped surface to create a second sloped face at exactly the same angle.

Follow these steps to create a sloped roof for the first box you created in this chapter:

1. **Click the corner that's farthest to the back, and then draw a short line along the blue axis.**

   A new line extends above the top of the boxes. SketchUp is ready for you to draw another line.

Tip: Press the up arrow to force the line to the blue axis, or wait until you see a tooltip that says "On Blue Axis", and then press and hold Shift. Pressing Shift locks your line to the blue axis.

---

2. **Draw a line down to the endpoint shared by the two boxes to create a triangular shape at the front of the box.**

   The angle of a sloped roof begins to take shape. Use Figure 4-5 as a reference for this second line.

3. **Repeat steps 1 and 2 to create an identical triangle on the box's right side.**

   As you draw the vertical line along the blue axis, hold down the Shift key to lock the inference on the blue axis. Then move the cursor to the top of the first line as shown in Figure 4-5 to set the height for the new line.

4. **Draw a ridgeline that connects the top point of each triangle.**

   Once the ridgeline is drawn, the back face and the sloped face fill in, creating the new roof.

Referencing a Sloped Surface

The first box you drew now has a handsome sloped roof. Suppose you want to create a sloped roof for the second box that continues along the same angle. You can draw this line the hard way, the inaccurate way, or the easy way. The hard way is to pull out SketchUp's protractor tool (see page 283) and to create a guideline that you use to create the new roofline. Well, that's not too hard, but it takes unnecessary steps and clicks. The inaccurate way is to change to a side view and just try to eyeball your roofline. You can get close, but it's unlikely you'll draw a truly accurate line. Creating your roofline the easy way takes only two clicks and a hover. Here are the steps:

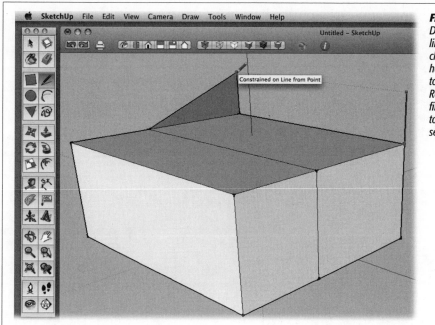

1. **With the Line (L) tool, click the point where your two boxes meet at the top.**

   A rubber band line appears, attached to the end of the Line cursor on one end and to the corner point on the other.

2. **Move the cursor over the sloping line above the first box and hover along the edge.**

   Don't click or do anything else; you're just expressing your interest in the angled line. SketchUp takes note when you hover over an edge or face.

3. **Move your cursor to extend that line across the vertical face of the second box, as shown in Figure 4-6.**

   When the line is at about the same slope as the roof line, it changes to a magenta color. This inference shows that the slope of the new line is identical to the line you hovered over in step 2. You can think of magenta as the parallel inference color.

4. **Press and hold Shift to lock the inference.**

   The thin magenta line turns into a thick magenta line. You can move your line cursor anywhere in the window, and the line stays locked to the roof's slope. You lock the inference to the sloped line with the Shift key, just as you locked inferences that followed the main axes.

5. **Click the box's right edge to finish the line.**

   Continue to hold Shift, and click any point along the right edge to complete the line.

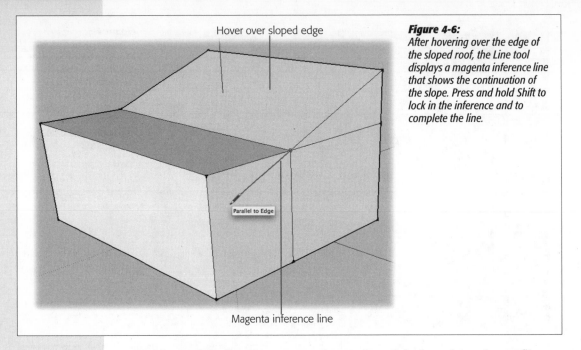

Hover over sloped edge

Figure 4-6:
*After hovering over the edge of
the sloped roof, the Line tool
displays a magenta inference line
that shows the continuation of
the slope. Press and hold Shift to
lock in the inference and to
complete the line.*

Parallel to Edge

Magenta inference line

6. **Use the Push/Pull tool to remove the portion of the box above the roofline, as shown in Figure 4-7.**

   Start by clicking the upper triangle, and then click on the back edge of the box to reference the back face. When you click the back face, the excess portion disappears as it's pushed out of existence.

It was easy to match the slope of the original roofline by using the magenta inference. You'd already drawn that second box, so it was simple to determine the endpoint for your new sloped roof. But what if you wanted to create a new 3-D shape by using that same slope? Perhaps you'd like to continue this roofline all the way to the ground. SketchUp gives you an easy way to figure out the dimensions of this new addition.

1. **Click the house's bottom corner, and then drag a line along the green axis.**

   When the line is oriented to the green axis, its color changes from black to green.

2. **Press and hold Shift to lock the green inference line.**

   Holding the Shift key locks the line to the green axis and changes it to a thick green line. Now you can move the Line cursor to any point in the drawing window without changing the line's orientation.

3. **Move the Line tool to the surface of the roof and then click.**

   Make sure your cursor is over the face of the sloped roof (as shown in Figure 4-8). When you click, SketchUp creates a line that's the perfect length to extend the slope of the roof to the ground.

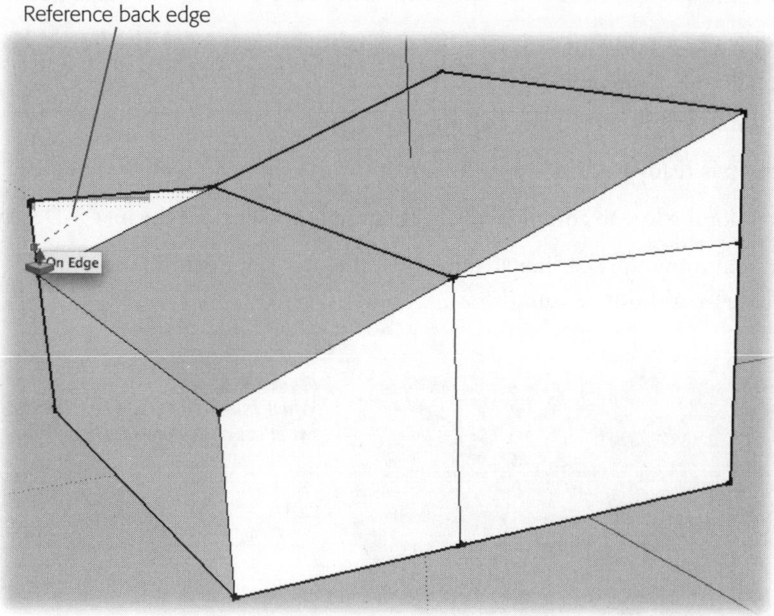

Reference back edge

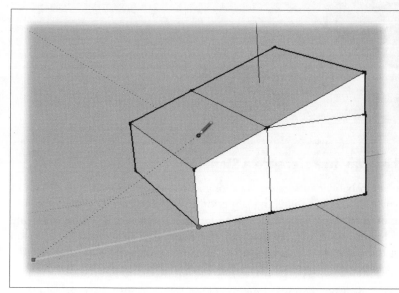

On Edge

Figure 4-7:
After creating the new slope line for the second roof, use the Push/Pull tool to push away the excess portion. Click and start your push, and then click the back edge of the box to remove the section entirely.

Figure 4-8:
By referencing the slope of the roof, you can draw a line exactly the right length to extend the roof to the ground. To reference the slope, make sure your tool is over the face of the roof (as shown here), not over one of its edges.

4. **Click the corner of the roofline to complete the new triangle.**

If you want to examine the new triangle you created, use the Orbit (O) tool. Inspection shows that it's a perfect extension of the other rooflines.

5. **Draw a line along the red axis, using the back of the box as a reference point.**

   Use Shift to lock this new line to the red axis, and then click the house's back edge to determine its length.

6. **Draw a line to connect to the bottom of the box.**

   SketchUp is ready to draw a new line, so all you have to do is click the corner.

7. **Draw a sloping line to complete the back triangle and enclose the new 3-D shape.**

   When you draw the last line (Figure 4-9), the top face forming the roof fills in, and the new addition is complete.

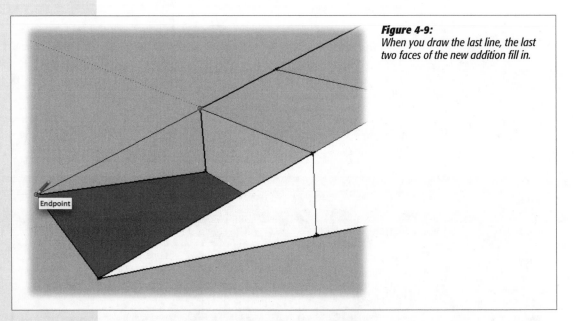

Figure 4-9:
When you draw the last line, the last two faces of the new addition fill in.

Endpoint

Yet Another Way to Reference a Slope

By now you're probably confident that as long as you have a sloped edge or face to reference, you can create a matching slope for any circumstance. That's true, but for the sake of complete disclosure, here's one more example. If you're following along doing the examples in SketchUp, use the Eraser tool to remove the addition you built in the last example. (For a tip on erasing several edges at once, see the box on the next page.)

In the previous example, you saw how to extend a line to just the right length to continue the slope of the roof. You can also use an inference to create a vertical line that's just the right height to continue the roof. As shown in Figure 4-10, the method is almost exactly the same. Click to start drawing a vertical line. When the line is blue, indicating it's aligned with the blue axis, press and hold Shift to lock in the inference. Then you can move your cursor to reference any point, edge, or face in your model. Move the cursor over the face of the sloped roof and then click; SketchUp references the slope of the roof and creates a vertical line of exactly the right height. Finish up by drawing an edge that connects the top points.

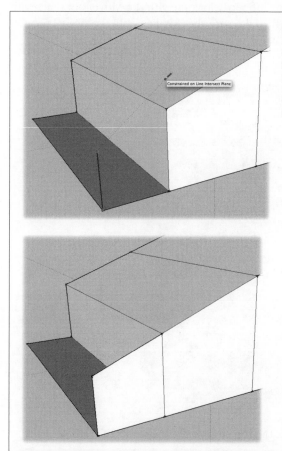

Figure 4-10:
Top: To create a vertical line that's exactly the right height to continue the roofline, press and hold Shift to lock the inference for the blue axis. Then click the face of the roof to reference the slope.

Bottom: After you draw the vertical, connect the top points for a perfect continuation of the roofline.

GEM IN THE ROUGH

Batch Erasing: The Smudge Technique

When you're drawing in SketchUp, you find that erasing edges is nearly as important as drawing edges. It's sort of like that old joke about how to sculpt an elephant—you get a piece of marble and then chip away everything that doesn't look like elephant. In SketchUp, after you've added and modified your model, you're often left with extra, shared edges in your model. Not only are they unnecessary, but extra edges also can lead to unexpected behavior later on. You can erase edges one at a time by clicking them with the Eraser tool, or you can erase multiple edges by clicking and dragging over all the edges you want to remove. As you drag over the edges, they're highlighted. When you release the mouse button, they disappear. Another method for batch erasing is to use the Select (space bar) tool to drag a selection window and then press Delete. When you drag to the right, SketchUp includes any entity entirely in the selection window in the selection. Drag to the left, and you select any entity partially in the selection window. If you accidentally erase an edge that the model needs, don't panic. Just press Ctrl+Z or ⌘-Z and try again.

Inference Locking with the Move Tool

Inference locking works with all of the drawing tools, including those that draw
lines and shapes. It also works with the tools that modify existing objects, such as
the Move tool. To get a feeling for inference locking with the Move tool, start with
a box like the one in Figure 4-11. Make sure the box has only six faces. If you're
using a model from the previous exercise, remove any extra shared edges.

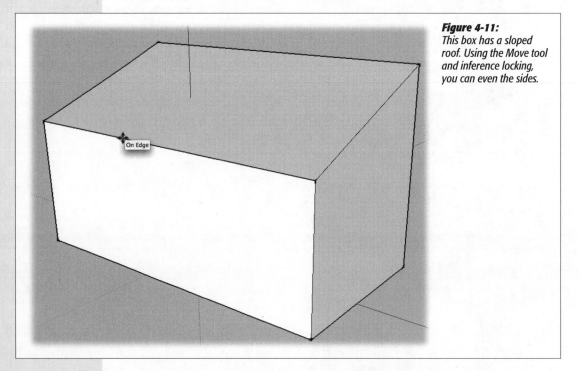

Figure 4-11:
*This box has a sloped
roof. Using the Move tool
and inference locking,
you can even the sides.*

1. **With the Move (M) tool, click the top edge of the short side of the box.**

   The entire edge is highlighted, and the edge moves as you move the cursor.

2. **Move the edge up, along the blue axis.**

   When the edge is moving along the blue axis, you see a blue dotted line and a
   tooltip that says "On Blue Axis".

3. **Press and hold Shift to lock the movement along the blue axis.**

   When you press and hold Shift, the dotted line becomes thicker, and movement is constrained to the blue axis. You can move the cursor to any point in
   the drawing area, and the edge continues to move along the blue axis.

4. **Move the cursor to the opposite edge, and click to reference the height of the opposite wall.**

When your Move cursor is over the opposite edge of the box, a tooltip appears saying "Constrained on Line Intersect Plane", as shown in Figure 4-12. This message is SketchUp's cryptic way of telling you that you're referencing the height of the opposite edge.

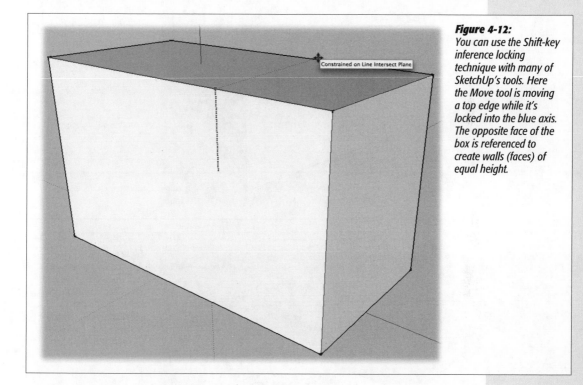

Constrained on Line Intersect Plane

Figure 4-12:
You can use the Shift-key inference locking technique with many of SketchUp's tools. Here the Move tool is moving a top edge while it's locked into the blue axis. The opposite face of the box is referenced to create walls (faces) of equal height.

If you want to experiment some more using the Move tool, try this exercise. You can use the box from the previous exercise, or create a new box similar to the one in Figure 4-13. Find the midpoint along one of the long edges, and draw a line from midpoint to midpoint, dividing the top of the box into two halves. Doing that divides the long edges into two parts, where each part has its own midpoint. Divide the two parts again, so that the top of your box looks like Figure 4-13.

Use the Move (M) tool to pull up one of the lines to create a peaked roofline. When the movement is along the blue axis, you see a blue dotted line and a tooltip message that says "On Blue Axis". Press and hold Shift to lock the movement to that axis. Click to complete the movement and the reshaping of the roofline. Next click one of the other lines in the roof, as shown in Figure 4-14. Pull it up in the same manner, locking it to the blue axis. Then move your cursor over to the first ridgeline and click. This creates two roof ridges of exactly the same height.

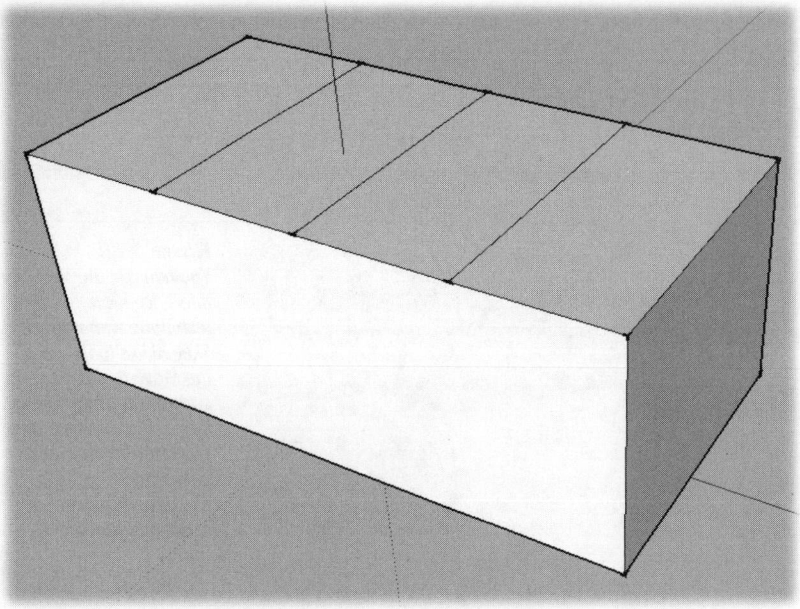

Figure 4-13:
The top of this box was divided into four parts. First, it was divided in half by drawing a line from midpoint to midpoint. Then each new section was divided in the same manner, from midpoint to midpoint.

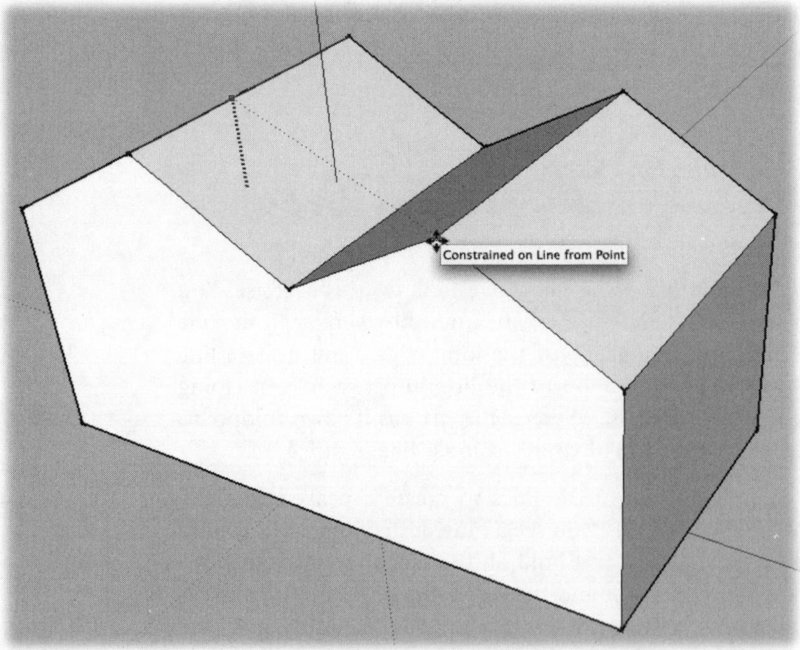

Figure 4-14:
As you pull the second roof ridge along the blue axis, hold down the Shift key to lock in the inference. Then reference the first ridge line to set the height of the edge.

Constrained on Line from Point

You can use inference locking as you move an entire face and all its edges. For example, click one of the middle roof faces. Begin to move the face along the blue axis, and lock the inference by holding Shift. Once the inference is locked, reference the opposite sloping face, as shown in Figure 4-15. Click the face, and you create a tall roof with a single, off-center ridgeline.

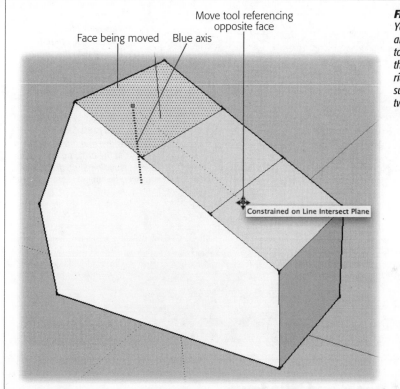

Face being moved Blue axis

Move tool referencing
opposite face

Constrained on Line Intersect Plane

Figure 4-15:
You can change the orientation of an entire face by using the Move tool and inference locking. Here the roof changes from two ridgelines and four sloping surfaces to a single ridgeline with two sloping surfaces.

Using Inference Locking with Shape Tools

If you've followed all the exercises in this chapter, you're probably a pro at locking inferences and referencing points, edges, and faces in your model. All that practice will come in handy as you work in SketchUp. This last example shows you how you can use references from one object, such as a house, to align shapes and faces that are completely unattached to that object. Again, this power comes from a combination of inference locking and SketchUp's click-move-click drawing method.

Start with a model that has a couple of sloped surfaces, like the house model from the previous exercises. Select one of the shape tools, like the Circle or Polygon tool. Notice that when you hold the shape tool over one of the surfaces of the house, the tool automatically orients itself to the surface underneath. Move to a different surface, and the tool snaps to that orientation. Move the tool to one of the sloped roof surfaces, and then press and hold Shift. Move the tool away from that surface, and then click-move-click to draw the shape in mid-air, away from the house model. When you're done, it should look something like Figure 4-16. The shape should be oriented to the same slope as the roof. Use the Orbit (O) tool to maneuver around and see the shape from different angles. If you want some more practice, draw shapes with the Rectangle and Polygon tools that are aligned to some of the other surfaces of the house.

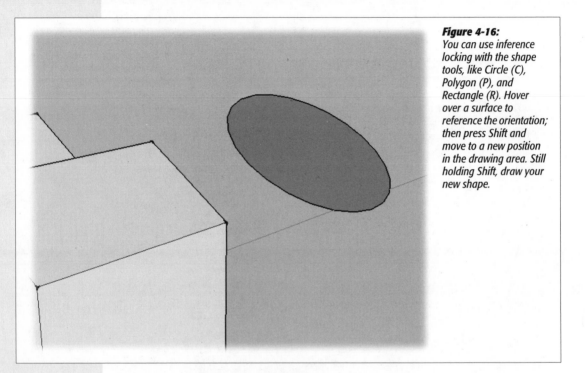

Figure 4-16:
You can use inference locking with the shape tools, like Circle (C), Polygon (P), and Rectangle (R). Hover over a surface to reference the orientation; then press Shift and move to a new position in the drawing area. Still holding Shift, draw your new shape.

Making Doors and Windows

When you're building a house in the real world, you spend a lot of time measuring and aligning the different elements. You may want to align several windows so they're at the same height. Perhaps you'd like to position a garage door so it's perfectly centered underneath the eaves. In the real world, that takes a lot of quality time with your tape measure. In SketchUp you can take advantage of computer-assisted shortcuts, most importantly, that old friend the inference.

For this exercise, start with a house-shaped box that looks like the one in Figure 4-17. You create and position openings for doors and windows. Later you'll create framing and trim for these features.

1. **With the Rectangle (R) tool, draw a front door on the house.**

   Position the door to the left of the midpoint, as shown in Figure 4-18. For this exercise, it's fine to eyeball the dimensions. Just drag out a rectangle that appears to be a reasonable size.

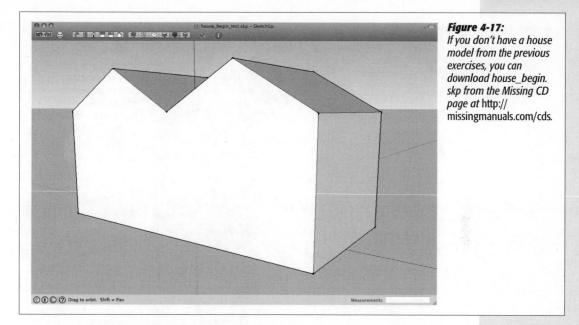

Figure 4-17:
If you don't have a house model from the previous exercises, you can download house_begin. skp from the Missing CD page at http://missingmanuals.com/cds.

2. **Hover over the door's upper-right corner, and then move horizontally to the right.**

   When you see a tooltip that says "Endpoint", move the cursor to the right. As you move the cursor horizontally, you should see a dotted inference line—if not, try moving up or down just a smidgen.

3. **Press and hold Shift to lock the inference.**

   The thin, dotted inference line becomes a thick, dotted inference line.

4. **Click-move-click to draw a window, with the top edge the same height as the door.**

   Your window can be square as is the one shown in Figure 4-18, or it can be rectangular. SketchUp displays a tooltip message when a rectangle is a square or a golden section.

5. **On the left side of your house, draw a large rectangle for a garage door.**

   You can place the garage door anywhere along the left side of the building. You'll position it precisely in the following steps.

6. **With the Select tool, click the garage door.**

   After you preselect the garage door, the face and edges show highlights.

7. **Choose the Move (M) tool and click the midpoint at the top of the garage door.**

   After you click the midpoint, the garage door moves with the cursor. It's constrained to moving along the face of the wall.

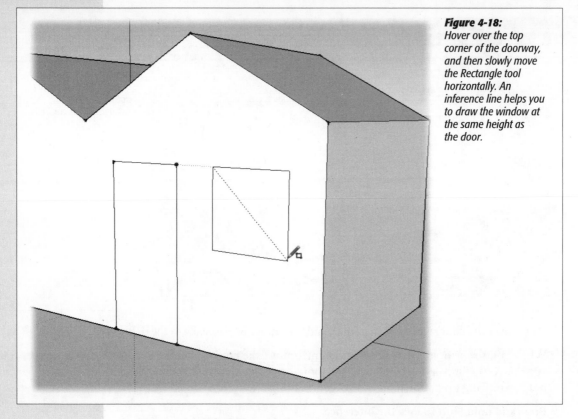

Figure 4-18:
Hover over the top corner of the doorway, and then slowly move the Rectangle tool horizontally. An inference line helps you to draw the window at the same height as the door.

8. Press and hold Shift, and then move the cursor to point at the peak of the garage, as shown in Figure 4-19.

   The garage door moves horizontally as you move the cursor.

9. Click to finish the move.

   The garage door is centered beneath the peak of the roof.

Using the Offset Tool

The world is full of symmetry—both natural and human made. This fact was not lost on SketchUp's software engineers; they created the handy Offset tool so you can easily copy and use the existing shapes and edges in your drawing. The Offset tool is in the toolbar, near the Move and Push/Pull tools, or you can choose Tools → Offset. For some tips and details about using the Offset tool, see the box on the next page. In this next exercise, you'll trim out the window and doors of your house model. *Trim out* is a carpenter's term for applying wood trim around something like a door or window. Trim hides the seams and provides a more finished look.

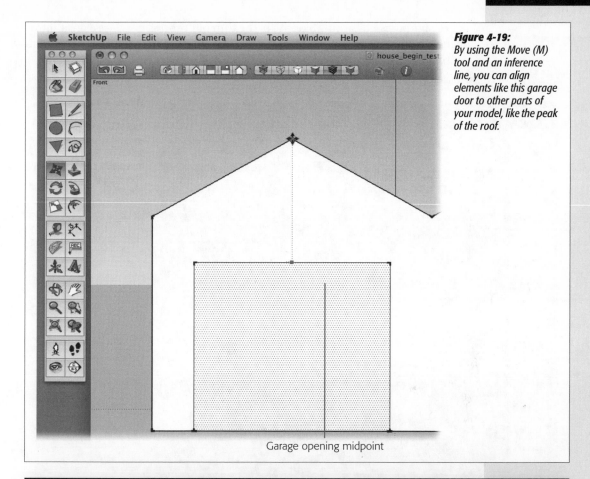

Figure 4-19:
By using the Move (M) tool and an inference line, you can align elements like this garage door to other parts of your model, like the peak of the roof.

Garage opening midpoint

UP TO SPEED

Saving Time with the Offset Tool

The Offset tool does more than simply copy and paste. The Offset tool lets you copy, paste, *and modify* with incredible speed. Consider a common architectural detail like the wood trim around windows. Perhaps it's a simple 1×4-inch piece of wood. You draw a rectangle for the window that's exactly the right dimensions. Then you need another rectangle (or two) with slightly different dimensions. With the Offset tool, you can select the rectangle for the window opening, and then enter a value such as 4" in the Measurements toolbar, and voilà—you've created window trim. Need to create window trim for 6, 12, or 24 more windows? Just double-click the window openings. The Offset tool remembers your last operation and applies that preset value to any thing you double-click.

Go ahead and try it using an empty or unused area of a SketchUp document. Change to Top view, and then create a 3-inch circle. Zoom in to get a good view. Grab the Offset tool and move it toward the circle. When you get close, you see a red square jump to the edge of the circle. That's the magic of auto-selection—SketchUp is always trying to figure out what you're going to do next. Drag slightly away from the circle, type 3", and then press Enter. A new circle appears around the original circle. Double-click the outer edge of the circle a couple more times. Each time you do, SketchUp creates a new circle 3 inches away from the perimeter of the last circle. When you're done, you have a perfectly formed target symbol like the one shown in Figure 4-20. Just add color, and you're ready for archery practice.

For the purposes of learning SketchUp, the trim out process provides a great introduction to the Offset tool. Before you use the Offset tool, make sure nothing in your model is selected by pressing Ctrl+T (Shift-⌘-A).

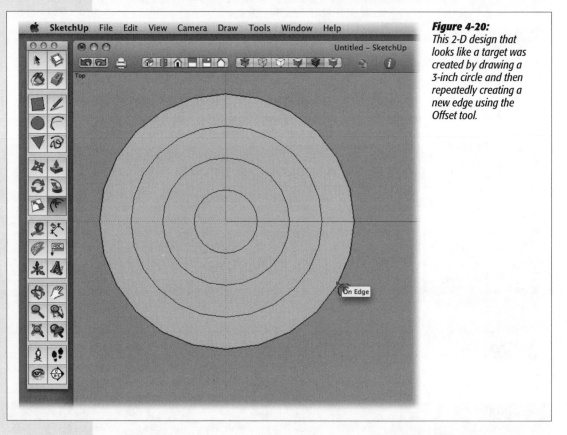

Figure 4-20:
This 2-D design that looks like a target was created by drawing a 3-inch circle and then repeatedly creating a new edge using the Offset tool.

1. **Select the Offset tool and then move the cursor over different parts of your house model.**

   As you move the cursor around your model, auto-selection kicks into action. Different faces are highlighted and a red square snaps to different edges. The square marks the target of the offset operation.

2. **Click once while the red square is on the edge of the window.**

   The square locks in place on the edge. Now as you move the cursor, you see another rectangle that indicates the shape to be created by the offset. Drag the cursor away from the opening to create an offset on the outside of the window opening, or drag it toward the center of the opening to create an offset inside. As you drag, the offset distance is displayed in the Measurements toolbar, as shown in Figure 4-21. If you want to be precise, you can type a value in the Measurements toolbar.

3. Move the cursor toward the middle of the window, and when you're happy with the size of the window trim, click once.

A new rectangle appears within the original window opening.

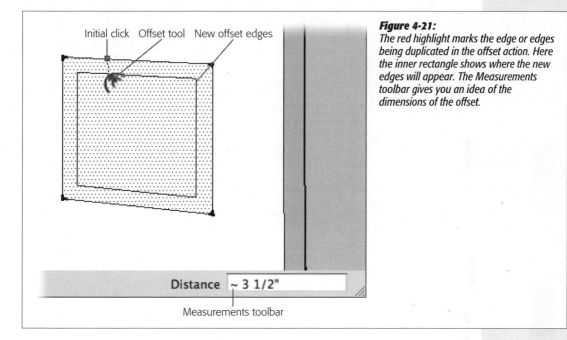

Initial click   Offset tool   New offset edges

Distance   ~ 3 1/2"

Measurements toolbar

Figure 4-21:
The red highlight marks the edge or edges being duplicated in the offset action. Here the inner rectangle shows where the new edges will appear. The Measurements toolbar gives you an idea of the dimensions of the offset.

4. Double-click the edge of the inner rectangle.

The Offset tool creates another rectangle inside of the window with the same offset distance.

5. Use the Push/Pull tool to push back the "glass" at the center. Then push back the frame about half that distance. Finally, pull out the trim so that it's about an inch or two in front of the surface of the house.

Adjust these features to taste for now. If you want, you can enter precise values in the Measurements toolbar.

Tip: When you're creating the trim and window frame details with the Push/Pull tool, it helps to change the camera view so you see the details from a slight angle. That makes it easier to judge the distance between the surfaces.

At this point the window trim looks pretty good. You've got an inset window frame and an outset window trim. For many buildings, the window and door trim are similar if not identical. When you look at the door, it's easy to see that it would look good with the same trim around the sides and top, but you don't really want trim on the bottom, where the door meets the floor. This calls for a little preselection before you apply the offset.

1. **With the Select (space bar) tool, preselect both sides and the top of the door opening.**

   Click one edge and then hold down the Ctrl (⌘ on a Mac) key. The arrow cursor displays a + sign to indicate that you can add elements to the selection. Click the other two edges to select them.

2. **Change to the Offset (F) tool, and then click the top edge of the door.**

   Because you preselected the edges of the door, the Offset tool automatically snaps to one of the three selected edges. Even if you hover over other parts of your drawing, it doesn't change the selection.

   When you click the top edge of the door, you see new offset lines for the three edges in the selection.

3. **Move the cursor over to the inside corner of the window trim.**

   With the selection locked in, you can move your cursor anywhere in the drawing window. In this case, you use the window trim as a reference to create the door trim.

4. **When you see a tooltip that says "Endpoint" (as shown in Figure 4-22), click the corner.**

   SketchUp creates an offset for the door trim that's similar to window trim. The three edges that were originally selected are still selected, making it easy to repeat the process to create the door frame.

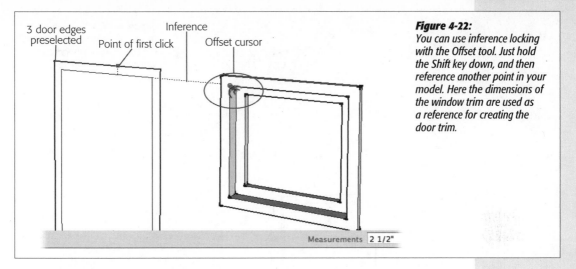

3 door edges
preselected

Point of first click

Inference

Offset cursor

Figure 4-22:
You can use inference locking with the Offset tool. Just hold the Shift key down, and then reference another point in your model. Here the dimensions of the window trim are used as a reference for creating the door trim.

Measurements 2 1/2"

5. **Again click the door's top edge.**

   The Offset tool goes into action, once again displaying new edges as you move the cursor.

6. **This time, move the cursor to reference the inside edge of the window frame and then click.**

   Another set of three lines appears, giving you an edge for the door frame.

7. **Press P to select Push/Pull, and then click the door opening.**

   After clicking, the face of the door moves back and forth as you move the cursor around the drawing area.

8. **Click the window opening.**

   When you click the window opening, Push/Pull uses that as a reference for the door and sets the door at the same depth in the wall.

9. **Click the door frame, and then click the window frame.**

   The door frame is the next section moving from the center to the outside of the door. You set its depth by referencing the window frame.

10. **Click the door trim, and then click the window trim.**

    The final clicks set the door trim so that it stands out from the wall the same distance as the window trim. Where you're done, your trimmed out door and window should look like Figure 4-23.

For consistency, you probably want to add trim to the opening for the garage door; however, it doesn't need an inset frame like the front door and window. You can trim out the garage door using the same technique you used for the front door. Preselect the two sides and the top edge, and then click the top with the Offset tool.

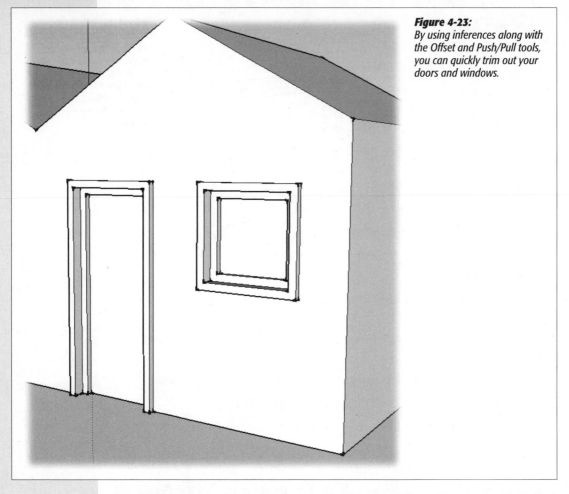

Figure 4-23:
*By using inferences along with
the Offset and Push/Pull tools,
you can quickly trim out your
doors and windows.*

Use the front door trim to size the trim for the garage door. You can use Push/Pull
to set the garage door back in the wall, and then use it to pull the trim out from the
wall surface.

Building a Roof with an Overhang

As you add details your model begins to look less like a modified shoebox and
more like a real house. Another detail that's important for real houses is a roof
with an overhang. The body of the roof holds beams and rafters that support the
roof, and the overhang protects the walls and siding from sun and weather. In the
real world the laws of gravity and nature seem to have more effect than they do in
SketchUp.

In this next exercise, you use the Offset tool to create a profile for your new roof, and then you use Push/Pull to give it shape. The first step is to modify the overall contour of the roof using the Move tool.

1. **Click the roof's left ridgeline, and move it down in along the blue axis.**

   When you move the ridgeline along the blue axis, you see a dotted blue line and a tooltip message that says "On Blue Axis".

2. **When you see the "On Blue Axis" tooltip, press and hold Shift.**

   The Shift key locks the movement of the edge to the blue axis.

3. **Click the house's left edge.**

   The roof flattens, eliminating the ridgeline.

4. **Erase the shared edge.**

   You no longer need the shared edge that divides the ridgeline; remove it now so it won't interfere with other parts of the model.

5. **Move the outside edge down just a bit.**

   Creating a slight slope here helps drain moisture and gives the building a bit of character, as shown in Figure 4-24.

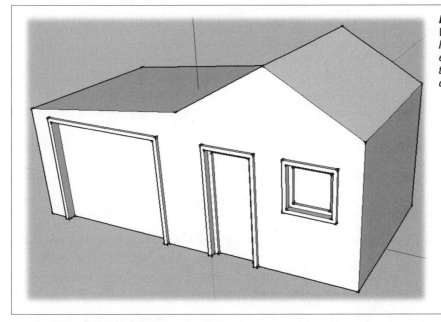

Figure 4-24:
When you adjust the roof line, make sure there's enough room between the roof and the garage door.

6. **At the front of the house, select the edges that define the roof's profile.**

   Your selection should include three lines at the top of the house.

7. **Use the Offset tool to offset the edges up.**

   You can eyeball this offset, or type dimensions. Something between 6 and 8 inches is appropriate for a roof.

8. **With the Line (L) tool, connect the edges between the original lines and the new lines created by the offset, as shown in Figure 4-25.**

   You close this new shape by drawing a line on each end. Once the shape is closed, the face fills in.

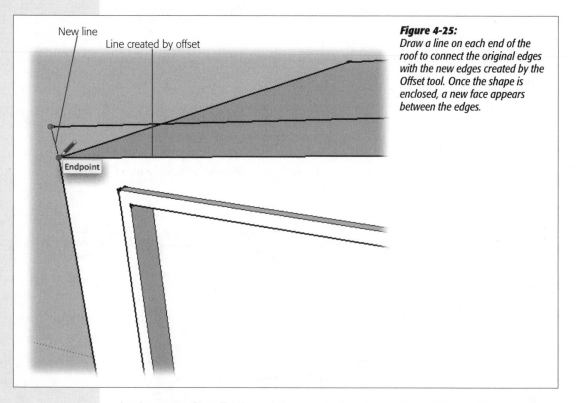

New line

Line created by offset

Endpoint

Figure 4-25:
Draw a line on each end of the roof to connect the original edges with the new edges created by the Offset tool. Once the shape is enclosed, a new face appears between the edges.

9. **Choose Push/Pull (P), and then push the new outline of the roof back to cover the rest of the house.**

   Click the new surface once with Push/Pull, and then push it to the back of the building. You can reference one of the back edges to temporarily align the roof with the back of the building.

10. **Pull out the overhang on the front.**

   Click the front face again, and begin to pull the face forward to create an overhang. A 9- or 10-inch overhang works well, but you can use any dimension you want.

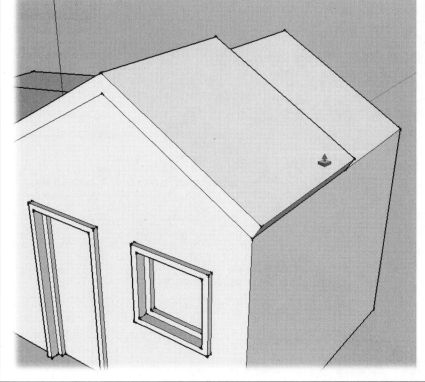

Figure 4-26:
Once the front face is complete, use Push/Pull to extend the new roof to the back wall of the building.

11. **Pull out the overhang on the sides and the back.**

    The overhang should be the same on all sides of the building. Use the Measurements toolbar to accurately create overhangs of equal dimensions. After you've pulled out all the overhangs, you may notice that the process leaves some extraneous lines.

Note: You can't just double-click to repeat the overhang distance. This is due to SketchUp's interior (white) and exterior (blue) face issues. For more details, see page 115.

---

12. **Change your view so you can see the bottom of the overhang, and then erase the extra lines.**

    As shown in Figure 4-27, delete the shared edges that separate faces on the same plane. Don't delete the edges where the roof changes angle; that also erases the faces.

13. **Orbit (O) around the place and admire your construction skills.**

    Unless you've gone off on a creative tangent, your model looks something like the house in Figure 4-28. You'll take care of the initial landscaping in the next few steps.

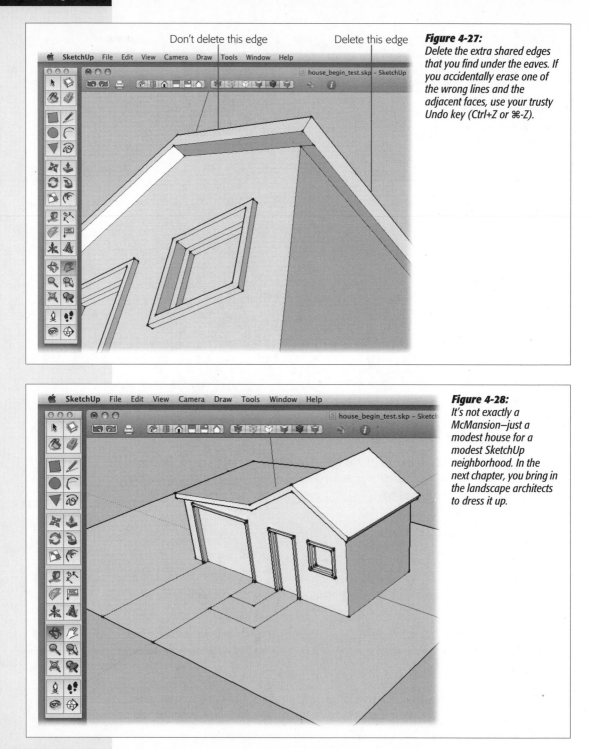

Don't delete this edge   Delete this edge

Figure 4-27:
Delete the extra shared edges that you find under the eaves. If you accidentally erase one of the wrong lines and the adjacent faces, use your trusty Undo key (Ctrl+Z or ⌘-Z).

Figure 4-28:
It's not exactly a McMansion—just a modest house for a modest SketchUp neighborhood. In the next chapter, you bring in the landscape architects to dress it up.

Initial Landscaping:
Front Walk and Driveway

You'll do some more extensive landscaping in the next chapter, but for now you can give your house a plot of earth and a couple of basic paths for cars and people. These basic features are created using the Rectangle and Line tools. You want to draw these elements at the ground level, so it's best to change to the top view before you begin. Once you've drawn the outline of the yard at ground level, the other shapes and paths will align to that surface.

1. **Change to the Top view.**

   This gives you a bird's eye view of your estate. You may want to zoom out a little so there's room around the house to create a yard. Press Z to change to the Zoom tool, and then drag to change the view.

2. **With the Rectangle (R) tool, click-move-click to draw a rectangle around the house to represent the yard.**

   Give yourself enough room for the kids and dog to play. And who knows, some day you may want to add a pool.

3. **Right-click (or Control-click) the face of the new yard, and choose Reverse Faces from the shortcut menu.**

   Because it's a two-dimensional shape, it's more than likely that your rectangular yard is displaying the blue face that indicates an interior. Reversing faces changes its color to white.

4. **Select the Line tool, and then draw two lines to create a drive from the garage to the edge of the yard.**

   Use Figure 4-28 as a reference for placing the edges of the driveway. It's easiest just to click the point where the garage door frame meets the yard.

5. **Use the Line tool to create the left edge of an L-shaped path from the door to the driveway.**

   Click the point where the front door meets the yard, and draw a short line toward the street. Then create another line segment that turns to the driveway, shown in Figure 4-29.

6. **Choose the Select (space bar) tool, and then select the two lines that mark the edge of the path.**

   When they're selected, the thin black lines become thick blue lines.

7. With the Offset (O) tool, click the selected lines, and then click the other corner where the front door meets the yard.

Your walkway has two edges and is the same width as the house's doorway.

8. **Save your model with the name** *house_finished.skp/*.

Not bad for a day's construction. You can use this model in the next chapter, where you tackle fence building and learn about the joys of SketchUp components.

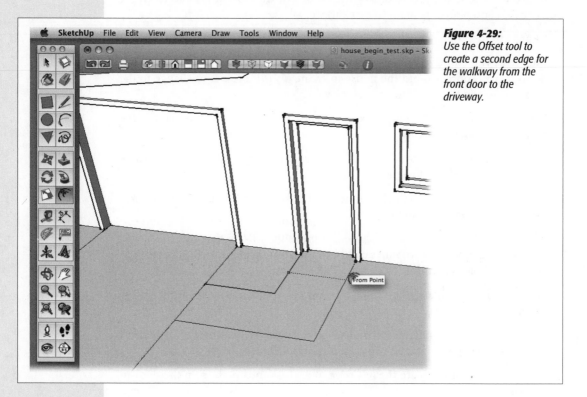

Figure 4-29:
Use the Offset tool to create a second edge for the walkway from the front door to the driveway.

Working Smarter with Groups and Components

SketchUp views the world as edges and faces. You might call them lines and surfaces, but then again, it's a computer program and you're a human being. It's natural that you'd like to organize those edges and faces into groupings that make sense to you. For example, some of the edges and faces in your house might form windows or doors or a roof. As you're working on that house model, you may want to hide the roof so you can look inside. Or you may want to show a client several different window styles. It would be a nuisance to have to select all of a window or roof's individual edges and faces every time you want to move it as a unit.

In this chapter, you learn two ways to collect those edges and faces into meaningful objects that are easier for you to work with. One method is to create a *group*, and the other method is to create a *component*. You'll learn how and when to use one or the other of these methods. Along the way you'll see how the Outliner keeps track of all the groups and components in your model. You'll learn how arrays can help you make multiple copies of objects. Most of the exercises focus on the job of building a simple picket fence.

Groups and components have many features in common, but components have some additional tricks up their sleeves. So it makes sense to take a look at groups first to explore the features they have in common.

Note: This group of exercises continues the SketchUp house project started in Chapter 4. You can use your own file or download *fence_begin.skp* from *http://missingmanuals.com/cds*.

Creating a Group

Have you ever noticed how sometimes one entity in SketchUp gets glued to another? Sometimes that's a good thing. When it's not, you can change this behavior by creating a group. A *group* is simply a collection of edges and/or faces. What you include in a group is entirely up to you. The entities in a group don't have to be connected, touching, or even close to each other. However, much of the time you do group adjacent edges and faces to together for the purpose of making them easier to handle.

Note: In SketchUp the word *entity* simply refers to any object in the drawing window that can be selected. A single edge or face is an entity. A group with lots of edges and faces is an entity, too.

In the next two exercises, you build a planter that fits next to the house. Along the way you'll see how helpful groups can be.

1. **With the Rectangle tool, begin to draw a new rectangle on the gray rectangle that represents the yard, and then type *4',1.5'*.**

   This size makes a planter that fits under the window on the right side of the house.

2. **With the Push/Pull (P) tool, begin to pull the rectangle up into a box; then type *1.5'*.**

   You have a large box in your yard, as shown in the top of Figure 5-1. Five of the faces are exposed above the yard. The bottom face is concealed unless you Orbit (O or middle mouse button) the entire model and look at it from underneath. Then you see that the box has no bottom face, just shared edges with the rectangle that forms the yard, as shown in the bottom of Figure 5-1.

Tip: If you Orbit around to see the bottom, make sure you come back to the surface for the next step. A quick way to do that is to use the View Previous button. Below the Orbit and Zoom tools in the toolbar, it looks like a magnifying glass with a back arrow.

3. **With the Select tool, triple-click the box.**

   When you triple-click the box, you select not only the box, but also the yard, the driveway, the walkway, and the entire house. That's because the box is connected to the yard, and the yard is connected to everything else. Remember, a triple-click selects all the connected faces and edges. You may think of the box as a separate entity, but to SketchUp, it's just a few of many connected faces and edges. There's a better way to make a planter that's not connected to everything else.

Tip: If you absolutely had to select the box in this situation, you could Ctrl-click (⌘-click on a Mac) to select all the faces. But there's a better way to build a box for your planter.

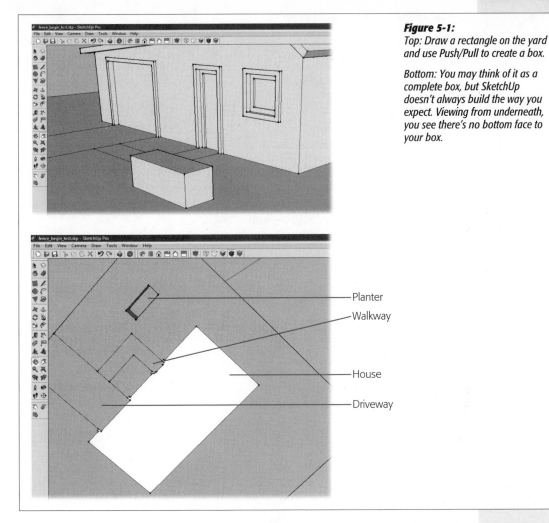

Figure 5-1:
Top: Draw a rectangle on the yard and use Push/Pull to create a box.

Bottom: You may think of it as a complete box, but SketchUp doesn't always build the way you expect. Viewing from underneath, you see there's no bottom face to your box.

Planter
Walkway

House

Driveway

4. **Click in an empty part of the drawing window or press Ctrl+T (⌘-Shift-A).**

   After you click on nothing or use the keyboard shortcut for Select None, nothing in your model is selected. If you use the click nothing method, which is faster, make sure you click *nothing* and that you don't click the yard surface.

5. **Press Ctrl+Z (⌘-Z) to undo the Push/Pull action.**

   Stop your undo actions when you're back to a rectangle on the surface of the yard. Back at square one, the next steps show a better way to build a planter that isn't attached to everything else in your model.

6. **With the Select (space bar) tool, click one of the edges of the rectangle.**

   The edge you click is highlighted, but the rest of the rectangle isn't selected. That'll change once you've grouped the rectangle.

---

7. **Select the face of the rectangle.**

   When you select the face of a shape like this rectangle, SketchUp automatically selects the edges that define the face.

8. **Choose Edit → Make Group.**

   The four edges and single face of the rectangle are now a group. Now if you click an edge, the entire group is selected.

9. **Choose Window → Outliner.**

   The Outliner displays a list of all the groups and components in your document (Figure 5-2). Right now the list shows one group—the one you just created. The solid square next to the word *Group* is the Outliner icon for groups. (The icon for components is four small squares.)

Note: The Outliner is covered in greater detail in Chapter 7.

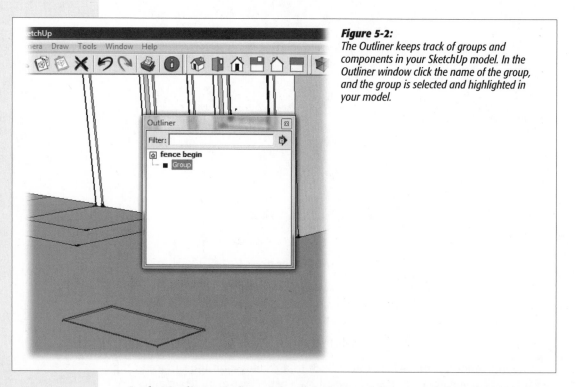

Figure 5-2:
The Outliner keeps track of groups and components in your SketchUp model. In the Outliner window click the name of the group, and the group is selected and highlighted in your model.

10. **In the Outliner window, right-click the word *Group*, and then choose Rename from the shortcut menu.**

    When you right-click the word *Group,* a shortcut menu appears listing more than a dozen things you can do with a group. Down at the bottom of the list is Rename.

11. Type *Planter* and then press Enter.

    In the Outliner your group is named Planter. It's not such a big deal when you've only got one group in your model. But imagine if you're working on a model of a college campus. It could be really helpful to organize buildings and the parts of buildings into groups.

12. Press M and then use the Move tool to move the rectangle around the yard and off of the yard.

    The entire rectangle, face and edges, moves as a single group. Moving the rectangle off the yard doesn't leave a hole in the yard rectangle.

13. With the Select (space bar) tool, double-click the rectangle.

    A dotted box (sometimes called a *bounding box*) appears around the rectangle. The rest of the SketchUp model is dimmed or grayed out. That's your signal that you've opened a group for editing. When you're in this mode, you can select individual faces and edges of the group and make changes.

14. Use Push/Pull (P) to begin to pull the rectangle up into a box. Then type *1.5′*.

    You've got a large box in your yard. Again! But now it's not connected to the rest of the yard, since it's a group unto itself.

15. With the Offset (F) tool, click one of the top edges of the planter and begin to move to the center. Then type *2′* and press Enter.

    An offset interior rectangular face appears on the top of the planter box.

16. With Push/Pull, begin to push the interior face down. Then type *1.2′*.

    This push "removes geometry" from the box, creating the hollow interior for the planter.

17. With the Select tool, click outside of the bounding box.

    The group closes, the bounding box disappears, and you're back in SketchUp's normal editing mode. You can use Edit → Close Group/Component to leave the group edit mode, but it's faster just to click outside the group.

18. Use the Move (M) tool to move the Planter group around the yard, and then place it under the window.

    It's easier to build the planter and then move it into place than to build it in place. The click-move-click method works as expected. It's easy to select and move the Planter group independently of the other faces and surfaces in your drawing.

Editing and Modifying a Group

So groups are great for organizing the edges and faces of an object. Once they're grouped, you can select and move them easily. But what if you want to make changes or additions to a group? You already did a little group editing in the previous exercise, when you double-clicked on the Planter group and pulled the rectangle up into a 3-D box. However, you're not limited to modifying what's already in a group; you can add a new planter to the Planter group as shown in these steps:

1. **With the Select (space bar) tool, double-click the Planter group.**

   The group opens up for editing. The rest of the model fades to gray.

Note: If there's a checkmark next to View → Component Edit → Hide Rest of Model, everything except the group disappears.

---

2. **Use the Rectangle tool to draw a 3 × 1-foot rectangle in front of the box.**

   The new rectangle appears in front of the box as shown in Figure 5-2.

3. **Select the face of the new rectangle and then choose Edit → Make Group.**

   A blue highlight appears around the newly created group.

4. **In the Outliner, right-click the new group and rename it *Small Planter*.**

   This time, the Outliner shows a dotted line branch leading to the new group, indicating that the Small Planter group is contained in the Planter group. In other words Small Planter is a subgroup of the Planter group. See Figure 5-3.

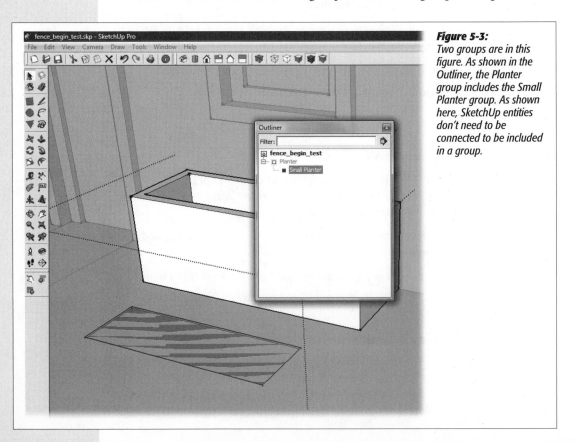

Figure 5-3:
Two groups are in this figure. As shown in the Outliner, the Planter group includes the Small Planter group. As shown here, SketchUp entities don't need to be connected to be included in a group.

5. **In the Outliner double-click Small Planter.**

   The subgroup opens for editing. You can double-click either the group or its name in Outliner to open a group for editing.

6. **Using Push/Pull (P), begin to pull the small rectangle up and then type *12*.**

   The small planter is now a 12-inch-tall box. It's time to hollow it out.

7. **Using the Offset tool, click the top edge of the box, and move the cursor to the middle. Then type *2*.**

   An offset interior rectangular face appears on the top of the planter box.

8. **With Push/Pull, begin to push the interior face down. Then type *11*.**

   The small planter is a miniature version of the first planter.

9. **Choose Edit → Close Group.**

   The Small Planter group is closed, and you're back in the Planter group. Everything except for the two planters is grayed out.

Tip: Another quick and easy way to close a group is to right-click outside of the group, and then choose Close Group.

---

10. **With the Select tool, triple-click the larger planter, and then choose Edit → Make Group.**

    A new group is created within the Planter group because you're still editing with the group.

11. **Right-click Group and choose Rename. Then type *Large Planter*.**

    Your Planter group contains two subgroups: Large Planter and Small Planter.

12. **Choose Edit → Close Group.**

    The Planter group closes, and you see your entire model.

    Notice what happens when you click different group names in the Outliner. You can select the entire group by clicking *Planter*. When you click *Large Planter* or *Small Planter,* the parent group automatically opens and the subgroup is selected.

13. **With the Move (M) tool, click anywhere on either of the planters. Move your cursor around the window and then press Esc.**

    The Planter group moves when you move your cursor. Both planters move with the group. Even though they aren't connected, they're both part of the Planter group. When you press Esc, the move is canceled and the planters return to their original position. If you want to move one of the planters independently, you have to open the Planter group for editing.

Now's a good time to practice opening and closing the Planter group and working with the subgroups. Try centering both planters under the house's window.

Remember, when you move an entity, you click a point like a corner and then click the exact point where you want the corner. This method is a good way to place the large planter against the house and the small planter against the larger. To center objects, find the midpoint on the object you want to move. Use the arrow keys to constrain the movement to a particular axis: right arrow = red, left arrow = green, up arrow = blue. With the movement constrained, you can move the cursor to find the midpoint on the window or on one of the planters. When you're done, your model looks like Figure 5-4.

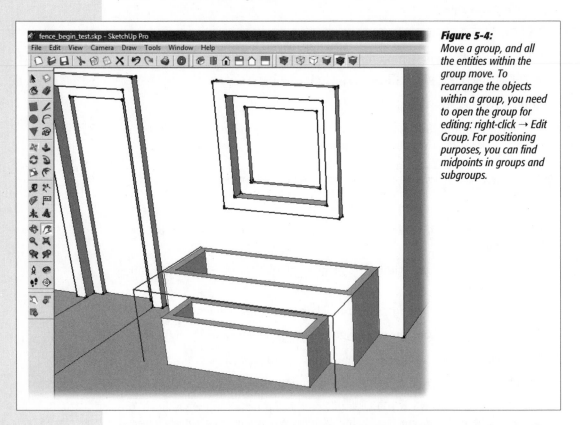

Figure 5-4:
Move a group, and all the entities within the group move. To rearrange the objects within a group, you need to open the group for editing: right-click → Edit Group. For positioning purposes, you can find midpoints in groups and subgroups.

If you followed the exercises so far in this chapter, you've got a good idea of how handy groups can be, especially if you're working on a large project with lots of entities. In fact you've just scratched the surface when it comes to groups and components. For example, right-click one of the groups in the Outliner and examine the shortcut menu (Figure 5-6). You see the same shortcut menu if you right-click in Outliner or if you click the object itself. From the menu you access a number of commands, some of which may be grayed out if they don't apply to the selected entity:

• **Entity Info** opens the Entity Info window for a group, where you can rename, hide, or lock the group. You can also change the way the group casts shadows, and move the group from one SketchUp layer to another. (Layers are covered in more detail on page 275.)

- **Erase,** as you might guess, deletes the group and any subgroups contained in that group from your model. In Outliner you can select and delete a subgroup within a larger group.

- **Hide** is a particularly handy command when your model becomes more complex. It's very helpful to be able to hide an entity such as a roof or wall to get a better view of other parts of your model.

- **Lock** is a safety feature. You can lock a group (or component). Once locked, it can't be changed or edited unless it's explicitly unlocked.

- **Edit Group** is the same as double-clicking on a group to open it in editing mode.

- **Explode** is used to "ungroup." While it sounds a little violent, it simply turns the grouped entities back into ordinary old SketchUp parts like faces and edges, or groups if the entity contains subgroups.

- **Make Component** turns a group into a full-fledged component (page 166). Keep reading this chapter for more details on the special features you find in components.

- **Unglue** changes the sticky behavior of components (see page 332 for details).

- **Reset Scale** returns a group or component to its original dimensions. You can change the dimensions of an entire group by using the Scale (S) tool. When this is done to the entire group or component, as opposed to opening and editing the group, you can undo the changes with the Reset Scale command.

- **Reset Skew** returns a group or component to its original dimensions. You can skew an entire group by making multiple changes with the Scale (S) tool. When you skew an entire group or component, as opposed to opening and editing the group, you can undo the changes with the Reset Skew command.

- **Intersect → Intersect with Model** changes how edges and faces are divided when entities meet. For more details see page 111.

- **Flip Along** repositions an object along one of the three major axes. As shown in Figure 5-5, Flip Along doesn't create a mirror image.

- **Soften/Smooth Edges** smoothes the angles formed where faces meet at an edge.

Figure 5-5:
A copy of the text on the left was repositioned using the Flip Along command. If the flip created a true mirror image, the F in the highlighted text would also be on the left side.

• **Zoom Extents** is great for zeroing in on a particular group or component. Similar to the Zoom Extents command that gives you a view of everything in your model, this command gives you a great view of the selected entity.

• **Rename** lets you give your group or component a new name, as explained in step 10 on page 160.

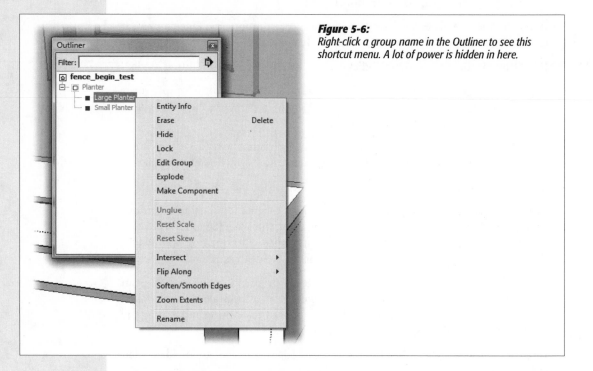

Figure 5-6:
Right-click a group name in the Outliner to see this shortcut menu. A lot of power is hidden in here.

Creating Components

Your house looks a little lonely here on its plot of earth with only a driveway and walkway. It could use a little dressing up. How about a fence to keep the kids and dog in the yard? If you followed the bench exercise in the first chapter, you saw that having SketchUp is like owning a lumber mill. You can whip up the materials you need for a fence in no time, starting with a basic fence board. Identical objects like fence boards or fence posts are perfect candidates for SketchUp components. Create one component, and you can use it over and over. Make a change to one fence board, and every fence board changes.

Note: This group of exercises continues a SketchUp project started earlier. If you need a file to work with, you can download *fence_begin.skp* from *http://missingmanuals.com/cds*.

1. **Zoom into an area slightly in front of the rectangle that designates the yard.**

   You may want to use Zoom (Z), Orbit (O), or the Pan (H) tools to find just the right spot.

2. **With the Rectangle (R) tool, draw a rectangle on the red/green plane at
ground level.**

It shouldn't be difficult to draw a rectangle at the same level as the yard. If you
have trouble, try orbiting around to a more downward view. This time you
don't want the new rectangle to be on top of the rectangle that represents the
yard—position it just in front of the yard.

3. **Type *6,1* and press Enter (Return on a Mac).**

Your rectangle takes on the dimensions of a 1×6-inch board. You don't need to
include the inches symbol when you use the "Architectural Design – Feet and
Inches" template. The long edge of the rectangle is parallel to the front of the
house. If for some reason the orientation is different, press Ctrl+Z (⌘-Z) to
Undo. Then reverse the order of the dimensions, typing in *1,6*.

4. **With Push/Pull, pull the rectangle up. Then type *4′* and press Enter.**

You just milled up a 4-foot, 1×6-inch fence board. You're going to need a lot of
them to keep the dog in the yard.

5. **With the Select (space bar) tool, triple-click the fence board.**

Triple-clicking selects all the faces and edges of the fence board. As shown in the
steps beginning on page 158, if the fence board is attached to any other objects,
triple-clicking selects all of the faces and edges of those objects, too. So, for
example, if in step 2 you drew the initial rectangle on top of the yard, instead of
in front of the yard, triple-clicking could end up selecting the yard, the walk-
ways, and the house. In that case, you're better off using the Select tool to drag a
selection window around the rectangle. For some tips on using this technique,
see the box on page 171.

6. **Press G.**

The G keystroke turns the selected items into a component and opens the Create
Component window, as shown in Figure 5-7.

In SketchUp you have two ways to turn multiple faces and edges into a single
element—groups and components. For the lowdown on when to use groups
and when to use components, see the box on page 190.

Note: It's a little odd that the G command creates components instead of groups. The name is a result of
the way SketchUp evolved from one version to the next. Just try to remember G for components not
groups. Mac users may prefer to use ⌘-G for groups and Shift-⌘-G for components.

---

7. **In the Name box, type *fence board*. In the Description box, type *4-foot 1x6
fence board* or some description of your choice, and then click Create.**

After you click Create, the window disappears, and your fence board is now a
component. As a result you see a special component highlight around the fence
board when it's selected.

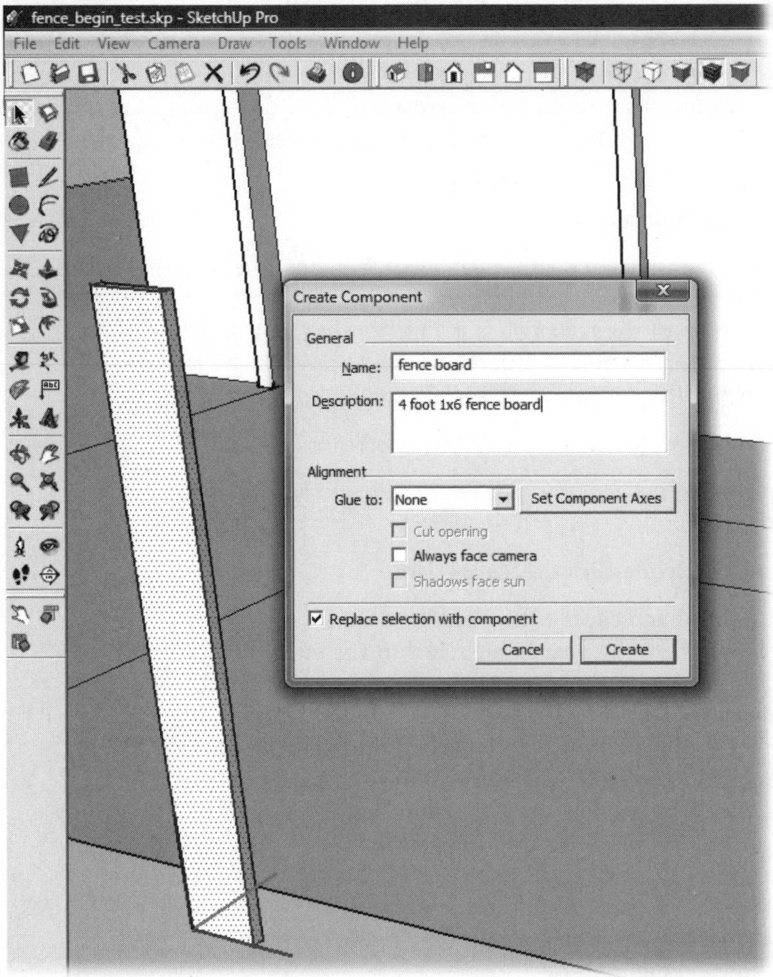

Figure 5-7:
Use the Create Component window to name and provide a description for your component. For many components the factory settings for Alignment and "Replace selection with component" work just fine.

8. **Select the Move (M) tool, and then hold the cursor over the fence board component.**

   When the Move tool is over the fence board, the component displays a high-light around its perimeter. The fence board shows the red crosses that you can use to rotate the component, as shown in Figure 5-8.

9. **Click to select the fence board, and then move it into the yard, to the right of the driveway.**

   The fence board moves as a single object, the same way a group moved.

Figure 5-8:
When it comes to selecting, moving, and rotating, components behave very much like groups. Click any part of the component to select or move it. Click one of the red crosses with the Move tool to rotate a component.

10. **Choose Window → Outliner.**

The Outliner opens showing <fence board>. Components appear bracketed in the Outliner list, and the icons for components and groups are different, as shown in Figure 5-9.

In many ways, components behave like groups, as described in the previous section. For example, you can select a component with a single click. Components display a blue highlight that envelops the entire component. As with groups, you can keep track of the components in the Outliner. To make changes to a component, you have to open it for editing. The next section shows how to build a fence the speedy way, by using an array.

Tip: You can find more details on creating different types of arrays in *Google SketchUp Cookbook* by Bonnie Roskes (O'Reilly).

Speeding Up Construction with Arrays

Once you create a component, it's easy to add a copy of it to your model. Open the Components window (Window → Components), and then click the In Model button (it looks like a house). *In Model* shows the components that are in your document.

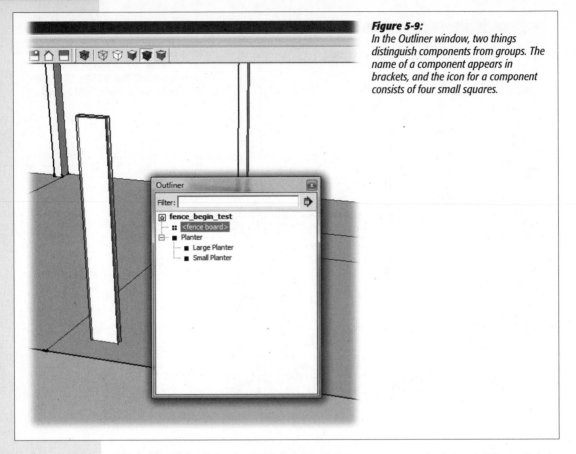

Click your fence board component in the Components window, and then click in the drawing area. If you built the bench covered in Chapter 1, you've already placed copies of components. In SketchUp-speak, the copies are called *instances* of the component. Placing components from the Components window is incredibly handy when you're adding a few windows to a house or adding benches to a public park. When you're building something like a fence, where you need dozens of fence boards perfectly spaced and aligned, there's a better method. You can create an *array* of fence boards. What's more, arrays aren't limited to components. In SketchUp if you can select it, you can create an array consisting of any number of identical objects. That means you can make an array of a single edge, a simple shape, a group, or a ridiculously complex component.

First here's a quick and easy way to make a single copy, and then in the following steps you learn how to create an array:

1. **Press M to select the Move tool.**

   You can also select the Move tool from the toolbar if that's handier. Once the tool is selected, your cursor changes to a cross with an arrowhead at each point.

UP TO SPEED

Selection Direction Matters

If you select objects in SketchUp in a willy-nilly manner, you may be in for some surprises. First, it's worth noting that the Select tool is one of the few SketchUp tools that use the click-drag method. Sure you can Shift-click to select multiple objects, but often it's faster to click and drag a selection window around several edges and faces to make your selection. However, this is where things get tricky. SketchUp behaves differently when you select from left to right than it does when you select from right to left.

- **Left to right selection** selects the faces and edges that are completely within the selection marquee. Google documents call this a *Crossing Selection.*

- **Right to left selection** selects all the faces and edges that are partially within the selection marquee. Google documents call this a *Window Selection.*

For a visual example of the differences, see Figure 5-10 and Figure 5-11. Once you get the knack of these two selection methods, you'll find that they're another SketchUp feature that speeds up your work. For example, when an ungrouped object (such as the fence post) is sitting on another object (such as the rectangle that designates the yard), it sticks to that surface. If you want to move the fence post to another location, it can be a sticky business (pun intended). You want to move all the faces and edges of the post, but you don't want to mess with the yard. Make your selection from left to right. Make sure that the only complete edges and faces within the marquee are those of the fence post, and you can safely extract the post from any adjacent objects.

As your models become more complex, either of these selection techniques can lead to disaster if you accidentally select part of your model before a Move or an Erase command. This is another good reason for protecting entities in groups or components and selecting them with single clicks or from the Outliner.

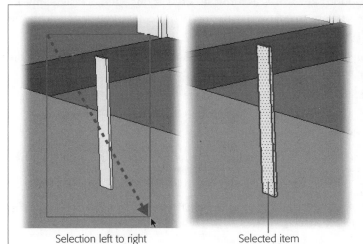

Selection left to right   Selected item

Figure 5-10:
When you drag from left to right with the Select tool, SketchUp selects all the edges and faces that are completely within the selection marquee. This technique is good for separating an object from background objects.

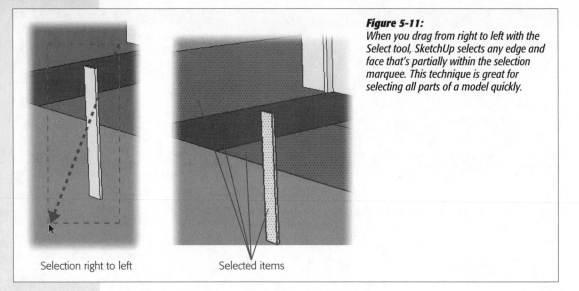

Selection right to left

Selected items

2. **Move your cursor over the fence board component.**

   In the lower-left corner, SketchUp displays hints for using the Move tool. In Windows, one hint says "Ctrl = toggle copy." On a Mac, it says "Opt = toggle copy." The hint means that you can use the Move tool to copy an object and then move the new copy to a new location.

3. **Press and release the Ctrl (or Option) key.**

   The Ctrl (or Option) key works as a toggle. Press it once and a + sign appears on the Move cursor, indicating that you're in copy mode, as shown in Figure 5-12. Press the toggle key a second time, and the + sign disappears.

4. **While the + sign is showing, click the fence board component, and move the copy along the red axis as shown in Figure 5-13.**

   Press and hold Shift to lock the movement to the red axis. The original fence board component stays put, and you place a second fence board in front of the house.

5. **Click to place the new fence board.**

   Don't press Enter or do anything else at this point. Now's the moment when you can perform some array tricks.

Note: You can duplicate any SketchUp entity using the Move tool's copy toggle. It doesn't have to be a component or even a grouped object.

---

6. **Type *20*, and then press Enter.**

   When you type *20*, the number appears in the Measurements toolbar, and SketchUp spaces your two fence boards so the center of one board is 20 inches from the center of the next board. In carpenter-speak, that's known as "20 inches on center." Sometimes you may see it written as "20" o.c."

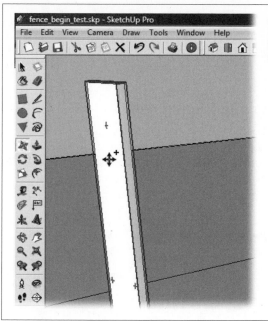

Figure 5-12:
*You can copy and move objects in one operation with the Move
tool. Press and release the copy toggle key—Ctrl on a PC or
Option on a Mac.*

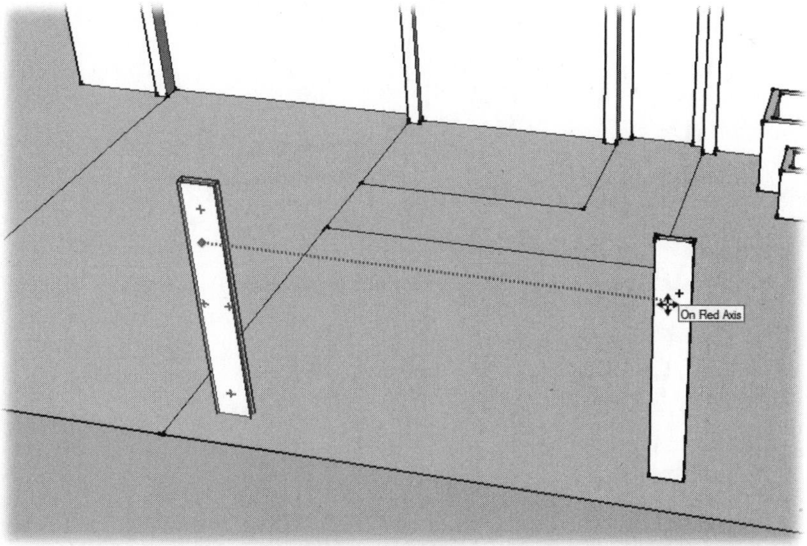

Figure 5-13:
*Here the copied fence
board is constrained to
movement along the red
axis. After you click to
place the new fence
board, you can type
changes to set the
distance between fence
boards or the number of
fence boards you want in
an array.*

Note: When you're using the Architectural Design – Feet and Inches template, SketchUp assumes you're
providing dimensions in inches unless you include a symbol, such as the foot symbol.

7. **Type *12* and then press Enter.**

After you type the number, the fence boards move so they're 12 inches on center. As long as you don't choose another command or tool, you can change the distance. This is handy when you're visually positioning objects and you don't know the exact measurement.

8. **Type *10x* and then press Enter.**

Instead of just one new fence board, you see 10 new fence boards, as shown in Figure 5-14. They're all spaced perfectly using the most recent measurement you typed. The x symbol is a signal to SketchUp that you want multiple copies of the item you're moving and copying. If you decide you need more or fewer fence boards, just type a new number followed by the letter x.

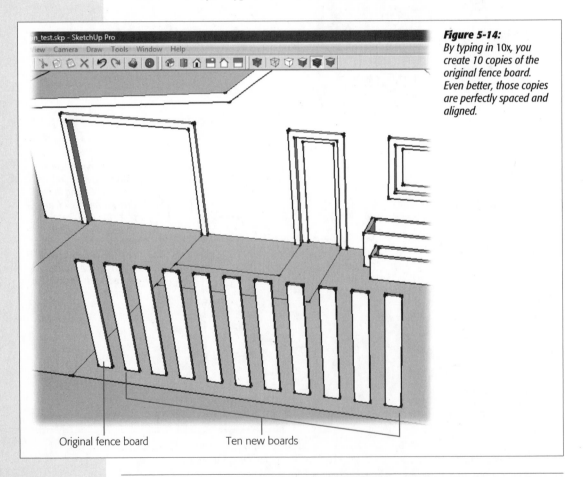

Figure 5-14:
By typing in 10x, you create 10 copies of the original fence board. Even better, those copies are perfectly spaced and aligned.

Original fence board   Ten new boards

Tip: When you create an array—like these fence boards—you can keep changing the distance between the elements and the number of elements. Just type your change. The change appears in the Measurements toolbar, and the changes appear in the drawing area. As soon as you choose another tool or command, you won't be able to change your array.

Like many features in SketchUp, arrays are simple in concept, but can save you a ton of time in practice. Not only do arrays help you to make multiple copies of a component, but they also do all the hard work of aligning and spacing them evenly. As you're working, remember that you can create an array of anything from a single edge to a component.

Creating an Array Between Two Points

Here's another handy trick. Suppose you know that you want your fence boards to stretch from the edge of the driveway down to the corner of the lot. Instead of trial and error, you can use some array magic to make the job easy.

1. **Press Ctrl+Z (⌘-Z) until you have only a single fence board component in your front yard.**

    If you did the previous exercise, chances are you've got a bunch of fence boards in the yard. Undo them or delete until you're back to one fence board component.

2. **Press M to select the Move tool, and then move it over the fence board component.**

    When you put the Move cursor over the fence board, you see the component highlights on the fence board. In addition to the blue envelope, you see red crosses at different points of the component. Move the Move tool over one of these crosses, and the tool changes to the Rotate tool. This gives you a quick and easy way to position and move a group or object with a single tool.

3. **Press and release the Ctrl key (Option on a Mac).**

    The + sign appears on the Move cursor, indicating that you're going to make a copy of the fence board and move the copy.

4. **Click the fence board, and then move the copy along the red axis to the end of the yard.**

    Hold the Shift key down to keep the fence board moving along the red axis, as shown in Figure 5-15.

5. **Type *12/* and then press Enter.**

    After you type 12/, SketchUp creates 12 copies of the original fence board and spaces the copies evenly between the original board and the board you placed at the corner of the yard (Figure 5-16).

Note: When you create arrays, you always have your original plus the number of copies you created. So if you type *12x* or *12/,* that means you have 13 fence boards.

---

6. **Type *20/* and press Enter.**

    As with the other array techniques, you can make adjustments up until you choose another command or another tool.

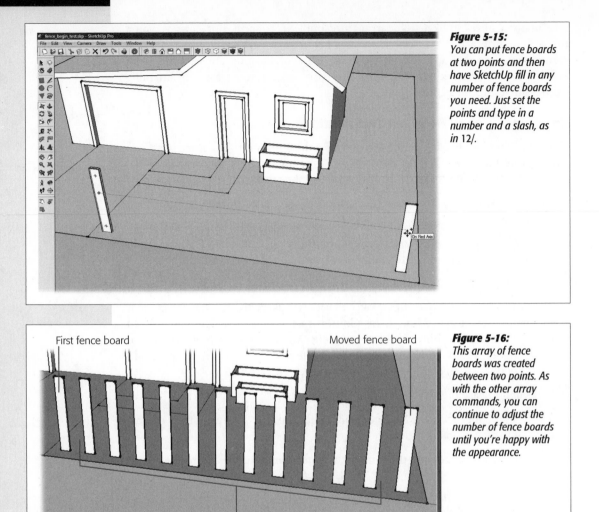

Figure 5-15:
You can put fence boards at two points and then have SketchUp fill in any number of fence boards you need. Just set the points and type in a number and a slash, as in 12/.

Figure 5-16:
This array of fence boards was created between two points. As with the other array commands, you can continue to adjust the number of fence boards until you're happy with the appearance.

First fence board

Moved fence board

Array created

Measurements toolbar

Editing Components

In some ways, editing a component is similar to editing a group, as explained on page 161. You can't just jump in and start moving edges or push/pulling the faces, since components live inside that protective envelope that enables you to select them with a single click. First, you must open the component for editing. You open components with a double-click or by right-clicking and choosing Edit Component. Then you can edit the edges and faces as you do other objects. Note one important difference when it comes to components: Any change you make to a component appears in *every other instance of that component*. This next exercise illustrates the point.

1. **With the Select (space bar) tool, double-click any one of the fence board components.**

   The component opens in editing mode. A bounding box appears around the component you're editing. The other entities in the modeling window are temporarily grayed-out or faded.

2. **With the Push/Pull (P) tool, click the face of the fence board, and then move the cursor back and forth.**

   As you make changes to the fence board component, all the other fence boards change, too. See Figure 5-17.

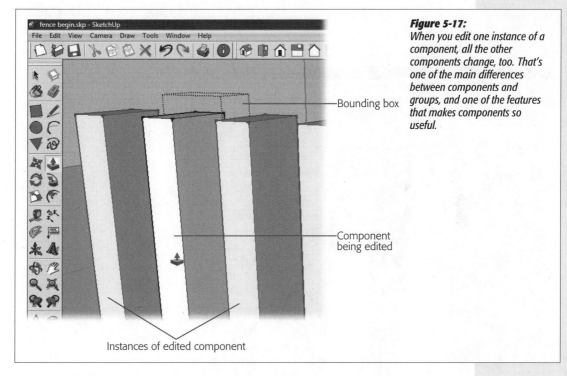

Bounding box

Component being edited

Instances of edited component

Figure 5-17:
When you edit one instance of a component, all the other components change, too. That's one of the main differences between components and groups, and one of the features that makes components so useful.

3. **Make the fence boards any thickness you like. If you liked the original thickness, press Esc.**

   The Esc key cancels the Push/Pull action and returns the fence board to its original shape. You're still in edit mode.

4. **Choose the Line (L) tool, and then click the midpoint at the top of the fence board.**

   The Line tool snaps to the midpoint of the top edge. A rubber band line runs from the midpoint to the tip of the Line cursor.

5. **Move the Line tool to create a diagonal line to one of the edges.**

   Choose an angle that looks like your basic picket fence.

6. **Draw another line from the top midpoint to the other edge.**

   Use an inference to make sure the two lines are symmetrical.

7. **Use Push/Pull to push away the excess corners, as shown in Figure 5-18.**

   Push the face of the section you want to remove, and click a back edge of the fence board to align the push action with that back face. The excess sections disappear.

8. **With the Select tool, click outside the component's bounding box.**

   You leave component edit mode. All the fence boards have a nice picket-shaped top.

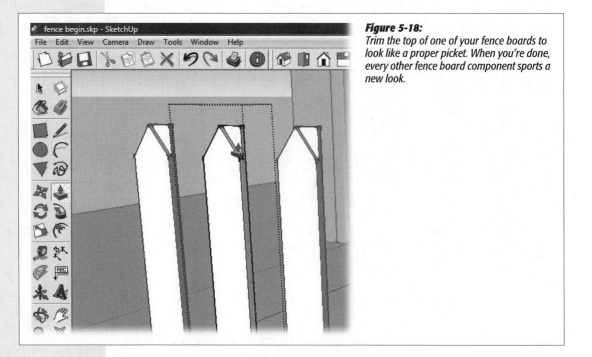

Figure 5-18:
Trim the top of one of your fence boards to look like a proper picket. When you're done, every other fence board component sports a new look.

Using the Make Unique Command

With the help of components and arrays, the front yard's fence is beginning to take shape. The fence boards look like fence board, but they're kind of floating in mid-air, not attached to anything. In the real world, fences have posts. These thicker pieces of lumber support the rest of the structure. You can turn one of your pickets into a fence post, but before you do that, you need to let SketchUp know that you only want to make changes to *one* fence board. You do that by using the Make Unique command.

Here's how you do it:

1. **With Select (space bar), right-click the fence post next to the driveway. From the shortcut menu (Figure 5-19) choose Make Unique.**

   After you choose Make Unique, nothing much appears to change, but rest assured, it has.

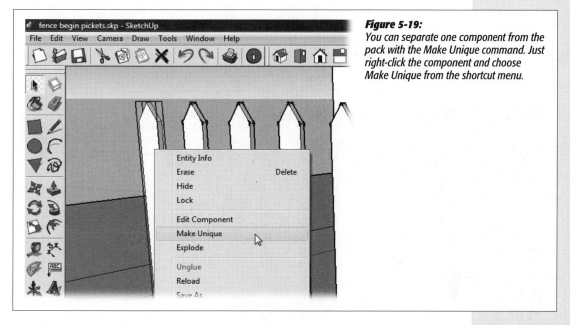

Figure 5-19:
You can separate one component from the pack with the Make Unique command. Just right-click the component and choose Make Unique from the shortcut menu.

2. **Double-click the fence board.**

   The fence board component opens for editing. That's right, the fence board is still a component.

3. **Use Push/Pull to pull the face about 5 more inches.**

   You want to turn this board into a 6×6-inch post. You can type 5 if you want to do it accurately, or you can eyeball it. The Push/Pull changes only affect the selected fence board.

4. **Use the Line (L) tool to draw a line separating the picket's point from the rest of the board.**

   The Line tool snaps to the angled endpoints on the picket.

5. **Use Push/Pull to remove the point.**

   Push the triangular face of the picket to the back edge of the post.

6. **Use the Orbit tool to get a good view of the top of the fence post.**

   In the next few steps you create a beveled top for the fence post.

7. Use Offset to create a new rectangle on the top of the post.

   Make the offset about a half inch in from the edge.

8. Select the Move (M) tool, and then press and release the Alt (⌘) key.

   This turns on the auto-fold toggle. To create a beveled top, SketchUp needs to add some new folds to the post. (For more details on auto-fold see page 118.)

9. Click the face of the rectangle centered in the top of the post, and pull it out slightly from the top.

   When you're done, your post should look similar to Figure 5-20. You may need to press the up arrow key to pull the face straight up parallel to the blue axis.

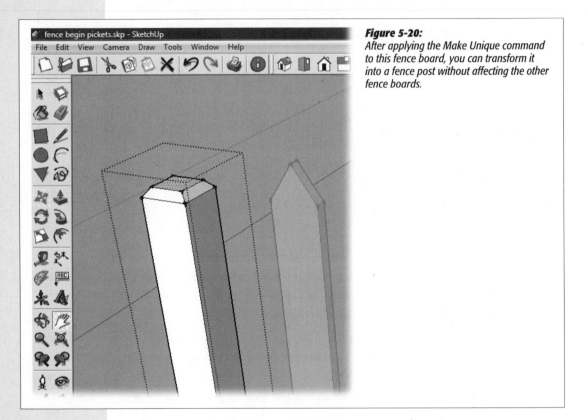

Figure 5-20:
After applying the Make Unique command to this fence board, you can transform it into a fence post without affecting the other fence boards.

10. Click outside the bounding box to leave component edit mode.

    Back out in the SketchUp modeling window, you see that the changes only affected the end post.

Exploring the Components Window

In the previous exercise, you made one of the fence board components unique, and then you modified it, turning it into a fence post. By making a component unique, you're actually creating a new component. You can verify this by opening the Components window (Window → Components) and looking for two board-like components. The Components window is a little deceiving—lots of features are packed into that little box. For example, it has three tabs: Select, Edit, and Statistics. Each leads to different tools and settings (Figure 5-21). It's worth learning about these features if you want to get the most out of your components. The Components window (sometimes called the Components Browser) remembers its last view. So if you close it when you're looking at the Statistics tab, that's what you see the next time you open the Components window.

Components Window: Select Tab

To find your fence components, make sure you're on the Select tab. Click the little Navigation button next to the house icon (shown in Figure 5-21), and then choose In Model. This option shows you all the components in your SketchUp model whether they're visible or not.

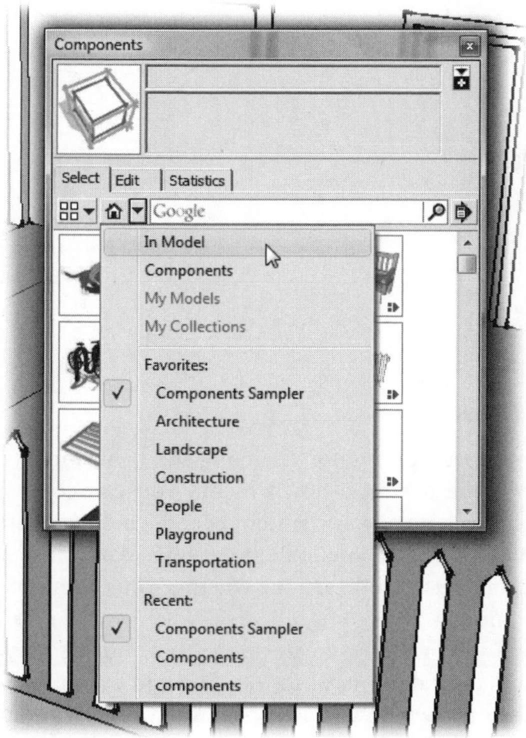

Figure 5-21:
Click the component Navigation button to choose a component library or to display the components in your SketchUp model. As a shortcut to the In Model components, you can click the button that looks like a house.

The In Model view may vary if you've been experimenting in your SketchUp document. If you've been following these exercises, you probably see two board-like components and your good friend Sang, similar to Figure 5-22. Click Sang, and in the description box you see that he's a member of the SketchUp development team. Click the board components, and you see that the one shaped like a picket is named "fence board," and the one that looks like a post is "fence board#1." SketchUp isn't very creative when it comes to naming new components, so now's a good time to rename that component to something like "fence post." Just click in the box at the top of the Components window and type in the new name. You can change the description, too. Something like *6x6x4 fence post* would be appropriate. (It's not unusual for carpenters to refer to a 4-foot 6×6 as a 6×6×4 even though the dimensions are mixed feet and inches.)

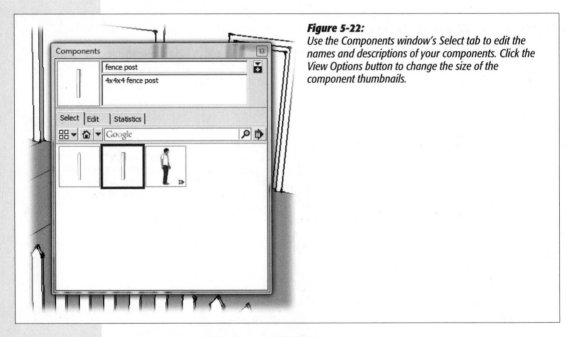

Figure 5-22:
Use the Components window's Select tab to edit the names and descriptions of your components. Click the View Options button to change the size of the component thumbnails.

Components Window: Edit Tab

On the Edit tab (Figure 5-23) you see options for changing the behavior of the selected component. Using the "Glue to" drop-down menu, you can control a component's "sticky" behavior. For example, you want doors and windows to stick to vertical walls. The options on the "Glue to" menu include None, Any, Horizontal, Vertical, and Sloped. A checkbox lets you determine whether your component cuts an opening in the face it's glued to. This option is great when you're making doors and windows. Not only will your window create an opening, but also if you reposition the window on the wall, you don't have to mess around cutting a new opening—the opening moves with the window. The other two checkbox options apply to two-dimensional components like Sang or 2-D trees. Ever wonder how Sang always faces the camera no matter how you change the view? He does that because the "Always face camera" option tells him to. The "Shadows face sun" option helps 2-D art to cast better-looking shadows. At the bottom, the Loaded From box tells you where the component came from. Components you created with this document are listed as "(Internal Component)".

Note: Sadly, the "Cut opening" feature works only on a single face; it doesn't work if you create realistic walls with two parallel surfaces. For details see page 330.

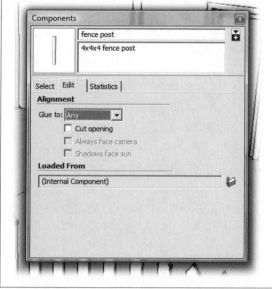

Figure 5-23:
Use the Edit tab to change the behavior of your components. For example, you can change the way components stick to the face of other objects in your model.

Components Window: Statistics Tab

Use the Statistics tab (Figure 5-24) if you want to see the numbers on your components. Perhaps the most useful number is the one in the lower-left corner. That number tells you how many times your component appears in the model. For example, in Figure 5-24 you see that there are 25 instances of the fence board component in the model. In addition, the Statistics tab tells you how many faces and edges are in the component, along with a slew of other details, many of which are covered later in this book.

Using the Flip Along Command

Back to fence building: You want a fence on both sides of the driveway, but you don't need to build a brand-new fence. You can use the Move/Copy technique that was covered on page 172. Here are the steps to copy the fence and then to flip it around so that it's oriented with the fence post next to the driveway.

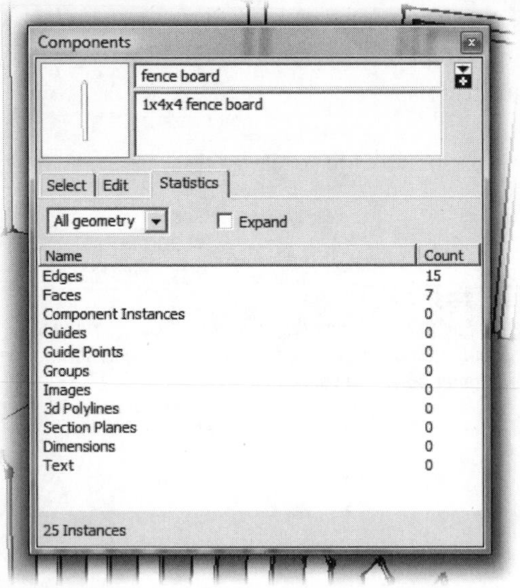

Figure 5-24:
The Statistics tab provides more information than you want to know about the components in your model. In the lower-left corner, you see how many instances of the selected component appear in the model—helpful when you need to order doors and windows for your new house.

1. **Use the Select (space bar) tool to select the post next to the driveway and some fence boards.**

   Choose enough fence boards to reach from the driveway to the left end of the yard. You can drag a marquee around the boards, or use the Shift-click method to make a selection.

2. **Choose the Move (M) tool, and then press the Ctrl (Option) key.**

   Pressing Ctrl (Option) turns on the copy toggle. You see a + sign on the Move cursor.

3. **Click the selected fence boards, and drag them across the driveway, as shown in Figure 5-25.**

   Your new fence is in place, but it'll look better with the thicker fence post next to the driveway.

4. **While the fence is still selected, right-click any of the boards.**

   A pop-up menu appears with several options, including Flip Along (Figure 5-26, top).

5. **Choose Flip Along → Red Direction.**

   Your fence changes its orientation so the thicker post is next to the driveway, as shown at bottom in Figure 5-26. When you use Flip Along, remember that it flips as shown in Figure 5-5. It doesn't mirror.

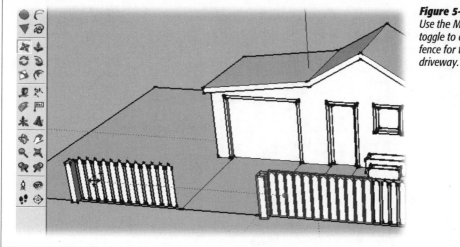

Figure 5-25:
Use the Move tool's copy toggle to create a section of fence for the left side of the driveway.

Note: In this example, you used Flip Along with a multiple selection. You can also use the command with any SketchUp entity including groups or individual components. When you flip a single component, SketchUp uses the axes defined by the component. You can change these axes when you create a component, so they may not always be the same as the axes in your model.

Exploding Components and Groups

Sometimes you may want to turn a component or group back into its individual parts and strip it of its special features. Suppose you have a fence where all the fence boards look the same except for one. You could create the fence using fence board components, and then simply modify the one that looks different. To make that change, you need to strip that one fence board of its component status. You could use the Make Unique command (page 178), which turns a component into a new component. Another option is to Explode one of the fence board components, which turns that instance back into separate edges and faces without creating a new component.

The process is easy. Just right-click the component, and then choose Explode from the shortcut menu (see Figure 5-27). Afterwards your component or group looks pretty much the same, except when you select it, you no longer see the special component highlights. After you've exploded the component, you can select the individual edges and faces with a single mouse click. You can modify it to your heart's content, with no effect on the other fence boards.

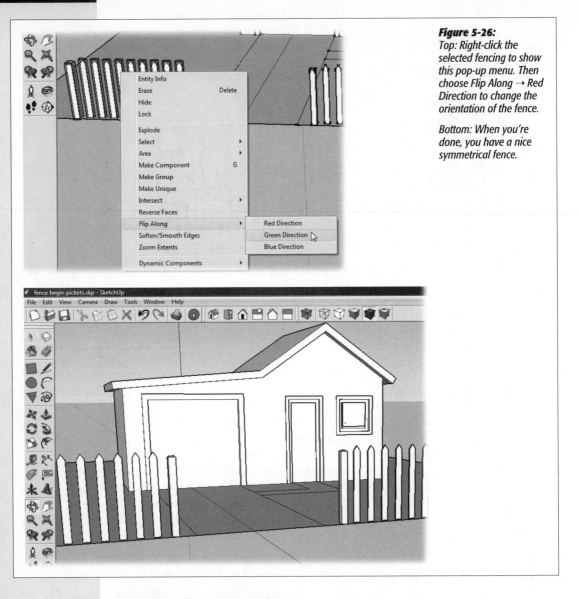

Figure 5-26:
Top: Right-click the selected fencing to show this pop-up menu. Then choose Flip Along → Red Direction to change the orientation of the fence.

Bottom: When you're done, you have a nice symmetrical fence.

Deleting Components

Deleting a component is completely different from exploding a component, as described in the previous section. Though exploding a component sounds somewhat violent, deleting a component has more serious consequences. When you delete a component, you remove the component from the list of components in the Components window, and you remove all the instances of that component from your drawing. Suppose you have a picket fence that's made up of 12 fence board components. If you delete the fence board component from the Components window, all 12 fence boards disappear, too. To delete a component, open the

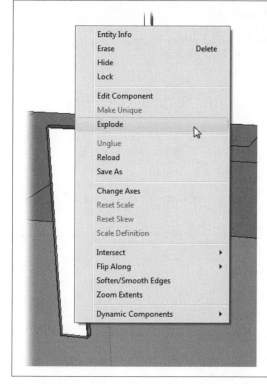

Figure 5-27:
You can turn a component back into its individual parts by right-clicking the component and then choosing Explode from the shortcut menu.

Components window (Window → Component). Then right-click the component you want to delete, and choose Delete from the shortcut menu, as shown in Figure 5-28. A message appears that says: "Warning! All instances will be deleted." Click OK, and the component disappears from the Components window, and all the instances of the component in your model disappear, too. If that's what you wanted—great. If not, you can undo the deletion with Ctrl+Z (⌘-Z), and everything is back to the way it was.

Purging Components

SketchUp keeps track of the components you add to your document. Even after you delete the component from the drawing window, SketchUp shows a copy in the In Model window and stores a copy of the component in the document file. SketchUp keeps it handy in case you want to pop it back in someplace. When you want to get rid of all the components except the ones that are actually in your document, follow these steps:

1. **Choose Window → Components.**

   The Components window opens. Three tabs are on the Components window, and you see whichever tab was displayed when the window was closed.

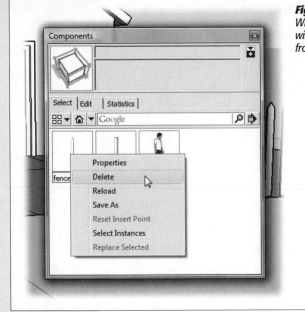

Figure 5-28:
When you delete a component from the Components window, you remove every instance of that component from your SketchUp drawing.

2. **Click the Select tab, and then click the In Model (house) button.**

   The Select tab displays components and on the right side shows the Details button, which looks like an arrow with a menu on top.

3. **Click the Details button and choose Purge Unused.**

   SketchUp removes from the document any components that aren't used in the drawing window; they no longer appear in the In Model display.

Using Dynamic Components

When you were browsing around in the Components window, you may have noticed lots of components. One of the great things about SketchUp components is that you don't have to create them all yourself. Need a sofa, a Doric column, or a 1972 Ferrari? You can find just about anything under the sun using the Components window's Search box (Figure 5-29). SketchUp searches Google's 3D Warehouse, which is filled with components developed by artists like you and shared under the terms listed at *www.google.com/intl/en/sketchup/3dwh/tos.html*.

With SketchUp 7, you can use dynamic components, which are smarter and even more useful than ordinary components. Continuing with your quest to fence in the dog and the kids, suppose you don't have time to model your own fence? Instead turn to the Components window and type *fence* in the Search box. SketchUp does a quick search in the 3D Warehouse and displays some likely candidates in the Components window. A couple of the fences have the Dynamic Component icon in the thumbnail's lower-right corner, as shown in Figure 5-30. Click the component, and you may see some additional details in the description box.

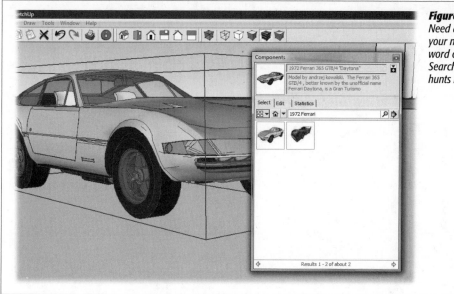

Figure 5-29:
*Need a component for
your model? Just type a
word or two in the
Search box and SketchUp
hunts it down.*

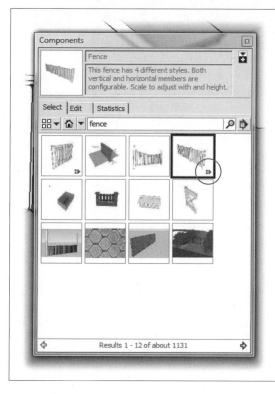

Figure 5-30:
*You can identify dynamic components by the special icon
(circled) in the lower-right corner of their thumbnail in the
Components window.*

When Should I Use Groups Instead of Components?

In SketchUp, groups and components share a lot of features. You create them and edit them in a very similar manner. You can hide, unhide, explode, and erase groups and components in the same way, too. So the question comes up, when should you use groups and when should you use components?

As a rule of thumb, use groups to create a unique entity, and use components when you want to reuse an entity either in your current model or in some future SketchUp project. Components provide many features you won't find in groups. Some of those features are described in this chapter, and more are covered in Chapter 10. For example:

- You can reuse components through the Components window.

- You can easily share them with other SketchUp modelers.

- Components provide detailed statistics, including the number of instances used in a model.

- Using the "Glue to" options, you can control components' sticky behavior (page 321).

- Components such as doors and windows can cut openings in other faces such as walls.

- Components help conserve your computer resources because your computer only has to keep track of the details of a single component. As a result, your SketchUp files are smaller and your work in SketchUp goes faster.

- You can customize two-dimensional components to always face the camera. (Using 2-D components in your models conserves computing power.)

You place components in your model in the same manner whether they're ones you made, or from the 3D Warehouse, or dynamic. Just click the component, and then click somewhere in your modeling window. One of the problems with off-the-shelf ordinary components is that they may not fit your project just right. For example, see the top of Figure 5-31. It's not unusual for stairs, fences, benches, bookshelves, or other components to look great but not quite fit the space you need to fill. If you're working with a standard component, you must open the component and make changes—not so with dynamic components. With dynamic components, fences can automatically add or remove posts and boards as you resize them. Stairs can add new treads when you stretch them.

Handling size changes is just one of the ways dynamic components are smarter than the average model. Component designers can add customizable features to their components. You, as the component user, can tweak these features by right-clicking the component and then choosing Dynamic Component → Component Options. The Component Options window opens (Figure 5-32), where you can customize the component. You'll find different options depending on the dynamic component you're using. It's the designer of the component who decides what features you get to tweak.

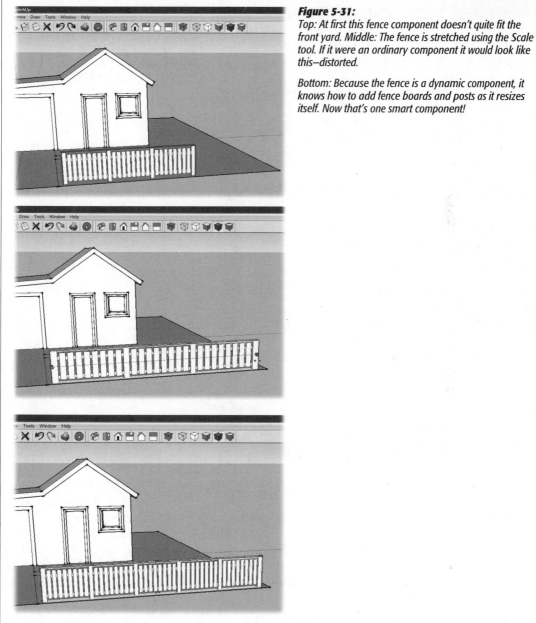

Figure 5-31:
Top: At first this fence component doesn't quite fit the front yard. Middle: The fence is stretched using the Scale tool. If it were an ordinary component it would look like this—distorted.

Bottom: Because the fence is a dynamic component, it knows how to add fence boards and posts as it resizes itself. Now that's one smart component!

That's not the only way that you, the dynamic component user, can make changes to a component. Some components let you interact with them. For a demonstration, you need assistance from your friend Sang. Drag him from the Components window into your model. If you don't see him in the Components window, just

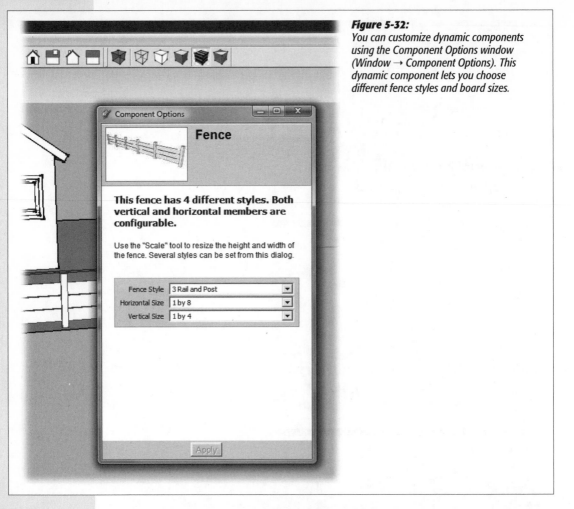

Figure 5-32:
You can customize dynamic components using the Component Options window (Window → Component Options). This dynamic component lets you choose different fence styles and board sizes.

type *Sang* in the Search box. He'll show up. Once Sang is in your model, go to Tools → Interact. Your cursor changes to a hand with a pointing finger. Click Sang's shirt, and it changes color. Each time you click, you see a new color. Again, it's the dynamic component designers who decide how you can interact with their components. It might be that you click the hood of a car and it opens so that you can see the motor. Doors and windows may open and close when you interact with them. The possibilities are many, and as time goes on, the SketchUp community is sure to come up with ever more intriguing components.

Tip: If you're interested in creating your own dynamic components, see page 459.

CHAPTER 6

Changing Styles and Applying Materials

The name "SketchUp" says a lot about how you might use the program. You can work quickly, with an end result that looks hand-drawn rather than like some polished special effect from George Lucas' Industrial Light and Magic. After all, you could have plenty of reasons to show someone a sketch rather than a photo-realistic image. From architects to advertising types, artists know that presenting sketches to their clients is a way of showing that the project is still in progress, open to suggestions and change. Photorealistic images and tightly drawn plans, on the other hand, imply that a project is finished and unchangeable.

By choosing different edge styles, you can give your model either a hand-drawn look or one that has machine-like precision. How and when you use different looks is up to you, but once you work through this chapter, you'll have the tools to create whatever look you want.

In this chapter, you'll learn how to change the whole look of your SketchUp project with just a mouse click or two. You'll delve into styles, which let you change the look of all the faces and edges in your model. You can make faces semi-transparent, so you can look through walls to see the inside workings of a model. Or you can apply materials that look like wood, metal, glass, or concrete.

Changing Face Styles

When you work in 3-D, you're constantly changing your view. It seems that something you want to see is either out of the picture or hidden by something else.

If you followed some of the earlier exercises, you've been orbiting around your model and jumping from Front view to Back, from Iso view to Top. Here are a couple more tricks to add to your model-viewing toolkit. For example, in some cases it's more helpful to see through your model than it is to view it from a different angle. Perhaps you need to select an edge on the back wall of your house. Use the X-ray (View → Face Style → X-ray) to make the faces semitransparent, or the Wireframe view (View → Face Style → Wireframe) to make the faces disappear entirely. Then with the Select tool, you can select an edge that's on your model's backside. The Face Style toolbar puts these and other views just a click away. If you set up your SketchUp environment using the suggestions on page 18, your toolbar looks like either the Mac or PC version shown in Figure 6-1.

Note: You can use any model for your Styles and Materials exploration. The examples in this chapter continue to use the same house model created in previous chapters. You can use your own model or download *materials_begin.skp* from *http://missingmanuals.com/cds*.

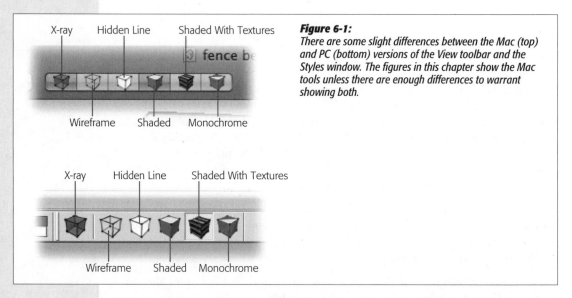

Figure 6-1:
There are some slight differences between the Mac (top) and PC (bottom) versions of the View toolbar and the Styles window. The figures in this chapter show the Mac tools unless there are enough differences to warrant showing both.

Click one of the buttons to change the way SketchUp displays the faces in your model. You can also access these same options under View → Face Style. Here's a rundown of the available choices:

• **X-ray.** The X-ray button works like a toggle. No matter which face style is showing, clicking the X-ray button gives you a view that shows semitransparent faces. In this view, you can select edges in the back of your model that would otherwise be hidden. Also, this view casts shadows. When you're done, just click the X-ray button again to go back to your previous style.

Note: The X-ray button is the only button in the Face Style group that works as a toggle. In the Mac toolbar, all the buttons change visually as if they're toggles, but only X-ray functions as a toggle.

- **Wireframe.** Similar to X-ray view, in Wireframe you can select edges that would otherwise be hidden (Figure 6-2). The difference is that no faces are in Wireframe and shadows aren't cast; the only entities you can see and select are edges. This view can help you understand a model's geometry, but it's limited in that you don't see and can't select faces in the usual way. As a result you can't use tools like Push/Pull in Wireframe.

Tip: In Wireframe view, double-clicking and triple-clicking selects edges in the normal way. Double-click an edge to select adjacent faces. Triple-click an edge to select all connected faces.

- **Hidden Line.** Use the Hidden Line view to show your model without any shading or textures. All faces are displayed using the background color. Shadows are displayed, and you can select both edges and faces.

- **Shaded.** If you've applied colors or materials to your model's faces, the Shaded view shows colors but no textures. Shaded is a great style to use when you're building your model; you can see and work with faces, edges, and shadows. Faces show a basic color, but they don't show any textures. This view is easier for you (and your computer!) because it's simplified and cleaner.

- **Shaded With Textures**. The most complete view, Shaded With Textures shows it all. In some cases, with complex models, this view may slow down your computer. If you find changing views, orbiting, or zooming painfully slow, consider using the Shaded view while you work. You can always use Shaded With Textures for printing or making presentations.

- **Monochrome.** As you might guess, the Monochrome view gives you the 1950s television view of your model—black, white, and shades of gray. At first glance, Monochrome looks similar to Hidden Line view, but the difference is that Monochrome displays shading. Monochrome lets you select both faces and edges.

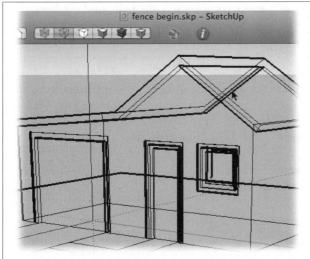

Figure 6-2:
Use the View toolbar to quickly change from one view to another as you work. The Wireframe view, shown here, and the X-ray view make it easy to select an edge that would otherwise be hidden from view.

You may want to work in one or two styles and use a completely different style for your printouts. When presenting a project to a client, you may jump back and forth between a few styles, showing your model from both inside and outside. Once you get used to the versatility of the face styles, you may find yourself changing fairly frequently. That's why it's helpful to have the Face Style toolbar visible as you work.

In the next section, you apply colors and materials to individual faces. Windows and Macintosh computers have quite different ways of working with colors, so this book handles them separately. If you're working on a PC, just read on. If you're working on a Mac, jump ahead to page 207.

Note: You can find some great practical techniques for working with both styles and materials in *Google SketchUp Cookbook* by Bonnie Roskes (O'Reilly).

Applying Colors and Materials (Windows)

When you use the Face Style toolbar (page 193) to change the look of your model, the changes you make apply to all the faces of the model. When you want to change the appearance of individual faces within your model, you change the color or materials of the face using the Paint Bucket (B) tool and the Materials window (Window → Materials), as shown in Figure 6-3.

Note: The tools for applying colors and materials are different on Macs and Windows. This section covers the Windows tools. If you're of the Mac persuasion, go to page 207.

---

1. **Click the Shaded face style button, or choose View → Face Style → Shaded.**

   Your model shows the base color for faces, but doesn't show textures. If you haven't applied color or textures to any faces, you won't see much of a change at this point. (To get the full picture for this exercise, make sure the X-ray button is toggled off.)

2. **Choose Window → Materials.**

   The Materials window appears, as shown in Figure 6-3. You use this window to apply both solid *colors* and *materials,* which mix colors and images to create a textured appearance. At the top you see a preview of the selected material and its name. Below that is the Collections drop-down menu. The individual colors or materials in the collection appear below the menu.

Note: You can also display the Colors window by selecting the Paint Bucket tool from the menu (Tools → Paint Bucket) or from the Tools palette or just by pressing B.

---

3. **From the drop-down menu, choose the Colors-Named collection.**

   The Colors-Named collection shows a variety of colors that are named with words and numbers.

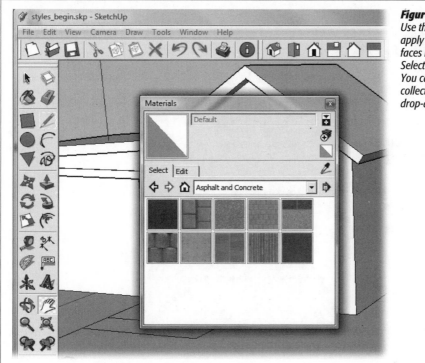

Figure 6-3:
Use the Materials window to apply colors or materials to the faces in your model. Click the Select tab to display materials. You can choose from different collections with the Collections drop-down menu.

4. **Scroll to the bottom and select 0135_DarkGray.**

   When you click a color or material, its name appears at the top of the Materials window, and a preview appears in the upper-left corner.

5. **Move your cursor over the house, and click the three faces that make up the roof.**

   When you click a face, SketchUp paints it with the selected color. The gray roof may show in slightly different shades depending on shadows and orientation, contributing to the 3-D effect.

6. **Click the Details button (Figure 6-4), and then choose "Open or create a collection".**

   The "Browse for Folder" window opens, where you can navigate through the folders on your computer.

7. **Navigate to a location where you want to save your new collection.**

   Click the triangle button to open folders, and then click a folder to select it.

8. **Click the Make New Folder button, and then type a name for your collection.**

   A new folder appears beneath your selected folder. As you type, the new name appears next to the folder icon. You can name it whatever you want, but *House Materials* works well for this exercise.

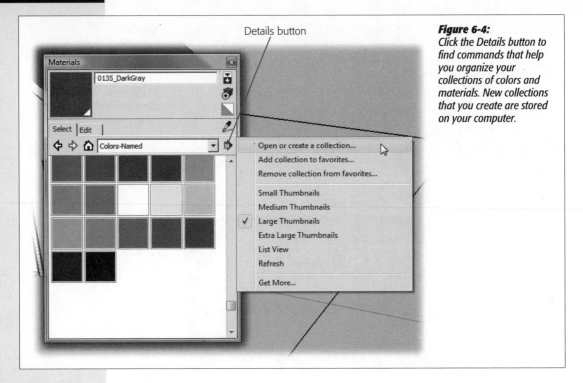

Figure 6-4:
Click the Details button to find commands that help you organize your collections of colors and materials. New collections that you create are stored on your computer.

9. **Click OK.**

The "Browse for Folder" window closes. Your new collection is already selected in the Collections window. It's empty at this point, so it doesn't have much to show.

10. **In the Materials window's upper-right corner, click the "Display the secondary selection pane" button.**

At the bottom of the Materials window, the secondary selection pane opens, as shown in Figure 6-5. It has similar controls to the top pane, including an In Model button and a Collections drop-down menu.

11. **Click the In Model button.**

Several color chips appear in the In Model collection. These may be colors applied to the house, or they may be colors applied to Sang, who may or may not be visible in your model.

12. **Find the color you applied to the roof, 0135_DarkGray, and drag the color chip up to your House Materials collection.**

When you hold the cursor over a color or material, its name appears as a tool-tip. Your House Materials collection now contains a copy of 0315_DarkGray. This collection is available whenever you use SketchUp for any model. By creating your own collections, you can save colors and materials that you know you want to reuse. The next time you need them, you won't have to search all over.

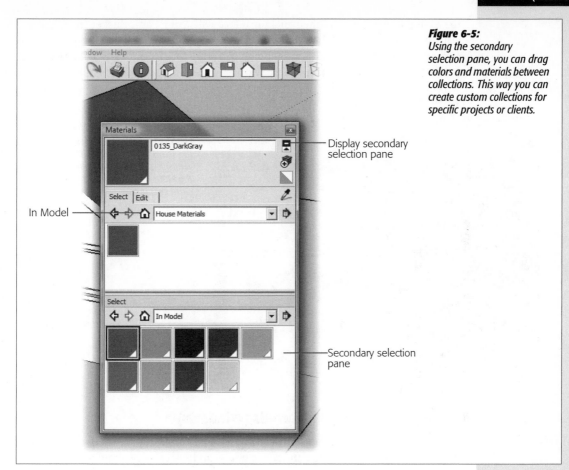

Figure 6-5:
*Using the secondary
selection pane, you can drag
colors and materials between
collections. This way you can
create custom collections for
specific projects or clients.*

13. **Use the Collections menu in the secondary selection pane to display Colors-
    Named, and then select 0133_Gray.**

    The lighter shade of gray appears in the preview at the top of the Materials window.

14. **Drag the 0133_Gray color chip to the House Materials collection.**

    A copy of 0133_Gray is now included in the House Materials collection. You
    can drag colors and materials between any of the collections to create copies.

15. **Apply 0133_Gray to the roof fascia.**

    The vertical trim at the edge of a roof is called *fascia*. On homes, it's usually made of
    wood. It can be painted to match the roof material or the other trim on the house.

Tip: If you preselect faces with the Select (space bar) tool, you can apply colors to several faces at once.
Just click with the Paint Bucket on any of the selected faces.

Now that you've applied a couple shades of gray to your roof, why not go ahead and
apply colors to the rest of your house model. It's just a matter of selecting the color in

the Materials window and then clicking a face with your Paint Bucket (B). Paint the walls and the trim. For the window surface, open the Translucent collection and choose Translucent_Glass_Blue, as shown in Figure 6-6. Don't worry about the yard. In the next section, you'll apply some textured materials for the landscaping.

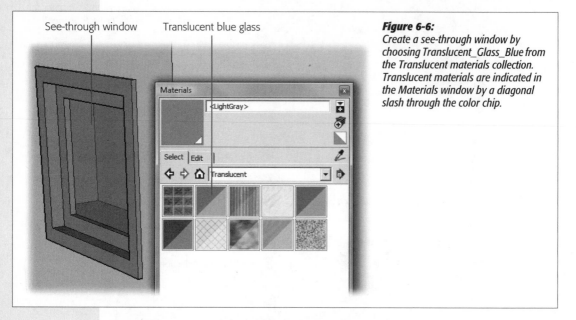

See-through window   Translucent blue glass

Figure 6-6:
Create a see-through window by choosing Translucent_Glass_Blue from the Translucent materials collection. Translucent materials are indicated in the Materials window by a diagonal slash through the color chip.

Finding and Applying Materials (Windows)

In real life, objects seldom appear as a single color. For example, wood almost always has a mixture of colors and textures. Materials can look like just about anything, from wood siding to a lawn. You add materials to the faces of your model to give it a more realistic appearance, or at least to hint at the underlying material. Some materials, like those for fencing, may have transparent areas. For those times when you want a solid, nontextured color, you can choose from the Colors or Colors-Named collections.

When SketchUp applies a material to a face, it takes a small image and repeats it many times over the surface. This process is called *tiling*. You may have seen it used on web pages where an image is repeated.

In Windows, you apply materials the same way you apply solid colors. For example, here are the steps to apply materials to the yard in your house model:

1. **In the Materials window (Window → Materials), use the Collections menu to choose Vegetation.**

   The Vegetation collection shows several natural textures, including a couple of grass options.

Tip: To get the full view of material textures, click the Shaded With Textures button or choose View → Face Styles → Shaded With Textures.

---

2. **Click Vegetation_Grass1.**

A sample of the grass texture appears in the preview at the top of the Materials window.

Tip: The names of materials that come with SketchUp are the same on PCs and Macs, so you can go ahead and specify materials by name when you're talking to your Mac-using colleagues.

---

3. **With the Paint Bucket, click the yard.**

The yard surrounding the house fills in with the green grass texture. (You didn't even have to use fertilizer!)

4. **In the "Asphalt and Concrete" collection, select Concrete_Aggregate_Smoke, and apply it to the driveway.**

The "Asphalt and Concrete" collection has several options that might work for the driveway. The Concrete_Aggregate_Smoke is light gray. (Only in SketchUp is it as easy to pave a driveway as it is to plant a lawn.)

5. **In the Stone collection, select Stone_Pavers_Flagstone_Gray, and apply the paving material to the walkway.**

Your walkway has an attractive stone texture.

6. **In the Groundcover collection, select Groundcover_gravel_1inch, and apply the gravel to the area between the front door and garage.**

At this stage, your yard should look something like Figure 6-7.

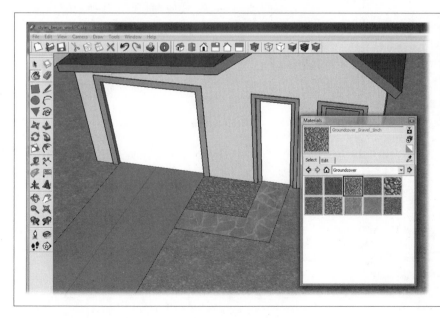

Figure 6-7:
Your house model gets dressed up with a variety of different materials. Browse the collections and try out different materials until you're happy with the results.

Materials go a long way toward dressing up your model. At this point, you may want to explore some of the material opportunities by adding materials to the house. Look under Roofing for different types of shingles and roofing materials. Look under "Brick and Cladding" for materials to apply to the sides of the house. You can choose one of the species in the Wood collection for the front and garage doors.

Mixing Your Own Colors and Materials (Windows)

Right off the bat, SketchUp gives you quite a few colors and materials to work with, but sooner or later you'll want more variety. You can use several ways to mix up your own colors. If you've ever selected colors in Adobe Photoshop or Illustrator, you'll feel right at home.

1. **Make sure the Materials window is open (Window → Materials) and then click the Create Material button.**

   The Create Material button is on the right side of the window, directly below the "Display the secondary selection pane" button. When you click the button, the Create Material window appears, as shown in Figure 6-8.

2. **Choose a color model from the Picker menu.**

   The Create Material window provides four different ways to mix and create colors: Color Wheel, HLS, HSB, and RGB.

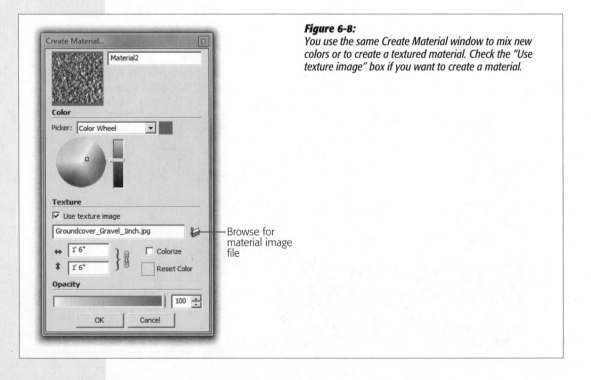

Figure 6-8:
You use the same Create Material window to mix new colors or to create a textured material. Check the "Use texture image" box if you want to create a material.

Browse for material image file

3. **Use the color model controls to mix a color.**

   If you're using the Color Wheel, click a color in the circle to select a hue, and then use the slider to the right to adjust the brightness.

   The controls for HLS (Hue Luminance Saturation), HSB (Hue Saturation Brightness), and RGB (Red Green Blue) color models are very similar. They consist of three sliders that affect the different aspects of the color model (Figure 6-9). Drag the sliders to create a color. As an alternative, you can type a numeric value in the boxes at the right. For example, if you work with a team of artists, you may be given an RGB color value to use for parts of a project. If someone says that the walls of the house should be the RGB color 79, 255, 80, then all you need to do is type numbers into the boxes to create the specified color.

4. **In the box at the top the Create Material window, type the name of your new color.**

   After you've created a color or a material, give it a unique name so you can find it and use it again.

   If all you're doing is creating a new color, your work is done. You can click OK to close the Create Material window. If you're creating a textured material, complete the rest of the steps.

5. **If you're creating a textured material, turn on the "Use texture image" box, and complete the rest of the steps.**

   The boxes and tools under Texture and Opacity are grayed out until you turn on the "Use texture image" box.

6. **Click the "Browse for Material Image File" button shown in Figure 6-8.**

   The Choose Image window opens, where you can navigate through the folders and files on your computer.

7. **Navigate to the material image file you want to use and then click Open.**

   The image is loaded in the Create Material window and a preview is displayed.

Tip: If your image is on the desktop or in an open folder, you can drag it right to the image box in the materials editor.

---

8. **Adjust the width and height dimensions (Figure 6-9) if necessary.**

   You can edit materials by changing width and height that the textured image covers. Use smaller numbers for a smaller pattern that repeats more frequently.

9. **Adjust the color if necessary.**

   After you've loaded a texture image, you may want to readjust the color. Turn on the Reset Color checkbox if you want to remove the current color. Use any of the color models to set a new color for the material.

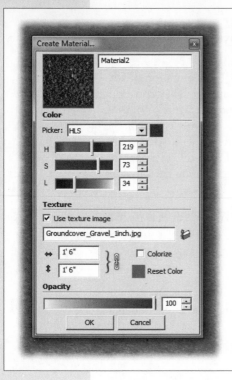

Figure 6-9:
Additional controls and boxes are activated when you check the "Use texture image" box. You can choose a texture image file and change the dimensions used to tile the image. You can also adjust the color and transparency of the material.

10. **Adjust the opacity if necessary.**

    Materials can be semitransparent. Use the Opacity slider to set the level. All the way to the right is 100 percent—completely opaque.

Tip: Shadows pass through materials that are less than 70 percent opaque. For more on shadows see page 381.

---

11. **Click OK.**

    SketchUp creates your new material and loads it into the Materials window, ready to go. To apply the material, just click one of your model's faces.

Finding New Materials (Windows)

SketchUp comes with quite a few different materials when you first install it. You can find additional materials on the Google SketchUp site or from other artists. If you're looking for something specific, try a Google search. Type something like *SketchUp materials bathroom tile* or *SketchUp materials redwood* and see what pops up. Materials are stored in image files.

Note: If you're talented at such things, you can create your own texture images to create a new material, and share them with others. Creating texture images is something of an art, and it isn't covered in this book.

Loading with the Eyedropper (Windows)

Sometimes when you're applying colors with the Paint Bucket (B), you want to load the bucket with a new color or texture. Sure, you can go back to the Colors window and hunt down the color you need. However, if the color is already applied to one of the faces in the model, you have a quick way to fill the Bucket with that color. Press Alt, and the bucket cursor changes to an eyedropper, as shown in Figure 6-10. Click the eyedropper on the face with the color or material you want to copy. Release the Alt key, and the bucket cursor reappears. You're all set to paint some new surfaces.

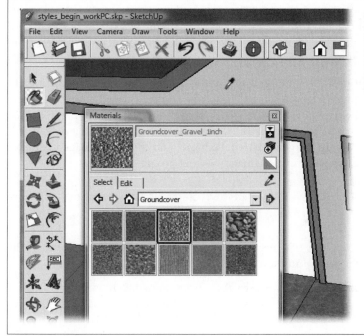

Figure 6-10:
When you're painting with the Paint Bucket (B), you can select colors and materials from your model. Press Alt, and the cursor changes to an eyedropper. Click the color or material you want to select.

Editing Materials (Windows)

Sometimes you want to make changes to materials. Perhaps the brick pavers aren't exactly the color you want. It's best to apply the material to a face in your model and then to make changes to that material. That way you don't change the original material, and it will still be available for other projects.

Note: You can download *edit_brick.skp* from *http://missingmanuals.com/cds* for your material editing experiments.

---

1. In the *edit_brick.skp* document, choose Window → Materials.

   The Materials window opens, showing the tab that was selected the last time you closed the window.

---

2. **Click the Select tab, and then click the In Model button (a house).**

   The materials used in the model are displayed.

3. **Click the red brick material.**

   The material's name, Brick_Basket_Two, appears at the top of the window.

4. **Click the Edit tab.**

   The Edit tab shows the settings for the selected red brick materials. The settings are divided into two parts—Color and Texture—the two elements that give a material its character.

   • **Color options.** The Picker drop-down menu lets you choose between the different color systems discussed on page 202. Mixing your color is a matter of selecting a hue from a color wheel or making adjustments with sliders. You can use the eyedropper buttons to load colors into the material.

   • **Texture options.** Use the texture options to load a texture image and to make adjustments to the image. The "Use texture image" checkbox determines whether or not a material uses a texture image. The file name for the image is shown below. Use the Browse button to find and load a new image. Click "Edit texture image in external editor", and the JPEG image file opens in a separate image-editing or image-viewing program.

Tip: Go to Window → Preferences → Applications to choose the program you want to use for image editing.

---

5. **Click the "Match Color of object in model" button, and then click one of the gray colors in the water fountain.**

   As you make color changes, you see the effects immediately in your model. If you want to undo the color changes, click the color swatch to the left of the eyedropper buttons.

   Of the two eyedropper buttons, you use the one on the left to load colors from objects in your model. Use the one on the right to select colors that are on your screen but not in the SketchUp model.

6. **In the width box (it's labeled with a double-headed arrow), type *12*.**

   The bricks in the texture image shrink. Changing the dimensions of a texture image is one of the easier ways to edit a texture. The tile size for the brick texture is 32".

7. **Click the chain links next to the dimension boxes and then, in the height box, type *32*.**

   The links icon changes to a broken link, and you can change the width-to-height proportion of the texture image.

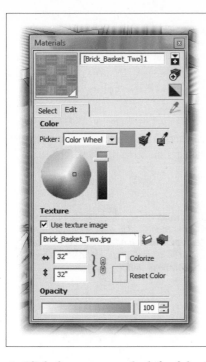

Figure 6-11:
Materials are made up of a color and a texture image. Use the Materials Edit tab when you want to make changes to either of these properties. Before you make changes to a material, apply it to a face in your model, and then change the material in your model.

8. Click the arrows to the left of the dimension boxes.

The arrows look more like labels than buttons, but clicking them resets the dimensions to the original values.

Applying Colors and Materials (Mac)

When you use the Face Style toolbar to change the look of your model, the changes you make apply to all of your model's faces. When you want to change the appearance of individual faces within your model, you change the color or materials of the face using the Paint Bucket tool and the Colors window.

Note: The tools for applying colors and materials are different on Macs and in Windows. This section covers the Mac tools. If you're of the Windows persuasion, go to page 196.

---

1. Click the Shaded face style button, or choose View → Face Style → Shaded.

Your model shows the base color for faces but doesn't show textures. If you haven't applied color or textures to any faces, you won't see much of a change at this point. (To get the full picture for this exercise, make sure the X-ray button is toggled off.)

---

2. **Choose Window → Materials.**

In SketchUp 7 the Colors window appears as shown in Figure 6-12. (Oddly, the name on the window is "*Colors*" not "*Materials*", as it is in the menu.) You use this one window to select both colors and materials. At the top of the window five buttons display different panels where you can choose colors or materials.

Note: The color and materials tools for Macs and Windows are different for a reason. The Mac version of SketchUp uses the Mac's accelerated graphics hardware. It also makes use of the Apple color system. The Color Picker in SketchUp extends Apple's version to include textures and SketchUp materials.

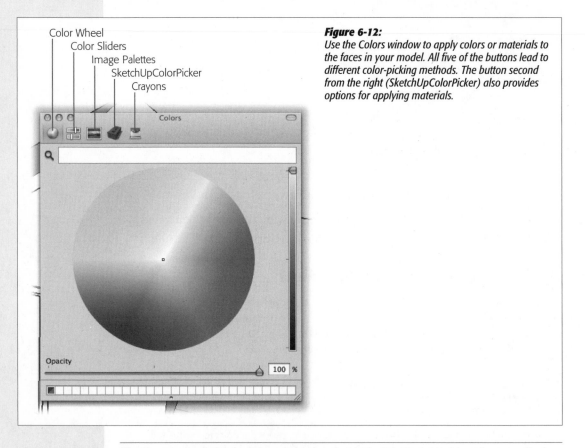

Color Wheel
Color Sliders
Image Palettes
SketchUpColorPicker
Crayons

Figure 6-12:
Use the Colors window to apply colors or materials to the faces in your model. All five of the buttons lead to different color-picking methods. The button second from the right (SketchUpColorPicker) also provides options for applying materials.

Tip: You can also display the Colors window by selecting the Paint Bucket tool from the menu (Tools → Paint Bucket) or the Tools palette, or just by pressing B.

3. **Click the rightmost button, which looks like a box of crayons.**

The panel underneath takes on the look of a box of crayons, as shown in Figure 6-13. This panel is the simplest of all the color pickers, providing a varied but limited selection of colors.

4. **Choose the middle gray-colored crayon named Iron.**

Iron is in the third row from the top, second crayon from the right. When you click a crayon, its name appears in the space above. When you select a color, the color appears in the preview bar above the color options.

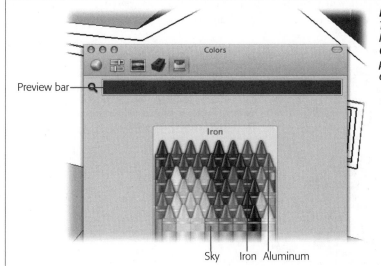

Figure 6-13:
The Crayons color view provides a limited number of named colors. Choose a color, and the name and a preview of the color appear at the top of the window.

5. **Move your cursor over the house, and click the three faces that make up the roof.**

When you click a face, SketchUp paints it with the selected color. The gray roof may appear in slightly different shades depending on shadows and orientation, which contributes to the 3-D effect.

6. **Drag the Iron color from the preview bar down to one of the small boxes at the bottom of the Colors window.**

These small boxes (Figure 6-14) make up your personal palette. You can store colors here and quickly retrieve them later without having to search all over. You can store textured materials in your palette, too. (Materials are covered on page 215.)

7. **Choose the light gray Aluminum (second row from top, rightmost), and apply it to the roof fascia and under the eaves.**

The vertical trim at the edge of a roof is called *fascia*. On homes it's usually made from wood. Fascia and the eaves can be painted to complement the roof material or to match the house trim.

Tip: If you preselect faces with the Select (space bar) tool, you can apply colors to several faces at once. Just click the Paint Bucket on any of the selected faces.

---

8. **Drag Aluminum to the second slot in the color palette at the bottom of the Colors window.**

   You can replace a color in the bottom palette by dragging a new color on top of it. In this case you want both Iron and Aluminum available, so drop the new color in an empty slot. You can reorganize this palette by dragging colors to different boxes. If you want to remove a color from the palette, drag one of the empty boxes to the color you want to remove.

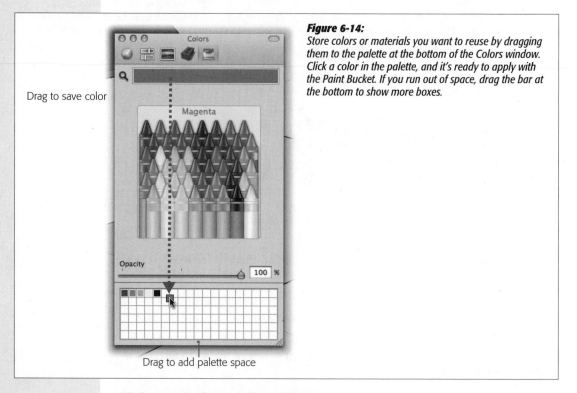

Drag to save color

Drag to add palette space

Figure 6-14:
Store colors or materials you want to reuse by dragging them to the palette at the bottom of the Colors window. Click a color in the palette, and it's ready to apply with the Paint Bucket. If you run out of space, drag the bar at the bottom to show more boxes.

Mixing Your Own Colors (Mac)

The Crayons are quick and easy to use, but they offer only a few colors. Soon you'll want more variety. For example, you can get more colors in several ways by using the Colors window. These color pickers may look familiar if you've used a color wheel or RGB values in other applications.

1. **If necessary open the Colors window (Window → Colors), and then click the Color Wheel.**

   The Color Wheel button is the first button from the left. The wheel in the center displays a wide range of colors. The slider on the right controls the brightness/darkness. The bottom slider controls the opacity/transparency.

2. **Drag the brightness/darkness slider (right) to change the colors in the wheel.**

   As you drag the slider toward the top, the colors in the wheel become lighter.

3. **In the wheel, click a color, and then if necessary make more adjustments with the brightness/darkness slider.**

   Using the color wheel to select a color is a trial-and-error process. Go back and forth adjusting the hue by clicking the wheel and then adjusting the brightness with the slider.

4. **With the Paint Bucket (B), click one of the house's walls.**

   The face of the wall changes immediately. As in real life, sometimes the color on the wall doesn't look the same as it did in your color palette. The solution is to mix up another color and repaint. You may want to store the final color in the palette at the bottom of the Colors window.

5. **Select a light blue color, and then set the opacity/transparency slider to about 40 percent, as shown in Figure 6-15.**

   The Opacity slider is at the bottom of the window. Adjust the opacity to taste. All the way to the right is 100 percent or completely opaque. Somewhere between 30 and 50 percent works well for windows and other glass objects.

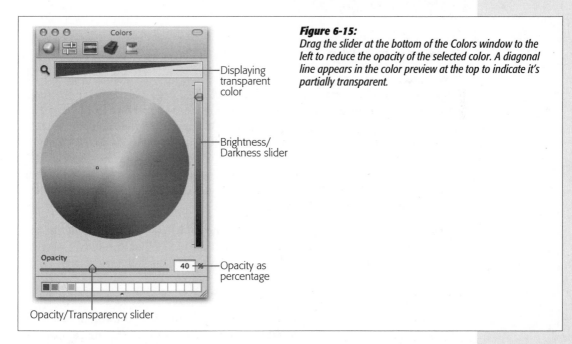

Figure 6-15:
Drag the slider at the bottom of the Colors window to the left to reduce the opacity of the selected color. A diagonal line appears in the color preview at the top to indicate it's partially transparent.

6. **With the Paint Bucket (B) click the face of the window.**

   The face is painted with the transparent blue color. You can see through the window into the house. You may need to use the Orbit (O) tool to get a good view of the back edges, as shown in Figure 6-16.

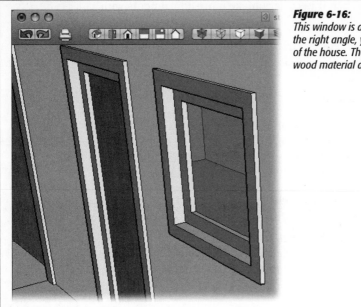

Figure 6-16:
This window is a transparent blue color. Viewing from the right angle, you can see the back corner and edges of the house. The front door and the garage door have a wood material applied.

Mixing colors with sliders

If you prefer, you can use the color sliders to mix up your colors (Figure 6-17). Click the second button from the right (Figure 6-12, page 208) to bring the sliders into view. These controls adjust the amount of red, green, and blue in the previewed color. Numerical values for red, green, and blue appear to the right of the slider. The RGB (Red Green Blue) color model is often used to specify colors shown on computer monitors. If you work with a team of artists, you may be given an RGB color value to use for parts of a project. If someone says that the walls of the house should be the RGB color 79, 255, 80, then all you need to do is type numbers into the boxes to use the specified color.

You can control the opacity/transparency of the colors you create by using the sliders. Just use the Opacity slider at the bottom of the box. When you have colors you want to save, store them in the palette at the bottom of the Colors window.

Choosing colors with image palette

Image palettes give you a unique way to serve up colors. Suppose you have a photo of a building with colors that you'd like to use. You can load the image into your image palette, and then click areas in the picture to make color selections. It doesn't have to be a photo—you can load a graphic image, like a company logo, into the image palette. The first time you display the image palette, you see SketchUp's spectrum image (Figure 6-18). It's similar to color models you've seen before and doesn't give you a clue as to the true usefulness of the image palettes.

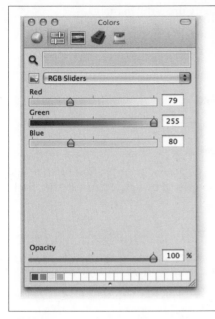

Figure 6-17:
Use the color sliders to mix a color to your taste. Here the green slider is dragged all the way to the right, while the red and blue sliders show lesser values. This makes green the predominant hue in the color.

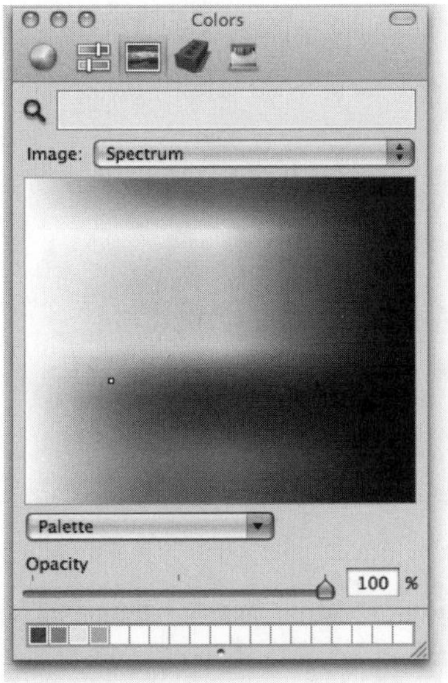

Figure 6-18:
Use the drop-down menu below the image to add new images to your collection of image palettes. Then use the drop-down menu at the top to select the image you want to use.

Follow these steps to load an image into the image palette:

1. **If necessary, open the Colors window (Windows → Materials). Then click the Image Palette button.**

    The Image Palette button is third from the right, as shown in Figure 6-12. The panel for the Image Palette appears, as shown in Figure 6-18.

2. **At the bottom of the window, click the Palette drop-down menu.**

   Several options appear on the menu, as shown in Figure 6-19. If you haven't yet added an image, a couple options are grayed out.

   • **New from File.** Load an image from a file on your computer or network.

   • **Rename.** Edit the name of a loaded image.

   • **Remove.** Remove an image from the image palette.

   • **Copy.** Make a copy of the selected image.

   • **New from Clipboard.** You can copy (⌘-C) an image or portion of an image from another program such as Photoshop or Preview. Then use this command to paste it into the image palette.

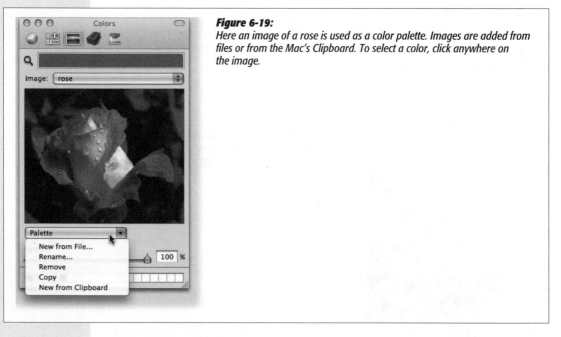

Figure 6-19:
Here an image of a rose is used as a color palette. Images are added from files or from the Mac's Clipboard. To select a color, click anywhere on the image.

3. **Choose "New from File".**

   When you choose "New from File", a Finder window opens where you can browse to find the image you want to load.

4. **Select the image you want to load and click Open.**

   SketchUp loads the image into the image palette and displays it in the preview. The image appears in the drop-down list at the top of the window.

5. **In the image, click a color and then use the Paint Bucket (B) to apply that color.**

   Once you load an image, you can click anywhere on that image to select a color. Use the Opacity slider if you want some transparency in the color. You can save selected colors in the palette at the bottom of the Colors window.

Finding and Applying Materials (Mac)

In real life, objects seldom appear as a single color. For example, wood almost always has a mixture of colors and textures. In SketchUp, materials are colors with a texture applied. Materials can look like just about anything from wood siding to a lawn. You add materials to your model's faces to give it a more realistic appearance, or at least to hint at the underlying material. Some materials such as those for fencing may have transparent areas.

When SketchUp applies a material to a face, it takes a small image and repeats it many times over the surface—a process called *tiling*. You may have seen it used on web pages where an image is repeated left and right as well as up and down a page.

You apply materials pretty much the same way you apply colors. There's just one extra step—first you choose a list. Click the button that looks like a brick to find the lists of materials. Then click the menu at the top to select one of the lists, as shown in Figure 6-20. Some of the lists are colors while others hold materials. Then you click to choose a material. A preview of the material appears at the top of the Colors window. Finally, click a face in your model to apply the material. If you want, you can adjust the transparency of materials using the slider at the bottom of the window. You can save materials along with colors that you plan to reuse in the boxes at the bottom of the Colors window.

Tip: To get the full view of material textures, click the Shaded With Textures button or choose View → Face Styles → Shaded With Textures.

Follow these steps to apply materials to bring your yard to life:

1. **Make sure the Colors window is open, and then click the SketchUpColorPicker button.**

   The SketchUpColorPicker icon looks like a brick, as shown in Figure 6-12. Hold your mouse over the brick for a second or two, and you see a tooltip that says "SketchUpColorPicker". When the Colors window displays the SketchUpColorPicker tools, you see the menu where you can choose one of the color/material lists.

Note: The PC version of SketchUp refers to these lists as *collections,* so don't be surprised if you see a reference to collections in some of Google's help tools.

---

2. **Use the menu to select the Vegetation list.**

   The Vegetation list shows several natural textures including a couple of grass options.

3. **Click Vegetation_Grass1.**

   A sample of the grass texture appears in the preview at the top of the Colors window.

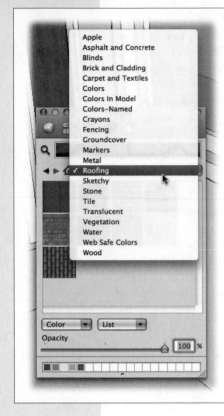

Figure 6-20:
The SketchUpColorPicker holds both colors and materials that you can apply to your model. From the menu at the top, you can choose from several collections with names such as Roofing, Groundcover, and "Carpet and Textiles".

Tip: The names of materials that come with SketchUp are the same on Macs and PCs, so you can go ahead and specify materials by name when you're talking to your PC-using colleagues.

---

4. **With the Paint Bucket, click the yard.**

   The yard surrounding the house fills in with green grass texture. You didn't even have to use fertilizer!

5. **Choose the "Asphalt and Concrete" list, and then select Concrete_Aggregate_ Smoke. Apply the material to the driveway.**

   The "Asphalt and Concrete" list has several options that might work for the driveway. Concrete_Aggregate_Smoke is light gray. Amazing—it's as easy to pave a driveway as it is to plant a lawn.

6. **Go to the Stone list to select Stone_Pavers_Flagstone_Gray, and then apply the paving material to the walkway.**

   Your walkway has an attractive stone texture.

7. **Use the Groundcover list to select Groundcover_gravel_1inch, and then apply the gravel to the area between the front door and garage.**

   The surface of the yard looks good. All it needs are some trees and shrubs.

8. As a finishing touch, choose a wood material from the Wood list, and apply it to the front door and the garage door.

At this stage your yard should look something like Figure 6-21.

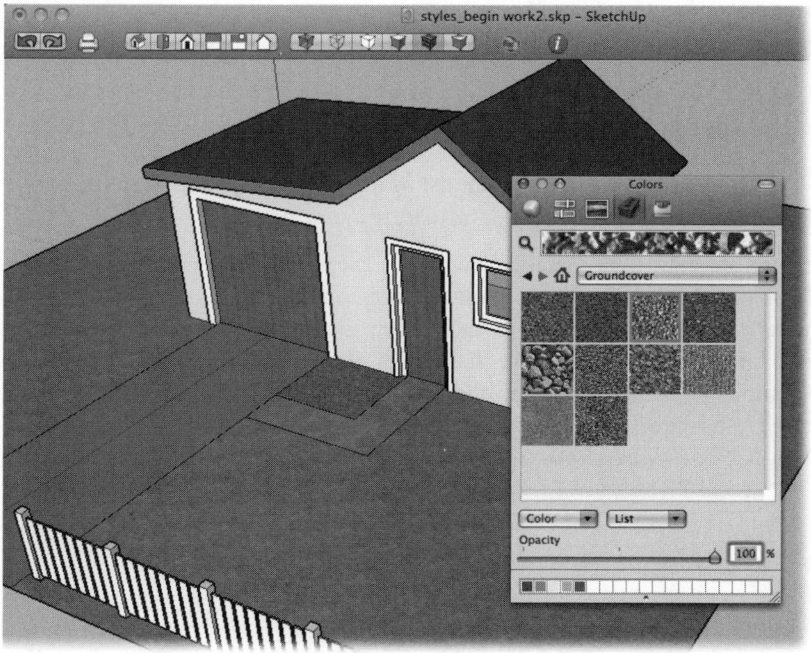

Figure 6-21:
After you apply materials to the yard surface, your house begins to look more at home.

Materials go a long way toward dressing up your model. At this point you may want to explore some of the material opportunities by adding materials to the house. Look under Roofing for different types of shingles and roofing materials. Look under "Brick and Cladding" for materials to apply to the sides of the house.

Adding New Materials (Mac)

SketchUp comes with quite a few different materials when you first install it. If you need more variety, you can find additional materials on the Google SketchUp site or from other artists. If you're looking for something specific, try a Google search for something like *SketchUp materials bathroom tile* or *SketchUp materials redwood* and see what pops up. (Materials are stored in image files.)

Here are the steps for adding a new material to your SketchUpColorPicker lists:

1. Make sure the Colors window is showing (Window → Materials) and displaying the SketchUpColorPicker.

The button for the SketchUpColorPicker is fourth from the left and looks like a brick.

2. **At the bottom of the window, click the pop-up menu on the left that says Color.**

   The menu opens displaying several options, including Edit, Remove, Duplicate, and New Texture.

3. **Choose New Texture from the menu.**

   A Finder window opens, where you can navigate to a folder holding the image files.

4. **In the Finder window, click the Open button.**

   The texture is added to the current list of textures and displayed in the preview. A box opens where you can give the texture a new name.

You can create your own materials and share them with others. Creating new textures and materials is something of an art and isn't covered in this book. However, if you want to tweak a material to make each tile cover a greater or smaller area, you can find the controls in the SketchUpColorPicker. Select the material you want to modify. Then at the bottom of the window, click the Color pop-up menu and then choose Edit. A new section opens at the bottom of the Colors window, as shown in Figure 6-22. You can type new dimensions for the tile's width and height.

Tip: The link to the right of the dimension boxes locks the dimensions, making them proportional. Click to break the link, and then you can enter nonproportional values in the Width and Height boxes.

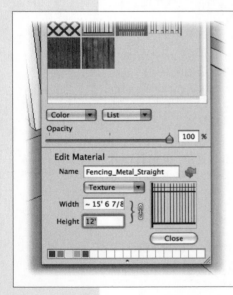

Figure 6-22:
You can edit materials by changing the width and height that the textured image covers. Use smaller numbers for a smaller pattern that repeats more frequently.

Loading with the Eyedropper (Mac)

Sometimes when you're applying colors with the Paint Bucket (B), you want to load the bucket with a new color or texture. Sure, you can go back to the Colors window and hunt down the color you need. However, if the color is already applied to one of the faces in the model, there's a quicker way to fill the bucket with that color. When you press ⌘, the bucket cursor changes to an eyedropper, as shown in Figure 6-23. Click the eyedropper on the face with the color or material you want to copy. Release the ⌘ key, and the bucket cursor reappears. You're all set to paint some new surfaces.

Figure 6-23:
When you're painting with the Paint Bucket (B), you can select colors and materials from your model. Press ⌘, and the cursor changes to an eyedropper. Then click the color or material you want to select.

Changing Face Styles: Take 2 (Mac and Windows)

Now that you've added a variety of colors and textures to your model, it's a good time to take another look at the effect of the different face style options. If you have the Face Style toolbar showing, simply click each button to compare the differences (Figure 6-24). To check out the way shadows are displayed with the different face styles, choose View → Shadows.

Working in the Styles Window

In SketchUp a *style* defines the look of face styles, edge styles, and backgrounds. The Styles window (Window → Styles) puts you at the artist's drawing board. You apply a style to your model by clicking one of the styles in the window (see Figure 6-26). By applying different styles, you give your model dramatically different looks. The Styles window also gives you tools to organize styles into collections. For example, if you work with teams of other SketchUp artists, you may want to collect all the styles used on a project into a single collection. When someone on the team develops a new style, he can store it in the collection where everyone has access to it.

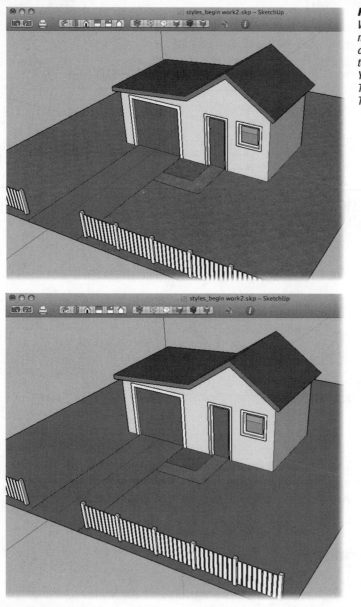

Figure 6-24:
*With colors and textures applied to your
model, you can begin to see the
differences between the face styles. The
top image shows the Shaded face style.
You see the base colors but no textures.
The bottom image is the Shaded With
Textures view.*

Note: In previous versions of SketchUp, style *collections* were called *libraries*. In SketchUp 7's menus,
they're called collections. In Google's documentation, you may still see them referred to as libraries.

Applying a New Style to Your Model

1. **Choose Window → Styles to open the Styles window.**

   The Styles window has three tabs and displays whichever tab you used last.

2. **Choose the Select tab.**

   SketchUp displays previews of several different styles. A drop-down menu above the previews determines which previews are shown.

3. **From the drop-down menu, choose the Assorted Styles collection (Figure 6-25).**

   The top of this menu always shows two choices: In Model and Styles. The In Model option displays styles for any style that you applied while viewing your model, even if it's not currently being used. To purge unused styles see page 224. The Styles option displays a folder view of all the collections.

   Beneath the In Model and Styles options, SketchUp displays named collections of styles. You can create your own styles and collections, so the content changes over time. Initially you see the styles that come with SketchUp. These include Assorted Styles, Color Sets, Default Styles, Sketchy Edges, Straight Lines, and Style Builder Competition Winners.

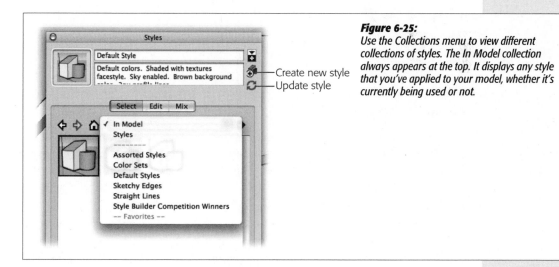

Figure 6-25:
Use the Collections menu to view different collections of styles. The In Model collection always appears at the top. It displays any style that you've applied to your model, whether it's currently being used or not.

4. **Click the "Pencil on Tracing Paper" style.**

   As soon as you click a style, it's applied to your model. The name and description appear at the top of the Styles window, and a thick highlight line marks the selected style.

5. **From the drop-down menu choose In Model.**

   You see the new style you're using listed in the In Model view of the Styles window. Any other styles you've used with the model are also listed.

SketchUp comes with dozens of styles in premade collections. These include collections named Assorted Styles, Color Sets, Default Styles, Sketchy Edges, Straight Lines, and Style Builder Competition Winners. The best way to get a feeling for the different styles and possibilities is to apply some of the styles to one of your models, such as the house model that's been used in this chapter. For variety, try some of the styles in the Assorted Styles collection. Then check out some of the styles in the Sketchy Edges collection. When you're done, you may want to go back to the Default Styles and choose the style named Default.

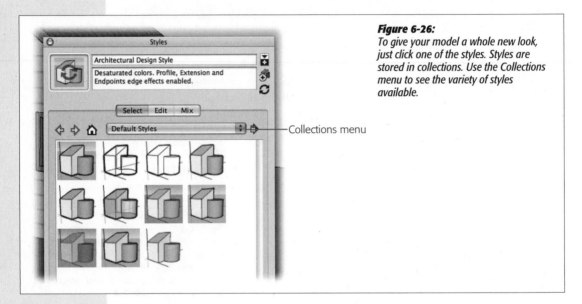

Figure 6-26:
To give your model a whole new look, just click one of the styles. Styles are stored in collections. Use the Collections menu to see the variety of styles available.

Collections menu

Organizing Styles

If you've already used the Components window, the Styles window probably feels a little familiar. At the top, the Styles window shows a preview and two text boxes: Name and Description. You're free to change the name or description just by typing in the boxes. You use the three buttons to the right of the preview area to manage your style collections:

- At the top, the **Display the secondary selection pane** button opens a new pane at the bottom of the Styles window that displays and lets you select styles (Figure 6-27). At first this may seem redundant, but actually it's helpful. The primary job of the Styles window is to apply styles. With the secondary selection pane showing, you can apply a style no matter which tab you're on in the Styles window.

- Click the **Create new Style** button to make a copy of the selected style. When you create a new style, you start with an existing style and make a copy using this command. After you've modified the style, you save it with the "Update Style with changes" command below.

• If you've made changes to a style, **Update Style with changes** saves those changes in the style. If you don't want to overwrite a style, you should make a copy using the "Create new Style" command above before saving changes with this command.

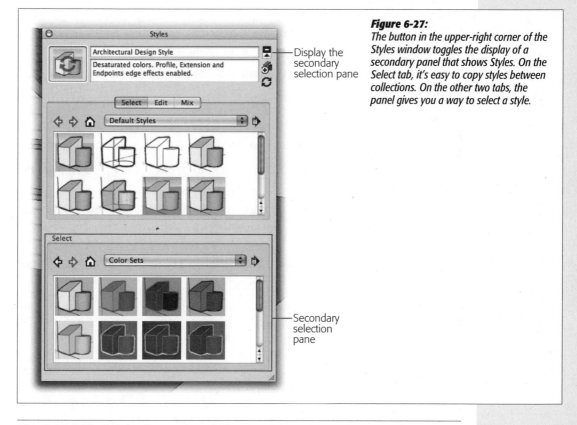

Figure 6-27:
The button in the upper-right corner of the Styles window toggles the display of a secondary panel that shows Styles. On the Select tab, it's easy to copy styles between collections. On the other two tabs, the panel gives you a way to select a style.

Tip: If you click the "Display the secondary selection pane" button, the secondary selection pane remains at the bottom of the Styles window no matter which tab you selected.

The three tabs in the Styles window are Select, Edit, and Mix. You use the first tab to select and organize your styles. The other two tabs let you modify and create new styles.

• Use the **Select** tab to preview and apply Styles to your model. You can view the Styles that you already used in your model, or you can view and organize all the Styles available.

• Use the **Edit** tab to modify the appearance of styles and create new styles.

• The **Mix** tab provides another method for modifying styles by combining the characteristics of one style with another.

Note: The Styles window remembers which tab was visible when it was closed and displays that tab the next time you open the window.

Purge Unused Styles from the In Model View

If you try several different styles as you're working on your model, all the styles you tried remain in the In Model view. If you'd like to clean house and get rid of the styles that you tried but didn't want to use, follow these steps:

1. **If it's not already open, go to Window → Styles to open the Styles window.**

   The Styles window has three tabs and displays whichever tab you used last.

2. **Choose the Select tab.**

   The Select tab is where you preview and select the styles you apply to your model.

3. **Click the In Model button (it looks like a house), or choose In Model from the Collections menu.**

   In the In Model view, you see a list that includes all the styles that are in your model. Any styles that you've applied since you created your model or since you last purged this list appear.

4. **To the right of the Collections menu, click the Details button and then select "Purge unused".**

   The icon for the Details button looks like an arrow with a small menu on top (see Figure 6-28). After you purge the unused styles from your list, SketchUp displays only the styles used in your model.

Editing and Modifying Styles

When you install SketchUp on your computer, it comes with a whole slew of styles. The variety of styles is remarkable. Some look like blueprints; others look like hand drawings on the back of an envelope. You can work in SketchUp for a long time using only these premade styles. Doing so will save you large chunks of time, because once you start tweaking styles using the Edit and Mix tabs in the Styles window, there may be no turning back.

Changing Edge Styles

Earlier in this chapter, you learned how to change the style of the faces in your model. When it comes to choosing styles for the edges, you have a lot more decisions to make. Here's where you determine just how "sketchy" you want your model to look. When you look at the collections of styles, it's obvious that there's a big difference between the Sketchy Edges styles and the styles that look more computer generated, such as the style SketchUp uses automatically. One of the goals of

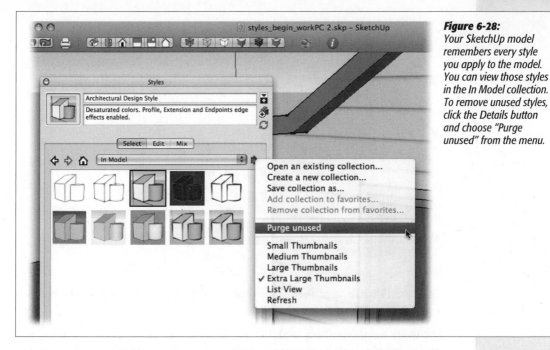

Figure 6-28:
*Your SketchUp model
remembers every style
you apply to the model.
You can view those styles
in the In Model collection.
To remove unused styles,
click the Details button
and choose "Purge
unused" from the menu.*

SketchUp, as you can tell by its name, is to produce artwork with a hand-drawn appearance. You can do so in a few different ways. Using the Edit tools, you change the way edges (lines) are drawn. The styles in the Sketchy Edges collection combine different effects to give drawings a random, human quality. These effects include doubling up on lines at endpoints, fading lines at junctions, using images to simulate lines with varying thickness, and so on.

Follow these steps to explore some of the options you use to change the appearance of edges:

Note: This exercise uses the same house model from the earlier exercises. If you need a new copy, you can use materials_begin.skp found at *http://missingmanuals.com/cds*.

1. **With your house model open in SketchUp, choose Window → Styles.**

   The Styles window opens, displaying the same tab as when you last closed it.

2. **Click the Select tab, and then use the Collections menu to choose Sketchy Edges.**

   You see a collection of SketchUp styles with a distinctly hand-drawn look.

3. **Click the Airbrush style.**

   Your model takes on the look of a hand-drawn sketch, as shown in Figure 6-29.

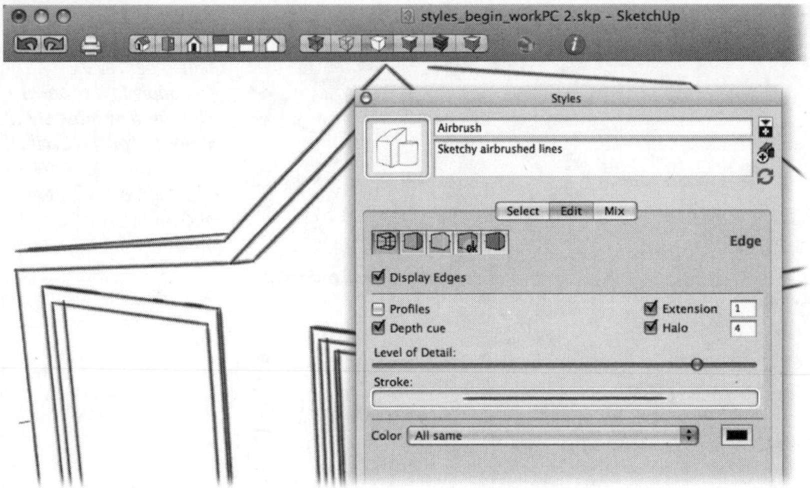

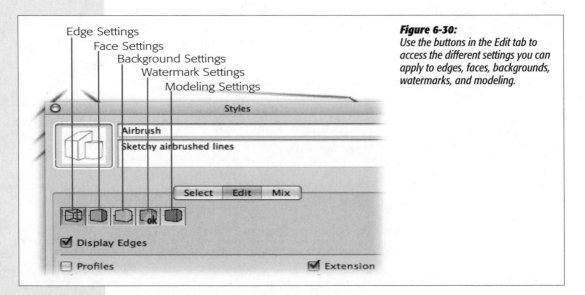

Figure 6-29:
The Airbrush style has a hand-drawn look that emphasizes edges over faces. This view is good when you're examining the effects of the Edge Settings.

4. **Click the Edit tab, and then with your cursor, hover over each of the buttons beneath the tabs.**

   The icons for the buttons look like boxes, as shown in Figure 6-30. When you hold the cursor over a button, a tooltip appears. The buttons are Edge Settings, Face Settings, Background Settings, Watermark Settings, and Modeling Settings.

Figure 6-30:
Use the buttons in the Edit tab to access the different settings you can apply to edges, faces, backgrounds, watermarks, and modeling.

5. **Click the Edge Settings button.**

   The Styles window changes to show the Edge Settings (Figure 6-31), where you customize the look of edges. Because you started with one of the Sketchy Edges styles, you see the related options. They include the following:

- **Profiles** emphasizes the outlines or outer edges of the major shapes in your model. A technique used by traditional artists, this reinforces some of the 3-D visual cues, while giving your model a hand-drawn appearance.

- **Depth cue** enhances the 3-D look of a drawing by making the lines that are nearer the viewer thicker, while the lines farther back are thinner.

- **Extension** emphasizes the hand-drawn look by extending lines slightly past their endpoint. Don't worry; this doesn't affect other aspects of SketchUp such as the position of inference lines. You can choose the distance of the extension by typing a number, measured in pixels, in the box next to Extension.

- **Halo** changes the way lines overlap in a drawing by ending the lines before the overlap. It's another effect that gives SketchUp models a distinctive hand-drawn look.

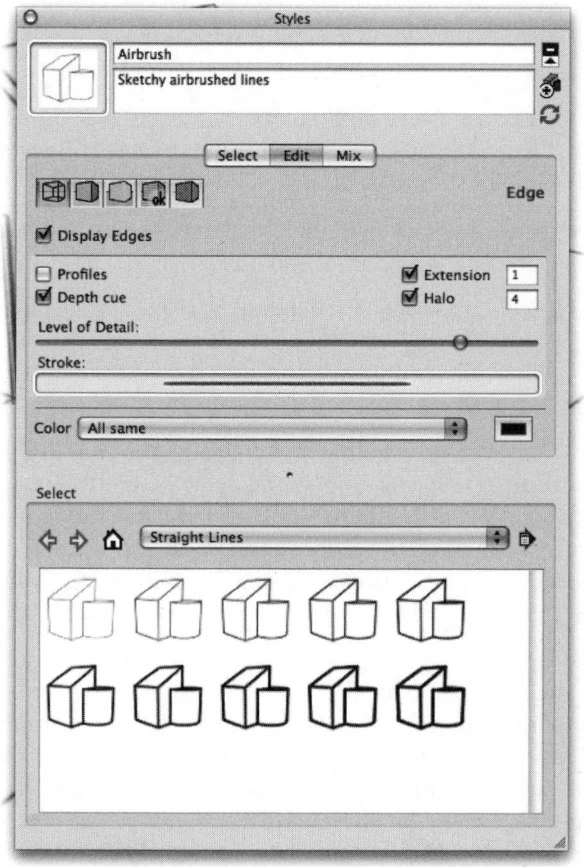

Figure 6-31:
You see different edge settings depending on whether you begin with a Sketchy Edges style or a standard edges style. This figure shows the edge settings that apply to Sketchy Edges.

6. **Choose various Edge Settings to get the hand-drawn look you desire.**

   To examine the effects of individual settings, turn all the checkboxes off, and then turn each back on by itself. Type a large number such as *20* into the Extension and Halo boxes to see their effects exaggerated. Drag the "Level of Detail" slider all the way to the left, and notice how it removes edges and the ends of edges from the model. Test the three settings in the Color menu: "All same", "By material", and "By axis".

7. **Click the "Display the secondary selection pane" button.**

   The secondary selection pane appears at the bottom of the Styles window, showing the Sketchy Edges styles.

8. **Select different sketchy styles, examine the Edge Settings and their effects, and choose which one you'd like for your drawing.**

   Notice how the styles show different hand-drawn lines in the Stroke box. These images are used in creating the unique look of the styles.

9. **From the Collections menu, select Default Styles and then select Default.**

   The Edge Setting options change. Some options such as Halo and "Level of Detail" are only available with Sketchy Edges. Other options such as Jitter and Endpoints are only available with standard edges.

   - **Endpoints** doubles up the stroke at endpoints, making corners and joints appear thicker and contributing to a hand-drawn look.

   - **Jitter** draws multiple lines, slightly offset at random, also providing a hand-drawn, traced-over appearance.

Choosing Face Settings for a Style

Earlier in this chapter, you saw how much face styles change the look of your model. When you edit or create a new style, you specify which face style is used. Click the Face Settings button (shown in Figure 6-30), and you see the face settings (Figure 6-32). You have a choice of all the face styles described on page 193. They include Wireframe, Hidden Line, Shaded, Shaded With Textures, Monochrome, and X-ray. X-ray is a toggle and can be used in combination with the other face styles.

In addition to letting you choose a face style, the Face Settings panel has a checkbox that lets you turn transparency on and off. Transparency uses more computer resources and may slow it down, so SketchUp gives you some options for making transparency work on your target machine. Use the "Transparency quality" menu to choose one of three options: Faster, Medium, or Nicer. Choose Faster if you need transparency but find that it slows your computer. Choose Nicer if you want the best-looking transparency effect your computer can provide. Medium, as you might guess, is for you middle-of-the-roaders.

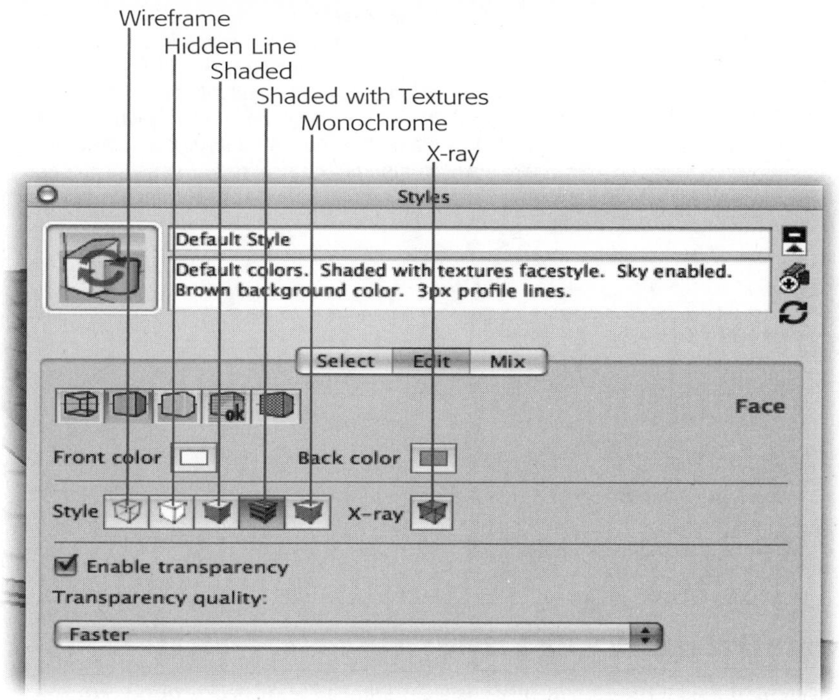

Wireframe
Hidden Line
Shaded
Shaded with Textures
Monochrome
X-ray

Figure 6-32:
Use the Face Settings panel to select a face style when you create a new style. The face style is used in combination with the styles defined in the Edge Settings, Background Settings, Watermark Settings, and Modeling Settings panels.

Styles

Default Style

Default colors. Shaded with textures facestyle. Sky enabled. Brown background color. 3px profile lines.

Select   Edit   Mix

Face

Front color   Back color

Style   X-ray

☑ Enable transparency
Transparency quality:

Faster

Tip: Tired of the colors SketchUp uses for the front and back side of faces? You can choose your own colors using the "Front color" and "Back color" buttons shown in Figure 6-32.

Adjusting Background Settings

Click the Background Settings button (Figure 6-33) to choose background options for your style. All styles always show a single background color. You can't turn off the background, but you can choose its color. Click the button to the right of the word *Background,* and the Materials (Windows) or Colors (Mac) window appears. Select a color to use for the background.

Other background options include Sky and Ground. If you don't want to show backgrounds for the Sky and Ground, turn off their checkboxes. SketchUp simulates sky and ground planes. The sky color is softly faded at the horizon. The ground plane includes a couple of extra options. You can adjust the ground's transparency using the slider. A checkbox controls whether the ground plane is visible when viewed from below the ground plane.

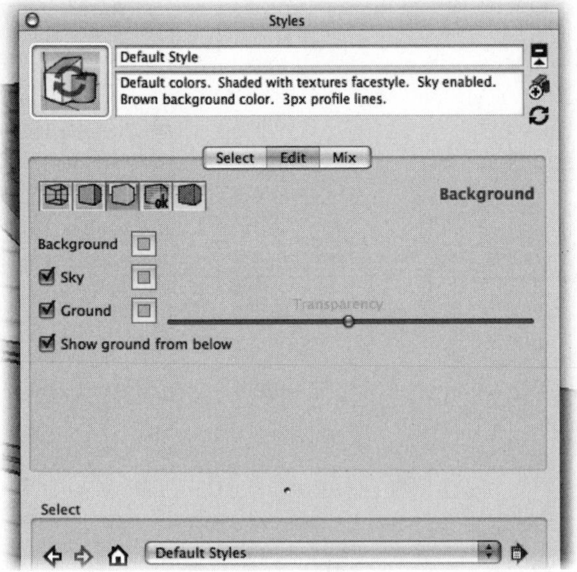

Figure 6-33:
Adjusting Background Settings is mostly a matter of choosing colors for the background, sky, and ground. Sky and Ground colors are optional, but all models use a single Background color, even if it's just white. Choose white if you want something inconspicuous.

Using a Watermark with a Style

In SketchUp a watermark can serve as a different type of background. For example, see Figure 6-34, where a watermark simulates a textured paper. Watermarks place an image in your SketchUp modeling window. You use the controls in the watermark settings to add the image file and to adjust the appearance of the image in SketchUp.

To add a watermark, follow these steps:

1. **In the Styles window, click the Edit tab, and then click the Watermark Settings button. Click the Add button.**

   The Choose Watermark window appears. Click the Select button to open a new window where you can browse for an image file to use as a watermark.

Note: If you need an image file for watermark experiments such as this exercise, you can find *paper_watermark.jpg* at *http://missingmanuals.com/cds*.

---

2. **After selecting an image file, click Next.**

   Two radio button options appear: Background and Overlay.

3. **Choose Overlay and then click Next.**

   The Overlay option places the watermark in front of your model, so that the edges of your model appear to be drawn on top of the watermark, as shown in Figure 6-34. The Background option displays the watermark image behind your model. Faces in your model hide the watermark.

   When you click Next, new options appear.

Figure 6-34:
*The "Pencil on light brown" style uses a
watermark that simulates a textured paper,
and the edge setting gives the look of a pencil
drawing.*

4. **Use the Blend slider to adjust the image. Leave Create Mask unchecked.
   Click Next.**

   Pulling the Blend slider to the right increases the visibility of the watermark,
   while moving it to the left fades it.

   The Create Mask option is used to create vignette-style effects.

   When you click Next, new options appear.

5. **Click the "Stretched to fit the entire window" radio button.**

   The stretched option takes a single image and extends it to cover the entire
   modeling window. This option is likely to distort the image, but with images
   such as the textured paper it doesn't look too bad. The "Tiled across window"
   option uses the image file at its original size and repeats the image to fill the
   modeling window. The "Positioned in the window" option shows the watermark at its original size one time in the window. This option works well for
   company logos or stern messages such as "Copyrighted Material."

6. **Click Finish.**

   The Choose Watermark window closes, and you return to the Watermark
   Settings as shown in Figure 6-35.

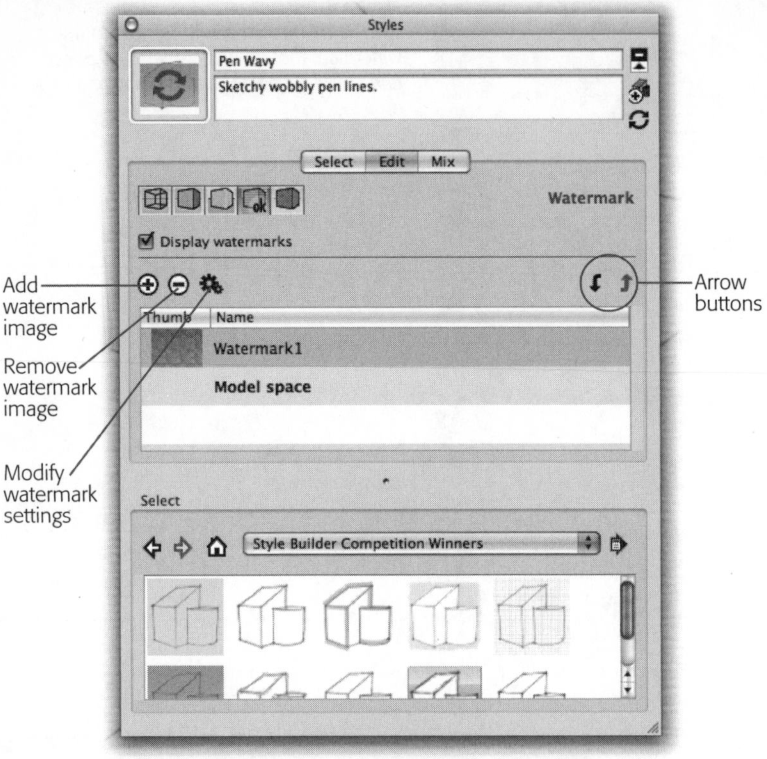

Figure 6-35:
*After you've added a
watermark, it appears listed in
the watermark settings. You
can use the + button again to
add more watermark images
or masks. Use the arrow
buttons to position the
watermark in front of or
behind the model or
other images.*

Even after you've finished adding a watermark, you can make changes to it. You
can add more than one image or mask to a watermark by clicking the + button and
repeating the previous steps. Use the arrow buttons (as shown in Figure 6-35) to
position the watermark images and the model in front of or behind each other. If
you want to make changes to the settings of a watermark image, click the button
that looks like a couple of gears. To remove a watermark image, click the image in
the list and then click the – button.

Changing the Modeling Settings for a Style

The modeling settings change how different entities appear in the modeling window. On the Styles window's Edit tab, click the Modeling Settings button
(Figure 6-36) to view the options. Use the six colored buttons at the top of the
Modeling Settings to choose the colors for different entities in the modeling window. For example, if you want to change the color of the highlights that indicate a
selected edge or face in your model to yellow, click the button labeled "Selected".
Then in the Materials (Windows) or Colors (Mac) window, choose yellow. Use
this technique to set colors for:

- **Selected.** The color of highlights that appear on selected edges as a thick line or
  appear on faces as dots.

- **Locked.** The color used to indicate locked components (page 244).

- **Guides.** The color used for guides that you create using the Tape Measure tool (page 281).

- **Inactive Section.** You can use section cuts to slice a model into parts so that you see a cross section of your model. Using this button, you can set the color for the Inactive portion of a section.

Note: Sections are covered in more detail on page 417.

- **Active Section.** The color used to highlight the active portion of a section.

- **Section Cuts.** The color used to define the active section plane's slice line (page 417).

- **Section cut width.** Enter a number (in pixels) to set the width of the section cut line (page 421).

Modeling settings

Change colors and highlights

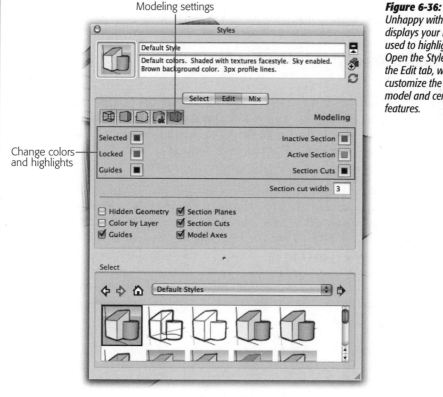

Figure 6-36:
Unhappy with the way SketchUp displays your model or the colors used to highlight different entities? Open the Styles window and click the Edit tab, where you can customize the appearance of your model and certain SketchUp features.

The rest of the Modeling Settings consist of checkboxes that show or hide SketchUp features. All of these options except for "Color by Layer" can also be found on the View menu.

- **Hidden Geometry.** Reveals items that you've hidden using the Outliner or pop-up menus. Hidden geometry appears with a cross-hatched pattern on the faces and dashed lines on the edges.

- **Color by Layer.** You can assign entities to different layers in SketchUp. Turn on this box to apply materials to geometry by layer, using the colors associated with the layer.

Note: Layers are covered in more detail on page 273.

- **Guides.** Displays guidelines and guide points (page 281). (Guides are sometimes called *construction lines*.)

- **Section Planes.** Displays Section Planes (page 417).

- **Section Cuts.** Displays Section Cuts (page 421).

- **Model Axes.** Display the red, green, and blue drawing axes (page 17).

Modifying Styles Using the Mix Tab

The Mix tab gives you another way to make changes to your styles. The way it works is unique and kind of clever. When you click the Mix tab, you see the settings shown in Figure 6-37. You're forgiven if you haven't got a clue about what you should do next. At the top of the Mix tab you see five sections labeled "Edge Settings", "Face Settings", "Background Settings", "Watermark Settings", and "Modeling Settings". SketchUp calls these sections *wells*.

In the bottom of the window, you see a selection pane with a Collections menu and styles. Suppose there's a style that has a watermark you want to use. You can easily add that watermark to any other style. First use the Select tab to select the style you want to modify. Then click the Mix tab. Use the Collections menu and the selection pane at the bottom of the Mix tab to find the Style with the watermark you want. Then drag that style onto the Watermark Settings well. SketchUp applies all the watermark settings from the dragged style to the style you're modifying. It's quick and easy to transfer any of the settings from one style to another.

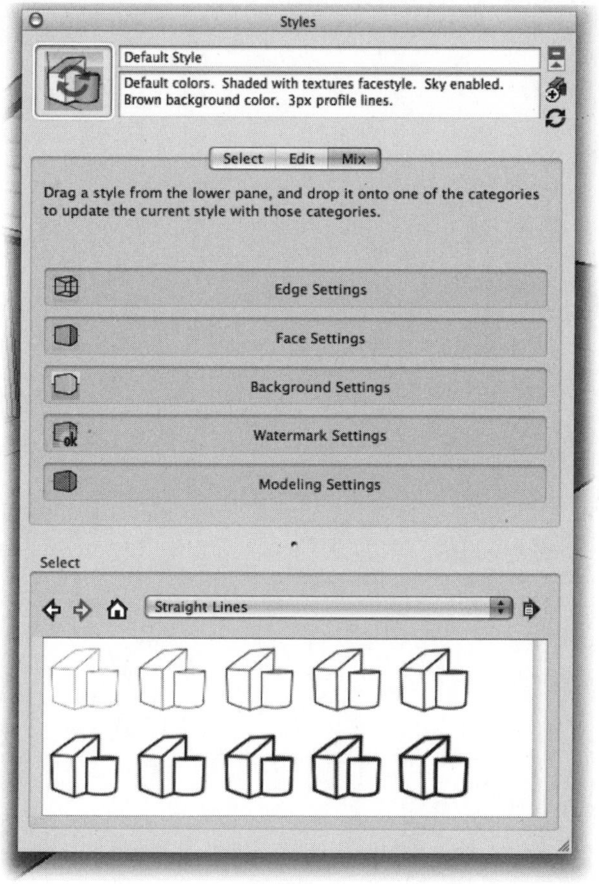

Figure 6-37:
The Mix tab lets you transfer style settings from one style to another. First use the Select tab to pick the style you want to change. Its name and description appear at the top. Then in the Mix tab, drag one of the styles shown in the bottom pane onto one of the settings wells above.

Organizing with Outliner and Layers

As models get more complicated, managing the different parts becomes a challenge. With complicated models, for example, you often want to hide one part of the model so you can work on another. As far as SketchUp is concerned, all edges and faces are equal. You may think of part of your model as a roof, a fence, or a wall, but to SketchUp, it's just a few edges and faces. It's up to you to decide how to organize those entities into something meaningful.

Your tool for the job is the Outliner. After you turn parts of your model into groups or components, the Outliner keeps track of them. You can define the relationships between parts of your model in a structured outline style, with one group nested inside of another. Using the Outliner, you can hide parts of your model and protect them from accidental changes. In this chapter, you build a set of entry stairs (like the one in Figure 7-1) and in the process learn how to use the Outliner to organize parts of your model.

Layers are another SketchUp feature that lets you organize parts of your model. Layers, covered on page 273, are used to show and hide parts of your model, but you need to use them with care. You'll find layer tips and warnings at the end of this chapter.

Note: You may find this chapter a little more challenging than some of the previous ones. To complete the staircase model in this chapter, you need to be able to adjust your view of the model (page 27), work with groups and components (page 157), and move entities with precision (page 44).

Organizing with Outliner

Your main tool for organizing the parts of your model is the Outliner, which keeps track of both groups (page 158) and components (page 166). (You first met both of these grouping tools in Chapter 5.) To recap, here are some of the benefits of groups and components:

- Groups keep faces and edges together, making it easy to move objects as one piece.

- Groups don't stick to other faces and edges, which helps you avoid accidental changes to your model.

- Groups can be as simple as a 2×4 or as complex as an entire floor of a skyscraper.

- Components are easily reusable. Design it once and you can use it many times.

- Components conserve computer resources when you need multiple copies or an object.

- Components are modifiable. Modifying a component changes all instances of that component.

- Both groups and components can contain other groups or components.

- Both groups and components can be locked to prevent accidental changes.

- Both groups and components can be hidden, giving you easier access to other parts of your model.

Figure 7-1:
In this chapter, you construct this set of stairs and use the Outliner to organize the stair parts.

The stairs in this example extend from a concrete step up to a landing. The landing includes a slanted roof that keeps rain off visitors at the door. Although fairly simple, the stairs and landing have a number of duplicate components and a few unique items. You can divide the entire project into two major elements: the stairs and the landing.

As far as SketchUp is concerned, you can tackle the different parts of this project in any order you want. For example, you could build the stairs suspended in mid-air and then build the landing. In real life, where gravity rules, it would be more sensible to build the landing, place the concrete step, and then build the stairs in between, so that's the order you'll use in this chapter.

The first step is to create the floor of the landing. It consists of a piece of plywood flooring that's framed around the bottom with 2×6 pieces of lumber. The framing helps hold the posts in place. (You may want to cover the plywood flooring with solid wood or some other more attractive floor covering, though that's not part of this project.)

1. **Start a new SketchUp document using the "Architectural Design – Feet and Inches" template.**

   When the template opens, you see Sang, the SketchUp model, standing near the Origin point, where SketchUp's axes meet. If you prefer a little more background color for your model, you could use the "Simple Template – Feet and Inches" (as shown in Figure 7-1).

Note: If you need a refresher on how to start a document using a particular template, see page 23.

---

2. **Using the Rectangle (R) tool, click the Origin, and begin to pull out a rectangle on the horizontal (red/green) plane. Then type the dimensions 6′6,4′ and press Enter (Return on a Mac).**

   The lower-right corner of the rectangle should be at the Origin. When you type the dimensions and press Enter, the rectangle takes shape. Its dimensions are 6 feet, 6 inches by 4 feet.

Tip: Remember, when you're using the Architectural Design – Feet and Inches template, you never have to enter the inches symbol. SketchUp assumes you're talking inches unless you say otherwise.

---

3. **Use the Push/Pull (P) tool and begin to pull the rectangle up, and then type 1 and press Enter.**

   The plywood flooring is now 1 inch thick.

4. **Choose File → Save and then name your new document Entry Stairway.skp.**

   It's always good to save your document early in your project and to continue saving each step of the way. If you think you may want to go back to an earlier stage in the project, save the file under a different name.

---

5. With the Select (space) tool, triple-click the plywood flooring. Then choose right-click → Make Group.

You've created the first group for the Entry Stairs project. It makes sense to use the group option for the floor of the landing, because there's no other object like it in the project. (If it's an element that you're going to reuse, you should create a component, as covered later in this exercise.)

6. Open the Outliner (Window → Outliner), right-click the word "Group", choose Rename from the shortcut menu, and then type *floor*.

The plywood flooring is the only object in your model at this point. When you turn it into a group, it's the only item named in the Outliner, as shown in Figure 7-2.

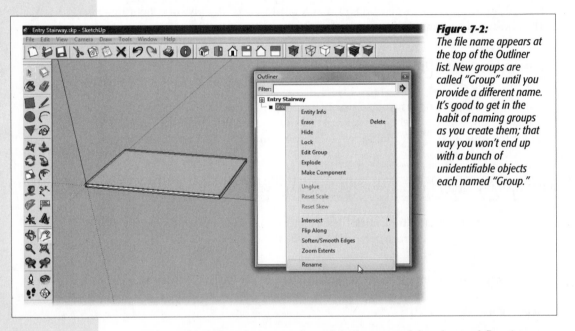

Figure 7-2:
The file name appears at the top of the Outliner list. New groups are called "Group" until you provide a different name. It's good to get in the habit of naming groups as you create them; that way you won't end up with a bunch of unidentifiable objects each named "Group."

7. Use the Orbit (O) tool to get a view of the bottom of the plywood flooring.

If necessary, use Zoom Extents (Shift+Z for Windows, ⌘-[for Macs) to get a good close view of the bottom of the flooring. In the next steps, you create a frame around the bottom of the landing.

8. On one of the long edges of the flooring, from a corner, begin to draw a rectangle, and then type *6′6,1.5* and press Enter.

Your rectangle is 6 feet, 6 inches long and 1.5 inches wide.

9. With Push/Pull, begin to pull the face of the rectangle down, and then type *5.5* and press Enter.

Now your rectangle looks like a 2×6 piece of lumber that's 6 feet, 6 inches long.

Carpenter's Glossary: Lumber used for construction typically is available either *rough* or *dressed*. Dressed lumber is planed smooth so its actual dimensions are less than the nominal dimensions. For example, a 2×6-inch piece of dressed lumber is actually 1.5×5.5 inches. In this project, you use the actual dimensions.

---

10. With the Select tool, triple-click the new framing piece and then press G.

Triple-clicking selects all the faces and edges of the 2×6. When you press G, the Create Component window appears (Figure 7-3), where you can provide a name and description for the component. You can also use this window to set the alignment and "Glue to" behavior of components.

11. Type *frame* in the component Name box; type *2x6 framing for landing* in the Description box; and then choose Create.

You don't need to make any changes in the Alignment section for this simple component. The main reason for turning this object into a component is that you need a duplicate for the back portion of this frame.

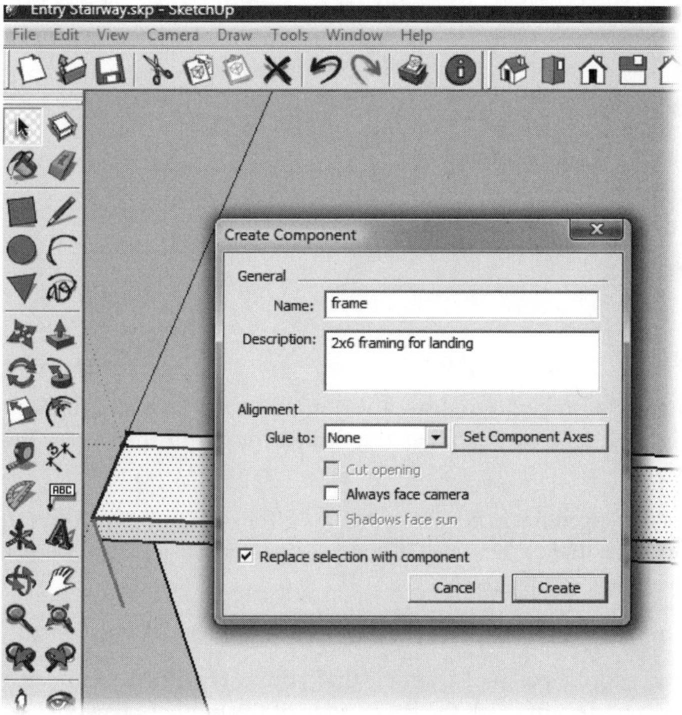

Figure 7-3:
Use the Create Component window to give your component a name and description. You can also use this window to set the alignment and "Glue to" behavior, although you don't need those options for this simple 2×6 piece of framing.

12. Use Orbit or the other camera tools to change to a view like the one in Figure 7-4.

    It's always good to plan ahead when you're building your model. An important part of preparation is to get the best view of the pieces you're moving, transforming, or shaping. In this case, you want to align a second piece of framing on the back end of the flooring. The easiest way is to move the corner of a new piece of framing to the corner of the flooring, as shown in Figure 7-4.

13. Choose the Move (M) tool and then press the Ctrl (Option) key.

    A + sign appears on the Move tool cursor when you press Ctrl (Option), indicating that the Move tool is in copy mode. Now when you click an object, the original stays behind and you place a duplicate elsewhere in your model.

14. Click the upper-right corner of the 2×6 frame, and then click the lower-right corner of the floor component.

    When you click the 2×6 frame, a new copy of the frame component is attached to the Move cursor. Clicking the corner of the floor component places the new frame board at that position. The second piece of the frame for the landing snaps into position.

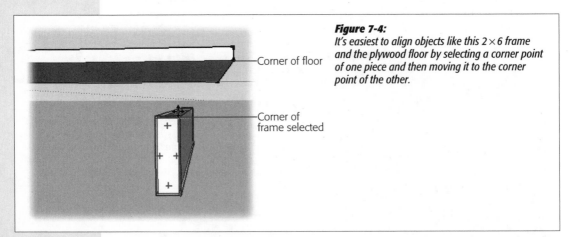

Figure 7-4:
It's easiest to align objects like this 2×6 frame and the plywood floor by selecting a corner point of one piece and then moving it to the corner point of the other.

Corner of floor

Corner of frame selected

15. Use the Rectangle tool to begin to draw a rectangle on the inside of the frame, as shown in Figure 7-5. Type *1.5,5.5* as the dimensions, and then press Enter (Return on a Mac).

    The rectangle is displayed near the end of the 2×6 frame. You want to create a rectangle that's taller than it is wide. If your rectangle is oriented differently, reverse the dimensions so they read *5.5, 1.5*.

16. Use Push/Pull to pull the rectangle to the edge of the opposite frame board.

    You have a new, shorter piece of framing that connects with the ends of the other pieces. For a perfect fit, click the inside edge of the lumber board.

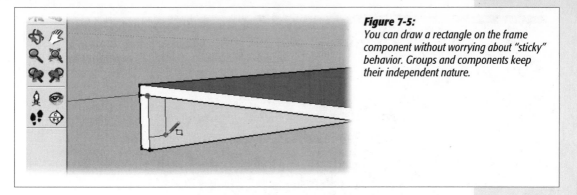

Figure 7-5:
You can draw a rectangle on the frame component without worrying about "sticky" behavior. Groups and components keep their independent nature.

17. Use Orbit or the other camera tools to view the floor from the opposite side.

    Maneuver until you have a view where you see the bottom of the plywood flooring and all three pieces of frame.

18. With the Select tool, triple-click the short piece of frame and then press G.

    The short piece was the last one you created. When you press G, the Create Component box opens.

19. Type *frame short* in the Name box, and then type *2x6 framing for landing sides* in the Description box. Then choose Create.

    You've created the model's second component. You have to give each component a unique name. The description is less important, but it can be helpful when your project becomes big and complicated.

20. Choose the Move (M) tool and then press Ctrl (Option).

    This key toggles the Move tool's copy mode. A + sign appears on the Move cursor.

21. Click the upper-left corner of the short frame component, and then click the upper-right corner of the frame board on the left, as shown in Figure 7-6.

    The move operation places a duplicate piece of framing at the end of the flooring. When you're finished, the frame around the bottom of the floor is complete, and it looks like Figure 7-6.

Creating a Group in Outliner

With the first part of your project finished, SketchUp's Outliner (Window → Outliner) shows a list of four components and one group (Figure 7-7). They're all listed under the file name, which is fine for the moment, but it might be helpful to group all these elements under the name "Landing". That will protect the group from inadvertent changes as you work with other parts of the model. For example, when the group is not in edit mode, it prevents you from accidentally dragging one of the framing pieces away from the floor.

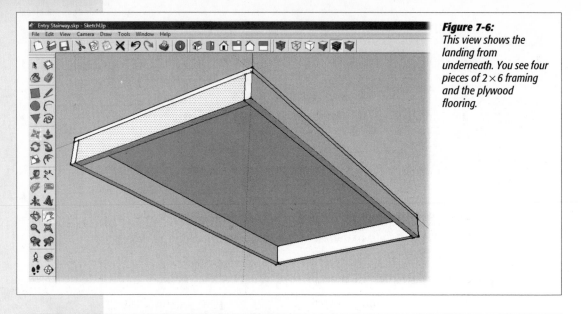

Figure 7-6:
This view shows the landing from underneath. You see four pieces of 2 × 6 framing and the plywood flooring.

Figure 7-7:
In Outliner, the icon indicating components is four small squares. The icon indicating a group is a larger solid square.

You can create the Landing group from within the Outliner. Select the four frame components and the floor group. Then right-click the selected names, and choose Make Group from the shortcut menu. In Outliner all the selected items move to the right a notch and "Group" appears above them. You can tell by the dotted line that the frame and floor items are contained in the group (Figure 7-8). Right-click the word "Group", and choose Rename from the shortcut menu. Then change the name of Group to *Landing*.

Locking a Group

If you'd like to give your group some added protection against inadvertent changes, you can *lock* the group. Once you lock a group, you must unlock it before you can make changes. To lock the group in Outliner, right-click the name, Landing, and then choose Lock from the shortcut menu. A small padlock appears on

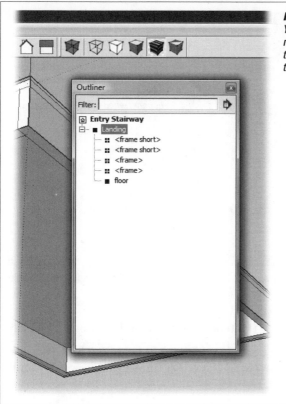

Figure 7-8:
*You can expand and collapse groups by clicking the +/- box
next to the name. Items inside a group are indented below
the group name and are connected to the group name by
thin dotted lines.*

the icon next to the word "Landing", and a similar padlock appears next to the
names of all items that belong to the group (Figure 7-9). When you select a group
that's locked, a red highlight appears, rather than the traditional blue highlight of a
group or component.

To unlock a locked group, right-click its name and then choose Unlock from the
shortcut menu. OK, so it's not exactly Fort Knox, but it does add a little more
security by saving you from yourself. Unlock the Landing group before you pro-
ceed with the rest of the exercise.

Note: You can individually lock any item in the Outliner list. So, for example, you could lock the floor
group in the Landing group, but leave the frame components unlocked.

Hiding and Unhiding in Outliner

In this next exercise, you create posts to support the landing, and you see how easy
it is to hide and unhide groups and components in the Outliner. When items are
well-organized in logical groups in the Outliner, it's much easier to use features
such as Hide and Unhide.

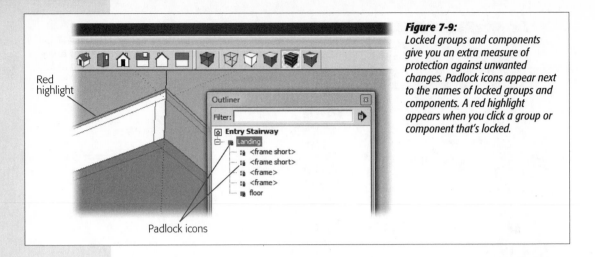

Figure 7-9:
Locked groups and components give you an extra measure of protection against unwanted changes. Padlock icons appear next to the names of locked groups and components. A red highlight appears when you click a group or component that's locked.

Red highlight

Padlock icons

Tip: Right-clicking an entity's name in the Outliner brings up the same shortcut menu as right-clicking the entity in the drawing window. Use whichever method is easiest to reach the Hide/Unhide and Lock/Unlock options.

---

1. **Use the Orbit (O) tool and Pan (H) tool to view the landing from underneath.**

   The next task is to create the posts that hold up the landing. The posts extend from the landing down to the ground, and they also extend upward from the landing to hold the small roof.

Tip: For this next step, to make sure you're not working inside the Landing group, click Entry Stairway in the Outliner.

---

2. **Using the Rectangle tool, begin to draw a rectangle on the floor group in the corner where two pieces of frame meet. Type *3.5,3.5* and then press Enter.**

   The dimensions 3.5×3.5 inches are the actual dimensions for most smooth-planed 4×4s that you find at the lumber yard.

3. **Pull the square out from the floor, type *7'6*, and then press Enter.**

   The post extends the right distance to reach the ground.

   You also want to pull the top of the post so that it extends above the landing; however, you can't select the top of the post because the landing is in the way. So you must take the extra step of hiding the landing before you Push/Pull the post.

4. **In Outliner, right-click the Landing group, and choose Hide from the shortcut menu.**

   The landing disappears and all you see is your 4×4 post.

5. Orbit around so you see the top of the post.

   Get a good view of the top, so you can operate on the top face with the Push/
   Pull tool.

6. With Push/Pull (P), click the top face and begin to pull it up. Then type *6'10*.

   Your post grows to a new height.

7. In the Outliner, right-click the Landing group, and choose Unhide from the
   shortcut menu.

   The parts of the Landing group reappear, and your post is positioned so that it
   extends above and below the landing (Figure 7-10). Perfecto!

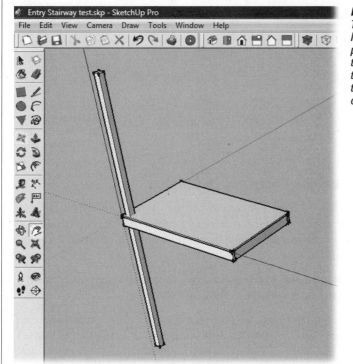

Figure 7-10:
This post extends above and below the landing's floor. You can position the post perfectly by drawing it on the bottom of the floor and pulling the bottom face out to the proper length. Use Outliner to hide the landing, and then you can pull the top of the post to the right length.

8. With the Select tool, triple-click the post and then press G. When the Create
   Component window appears, type *post front* in the Name box and *4x4 post 14
   feet, 2 inches* in the Description box and then press Create.

   Your new component is listed in Outliner. You made the post a component instead
   of a group because you need a 4×4 post of exactly the same height for the other side
   of the landing. Sure, you could duplicate a group or create a brand-new post for the
   job, but using components reduces the size of your SketchUp document and uses
   less computer horsepower. Smaller and faster—that's what you want.

9. **Use the Move (M) tool in copy mode to drag a duplicate post to the other side of the landing.**

Press Ctrl (Option) to toggle copy mode. It's best to view the landing from underneath to position the post so it's in the corner of the frame, as shown in Figure 7-11.

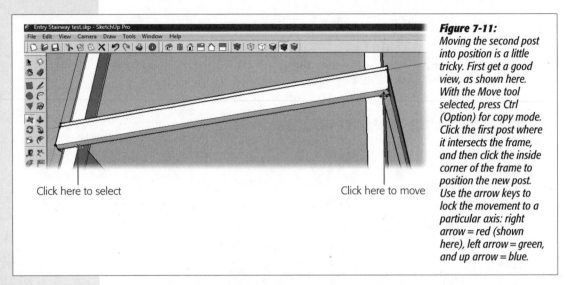

Click here to select   Click here to move

Figure 7-11:
Moving the second post into position is a little tricky. First get a good view, as shown here. With the Move tool selected, press Ctrl (Option) for copy mode. Click the first post where it intersects the frame, and then click the inside corner of the frame to position the new post. Use the arrow keys to lock the movement to a particular axis: right arrow = red (shown here), left arrow = green, and up arrow = blue.

Using the Make Unique Command in Outliner

The posts in the back are 1 foot, 2 inches taller than the ones in the front. They're designed to hold the small roof at an angle so rainwater runs off. The easiest way to create the back posts is to make another instance of the front post. Then you can make that instance unique.

1. **Repeat the last step in the previous exercise to create yet another post, and move it to one of the back corners of the landing.**

The Move tool leaves the original post in place and puts a duplicate on the back of the landing. Each copy of a component is an instance (page 169) of that component.

2. **In Outliner, right-click the duplicated component and choose Make Unique (Figure 7-12).**

The Make Unique command turns the selected component into a separate new component. This new component, <post front#1>, is no longer an instance of the original post component.

Note: Sometimes when you're working in the drawing window, it's quicker to right-click a component and choose Make Unique from the shortcut menu.

---

3. Right-click <post front#1>, and then choose Rename from the shortcut menu. Then type *post back* and press Enter.

It helps to give your new component a descriptive name.

4. Use the Select (space bar) tool to double-click to open the post in Edit Component mode.

The post back component opens in edit mode, and you can change the dimensions of the post.

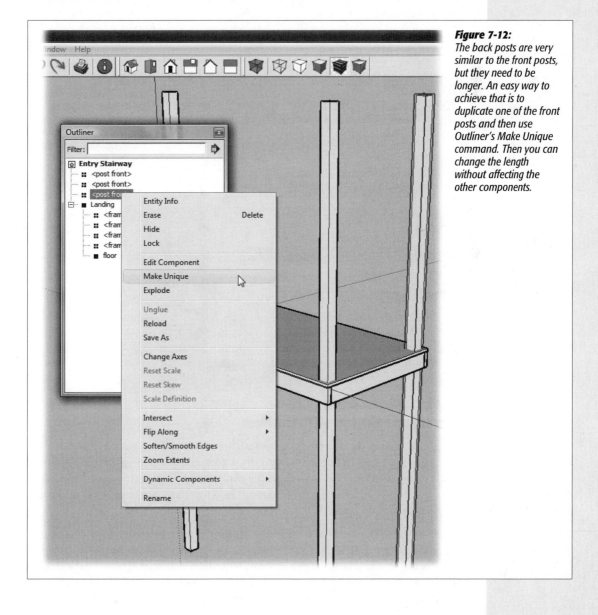

Figure 7-12:
The back posts are very similar to the front posts, but they need to be longer. An easy way to achieve that is to duplicate one of the front posts and then use Outliner's Make Unique command. Then you can change the length without affecting the other components.

5. **Using Push/Pull (P), start to pull the top face of the post up, type _1'2_ and then press Enter.**

Because you made a unique component, the front posts won't be affected.

6. **Click outside of the component (or choose Edit → Close Component/Group).**

Clicking away from the component closes the component so it's no longer being edited.

7. **Use the Move (M) tool in copy mode to position a new copy of the back post in the last corner.**

Now you have two instances of <post back> in your model (Figure 7-13).

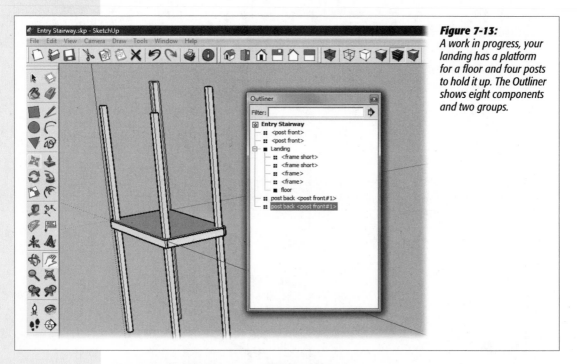

Figure 7-13:
A work in progress, your landing has a platform for a floor and four posts to hold it up. The Outliner shows eight components and two groups.

Reorganizing Groups with Outliner

There's no reason the four post components shouldn't be part of the Landing group. Moving items in and out of groups is a simple drag operation. In Outliner, Ctrl-click (⌘-click on a Mac) each of the four posts to select them, and then drag them on top of the Landing group name. The four posts are now listed under the Landing group as shown in Figure 7-14.

The next step in the construction of the landing is to create two 4×4 beams that reach across the top of each set of posts. If you've been following the steps up to now, this one is a cinch. Click the Right view button and then draw a vertical 3.5× 3.5-inch square on the top of one of the posts, and then Push/Pull to create a beam. Click the edge of the opposite post for alignment, as shown in Figure 7-15.

Figure 7-14:
Here the four posts were added to the Landing group. Reorganizing your groups in Outliner is a drag-and-drop affair.

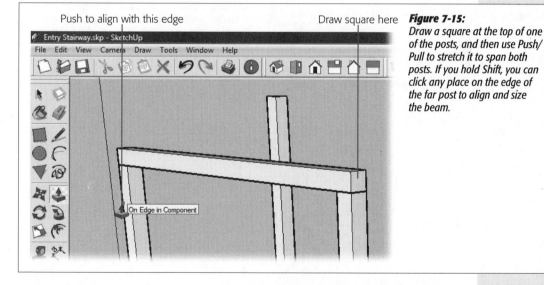

Push to align with this edge

Draw square here

Figure 7-15:
Draw a square at the top of one of the posts, and then use Push/ Pull to stretch it to span both posts. If you hold Shift, you can click any place on the edge of the far post to align and size the beam.

You need an identical beam to span the back posts, so it makes sense to create a "beam" component. Triple-click to select the entire beam and then press G. Name your component *beam* (unless you want to get creative), and give it a description like *4x4 roof beam*. Then use the Move (M) tool in copy mode to create a copy, and place it over the back posts. Then, to keep things organized, look in Outliner and drag your beams into the Landing group.

Building a Small Angled Roof

The roof for this landing is pretty simple. It consists of four 2×4s that serve as rafters and a single piece of plywood for the roof. The only thing that's slightly tricky about it is the angle, but SketchUp has some tools to help with that.

1. **Click the Back view button.**

   The view changes so the taller posts are closest to you.

2. **Using the Rectangle (R) tool, draw a vertical rectangle beginning at the corner of the top beam, type *1.5,3.5* and press Enter (Return on a Mac).**

   Your 2×4 rafter has actual dimensions of 1.5×3.5 inches.

3. **With Push/Pull (P), push the rafter so it extends way beyond the lower beam (as shown in Figure 7-16).**

   You don't have to be precise about the length, because you will trim the end later. The rafter extends horizontally into space. In the next steps you rotate it into place.

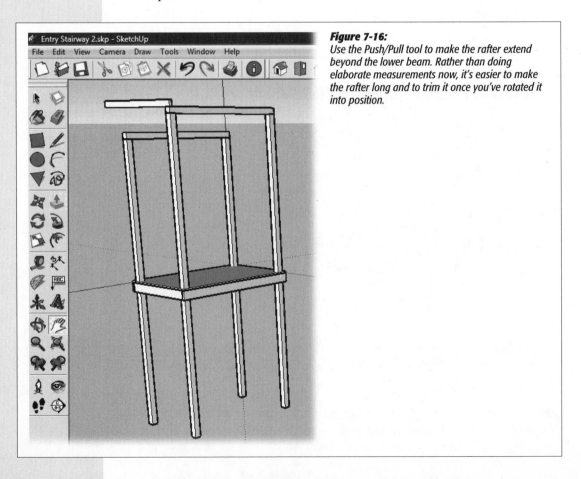

Figure 7-16:
Use the Push/Pull tool to make the rafter extend beyond the lower beam. Rather than doing elaborate measurements now, it's easier to make the rafter long and to trim it once you've rotated it into position.

4. Triple-click the rafter and then press G. Name the component *rafter* and type *2x4 rafter* in the Description box. Then click Create.

5. With the Rotate (Q) tool, click the point where the rafter meets the inside edge of the top beam.

   You want the rafter to rotate around this point.

6. Drag the Rotate tool to the left along the bottom end of the rafter and then click. Then move the cursor toward the lower beam. Click when the rafter rests on the lower beam.

   As you move the cursor, the rafter follows, rotating around the first point you clicked. When you're done, the top of the landing looks like Figure 7-17.

7. Double-click to open the rafter component in edit mode.

   The rafter component opens for editing. You may want to zoom in a bit to get a good view of the end of the rafter as you trim it in the next step.

8. With the Line tool, draw a vertical (parallel to the blue axis) trim line about an inch or two from the beam.

   You can draw a line flush with the end of the beam or one that lets the rafter extend slightly beyond the beam as in Figure 7-17.

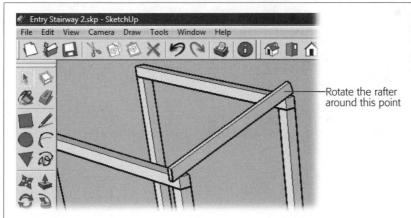

Figure 7-17:
When it's positioned and trimmed, a rafter looks like this. The landing uses four instances of the rafter component.

Rotate the rafter around this point

9. Use Push/Pull to lop off the unneeded portion of the rafter, and then click outside of the component to leave edit mode.

   Push on the face of the unneeded portion, and then click the back side of the rafter.

Creating an Array of Rafters

You first met SketchUp arrays on page 168, where you used them to build a fence. You can use an array here to duplicate and position the rafters. It all starts with the

Move tool in copy mode. After you move and place a second rafter, you use the / key to create an array of rafters in between the first two.

1. **Choose the Move tool and press Ctrl (Option).**

   A + sign appears on the Move tool cursor to indicate it's in copy mode.

2. **Click the rafter and move a copy to the opposite end of the beam.**

   You have rafters at both ends of the roof, and all you need to do is add some in between. For tips on how to accurately move and position the rafter, you may want to refer to the explanation for moving beams in Figure 7-11.

3. **Type *3/* and press Enter (Return).**

   SketchUp creates two new rafters and spaces them evenly in between the others, as shown in Figure 7-18.

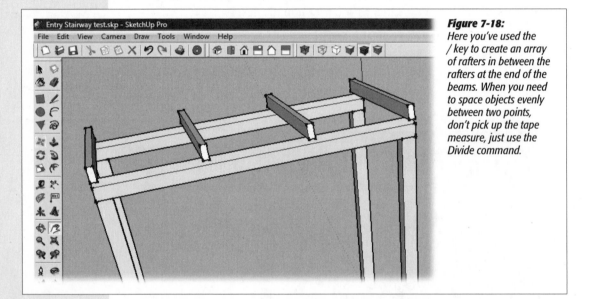

Figure 7-18:
Here you've used the / key to create an array of rafters in between the rafters at the end of the beams. When you need to space objects evenly between two points, don't pick up the tape measure, just use the Divide command.

Putting a lid on it

The last step for this little roof is to place a piece of plywood on top. The easiest way to create a 1-inch piece of plywood for the roof that's angled just right is to use the Line (L) tool to draw a rectangle that reaches from rafter corner to corner. Then select the three edges that aren't next to the house, and use the Offset (F) tool to create a 4-inch overhang on the two sides and the front. You don't want to offset the back side, because it's up against the house. After using Offset, you may need to do a little cleanup work with the Line tool to connect the edges on the back corners.

Finally, use Push/Pull (P) to pull the face up an inch. Your plywood face may be divided into a couple of faces where the rafters or the Offset tool create unwanted edges. If that's the case, just pull up the faces to the same 1-inch level and then use the Eraser (E) to delete the extra edges. Check all the sides and the bottom when you're removing unneeded edges. If on inspection, you have some missing faces, use the Line (L) tool to retrace the edges. After an operation like creating this plywood roof, you may need to do some cleanup using right-click → Reverse Faces or the Eraser (E). Your completed roof looks like Figure 7-19.

After you've finished creating the piece of plywood that serves as the roofing, triple-click it and choose Edit → Make Group. Then rename the group *roofing*. By turning the plywood roofing into a group, you make it appear in the Outliner, where you can organize it along with the other parts of the landing.

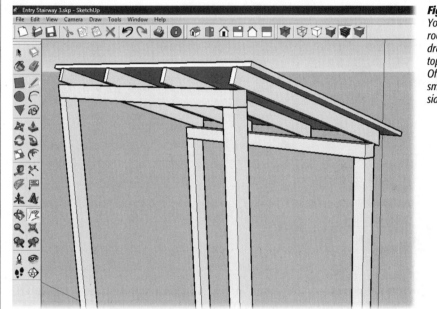

Figure 7-19:
You create the plywood roof for the landing by drawing a rectangle on top of the rafters. Use the Offset tool to create a small overhang on the sides and front.

Drawing Guides with the Tape Measure

One side of the landing leads to the front door of the house, and another side of the landing leads to the stairs (Figure 7-1). The remaining two sides have 2 × 4 railings. The top of the high railing is 32 inches from the floor of the landing. The top of the lower railing is 16 inches from the floor. Before you make the railings, you use the Tape Measure (T) tool to place guides to mark their position. You may have used guides in two-dimensional drawing programs such as Adobe Photoshop or Adobe Illustrator. The guides you draw with the Tape Measure are similar to those, but because you're drawing a guide in 3-D space, you need to attach it to something. So in SketchUp, you click an edge in your model and then move the Tape Measure away from that edge. As you move, the tape measure displays the distance between the edge and your cursor. To set a guide, click again. A dashed guideline appears that runs parallel to the edge you first clicked.

Here are the steps for creating guides for the landing's railing:

1. **In your *Entry Stairway.skp* document, press T or select the Tape Measure tool from the toolbar.**

   In the modeling window the Tape Measure tool looks remarkably like a tape measure with a plus sign next to it. Click anywhere and drag the cursor, and the distance appears in the Measurements toolbar and in the tooltip attached to the cursor. The little diamond-shaped selection point near the end of the Tape Measure snaps to edges, points, and intersections. When it snaps to an edge, you see a square. When it snaps to a point, you see a circle. When it snaps to an intersection without an edge, you see an X, as shown in Figure 7-20. SketchUp can't create a guide from an intersection, so first you need to create an edge where the post passes through the floor of the landing.

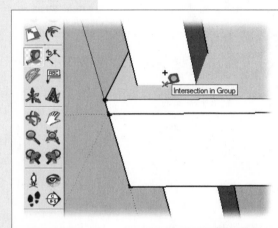

Figure 7-20:
Here the cursor on the Tape Measure has snapped to an intersection where there's no edge. The × is a reminder that the Tape Measure can't create a guide from this selection point. First you must draw an edge along this intersection.

2. **In Outliner right-click the "floor" group, and then choose Intersect → Intersect with Model from the shortcut menu.**

   Edges appear where the posts pass through the landing's floor.

Tip: Selecting or right-clicking a group or component in Outliner is the same as selecting or right-clicking it in the modeling window.

---

3. **With the Tape Measure, select the edge and then move the cursor up the post. Type *16* and press Enter (Return).**

   A guideline appears 16 inches from the floor. The Tape Measure is similar to the drawing tools. Type a measurement, and it appears in the Measurements toolbar. This gives you a quick way to accurately create guidelines. You can change the measurement by simply typing a new number, as long as you haven't selected another tool or command.

Tip: Sometimes you just want to measure a distance and don't need to create a guide. Use the Ctrl (Option) key to toggle between Tape Measure's two modes. The cursor shows a + sign when it's in guide-creating mode. When no + shows, Tape Measure is in measure-only mode. In either case, the distance appears in the Measurements toolbar.

4. Click again on the edge where the post meets the floor. Move the cursor up the post, type *32*, and then press Enter (Return).

   A second guide appears 32 inches above the landing's floor.

5. Zoom in a bit and then using the Rectangle (R) tool, start drawing a rectangle from the point where the 16-inch guide meets the corner of the post. Type *1. 5,3.5*, and then press Enter (Return).

   A rectangle appears on the post, as shown in Figure 7-21. The top of the rectangle is 16 inches from the landing's floor. At 1.5×3.5 inches, the rectangle is the actual dimensions of a smooth-planed 2×4.

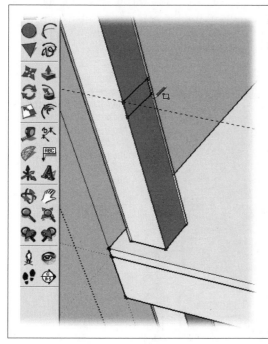

Figure 7-21:
The Rectangle cursor snaps to the guideline the same way it snaps to other edges and points in your model.

6. Use Push/Pull (P) to pull the 2×4 so it extends to the post on the other side of the landing.

   Click the edge of the right post to align the end of the 2×4 rail.

7. Triple-click the rail and then press G. Type *front rail* in the Name box, and type *2x4 front rail for landing* in the Description box.

   You can use an instance of this component to create the top rail, which has the same dimensions.

8. **Use the Move (M) tool in copy mode to create a top rail aligned to the guide 32 inches from the landing's floor.**

   When you're done, two rails are at the front of the landing, as shown in Figure 7-22. Use the Ctrl (Option) key to put Move into copy mode. Press the up arrow key to lock the move to the blue (vertical) axis.

9. **Use the techniques in the steps above to create an upper and lower rail for the right side of the landing.**

   This completes the construction of the landing. Next up, you build some stairs.

10. **Choose File → Save or File → Save as to save your document.**

    Sometimes it's helpful to save your SketchUp project at different stages of progress. So occasionally you may want to use the Save As command and then save your work using sequential numbers such as Entry Stairway 1.skp, Entry Stairway 2.skp, Entry Stairway 3.skp, and so on.

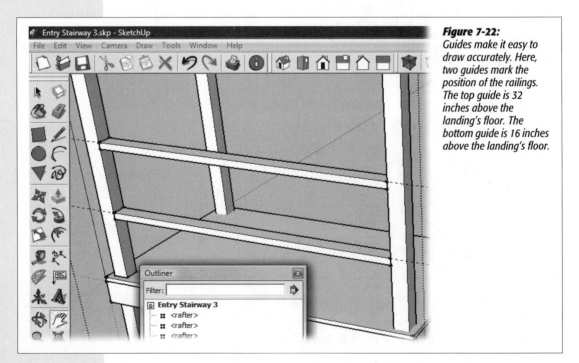

Figure 7-22:
Guides make it easy to draw accurately. Here, two guides mark the position of the railings. The top guide is 32 inches above the landing's floor. The bottom guide is 16 inches above the landing's floor.

Erasing and Hiding Guides

It can be distracting to have lots of leftover guidelines in your model. If you know you won't need a particular guide again, it makes sense to delete it. To delete a guide, press E to switch to the Eraser tool, and then click the line you want to erase. If you want to erase more than one guide, you can click and drag the Eraser over the lines.

Hiding guides

What if you don't want to erase the guidelines permanently; you just want to hide them for a while? To hide guidelines, choose View → Guides. The Guides option on the View menu displays a checkmark when guides are visible. Click to remove the checkmark, and all guides are temporarily hidden.

Creating a Nested Group in Outliner

Now that the landing is finished, it's a good time to reorganize the entities in the outline. For example, the beams, rafters, and roof form a discrete element in the model. At times you may want to hide the roof so you can see other elements. You can create a Roof group that's nested inside the Landing group.

1. **In Outliner select the two beams, and then choose Edit → Make Group.**

   A new group (cleverly called Group) appears nested inside the Landing group.

2. **Right-click Group and then choose Rename from the pop-up menu. Type** *Roof* **as a new name.**

   The new Roof group contains two beams. It's time to put the rest of the roof inside the group.

3. **Drag the four rafter components and the roofing group into the Roof group.**

   When you're finished with reorganization, your Outliner looks like the bottom image in Figure 7-23.

You can create and rearrange your groups and nested groups on the fly. Use the Outliner to organize your model in any way that might be helpful while you're working. For example, you may want to group the landing's floor and floor framing into another nested group in the Landing group.

Building Stairs: The Divide and Conquer Method

Talk to any carpenter and she'll tell you, you won't enjoy designing and building stairs unless you like geometry and division. To build stairs in the real world, you need to:

• Measure the horizontal distance the stairs travel.

• Measure the vertical distance the stairs travel.

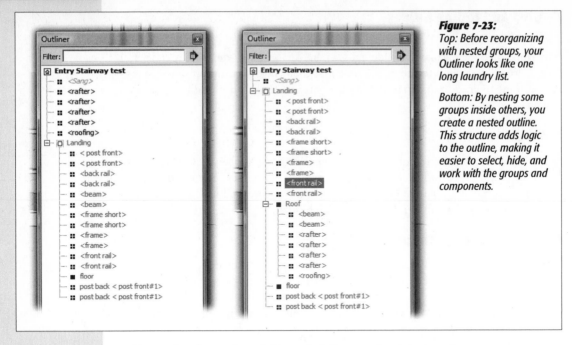

Figure 7-23:
Top: Before reorganizing with nested groups, your Outliner looks like one long laundry list.

Bottom: By nesting some groups inside others, you create a nested outline. This structure adds logic to the outline, making it easier to select, hide, and work with the groups and components.

- Determine the angle and the angled distance the stairs travel.

- Determine the number of steps the stairs require.

- Calculate the vertical distance between the steps, known as the *rise*.

- Calculate the horizontal distance between the steps, known as the *run*.

If that doesn't sound like fun to you, perhaps you aren't among that group of humans who enjoy geometry and division. In that case, you'll love how SketchUp does the work of stair building for you. The tool that does the hard work is the Divide command. Once you know the horizontal and vertical distances the stairs span, SketchUp does all the other calculations automatically. Keep in mind that when you build stairs, you need to follow the standards for your community; see the box on the next page.

In this example, the stairs reach from the middle of the concrete step to the middle of the landing frame. Building from the ground up, it makes sense to create and position the concrete step before building the stairs. So mix up some concrete and follow these steps:

1. **In the *Entry Stairway.skp* document, change to Top view (Camera → Standard Views → Top), and then with the Rectangle (R) tool begin to draw a rectangle. Type *2′,4′* and then press Enter (Return).**

   SketchUp draws a 2 × 4-foot rectangle on the ground level.

CONSTRUCTION TIP

Stairway to Success

The trickiest part of designing and building stairs is designing the *stringer*. This is the point where the rise and fall for each step must be calculated along with determining the total number of stairs. Designing and building stairs is a safety issue, too, so standards and codes apply. In the U.S., the Occupational Safety and Health Administration (OSHA) defines the minimum standards for stairs in the workplace. When you're designing and building stairs, it's important to check your community building code because different communities use different standards, and they're usually stricter than OSHA's minimum standards.

Carpenters use some general guidelines. The treads for residential outdoor stairs such as these are often about 9 to 12 inches in width. This dimension provides solid footing without requiring a long stride to reach the next step. Sometimes a portion of the tread slightly overlaps the step below, making each tread slightly longer then the run. Rise is usually between 5 and 8 inches. OSHA's standard for the angle formed by the stairway to the horizontal surface is 30 to 50 degrees; however 30 to 40 degrees is a more comfortable angle for residential exterior stairs, such as the ones in this chapter.

2. **Using Push/Pull (P), begin to pull the step up. Type 6 and then press Enter.**

   The concrete step is 6 inches tall. Because you drew the first rectangle in Top view and then pulled the step up, the bottom of the step is properly aligned to the ground level in the model. The ground level is the plane formed by the red and green axis guides.

3. **Triple-click the concrete step and choose Edit → Make Group. Then in Outliner right-click the new group and choose Rename. Type *concrete step* and press Enter.**

   The faces and edges are all grouped together and named "concrete step."

4. **Change to Front view by clicking a button or by choosing Camera → Standard Views → Front.**

   At this point you may notice a problem with the landing. The posts and the landing frame extend beyond the ground level. This little problem occurred when you created the posts by pulling them down from the landing. In the next step, you'll level things up.

5. **In the Outliner, click to select the Landing group.**

   All the parts of the landing are selected.

6. **With the Move (M) tool, click the bottom edge of one of the Posts and press the up arrow.**

   The entire landing moves with the Move tool cursor, as shown in Figure 7-24. Pressing the up arrow locks the movement to the blue axis.

7. **Click the bottom of the concrete step.**

   The bottom of the step and the landing are now both aligned to the ground level.

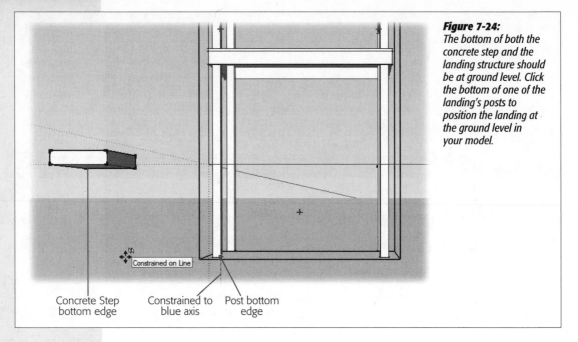

Figure 7-24:
*The bottom of both the
concrete step and the
landing structure should
be at ground level. Click
the bottom of one of the
landing's posts to
position the landing at
the ground level in
your model.*

Constrained on Line

Concrete Step
bottom edge

Constrained to
blue axis

Post bottom
edge

Next you move the step the proper distance from the Landing. Hope you're
feeling strong. That concrete is heavy.

8. **Deselect the Landing group. Then using the Move tool, click the lower-right corner of the concrete step, and then click the Origin point, where all the axes meet.**

   The step moves to the Origin point.

9. **Click the lower-left corner again; then press the right arrow key. Begin to move
the step to the left, and then type *8'2*. Press Enter.**

   The concrete step moves into position, ready to support the stairs. In this case,
   the distance between the concrete step and the landing is dictated by the design
   of the house (Figure 7-1). The stairs need to reach the ground a reasonable distance before the garage door.

Using Divide to Build Stair Stringers

Using the Tape Measure (T) tool described on page 281, measure the right angle
formed between the midpoint of the concrete step and the midpoint of the landing's frame. You need to know both the vertical and horizontal distances spanned
by the stairs. So click the top edge of the concrete step, and then press the up arrow
to lock the cursor's movement to the blue axis. Then move the cursor over to the
midpoint of the landing's frame. As you can see in Figure 7-25, a tooltip appears
displaying the distance. For the model in this section, that distance is 6' 9 1/4". (If
your measurements vary by an inch or two, don't worry about it. Follow these
steps and SketchUp makes the stairs to fit.) You might as well click to place a guide

marking the midpoint; it may come in handy later. To measure the horizontal distance, click the edge of the landing's frame, and press the right arrow to lock the cursor's movement to the red axis. Then click the midpoint of the concrete stone. Tape Measure reports the horizontal distance is 9' 2".

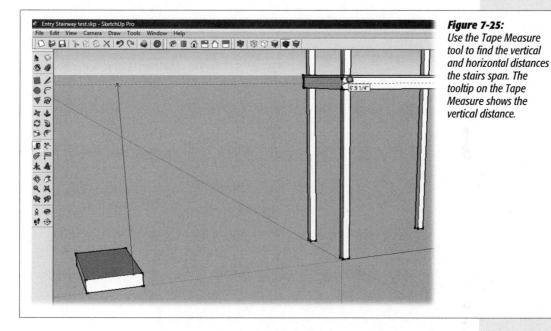

Figure 7-25:
Use the Tape Measure tool to find the vertical and horizontal distances the stairs span. The tooltip on the Tape Measure shows the vertical distance.

Armed with these two measurements, the vertical and horizontal distance, you can create your stairs. SketchUp does the rest of the calculations courtesy of the Divide command. It's easier to build the steps first and then place them in the model, so begin your drawing in front of the concrete step and the landing.

1. **Using the Rectangle tool, begin to draw a rectangle. Type *9'2,4'*, and then press Enter (Return).**

   Your measurements provided the horizontal distance the stairs must travel: 9 feet, 2 inches. You want the stairs to be as wide as the landing: 4 feet.

2. **With the Select (space bar) tool, right-click the front edge and choose Divide from the shortcut menu. Then move the cursor left or right to adjust the division. Click when the tooltip says "11 segments".**

   SketchUp displays red squares to mark the division of the edge. As you move the cursor to the right, SketchUp displays fewer segments; move it to the left, and the tooltip shows more segments. Below the number of segments, you see the Length and a measurement in inches. The number showing will be the run for your stairs and roughly the size of the stair tread. As explained in the box on page 261, you want your run to be between 9 and 11 inches.

3. Choose the Line (L) tool, and then move it along the divided edge. When you see a tooltip that says "Endpoint", draw a perpendicular line to the opposite edge.

   Your line creates a new face in the rectangle that looks suspiciously like a stair tread.

4. Continue to draw lines at the endpoints to divide the large rectangle into 11 faces, as shown in Figure 7-26.

   If you have trouble drawing a line on axis, press the left arrow to lock the cursor's movement to the green axis.

   When you're finished, you're done with the horizontal work. The next steps go vertical.

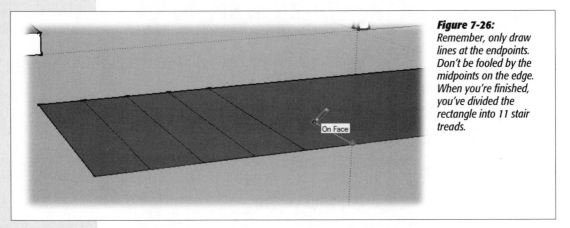

Figure 7-26:
Remember, only draw lines at the endpoints. Don't be fooled by the midpoints on the edge. When you're finished, you've divided the rectangle into 11 stair treads.

5. With the Line (L) tool, start to draw an edge from the front right corner of the rectangle along the blue axis. Type the height for the stairs.

   Press and release the up arrow to lock the line to the blue axis. The height for the model in the figures is *6'9.25*. Your mileage may vary.

6. With the Select tool, right-click the new vertical edge, and then choose Divide from the pop-up menu. Type *11* and press Enter.

   This one's easy: you already know that you have 11 steps and need to measure 11 vertical positions. The Divide command does the work of figuring out just how much rise is required. The line divided into 11 segments serves as your measuring stick.

7. With Push/Pull (P), click the face closest to the divided vertical edge, and then pull the face up to the top of the line.

   Your top stair step snaps into place.

8. Continue to pull the rest of the steps into position, as shown Figure 7-27.

   At this point, your rectangle is Push/Pulled into a shape that looks remarkably like a set of stairs.

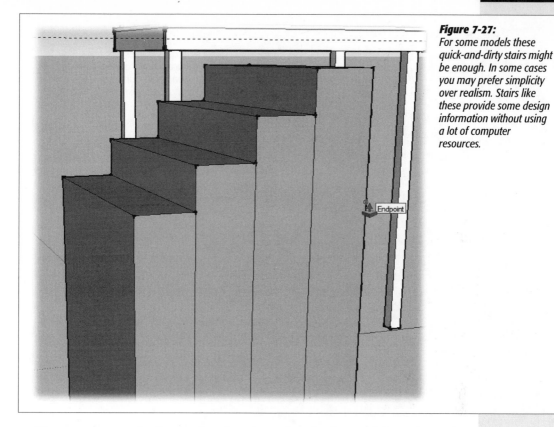

Figure 7-27:
For some models these quick-and-dirty stairs might be enough. In some cases you may prefer simplicity over realism. Stairs like these provide some design information without using a lot of computer resources.

9. **Clean up your stairs by erasing the extra edges in the model, as shown in Figure 7-28. If necessary reverse the faces (right-click → Reverse Face).**

    Make sure to erase the extra edges on the back of the stairs that were created during the Push/Pull operation.

At this stage the stairs are the right dimensions to drop in place—4 feet wide. If you want, go ahead and use the Move tool to put them temporarily in position. When you're finished checking them out, bring the stairs back out in front of the landing. For some models where you want to limit the detail, quick-and-dirty stairs like these may be fine. For this model, you'll create a few more stair details. If you take another look at the stairs in Figure 7-1, you see that they're made from two stringers and 11 treads for the steps. The stringers are made from 2-inch lumber. In the next steps, you'll trim your stair stringer down to size and turn it into a component.

1. **Using the Move (M) tool, click the face of the stairs, and then begin to push back (Figure 7-29). Press the right arrow key to lock the movement to the green axis. Type *3'10* and then press Enter (Return on a Mac).**

    The stairs were 4 feet wide. Trimming them down by 3 feet 10 inches creates a stair stringer that's 2 inches wide. If you have any leftover edges or faces that aren't part of the string, clean them up with the Eraser (E).

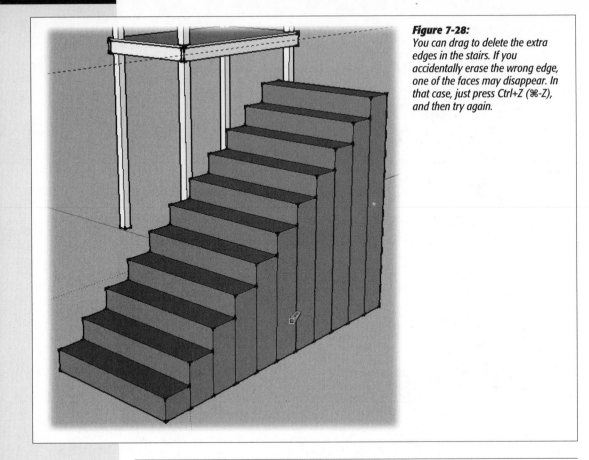

Figure 7-28:
You can drag to delete the extra edges in the stairs. If you accidentally erase the wrong edge, one of the faces may disappear. In that case, just press Ctrl+Z (⌘-Z), and then try again.

Note: Lumber used for construction is usually available either rough or dressed. Dressed lumber is planed so its actual dimensions are less than the nominal dimensions. So far in this chapter, most of the lumber was planed. For the stringers, you're specifying rough lumber with actual dimensions that are close to the nominal 2 inches. The stringers are hidden from view and touch, so rough lumber doesn't present an aesthetic problem. The stairs can benefit from the extra strength of thicker lumber, too.

2. **With the Line (L) tool, hover over the top stringer's first inside corner as shown in Figure 7-30. Move on the red axis to the edge and click the edge.**

   An inference line appears as you move the cursor back to the edge.

3. **Move to the bottom edge of the stringer, and find an inference from the bottom inside corner, as shown in Figure 7-30. Click the bottom edge of the stringer.**

   A diagonal line marks the angle for the bottom edge of your stringer. Get out the power saw.

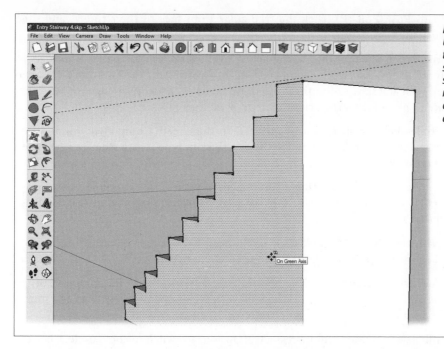

Figure 7-29:
Use the Move (M) tool to turn your 4-foot-wide stairs into a 2-inch-wide stair stringer. Here, the moving face is constrained to motion along the green axis.

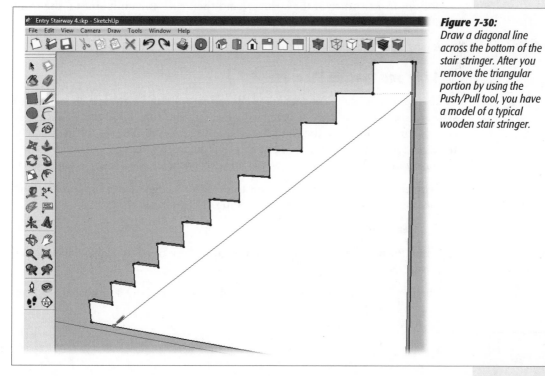

Figure 7-30:
Draw a diagonal line across the bottom of the stair stringer. After you remove the triangular portion by using the Push/Pull tool, you have a model of a typical wooden stair stringer.

4. With Push/Pull (P), click the triangular front face of the stringer, and then click the back edge.

    The excess material that was attached to the stringer disappears. It now looks more like a real piece of lumber sawn into a stringer. And you don't even end up with any sawdust on the ground. If you have any leftover edges or faces that aren't part of the string, clean them up with the Eraser (E).

5. Triple-click the stringer and press G. In the Create Component window, for the name, type *stringer* and for the description, type *2-inch stair stringer.* Then choose Create.

    You've created a new stringer component. For these stairs you need two stringers. Wider stairs often use more stringers to provide support in the middle of the tread.

6. With the Move (M) tool, click the bottom-back corner of the stringer. Then click the midpoint on the back of the concrete step.

    The stringer is installed. The bottom edge is aligned with the midpoint of the concrete step. The top edge is aligned with the midpoint of the landing's frame. The back edge of the stringer is flush with the back edge of the landing.

7. Still using the Move tool, press Ctrl (Option) to switch to copy mode. Click the bottom-front corner of the stringer, and then click the midpoint on the front of the concrete step.

    A new stringer is positioned on the other side of the concrete step.

Making and Placing Stair Treads

Your landing and stair stringers are in place, just waiting for the last element—the stair treads. Measure your stringer to determine the *run,* the distance each step covers horizontally. For the model in the figures, the distance is 10 inches. The treads are going to be an inch wider, and their exposed edge will be rounded over. Because you need 11 identical treads, it makes sense to create a single component.

1. With the Rectangle (R) tool, begin to draw a rectangle on the ground next to the stairs. Type *11,4'* and then press Enter (Return on a Mac).

    The treads are 11 inches wide and 4 feet long.

2. Using Push/Pull (P), begin to pull the face of the tread up. Type *1.5* and then press Enter.

    The tread is 1.5 inches thick, the actual dimension of 2-inch lumber that's been planed smooth.

3. Use Orbit (O) and the other view tools to get a good close view of the end of the tread, like the one shown in Figure 7-31.

You need to be close enough to the end of the tread that you can identify its midpoint.

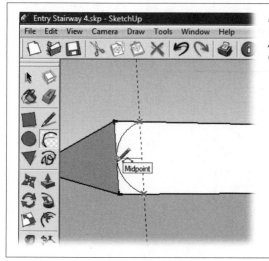

Figure 7-31:
The stair treads have a round edge that you can create using the Arc tool (A) shown here and the Push/Pull tool (not shown). You can create a half-inch guideline, or you can eyeball the distance.

4. With the Arc tool, click the tread's edge about a half inch from the end.

If you want to be precise, use the Tape Measure (T) tool to add a guide at the half-inch point, as shown in Figure 7-31. Otherwise you can eyeball the distance.

5. Click the tread's opposite edge, and then click the midpoint at the end.

A curved edge forms an arc on the end of the tread.

6. With Push/Pull, click the corner face, and then click the back edge of the tread.

Remove both the top and bottom corners to create a round nose on the front of the tread.

Tip: You can use the Eraser (E) with the Soften/Smooth modifier key (Ctrl for Windows; Option for Mac) to soften the edge in the curve.

---

7. Triple-click the tread and then press G. In the Create Component window, name the component *tread,* and for the description, type *2-inch stair tread.* Then click Create.

8. Using the Move (M) tool, click the bottom-right corner of the stair tread, and then click the corner formed by the stringer, as shown in Figure 7-32.

When you move the corner of the tread to the corner of the stringer, the treads snap into place.

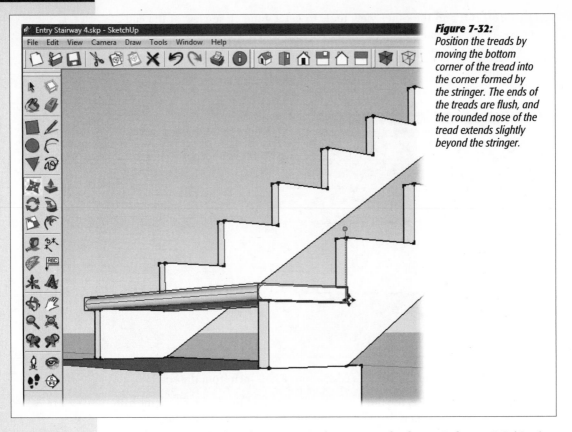

Figure 7-32:
Position the treads by moving the bottom corner of the tread into the corner formed by the stringer. The ends of the treads are flush, and the rounded nose of the tread extends slightly beyond the stringer.

9. **Use the Move (M) tool in copy mode. Press and release Ctrl on a PC (Option on a Mac). Copy and place the rest of the stair treads.**

    As you place the stair treads, you may find that you inadvertently select the stringer. You can minimize this by right-clicking the stringer Outliner and then choosing Lock from the pop-up list. A padlock appears next to the stringer, and the outline in the modeling window turns to red (instead of blue). With the stringer component locked, you can't select it with the Move tool.

Tip: You can use an array to place the stair treads quickly. Move the second tread into place and then type *10x*.

Building the stair's railing

The railing for the stairs matches the railing at the top of the landing. There are two 4×4 posts that support the railing. One post is on the sixth or middle step, and the other is on the bottom step. The top rail is a 2×6 (actual dimensions 1.5× 5.5 inches). The top rail rests on top of the posts. The bottom rail is a 2×4 (actual dimensions 1.5×3.5 inches). The bottom rail meets the posts at an angle, about 16 inches above the tread.

The techniques for building the railing are very similar to those used building the landing's railing, so only an abbreviated version appears here. If you need extra help, review the more complete steps described on page 255.

- Create posts by drawing a 3.5 square on the treads, and use Push/Pull (P) to make them about 36 inches tall. (You'll trim them later.)

- Use the Rectangle (R) tool or Line tool to draw the 1.5×3.5 lower rail on the post at the landing. The top of the rail should be 16 inches from the floor of the landing.

- Use Push/Pull (P) to pull the bottom rail out horizontally. Make it too long. (Later you rotate it into position and trim it.) Turn it into a group named *stair rail bottom*.

- The railings should be oriented to the same angle as the bottom edge of the stairs. Use the Protractor to measure that angle. See page 283 for details on measuring angles with the Protractor.

- Use Rotate (Q) to tilt the bottom rail into place. Type the angle you measured in the preceding step. The rail passes through the posts with its top face 16 inches from the tread. Create a guide on the bottom post if you want to be precise.

- Double-click the bottom rail to open the group in edit mode for some cleanup operations. Right-click and use the Intersect → Intersect with Model command to break the railing into smaller segments where it meets the posts. Use Push/Pull to trim the excess at the end of the rail. Use the Eraser (E) to remove unwanted edges on the posts. If you lose faces in either the rail or the posts, trace over the edges with the Line (L) tool to bring the faces back.

- At 1.5×5.5 inches, the top rail is wider than the posts. Draw the rectangle on the face of the post so that its top edge is 32 inches above the landing floor. Use the rectangle's midpoint to center it on the post.

- Follow the same steps described above to tilt the top rail into place. Use Intersect → Intersect with Model, the Eraser, and the Line tool to clean up the extra edges and faces.

- As a final touch, you may want to bevel or trim the ends of the top rail to give it a more finished look.

Note: If you want to see a model for comparison, you can find *entry_stairs_finished.skp* at *http:// missingmanuals.com/cds*.

Using Outliner's Filter

You've added a bunch of new components and groups to your model, and the names are all showing in the Outliner. Your landing parts are carefully organized in a group named Landing. It makes sense to do the same with the stairs.

---

1. Open the Outliner window (Window → Outliner), and then click the Details button and choose Expand All.

   All the groups and components in your model appear in the Outliner list. If any groups or components were collapsed, they expand completely. Use the menu under the Details to expand and collapse the Outliner list and to sort the list by name.

2. In the Filter box at the top of Outliner, type *tread*.

   All the items except for the 11 instances of tread disappear from the Outliner.

3. Select all the treads and then right-click the selection. From the shortcut menu, choose Make Group.

   You see a blue highlight on the selected tread components. You can right-click any part of the blue selection highlight. The menu displays the same options you see if you right-click the components in the modeling window.

   The treads are contained in a new group called Group.

4. Right-click Group and choose Rename. Type *Stairs* as the new name.

   The group Stairs and its contents, the treads, are the only items in the Outliner, shown in Figure 7-33. It's still being filtered by the word "tread".

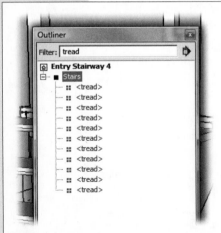

Figure 7-33:
Here the word "tread" is entered in the Filter box. The Outliner displays all the items with "tread" in the name. The treads are contained in the Stairs group.

5. In the Filter at the top, type *stringer*.

   The Outliner shows the two stringers. If one of the stringers is still locked from the previous exercise, unlock it now.

6. Select the two stringer instances, and then select and delete the word "string" in the Filter.

   When you delete the word in the Filter box, the Outliner displays all the elements in the outline. The two stringers remain selected.

7. Drag the stringers and the concrete step into the Stairs group.

All the groups and components are now in one of two groups: Landing or Stairs.

That wraps up the construction of the Entry Stairway and the exploration of the Outliner. The Outliner serves several functions in SketchUp. It gives you a way to organize parts of your model in a logical way. The Outliner is great for hiding and unhiding parts of your model. With complicated models, it's often easier to select a group or component in the Outliner than it is to select it in the modeling window. The same is true when you want to right-click an entity to use a command from its shortcut menu.

Working with Layers

SketchUp layers are another way you can organize your model. You may have used layers before in a CAD (computer aided design) program or in two-dimensional art programs like Adobe Photoshop or Illustrator. At the outset it's important to understand that SketchUp's layers are different from those programs. In other programs, you may use layers to group objects, and then you work on those objects in their respective layers. That may not be the best way for new SketchUp artists to work, since layers don't protect parts of your model from accidentally changing.

Adding, Naming, and Deleting Layers

You can use two primary tools when it comes to working with layers: the Layers window and the Entity window. You use the Layers window to create, name, and remove layers. You use the Entity window to move entities (preferably groups or components) to a particular layer. Here are the simple steps for creating and naming a new layer.

1. Choose Window → Layers.

The Layers window appears, as shown in Figure 7-34. The first layer in SketchUp is always there and it's named Layer0.

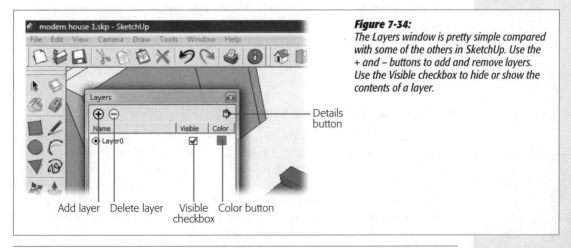

Figure 7-34:
The Layers window is pretty simple compared with some of the others in SketchUp. Use the + and – buttons to add and remove layers. Use the Visible checkbox to hide or show the contents of a layer.

Details button

Add layer   Delete layer   Visible   Color button
                          checkbox

2. **Click the + (plus) button.**

   A new layer is created. As you create them, SketchUp numbers your layers sequentially, starting at 0. So the second layer in your model is named Layer1. When you create a new layer, the layer name is already selected so you can rename it by simply typing the new name.

Note: Starting a count at 0, as in the case of SketchUp layers, is a computer programmer thing. It makes sense to programmers, but leaves the rest of the world puzzled.

---

3. **Type *Furniture* and then press Enter (Return on a Mac).**

   You now have a new layer named "Furniture". You can use any name you want for layers that you create, but you can't rename Layer0.

   If you want to rename an existing layer, double-click the layer name, and then type the new name.

4. **Click Layer0 and then click Furniture.**

   The individual layers are highlighted when you click the name. You need to select a layer in this manner before you can remove the layer.

5. **With the Furniture layer selected, click the – (minus) button.**

   The Furniture layer disappears. Your Furniture layer didn't contain anything, so deleting the layer didn't change your model. If content had been on the layer, SketchUp would have warned you with the message box shown in Figure 7-35. The message box gives you three options:

   • **Move contents to Default layer.** Use this option to move the contents to Layer0—generally a good move, especially if you're planning on making any changes to the content.

   • **Move contents to Current layer.** You can use this option to send the contents to a layer other than Layer0.

   • **Delete contents.** Use this option to delete all the entities on the layer at the same time you delete the layer.

Tip: If your workspace is tight, use the Layers toolbar to select the current layer. In Windows, choose View → Toolbars → Layer. On a Mac, Ctrl-click the top of the document window and choose Customize Toolbar.

Moving Entities to a New Layer

The main reason for creating a layer is to show and hide several entities at the same time. For example, you may have a house model with lots of furniture components inside. The furniture looks great in your house, but it really slows things down when you work on your model. Even with today's fast computers, it takes quite a bit of graphics horsepower to render all those detailed components. So if you put all your furniture components on a layer named "Furniture", you can hide all your furniture

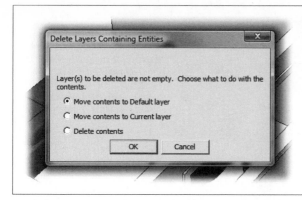

Figure 7-35:
If you try to delete a layer with contents, SketchUp displays this message box giving you the options to move the contents to a different layer or to delete the contents along with the layer.

with one click while you're working. Then you can bring it back when you're printing or making a presentation. With architectural models, landscape components are another part of the model that's frequently moved to a separate layer.

Note: In SketchUp, an *entity* is anything that can be selected. An entity can be a line, a face, a group, or a component. You can examine an entity using the Entity Info window (Window → Entity Info).

You may be tempted to place different parts of a building on separate layers, such as the roof or different floor levels. However, if you're coming to SketchUp from a program such as Photoshop, it's important to understand the way SketchUp layers are different. Being on a separate layer doesn't protect those entities from being changed accidentally. It's best to use layers for self-contained groups or components such as furniture and trees. Remember, if you want to show and hide something like your roof or the second-storey walls, you can always right-click or use Outliner to hide and unhide groups and components.

With those warnings out of the way, here are the steps for moving a group or component to a new layer:

1. **With the Select (space bar) tool, click the group or component you want to move.**

   Shift-click to select more than one entity. You may select the entity you're moving in the modeling window, or you can select it in the Outliner.

2. **Choose Window → Entity Info.**

   The Entity Info window appears. At the top is a drop-down menu named Layer. If you right-click a group or component in the Outliner window, you can choose Entity Info from the shortcut menu.

3. **Click the Layer drop-down menu and choose the destination layer.**

   When the menu closes, the layer for the selected group or component is displayed as shown in Figure 7-36.

Tip: If you don't know which layer a group or component is on, you can always select it and then open the Entity Info window. The name of the layer is shown in the Layer menu.

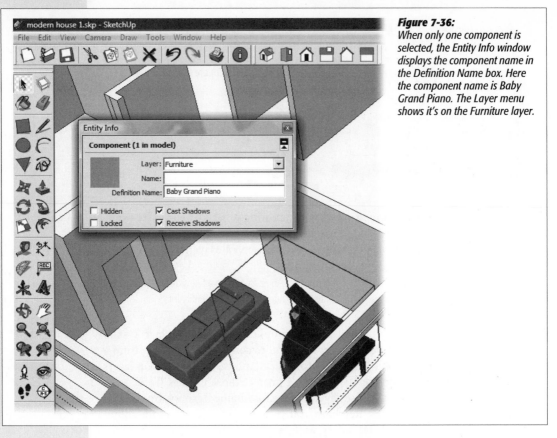

Figure 7-36:
When only one component is selected, the Entity Info window displays the component name in the Definition Name box. Here the component name is Baby Grand Piano. The Layer menu shows it's on the Furniture layer.

Setting the Active Layer and Hiding Layers

If you're new to SketchUp, it's easiest to always work in Layer0 and keep it as the active layer. If you find it necessary to make another layer the active layer, click the radio button next to the layer name. In Figure 7-37 the Furniture layer has been selected as the active layer and Layer0 has been hidden. While the Furniture layer is active, any objects drawn will be placed on the Furniture layer.

To hide a layer, turn off the Visible checkbox to the right of the layer name. You can hide several layers at a time, but you can't hide the active layer.

Viewing Layers by Color

You can assign colors to different layers. This gives you a quick and easy way to figure out which entities are on which layers. Click the Details button and choose "Color by layer" from the menu. Then in your modeling window, entities take on the colors assigned to their layers, as shown in Figure 7-38. You turn off "Color by layer" by using the same menu.

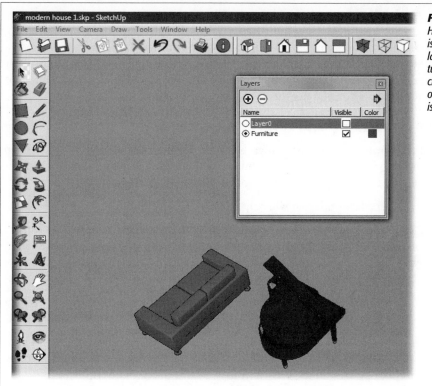

Figure 7-37:
Here the Furniture layer
is selected as the active
layer. Layer0 is hidden by
turning off the Visible
checkbox. As a result,
only the furniture
is showing.

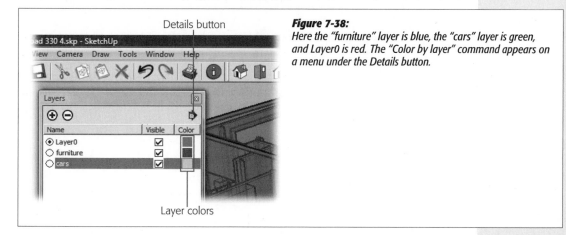

Details button

Layer colors

Figure 7-38:
Here the "furniture" layer is blue, the "cars" layer is green,
and Layer0 is red. The "Color by layer" command appears on
a menu under the Details button.

You can change the color assigned to a layer by clicking the colored square. SketchUp shows the standard color tools for your system. Windows and Macintosh use different color systems. (See page 196 for details on Windows colors; see page 207 for details on Mac colors.)

Purging Layers

If you have lots of layers in your model and some are empty and unneeded, you can get rid of the empty layers with the Purge command. In the Layers window, click the Details button and choose Purge from the menu. SketchUp deletes all the layers that have no content. You don't have to worry about SketchUp deleting part of your model when you use this command.

Tips for Working with Layers

If all the warnings in this section gave you the feeling that working with layers can get you into trouble—good! It's awfully easy to make unwanted changes when part of your model is on one layer and another part is on a different layer.

Here are some layer tips that will help you stay out of trouble:

- If you're new to SketchUp, keep Layer0 as the active layer when you work. If you don't follow this rule, it's easy to end up with entities scattered on different layers. Later when you're used to working with layers, you can explore some other layer techniques.

- Do all your editing and modeling work on Layer0. This rule is really just a reiteration of the first rule; it keeps you from making accidental changes to your model.

- Before you move entities to another layer, group them or turn them into a component. This helps prevent those accidental changes. In a way, it puts a protective envelope around the entities you move to a different layer.

- Use layers to show and hide parts of your model. This is the primary use for layers in SketchUp.

- Use Layers to organize discrete objects such as furniture or trees. That way you're less likely to foul up the main, more complex part of your model.

- Be careful about putting connected entities on different layers. For example, if you keep the different levels of a building on separate layers, it's very easy to make accidental changes.

Part Three: Advanced Construction Techniques

3

Drawing a Hipped Roof and Using Follow Me

The world is full of patterns and symmetry. Several SketchUp tools, including the Follow Me tool, take advantage of this happy fact. In earlier chapters, you saw the Push/Pull tool in action. Push/Pull takes a two-dimensional shape and expands it into a three-dimensional object. The process is called *extrusion*. Follow Me is another SketchUp tool that extrudes 2-D shapes. The difference is that Follow Me extrudes shapes along a path, rather than just in a straight line. In this chapter, you extrude the profile of a roof around the top edge of a building. Like other SketchUp tools, the Follow Me tool is a great timesaver. You provide the minimum amount of information needed to define the shape of the roof, and SketchUp takes that information and draws it with all the proper edges, faces, corners, and angles.

This chapter also explores the Protractor tool. You use the Protractor to measure angles and to create angled guides in your model. For those cases when you can't simply align an edge along one of the main axes, the Protractor tool comes in handy. The hipped roof created in this chapter is just one of those cases. So roll up your sleeves. Find the Follow Me and Protractor tools in your SketchUp toolbox. It's time to build a roof.

Making Construction Lines

Before you can build a roof, you need a building and a plan. The simplest shapes will do the trick, so this section starts off by making a couple of building-shaped boxes. Then using the Tape Measure tool, you place some guides that you'll use to draw the profile shape for a hipped roof.

1. **Choose File → Open to create a new SketchUp document.**

    A new document opens and Sang, the SketchUp model, greets you. It's probably best to hide or delete him at this point. You don't need anyone looking over your shoulder.

Note: The figures in this chapter use the "Simple Template – Feet and Inches", but you can also use the "Architectural Design – Feet and Inches" template. If you need a refresher on how to open a document using a particular template, see page 23.

---

2. **Using the Rectangle (R) tool, begin to draw a rectangle. Type *20',30'* and then press Enter (Return on a Mac).**

    A rectangle appears on the plane formed by the green and red axes.

    Starting at the rectangle's upper-right corner, draw a second rectangle. Type *20',10'* and press Enter.

    You've got the beginnings of an L-shaped floor plan, as shown in Figure 8-1.

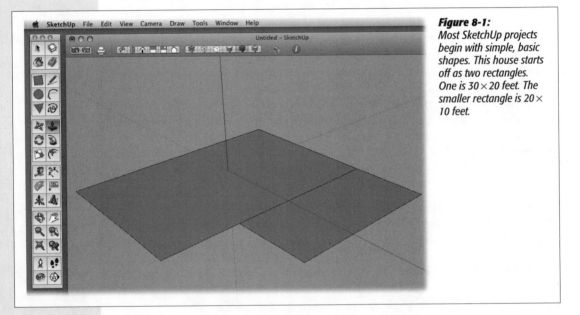

Figure 8-1:
Most SketchUp projects begin with simple, basic shapes. This house starts off as two rectangles. One is 30×20 feet. The smaller rectangle is 20× 10 feet.

3. **With Push/Pull (P), begin to pull the large rectangle up vertically, along the blue axis. Type *10'* and then press Enter.**

    The large rectangle pops up to a story-size, 10-foot height.

4. **Still using Push/Pull, double-click the small rectangle.**

    The small rectangle duplicates the last Push/Pull action moving the same distance and the same direction. You may have to reorient the faces after you've pulled up the second box.

5. **With the Push/Pull tool still selected, press the Ctrl (Option) key.**

   A + sign appears on the Push/Pull cursor, showing that it's now in copy mode. See the top of Figure 8-2. The copy mode for Push/Pull is similar to the copy mode with the Move tool. Using Push/Pull in copy mode is similar to using the Move tool in copy mode. The original shape or entity stays put, and Push/Pull creates new edges and faces. In this case, it's a great way to create a second story.

6. **Click the top face of the box and begin to pull up. Then type *10'* and press Enter.**

   The larger box now appears to be a two-story building with a horizontal edge separating each floor. Because you used the copy mode with Push/Pull, a horizontal edge is between the top and bottom stories.

7. **Use the Eraser to remove the extra vertical line on the side of the second story.**

   It's always best to remove any unneeded edges as you see them. This edge could cause trouble when you create the roof.

8. **With the Tape Measure (T) tool, click the top edge of the second story, and begin to move vertically (parallel to the blue axis). Type *10* and then press Enter.**

   Make sure there's a + sign showing on the Tape Measure tool. When there's a + sign showing, the Tape Measure creates guides in your model. If the + sign isn't showing, press Ctrl or Option to toggle copy mode on.

   Before you click, you should see a red dot at the cursor's selection point indicating that it's on the edge. Then as you move the cursor, you see a blue, dashed line when the Tape Measure is moving on the blue axis.

Note: There's no need to include the inches symbol when you're working in the "Architectural Design – Feet and Inches" template.

---

9. **With the Tape Measure tool, click the right edge of the building, and then move horizontally, parallel to the red axis. Type *12* and press Enter.**

   As shown in Figure 8-4, (page 286) the two guides intersect at a point 10 inches above the roof and 12 inches to the right of the second story. As you move the Tape Measure, the distance appears in a tooltip. Still, it's usually faster and more accurate to type distances when you're placing guides in your model.

Using the Protractor Tool

SketchUp inferences are great as long as you're drawing lines along one of the main axes, but they're not as much help when you're drawing angles. That's a job for the Protractor tool. The Protractor is similar to the tape measure; you can use it to measure and to create guides.

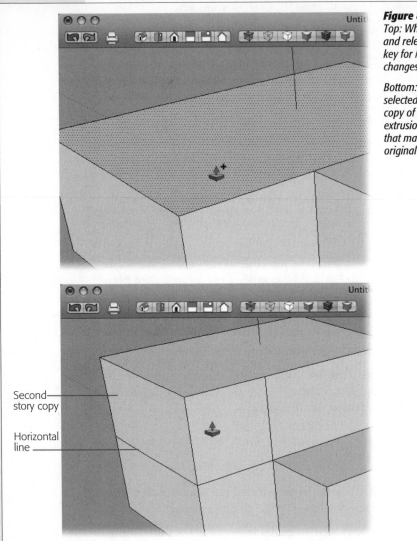

Figure 8-2:
Top: While using Push/Pull, press and release the Ctrl key (Option key for Macs), and the tool changes to copy mode.

Bottom: Instead of just moving the selected face, Push/Pull makes a copy of the face and uses it for the extrusion. Notice the horizontal line that marks the position of the original face.

Second-story copy

Horizontal line

It takes three clicks to place a guide in your model using the Protractor. The first click sets the corner of the angle; or if you think of the 360-degree arc of a circle, that first click is the center of the circle. The second click sets a reference guide. This line isn't permanent; it's only displayed while you're measuring the angle. As you move the cursor between the second and third click, the Measurements toolbar shows (in degrees) the angle between the reference line and your cursor. You can create a guide by clicking, or by entering a value for the angle, as shown in Figure 8-3. Values can be expressed in degrees down to one tenth of a degree. Or, angles can be expressed in architectural slope notation. If you're unfamiliar with that notation, see the box on page 288.

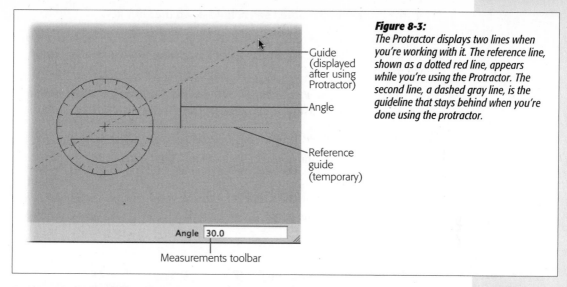

Figure 8-3:
The Protractor displays two lines when you're working with it. The reference line, shown as a dotted red line, appears while you're using the Protractor. The second line, a dashed gray line, is the guideline that stays behind when you're done using the protractor.

Guide (displayed after using Protractor)

Angle

Reference guide (temporary)

Angle 30.0

Measurements toolbar

Protractor Modifier Keys

The Protractor has two modifier keys. If you need a reminder, you find them listed in the status bar hints in the lower-left corner:

- **Guide Mode** (Ctrl for Windows; Option for Macs). As with the Line tool, you can use the protractor to simply measure an angle, or you can use it to place a guide. Press Ctrl (Option) to toggle between the mode that creates guides and the one that doesn't.

- **Lock Orientation** (Shift). When you move the Protractor around your model, it snaps to orient itself with the faces under the cursor, and it displays a color relative to the axis (red, green, or blue). You can lock the Protractor's orientation by pressing and holding Shift before your first click. Then, you're free to move it around the modeling window without the Protractor changing orientation.

In the next few steps, you use the Protractor tool to create the angle of the hipped roof, and then you draw in the profile shape that's used to create the roof.

Tip: The cursor for the Protractor and the Rotate tool are nearly identical, and they're located close to each other on the toolbar. If either tool seems to be misbehaving, double-check to make sure you selected the tool you want.

---

1. **Choose the Protractor tool and then move it over the different faces of the building.**

   The cursor automatically orients itself to the faces of the building, and the cursor changes color to indicate an axis.

2. **While the Protractor is colored green, hold down the Shift key.**

    The Protractor is locked to the green axis. Now you can move the cursor away from the face of the building, and it keeps its orientation and its green color, as shown in Figure 8-4.

3. **Move the center of the Protractor over the point to the right of the building, where the two Tape Measure guides intersect, and then click.**

    The Protractor tool requires three clicks. The first click marks the center point.

4. **Move along the horizontal construction line and then click again.**

    The Protractor (Figure 8-4) displays a line as you move away from the point of that first click. When you click, SketchUp displays a line that's used as a reference as you determine the angle. This line doesn't remain after you're finished with the Protractor.

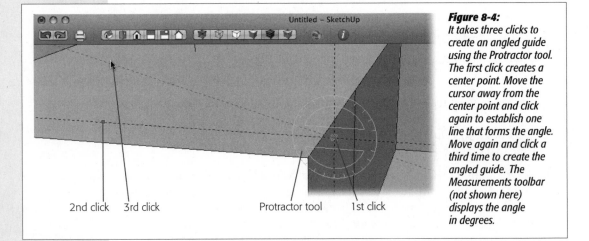

Figure 8-4:
It takes three clicks to create an angled guide using the Protractor tool. The first click creates a center point. Move the cursor away from the center point and click again to establish one line that forms the angle. Move again and click a third time to create the angled guide. The Measurements toolbar (not shown here) displays the angle in degrees.

2nd click   3rd click   Protractor tool   1st click

5. **Release the Shift key and move the cursor up along the blue axis, and then type 2:12.**

    SketchUp draws the guide at an angle that rises 2 vertical inches for every 12 horizontal inches it spans.

    Releasing the Shift key lets you move the cursor off-axis. As you move, SketchUp displays the value of the angle in the Measurements toolbar (Figure 8-5). The value, typed as 2:12, expresses the angle in architectural slope notation. For more details, see the box on page 288.

6. **With the Line (L) tool, click the midpoint of the front edge of the roof; then press and release the up arrow key. Move the cursor vertically and then click a second time when the cursor reaches the angled guide that was created by the Protractor.**

    This line (shown in Figure 8-6) is one edge of the shape that you'll extrude to create the hipped roof.

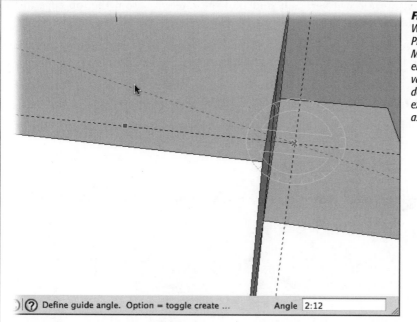

Figure 8-5:
When you work with the Protractor, you use the Measurements toolbar to enter precise values. The value can be expressed as degrees, or it can be expressed in slope notation, as in 2:12.

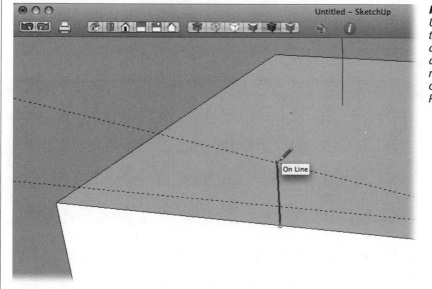

Figure 8-6:
Use the midpoint in the top edge of the building as a starting point. Then draw a vertical line that reaches up the guide created by the Protractor tool.

7. Continuing with the Line tool, click the point where the two Tape Measure guides intersect.

   This point is also the one that you first clicked with the Protractor.

8. **Next move down vertically and find the inference from the top edge of the building.**

   If necessary you can lock the line on the blue axis by pressing the up arrow key, and then click the corner of the roof.

9. **Move the cursor back to the starting point—the midpoint on the front edge of the roof.**

   The face fills in, forming a roof profile that extends from the eaves to the ridge of the roof, as shown in Figure 8-7.

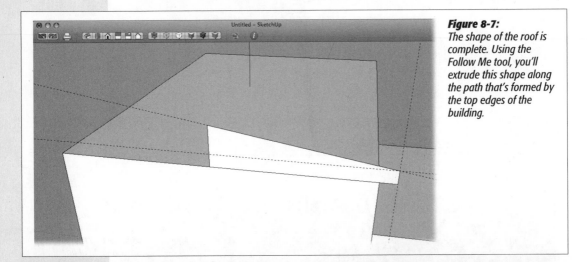

Figure 8-7:
The shape of the roof is complete. Using the Follow Me tool, you'll extrude this shape along the path that's formed by the top edges of the building.

ARCHITECT'S TOOLBOX

Architectural Slope Notation

Architects use a standard form of notation to indicate the rise and run of a slope. For example, a 2:12 slope rises vertically 2 inches for every 12 inches it covers horizontally. When you're using the Protractor tool, the Measurements toolbar accepts angle measurements in either degrees or slope notation. If you're using degrees, you don't need to enter any special units of measure. If you want to use slope notation, the presence of the colon (:) is enough for SketchUp to understand.

Using the Follow Me Tool

You use the Follow Me tool to extrude a two-dimensional shape along a path. As you see, with this project the path can take a few corners, and the extruded shape follows suit, creating corners and angles as needed. In the previous steps, you created a simple building-shaped box and the profile of a roof—or more accurately, the profile of half a roof. In the next steps, with the Follow Me tool, you extrude that path around the top edge of the building.

1. Click the Follow Me tool in the toolbar or choose Tools → Follow Me.

   The cursor changes to the Follow Me tool. The hint in the status bar says "Select face to extrude." When you hold the cursor over different faces in your model, a highlight of blue dots appears on the faces.

2. Click the face that's the profile of the roof.

   After you click the face, the shape is attached to the cursor. It's similar to using the Push/Pull tool. When you hover over an edge like the top edge of the building (Figure 8-8), the edge displays a highlight, and the extruded shape follows, perpendicular to the selected edge.

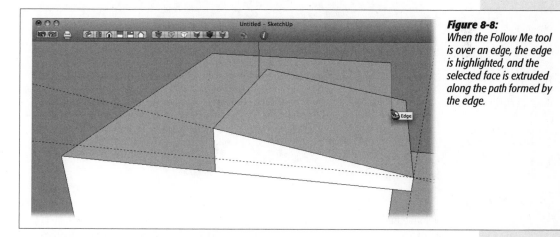

Figure 8-8:
When the Follow Me tool is over an edge, the edge is highlighted, and the selected face is extruded along the path formed by the edge.

3. Move the cursor all the way down the edge on the right side of the building, and then turn the corner and follow the back edge of the building.

   As you turn the corner at the back of the building, the extruded face turns to follow the new edge, forming perfect angles and sloped faces. It may take a little practice to move the cursor along the edge.

4. Turn the far corner and move the cursor back toward the front of the building.

   Each time you move the cursor over a new edge, the roof shape follows, creating clean edges and a well-shaped roofline.

5. Turn the corner and then move the cursor across the front edge of the building, finishing up at the closest corner.

   When the extruded shape passes the midpoint at the front edge of the building, some excess geometry appears. SketchUp isn't yet aware that you're near the end of the line with the Follow Me tool. When you click the building's front corner, SketchUp figures it all out and creates the proper edges and faces for a perfect roof, as shown in Figure 8-9.

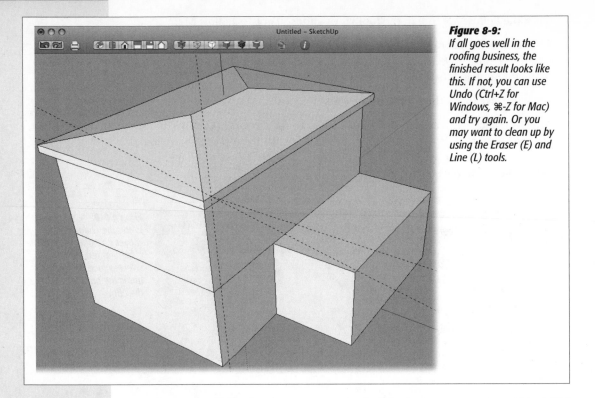

Figure 8-9:
If all goes well in the roofing business, the finished result looks like this. If not, you can use Undo (Ctrl+Z for Windows, ⌘-Z for Mac) and try again. Or you may want to clean up by using the Eraser (E) and Line (L) tools.

Tip: If your extruded roof doesn't come out as expected, make sure no extra edges or faces are in your model that interfere with the Follow Me tool. Make sure the profile is touching the path—in this case, the top edge of the roof. At the end of the Follow Me action, you may want to zoom in to make sure you're clicking the corner of the roof and not one of the guides. If you continue to have problems, try the preselection technique described in the next section.

If your results don't look like Figure 8-9, then it's possible that the last point you clicked wasn't the corner of the building—perhaps it was the corner of the roof. If that's the case, it's likely you have some extra lines and extra geometry in your roof. You can undo the Follow Me operation by pressing Ctrl+Z (⌘-Z on a Mac). Then take another crack at it. When you get to that last point, try to make sure you're clicking the corner of the building and not the edge of the roof or one of the guides. You should see a tooltip that says "Endpoint".

An alternative solution is to clean up the excess architecture in your roof. Use the Eraser (E) to remove extra edges. Then if you have missing faces, use the Line (L) tool to trace over some of the edges until the faces appear. As you work in SketchUp, you'll find many other instances where your models need some cleanup, so a little practice at the art is never wasted.

Preselecting the Path for the Follow Me Tool

You can use a faster way to create the perfect, hipped roof. When you move the Follow Me cursor over the edge of the building, you're showing SketchUp the path you want to follow. What if you show SketchUp the path before you apply the Follow Me tool? Here's how it works:

1. **Press Ctrl+Z or ⌘-Z until you're back to the point before you used Follow Me.**

   Your model should look like Figure 8-7.

2. **With the Select (space bar) tool, Ctrl-click (Option-click) the edges all the way around the top of the roof.**

   As you click, the selected edges show a blue highlight. Be sure to select both segments of the edge in the front. (SketchUp divided that front edge when you drew the vertical line from the midpoint to create the roof profile.)

3. **Choose the Follow Me tool from the toolbar or from the menu Tools → Follow Me.**

   When you change tools, the highlight disappears from the selected edges, but don't worry. SketchUp remembers.

4. **Click the profile shape of the roof.**

   Bang! SketchUp draws the entire roof, making perfect corners all the way around. The result looks exactly like Figure 8-9.

One more path to hipped roof nirvana

Believe it or not, you can use an even faster way to build your roof. You can select all the edges in a closed shape like the top of this building by clicking a face. It's easier than selecting every edge, and it makes building the roof a two-click operation.

1. **Press Ctrl+Z or ⌘-Z until you're back to the point before you used Follow Me.**

   Your model should look like Figure 8-7. Yes. Back here again.

2. **With the Select (space bar) tool, click the building's top face.**

   When you select a face (as shown in Figure 8-10), SketchUp automatically selects the edges that form the face.

3. **Choose the Follow Me tool from the toolbox or from the menu Tools → Follow Me.**

   When you change tools, the highlight disappears from the selected face.

4. **Click the profile shape of the roof.**

   SketchUp draws the entire roof, and again the results look exactly like Figure 8-9.

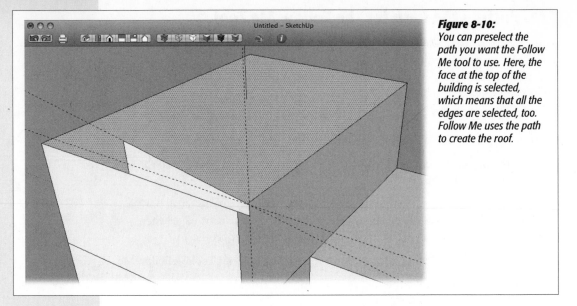

Figure 8-10:
You can preselect the path you want the Follow Me tool to use. Here, the face at the top of the building is selected, which means that all the edges are selected, too. Follow Me uses the path to create the roof.

So you have three ways to extrude the roof shape around the edge of a building. Now it may have seemed a little repetitive drawing the hipped roof three times. But each method for selecting the path is useful. With some models, you'll have to carefully follow the path with the Follow Me cursor. With other models, you can manually select different edges to identify a path. Thankfully, on many models, especially buildings, one click on a face does the trick by automatically selecting the adjacent edges.

Practice using the Follow Me tool with different shapes such as the molding shown in Figure 8-11, and you'll be a pro in no time. You can experiment with different types of paths, too. On page 298, you see how to use the Follow Me tool like a lathe.

Note: Save a copy of the model you made in this chapter with the name *hipped_roof_finished.skp*. You can use it in the following chapters.

The Follow Me tool is capable of other tricks, too, as you'll see in the rest of this chapter. The ability to extrude a profile along the path has some surprising uses.

Making Spheres with Follow Me

Follow Me might not be the first SketchUp tool that jumps to mind when you need to create a sphere, but it works great. All you need are two circles on perpendicular planes. It's best if the "path" circle is slightly larger than the circle being used as the profile. The circles need to have exactly the same center point, as shown in Figure 8-12. With those ingredients, you can create a circle with a single click of Follow Me.

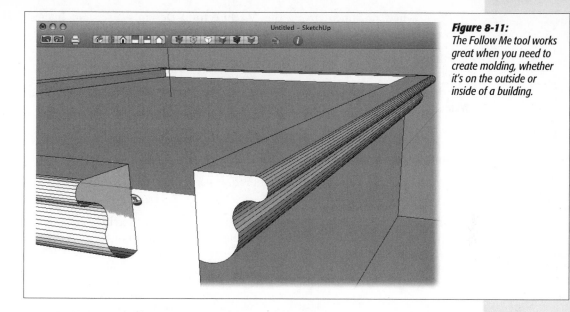

Figure 8-11:
*The Follow Me tool works
great when you need to
create molding, whether
it's on the outside or
inside of a building.*

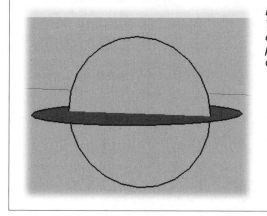

Figure 8-12:
*You can use the path of one circle to extrude the profile of
another circle. The trickiest part is creating two circles that are
perpendicular to each other and aligning them both on the same
center point.*

The cursor for the Circle tool looks like a pencil. At the point of the pencil is a circle that changes color depending on its orientation. If you experiment a little with the Circle (C) tool in an empty document, you notice that the circle likes to snap to one of the three axes. If you move the circle down below SketchUp's horizon and have a slightly downward view, the Circle cursor usually snaps to the blue axis. That means the circle will be drawn on the ground, perpendicular to the blue axis. Move the cursor above the horizon line, and it usually snaps to either the red or green axis, depending on your view.

Tip: Want the Circle tool to align to a different axis above the horizon? Use the Orbit (O) tool to change your view so it's closer to a perpendicular angle with that axis. It doesn't have to be perfectly perpendicular—just closer.

1. Open a new document using the "Architectural Design – Feet and Inches" template.

   Hide or delete Sang, the SketchUp model. You won't need his services for this project.

Note: These steps work best if you don't change your view after you open the template.

---

2. Use the Circle (C) tool and begin to draw a circle on the blue axis. Type *5'* and press Enter (Return on a Mac).

   SketchUp draws a circle with a 5-foot radius perpendicular to the blue axis. This is your "path" circle.

   Draw your circle so that it doesn't intersect with any of SketchUp's axis lines. The area in between the solid red and green lines, as shown in Figure 8-13, is a good spot.

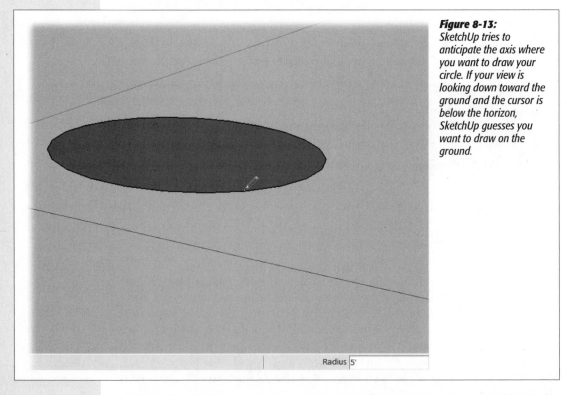

Figure 8-13:
SketchUp tries to anticipate the axis where you want to draw your circle. If your view is looking down toward the ground and the cursor is below the horizon, SketchUp guesses you want to draw on the ground.

Radius 5'

3. Move the Circle cursor above the horizon line, and then press and hold the Shift key.

   When you move the cursor above the horizon, the circle snaps to the green axis. Holding Shift locks the circle to the axis, so even when you move back down below the horizon line, the circle displayed on the cursor stays green.

4. Still holding Shift, move the cursor to the center of the circle, as shown in Figure 8-14, and then click.

   When the cursor is over the center point of the "path" circle, a tooltip appears that says "Center". Clicking sets the center point for the new "profile" circle.

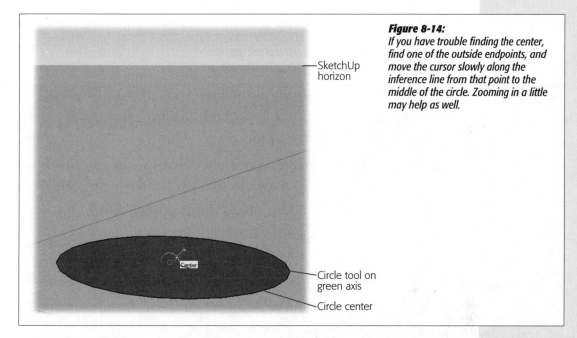

Figure 8-14:
If you have trouble finding the center, find one of the outside endpoints, and move the cursor slowly along the inference line from that point to the middle of the circle. Zooming in a little may help as well.

SketchUp horizon

Circle tool on green axis

Circle center

5. Release the Shift key and move the cursor away from the circle's center point. Then, type *4.5'* and press Enter.

   A new circle appears with a 4.5-foot radius. This is your "profile" circle—its curved profile will be extruded along the circular path.

6. Using the Select (space bar) tool, click the face of the first circle—the "path" circle.

   The face of the circle displays blue dots to show that it's selected. Clicking the face of the circle also selects the path along the edge of the circle.

7. Select the Follow Me tool, and then click the second circle—the "profile" circle.

   When you select the Follow Me tool, the highlight disappears from the "path" circle, but don't worry. SketchUp has already registered this circle as the path for the Follow Me tool. When you click the second circle, the profile is extruded along the path, and after a 360-degree trip, it becomes a sphere. Because the first circle was slightly larger, your sphere looks a little like Saturn at this point.

8. **With the Eraser (E), click the edge of the Rings of Saturn.**

   One click is all it takes to erase the first circle that you used as a path. Using a larger circle as the path makes it easier to delete it when it's no longer needed. If you're wondering why you shouldn't use two circles of the same size, see the box below.

Note: Technically, this exercise creates a faceted object that resembles a sphere. If you turn on Hidden Geometry (View → Hidden Geometry), you can see the facets.

FREQUENTLY ASKED QUESTION

The Big Profile Circle

Why draw circles of different sizes when creating a sphere?

In the example on page 292, you use two circles to create a sphere. The steps say to make one circle larger than the other. At the end of the process, you delete the larger circle you used as the path. Why can't you make both circles the same size? Well, you can make both circles the same size, and the method still creates a sphere. You can even make your "path" circle smaller than the "profile" circle, and you get the same result. The reason a larger circle is recommended has less to do with drawing the sphere and more to do with removing excess geometry from your model (Figure 8-15). When you're done with your sphere, you don't want the extra circle in the model. It's unnecessary, it slows things down, and it might cause unintended consequences down the road. The main reason for using a "path" circle that's larger is that the larger circle is easier to see and remove with the Eraser tool.

Ideally, you want your models always to have the minimum number of edges and faces needed to do the job. With fewer entities to keep track of, SketchUp works faster and your SketchUp files remain smaller. It may not seem like such a big deal at first, but what if your sphere ends up inside a component that's repeated 40, 50, or maybe even 100 times in a model? That one unnecessary circle begins to take up a lot more computer horsepower. And what about the unintended consequences? If you have edges and faces in your model that you're unaware of or have forgotten about, you may get confused if SketchUp uses those entities to provide inferences.

Using a Reference Object to Draw a Sphere

Sometimes when you draw that second circle for the profile, it's awkward fiddling around with the views to get the Circle tool oriented properly. If that's the case, use another surface in your model as a reference, as shown in Figure 8-16. If you don't have any other objects in the model, it's easy enough to draw a simple box to do the job. For example, use the Rectangle tool to draw a rectangle, and then Push/Pull it up into a box. Then with the Circle tool, hold the cursor over one of the faces of the box. Press and hold the Shift key to lock the Circle tool to that axis. Find the center point of the "path" circle and draw the "profile" circle. Extrude the profile as you did in the previous example, by clicking the Select tool on the face of the "path" circle and then clicking the Follow Me tool on the face of the "profile" circle. If you created a reference box specifically for the sphere job and no longer need it, just triple-click the box and press Delete.

Extra geometry

Figure 8-15:
*Both these circles are displayed using View → Hidden
Geometry.*

*Top: This sphere was created with two circles of the same
size. You can see the extra geometry that exists when the
"path" circle isn't deleted.*

*Bottom: The same circle is less complex when the "path"
circle is removed.*

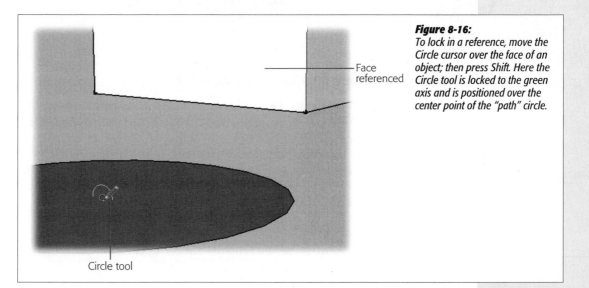

Face
referenced

Circle tool

Figure 8-16:
*To lock in a reference, move the
Circle cursor over the face of an
object; then press Shift. Here the
Circle tool is locked to the green
axis and is positioned over the
center point of the "path" circle.*

Using Follow Me As a Lathe

Many architectural details and other objects are created on lathes. If you've ever seen a lathe in action, you know that that they take raw material and spin it around. Knives shave away portions of the material to create complex shapes. That's exactly the same thing that the Follow Me tool does when it follows a circular path, as shown in Figure 8-17.

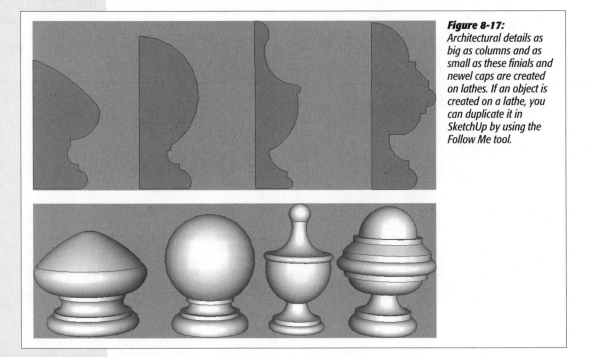

Figure 8-17:
Architectural details as big as columns and as small as these finials and newel caps are created on lathes. If an object is created on a lathe, you can duplicate it in SketchUp by using the Follow Me tool.

Making Complex Profiles Follow a Path

The earlier examples have all shown how easy it is to add geometry to your models when using the Follow Me tool. You can also use Follow Me to remove geometry from an existing object. In this next exercise, you build a planter. It looks a little like one of those concrete planters that might appear in an Italian garden. First you add molding to the top of the planter. Then you remove a curved section from the middle of the planter. This second step shows that the path and the profile don't necessarily need to be connected to each other.

Follow these steps to go into the garden furnishings business:

1. **Open a new document using the "Architectural Design – Feet and Inches" template.**

    Again, you can send Sang, the SketchUp model, on an errand while you tackle this project. Select and delete him, or right-click and choose Hide from the menu.

2. **Using the Rectangle (R) tool, draw a rectangle.**

   A 4-foot square works well, but the size isn't that important for this example, so you're free to be creative.

3. **With Push/Pull (P) click the face of the rectangle, and pull it up into a box.**

   This box serves as the basic shape for the planter before you add ornamentation. It should look something like Figure 8-18.

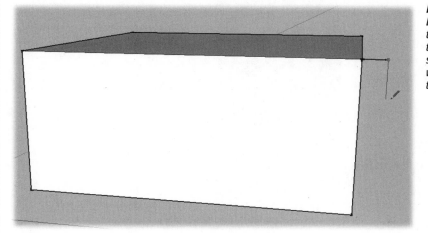

Figure 8-18:
Draw a rectangle off the top edge of the box using the Line (L) tool. This shape, after it's modified, will add geometry to the model.

4. **With the Line (L) tool, click the closest top corner. Draw a line in the red direction, and then draw a connecting line down in the blue direction.**

   You could also use the Rectangle tool for this job, but sometimes it's easier to control the orientation with the Line tool.

5. **Finish the rectangle by drawing another line back to the edge of the box.**

   When you're done, you have a rectangle hanging off the top edge of the box.

6. **Choose the Freehand tool and then draw an irregular line that bisects the small rectangle from top to bottom.**

   Here's another place where you can let your creativity take over. Draw a profile that you'd like to see turned into molding.

7. **Use the Eraser to erase the excess outer edges of the profile, as shown in Figure 8-19.**

   Click or drag across the rectangle's three outside edges to remove the excess portion. What's left is the profile to be extruded with the Follow Me tool.

8. **With the Select (space bar) tool, click the face on the top of the box.**

   Selecting the face automatically selects the four top edges of the box.

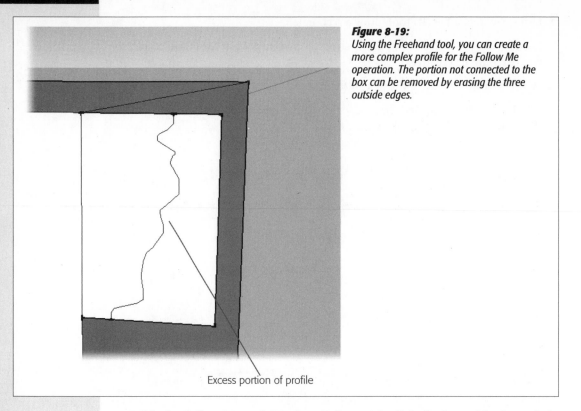

Figure 8-19:
Using the Freehand tool, you can create a more complex profile for the Follow Me operation. The portion not connected to the box can be removed by erasing the three outside edges.

Excess portion of profile

9. **With the Follow Me tool (Tools → Follow Me), click the face of the irregularly shaped profile.**

   The irregular face is extruded all the way around the box, creating something that looks like a piece of architectural molding (Figure 8-20).

10. **Use the Arc (A) tool to draw an arc at the corner of the planter.**

    Make sure the arc is on the face of the box, as shown in Figure 8-21. The portion inside the arc will be removed. This arc, or whatever shape you draw here, could touch the bottom of the box; however, for this exercise keep at least a couple of inches away from the bottom.

11. **With the Orbit (O) tool, change the view so that you can see the bottom of the planter and then, with the Select (space bar) tool, click once on the bottom.**

    The bottom of the planter displays a highlight. If you've followed the instructions above, the profile formed by the arc doesn't touch the bottom of the planter.

12. **Choose Follow Me and click the semicircle formed by the arc.**

    Geometry is removed from the box as the semicircle profile cuts its way along the path. Even though the profile and the path aren't touching each other, the Follow Me operation works as it did in other cases.

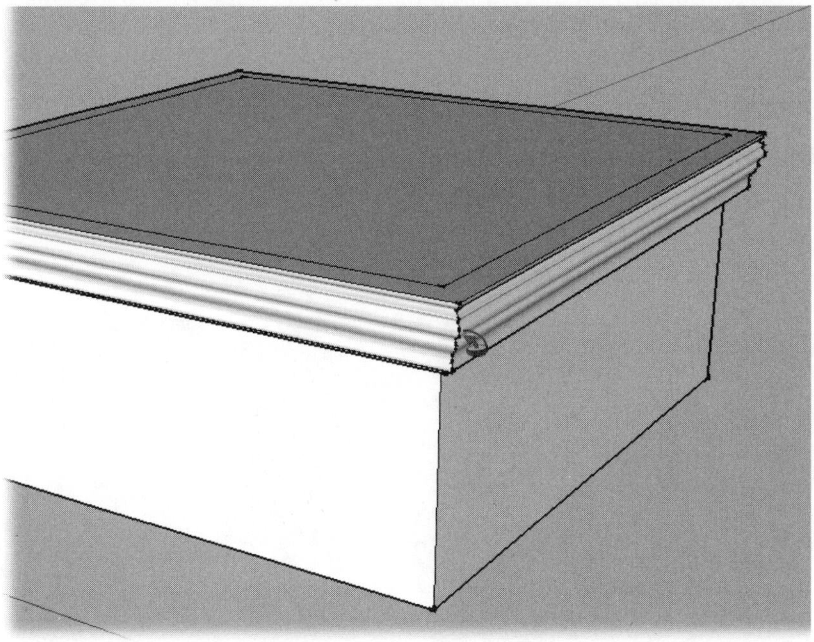

Figure 8-20:
In concept, this project is
a garden planter, but you
can use this same
technique to create
interior or exterior
molding.

Figure 8-21:
Even though there's no
connection between the
selected path (the bottom
edges of the planter) and
the profile (the semicircle
formed by the arc), the
Follow Me tool will
still work.

13. Use Orbit or other view tools to view the top of the planter. Then use Offset to create a new smaller box in the top of the planter.

    This smaller box must be narrower than the cutout created when you removed geometry in step 12.

14. With Push/Pull, push the new smaller face down into the box.

    Your planter now has an opening to hold soil and plants, as shown in Figure 8-22.

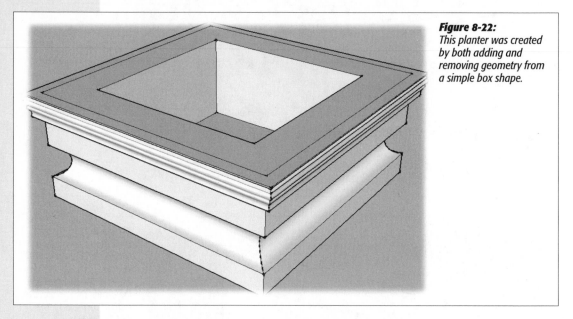

Figure 8-22:
This planter was created by both adding and removing geometry from a simple box shape.

The steps above show that the Follow Me tool can be used to both add and remove geometry as it follows a path. It's also good to keep in mind that Follow Me works even when the profile and the path aren't touching each other.

Following Complex or Irregular Paths

Up to this point, all the Follow Me examples used a closed path. The paths were either rectangular or circular. In this next example, you use Follow Me on an open path that curves in two different directions.

1. Open a new document using the "Architectural Design – Feet and Inches" template.

    Hide or delete Sang, the SketchUp model.

2. With the Arc (A) tool, draw a gentle arc on the ground.

    Think serpentine wall here—something that might look stunning in an art museum's garden. It takes three clicks to create an arc. First you set the two endpoints. Then you set a point that determines the curve. As usual, the Measurements toolbar helps you be precise. After your first click sets a starting point for your arc, you can type a precise distance to the other endpoint. Press Enter (or Return) to set the point, and then you can type a measurement for the "bulge," as SketchUp calls it.

3. **Click the endpoint of the arc, and draw a second arc from the end of the first.**

These two arcs form the path that's used by the Follow Me tool.

The technique for drawing a second connected arc is a little different. As usual, SketchUp is anticipating your next move. Instead of drawing a straight line first, as in step 2, SketchUp shows you an arc as you move the cursor (Figure 8-23). Double-click to draw that arc. When you pause, you're likely to see a tooltip that says "Tangent at vertex". Not only is SketchUp guessing that you want to draw a second arc, it's guessing that you want a nice, smooth curve where the two arcs meet. Wherever you move the cursor, SketchUp works to create two arcs that are tangential at the point where they meet. If you like what SketchUp's showing, double-click. If that's not what you want, you can create your second arc the same way you created the first one. Click to set the end, and then click again to set the bulge.

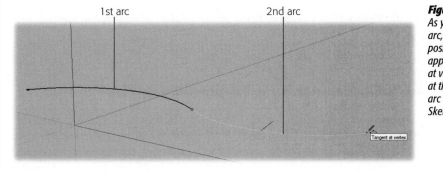

1st arc   2nd arc

Tangent at vertex

Figure 8-23:
As you draw a second arc, the tool snaps to position and a tooltip appears saying "Tangent at vertex". Double-click at this point to draw the arc displayed by SketchUp.

4. **Using the Line (L) tool, click the starting point of the first arc and then draw a line along the blue axis.**

If necessary you can press the up arrow to lock the Line tool to the blue axis.

5. **Continuing with the Line tool, draw a line along the red axis.**

This new line is perpendicular to the first.

6. **Still using the Line tool, start to draw down along the blue axis. Press Shift to lock the line to the blue axis, and then move the cursor over the starting point of the first arc and click (Figure 8-24).**

The length of the line is equal to the first line that was drawn on the blue axis.

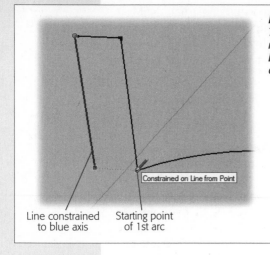

Figure 8-24:
The profile that is extruded along the arcing lines begins as a rectangle. Here, the Shift key is held down to lock a line on the blue axis, while the starting point is used as an inference establishing the line's length.

Constrained on Line from Point

Line constrained
to blue axis

Starting point
of 1st arc

7. **Draw a line back to the starting point to complete the rectangle.**

   The face of the rectangle fills in when the last line is drawn.

8. **Use the Arc (A) and Line (L) tools to sculpt a profile for your wall.**

   Go ahead and be creative, or try to duplicate the profile shown in Figure 8-25.

9. **Use the Eraser (E) to remove extra pieces of the original rectangle that aren't needed.**

   You can click individual edges, or drag to remove more than one edge at a time. You want one solid face when you use the Follow Me tool, so erase any interior, shared edges that appeared as you sculpted your wall.

10. **With the Select (space bar) tool, click to the right of the arcs and drag back to the left to select the two arcs that form the path.**

    Make sure none of the wall profile is included in the selection.

    When you drag from right to left, the Select tool selects any edge that is partially inside of the selection box. (Drag the Select tool the opposite way, from left to right, and it selects only edges that are completely in the selection box.)

11. **Choose the Follow Me tool (Tools → Follow Me), and click the face of the wall profile.**

    When you choose the Follow Me tool, the highlight on the path disappears, but SketchUp still knows to use the two arcs as the path. When you click the wall profile, the shape is extruded along the curved path. That completes the wall, but you can go ahead and dress it up as shown in (Figure 8-26) by adding people components (Window → Components) and snazzy SketchUp styles (Window → Styles).

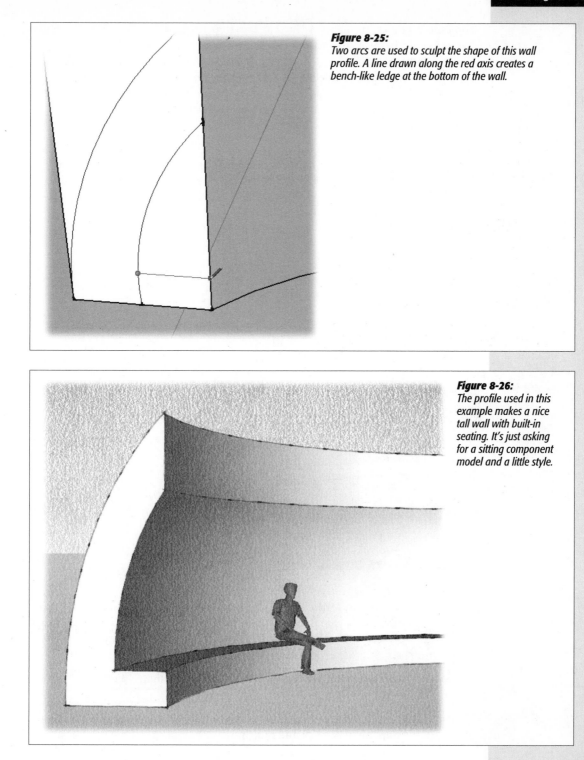

Figure 8-25:
Two arcs are used to sculpt the shape of this wall profile. A line drawn along the red axis creates a bench-like ledge at the bottom of the wall.

Figure 8-26:
The profile used in this example makes a nice tall wall with built-in seating. It's just asking for a sitting component model and a little style.

Something interesting happens in that last step when you click the wall profile. Even though the profile wasn't drawn perpendicular to the arced path, SketchUp flips the profile around so that it's perpendicular before extruding the profile. Figure 8-27 shows the profile before and after the Follow Me operation. As you use the Follow Me tool, it's important to keep in mind that the extruded profile is always perpendicular, even if it wasn't drawn that way at the start.

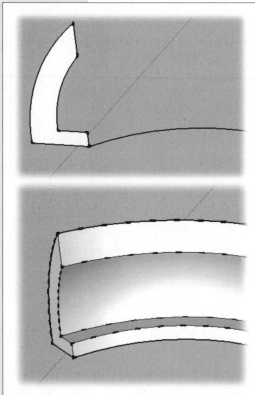

Figure 8-27:
Top: To begin with, the profile that's extruded along the curved path isn't perpendicular to the path.

Bottom: SketchUp automatically turns it so that it's perpendicular before it's extruded.

Making Stairs and a Railing

In this last example, you use the Follow Me tool to extrude a shape along a path that twists and turns and travels along different axes. You've probably seen plenty of examples of round metal handrails like the one modeled in Figure 8-32 (page 310). In this project, before you make the handrail, you'll learn another quick way to design steps.

1. **Open a new document using the "Architectural Design – Feet and Inches" template.**

   Send Sang, the SketchUp model, to the unemployment line for this one. Select and delete him, or right-click and hide him.

2. **With the Rectangle (R) tool, begin to draw a rectangle on the ground. Then type** *12′,12′*.

   You may need to Orbit (O) around to a view that looks down to make sure your rectangle is drawn on the ground plane.

3. **Use Push/Pull to pull the rectangle up into a box.**

4. **With the Line (L) tool, draw a profile that represents the run and rise for the stairs.**

   If you want to be precise, you can type in values as you draw your lines. However, you don't have to sweat over it too much. Focus on the techniques now, and worry about precision later when you create your masterpieces.

   That little backward L shape (Figure 8-28) is all you need to create stairs in this example, which uses SketchUp's array feature.

5. **With the Select tool, click the vertical line (the rise), and then press Shift as you click the horizontal line (the run).**

   The two lines show a blue highlight when they're selected.

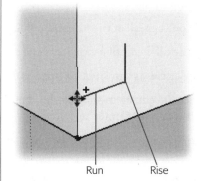

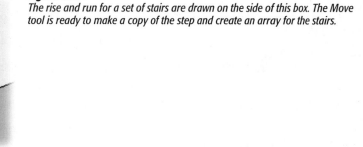

Figure 8-28:
The rise and run for a set of stairs are drawn on the side of this box. The Move tool is ready to make a copy of the step and create an array for the stairs.

Run   Rise

6. **Choose the Move tool (M) and press Ctrl (Option).**

   When you toggle the Ctrl key (Option on a Mac), the Move tool's cursor displays a + sign indicating that it's in copy mode.

7. **With the Move tool, click the left endpoint of the selected lines.**

   A copy of the two lines is attached to the move cursor.

8. **Click the top endpoint of the rise line.**

   At this point, you have two steps drawn on the side of the box (Figure 8-29). Using SketchUp's array feature, it's easy to make more.

9. **Type *4x* and then press Enter.**

   SketchUp creates four steps. That gives you four copies plus your original for five total steps.

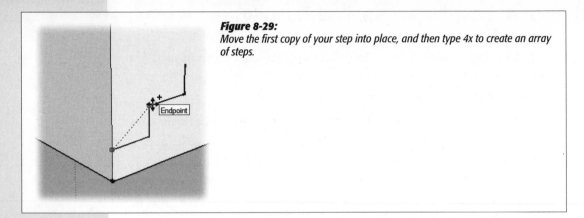

Figure 8-29:
Move the first copy of your step into place, and then type 4x to create an array of steps.

Endpoint

10. Using the Line (L) tool, draw a line from the top stair to the back of the box.

    The line divides the face of the box into two separate faces.

11. If necessary, use Push/Pull to adjust the size of the box.

    You box doesn't have to be exactly like the one shown in Figure 8-32, but size it so that the stairs lead to the upper level of the building.

12. Using the Circle (C) tool, draw a small circle on the wall at the top of the stairs.

    Don't make the circle too large. It should be the diameter of a circular handrail.

13. Using the Line (L) tool, click the center of the circle, as shown in Figure 8-30.

    You may need to zoom in on the circle to get the cursor to snap to the center. When you're at the right spot, a tooltip appears saying "Center".

14. Draw a line along the red axis. Press the right arrow key, and then click the back-right corner of the landing.

    Pressing the right arrow locks the Line tool on the red axis. Clicking the back corner of the steps sets the distance of the line using the corner as an inference.

15. Move the Line cursor along the green axis, and toggle the left arrow key. Then click the front corner of the landing.

    A new horizontal line appears. You see the path for two segments of the railing that enclose the landing.

16. Using the Line (L) tool, draw a line that follows the angle of the steps, as shown in Figure 8-31.

    You may need to use the Orbit (O) and Pan (H) view tools to get a good view of the stairs for this line. Hover over the corner of the bottom step to coax an inference from that corner, and then move the cursor slowly away from the stairs. When you're happy with the angle and distance, click to set the line. (In this case you're just eyeballing the angles and distances. For a finished project, you'd want to spend more time using precise measurements.)

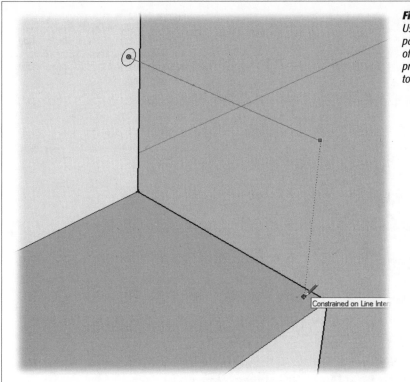

Figure 8-30:
Use the Line tool to create a path for the railing. The corners of the landing and the steps provide inferences you can use to set the length of your lines.

Constrained on Line Inter

17. **Draw a line from the end of the rail to the ground.**

    The path for the railing is complete, as shown in Figure 8-31.

Tip: For a really smooth-looking rail, choose the Eraser (E) and then press the Soften/Smooth modifier key (Ctrl or Option) as you click the lines where the railing changes angles.

---

18. **With the Select (space bar) tool, click the line segment that goes to the ground; then press Shift as you click the other three segments.**

    When you press and hold Shift, the Select cursor displays a +/– sign, indicating that your clicks add and remove entities from the selection.

19. **With the Follow Me tool (Tools → Follow Me), click the small circle on the side of the building.**

    The circle profile is extruded along the path formed by the lines, creating a round railing that looks like a metal pipe. At some point, the extruded pattern (a circle) runs along each of the major axes (red, green, and blue).

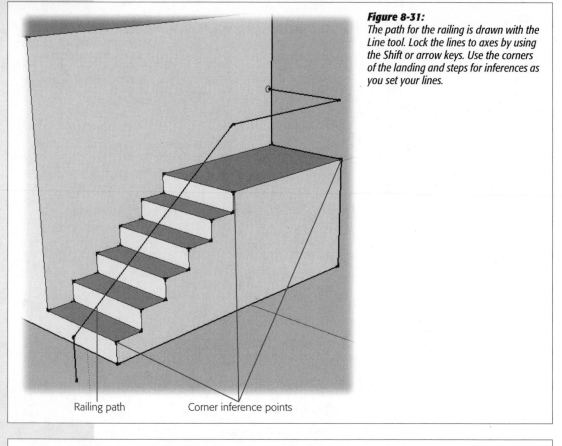

Figure 8-31:
The path for the railing is drawn with the Line tool. Lock the lines to axes by using the Shift or arrow keys. Use the corners of the landing and steps for inferences as you set your lines.

Railing path   Corner inference points

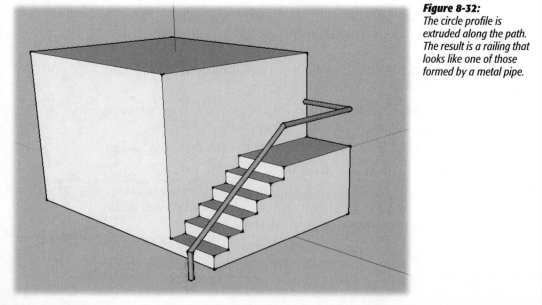

Figure 8-32:
The circle profile is extruded along the path. The result is a railing that looks like one of those formed by a metal pipe.

Advanced Techniques for Groups and Components

Groups and components are such an integral part of SketchUp that they're used in just about any project you're likely to tackle. That's why you've seen them in Chapter 1 and throughout this book. Chapter 5 covered components and Chapter 7 showed how the Outliner keeps a running list of groups and components, including their relationships when they're nested inside of each other.

This chapter explores more advanced techniques for working with and managing components. You'll explore the mysteries of SketchUp entities' sticky behavior and learn how that's different from components' "glue to" options. (Yes, they're two different subjects.) You'll learn how to use collections to organize and store the components you use the most, as well as tips for managing the components in folders on your own computer or network. Along the way you'll learn how to share components and how to move components between two computers—like an office computer and a home computer.

Making Groups and Components

You can create groups and components in any of several ways. In this section, you'll try the different commands so you can settle on the ones that work best for your style, computer equipment, and the job at hand. For example, if you're a one hand on the keyboard and one hand on the mouse artist, you may find that the keyboard shortcuts work best for you. Then again, many people prefer the speed of right-clicking a selection and choosing either Make Group or Make Component from the shortcut menu. Using the commands from the main menu bar is the slowest and least popular method. However, when you know a command exists but can't remember where it is, menus are a good last resort for hunting down the culprit. Here are the different ways you can create groups and components:

Making groups:

- Keyboard shortcut: ⌘-G (Mac).
- Right-click → Make Group (Windows); Control-click → Make Group (Mac).
- Edit → Make Group.

Making components:

- Keyboard shortcut: G (Windows); G or Shift-⌘-G (Mac).
- Right-click → Make Component (Windows); Control-click → Make Component (Mac); see Figure 9-1.
- Click the Make Component (Component Maker on the Mac) toolbar button.
- Edit → Make Component.

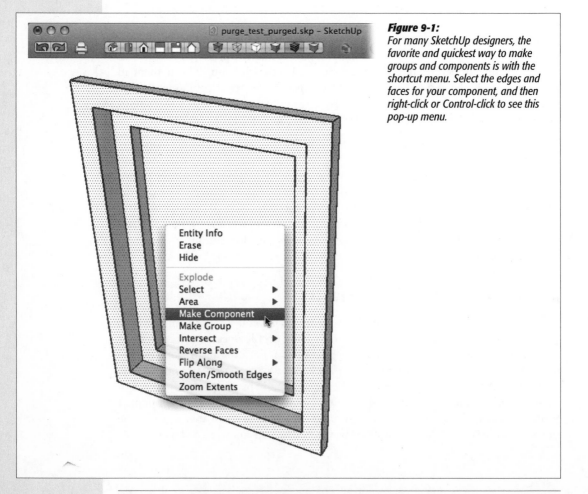

Figure 9-1:
For many SketchUp designers, the favorite and quickest way to make groups and components is with the shortcut menu. Select the edges and faces for your component, and then right-click or Control-click to see this pop-up menu.

Note: Yes, it's a little confusing that the G key creates components rather than groups, but that's just the way it is. If you learn to live with it, your SketchUp career will be much easier. If you're unable to accept it, you can always create custom keyboard shortcuts that work for you (page 31).

The earlier chapters in this book pointed out the many benefits of groups and components. They make it easy to show and hide parts of your model (page 245). They give you the ability to nest parts of your model inside of other parts. For example, stair treads can be nested inside of a stairway group (page 259). One major advantage that groups and components bring to SketchUp is the way they affect "sticky" behavior, as explored in the next section.

Understanding SketchUp's Sticky Behavior

If you've been following the exercises up to this point, no doubt you've experienced SketchUp's "sticky" behavior. When edges and faces come in contact with each other, they tend to weld themselves together in a way that makes it difficult to separate the entities. In these next steps, you'll deliberately experiment with SketchUp's sticky behavior, and then by creating a grouped object, you'll see how to overcome this natural tendency in SketchUp:

Note: The exercise in this section uses the house model that was designed in Chapter 8 (shown in Figure 9-2). You can use your model or you can download *advanced_components_begin.skp* from *http:// http://missingmanuals.com/cds*.

1. **Using the Rectangle (R) tool, begin to draw a rectangle in front of the house. Then type *10',3'* and press Enter (Return on a Mac).**

   A rectangle appears in front of the house. Make sure none of the rectangle's edges touches the house model.

2. **With Push/Pull (P), begin to pull the rectangle up and then type *2'* and press Enter.**

   Your planter box begins to take shape.

3. **With the Offset (F) tool, click the top edge of the box and, on the top surface, begin to move to the inside of the rectangle. Type *6* and then press Enter.**

   The Offset tool creates an additional face on the top of the box.

4. **With Push/Pull (P), click the center face in the top of the planter and begin to push down. Then type *2* and press Enter.**

   At this point the planter looks like the one in Figure 9-2. You can easily select it with a triple-click because it isn't touching any other surfaces. You're going to place this planter against the house, so it doesn't need a back wall.

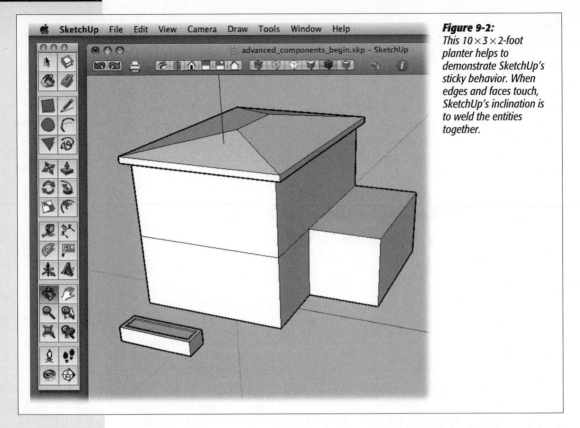

Figure 9-2:
*This 10 × 3 × 2-foot
planter helps to
demonstrate SketchUp's
sticky behavior. When
edges and faces touch,
SketchUp's inclination is
to weld the entities
together.*

5. With Push/Pull (P), click the interior face of the planter's back wall. Push back and then click one of the back edges.

   After the interior face of the planter wall is aligned with the exterior face as shown in Figure 9-3, the wall disappears.

6. Using the Select (space bar) tool, triple-click the planter.

   The entire planter is selected; because the planter isn't connected to any other entities, nothing but the planter is selected.

7. With the Move (M) tool, click the lower-right back corner of the planter (Figure 9-4), and then click the bottom edge of the house's wall.

   The planter moves so that the back face of the planter is against the wall of the house. The bottom of the planter is aligned with the bottom of the house. The planter remains selected.

8. Still using the Move tool, click one of the planter's faces, and move the cursor in different directions around the modeling window.

   The planter is "stuck" to the wall of the house (Figure 9-5). It moves easily back and forth along the red axis. When you move the planter along the green axis, it actually pulls the wall out, distorting the shape of the wall.

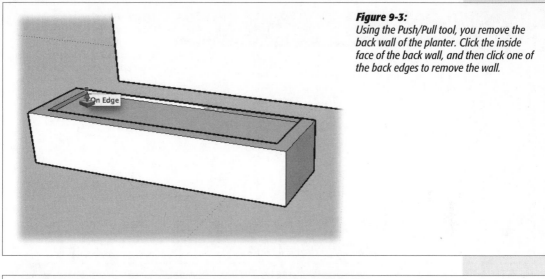

Figure 9-3:
Using the Push/Pull tool, you remove the back wall of the planter. Click the inside face of the back wall, and then click one of the back edges to remove the wall.

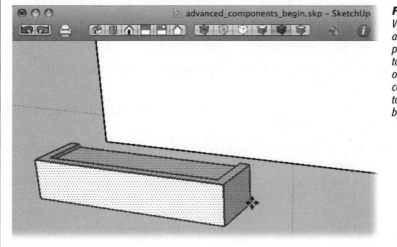

Figure 9-4:
When you're moving entities, it's always best to match a specific point on the object being moved to a specific point on another object. Here the lower-right back corner is selected with the Move tool. It will be moved to the bottom edge of the house's wall.

Don't confuse the sticky behavior of ungrouped entities with the glue-to behavior of components. They're two different things, as explained in the box on page 319.

9. **Press Ctrl+Z (⌘-Z).**

The planter is back in front of the house, not touching the rest of the model. The planter is still selected.

10. **Right-click the planter and choose Make Group from the shortcut menu.**

An extra highlight appears around the planter indicating that it's now a group. You may want to go ahead and give it a creative name like *Planter*.

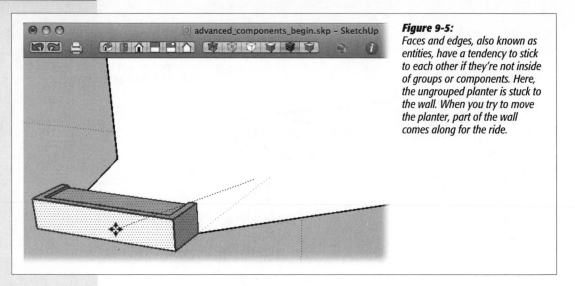

Figure 9-5:
Faces and edges, also known as entities, have a tendency to stick to each other if they're not inside of groups or components. Here, the ungrouped planter is stuck to the wall. When you try to move the planter, part of the wall comes along for the ride.

11. **Choose the Move (M) tool, and then click the lower-right back corner of the planter. Click the bottom edge of the house.**

    The planter snaps to the edge of the house as before.

12. **Still using the Move tool, click one of the planter's faces, and move the cursor in different directions.**

    This time you can move the planter in different directions without bringing parts of the house along with it.

The behavior of the planter as a grouped object is dramatically different from the behavior of the planter when it was just a collection of selected edges and faces. So the lesson here is simple but important to keep in mind. If you don't want parts of your model to stick to each other, keep them in groups or components. You're still able to align them with other parts of your model; the difference is they won't weld together in a way that makes your model difficult to manage.

Unsticking Sticky Entities

If you want to keep the entities in your SketchUp model from sticking to each other, the best thing to do is to select the edges and faces that make up a logical object and then combine those entities in a group (right-click → Make Group) or in components (right-click → Make Component). Groups and components offer many other benefits, but controlling sticky behavior is at the top of the list.

So what do you do if you've created a model (or one is passed along to you) and the logical objects in the model weren't grouped? That's the situation with the house model used in this exercise, and you need a way to take care of the problem after the fact. Logically, the roof, garage, and maybe even the individual floors should be separate groups. Go ahead and try to grab the roof and move it to another location. The walls of the second floor are stuck to the bottom of the roof. The result looks like Figure 9-6.

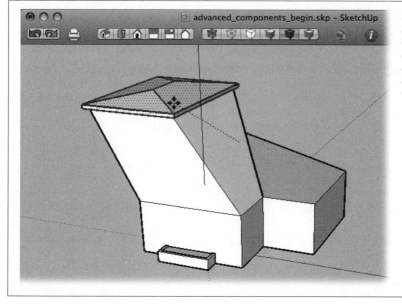

Figure 9-6:
Logically, the roof is a separate element from the walls of the house, but SketchUp doesn't know that unless you turn the roof into a group or a component.

The cure is to select the edges and faces (also known as *entities*) that make up your roof, and then turn them into a group. Sometimes it can be a little tedious to find all those edges and faces, and you have to be careful not to include the wrong edges and faces in the selection. Using the house roof as an example, here are some procedures to follow:

1. **Click the Front view on the View toolbar, or choose Camera → Standard Views → Front.**

   SketchUp shows you the Front view of the house with the planter.

2. **With the Select (space bar) tool, starting to the left and above the roof, drag a selection window around the entities that make up the roof.**

   When you drag from left to right, the entities that are completely within the window are selected (as shown in Figure 9-7).

3. **On the View toolbar, click the X-ray button, or choose View → Face Style → X-ray.**

   The faces in the model become semitransparent, making it easier to see the edges in your selection (Figure 9-8). Because you're able to see through the house, you can tell without changing your view whether the back edges or faces are selected.

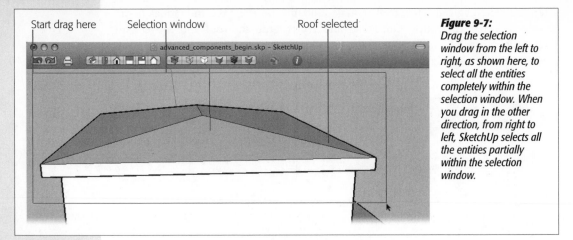

Start drag here   Selection window   Roof selected

Figure 9-7:
*Drag the selection
window from the left to
right, as shown here, to
select all the entities
completely within the
selection window. When
you drag in the other
direction, from right to
left, SketchUp selects all
the entities partially
within the selection
window.*

4. **Right-click the selection and choose Make Group from the shortcut menu.**

   The entities that make up the roof become a group, and SketchUp highlights
   the group. When you click any part of the group, you select the entire group.

   Tip: If you're creating lots of groups, it's best to rename them as you create them. That way, they're easier
   to keep straight.

   ---

5. **With the Move (M) tool, click the roof and move it away from the top of the
   house.**

   As expected, because the roof is grouped, it moves as a single unit and doesn't
   bring parts of the house walls as you move. Now you can look down into the
   second floor of the house. Moving or hiding the roof is a great way for you to
   examine separate floors in a model.

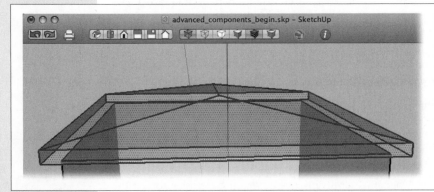

Figure 9-8:
*Use the X-ray view to
double-check your
selection before making
a group or component.
Make sure that all the
edges you want in your
group are highlighted
and also that you don't
catch any unwanted
edges in the selection.*

It's much easier to group your model as you build it, as opposed to separating an existing model into groups after the fact. Still, sometimes you need to divide and conquer after the fact, so a little practice never hurts. Go ahead and separate the garage from the rest of the house. Here are a couple of tips to keep in mind:

- Drag your selection window from left to right. That way, only entities entirely inside of the selection window are selected.

- Remember that it's easiest to see selected entities when you're in X-ray mode.

UP TO SPEED

Sticky Behavior vs. "Glue to" Behavior

These two SketchUp terms seem similar but describe entirely different behaviors, and it's worth noting the difference. When SketchUp designers refer to sticky behavior, they're talking about the way edges and faces stick to each other. Place an ungrouped box flush against a surface, and you find that they're welded together. Moving one distorts the other. (This chapter explores sticky behavior beginning on page 313.)

SketchUp's gluing or "glue to" behavior is a different phenomenon. When you create a component in SketchUp, as described on page 321, you can adjust settings that control

the natural alignment of the component. For example, you probably want doors and windows to glue to walls. So you change their settings to glue to vertical surfaces. Other components like trees, furniture, and people you want to glue to a horizontal surface.

To avoid confusion, remember that sticky behavior describes the way ungrouped entities naturally stick to each other. "Glue to" behavior is limited to the alignment properties that you set when you create components and import image objects. For more on imported images, see page 452.

Editing a Group

When you click a group, you select the entire group. If you want to make changes to the edges and faces inside of a grouped object, you have to open it in edit mode. As usual in SketchUp, you have more than one way to get to the same place:

- **Right-click → Edit Group (Control-click → Edit Group).** Use the Select (space bar) tool to select the group, and then right-click it in the modeling window. As an alternative, you can right-click the name of the group in the Outliner window.

- **Double-click the group.** This technique is a quick and easy way to open a group for editing, especially if you're comfortable double-clicking.

- **Edit → Edit Group.** This is the longest route to opening a group for editing, but you can be confident that the menu command is always there when you need it.

Hiding the Rest of the Model while Editing Groups and Components

Typically when you open a group for editing, the rest of the model is faded, and the group (or component) is the only part of the model that's displayed in sharp colors. You can use another way to edit groups and components. You can have

---

SketchUp completely hide the rest of the model while you're editing, making it easier to focus your attention on the group that you're editing; it also gives you a handy way to determine exactly what's included in your group.

1. **In your model of the house, with the Select (space bar) tool, right-click the roof group and then choose Edit Group.**

   The roof of the group opens for editing. The rest of the model is faded.

2. **Choose View → Edit Component → Hide Rest of Model.**

   Everything in the modeling window disappears except for the entities that are part of the group that's being edited, as shown at the bottom of Figure 9-9. You may think it's a little misleading that this command is hidden under Edit Component, and you're right. It's good to keep in mind that many commands that work with components also work with groups, and vice versa. When in doubt, try it out. If something unexpected happens, you can always reverse it with the Undo key (Ctrl+Z or ⌘-Z).

3. **Click the X-ray view button on the toolbar or choose View → Face Style → X-ray.**

   You see the lines and edges that make up the roof. If you look carefully in the middle of the group, you see some unneeded edges. They were left behind after the Follow Me tool created the roof.

4. **Using the Eraser (E), remove the extra edges.**

   If you accidentally erase something the roof needs, press Ctrl+Z (⌘-Z) and try again.

5. **Choose View → Edit Component → Hide Rest of Model.**

   Unless you want to continue to edit your components with the rest of the model hidden, choose this menu command to remove the checkmark next to "Hide Rest of Model".

In this example, you used two tools that make it easy to clean up your groups and components: the "Hide Rest of Model" command and the X-ray style. When you hide the rest of the model, it's obvious what edges and faces are included in a group or component. Using the X-ray style, you can easily view all the edges and faces in your model from almost any viewpoint.

Hiding similar components

There's also a second command under View → Edit Component that applies only to components. When you edit components, SketchUp shows all the other instances of that component, even if you've selected "Hide Rest of Model". If you only want to focus on the single components you're editing, choose View → Edit Component → Hide Similar Components. Then everything disappears except the component that's open for editing.

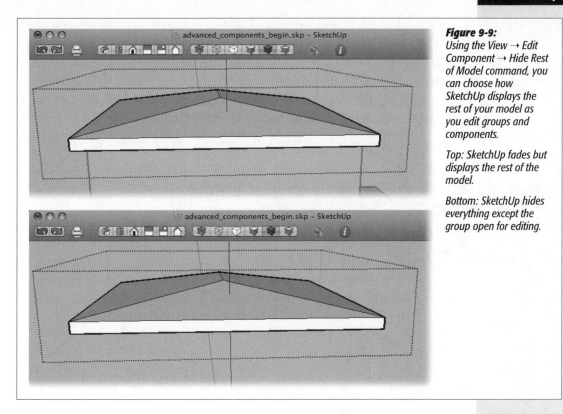

Figure 9-9:
*Using the View → Edit
Component → Hide Rest
of Model command, you
can choose how
SketchUp displays the
rest of your model as
you edit groups and
components.*

*Top: SketchUp fades but
displays the rest of the
model.*

*Bottom: SketchUp hides
everything except the
group open for editing.*

Creating Components with "Glue to" Options

When you create new components, it usually works best to build them in place. In this next example, you create a window component. The first step is to draw the window in a wall. That way SketchUp knows how the component is oriented in the modeling window. In addition, when you create a component, you can tell SketchUp what types of surfaces it should adhere to and align with. In the following steps you see how to align a component by setting its "Glue to" properties:

1. **With the Rectangle (R) tool, start to draw a rectangle on the front of the house. Then type *4',3'* and press Enter (Return on a Mac).**

    A window-like rectangle appears on the front of the house.

2. **With the Offset tool, click the edge of the window and start moving in; then type *3* and press Enter.**

    SketchUp creates a new face 3 inches inside of the original rectangle. The 3-inch offset forms part of the window trim. (Remember, you don't have to type the inches symbol when you're using the "Architectural Design – Feet and Inches" template.)

3. Still using the Offset tool, double-click the line created by the last Offset command.

   This inside rectangle forms the window frame. Double-clicking with the Offset tool repeats the last command. In this case, you create another face that's 3 inches inside of the previous edges.

4. Using Push/Pull (P), push the windowpane back 6 inches, push the window frame back 3 inches, and pull the window trim out 2 inches.

   When you're done, the window looks similar to the one in Figure 9-10.

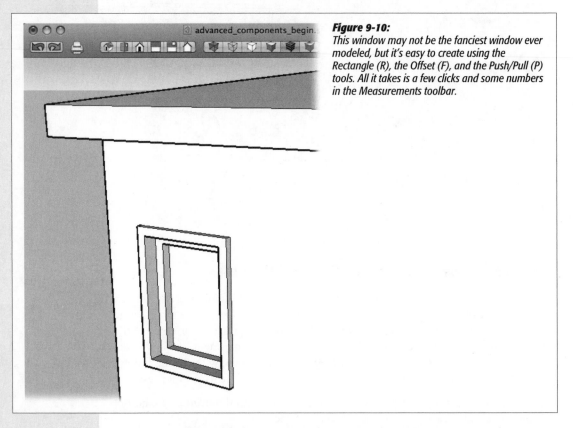

Figure 9-10:
This window may not be the fanciest window ever modeled, but it's easy to create using the Rectangle (R), the Offset (F), and the Push/Pull (P) tools. All it takes is a few clicks and some numbers in the Measurements toolbar.

5. On the toolbar, click the X-ray view button, or choose View → Face Style → X-ray.

   When you're in X-ray view, you can see all the edges in your model. This view makes it easier to see the edges that are highlighted as you make a selection.

6. Using the Select (space bar) tool, drag from left to right to create a selection window around the model's window.

7. **Right-click the selection and choose Make → Component.**

The Create Component window appears (Figure 9-11), showing options divided into three groups: General, where you can enter a name and description; Alignment, where you can change several options including "Glue to" properties and "Cut opening". The third group doesn't have a title and shows only one checkbox: "Replace selection with component".

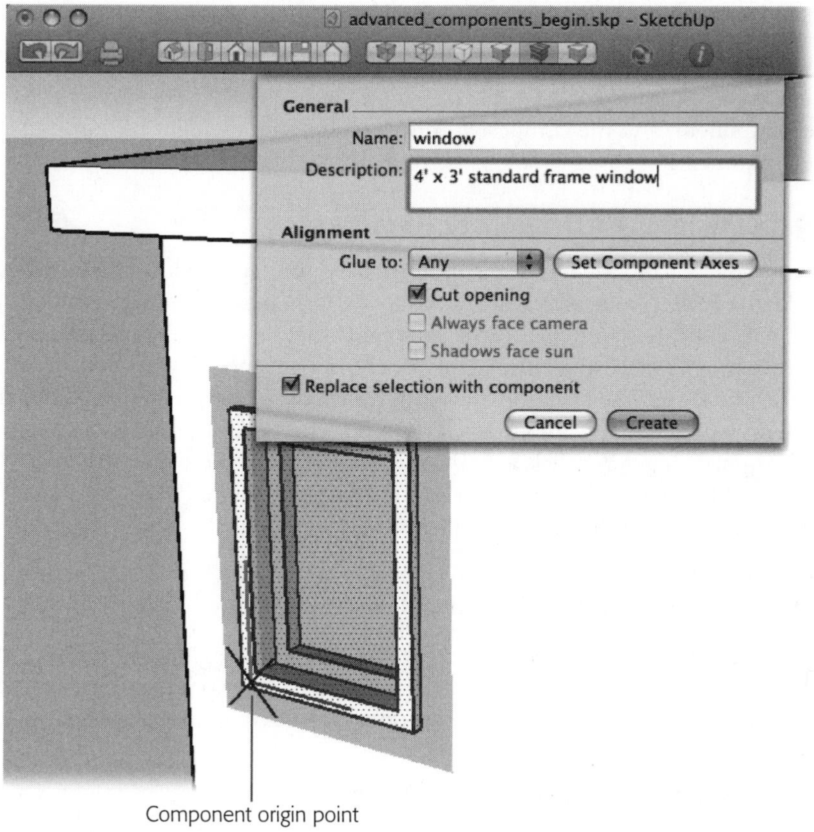

Figure 9-11:
The Create Component window looks a little different on a Mac than in Windows, but it has all the same settings. Each component has its own Origin point that's used to align the component in other models.

Component origin point

8. **Type *window* in the Name box and *4' x 3' standard frame window* in the Description box.**

Descriptive names are very helpful when you work with components. If you're in a great rush, you can skip the description.

9. **Click to open the "Glue to" menu, and then choose Any from the options shown.**

The "Glue to" options include None, Any, Horizontal, Vertical, and Sloped. By choosing the Any option, you make sure that your window component will adhere to vertical, horizontal, or sloped surfaces.

10. Leave the "Cut opening" and "Replace selection with component" boxes turned on. Choose the Create button.

    The "Cut opening" option creates openings for components such as doors and windows. It's described in more detail on page 330. When the "Replace selection with component" box is turned on, SketchUp turns the selection in the modeling window into an instance of the component.

11. On the toolbar, click the X-ray button.

    The faces in your model become opaque.

The window is a single component, similar to the planter and roof in the previous exercises. When you click the window, a single click selects all the edges and faces in the component, and the component displays an extra highlight box around the entire component.

Using a Component's Origin and Axes

Your component displays an Origin point where red, green, and blue axis lines meet (Figure 9-11). Your window component's Origin is in the lower-left front corner. This point lets you align the component when it's placed in other models. When you want to place an existing component in your model, you click the component in the Component window (Window → Component). At that point, the component is attached to your cursor. The point where it's attached is the component's Origin. When you click a point in the SketchUp modeling window, you place the component in the larger model. In other words, the Origin for the component is positioned at the point you clicked in the model.

You can change the position of the Origin by clicking the Set Component Axes button. That's not something you need to do for this window.

Don't be concerned when you see that the green and blue axes are swapped in components. It won't have an effect when they're inside a larger model. The technical reason for this axis swap has to do with the way dynamic components are built.

Copying and Placing Components

There's no big mystery when it comes to copying and pasting components. The process is similar to that in most other programs, including your word processor. Select the component you want to copy. You can perform the Copy command in a couple of ways:

- Keyboard shortcut: Ctrl+C (Windows); ⌘-C (Mac)

- Edit → Copy

By copying the window component, you place it on your computer Clipboard. Then you can paste the copy into your model in a similar fashion:

- Keyboard shortcut: Ctrl+V (Windows); ⌘-V (Mac)

- Edit → Paste

There's another method that you used in some of the earlier examples. You can use the Move (M) tool in copy mode: toggle key Ctrl (Windows) or Option (Mac).

Tip: You may expect to see the Copy, Paste, and Cut commands on the shortcut menu that you bring up with a right-click, but that's not the case in SketchUp. If you're looking for "cut and paste" speed, the keyboard shortcuts are your best bet.

---

1. **With the Select (space bar) tool, click the window component and press Ctrl+C (⌘-C).**

   SketchUp places a copy of the window component on the Clipboard.

2. **Press Ctrl+V (⌘-V).**

   A copy of the window component is attached to the cursor.

3. **Move the cursor to different faces on the house model.**

   The window snaps to any face in the model, even the sloped face of the roof.

4. **Click to place the window next to the first window you created.**

   The copy of the window component is glued to the wall next to the original.

At this point, you can continue to place window components in your model simply by pressing the Paste keyboard shortcut and clicking the surface of your house. The problem is, you're not being very precise about the placement, so erase any windows you may have placed in your model except for the first one. Naturally SketchUp provides ways for you to place components quickly and precisely, as you'll see next.

Using Guides to Place Components with Precision

When you want to place entities with precision, think of the Tape Measure tool. Using the Tape Measure, you can place guides in your model. You can then align other entities along those guides. SketchUp arrays (described in this next example) also give you a way to quickly create aligned and evenly spaces entities. These entities can be groups, components, or even a single edge.

1. **With the Tape Measure (T) tool, click the edge between the first and second floors, and then click the bottom edge of the window frame where it touches the face of the wall.**

   Make sure you click the point where the window frame touches the wall (Figure 9-12), or you'll have trouble aligning the rest of the windows.

2. **Still using the Tape Measure, click the wall's left edge, and begin to move toward the center of the wall. Type _12_ and then press Enter.**

   SketchUp creates a guide that's 12 inches from the left edge of the wall.

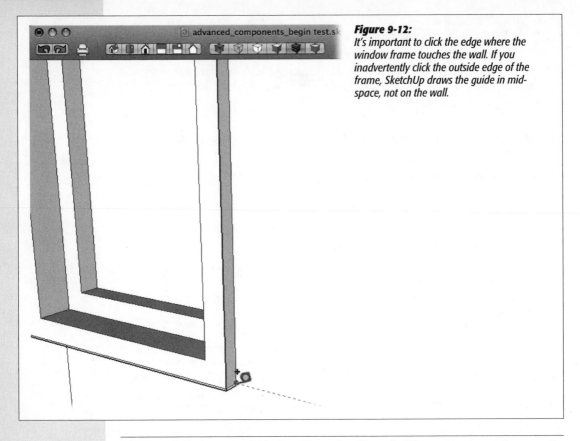

Figure 9-12:
It's important to click the edge where the window frame touches the wall. If you inadvertently click the outside edge of the frame, SketchUp draws the guide in mid-space, not on the wall.

Tip: Use Ctrl (Option) to toggle the Tape Measure's guide mode. When a + appears on the cursor, the Tape Measure creates guidelines.

---

3. **Use the Tape Measure to click the right edge of the wall, and begin to move to the center of the wall. Type *12* and then press Enter.**

   SketchUp creates a guide 12 inches from the wall's right edge.

4. **Click the lower-left corner of the window component where it meets the wall, and then click the guides where they intersect on the left side of the wall.**

   The window is placed on the horizontal line, precisely 12 inches from the wall's left edge.

5. **Choose the Move (M) tool and then press Ctrl (Option).**

   A + sign appears on the Move tool's cursor, indicating that the Move tool is in copy mode.

6. **Click the window component's lower-right corner where it meets the wall.**

   A copy of the window component is attached to the Move cursor, as shown in Figure 9-13.

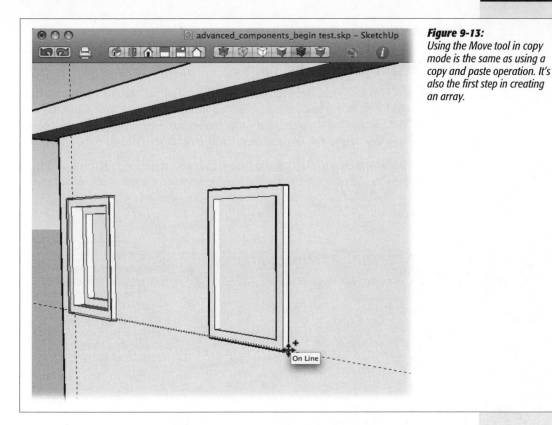

Figure 9-13:
Using the Move tool in copy mode is the same as using a copy and paste operation. It's also the first step in creating an array.

7. **On the right side of the wall, click the intersection of guides.**

   The copy is placed on the horizontal guide, exactly 12 inches from the edge of the wall.

8. **Type *3/* and then press Enter.**

   SketchUp creates an array of evenly spaced windows between the original and the copy. The wall has four windows: the first window and the three windows created by the Array command. Until you enter another command or choose another tool, you can continue to change the number of windows.

9. **Type *4/* and then press Enter.**

   SketchUp shows five windows on the wall: the original and the four created by the Array command. Choose a number of windows that looks good to you on the wall.

In this example, you create an array of windows between the original and the copy by using the forward slash symbol (/), meaning "divide by." You can also create an array using the multiply symbol (x). Here's how it works. Follow the steps above to move a copy of the window a short distance, say 10 inches. Then at step 8, type *4x* and press Enter (Return on a Mac). Instead of placing the array of new windows between the original and the copy, SketchUp positions the new windows every 10 inches.

Note: SketchUp's Array feature is described in more detail on page 169.

The Effects of the "Glue to" Options

At this point you can examine the effect that the "Glue to" options have on your components. Remember, back on page 323, you chose Any as the "Glue to" setting. You already saw how your window components were ready to snap to any face of the house whether the faces were vertical walls or the sloped roof.

Now with the Move (M) tool, click the face of the wall with the windows, and then pull it forward in the modeling window. Notice how the windows stay glued to the face of the wall. Wherever that wall goes, the window components follow (Figure 9-14).

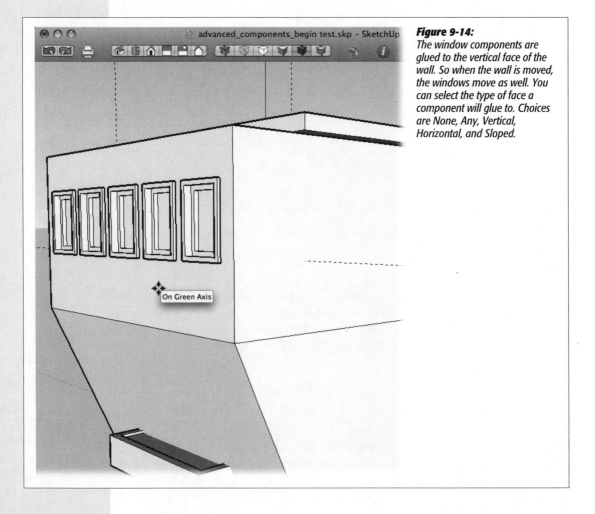

Figure 9-14:
The window components are glued to the vertical face of the wall. So when the wall is moved, the windows move as well. You can select the type of face a component will glue to. Choices are None, Any, Vertical, Horizontal, and Sloped.

Click one of the windows, and drag it to a new position. Because of its glued-to nature, the window wants to move along the plane of the face that it's glued to. Drag the window to the side of the house, so that it doesn't touch the face of the wall. Then with the Move tool, click and move the face of the wall. The window still moves with the wall, even though it's no longer on the face—all because of its glued-to status. When you're done experimenting, press the Undo key (Ctrl+Z for Windows; ⌘-Z for Mac) until you return to the point where you have several windows on the face of the wall.

Ungluing a Component

A time will come when you want to unglue a component from the face it adheres to. Right-click one of the windows on the face, and then choose Unglue from the pop-up menu. The window doesn't move, but it does look changed, as shown in Figure 9-15. The unglued window is different from the other glued components in three ways:

- Once the window is unglued, it no longer moves with the face of the wall. The unglued window stays in position while the wall and other windows move.

- It's also easier to move the unglued window into any position within the modeling window.

- The unglued window no longer cuts an opening in the face of the wall.

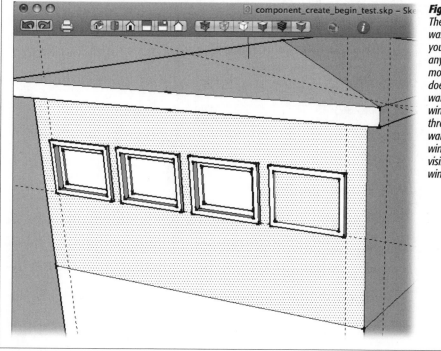

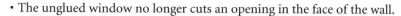

Figure 9-15:
The window on the right was unglued. That means you can drag the window anywhere in the modeling window, and it doesn't move when the wall moves. The unglued window no longer cuts through the face of the wall, so, unlike the other windows, the wall is visible through the window frame's opening.

Note: If you unglued one of your window components, use Undo (Ctrl+Z or ⌘-Z) to restore it to its glued glory before continuing with the examples in this chapter.

Component's Cut Opening Option

When you created the window component (page 323), the "Cut opening" option was checked, as shown in Figure 9-16. As a result, the windows created an opening when the glass pane was pushed back into the model. As you might guess, the "Cut opening" option is great for creating doors, windows, and a lot of other components; however, it does have one major drawback. In the real world, walls aren't paper-thin. They have a surface on each side and some sort of framing in the middle, often 2×4 or 2×6 lumber. The cut opening feature only cuts openings in the single surface that it's glued to. As handy as the cut opening feature is for making quick-and-dirty models with simple exterior faces, it isn't very helpful when you're making a more realistic model that includes interior floor plans. In those cases, you're going to have to do more work and cut your own openings for windows.

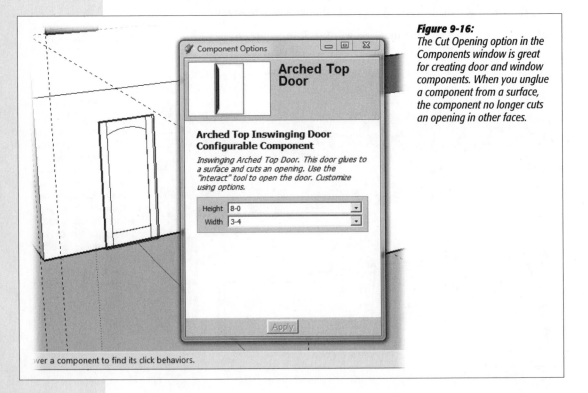

Figure 9-16:
The Cut Opening option in the Components window is great for creating door and window components. When you unglue a component from a surface, the component no longer cuts an opening in other faces.

Placing Components in Your Model

Components are an important part of SketchUp. It's likely that many of your models will include both components that you create and readymade components that you find in SketchUp or the 3D Warehouse:

1. **Choose Window → Components.**

   The Components window opens.

2. **In the Components window, click the In Model button (Figure 9-17).**

   The Components window shows the components that are in your model. You see your window component. You may or may not see Sang, depending on how you disposed of him. You don't see the planter that you created at the beginning of this chapter (page 313), because the planter is a group, not a component.

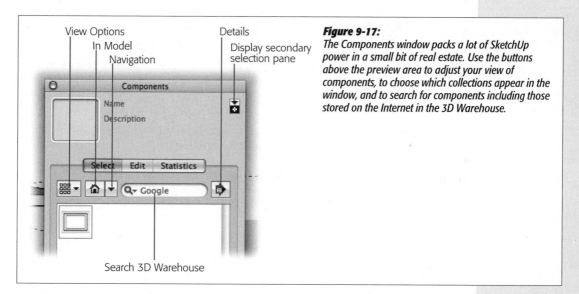

View Options
In Model
Navigation

Details
Display secondary
selection pane

Components

Name
Description

Select Edit Statistics

Q▾ Google

Search 3D Warehouse

Figure 9-17:
The Components window packs a lot of SketchUp power in a small bit of real estate. Use the buttons above the preview area to adjust your view of components, to choose which collections appear in the window, and to search for components including those stored on the Internet in the 3D Warehouse.

3. **Click the window component and place a couple more windows on both sides of the house on the second floor.**

   The number of windows and how carefully you want to place them is up to you. Use the Orbit (O) and other view tools to maneuver around your model. If you're going for precision, use the Tape Measure (T) to create guides and the Array feature to add copies.

4. **Place two windows on the roof as skylights.**

   At this point, you run into a "gotcha!" The windows appear to align with the surface of the roof, but notice that they don't cut an opening in the face of the roof. The edges and faces of the roof are inside of a group. For the window component to do its cut-opening magic, you need to open the group for editing and place the window inside of the group.

Tip: A window or door component cannot cut an opening in a wall if the wall's face is inside of a group or component and if the window or door is on the outside. You must open the component, and then place the door or window on the wall.

5. **Use the Select (space bar) tool to select the windows and then press Delete.**

   The windows disappear from the model. You can use Shift-click to select both windows at once before you press Delete.

6. **Right-click the roof and choose Edit Group from the shortcut menu.**

   The Group opens for editing. The rest of the model is faded. If you have set View → Hide Rest of Model, then all you see is the roof group.

7. **Click the window component and then click the roof. Place two windows on the roof.**

   The window components are now glued to the roof surface and cut an opening in the roof.

As your models become more complex, it becomes second nature to open groups and components for editing. Sometimes you want to make changes, and other times you want to add new elements to the group or component. In this example, you made changes to a group. Those changes only affect that group. As you see later in this chapter (page 336), when you make changes to components, those changes affect all the other instances of that component.

Exploring the Components Window

As far as components are concerned, the Components window is Grand Central Station. That's where you find all the components in your model and where you hunt for premade components. In the next few steps you add premade door components to your model. In the process, you make a visit to the 3D Warehouse—think of it as Home Depot for SketchUp.

1. **Click the Navigation button and then choose Architecture from the drop-down list.**

   When you click Architecture, several collections of architectural components are displayed in the preview window.

   The Navigation list shows collections of components (Figure 9-18). Click one of the collections' names to see the components it holds. At the top of the list, you see the familiar In Model option. Further down the list, you see collections grouped under "Favorites" and "Recent". You add and remove collections from your Favorites list by using the commands under the Details button on the Components window. The Recent list keeps track of collections that you've used recently.

2. **Click the View button and choose List View.**

   In the drop-down menu, you see several options:

Figure 9-18:
When you click the Navigation button in the Components window, you see a list of all component collections. At the top of the list, the In Model collection shows the components that are stored in your SketchUp document. The other collections may be stored on your computer or at the Google 3D Warehouse.

- **Small Thumbnails** displays icon-sized images representing the collection or the component.

- **Large Thumbnails** displays larger, but still icon-sized, images representing the collection or the component.

- **Details** shows on the left the icon for the collection or component. On the right is descriptive text, which may include a link to a website with even more information about the collection or component.

- **List View** shows no image, just a few words to describe the collection or component. When you need to cut through the clutter, the list view can help.

- **Refresh** is similar to your browser's refresh button. Choose Refresh when you want SketchUp to reread and redisplay the component or collection info.

3. **Choose "DC Doors and Windows".**

"DC" stands for dynamic components, so you see several door and window components that offer special features. For example, you may be able to change the dimensions of the components, or you may be able to open and close them in your model. If you're in Details view, make sure you click the icon, not the text. If you click the text, SketchUp opens the 3D Warehouse in your web browser.

4. **Choose Door Arch Top from the list.**

SketchUp downloads the component from the 3D Warehouse. Briefly you see a progress bar on the screen, indicating that SketchUp is downloading the component from the 3D Warehouse. When the download is complete, the component is already attached to your cursor, so all you have to do is click in your model to place the component.

Note: SketchUp's 3D Warehouse is a website: *http://sketchup.google.com/3dwarehouse/*. The Search box in the Components window searches the component collections on your computer and the ones in the 3D Warehouse. If you don't find what you want using the search function in the Components window, check the website. The two don't always show the same results.

---

5. **Click the bottom edge of the wall next to the garage.**

The door component is placed in the wall.

6. **Right-click the component and then choose Dynamic Component → Component Options.**

The Component Options window displays an image of the component and its name at the top. With most components, you see text that explains how the component works and what options you can change (Figure 9-19). Below that are controls for making changes to the component.

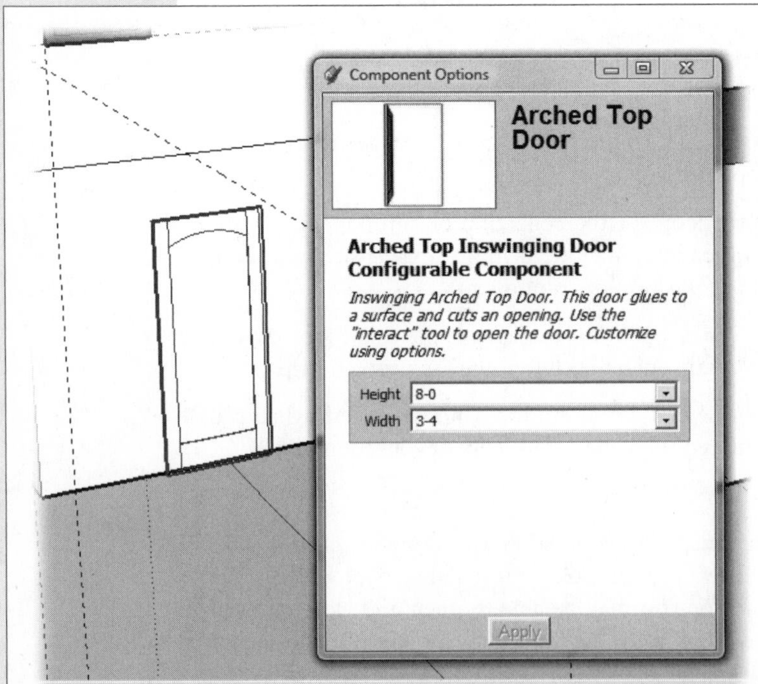

Figure 9-19:
The Component Options for the Arched Top Door explain that it's an inswinging door that glues itself to the surface and cuts an opening. When clicked with the Interact tool, the door opens and closes. Use the drop-down menus to change the width and height of the door.

7. Click the Height menu and choose 8. Then click the Width menu and choose 3-4. Click Apply and close the Component Options window.

The door changes dimensions according to your specifications.

8. Choose Tools → Interact and then click the door (Figure 9-20).

When you choose Interact, the cursor changes to a finger with a highlight on the end. When you click the door, it opens or closes.

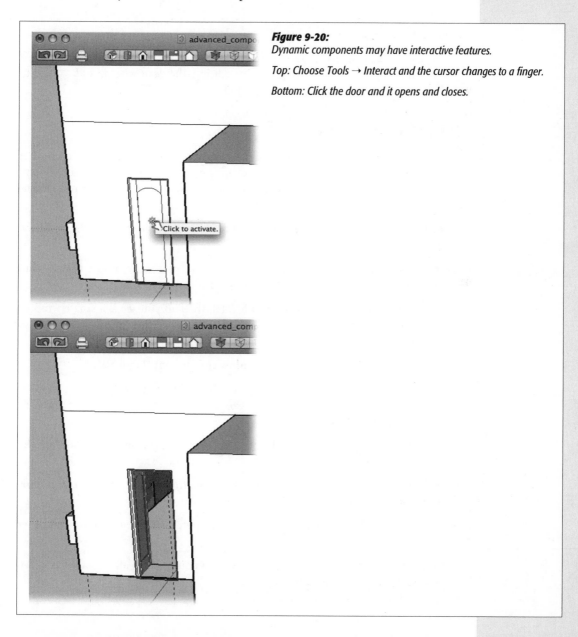

Figure 9-20:
Dynamic components may have interactive features.

Top: Choose Tools → Interact and the cursor changes to a finger.

Bottom: Click the door and it opens and closes.

9. **Double-click to open the garage group for editing.**

   If you open the garage in edit mode before you hunt down a garage door, you'll save some time and a click or two.

10. **In the Search box of the Component window, type** *one car rolling garage door.*

    SketchUp searches the online 3D Warehouse for a component that matches your description. When it finds a match, it shows the component in the Components window.

11. **Click the garage door and then click to place it on the face of the garage.**

    The garage door snaps to the surface of the garage and cuts a hole in the face. If you hadn't opened the garage group for editing, the door would not be glued to the face and it wouldn't cut an opening.

Editing Components

As explained earlier, editing a component is different from editing a group in that the changes you make to a component change every instance of that component. You've got lots of window components in your house, so they present an opportunity to see this principle in action:

1. **Right-click (or Control-click) any one of the windows in your model and then choose Edit Component.**

   The window component opens for editing. The rest of the model fades. As an alternative, you can double-click a component to open it for editing.

   If you have set View → Hide Rest of Model, then all you see is a single window component. For this example, it's best if you can see the rest of the model, so change your view, at least for a moment.

2. **Zoom in to a close-up view of the window component (Figure 9-21).**

   You can use several handy zoom tools. If you have a scroll wheel on your mouse, that may be the easiest. You can also click with the Zoom (Z) tool, or drag with the Zoom Window tool.

3. **With the Rectangle (R) tool, draw a small rectangle on the middle of the window's frame.**

   Make the rectangle about half the height of the frame, so it can serve as a horizontal piece of sash, as shown in Figure 9-21.

4. **With Push/Pull (P), pull the rectangle and then click the frame on the other side of the window.**

   Notice that as you make changes to the open component, all the other components change at the same time.

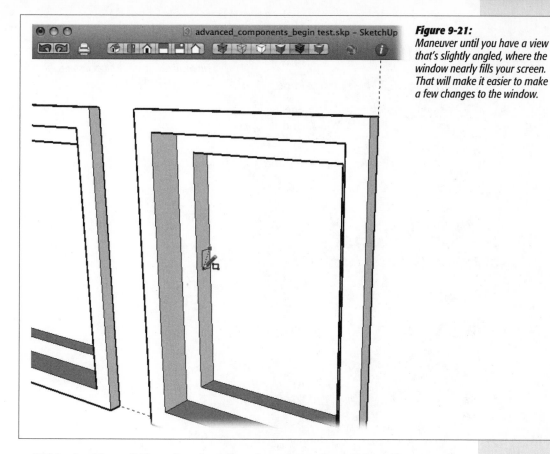

5. **With the Move (M) tool, select the edge where the windowsill meets the window frame, and then pull the edge up in the blue direction (Figure 9-22).**

   You're creating a slope for the windowsill. That should help it to drain water when the storms hit SketchUp land.

6. **Open the Materials window (Window → Materials), and change the color of the windowpane to a blue translucent color. Change the color of the frame to gray or some other color of your choice.**

   The technique for applying colors is different for Windows (page 196) and Mac (page 207).

7. **When you're happy with the modifications, click outside of the component or choose Edit → Close Group/Component.**

   The window component closes and all the instances of the window component reflect the changes just made.

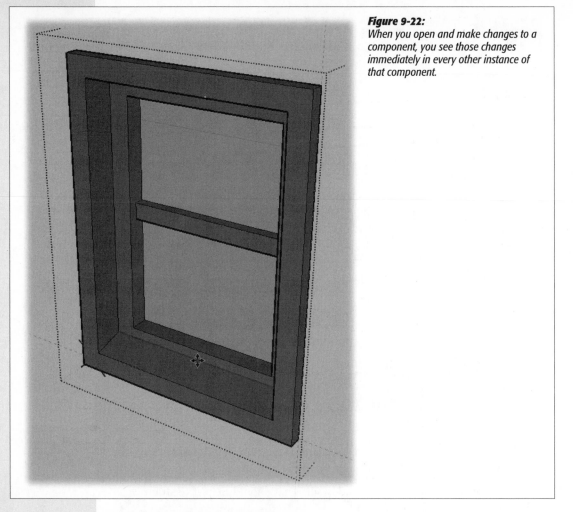

Figure 9-22:
When you open and make changes to a component, you see those changes immediately in every other instance of that component.

Making Components Unique

The changes made to the windows look fine all the way around the sides of the house, but there's a problem with the two windows that serve as skylights. They're sure to catch water and, once they do that, they're sure to leak. Some modifications are in order; however, because the skylights are instances of the window component, any changes you make will affect the other windows. The solution? Before you make your changes, make the two skylight windows unique. Here are the steps:

1. **Right-click (or Control-click) the roof, and then choose Edit Group from the shortcut menu.**

   You need to open the roof group for editing before you can make changes to the skylights.

2. **With the Select (space bar) tool, click the first skylight and then Shift-click on the second.**

   Both skylight components are selected, and they show the selection highlight.

3. **Right-click one of the window components, and then choose Make Unique from the shortcut menu (Figure 9-23).**

   The two skylight windows are no longer instances of the window component. Look in the Components window (Window → Components), and you see the original window component, named "window". A second component is called "window#1". That's the name SketchUp gives the new component it created as a result of the Make Unique command.

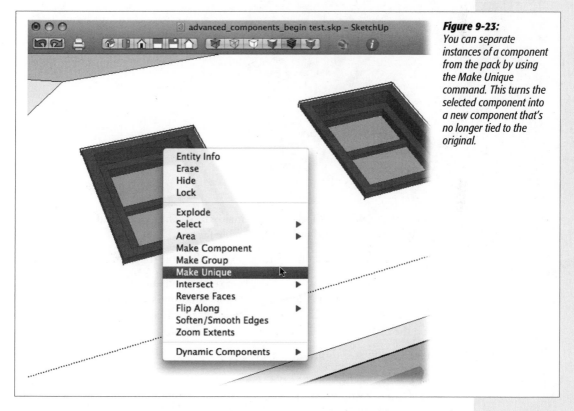

Figure 9-23:
You can separate instances of a component from the pack by using the Make Unique command. This turns the selected component into a new component that's no longer tied to the original.

4. **Double-click one of the window#1 components to open it for editing.**

   The component opens and the rest of the model is grayed out. Changes that you make to this component appear in the other skylight but not in the other window components.

5. **With the Line tool, trace the inside edges of the window frame from corner to corner.**

   One line may be all it takes for the face of the window to fill in.

---

6. Using the Offset (F) tool, click the edge of the window frame, and begin to move in toward the center of the window. Type *4* and then press Enter (Return on a Mac).

A new inset face appears in the center of the window, as shown in Figure 9-24.

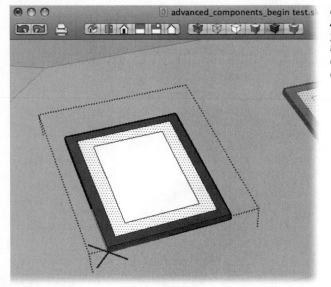

Figure 9-24:
After making the windows on the roof unique, you can go ahead and make modifications to turn them into a skylight. This figure shows one of the in-between stages on the way to creating a skylight.

7. Choose the Move tool and click the inside face. Then press and release the Alt key (⌘ on the Mac) and pull up the inside face.

Pull the surface up so that it creates the kind of bubble shape you see on skylights.

The Alt (⌘) key toggles auto-fold, so SketchUp creates the necessary folds to distort the face of the windowpane. Double-diamonds appear on the Move cursor when it's in auto-fold mode. If you have trouble pulling the window up along the blue axis, press and release the up arrow.

8. Choose the Eraser tool. Then press and hold Ctrl (Option), and click the lines in the skylight "glass."

Ctrl (Option) smoothes the edges as you click them, which gives the skylight glass a nice curved effect (Figure 9-25).

Tip: Want to unsmooth an edge? Use the Eraser tool and press Shift+Crtl (Shift-Option) as you click edges that were previously smoothed.

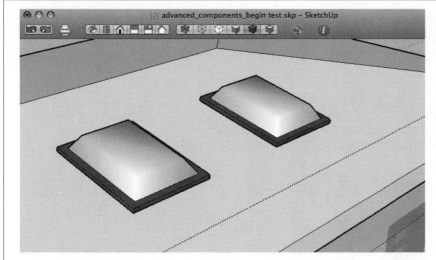

Figure 9-25:
By using the smooth option (Ctrl in Windows, Option on a Mac) with the Eraser tool, you can create a curved skylight for the roof. With the curved glass, the skylights look like they'll be waterproof when the next big storm comes along.

Note: To follow SketchUp best practices with this model, remove the extra faces and edges in the window#1 component. The easiest way to do so is to right-click the curved glass and choose Hide from the pop-up menu. Then go to work with the Eraser (E), erasing the leftover window frame and panes. You have lots of edges to dispose of, but be careful not to erase the outside frame that's used in the skylight. When you're done erasing unneeded geometry, go to Edit → Unhide → Last and the skylight glass reappears.

9. **Choose Edit → Close Group/Component twice.**

   First you close the window#1 component. The repeated command closes the roof group. As an alternative, you can click outside of the components in the modeling window. Once all the components are closed, you no longer see dotted lines surrounding the groups or components.

At this point the house model is beginning to show a little character. To dress it up even more, you can continue adding premade components. The next sections focus on more techniques for working with and managing your components.

Renaming Your Component

When you use the Make Unique command, SketchUp keeps the original name and adds numbers. That's enough detail to identify the new component in the Components window, but "window#1" isn't a very accurate name for your newly created skylight. To change the name and description, open the Components window (Window → Components). Click window#1 and then, at the top of the window, type the name and description you want to use for your component, as shown in Figure 9-26.

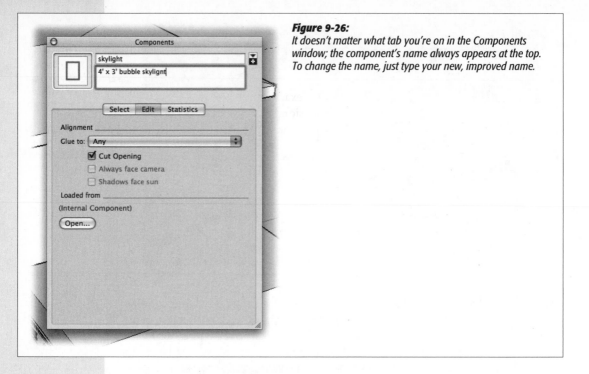

Figure 9-26:
It doesn't matter what tab you're on in the Components window; the component's name always appears at the top. To change the name, just type your new, improved name.

Saving Components for Reuse

You're the creator of the newly named "skylight" component. It wasn't one of the components that you retrieved from a collection or the 3D Warehouse. So at this point the only place the skylight component exists is inside of this SketchUp document. With a decent chance you'll need a skylight again, it makes sense to save it where you can reuse or even modify it for some other purpose.

1. **In the Components window (Window → Components), click the Select tab.**

   The Select tab shows your components as thumbnails, a list of names, or longer descriptions, depending on the View Options (Figure 9-17). Choose the view you like best.

2. **Click the In Model button.**

   SketchUp displays the components that are in your model. If you added components to your model but later deleted them, they'll show here, too.

3. **Right-click the skylight component, and choose Save As from the shortcut menu.**

   A file browser window opens. Use the browser to find a folder where you want to store your SketchUp components. If this is your first component, you may want to create a special SketchUp Components folder. Over time, it's likely that you'll want to create subfolders to hold different types of components: windows and doors, landscape furniture, people, and pets. It's your collection, so organize it in a way that makes sense to you and provides room for growth.

4. **Click the Save button.**

SketchUp saves components in files that are exactly the same as any SketchUp document. In fact, the files have a .skp extension. That means you can use any SketchUp document as a component, and you can open any component file as a SketchUp document.

Purging Unused Components from Your Model

SketchUp keeps track of all the components in your model. Click the In Model button (Figure 9-27), and you see a list of all the components that are currently in your model. If you added a component, then decided you didn't need it and deleted it, you'll still see the component in the list. What's more, SketchUp keeps a copy of the component saved in your document, so it's ready to use if you need it. Complex components dramatically increase the size of your documents, so if you're not using and not planning to use components, it makes sense to get rid of them. To purge your SketchUp document of any component that isn't actually used in your model, click the Details button and then choose "Purge unused".

It's a good idea to purge your SketchUp documents of unneeded components and colors before you save a final copy or email it to a colleague. It keeps the file size to a minimum, and it keeps everything neat and tidy.

Tip: There's a similar "Purge unused" command in the Materials window. It makes just as much sense to purge your document of unneeded materials. In Windows, click the Select tab and then choose Details → Purge Unused. On a Mac, go to Window → Materials. Instead of a Materials window, you see a window named Colors that's part of the Mac's standard color system. Click the SketchUpColorPicker—it looks like a brick. At the bottom of the window, click the List pop-up menu and choose Purge Unused. If you want to purge your document of materials, components, and empty layers, go to Window → Model Info → Statistics and click Purge Unused.

Creating a Collection

SketchUp stores components in collections. When you first use SketchUp, you see the collections that came with the program, and you see additional collections that are stored in the 3D Warehouse. As you create your own components, you'll want to start creating your own collections. You can organize your collections however you want—by object, by client, or by project. It's up to you. Suppose you want to create a new collection named My Windows for the window and skylight created in this chapter. Here are the steps:

1. **In the Components window (Window → Components), click the Select tab.**

The Select tab shows your components as thumbnails, a list of names, or using longer descriptions, depending on the View Options setting.

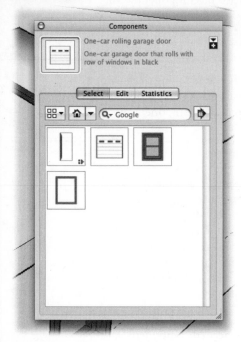

Figure 9-27:
Click the In Model button and SketchUp shows all the components in your document. Here SketchUp shows window, arch top door, garage door, and the skylight components.

2. **Click the In Model button, as shown in Figure 9-27.**

   SketchUp displays the components in your model. If you added components to your model but later deleted them, they'll show here, too.

3. **Click the Details button and choose "Open or Create a Local collection"; "Create a new collection" on a Mac.**

   A standard file browser window opens, where you can navigate through your folders and create new folders. Find or create a folder named *My Windows* where you want to store your windows.

4. **Select the My Windows folder and then click Open.**

   SketchUp creates a new collection named My Windows.

5. **In the upper-right corner, click the "Display the secondary selection pane" button.**

   A new pane opens at the bottom of the Components window. With two panes open in the Components window, you can drag components from one collection to another.

6. **In the drop-down menu in the secondary pane, choose the My Windows collection.**

   Nothing yet is in the My Windows collection.

7. **Drag the "skylight" and "window" components into My Windows.**

SketchUp saves copies of the skylight and window components in the My Windows folder as .skp files. The next time you use SketchUp for this or any other document, you'll find the two windows in the My Windows collection (Figure 9-28).

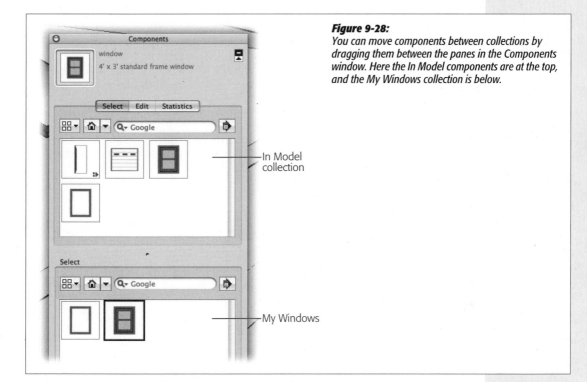

Figure 9-28:
You can move components between collections by dragging them between the panes in the Components window. Here the In Model components are at the top, and the My Windows collection is below.

Sharing SketchUp Components

You can move SketchUp components between computers or share them with colleagues in many ways. Because SketchUp components are SketchUp (.skp) documents, you can shuffle them in and out of your collection folders using your computer's file management tool: Windows Explorer or the Mac Finder. Want to move components between your home and office computer? Copy them to a thumb drive or email them to yourself; then place them inside of one of your component collection folders.

If you work on a computer network and want to share components with your colleagues on the network, create collections in a public or shared folder. That way everyone with permission to access the folder can access the same components.

Swapping Components in Your Model

It's easy to swap one component for another in your model. Or if you prefer, you can replace every instance of a component with a different component. In this example, you replace one of your window components with a window from the 3D Warehouse. The first step is to find a likely candidate that's roughly the same size as your 4 × 3-foot window.

1. **In the Components window (Window → Components), choose the Select tab and then in the Search box, type** *double hung window 35 x 58.*

    SketchUp hunts around the 3D Warehouse and presents any candidates that meet your description (Figure 9-29).

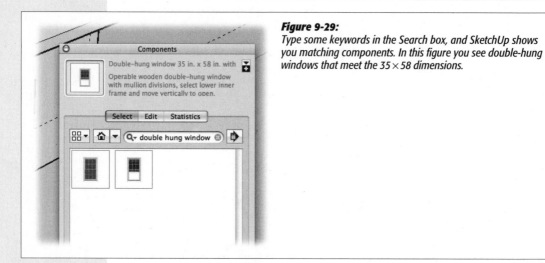

Figure 9-29:
Type some keywords in the Search box, and SketchUp shows you matching components. In this figure you see double-hung windows that meet the 35 × 58 dimensions.

2. **Click a window and then press Esc.**

    When you click a window, it's downloaded and then added to your In Model collection. The window is automatically attached to your cursor. Pressing Esc removes the window from your cursor, but it still appears in the Components window's In Model view.

3. **With the Selection tool, click one of the windows in your model.**

    A selection box appears around the selected window.

4. **In the Components window, click the In Model button.**

    SketchUp shows all the components in your model, including the newly added window from the 3D Warehouse.

5. **In the Components window, right-click (or Control-click) the new window, and then choose Replace Selected from the context menu.**

    The selected window in your model is swapped for the new window.

The Replace Selected command works great if you want to swap just a few components at a time. There's an even better way if you want to swap all the instances of a component at once.

Tip: When you swap components, SketchUp uses the component's Origin as a reference for placing the new component in the model. (For details on a component's Origin, see page 323.) The new component's Origin is placed in the same spot as the previous component's Origin. If the Replace Selected or Reload commands aren't behaving the way you expect them to, check to see if the components' Origin and axes are oriented differently.

Swapping Components Using the Reload Command

Suppose you want to show a client a house with a few different window styles. Using the Reload command, you can change all the instances of a window component with a single command (Figure 9-30). The only caveat is that the new window component must be stored on your computer or on your network where you can find it with a file browser. Here are the steps to swap the window you created with the double-hung window from the 3D Warehouse:

1. **In the Components window (Window → Components), right-click (or Control-click) the new double-hung window.**

    A context menu pops up with several different options.

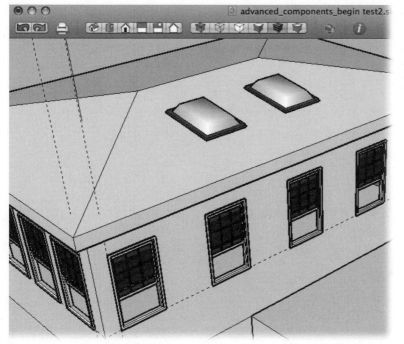

Figure 9-30:
Use the Reload command when you want to swap all the instances of a component for another component. Here the window you created in this chapter is swapped for a window from the 3D Warehouse.

---

2. **Click Save As.**

A file browser window opens where you can navigate through the folders on your computer or network.

3. **Find the My Windows folder and then click Save.**

SketchUp saves a copy of the double-hung window as a .skp file in your my Windows folder. You can save it with a different file name if you want.

4. **In the Components window, right-click (or Control-click) the window component you created earlier, and then choose Reload from the pop-up menu.**

A file browser window opens, similar to the one in step 2. Make sure you're viewing the In Model collection, or you won't see the Reload command.

5. **Navigate to the My Windows folder, and then double-click the double-hung window.**

SketchUp replaces all the window components in the model with the double-hung window. Because it's no longer in the model, the original window is no longer listed in the In Model collection.

The Reload command is a great way to demonstrate changes in a model. It usually works best when the components are similar in size, shape, and orientation. However, you have no restrictions on the components you can swap. If you'd like to swap a window with a pickup truck component, you're free to do so. Your architecture career may suffer, but you could do it.

CHAPTER 10

Matching Your Photos in SketchUp

Google SketchUp is far from being a one-trick pony. As you saw in earlier chapters, SketchUp lets you quickly design models from scratch and determine the dimensions as you work. But say you already took a photograph of what you're trying to model. Wouldn't it be great if you could just show the picture to SketchUp and say, "I want this. Same shape. Same size. Just do it." It may not be quite that easy, but you *can* use a photograph as a reference when you create a 3-D SketchUp model. Using a little magic called Photo Match, SketchUp identifies the perspective and focal length of the photograph. Then it recreates that view in the modeling window. Using the drawing tools, you trace over parts of the image to create edges and faces of a three-dimensional model. You can use the original photo to create textured surfaces in your model, or you can use the standard SketchUp methods to add details.

This chapter shows you how to do it all. It begins with a detailed explanation of Photo Match and some tips to consider when you're shooting photos for Photo Match. Then, in the exercises, you get to see Photo Match in action as you create a model of the famous Villa Savoye, located in Poissy, outside of Paris, which was designed by the noted architect Le Corbusier.

How Photo Match Works

When you work in SketchUp, you create three-dimensional models using a two-dimensional tool—your computer's monitor. SketchUp provides visual clues that simulate the perspective you see in the real world and vanishing points that artists have used for centuries. The blue, red, and green axes also give you reference points, so you can identify three-dimensional directions even though you're looking at a two-dimensional computer screen. Your view of the SketchUp model is called the camera view because it's similar to looking at a scene through a camera lens.

Now consider a photograph of a building. A photo is a view of a scene through a camera lens. It's very similar to a single view within SketchUp's modeling window. Within that scene, you can probably identify a vertical line that's the same as SketchUp's blue axis line. With some photos, you may also be able to trace lines that represent the red and green axis lines. If it's easy to find axis lines in a photo, it's probably a good candidate for Photo Match.

Tip: If you can't find horizontal lines at a right angle to each other in the photograph, you may have a problem using it in Photo Match. See the next page for tips on photos that work well with Photo Match.

In a nutshell, here's how Photo Match works:

1. You take a photo of a building or other object that you want to model. The photo in Figure 10-1 is a nearly perfect candidate for Photo Match.

2. You import that photo into the SketchUp modeling window by using a special matching mode. The steps on page 353 explain how to import a photo for Photo Match.

3. Using calibration tools in matching mode, you help SketchUp identify the blue, green, and red axes in the photo. In the process, you're also helping to identify a point that's similar to the Origin point in SketchUp's modeling window. The calibration process gives SketchUp the information it needs to set up a SketchUp camera view (perspective and focal length) that matches that of the photo. On page 355, you see the steps for calibrating an image for Photo Match.

4. Once the calibration is complete, you can trace over some of the lines in the photo to create edges and faces for the three-dimensional model. The exercise on page 371 shows an example of tracing over an imported Photo Match image to create three-dimensional objects.

5. Since you already have a photo of the structure, why not use that image as a texture for the faces in the model? The quality of the results depends on the photo. For details on the process, see page 369.

6. As an alternative to using a photo texture, you may want to use the image to help you create three-dimensional features attached to your structure. The steps on page 371 give you an opportunity to do that.

Once you've created the front of your model, you'll often repeat this process to create the back faces and sometimes the top of your model.

For Photo Match to figure out the focal length for a particular camera view, it needs to identify parallel lines on both the red and green axes, and it needs to identify the *vanishing point* for those parallel lines. The classic vanishing point example is a set of train tracks. When you stand on the tracks and look down the line,

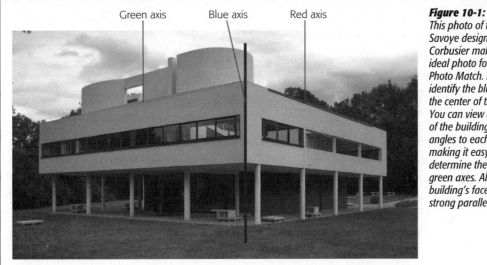

Green axis   Blue axis   Red axis

Figure 10-1:
This photo of the Villa Savoye designed by Le Corbusier makes an ideal photo for use with Photo Match. It's easy to identify the blue axis in the center of the image. You can view two faces of the building at right angles to each other, making it easy to determine the red and green axes. Also, the building's faces have strong parallel lines.

it appears that the tracks meet at some point in the distance—that's the vanishing point. (Now get off the tracks before a train comes.) SketchUp analyzes the distance between the parallel lines at different points along the axes. From these details, Photo Match can create the proper perspective and focal length for the camera view in the SketchUp modeling window.

Shooting Photos for Photo Match

You use SketchUp's Photo Match feature to help you draw a three-dimensional model using a two-dimensional photograph as a reference tool. It's not surprising that some photos work better than others. For example, a photo taken with an extremely wide angle lens may be so distorted that straight lines appear to be curved. Not helpful. If the object you want to recreate in three dimensions is very small in a photo, you may not have enough useful detail. That's often the case in photos where a building isn't the main subject. To get the best results when taking photographs for Photo Match, you need to shoot carefully and follow these guidelines:

- Keep in mind that you want to be able to identify the blue, green, and red axes within the photo.

- Photo Match works best with models that have parallel lines, like buildings with rectangular windows. SketchUp can use these lines to determine the perspective or focal length of the camera view. Roof lines may work well depending on how the roof relates to the face of the building's walls. The line where a building meets the ground is often uneven, so it's not much use.

- Shoot the building from the corner so that you can see two faces of the building. Ideally you want that corner to be in the center of the photo.

- Shoot with a normal-view lens to avoid distortion, like the equivalent of a 50mm lens on a 35mm film camera. Don't zoom in to a telephoto view or zoom way out to a wide angle or fisheye view.

- Get close enough to the building so that you shoot a reasonably high resolution image, but not so close that you have to use a wide angle lens that distorts the lines.

- Lines that are straight in the object should appear as straight lines in the photograph.

Some photos are almost always difficult to work with in Photo Match. Here are some of the types of photos that don't work and why:

- **Foreground objects blocking the view.** When using Photo Match, you need to be able to find straight, relatively long lines that run vertically and horizontally in the picture. When identifying horizontal lines, you need to find lines at right angles—think of your SketchUp models with their red and green axes.

- **Photos taken from high above or way below a building.** These angles distort the image. Ideally you want the camera and the subject to be roughly at the same level.

- **Cropped images or images where the margins are expanded.** These don't provide a true perspective, because the center of the photograph has been artificially changed. Photo Match uses the center of photographs to recreate the perspective and to determine the focal length of SketchUp camera view.

- **Perspective-corrected photos.** That is, photos where the camera's natural perspective has been changed. You might change perspective on a camera with a perspective correction lens or by adjusting the plane on special "view" cameras. You can also do this type of correction in software like Photoshop. These types of images may look great, but they don't give SketchUp the information it needs to determine perspective and focal length.

- **Spliced images.** These are panoramic images or stitched images created by splicing several photos together. The process used to create these images so that their edges match warps the images to the point that they're not useful for Photo Match.

- **Head-on images of a single face of a building.** SketchUp needs to place the blue, green, and red axes over the image. A straight-on photo of a building only provides references to two axes, making it difficult or impossible to determine the perspective and focal length for SketchUp's camera view.

- **Super high resolution images.** Such images may cause a problem because they increase the size of the SketchUp file.

Note: Bonnie Roskes' *Google SketchUp Cookbook* (O'Reilly) has some great recipes for photo match techniques.

Importing a Photo for Photo Match

After you've captured the perfect photo, according to the process described on page 351, you want to import the photo into SketchUp. In this example, you import a photo of the Villa Savoye, shown in Figure 10-1, so that it can be used with Photo Match. You can download a copy of the photo, named *villa_savoye_front.jpg*, from *http://missingmanuals.com/cds*.

1. **Open a new SketchUp document by using the "Architectural Design – Feet and Inches" template.**

   You can hide or remove Sang, the SketchUp model, from the modeling window.

2. **Choose Camera → Match New Photo.**

   The "Select background image file" window opens. In Windows it looks like Figure 10-2. Macs display a similar window for finding and opening files.

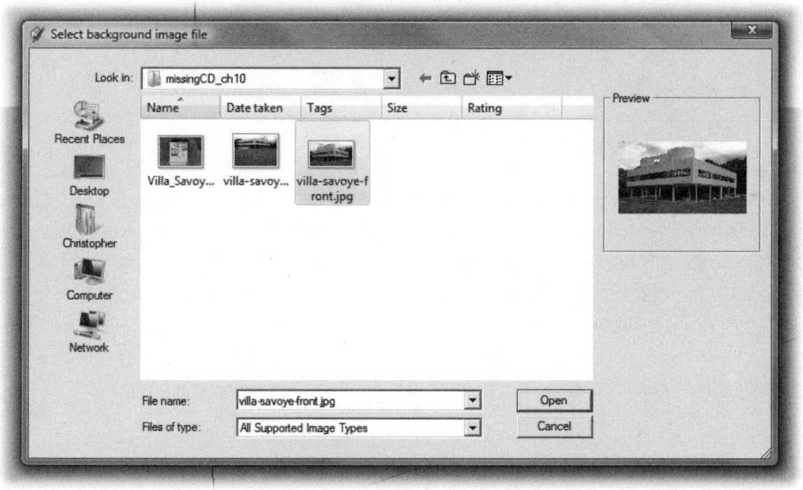

Figure 10-2:
Use the "Files of type" menu to choose a specific image format such as JPEG. To display all the types of image files that SketchUp can import, choose All Supported Image Types as shown here.

3. **Navigate to the folder holding your photos, and then select *villa_savoye_front.jpg* and click Open (Import on a Mac).**

   The imported image showing the front of Villa Savoye appears in the modeling window. A grid and several axes and control lines appear superimposed on the image as shown in Figure 10-3. The Match Photo window (Figure 10-5) automatically opens.

Figure 10-3:
When you import an image to use for Photo Match, SketchUp puts a lot of grid lines and controls over the image. Don't be intimidated; using the grid lines and controls is easier than it looks at first glance.

Note: The maximum size of an image that SketchUp can import is 1024 × 1024 pixels. SketchUp automatically shrinks files that are larger than this size when it imports them. The folks at Google say you'll get the best results by resizing images before you import them, rather than letting SketchUp do the job. They recommend using a program like Photoshop that uses a scaling method called *bicubic resampling*. As of SketchUp 7 you can override this file size limitation by going to Window → Preferences → OpenGL (SketchUp → Preferences → OpenGL) and turning on the "Use maximum texture size" checkbox. When you make this change, SketchUp warns that that this setting may slow your computer.

An Alternative Method for Importing Images

Another command you can use to import photos into SketchUp is File → Import. This option brings up a similar file browser box, but the difference is that this generic import file box lets you choose how you want to use the imported file. As shown in Figure 10-4, your options are:

- **Use as image.** This option lets you place an image anywhere in the SketchUp modeling window. It looks a little like a two-dimensional billboard. You can move it and anchor it to any location, and you can resize it with the Scale tool. Interestingly, you can view the image from either side, but the back side is a mirror image of the front.

- **Use as texture.** Choose this option when you want to load an image to be used as a texture. After you click Open (or Import on a Mac), the image is loaded in the paint bucket cursor, ready to apply to any face in SketchUp.

- **Use as New Matched Photo.** Use this option when you want to import an image to assist you in creating a three-dimensional model. SketchUp loads the image as a background, just as described in the previous steps.

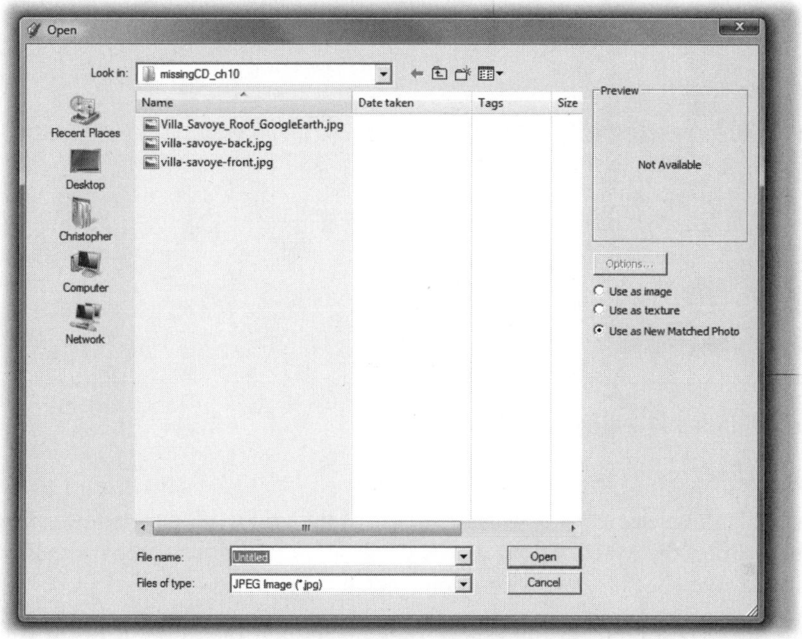

Figure 10-4:
As an alternative, you can import a photo using the File → Import command. The only difference is you need to choose how you want to use the image. Choose "Use for Photo Match" when you want to create a 3-D model using a photo as reference.

Calibrating the Photo Match Image

After you've imported an image for Photo Match, as described on page 353, the Match Photo window appears on your screen (Figure 10-5). Many of the other menu commands are grayed out, meaning you can't use them. That's the case until you click the Done button in the Match Photo window. The assumption is that the first and most important thing you need to do at this moment is to calibrate the photo. If that's not the case, you can click Done and then reopen the Match Photo window later by choosing Camera → Edit Matched Photo → *villa_savoye_front.jpg* (or the name of your imported photo).

Photo Match needs your help identifying a few key elements in your photo. Armed with that information, SketchUp can set up a camera view that matches the photo, making it easy for you to trace over the two-dimensional image to create a three-dimensional model.

Here are the elements that Photo Match needs identified:

- Origin point.
- Blue axis.

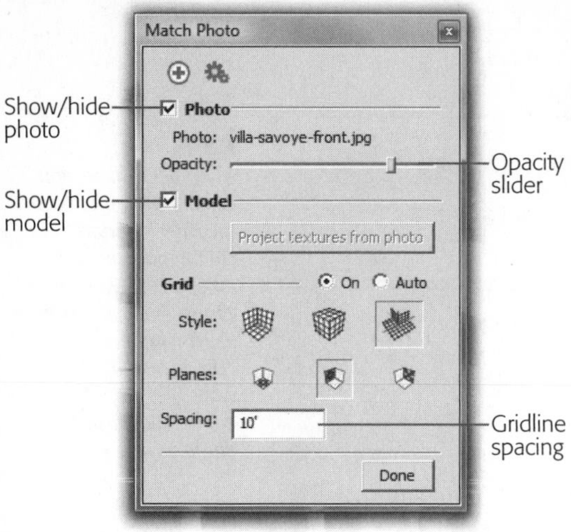

Figure 10-5:
You use the Match Photo window as you calibrate SketchUp to work with an imported photo. The settings let you show and hide the photo and your model as well as the appearance of the gridlines shown over the photo. When you choose Done, the grid disappears.

- Parallel lines on the green axis.

- Parallel lines on the red axis.

You identify these elements by dragging parts of the grid that's superimposed over the image when the Match Photo box is displayed. Follow these steps to calibrate the Villa Savoye photo for use with Photo Match:

1. **Find the Origin point in the Photo Match grid, and then drag it to the lower corner of the Villa Savoye structure, as shown in Figure 10-6.**

    As you drag the Origin, the grid rearranges itself over the image. When the Origin is in place at the corner of the building, the blue axis runs along the front corner of the building, as shown in Figure 10-6. If your mouse has a scroll wheel, it may help to zoom in to get a better view of the corner and the blue axis. You don't need to worry about any of the other lines at this point—you'll deal with them in later steps.

2. **Find the two red, dashed registration lines with the boxes on the ends. Drag the boxes to arrange the top line along the top edge of the building, as shown in Figure 10-7.**

    As you drag the control boxes, the other lines in the grid change position over the photo. For example, the blue axis pivots around the Origin point. Don't worry about the other lines, just work to get the registration in position. Once all the registration lines are in place, the rest of the grid will shape up just fine.

Tip: To quickly zoom out so you can see the entire building, right-click the picture, and then choose Zoom Matched Photo.

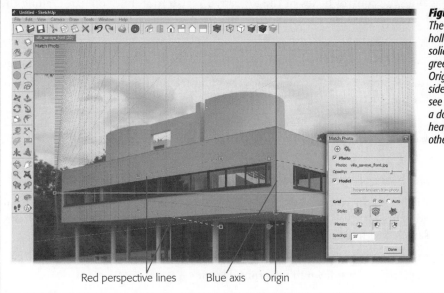

Figure 10-6:
The grid's Origin is a hollow, yellow square. A solid red and a solid green line lead into the Origin. On the opposite side of the Origin, you see a dotted red line and a dotted green line heading off in the other direction.

Red perspective lines   Blue axis   Origin

Red registration line   Control box

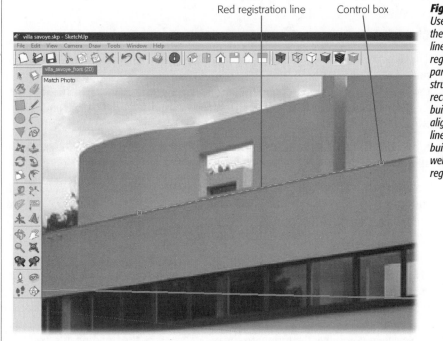

Figure 10-7:
Use the control boxes on the ends of the dashed lines to arrange the registration lines along parallel lines in the structure. The rectangular faces of the building are perfect for aligning the registration lines. The windows in this building would also work well for aligning the registration lines.

3. Drag the control boxes of the lower red registration line to align it along the bottom edge of the windows.

It's not necessary to position the boxes at the corners of the building, just align them on the edges you know to be parallel to the first line.

4. Repeat steps 2 and 3, to align the green registration lines along the other face of the building.

The purpose of positioning these registration lines is to identify two lines that you know are parallel. By identifying these lines, you give Photo Match the information it needs to position the SketchUp camera in the modeling window.

5. Double-check the alignment of the origin, and the registration lines.

At this point, you may want to zoom in on each of the lines and make small adjustments. The order doesn't matter; just make adjustments until you're satisfied with the results.

6. Move the Origin point to the right-back corner of the building, and then drag the Origin point down to the ground level.

The blue axis may not be perfectly aligned with the back corner of the building, due in part to distortion in the photo. A dotted line extends next to the columns (called *pilotis*).

7. Right-click the image and choose Rotate 90 Right.

The axes rotate 90 degrees around the Origin point. What you see depends on the original orientation of the axes around the Origin, but it's likely that one of the lines (red or green) emanating from the Origin changes from dotted to solid, making it easier to see. If you don't see a solid line, right-click and choose Rotate 90 Right a second time.

8. Move the Origin to the back corners of the building, and double-check the alignment of the axes.

You can move the Origin to different positions in the photo. When you do, you should see a red or green line emanating from the Origin. Check to see if this line is aligned with an edge in the photo, such as the bottom of Villa Savoye. If the red or green line is dotted, right-click and choose Rotate 90 Right until you see a solid line.

Adjusting the registration lines is one of those processes where you tweak the position of the lines, change your view, and tweak a little bit more. Some photos are easier to work with than others, but you'll seldom get everything lined up perfectly. It's just the nature of photos and camera lenses to introduce some distortion into pictures. For example, when you move the Origin to the back corners of the building, it's likely that the blue axis line will be slightly skewed. Still it's worthwhile spending some time to do the best you can with your image.

Adjusting the Grid

Measurements are important in SketchUp whether you create a model from scratch or from a photo. When you type *20'* in the Measurements toolbar, you want SketchUp to respond accurately. So when you're creating a model from a photograph and Photo Match is setting up the camera view, how do you set the scale for measurement? You do that by adjusting the grid that's superimposed over the photo to match something of known height.

In addition to the thicker axis lines, you see lighter, dotted grid lines over the photo. These grid lines form squares, like graph paper, along the axes in the modeling window. By setting the grid spacing in the Match Photo box, you establish the measurement system for the model. Sometimes you know exact dimensions of a building, and other times you may have to make an estimate from the photograph. With Villa Savoye, you can estimate that the height from the ground to the top wall is about 20–22 feet. To adjust the grid, you tell SketchUp the size each square represents. Then in the photo, you adjust the grid itself to match. It's easier to understand by actually doing it. Assuming that the height of Villa Savoye is 20 feet, here are the steps:

1. **Drag the Origin back to the right-back corner of the building.**

   The right-back corner gives you a clear view of the height of the building. Place the Origin all the way down on the ground for this operation.

2. **In the Match Photo window, type *20'*.**

   Remember to enter the unit symbol for feet, otherwise SketchUp assumes you're talking inches.

3. **Drag the blue axis line so that one square in the grid reaches from the ground to the top of the wall, as shown in Figure 10-8.**

   When your cursor is over the blue axis line, it changes to a double arrow. When you drag, the axis line doesn't actually move, but the size of the grid squares grows or shrinks, depending on the direction of the drag. You know that one corner of the grid begins at the Origin, so you want to position the next horizontal line at the top of the wall.

Tip: Sometimes it's difficult to see the grid lines over a photo. In addition to whatever is going on in the photo, you see axis lines and the registration lines, which appear brighter and bolder than the grid lines. If you're having trouble seeing the grid lines, use the Opacity slider in the Match Photo window. Drag the slider to the left. As the photo disappears it becomes easier to see the grid lines.

---

4. **In the Match Photo window readjust the Opacity of the photo and then click Done.**

   If you made changes to the opacity of the photo, you want to bring it back to its fully opaque glory for the next exercise, "Applying an Image to a Model" on page 369. Adjusting the grid is the last step for calibrating the photo, so when you choose Done, the grid and all the other calibration apparatus disappear.

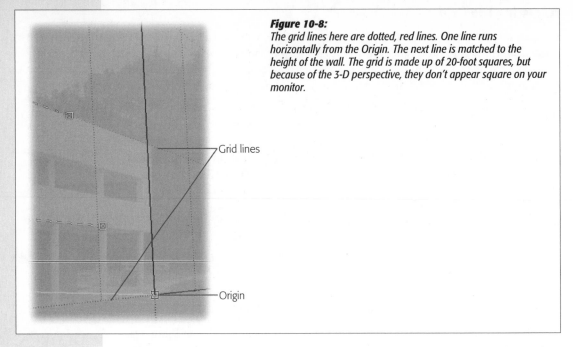

Figure 10-8:
The grid lines here are dotted, red lines. One line runs horizontally from the Origin. The next line is matched to the height of the wall. The grid is made up of 20-foot squares, but because of the 3-D perspective, they don't appear square on your monitor.

Grid lines

Origin

The Match Photo window is still on the screen, but its name is changed to Sketch Over.

If you need to bring it back later for adjustments, choose Camera → Edit Matched Photo. You can also click the gears icon in the upper-left corner of the Sketch Over window.

With the grid properly adjusted, you can use the measurements that appear in the Measurements toolbar as references. And you can be confident that when you type measurements for dimensions, moves, and push/pull operations, they'll be to scale.

Building a Model from a Picture

With the SketchUp modeling window and camera view all set up, you can create a three-dimensional model by tracing over the picture. Always begin your Photo Match modeling at the Origin and build from there. If you start drawing at some other point, it's deceptively easy to create entities that look good from one angle, but are actually way off in space. In the case of the Villa Savoye, you have a photo of the back of the building, too (*villa_savoye_back.jpg*). To use both the front and back images, you need a common reference point. The right-back corner in the front image works well, because you can see it in both photos.

Villa Savoye is obligingly rectangular, so the best tool to grab is the Rectangle tool. You draw the back wall, and then using the Push/Pull tool, you can create a box the size of the building by using the reference points in the photo.

Follow these steps to build your Villa Savoye model:

1. **With the Rectangle (R), click the Origin, and then draw a rectangle for the back wall of Villa Savoye as shown in Figure 10-9.**

   Your rectangle looks distorted because of the perspective. At this point, you can just make a rough guess about the location of the hidden back corner of the building. The important thing is that the rectangle is on the back plane.

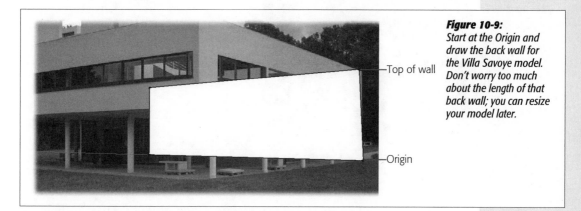

—Top of wall

—Origin

Figure 10-9:
Start at the Origin and draw the back wall for the Villa Savoye model. Don't worry too much about the length of that back wall; you can resize your model later.

2. **With the Pan (H) tool, drag to move the photo and the model. Then with the Orbit (Q) tool, drag to change the camera view.**

   When you use the Pan (H) tool or the Zoom (Z) tool to reposition the model and the picture, you remain in the Sketch Over view, and the photo is still visible. However, if you use the Orbit or one of the other view tools, the photo disappears. That happens because you've moved the position of SketchUp's camera.

3. **In the upper-left corner, above the modeling window, click the name of the photo, *villa_savoye_front.jpg.***

   When you click the name of the photo, the image returns and SketchUp moves the camera back to the Sketch Over position. The words "Sketch Over" appear beneath the photo's name, as shown in Figure 10-10.

4. **With Push/Pull (P), click the face of the rectangle, and pull the face to the front edge of the building.**

   Match the top-front corner of the box with the building in the photo. You can hide the model by turning on the Model checkbox in the Sketch Over window. The Sketch Over window and the Match Photo window are the same beast. There's just a different name at the top of the window, depending on what you're doing. If the Sketch Over window isn't visible, you can bring it back with Window → Photo Match.

Tip: It may be helpful to change to X-ray view as you're extruding the box with Push/Pull.

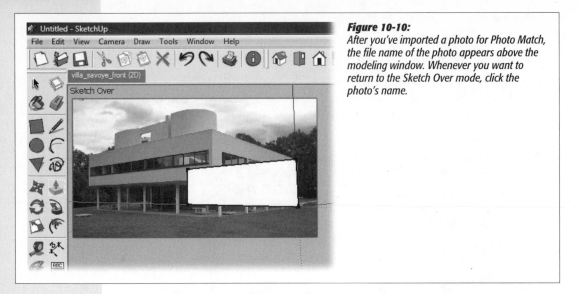

Figure 10-10:
After you've imported a photo for Photo Match, the file name of the photo appears above the modeling window. Whenever you want to return to the Sketch Over mode, click the photo's name.

5. In the Sketch Over window, click the button named "Project textures from photo".

The image from the photo is superimposed on the faces of the box, as shown in Figure 10-11. In the figure, the box extends beyond the edge of the photo. This problem occurred because in step 1 it was hard to figure out exactly where the hidden back corner was. It's not a big problem, though, because you can easily fix it with the Push/Pull tool.

Figure 10-11:
Here the photo is projected onto the two faces of the box. The Opacity slider is adjusted so that the part of the photo not projected on the box is faded. Notice how the left side of the box extends beyond the edge of the building.

6. **Orbit around to get a view of the left side of the box; then use the Push/Pull tool to adjust the box's size.**

When you change view, the background photo disappears, but the image projected on the box remains (Figure 10-12), which makes it easy to resize the box to fit the image. If the top or other sides of the box need adjusting, you can make those changes now.

Note: Some parts of the photo such as the columns (pilotis) may appear distorted, and the corners may not match up perfectly. Most photos have some degree of distortion. You can improve some of these problems with small tweaks. In the case of the pilotis, it makes sense to create 3-D models rather than using the image.

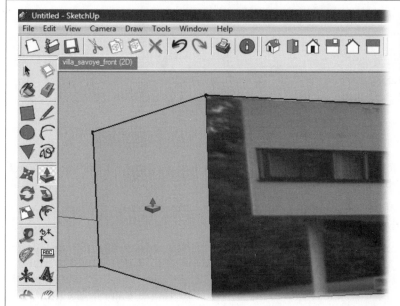

Figure 10-12:
With the photo projected onto the box, it's easy to resize the box to match the photo. Here the Push/Pull tool is moving the face to match the end of the building in the photo.

7. **Use the Orbit (Q) tool to maneuver around to the back of the building.**

Find an angle that shows the back corner centered in the window, with both faces that were previously hidden now in view.

8. **In the Sketch Over window, click the New Matched Photo button.**

The New Matched Photo button looks like a + sign. When you click the button, a file browser window appears. In Windows it looks like Figure 10-13.

9. **Find the photo file *villa_savoye_back.jpg* and click the Open button.**

The photo of the back of Villa Savoye appears as the background in the SketchUp modeling window along with the calibration grid. Now two photo file names appear as tabs above the modeling window.

New Matched Photo

Figure 10-13:
*Using the New Matched
Photo button, you can
add more than one
photo to a SketchUp
document. Here a photo
of the back side of Villa
Savoye is added.*

10. **In the Sketch Over window, turn on the checkbox next to Model.**

Your model, which at this point is a basic box, disappears. Don't worry; you'll bring it back later.

11. **Repeat the steps to calibrate this image (described on page 355) and to adjust the grid (described on page 359).**

This image for the back side of the building needs to be calibrated to the SketchUp model. The steps to do so are identical to the steps used to calibrate the first image. Line up the red and green registration lines on parallel lines in the photo. Move the Origin to the same corner used to calibrate the front view. From the back, that's the left corner. You don't have to enter a new grid size in the Match Photo window, because SketchUp remembers the grid size. You do have to drag the blue axis to adjust the grid in this view to match this image.

12. **After you've calibrated the photo, turn on the Model checkbox in the Match Photo window.**

The box reappears and it should match pretty closely with the photo as shown in the bottom of Figure 10-14. If necessary, you can make adjustments to the model or to the photo calibration.

13. **Click the "Project textures from photo" button.**

The image from the back of the building is projected on the back sides of the box.

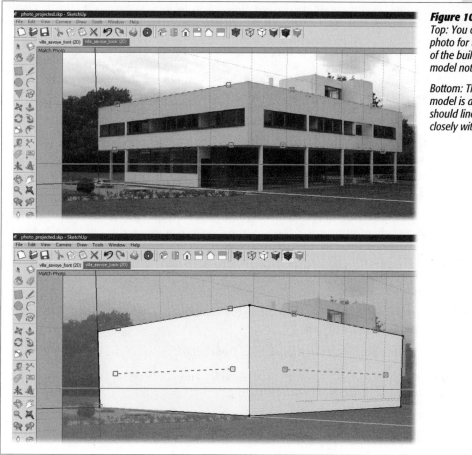

Figure 10-14:
Top: You calibrate the photo for the back side of the building with the model not displayed.

Bottom: Then when the model is displayed, it should line up pretty closely with the photo.

14. Use the Orbit (Q) tool to view your model from different sides.

You can continue to tweak the model and the way it's projected over the box.

- To reposition the image over the box, click the Edit Matched Photo button (it looks like gears) in the Sketch Over window. Then adjust the green and red registration lines.

- To resize the box, use the Push/Pull tool on one of the faces.

At this point, you have a box that's dressed up with the projection of photos on four faces. It's not perfect, but it shows promise.

Adding 3-D Details to Your Model

Sometimes photo projection doesn't give you satisfactory results, and you're better off using your 3-D modeling skills. That's the case with the bottom portion of Villa Savoye. The pilotis look okay when you view them from the original angle of the photo, but as you rotate the image, they begin to look skewed, due to the distortion of the photograph. Cylindrical columns aren't hard to produce and copy in SketchUp, so you're better off recreating them. That way they'll look good from every angle.

1. **Using the Orbit tool, change the view so you can see the bottom of the model. Then with Push/Pull push the bottom of the box up.**

   Align the bottom of the box with the bottom edge of the building. When you're done, none of the columns is visible.

2. **With the Circle (C) tool, begin to draw a circle on the bottom of the box, near the corner, and then type *4*.**

   Your circle has a 4-inch radius, which, with the help of Push/Pull, you can turn into columns that are 8 inches in diameter. You don't have to worry too much about where you create the column—later you'll use the photo to help you position it.

3. **Using Push/Pull, begin to pull the bottom of the column down, and then click the Origin.**

   By clicking the Origin, you align the bottom of the column with the ground level, as shown in Figure 10-15.

4. **Click the photo name *villa_savoye_front (2D)*.**

   The background photo becomes visible, and the view changes to the Sketch Over view of the front of the building.

5. **With the Move (M) tool, position the column at the front of the building.**

   Move the column so that it's directly over the column in the photo.

Tip: When you notice differences between your model and the background photograph, make your decisions based on your end-product. Here it's more important that the columns are lined up properly with the model than that they're exactly lined up with the columns in the photo. You're using the photo as a reference, but you don't have to follow it slavishly.

---

6. **Still using the Move (M) tool, press and release the Ctrl (Option) key. Then move a copy of the column to the left corner of the model.**

   If necessary use one of the arrow keys to lock the movement along an axis. Place the copy over the image of the column in the photograph.

7. **Before doing anything else, type 4/ and press Enter.**

   SketchUp creates an array, so you have five columns, or pilotis, along the front of the villa. (To create an array, type the number and the divide sign immediately after making a copy.)

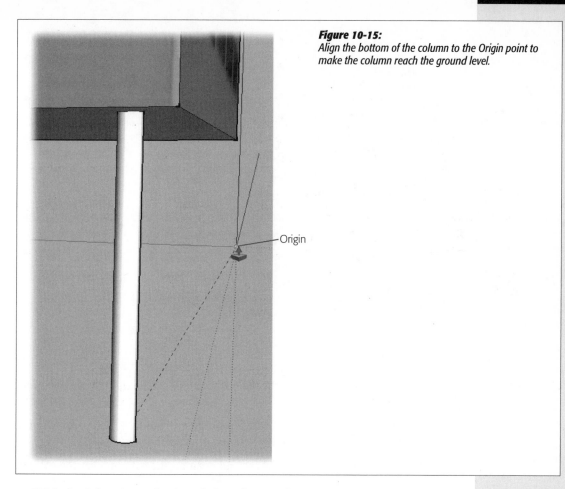

Origin

8. **With the Select (space bar) tool, drag from right to left over the bottom of the
column at the front corner.**

    The column displays a selection highlight. By dragging the selection window
    from right to left, you select any entities partially within the selection window.
    This movement selects the entire column.

9. **Press Shift as you drag from right to left over the column on the left corner.**

    The columns on both ends are now selected, as shown in Figure 10-16.

10. **Click the tab with the photo name "villa_savoye_back (2D)".**

    The view changes to the Sketch Over view of the back of the building. You can
    see the five columns, because the model appears over the photograph. The two
    columns on the ends are still selected.

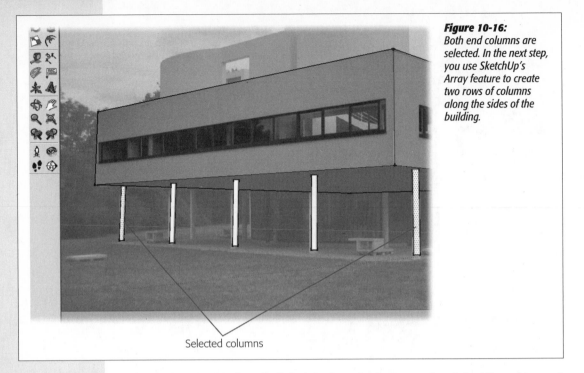

Figure 10-16:
Both end columns are selected. In the next step, you use SketchUp's Array feature to create two rows of columns along the sides of the building.

Selected columns

11. **With the Move (M) tool, click the selected column on the right. Then press and release Ctrl (Option).**

    Pressing the toggle key puts the Move tool in copy mode. When you move the cursor, copies of both the selected columns move with the cursor.

12. **Move to the back corner of the house and position the column over the column in the photo. Then click.**

    When you click the photo, you place two columns at the back of the house.

13. **Type 4/ and then press Enter.**

    SketchUp creates an array of columns along both sides of the house.

14. **Use the Orbit (Q) tool to examine the column placement.**

    You see five columns placed at the front of the building and two rows of columns along the sides. The placement of the columns should be uniform.

If the columns are all properly positioned, great! You're ready to head up to the roof to do some more work. If you're not happy with the columns, you can select and reposition some of them or start over. Remember that there's always a little distortion in the photos. So if you weren't happy with placing some of the columns directly over the columns in the photos, make some adjustments when you try again.

Applying an Image to a Model

You may have noticed from the photo that a lot is going on up on the roof at Villa Savoye, which has some interesting curved walls and openings. The Front and Back view don't give you the whole picture, but Google Earth satellites do. In this next section, you apply a photo of the roof to the top of your model. Then you use the image to help you recreate that detail on the top of the villa. Instead of importing this image as a matched photo, you import it as a texture:

1. Click the "villa_savoye_front (2D) tab".

   When you change your view in the next step, the photo disappears, but remember which side of the building is the front with the curved walls.

2. Use the Orbit (Q) tool to view the roof of the building.

   Rotate the view so that the front of the building is pointed toward the bottom of your computer screen.

3. Choose File → Import.

   A file browser window opens. In Windows it looks like Figure 10-17.

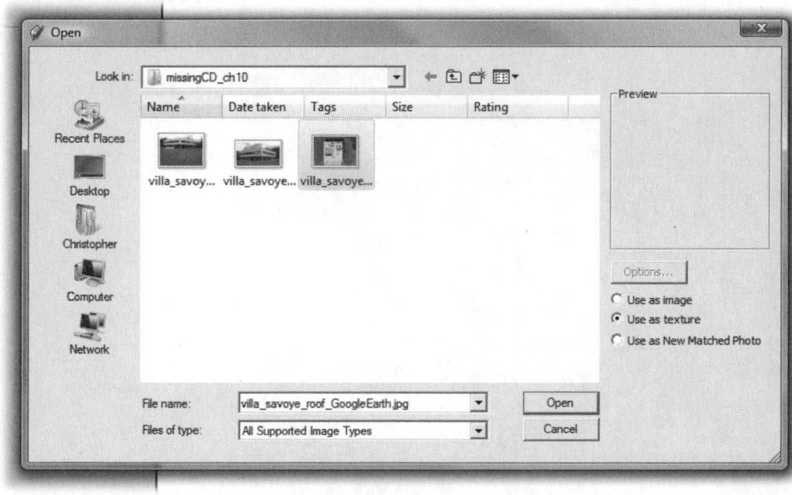

Figure 10-17:
You can import the photo of the roof as a texture file. This way, you don't have to calibrate it, but you do have to resize it and position it on the roof of the model.

4. Find and select the file named *villa_savoye_roof_GoogleEarth.jpg*. Click the "Use as texture" radio button and then click Open.

   The image you're importing is attached to the cursor.

   If you don't see the file where you saved it, make sure the "Files of type" menu (Format on a Mac) is set to either JPEG or All Supported Image Types.

5. **Click the roof's upper-left corner and then click its right edge.**

   The first click anchors one corner of the image. The second click applies the texture to the face of the roof. The photo isn't oriented or sized properly.

6. **With the Select tool, right-click the photo and choose Texture → Position.**

   The imported photo is tiled on the screen. You see pushpin markers at the corners of the image (Figure 10-18). Each of the pins is a different color and has an icon next to it. One icon, a cross with four arrows, looks like the Move tool. Drag that icon to move the image on the screen. Another icon is a circle. Click that icon to rotate the image. The last two icons show skewed rectangles. You can use these controls to change the photo's orientation to the face of the roof.

Tip: After you use one of the position tools, SketchUp returns to its standard modeling mode. If you want to make more changes to the texture image's position, use the Select tool to right-click the photo, and choose Texture → Position again.

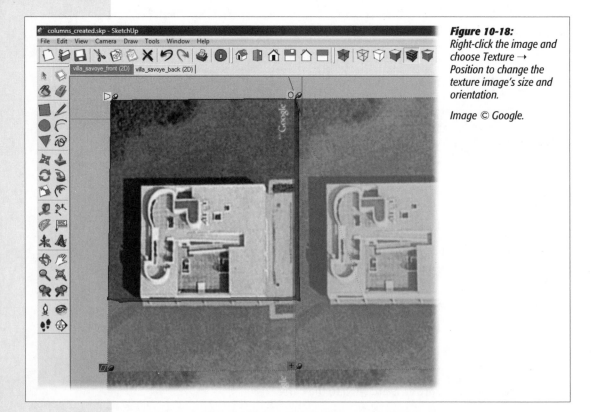

Figure 10-18:
Right-click the image and choose Texture → Position to change the texture image's size and orientation.

Image © Google.

7. **Click the circle icon and spin the image so that the curved walls face the bottom of the computer screen.**

   When you click the Rotate icon, a protractor style tool appears, making it easy to tell when you've rotated the image 90 degrees.

8. **With the Select tool, right-click the image and choose Texture → Position.**

   The tiled image appears again. Pushpins mark the corners of one of the images.

9. **Right-click once more and then click Fixed Pin.**

   The fixed pin mode is deselected, and the checkmark next to Fixed Pin disappears. This means you're in free-pin mode and can reposition the pushpins.

Tip: In free-pin mode, you can move the pins to different positions in the photo by using the click-move-click method. To position a pinned point of the image on a particular point of your model, drag the pin. First you click-move-click to mark positions in the photo. Then you drag to stretch the image into position over your model.

---

10. **Click one of the pushpins, and then click again at the corner of the roof in the image. Place each of the pins on a different corner of the roof.**

    You move the pins using the click-move-click method. When you're finished, the four pins mark the corners of the roof in the image.

11. **Drag the pin next to the Move icon to the nearest corner of the model. Drag each of the pins to the corner of the model.**

    As you drag the pins, the image twists and distorts, but when you're finished, the photo of the roof is positioned on top of the model, as shown in Figure 10-19.

12. **Right-click and then choose Done from the shortcut menu.**

    When you click Done, you return to SketchUp's standard model editing mode. The Villa Savoye has images applied to all four sides and the roof, as shown in Figure 10-20.

Tip: If you make a mistake while positioning a texture, it's best to right-click (⌘-click) and choose either Undo or Reset. If you use Ctrl+Z (⌘-Z) to undo, you lose the entire positioning operation and have to start from scratch.

Creating 3-D Details from a Texture Image

The photo creates a fine map of the top of the building when you look straight down from the sky—that's the Google satellite view. It doesn't do much for the model when viewed from the ground level. So, this is another case where it makes sense to use the image as a guide to model three-dimensional elements.

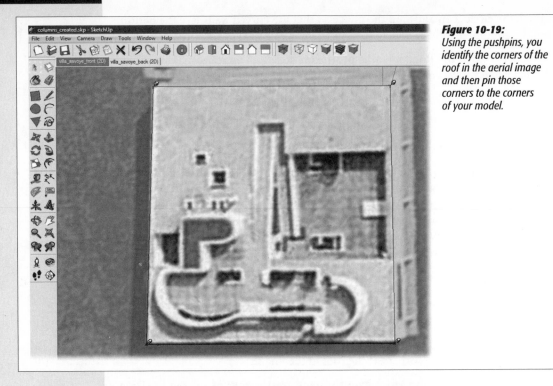

Figure 10-19:
Using the pushpins, you identify the corners of the roof in the aerial image and then pin those corners to the corners of your model.

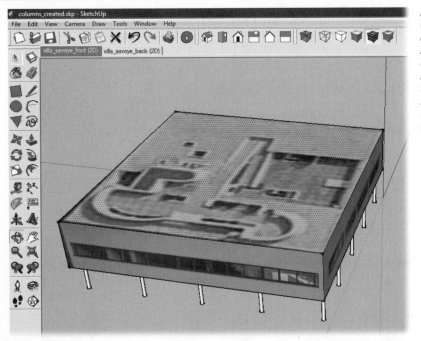

Figure 10-20:
Once the texture image is applied and positioned, it looks like this. In some cases just applying an image may be enough. In this case you can use the image as a reference for creating 3-D details for the Villa Savoye model.

You've learned earlier in the book all of the SketchUp skills required to build up the wall on top of the Villa Savoye. You need to use the Line and Arc tools (page 57), the Offset tool (page 144), and the Push/Pull tool (page 103).

- Use the Line (L) and Arc (A) tools to trace the lines of the roof wall.

- Shift-click with the Select (space bar) tool to select all the lines except for the "P" shape.

- Use the Offset tool to offset the lines 6 inches.

- Use the Line tool to connect the ends of the two lines.

- Select the "P" shaped portion of the wall.

- Use the Offset tool to create new lines 6 inches inside the "P" shape (Figure 10-21).

- Use the Eraser to remove the inside lines of the wall.

- Use the Push/Pull tool to pull the wall up. Click the "villa_savoye_front (2D)" tab, and then use the photo as a guide for the height of the wall.

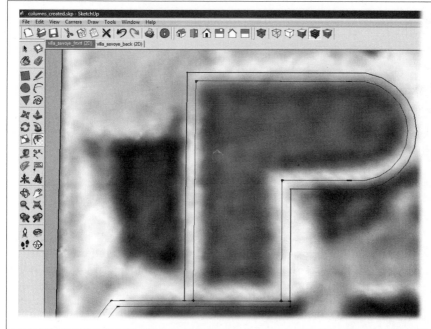

Figure 10-21:
To create the walls on top of Villa Savoye, you trace a single-line outline of the walls with the Line and Arc tools. Then using the Offset tool, you can create walls that are 6 inches thick and that are ready to Push/Pull up to their proper height.

While you're in Sketch Over view, you could right-click the wall surfaces and then choose Project Photo to create a texture for the roof walls. The problem is the photo textures don't work that well for these surfaces, especially when you view the model from different angles. A better choice is to select the wall surfaces and then to use the paint bucket to paint the walls white.

Creating 3-D Details for the Bottom of Villa Savoye

You can add detail to the bottom of the building, too. Start off by orbiting around to view the bottom; then draw a rectangle at the back. Start your rectangle on the edge where there are no columns, and draw it back toward the middle of the building. Use Push/Pull to pull the bottom so that it's aligned with the bottom of the columns, as shown in Figure 10-22.

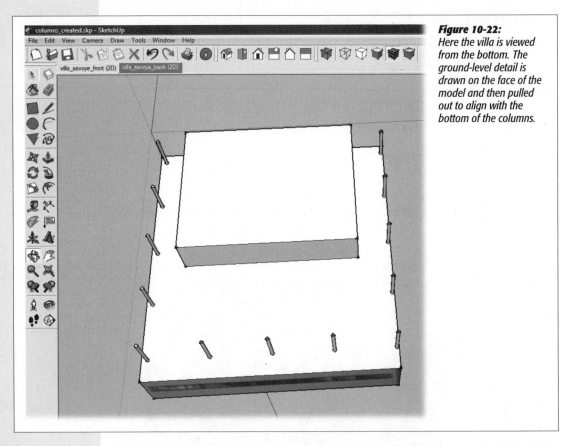

Figure 10-22:
Here the villa is viewed from the bottom. The ground-level detail is drawn on the face of the model and then pulled out to align with the bottom of the columns.

Click the "villa_savoye_back (2D)" tab to see the new detail from the back of the building. Some of the faces show the photo projected on the new geometry. If you want to project the image on additional faces, preselect the face with the Select (space bar) tool. Then right-click the face and choose Project Photo. See Figure 10-23.

Use the Push/Pull tool to position the walls of the ground floor. The photo gives you clues for the position of the walls. The ground floor has a curve at the front of the building. Draw a curve with the Arc tool, and then use Push/Pull to align the new section with the rectangular section (Figure 10-24).

Figure 10-23:
You can project the photo image onto the faces at the bottom of the building, even if the faces are set in from the other walls. Use Push/Pull to adjust the geometry of the model to match the building.

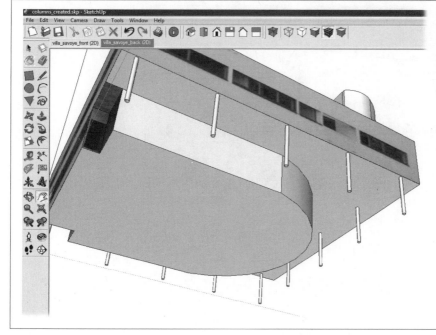

Figure 10-24:
The ground floor of Villa Savoye is curved at the front of the building as you can see in this view from the bottom of the building.

When you're done, you can view your model in Sketch Over view with the photo in the background (top: Figure 10-25). Or you can view it as a model with photo textures applied to some of the surfaces, as shown at the bottom of Figure 10-25.

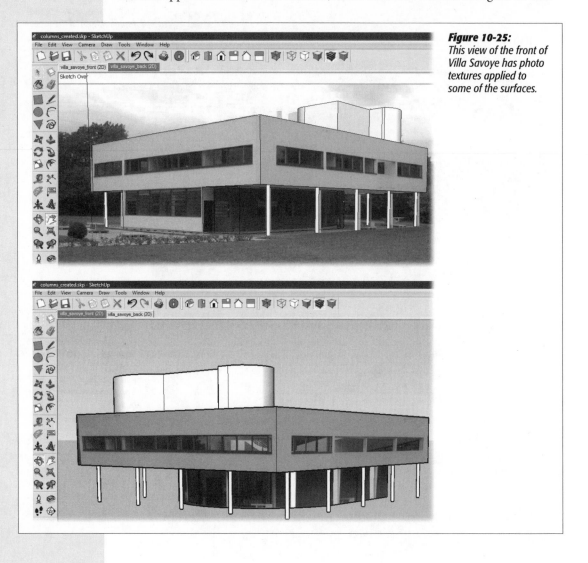

Figure 10-25:
This view of the front of Villa Savoye has photo textures applied to some of the surfaces.

Finding Models with Photo Textures

If you're interested in seeing some other models that use photo textures, just head over to Google's 3D Warehouse *http://sketchup.google.com/3dwarehouse/*. Browse through the collections where you'll find buildings, cities, furniture, people, and cars. Check out some of the "Cities in Development" in the 3D Building Collections. Inside you'll find many examples of simple models that use photo textures to give the appearance of detail. You can download models and examine them in SketchUp (Figure 10-26). You can see more details on using the 3D Warehouse on page 451.

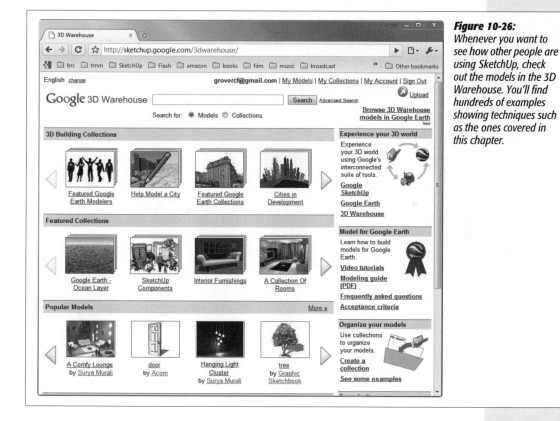

Figure 10-26:
Whenever you want to see how other people are using SketchUp, check out the models in the 3D Warehouse. You'll find hundreds of examples showing techniques such as the ones covered in this chapter.

Part Four:
Adding Realism
and Movement

4

Adding Shadows and Placing Your Model in Google Earth

As mentioned earlier, some challenges come with using a two-dimensional tool (your computer screen) to build and display three-dimensional models. This chapter focuses on a great, easy-to-use tool that makes it easier to meet the challenge and makes your models look great—shadows. You may not think about it in your day-to-day life, but shadows provide a ton of visual information about distance, position, and depth. You instinctively process that information to cope with your three-dimensional environment. By adding shadows to your SketchUp models, you communicate valuable messages to your audience in a way that they instinctively understand. And of course those shadows make your models look oh-so-much cooler.

The good news is that SketchUp shadows are easy to add. You don't need to pull out a No. 2 pencil and laboriously add shading at just the right angles to your model. You don't even have to add and position light sources in your 3-D modeling window (as you do with other 3-D graphics programs). In SketchUp, adding shadows to your model is almost as easy as flicking a light switch.

Flicking the Light Switch

SketchUp has a single light source: the sun. It's either on or it's off. This simplifies using light and shadows, but you may be surprised about the level of control you have over the results. You can control the angle of shadows (page 384), and you can control the strength of the shadows (page 391). You can even control the way individual edges, faces, groups, and components cast and display shadows by using the Entity Info window (page 392).

Before moving on to those issues, here's the user manual for flicking on the sun:

Note: This chapter uses the Villa Savoye model that was the subject of Chapter 10. You can use your own model from those exercises, or you can download *villa_savoye_ch11_begin.skp* from *http:// missingmanuals.com/cds*.

---

1. **Open *villa_savoye_ch11_begin.skp*.**

   The Villa Savoye model opens in your modeling window.

Note: You can use whatever SketchUp style (Window → Styles) you want with shadows for different effects. The style shown in Figure 11-2 is the Simple style found under Default Styles. Styles are covered in detail on page 193.

---

2. **Choose Window → Shadows.**

   The Shadow Settings window opens, as shown in Figure 11-1. At the top you see a checkbox named Display Shadows. It has two sliders: Time and Date. Next to the sliders are text boxes displaying the time and date information.

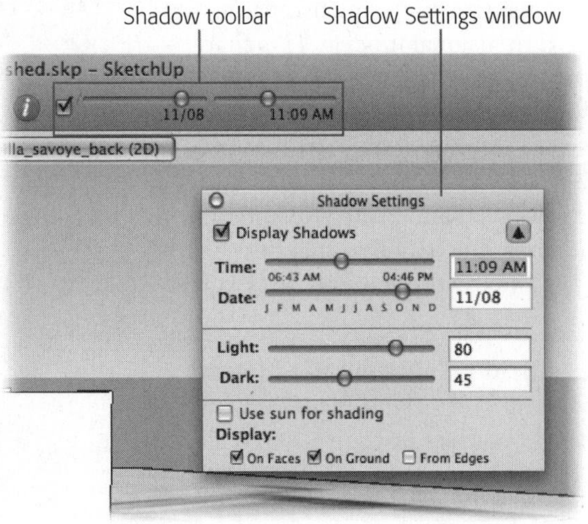

Figure 11-1:
You can manage your shadows with the Shadow Settings window, or you can display a special Shadow toolbar. The toolbar doesn't provide all the shadow settings, but it does let you turn shadows on and off, and control the shadow angle by setting the time and date.

3. **At the top of the Shadow Settings window, turn on the Display Shadows checkbox.**

   That's it! You flicked the switch and the light (sun) turned on. Parts of your model display shadows on SketchUp's virtual ground plane, as shown in Figure 11-2. You may want to orbit around your model to appreciate the shadow from different angles.

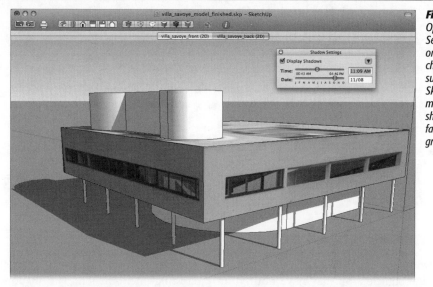

Figure 11-2:
*Open the Shadow
Settings window and turn
on the Display Shadows
checkbox to turn on the
sun. Most of the
SketchUp faces in your
model automatically cast
shadows on the other
faces and on SketchUp's
ground plane.*

UP TO SPEED

Adding Shadow Control to Your Toolbar

If you plan to do a lot of shadow tweaking, you may find it handy to add the Shadow toolbar to your SketchUp workspace. The toolbar lets you turn shadows on and off, and lets you adjust the shadow angle by setting the time and date. For more detailed controls, you need to use the Shadow Settings box.

The toolbar looks a little different on Macs (Figure 11-1) and on Windows (Figure 11-3). The process for adding the toolbar is slightly different, too.

For Windows, go to View → Toolbars → Shadow. The Shadow toolbar appears with your other toolbars. You can drag the tab on the left side of the toolbar to position it in your workspace. You can drag your toolbars away from their docking position and use them like floating palettes.

For Mac, go to View → Customize Toolbar to open the toolbar options. The Shadow tools are in the top row. Drag the tools to a spot at the top of the SketchUp document window. Then click Done. Once you've done that, you'll see the Shadow tools every time you create a new document.

Figure 11-3:
You can manage your shadows with the Shadow Settings window, or you can display a special Shadows toolbar. On PCs, the Shadow toolbar looks like this.

Limitations of SketchUp Shadows

Having a single light source puts some limitations on SketchUp shadows. Other 3-D programs let you place lights where you want them and direct that light in different ways. With more complicated lighting and shadow systems, you can, for example, have a car with shining headlights or a lamp on a table to cast light. When your only light is the sun and there's no way to reposition it, you face obvious limitations. One of those problems is lighting the interior of a building. Some of the common workarounds are either to hide the roof or to apply a material with less than 70 percent opacity to the roof.

On top of the limitations, there's a phenomenon that some SketchUp users call the "infamous shadow error". When SketchUp's camera is entirely within a shadow, as it is in most interiors, other shadows may appear inverted, fragmented, or just plain wrong. When this occurs, the only solution is to move the camera outside of the shadow.

Changing Shadow Angles

If you occasionally abandon your computer screen and explore the world outside of the cubicle, you may have noticed an interesting phenomenon. The shadows created by the sun change their size, shape, and location depending on the time of day and the day of the year. It's remarkably different from that fluorescent lighting in the cubicle. The world inside the SketchUp modeling window is like the great outdoors. Shadows change according to the time, and you, the architect of the 3-D SketchUp universe, get to control time, space, and the way your shadows look. Kidding aside, time of day is a very convenient way to control shadows. Lots of SketchUp models are buildings that already exist or that are in the planning stages, so the angle of light and the path of shadows play a big part in planning and design. For example, you want sun decks and patios to take advantage of sunny summer days. You want certain windows and skylights to let the warming sun through in the winter, but shield you from excess heat in the summer. You can study these effects in your SketchUp model.

For models that aren't anchored to a particular spot, the location, date, and time of day may not be critical. Still, for those models, it's easy to control the angle of shadows using the Time and Date controls and by rotating the model inside SketchUp.

Changing Shadows Using Time Controls

If you haven't already experimented with the Time slider, go ahead and drag it now. Position it all the way to the left, and your model turns dark. Nudge it slightly from the left, and the shadows take on the appearance of sunrise (Figure 11-4). The time for sunrise is displayed beneath the slider. Drag the slider to the right, and you pass through the middle of the day until you reach sunset. The time for sunset is displayed on the right of the slider. If you prefer to type in a specific time, just click in the box to the right of the time slider, and type a time such as *3:10 PM*.

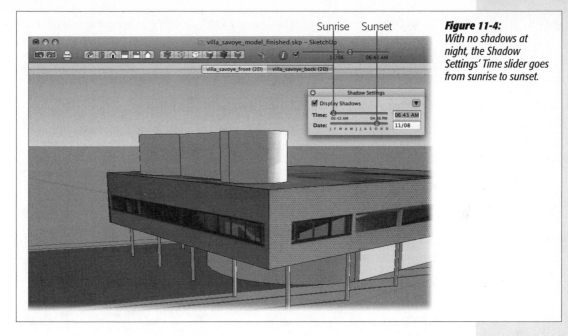

Sunrise   Sunset

Figure 11-4:
*With no shadows at
night, the Shadow
Settings' Time slider goes
from sunrise to sunset.*

The Date slider works in the same manner. Drag the slide back and forth, and you see the seasonal changes in the shadow. If you prefer, you can type in a specific date such as the summer solstice for the northern hemisphere: *06/21*. Your model takes on the appearance it would have on the shortest day of the year.

Changing Shadows by Changing Location

The actual moment in time is just one factor determining the angle of shadows. The model's location on the face of the planet is another. As far as SketchUp is concerned, every model is located at a specific geographic location identified by longitude and latitude. (It's latitude that really affects the shadow angle, while the longitude affects sunrise and sunset for different time zones.) If you haven't made any changes, SketchUp starts your model off in Boulder, Colorado. Why Boulder? That was the hometown of @Last Software, the company that originally developed SketchUp.

Here are the steps for changing the geographic location of your model:

1. **Choose Window → Model Info.**

   The Model Info window stores all sorts of details related to the SketchUp document with the Villa Savoye model (Figure 11-5). On the left side of the Model Info window, you see different info categories such as Animation, Dimensions, and Location.

Tip: The Model Info details are specific to a single SketchUp document, but you can store details inside of a SketchUp template so you don't have to make the same changes every time you start a model. For example, if most of your models are located in Bangor, Maine, you can save that information in your template. For details on templates see page 23.

2. **On the left side of the Model Info window, click Location.**

   The Model Info window changes to display Location settings, including Country, Location, Latitude, and Longitude.

3. **Under Geographic Location, click the Country drop-down menu and choose France.**

   The Country setting changes to France, and you may notice an immediate change in the angle of the shadows in your model. Another change takes place, but you won't see it until you click the menu—the names in the Location menu change to show specific cities and places in France.

4. **Click the Location drop-down menu and choose Paris.**

   The Location changes to Paris, and you may notice changes in the shadows in your model.

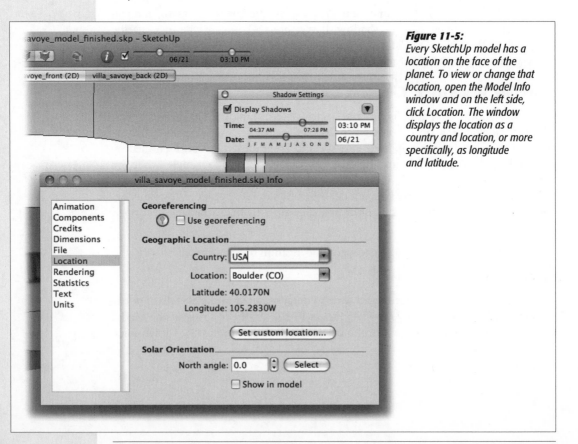

Figure 11-5:
Every SketchUp model has a location on the face of the planet. To view or change that location, open the Model Info window and on the left side, click Location. The window displays the location as a country and location, or more specifically, as longitude and latitude.

When you choose a Country and Location from the drop-down menus, SketchUp fills in the longitude and latitude details for you. On the other hand, if you have a specific longitude and latitude, you can provide the details and bypass the Country and Location menus. Just click the "Set custom location" button. A new window appears, like the one in Figure 11-6. When you set a custom location, you have the option of providing a country and name for the location. Use the drop-down menu at the bottom of the box to set a time zone for the location.

Tip: Need to find the longitude and latitude for a city or famous place? The Web can give you an answer quickly. Google is a great place to start. Lots of directories include geographic location details, and of course Google Earth and Wikipedia often have the information you need.

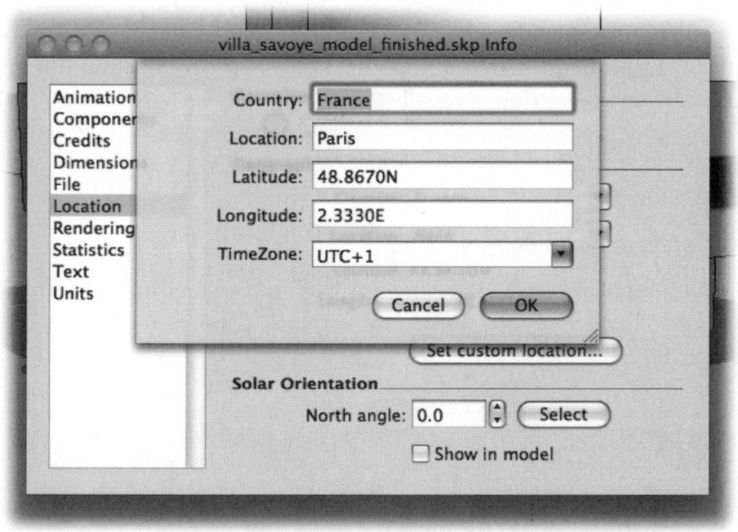

Figure 11-6:
If you have the longitude and latitude for your model's location, you can set a custom location. The custom location box lets you provide a country and name in addition to the geographic location.

Positioning Your Model by Pointing North

If you want to accurately study shadows and light, your building, landscaping, and other structures need to be properly oriented to the compass. For this to work, SketchUp needs to know which direction is north. When you first start a document, SketchUp assumes that the solid green line starting at the Origin points north. If you create your models with this in mind, you're in good shape. If you're working with an existing model, you can manually set the "North angle" option in a couple of ways:

1. **Open your model in SketchUp.**

   You can use any model for this example, including the Villa Savoye model.

---

2. **Click the Top view button (or choose Camera → Standard Views → Top).**

You don't have to use a perfect top-down view to set the north angle, but usually it's easier with a view that looks down on your model.

3. **Click the Model Info button (blue circle with the letter i) or choose Window → Model Info.**

The Model Info window stores the north angle information with the other Location details.

4. **On the left of the Model Info window, click Location.**

The Model Info window shows the location info for your model. At the top you see the Country and Location details (described in the previous section). At the bottom you see the Solar Orientation settings.

You have two ways to show SketchUp which direction is north. You can type a value in the "North angle" box, or you can draw a north-pointing line over your model. The second option is usually the easiest.

5. **Click the Select button.**

Your cursor changes to a compass.

6. **Click one point in your model.**

This point is the starting point for your north-pointing line. As you move the cursor, a rubber band line stretches from the clicked point to the cursor, as shown in Figure 11-7.

Figure 11-7:
To set the North angle manually, you create a line that points north. Here the line starts with the compass at the building's lower-right corner and stretches toward the window's upper-left side.

7. **Click a second point that is due north of the first.**

   The process is exactly like the click-move-click method you use to draw an edge in SketchUp. The difference is you're not creating a permanent, visible line in your document. After the second click, a new number appears in the North angle box, and SketchUp knows which direction is north.

8. **Turn on the "Show in model" checkbox.**

   An orange line appears in your model. It starts at the Origin and extends north. The other axes in your model, including the green axis, are unchanged.

Using Google Earth to Set Geographic Locations

SketchUp and Google Earth have a special relationship—you can use these tools together in all sorts of ways. As explained in the previous section, SketchUp uses the geographic location of a model to determine the angle of the shadows it casts. What better tool is there to determine a geographic location than Google Earth? Sure you can type the name of a country and city and get a general location for your model, but you have an even more precise way to put your model on a specific place. Here are the steps to set the location for Villa Savoye.

Note: Like SketchUp, Google Earth comes in two versions. One version is free. Google Earth Pro costs $499 and provides additional features. You can use the free version to set geographic locations in SketchUp as described in this section. To download Google Earth, go to: *http://earth.google.com*.

---

1. **In SketchUp, open the file *villa_savoye_geo_begin.skp*, and then click the Top view button.**

   This SketchUp document contains a simple model of the Villa Savoye. It's similar to the model created in Chapter 10 and used in the previous example.

2. **Start up Google Earth, and then choose View → Sidebar.**

   Make sure the word "Sidebar" is checked and that the sidebar is open on the left side of the window.

3. **In the Google Earth sidebar, in the Search pane, click the "Fly to" tab.**

   You see a text box and a button with a magnifying glass.

4. **In the text box type *Poissy, France, Villa Savoye.***

   The earth spins and Google Earth zooms in on Poissy, France. You should be close enough to identify Villa Savoye from the air.

Note: Villa Savoye is easy to find because it's a famous building. For less famous locations, you can type a street address.

---

5. **Use Google Earth view tools to change the view so that the building fills most of the window, as shown in Figure 11-8.**

   The cursor looks like a hand when it's over the image in Google Earth, and you can drag to position the image in the window. If you have a mouse with a scroll wheel, you can use that to zoom in and out on the image. Otherwise, use the slider on the right side of the window, but don't zoom in so far that the view changes to a horizontal angle.

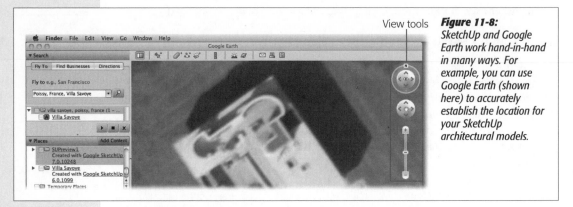

View tools

Figure 11-8:
SketchUp and Google Earth work hand-in-hand in many ways. For example, you can use Google Earth (shown here) to accurately establish the location for your SketchUp architectural models.

6. **In SketchUp, click the Get Current View button, or choose Tools → Google Earth → Get Current View.**

   SketchUp downloads an image from Google Earth and displays it as a background in SketchUp. This image is locked so you won't accidentally move or delete it as you work. At the same time that the image is imported, SketchUp changes the Location settings in the Model Info window. You can check this by going to Windows → Model Info and clicking Location. The Villa Savoye model isn't positioned perfectly in the image, so you need to adjust it to the proper orientation.

   Something else occurs when you click Get Current View, but it's not quite as apparent. SketchUp downloads a Google Earth terrain layer that matches the photo snapshot. This is a three-dimensional object that maps the peaks and valleys of the land. The snapshot and the terrain are each placed on a SketchUp layer. The snapshot is automatically visible, but the terrain is not. To view the terrain, choose Tools → Google Earth → Toggle Terrain.

7. **Triple-click the Villa Savoye model.**

   All the edges and faces in the model are selected.

8. **With the Move (M) tool, click a corner of the model, and then click again to position the corner over the proper corner in the Google Earth image.**

   With one corner of the villa in position, all you need to do is rotate the model into place.

9. **With the Rotate (R) tool, click the correctly positioned corner again. Then move the cursor vertically along an edge of the model and click again.**

   After the second click, the villa model rotates around the corner as you move the cursor.

10. **Rotate the model until it is properly positioned over the photo and then click.**

    The model is positioned over the photo (Figure 11-9), and even more importantly, it's positioned accurately in relationship to the sun and shadows. If you're through with the photo and want to hide it, follow the next two steps.

Tip: Sometimes as you move and rotate your model into position, you may end up aligning a top part of the model with the photo on the ground plane. The result is, your model seems to be buried underground. If that happens, just use the Move tool to place the model above ground.

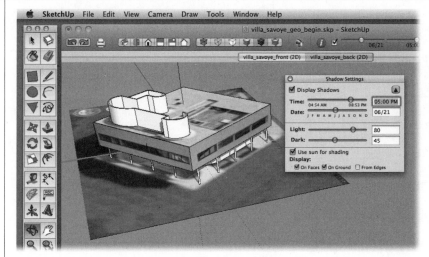

Figure 11-9:
SketchUp snatches the current view from Google Earth and places it in your model as a black-and-white image. The quality isn't great, but it's good enough for you to accurately position a model for a shadow study.

11. **Right-click the photo and then choose Unlock.**

    The imported photo is unlocked. At this point you can hide or delete it.

12. **Right-click the photo and then choose Hide.**

    The photo disappears from view. If you ever want to bring it back, you can use the Outliner to find the image. Right-click its name and then choose Unhide.

Controlling the Strength of the Shadows

For all the valuable information shadows communicate about position, depth, and distance, they also have an aesthetic value. In that role, it's important that you, the designer/artist, can control the visual effect. In some cases, you may want strong,

---

midnight-black shadows, while in other cases a lighter touch is needed. SketchUp provides two slider controls that affect the appearance of the sunlight and shadows. To see these sliders, click the triangle shaped button in the upper-right corner (Figure 11-10). The Shadow Setting window expands to show more controls, including sliders for Light and Dark.

- **The Light slider** controls the quality of the sunlight. Drag the slider to the left, and the sunlight becomes weaker. Drag the slider to the right, and the sunlight becomes stronger. This control has the greatest effect on surfaces that are not in shadow.

- **The Dark slider** controls the quality of the shadows. Drag the slider to the left, and the shadows become stronger and darker. Drag the slider to the right, and the shadows are weaker and lighter. This control only affects the parts of the modeling area that are in shadow.

If you don't want to use the slider, you can type values directly into the box to the right of either slider.

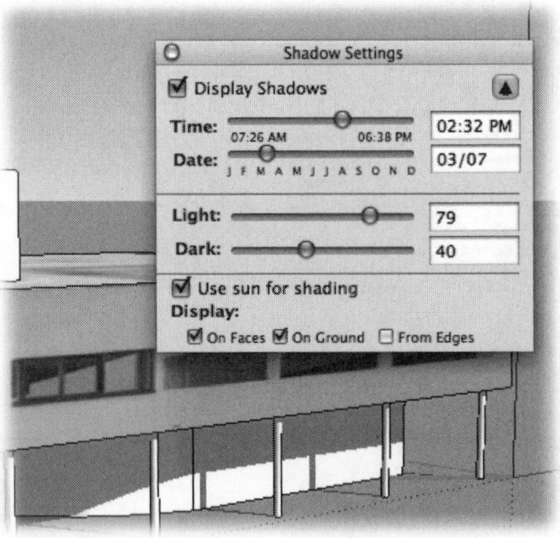

Figure 11-10:
Click the triangular Expand button at the upper right of the Shadow Settings window to see additional options for controlling shadows in your model.

Choosing Whether Faces and Edges Cast Shadows

You get to choose what entities in your model cast shadows. When SketchUp creates a new document, the settings are pretty good, but if you have special needs for a model, you can make changes. At the bottom of the Shadow Settings box, you see three checkboxes:

- **On Faces.** Usually you want this option turned on, so shadows appear on the faces in your model. That means any faces like walls and doors display shadows that happen to fall on them.

- **On Ground.** If you don't specifically create a ground plane for your model, SketchUp considers the horizontal plane at the level of the Origin the ground plane. When this checkbox is turned on, shadows appear on the ground plane. One time you want this option turned off is if you model your own terrain in SketchUp. In that case leave On Faces turned on. Then your shadows appear on the faces of the terrain.

- **From Edges.** Usually a single edge doesn't cast a shadow, and most of the time that works best. However, if you're using edges to represent something like a telephone line or thin cables like those in Figure 11-11, and want them to cast shadows, turn on the From Edges box.

Tip: Choosing the option to cast shadows From Edges puts a strain on any computer that lacks an extremely powerful graphics card. Sometimes this can stop your computer dead in its tracks while it makes calculations for all the shadows.

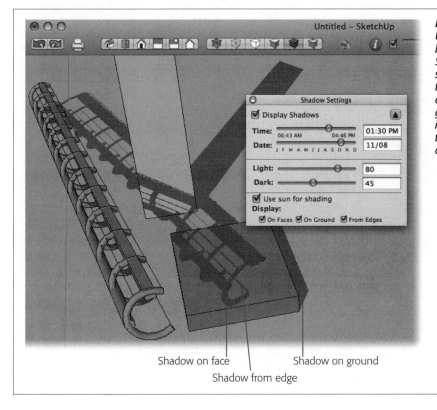

Figure 11-11:
Use the checkboxes at the bottom of the Shadow Settings window to control shadows in your model. In this image, shadows appear both on the ground plane and on faces in the model. In addition to faces, single edges also cast shadows.

Shadow on face   Shadow on ground
Shadow from edge

Using Sun for Shading

You see one more checkbox in the Shadow Settings window: "Use sun for shading" (Figure 11-10). This checkbox is a little different from the others; it doesn't affect objects that cast shadows on other objects. Instead it adds a little more 3-D definition to objects by creating highlights and lowlights. This option works when Display Shadows is turned off. Surfaces that face the sun are lightened, and surfaces away from the sun are darkened, but no shadows are cast on other faces. If you want to enhance the 3-D nature of a non-architectural model, explore this option.

Creating Windows That Transmit Light

In SketchUp, faces that are less than 70 percent opaque do not cast shadows. That means you can create windows that let sunlight pass through into your models, provided the sun is at the correct angle (Figure 11-12). To make a face that doesn't cast a shadow, make sure it is less than 70 percent opaque.

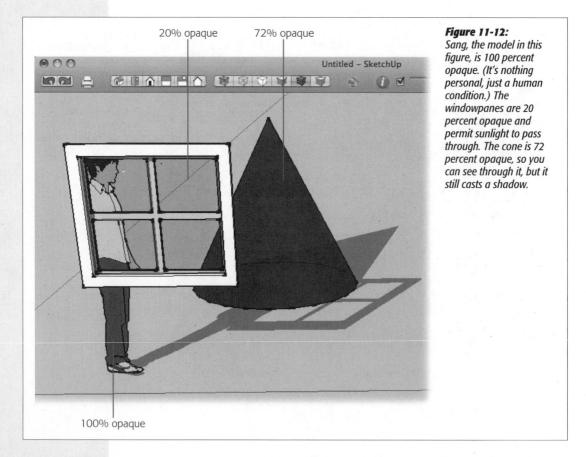

20% opaque   72% opaque

Untitled – SketchUp

100% opaque

Figure 11-12:
Sang, the model in this figure, is 100 percent opaque. (It's nothing personal, just a human condition.) The windowpanes are 20 percent opaque and permit sunlight to pass through. The cone is 72 percent opaque, so you can see through it, but it still casts a shadow.

Turning Shadows On and Off for Individual Entities

If you really want to fine-tune the way your SketchUp model displays shadows, you can decide whether individual entities cast shadows or display shadows. Since an entity in SketchUp can be a single edge or face, or a complex group or component, you have tremendous power over the shadow casting and receiving in your model. Initially all faces and edges are set to cast and receive shadows; however, edges only cast shadows if you turn on the From Edges option (page 393).

Here are the steps to change the shadow settings for an entity so it doesn't cast or receive shadows:

1. **Right-click the entity, group, or component, and then choose Entity Info from the shortcut menu.**

   The Entity Info window appears.

2. **In the upper-right corner, click the triangular Expand button.**

   The Entity Info window expands to display additional settings, including checkboxes for Cast Shadows and Receive Shadows (Figure 11-13).

3. **Turn off the Cast Shadows and Receive Shadows checkboxes.**

   When Cast Shadows is turned off, the entity no longer creates shadows on the ground or other faces. When Receive Shadows is turned off, the entity no longer displays shadows that fall on it.

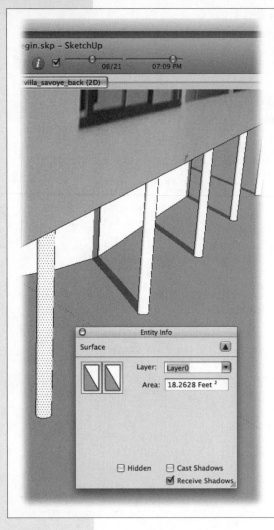

Figure 11-13:
The Entity Info window was used to change the shadow settings for the closest column in this figure. It no longer casts shadows on the ground or on other faces in the model.

CHAPTER 12

Saving Views and Animating with Scenes

If you've worked in SketchUp for a while, you're probably comfortable with the idea that you view your three-dimensional model and its world through a camera. It's as if you're running around the city shooting pictures. Move to a different position, and the view in your lens changes. This chapter pushes the whole camera view metaphor to the limit. You learn how to save the views of your model in scenes. That way, you can jump back to that camera view with the click of a button.

It's hard to appreciate the beauty of three-dimensional objects and environments that you create with a static camera view. To really see and understand the environment, you need to move the camera and to view objects from different angles. Naturally SketchUp gives you some impressive ways to move the camera and animate your views. With SketchUp it's pretty easy to create a walkthrough or a flythrough of your model. Friends and colleagues will not only be wowed by your 3-D modeling skills, but they'll also be impressed with your computer animation savvy, too. It all starts with creating a scene—but in a good way.

Creating a Scene

When you work in SketchUp, you're constantly jumping from one view to another. You need to see your model from different angles to understand the relationship of the entities as you create them. More importantly, you need to make sure that construction is proceeding as planned. If you try to do all your building from a single view, it's awfully easy to make mistakes. So you use the standard camera views or the Orbit tool to see your model from different angles. Sometimes those standard camera views aren't going to show what you want. In that case, you can save a view in a scene. Then anytime you want to view your model from that angle, all you have to do is click the scene's tab.

Note: The exercises in this chapter use the model in *modern_house_scenes_begin.skp,* which you can find at *http://missingmanuals.com/cds.*

1. **Open *modern_house_scenes_begin.skp.***

   This SketchUp document is a model of a simple house with the stairs and landing, like the one created in Chapter 7.

2. **Using the Orbit (O) tool, change the view so you have a pleasant view of the right corner, with the stairs.**

   A nice 45-degree angle of the corner works well.

3. **Choose Window → Scenes.**

   The Scenes window opens, as shown in Figure 12-1. No scenes are listed in the window, unless you've already added a scene.

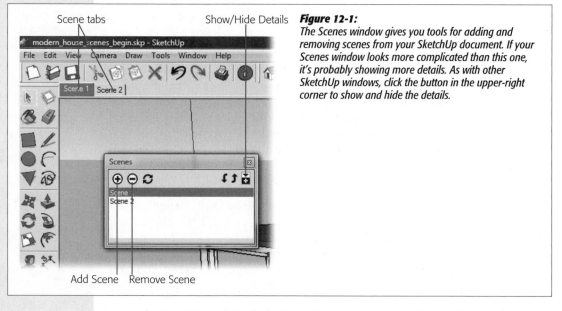

Figure 12-1:
The Scenes window gives you tools for adding and removing scenes from your SketchUp document. If your Scenes window looks more complicated than this one, it's probably showing more details. As with other SketchUp windows, click the button in the upper-right corner to show and hide the details.

4. **In the Scenes window click the Add Scene button—it looks like a + sign in a circle.**

   SketchUp adds Scene 1 to the list in the Scenes window.

5. **Using the Orbit (O) tool, change the view so you have a view of the model's left corner.**

   Actually, you can use any other view you'd like. For dramatic effect it's best to choose a view that's noticeably different from the first.

6. **In the Scenes window click the Add Scene button.**

   SketchUp adds Scene 2 to the list in the Scenes window. If you want, you can keep on adding scenes that show different views of your model.

7. **Using the Orbit (O) tool, change the view so you have a view of one of the back corners of the model.**

   Again, feel free to substitute any view that's different from the first two.

8. **In the Scenes window click the Add Scene button.**

   SketchUp adds (you guessed it) Scene 3 to the list in the Scenes window (Figure 12-2). If you want, you can keep adding scenes that show different views of your model.

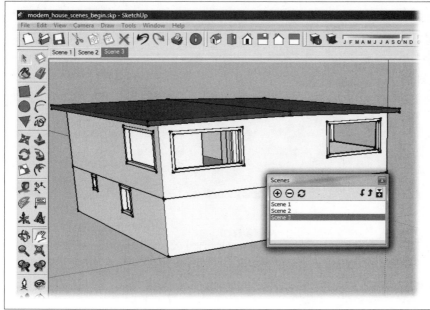

Figure 12-2:
Each time you add a scene to your document, SketchUp adds the scene to the list in the Scenes window and adds a scene tab above the modeling window.

9. **In the Scenes window double-click Scene 1, then double-click Scene 2, and then double-click Scene 3.**

   When you double-click Scene 1, the SketchUp view moves slowly from the current view to the view saved in Scene 1. The same thing happens when you click any of the scenes in the list.

Congratulations! You just animated your SketchUp model. It's as if you have a movie camera mounted on a crane and you, the director, are moving the camera from one location to another. Film folks call this a dolly shot or crane shot. By clicking the scene name in the list, you manually jump to a new camera view. SketchUp can automate this process for you.

Changing Scenes

Why do I see a warning box when I create a new scene?

Occasionally when you create a scene, an ominous warning pops up, demanding attention before you can go on (Figure 12-3). Here's what's going on: SketchUp keeps track of the Styles you're using. When you choose a style and then make changes to the style, SketchUp takes note. The change could be something like turning on shadows or hiding guides. When you create a scene, SketchUp remembers the style used in the scene. However, if you made changes to the style but haven't saved those changes, SketchUp gets confused. Later when you show this scene, do you want to see the original style? Do you want to see the changed style? Usually you want to see what you're viewing at the moment in the modeling window, and that's the changed style. The problem is SketchUp can't show you what you see in the modeling window unless you save the style and its changes. So it gives you a few choices via radio button:

- **Save as a new style.** Choose this option when you want the scene to show the style with changes. SketchUp automatically creates a new style to match what you see in the modeling window.

- **Update the selected style.** This option also saves the view that you see in the modeling window. The difference is that it saves the style changes to the original style. That means any other scenes that use that style will look different, too.

- **Do nothing to save changes.** If you choose this option, the scene won't match what you see in the modeling window. SketchUp doesn't create a new style and doesn't change the existing style.

At the bottom of the warning box is a checkbox where you can tell SketchUp "Quit bugging me with this annoying question." That's not exactly what the label says, but that's what it means. Turning on this box is the same as always choosing the "Do nothing to save changes" option. In this case, you're responsible for remembering when you've made changes to styles and making sure that the scenes are saved with the look that you want.

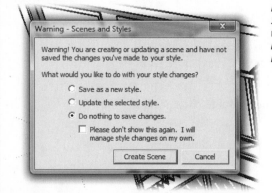

Figure 12-3:
Sometimes when you create a scene, SketchUp flashes this warning box. It's telling you that you changed the style used in the scene and asking if you want to save the changes you made to the style.

Playing the Scenes Animation

When you're working in SketchUp, it's great to be able to click a scene to jump from one predesigned view to another. When you're making a presentation, you may prefer to have SketchUp automatically show one view and then move to the next.

That's a cinch; just choose View → Animation → Play. An even quicker way to play the animation is to right-click any of the scene tabs and then to choose Play from the shortcut menu. You can choose which scenes are included or excluded from the animation, as explained on page 407.

Tip: If the little window with the video control buttons (shown in Figure 12-4) isn't visible, you can start and stop the animation using the same menu command: View → Animation → Play.

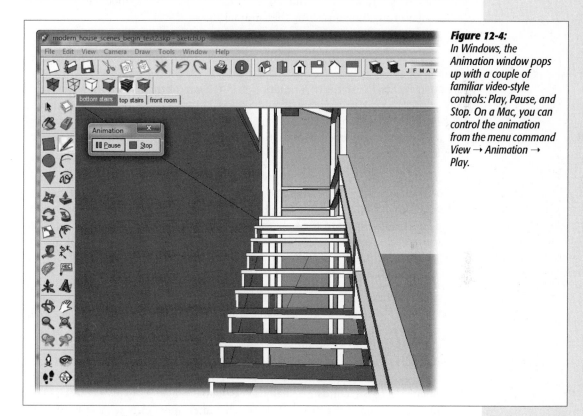

Figure 12-4:
In Windows, the Animation window pops up with a couple of familiar video-style controls: Play, Pause, and Stop. On a Mac, you can control the animation from the menu command View → Animation → Play.

SketchUp automatically changes from one view to the next, with a short pause at each. Scenes play from the top of the list to the bottom. The animation loops, so after SketchUp shows the last scene in the list, it goes back to the first and starts again.

Note: The steps for exporting your animation as video files are included in the chapter on exporting to different file formats, page 443.

Changing the Animation Timing

SketchUp's timing for animations works pretty well for many projects, especially considering that you didn't have to make any decisions or do much of anything to animate your model. The camera takes a couple of seconds to move from one camera position to another and then pauses at each camera position for 1 second. For the animation to work smoothly, make sure that your camera positions are roughly equal distances apart. Otherwise it may look as if the camera is leisurely moving to one spot and then racing to the next. If your camera positions are too far apart, it looks like your animation is running in fast forward. When these things start to annoy you, it's good to know that you have some control over the timing of your animation. The control is pretty limited, which is unfortunate if you want to micro-manage your animations, but it may be good news if you'd rather spend your time modeling than animating.

To change the timing in your animation, choose View → Animation → Settings. This command opens the Model Info window, which you may remember from previous chapters (Figure 12-5). The left side of the Model Info window lists features that you can fine-tune. Animation is at the top of the list, and it's automatically turned on. You can control only three animation properties, and they're applied to the entire animation. You may have to compromise a little, using timings that work best for the overall animation but that aren't exactly what you want for individual transitions.

- Use the **Enable Scene transitions** checkbox to control whether the camera smoothly moves to new camera positions or jumps to a new position. When the box is turned on, the motion is animated. When the box is turned off, the camera cuts immediately to the new camera view. For many reasons, you may not want to use transitions. If you have a big SketchUp model, it takes a lot of time to move from one location to another. Sometimes you only want to zero-in on a couple of views in a model, and the transition between isn't necessary.

- Use the **seconds** box to set the time it takes for the camera to move to a new position. This option is only available when "Enable scene transitions" is turned on. You have to make the duration of the transition match your subject, the distance traveled, and your audience's patience. Too fast, and they won't understand what they're seeing. Too slow, and they'll be leaning forward in their chairs urging the camera to move faster. To create a walkthrough for a typical residence, 2 to 5 seconds is usually a reasonable range. As explained earlier, it's important to make the distances between camera positions relatively uniform. You can't control the timing to move between individual scenes, so it may take trial and error to get the camera movement just right.

Tip: It's best to think of the "seconds" timing as an estimate, particularly if your scene includes complex models, materials with textures, transparency, and shadows. The timing does depend on the power of your computer and graphics card.

- Use the **Scene Delay seconds** box to set how long the camera pauses at each camera position. Again, this option is a matter of taste. You may not want the camera to pause at all. If that's the case, set seconds to 0. If you want your audience to focus on each view, change the setting to 1, 2, or 3 seconds.

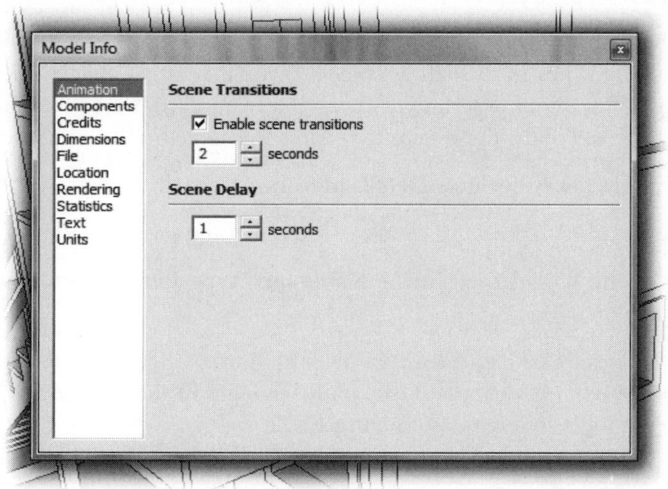

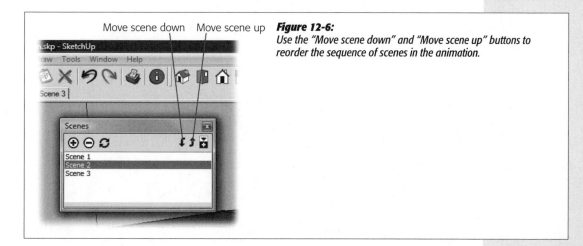

Figure 12-5:
If you're not happy with the timing that SketchUp automatically applies to transitions in your animation, you can change the settings in the Model Info window. The animation options are at the top of the list of options at left.

Whatever settings you choose, make sure you preview your animation before unveiling it to the public. It's also wise to test it out on a few folks who are unfamiliar with the project. They may give you valuable input about the pace and timing of the animation.

Changing the Order of Scenes

You may not always create scenes in the order that you want to view them, especially with larger models and more elaborate animations. When you want to change the order of scenes, all you need to do is change their position on the list in the Scenes window. In the upper-right corner are two arrow buttons: "Move scene down" and "Move scene up." Select a scene and then click one of the buttons to reorder the list (Figure 12-6).

Move scene down   Move scene up

Figure 12-6:
Use the "Move scene down" and "Move scene up" buttons to reorder the sequence of scenes in the animation.

Renaming Scenes

Perhaps you find the names "Scene 1", "Scene 2", and "Scene 3" somewhat uninspired. If your model becomes even slightly complex, you'll want to change those names to something a little more descriptive. To do that, you need a more detailed view in the Scenes window. Follow these steps to rename the scenes in the animation:

1. **In the Scenes window, click the Show Details button.**

   The Scenes window expands, showing a couple of text boxes and several checkboxes.

2. **In the list, click Scene 1, and then in the Name box, type *Entry Stairs*. Then press Enter (Return on a Mac).**

   The name change doesn't take effect until you press Enter or click somewhere outside of the Name box. At that point, the name changes in the list and in the scene tabs above the modeling window (Figure 12-7).

3. **Click Scene 2 and type *Garage*.**

   In addition to changing scene names, you can add a description for the scene. Often a description isn't necessary, but it's a place you can stash some additional info if you want.

4. **Click Scene 3 and type *Back Corner*.**

   Now all three scenes have descriptive names.

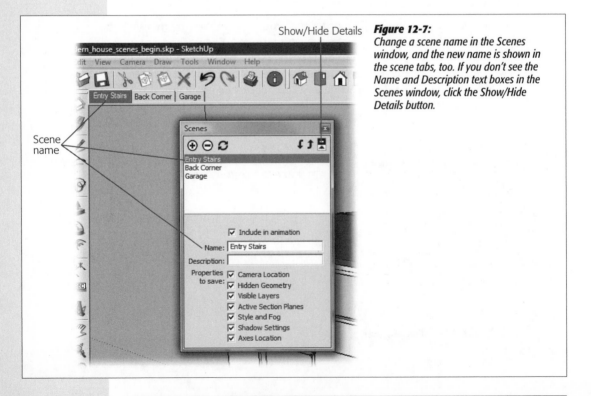

Show/Hide Details

Figure 12-7:
Change a scene name in the Scenes window, and the new name is shown in the scene tabs, too. If you don't see the Name and Description text boxes in the Scenes window, click the Show/Hide Details button.

Scene name

Deleting (Removing) Scenes

Removing a scene is easy. The only gotcha is that once you remove a scene, you can't bring it back with an Undo command. In fact you can reverse or repeat few actions related to scenes by using the standard commands. That aside, you can use a couple of easy ways to delete or remove scenes from your document:

- Right-click a scene tab, and choose Delete from the shortcut menu. Windows systems display an alert box, asking if you really want to delete the scene. On Macs, the scene disappears in a poof of virtual smoke!

- Select the scene in the Scenes window, and click the Remove Scene button. When you use this method, both Windows and Mac computers double-check to make sure you really want to delete the scene.

Once the scene is gone, SketchUp moves on to the next scene on the list in the Scenes window.

Turning Scenes into Video

When you're happy with your animation, you can export it to a video file. You can show video files on websites, email them to colleagues, and burn them to DVDs. Windows computers use the Video for Windows .avi format, and Macs use the QuickTime (.mov) format. Your video shows the scenes as they're displayed when you use the View → Animation → Play command. If your model is complex and includes textures, transparencies, and shadows, you may find that the video plays faster than the animation inside of SketchUp. To export an animation to video, choose File → Export → Animation. The Export Animation window opens, where you choose a name and location for saving the file. Click the Options button to see the Animation Export Options window, where you can change the image size and other features of the video (Figure 12-8). For the complete details on exporting animations and other types of files, see Chapter 13.

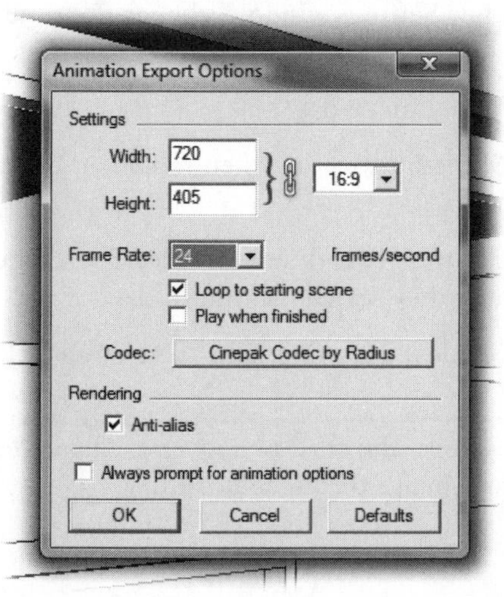

Figure 12-8:
When you export an animation, you can change the size of the video image, the number of frames per second, and the method used to encode the video. For all the details see page 443.

Studying Shadow Movement with Scenes

As every director from David Lynch to Quentin Tarantino knows, movie directors get to control both time and space. Here's an exercise that shows how to use SketchUp scenes to show time changes in your animations.

Chapter 11 explained how to add shadows to your model that change according to the time of year and the time of day (page 384). By combining scenes with shadows, you can create shadow study animations. Here are the steps, using the model from the previous exercises in this chapter:

1. With *modern_house_scenes_begin.skp* open in the modeling window, click the Display Shadows button or choose View → Shadows.

   The house model casts shadows on the ground plane. Shadow patterns appear inside the model, too, where light comes through the windows.

Note: See page 18 for details on how to display the Shadows toolbar for your computer.

---

2. Using the Shadow toolbar or the Shadow Settings window (Window → Shadows), set the date to *June 21* and the time to *6:00 am.*

   If you're using the toolbar, you may not be able to set the time and date with precision. Ballpark timing is good enough for this example.

3. In the Scenes window click the Add Scene button—it looks like a + sign in a circle.

   SketchUp adds new scene to the Scenes list.

4. In the Scenes window, click the Show Details button (Figure 12-7). Then in the Name box, type *Shadow Morning.*

   Your scene displaying shadows has an appropriate name.

5. Using the Shadow toolbar or the Shadow Settings window, change the time to *6:00 PM.*

   The angle of the shadows changes with the time of day.

6. In the Scenes window click the Add Scene button, and then rename the scene *Shadow Evening.*

   Now you have two scenes in your model at two different time. The shadow angles are different in each scene, because they match the time of day.

7. In the Scenes window double-click Shadow Morning, and then double-click Shadow Evening.

   As you click the different "Shadow" scenes, the shadow moves gradually to a new position, showing how the shadows change throughout the day.

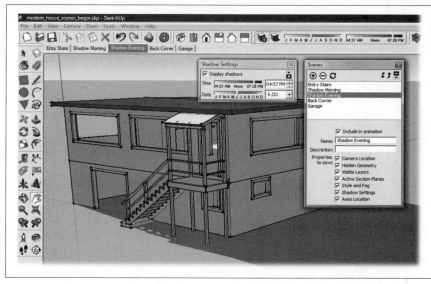

Figure 12-9:
Animations are great for shadow studies. You can view your model from different angles and create animations that show how shadows change throughout the day or from one season to the next.

Shadow studies are important when you're designing a house or yard. For example, if you're building a deck, you may want to make sure that in the summer months, part of the deck is always in the shade. To display accurate shadows in SketchUp, in addition to setting the date and time of day, you need to position your model on the face of the Earth, as explained on page 385.

Including or Excluding Scenes in an Animation

If you've followed along with all the exercises in this chapter, your Scenes window shows five named scenes. The animation shows all five scenes. What if you want to watch an animation that shows just the two shadow animations? Sure, you could delete the other three scenes, but perhaps you'd like to keep those views around for modeling purposes. The expanded Scenes window displays a little checkbox labeled "Include in animation" (Figure 12-10). Make sure it's turned on for the scenes you want in your animation and turned off for the scenes you want to exclude. So if only the two shadow scenes are checkmarked, all you see when you choose View → Animation → Play are the two scenes in the shadow study. The names of scenes not included in the animation are enclosed in parentheses on the scene tabs and in the list in the Scenes window.

What's Saved in a Scene

As shown in the previous example, SketchUp scenes save more than just the camera position. In that case, the scenes saved the position of shadows at different times of the day. To see the variety of properties saved in a scene, click the Show Details button in the Scenes window. Under the Name and Description boxes, you see the following checkboxes that toggle on and off the properties saved in a scene (Figure 12-10):

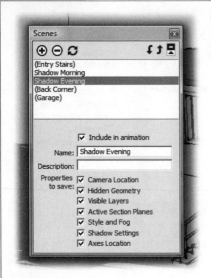

Figure 12-10:
You may not want every scene you create to show in your animation. Choose which scenes are shown by turning on the "Include in animation" checkbox. Scenes in parentheses haven't been included in the animation.

- **Camera Location.** Turn on this box to save the camera position with the style. If this box isn't turned on, the other properties are saved, but the camera position doesn't change from the previous position. If the thought of saving a scene without a camera view seems confusing, see the box on page 410.

- **Hidden Geometry.** You hide entities in SketchUp by right-clicking the entity and choosing Hide from the shortcut menu. When you turn on this property, SketchUp remembers which entities are hidden and not hidden at the time the scene is created. Later when you select the scene tab, the same entities will be hidden and unhidden. So, for example, you can create a scene called *Hide Barn;* then when you click that scene tab, the barn disappears.

Tip: This property doesn't affect the View → Hidden Geometry menu option. That command works as usual, giving you an opportunity to view hidden geometry in any scene.

- **Visible Layers.** This checkbox saves details about layers that are visible and not visible in the scene. (See page 273 for more about working with layers and visibility.)

- **Active Section Planes.** Section planes are used to display cross-section views of your model. Use this checkbox to store the view created by a section plane in the scene. (For more details see page 417.)

- **Style and Fog.** Styles and fog change the appearance of your model without changing the entities in the model. You can save style and fog settings in a scene. (Styles are covered on page 193.)

- **Shadow Settings.** As shown in the previous section, you can save shadow details in a scene. That includes the specific date and time that affects the angle of the shadow. For details on shadows, see page 381.

- **Axes Location.** Turn on this box to display the drawing axes and their position in the scene.

To choose individual properties in a scene, follow these steps:

1. **Arrange your camera view and all the visual properties the way you want them for the scene.**

   Make sure the camera view, styles, and shadows appear the way you want to save them in the scene.

2. **In the Scenes window click the Add Scene button, and then type a name for the scene in the Name box.**

   A descriptive name may include the subject that's viewed, but it's also helpful to name the properties saved in the scene. For example, you may want to name a scene: "CAM Front SHADOW 5pm." In Windows, the scene tabs expand to accommodate the name. A descriptive scene name makes it easy to understand what's included in a scene without viewing it.

3. **If necessary, click the Show Details button in the Scenes window to see the "Properties to save" list.**

   The Show/Hide Details button acts as a toggle.

4. **Under "Properties to save", turn on the checkboxes for properties you want to save.**

   Make sure a checkmark is next to any of the properties that you want to save in the scene. SketchUp saves the settings for all of the checked properties. In the future, anytime you select the scene, SketchUp applies these visual properties.

Tip: SketchUp saves the visual properties when scenes are created and when they're updated (see page 407). Just changing the checkboxes without creating a new scene does nothing. For example, if you select a scene in the Scenes window and turn off the Shadow Settings, it won't have any effect on the selected scene. However, those settings are applied the next time you click the Add Scene button.

When you're starting out, you probably want to save all the properties in the list, and that's the way things are set up if you don't make any changes. As you become more experienced working with scenes, you may want to tweak these settings for special projects or for special effects. For example, you could create scenes that don't change anything except the Style and Fog properties. That way you could apply several different styles to your model simply by clicking a scene tab.

Saving a Scene

How can I save a scene without saving a camera location?

Sometimes new SketchUp builders and modelers have a tough time wrapping their brain around the concept of saving a scene without saving a camera position. What exactly are you saving in the scene? The short answer is, you're saving any other visual property that's checkmarked on the "Properties to save" list. Suppose you save a scene and all that's turned on are the shadow settings for July 21 at 3:00 p.m. and name the scene *Shadow Summer Afternoon*. Whenever you select that scene tab, the only thing that changes in your view of the model is the angle of the shadows. If prior to that your view of the model didn't display shadows, shadows appear when you click the Shadow Summer Afternoon tab. If prior to clicking the Shadow Summer Afternoon tab, shadows are displayed but for a different time and date, you see the shadows change to match July 21 at 3:00 p.m. It's the same with the other visual properties saved in scenes. You can use tabs to apply different SketchUp styles, to hide and show hidden geometry, or (as covered on page 417) to show and hide cross-section views of your model using section planes.

What's Not Saved in a Scene

Sure, it's important to understand what properties are saved in a scene—it's just as important to understand what's not saved. Scenes save the properties related to the appearance of your model, but they don't save the model itself. If you save a scene and then change, move, or delete the model within that view, the scene will look different than it did when you saved it. In other words, scenes don't save your model's *state*. So saving scenes isn't a way to save multiple versions of a model at different points of construction. The best way to do that is to save multiple SketchUp documents and to save them with names such as *Guggenheim Museum 1, Guggenheim Museum 2,* and so on. You may want to replace the numbers with dates, times, or whatever tracking system works for your project.

This issue of "what's not saved" sometimes trips up new SketchUp builders. They're surprised to return to a scene and find that it doesn't look exactly as it did when they saved it. Just remember that scenes may save camera position and other visual properties, but they don't save the model itself.

Updating Scene Details

Making changes to a previously saved scene is a lot like creating a scene:

1. **Choose the scene you want to edit by clicking the scene tab.**

   You can also double-click the scene in the Scenes window.

2. **Arrange the visual properties the way you want.**

   Often you'll just be updating a single visual property such as shadows or styles. If that's the case, just make sure those properties are set the way you want.

3. **Click the Update Scene button, shown in Figure 12-11.**

The Scene Update window appears (also in Figure 12-11). The Scene Update window looks a lot like the "Properties to save" section of the Scenes window and does pretty much the same job.

4. **Turn on the visual properties you want to update in the scene, and then click Update.**

SketchUp changes only the properties that are turned on; it leaves the other properties as they were before the update.

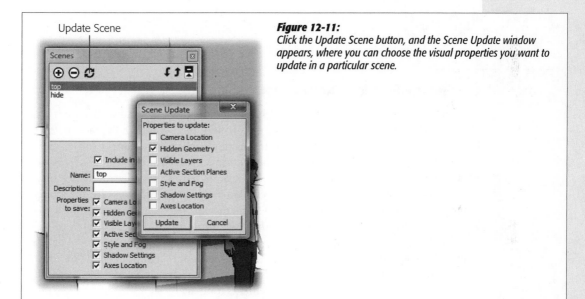

Figure 12-11:
Click the Update Scene button, and the Scene Update window appears, where you can choose the visual properties you want to update in a particular scene.

More Ways to Move the Camera

Often the camera position is the most important property being saved in a scene. If you've been working in SketchUp for a while, you're probably pretty experienced at placing the camera where you want it for a particular view. The standard camera views (Camera → Standard Views) or the buttons on the View toolbar give you a great start. Then you can use those old friends the Orbit (O), Pan (H), and Zoom (Z) tools to fine-tune the view. SketchUp has three other tools, known as the Walkthrough tools: Position Camera, Walk, and Look Around. These tools help you set up specific views in your model, and they work great in combination with scenes.

Tip: Don't forget about the Previous and Next view buttons as you're working to set up views and scenes. The Previous button is especially helpful if one of the Walkthrough tools doesn't give you the view you want. Just click Previous and give it another try.

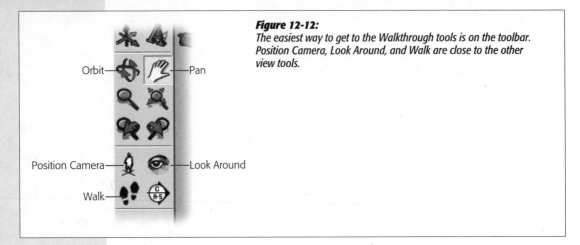

Figure 12-12:
*The easiest way to get to the Walkthrough tools is on the toolbar.
Position Camera, Look Around, and Walk are close to the other
view tools.*

Orbit — Pan

Position Camera — Look Around

Walk

Using the Position Camera Tool

If you're a photographer, the ideas behind the Position Camera tool are pretty easy
to grasp. Imagine you've got a camera on a tripod. First you click to place the tripod
at a certain position in your model. If you don't make any changes to the camera
height, your view is 5 feet, 6 inches above the surface you clicked. That's a pretty
good height to get a person's eye view. If you want a bird's eye view of the scene, you
may want to type in *24'* and press Enter. You need to enter the new height immediately before or after using the Position Camera tool. The height appears in the Measurements toolbar, and the camera height zooms up to the 24-foot level. The
Measurements toolbar uses SketchUp's imaginary ground plane as a point of reference. So keep this in mind if you're on the second floor of a building and you want to
move up 8 feet to see the third floor. In that case, you want to add 8 feet to the current "eye height" shown in the Measurements toolbar.

You can choose the direction and angle of your view at the same time that you set
the camera position. It's a two-step operation. Click to place the camera on a surface, and then before you let go of the mouse button, drag in the direction you
want to view. You see a dotted line extending from the clicked point to the mouse
cursor. This line is a guide to use while you're establishing the view. When you let
go of the mouse button, the line disappears, and your camera view is established.
This technique literally places the camera on the surface you click, changing the
"eye height" value. You may find it easier to adjust the view with the Look Around
tool, which becomes available after you place the camera.

Setting the Field of View

When you view a scene through a camera, your view is limited by the type of lens
on the camera. A wide angle lens shows you more than a narrow telephoto view
(Figure 12-13). SketchUp works the same way. When viewing interiors, the view is
already limited by the walls. Photographers often use a wider angle lens for interiors
because it helps to define the space and the relationship of objects better. A view of
about 60 degrees is fairly close to a person's natural view and works well for interiors.

For exteriors, photographers often choose a narrower filed of view, something around 30 or 35 degrees is similar to a standard 50mm camera lens.

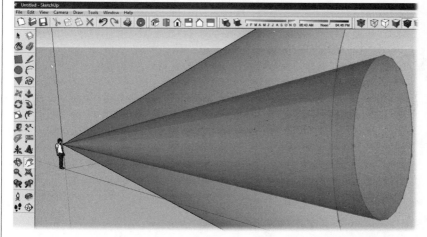

Figure 12-13:
You can think of field of view as a cone with the pointy end at eye level. In this figure, Sang's 30-degree field of view is shown as a blue cone. His 60-degree field of view is shown as a yellow cone, similar to a 30mm lens on a standard SLR film camera.

To change the current field of view, choose Camera → Field of View, and then type a value. The value appears in the Measurements toolbar, as shown in Figure 12-14. You can supply a field of view in degrees, such as *30 deg* for 30 degrees. Or you can provide a camera lens value such as *50mm* for a 50-millimeter lens. Use whichever unit system you understand best; SketchUp handles the conversion for you. The "Field of View" values are saved in scenes along with the other camera position properties.

Looking Around

If you continue with the camera-on-a-tripod metaphor, it's easy to understand how the Look Around tool works. After you've placed your virtual camera and tripod in a position, you use the Look Around tool to pan left and right and to tilt up and down. The camera stays in the same location; you're just pivoting to see a different view. Click the Look Around tool in the toolbar or choose Camera → Look Around, and your cursor changes to a pair of eyeballs. Just drag to change the view. The action feels similar to using the Orbit tool, but to avoid frustration, keep in mind that when using Look Around, the camera doesn't change position; it just pivots in place.

Walking the Camera

Like other SketchUp tools, the Walk tool helps you do a very specific task. You use the Walk tool to move around your SketchUp model in a way that mimics a person walking from one place to another:

1. In *modern_house_scenes_begin.skp,* move to a camera view where you can see the front stairs.

   For this exercise, you can use a fresh copy of the file, or you can use the version you modified during the previous exercises in this chapter.

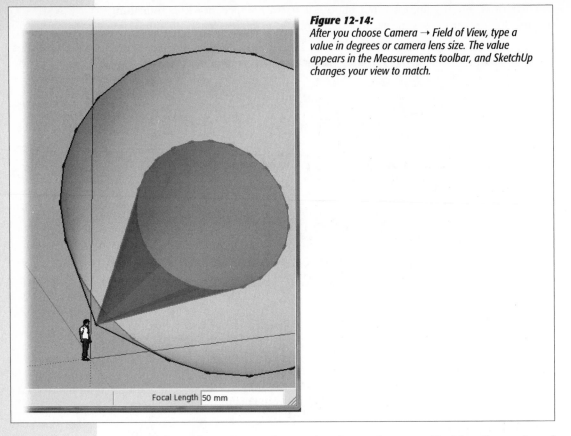

Figure 12-14:
After you choose Camera → Field of View, type a value in degrees or camera lens size. The value appears in the Measurements toolbar, and SketchUp changes your view to match.

Focal Length 50 mm

2. **Click the Position Camera button (or choose Camera → Position Camera), and then click a spot in front of the stairs.**

   Choose a spot where you'd begin to walk up the stairs. After you click a position, your cursor automatically changes to the Look Around tool. The cursor looks like a couple of eyeballs. If you click directly on the ground, the Measurements toolbar shows that the eye height is 5' 6". (If you've changed the eye height, type *5'6"* in the Measurements toolbar now.)

3. **Drag the Look Around tool until you have a view of the stairs.**

   Shoot for a head-on view of the stairs, where you're looking neither up nor down.

4. **Choose Camera → Field of View, and then type *50 mm*.**

   The view changes to a 60-degree angle and at this point should look similar to Figure 12-15.

5. **Choose Window → Scenes and then click the Show Details button. Make sure all the checkboxes under "Properties to save" are turned on.**

   In this example, you want to save the camera position and all the other visual properties.

6. Click the Add Scene button.

SketchUp saves the camera view and other visual properties in the scene.

7. Click in the Name box and type *bottom stairs.*

The new scene is renamed. The new name appears in both the Scenes window list and on the scene tab above the modeling window.

8. Click the Walk tool and continue to press the mouse button. Then drag the cursor forward in the direction of the stairs.

The camera walks forward as you drag the cursor. When the camera position hits the first step of the stairs, you notice a little jump up. The camera actually steps up the stairs. You notice the same stepping action all the way up the stairs until you reach the landing.

Tip: You don't have to keep the "walking feet" on a ground surface. In fact, it's best to put the feet icon at about eye level in the direction you want to walk. When you use the Walk tool, SketchUp places a cross near the center of the window. Move the feet cursor above the cross to walk forward and below the cross to walk backward. Move to the left or right of the cross to walk in either of those directions. When the feet are on top of the cross, motion stops.

---

9. **When you get close to the front door, begin to angle the cursor toward the door opening. When you're slightly angled toward the door and looking into the front room, release the mouse button.**

If you gradually turn toward the door opening as you move close to it, you can mimic the movements of a person about to enter the door. It may take a while to get the hang of walking with the Walk tool. It's easy to get lost, especially if you find yourself walking through walls.

10. Click the Save Scene button.

SketchUp saves the camera view and other visual properties in the scene.

11. Click in the Name box and type *top stairs.*

The second scene is renamed to "top stairs".

12. Click the Walk tool again, and drag to enter the front room of the house.

Things are a little barren in the house. No furniture or fixtures, but it makes a good maze to practice your walkthrough skills.

13. Click the Save Scene button, and rename the new scene *front room.*

14. Click the "bottom stairs" tab.

The scene and view change to the view at the bottom of the stairs.

15. **Right-click one of the scene tabs, and choose Play from the shortcut menu.**

The animation runs, showing each of the scenes you saved. The camera moves smoothly from one saved scene to another. For example, you don't see the bumping of each stair step; instead the camera moves smoothly from the bottom of the stairs to the top.

Tip: For a smooth, fluid motion, remember to make the camera distances between scenes consistent.

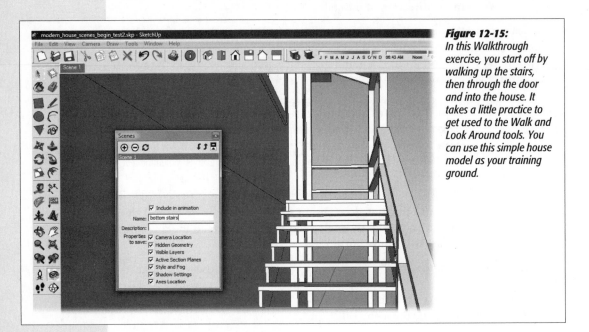

Figure 12-15:
In this Walkthrough exercise, you start off by walking up the stairs, then through the door and into the house. It takes a little practice to get used to the Walk and Look Around tools. You can use this simple house model as your training ground.

Using the Walk tool modifiers

As you use the Walk tool, glance down at the status bar, and you see hints about the related modifier keys. If you'd rather run than walk, press Ctrl. Generally the Walk tool just moves forward and backward. When you want to move up and down or sideways, press Shift. When you first use the Walk tool, it stops when you hit a wall. You may notice the cursor change into the shape of a person and jiggle back and forth, indicating a collision. Want to walk through walls without interference? Press Alt as you use the Walk tool.

Walk On

The *modern house* model is a good place to experiment with the Walkthrough tools and creating animations. If the rooms are too barren and indistinguishable from each other, go to the 3D Warehouse, and hunt down some furniture and appliances. Practice moving from room to room and creating animations with smooth transitions.

View Cross-Sections with Section Planes

In the previous section, you learned how to walk through walls by using the Walk tool. That's nothing compared with what you can do with the Section tool. Using section planes, you can slice into a model like it's a layer cake, displaying a cross-section of its innards. The effect is cool in a still image, but it's especially impressive in an animation.

Note: You don't have to be working with scenes to use section cuts and section planes. They're available anytime you're working in SketchUp.

---

1. **Open a fresh copy of *modern_house_scenes_begin.skp*.**

   You can find a copy of this SketchUp document at *http://missingmanuals.com/cds*.

2. **Choose Window → Outliner.**

   The Outliner shows that this document has three groups: house, landing, and steps.

3. **Double-click the "steps" group.**

   The "steps" group opens for editing. You aren't really editing when you use section planes to create section cuts in your model. However, you can't apply a section plane to a closed group.

4. **Click the Section Plane button (or choose Tools → Section Plane).**

   The cursor changes to a green square with a diamond in the center. As you move the cursor, the square snaps to align with faces and surfaces.

5. **Click a vertical face of the stair stringer.**

   A section plane appears at the point where you clicked. After you add a section plane, usually the first thing you want to do is move the plane; however, you can't just click it with the Move tool. If you try, you end up moving parts of your model. Instead you need to explicitly select the section plane before you move it.

6. **Using the Select (space bar) tool, click the section plane.**

   The section plane displays blue highlights, as shown in Figure 12-16.

7. **Using the Move (M) tool, click the section plane. Then move the plane back toward the house and click again.**

   As the section plane moves back toward the house, it hides the front portion of the stairs, creating a cutaway view of the stairs.

8. **Right-click the section plane, and choose Reverse from the shortcut menu. Again right-click the section plane, and choose Reverse from the shortcut menu.**

   The portion of the stairs that was visible is hidden, and vice versa. The command reverses what is visible and what is hidden by the section plane. After your double-reverse, the portion of the stairs closest to the house is visible.

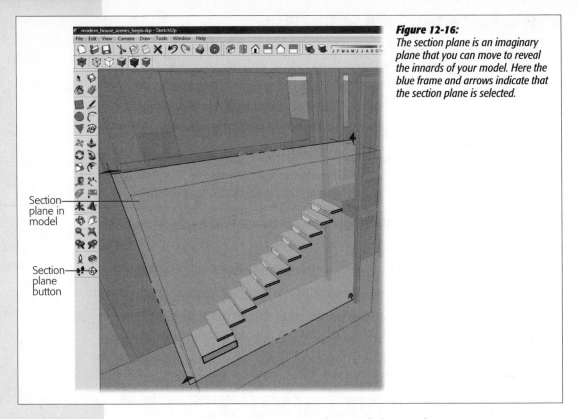

Figure 12-16:
The section plane is an imaginary plane that you can move to reveal the innards of your model. Here the blue frame and arrows indicate that the section plane is selected.

Section plane in model

Section plane button

9. **Right-click away from the section plane and choose Close Group.**

   The "stairs" group closes and you see the entire house model in its full glory. The section plane and the section cut are still visible.

Note: section *plane* refers to the selectable object that controls the cutaway effect. section *cut* refers to the visual cutaway effect created by the section plane.

---

10. **Go to View → Section Planes.**

    In the View menu the checkmark next to Section Planes disappears. In the modeling window the section plane disappears, too.

11. **Go to View → Section Cuts.**

    In the View menu, Section Cuts is deselected. In the modeling window, all traces of the section plane and the section cut are gone. You can bring them back anytime using the same commands.

Section planes, like animations, are one of those SketchUp effects that are bound to get oohs and aahs from an audience. They're not only cool, but they're also a great way to provide extra information about your model, whether it's a building, a piece of furniture, or the latest hydrogen fuel cell–powered automobile.

Rotating a Section Plane

When you first create them, section planes snap to the faces in your model. But you don't have to settle for that. You can use most of the tricks you use to orient and create rectangles, ovals, and polygons. That includes using the Shift key to lock the section plane to a particular orientation and then moving it elsewhere. Once you've created a section plane, you can use the Rotate (R) tool to change the angle. To give it a try in *modern_house_scenes_begin.skp*, double-click the "house" group. Then create a section plane that's aligned with the plane of the left side of the house. Select it and push it back partway into the model. When you're done, it should look like Figure 12-17.

Tip: If you need more details on how to create a section plane, see the exercise on page 417.

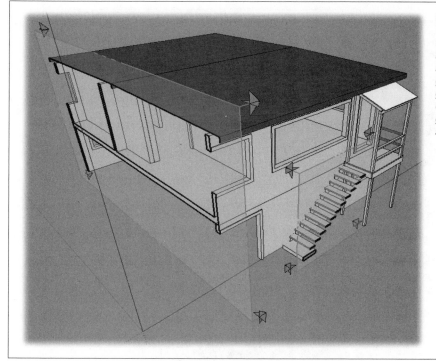

Figure 12-17:
You can view two section cuts at the same time, as long as the cuts are inside of separate groups. Here the "stairs" group shows a section cut, and the "house" group shows a section cut.

To rotate the section plane in the house group, follow these steps:

1. **Make sure that you're inside of the "house" group, and then click one of the section plane handles.**

   You want to be inside of the "house" group, but not inside of its subgroups. When you're at the right level, you should be able to select the section plane without any other entities being selected.

2. **Click the Top view button, or choose Camera → Standard Views → Top.**

   You see the roof of the house, and the section plane is still selected.

3. **With the Rotate (R) tool, hold the cursor over the ground, and then press and hold Shift.**

   The Rotate tool is locked to the ground plane.

4. **Move the cursor to the top edge of the section plane and then click.**

   This click sets the first point for the rotate action. Release the Shift key.

5. **Move the cursor down the top edge of the section plane and click again.**

   Now when you move the cursor, the section plane pivots around the first point you clicked, as shown in Figure 12-18.

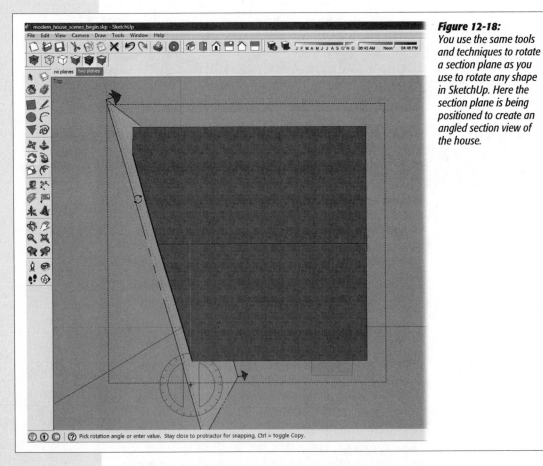

Figure 12-18:
You use the same tools and techniques to rotate a section plane as you use to rotate any shape in SketchUp. Here the section plane is being positioned to create an angled section view of the house.

6. **Type *45* and press Enter (Return on a Mac).**

   The section plane is rotated to a 45-degree angle.

7. Use the Orbit tool to view the house from roughly the same angle as the section plane. Then use the Move tool to push the plane back and forth.

As you move the plane, the 45-degree, angled section cut moves back and forth across the model. As shown in Figure 12-19, this second section plane has no effect on the "stair" group.

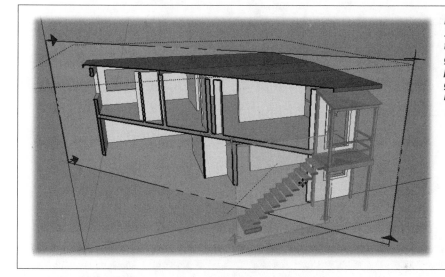

Figure 12-19:
Section planes only affect the entities within their group. Here the section plane crosses the "stairs" group, but it has no effect.

Saving Section Planes and Section Cuts in Scenes

Use the View menu to show or hide section planes and section cuts in your SketchUp modeling window. (See the note on page 418 for the definition of section planes and section cuts.) For example, if you want to show a section cut without the section plane apparatus, go to View → Section Plane to deselect the Section Plane option in the menu. The result looks like Figure 12-20. When you have the look you want, you can save the settings in a scene. Open the Scenes window (Window → Scenes), and make sure that under "Properties to save" the Active Section Planes option is turned on. Click the Add Scene button and you're done.

Keep in mind that you're saving the visibility or invisibility of the section plane and section cut in that scene. You're not saving the position of the plane. If you move a plane after you've saved a scene, your scene won't look like it did when you saved it.

Copying a Section Plane

The easiest way to create a second section plane inside of a group is to duplicate the first one. Select the section plane; then, using the Move (M) tool, press the Ctrl (Option) key. That puts the Move tool in copy mode. When you move the cursor, you see the small Section Plane icon. Click a new position, and SketchUp creates the second section plane, as shown in Figure 12-21.

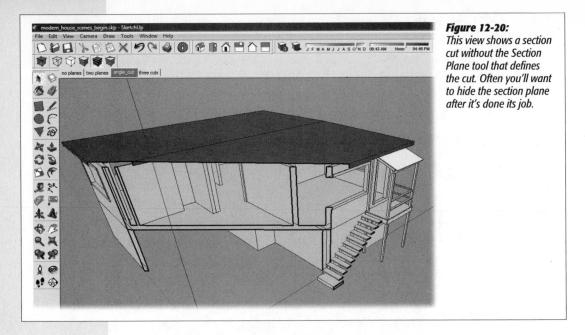

Figure 12-20:
This view shows a section cut without the Section Plane tool that defines the cut. Often you'll want to hide the section plane after it's done its job.

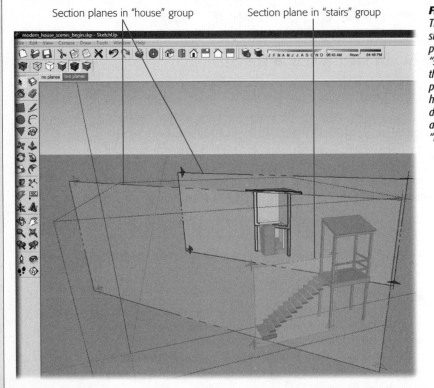

Section planes in "house" group   Section plane in "stairs" group

Figure 12-21:
This SketchUp view shows three section planes: one in the "stairs" group and two in the "house" group. The plane with the blue highlights is active and determines what's visible and not visible in the "house" group.

Setting the Active Section Plane

Within a group, only one section plane can be active at a time, which also means only one section cut is visible. To make a section plane active, right-click the plane, or better yet the plane handles; then choose Active Cut from the shortcut menu.

So if only one section plane can be active at a time, why would you want to have two planes within a group? As far as scenes are concerned, section planes are static objects, like your model. When you save a scene with the Active Section Planes property turned on, SketchUp remembers which section plane is active. So if you want one scene to show the house with a section cut at a 45-degree angle and another scene to show a section cut that's perpendicular to the front wall, you need to have two section planes inside of the house group. Before saving the scene, make sure the correct section plane is active.

Tip: You can show more than one section cut in the modeling window or in a scene as long as the section cuts are inside of different groups. When you have two section planes in a single group, only one can be active and visible at a time.

Part Five: Saving, Printing, and Sharing Projects

5

Importing, Exporting, and Printing

You'll find many reasons to import files from other programs into SketchUp. For example, you've already learned how to use files containing two-dimensional images for textures (page 369) and photo matching (page 353). This chapter details the different types of two-dimensional and three-dimensional files that you can import into SketchUp.

Note: This chapter focuses on the techniques for importing files. Other chapters go into much more detail about what to *do* with the files once they're in SketchUp.

The flip side of importing is exporting. You can create new files by exporting your 3-D model or 2-D image out of SketchUp, and you'll have plenty of occasions to do so. You may want to place your model on the map in Google Earth. Or you may want to create a 2-D image to paste into a document or to email to a colleague. And if you have SketchUp Pro, you can even export a model so someone else can open it in AutoCAD or another 3-D design program.

Printing images from SketchUp is basically just another form of exporting. It just happens that the end product is a printed page instead of a computer file. This chapter explains how to print from SketchUp. (For details on using SketchUp Pro's Layout program, see page 499.)

Importing 3-D Models

Importing 3-D models into SketchUp isn't all that difficult. The import/export business gets dicey in only a couple of places. For example, when one program doesn't understand the features saved by a different program, problems can crop up.

One way to avoid that is by saving files in common, well-understood file formats. SketchUp reads 3-D graphics files from several different sources, as shown in Table 13-1. Other problems can occur when you try to import huge files or files with supercomplex geometry. These types of files gobble up your computer resources and cause slow and erratic behavior in SketchUp.

Table 13-1. Types of 3-D files you can import into SketchUp

File Type	Extension	Note
Autodesk 3D Studio Max	.3ds	Readable by many 3-D graphics programs and used as the common denominator for exchange. 3D Studio Max is a popular program for creating professional quality 3-D models. It's used in everything from computer games to feature films. Its native file format is .max, but it can import and save .3ds files.
Autodesk AutoCAD	.dwg, .dxf	Supports both 2-D and 3-D graphics. AutoCAD is the de facto standard for architects. The relationship between SketchUp and AutoCAD is an important feature. Files with the .dxf extension are AutoCAD Interchange Files.
Digital Elevation Model	.dem	Used by the U.S. Geological Service and others to define topography, .dem files are typically used to create terrain in SketchUp models. The .dem file format varies depending on the program that creates the file, and SketchUp cannot open them all.
Google SketchUp	.skp, .skb	SketchUp can import other SketchUp files into a document. (Components are actually .skp files.) The files with the .skb extension are backup files.

You can save time and minimize your aspirin consumption by preparing files in their native programs before importing them into SketchUp. The following sections provide tips for preparing specific file formats. As a rule of thumb for all files that are destined to be imports, keep them simple and small. For example, if you only want to import the university gymnasium, don't import the entire campus. Save the gym by itself first. Also, where possible eliminate extra details that you won't need in SketchUp. For example, you may want to eliminate layers, text, dimension marks, and hatching.

Importing SketchUp SKP and SKB Files

Naturally the easiest file format to import into your document is one of the native SketchUp formats: *.skp* or *.skb*. When you save models and components, SketchUp automatically saves them in the .skp format. When you import a SketchUp document, it automatically becomes a component in the host document. You can import any .skp file into your document by using the File → Import command. Initially SketchUp assumes you want to open a SketchUp file. To choose any other file formats, use the drop-down menu in the file browser window.

Tip: You can drag a SketchUp file directly into a SketchUp document. The result is the same as File → Import.

Files saved with the .skb extension are backup files. As you work, SketchUp automatically saves backup files. Should lightning strike or if Cuddles your bulldog pulls the computer power plug out of the its socket, you can use the .skb files to recover at least part of your work. You can adjust the settings for backups in SketchUp Preferences: Windows → Preferences in Windows or SketchUp → Preferences on a Mac. The menu is named "Files of type" in Windows or "Format" on Macs. When the Preferences window opens, at left choose General, as shown in Figure 13-1.

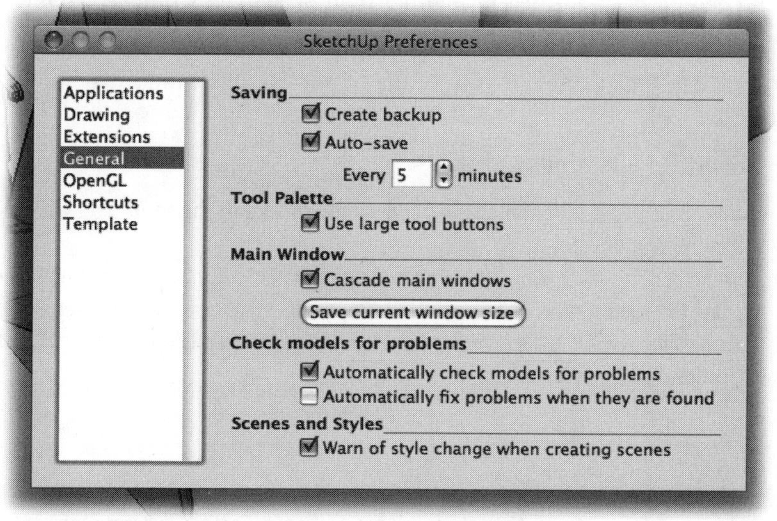

Figure 13-1:
The settings for automatically creating backup files are in the Preferences window under General. It's a good idea to create backups, so keep the Create Backups checkbox turned on, and then decide how frequently you want SketchUp to update the backup file.

Importing AutoCAD 3D DWG or DXF Files

Prepare your CAD files before importing them into SketchUp. Simplify the files as much as you can before bringing them into SketchUp, by eliminating unneeded elements from the files. Use the AutoCAD Purge command to remove unplaced blocks and layers. That way you only import details that you actually need in SketchUp, and your computer won't expend its power on nonessential details. If you need XREF (cross-referenced) information to be available in SketchUp, you must bind it into the AutoCAD file.

1. **Choose File → Import.**

   A file browser window opens; the Windows and Mac versions are slightly different.

2. **Using the "Files of type" or Format drop-down menu, select "AutoCAD files (*.dwg, *.dfx)".**

   This menu narrows down which files you see in the file browser window.

3. **Click Options, and then using the Units drop-down menu, choose the units of measure for the file you're importing.**

   You're giving SketchUp an idea of the scale for the file you're importing. See the box on the next page for more details.

4. **Navigate to the file you want to bring into SketchUp, and then click Open (Import on a Mac).**

   Depending on the complexity of the AutoCAD file you're importing, it can take several minutes to import and convert a file. Programs like AutoCAD handle lines and geometry in a different manner than SketchUp, so more is going on behind the screen than you might guess.

   Once SketchUp digests the file, you see the Import Results window, as shown in Figure 13-2.

5. **In the Import Results window click OK.**

   The window disappears and SketchUp displays the model in the modeling window.

Tip: If you don't immediately see the model in SketchUp, the imported model may be way off in some distant frontier. Click the Zoom Extents button, which shows you all of the entities in your SketchUp universe. If there's something way off in the distance, the entities on your screen become very small, but at least you can track down your new import.

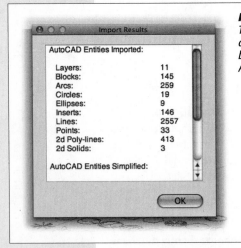

Figure 13-2:
Take time to peruse the Import Results window after you import artwork. Not only do you see a tally of the entities that were imported, but also if there were any problems, you see those noted under AutoCAD Entities Simplified and AutoCAD Entities Ignored.

Importing 3DS Files

So many programs can read and write in the .3ds file format that it's a lingua franca for communicating 3-D information when better options aren't available. The steps for importing .3ds files are similar to those described previously for .dwg files:

- Prepare your file for import by eliminating all the elements that won't be needed in your SketchUp model.

Dealing with CADs

How do I import a CAD file at the proper scale?

When you import a CAD file, take full advantage of the accuracy of the original plan. To apply the appropriate scale when you import CAD files, click the Options button in the file browser window. An Options window opens that's specific to the file's format, like the one in Figure 13-3. Select the scale from the Units drop-down menu. At the same time,

you can choose other settings, such as "Preserve drawing origin", "Merge coplanar faces", or "Orient faces consistently". (Warning: The latter two options have been known to cause problems in some SketchUp models.) Click OK to close the Options box, and then click Open (Import on a Mac) to close the file browser window and import the file.

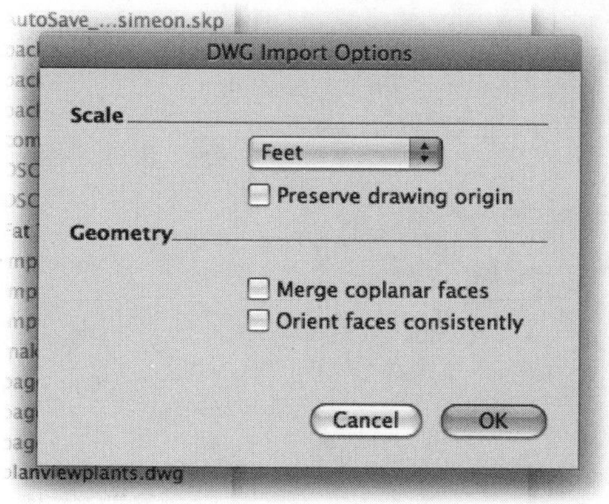

Figure 13-3:
Click the Options button as you're importing files to set the scale. Here in the Import Options window for AutoCAD files, you can choose the units of measure for the file being imported.

- If the 3DS file is textured, the images (usually JPGs) must be stored in the same folder as the 3DS file.

- Use the File → Import command to open a file browser window.

- Use the "Files of type" or Format drop-down menu to choose "3DS Files (*.3ds)".

- Click the Options button to set the import options such as the units of measure to use. Click OK to close the Options window.

- Click Open (or Import) to import the file. If it's a complex file, the importing process can take several minutes.

- View the notes in the Import Results window and then click OK.

- The model appears in the SketchUp window. If it isn't immediately visible, try using Zoom Extents (Camera → Zoom Extents) to find the model.

Models created in other programs such as 3D Studio Max can be very complex, so SketchUp can end up with a lot of edges and faces to analyze and account for. While they can trade document files, programs like SketchUp and 3D Studio Max are designed for very different types of projects. Models with a high polygon count, like the antelope in Figure 13-4, can consume a lot of computer resources and slow SketchUp to a crawl.

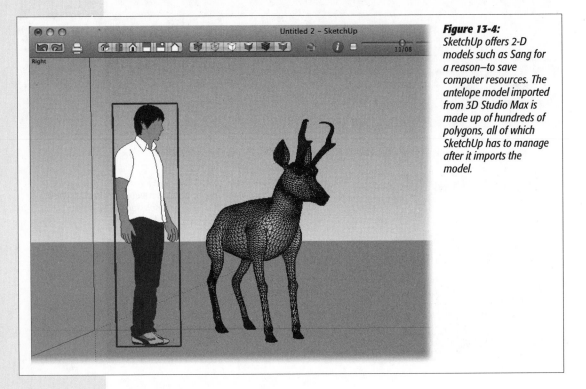

Figure 13-4:
SketchUp offers 2-D models such as Sang for a reason—to save computer resources. The antelope model imported from 3D Studio Max is made up of hundreds of polygons, all of which SketchUp has to manage after it imports the model.

Importing 2-D Images

You can import 2-D graphics into SketchUp for a number of reasons. You can use them as textures for materials or as templates for creating 3-D models. In some cases, you may keep the 2-D image in the model.

When you import 2-D images, you should do your image editing, cropping, and scaling in the native program such as Photoshop, Fireworks, or iPhoto. Crop your image to remove any unneeded portions. SketchUp doesn't import images that are larger than 1024 × 1024 pixels. If an image is larger than that, SketchUp automatically scales it down. Your image editing software can probably do a better job at scaling the image than SketchUp, so you might as well downsize your image in its native program. (If possible, use bicubic resampling if you see it listed among the scaling options.)

Tip: If you want to force SketchUp to import images larger than 1024 pixels, go to Windows → Preferences → OpenGL (SketchUp → Preferences → OpenGL), and then turn on "Use maximum texture size". Depending on your computer and graphics card, though, these images can dramatically slow your system.

The basic steps for importing 2-D graphics are pretty much the same regardless of the file format:

1. **Choose File → Import.**

   A file browser window opens where you can navigate through your file and folder system.

2. **Use the "Files of type" or Format drop-down menu to select the file type you want to import.**

   The types of 2-D image files SketchUp imports are shown in Table 13-2. This menu determines which files you see in the file browser window. You can also choose "All Supported Image Types" to see all possible 2-D files that SketchUp can import.

3. **In the Format drop-down menu, choose how you want to use the image.**

   As shown in Figure 13-5, the menu provides three options: "Use as Image", "Use as Texture", and "Use as New Matched Photo".

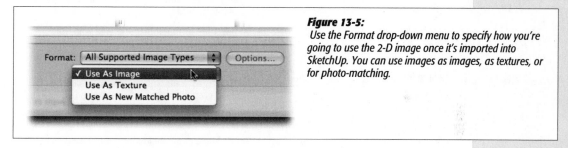

Figure 13-5:
 Use the Format drop-down menu to specify how you're going to use the 2-D image once it's imported into SketchUp. You can use images as images, as textures, or for photo-matching.

4. **Navigate to the folder where your file is stored, and then select the file. Click Open (Import on a Mac).**

   SketchUp imports the file, which may take some time if it's complex. Once it's been imported, you may see an Import Results message box. Your cursor changes to an arrow.

5. **Display and position the imported image in your model.**

   The method you use to display the image depends on the import option you chose in step 3:

   • **Use As Image.** Click two points to position and size your image in the modeling window. Once you've clicked in the modeling window, moving the cursor stretches your image. This method is similar to creating a rectangle. Once you set the two points, your image is a rectangular object that's visible from both sides.

   • **Use As Texture.** If you chose this option, the cursor changes to a paint bucket. Click a face to apply the photo as texture.

   • **Use As New Matched Photo.** Follow the steps for using a photo as a reference for creating a new model on page 353.

Table 13-2. Types of 2-D files you can import into SketchUp

File Type	Extension	Note
Adobe Reader (portable document file)	.pdf	If the PDF file has multiple pages, only the first page is visible in the modeling window. This option is only available on Mac.
AutoCAD	.dwg, .dxf	The .dwg and .dxf file formats support both 2-D and 3-D graphics. AutoCAD is the de facto standard for architects. The relationship between SketchUp and AutoCAD is an important feature.
JPEG Image (Joint Photographic Experts Group)	.jpg	JPG files are relative small because the format uses a "lossy" compression technique. Some photographic detail may be lost when the file is compressed.
Photoshop	.psd	Photoshop is the de facto standard for editing photos and other 2-D graphics.
Piranesi	.epx	Piranesi is a program that's used to create high-quality artistic renderings. This option is only available on a Mac.
Portable Network Graphics	.png	A newer file format that works well with both photographic images and line art. Compresses images without losing detail.
Tagged Image File	.tif, .tiff	A "lossless" raster image file format.
Targa File	.tga	A raster graphic image file format originally defined by AT&T and used by Truevision for their video graphics cards.
Windows Bitmap	.bmp	An early raster image file format not used as much in recent years.

Importing 2-D AutoCAD DWG and DXF Files

AutoCAD files can contain either 2-D or 3-D information. As in all other cases, you want to prepare the files as much as possible in the native program before importing them into SketchUp. Here are some of the things to do to prepare AutoCAD .dwg and .dxf files before you import them:

- Remove entities from the CAD file that you won't be using in SketchUp.

- Move the objects you need close to the Origin in the CAD program.

- If you need to use XREF (cross-referenced) information from AutoCAD in SketchUp, you must bind it into the AutoCAD file before importing. Otherwise SketchUp won't import any XREF information.

- Use the AutoCAD Purge command to remove memory-consuming but unplaced blocks.

UP TO SPEED

Vector vs. Bitmap Images

The world of 2-D computer graphics offers two systems for storing and displaying images: vector graphics and bitmaps (technically called *raster* graphics). Computers store vector graphics as a bunch of formulas. Vector graphics are relatively modest in size compared with bitmaps and they're scalable. In other worlds if you draw a tiny water fountain and then decide to scale it 500 percent, your scaled drawing will still look like a nice, crisp water fountain, only much bigger.

In contrast, computer programs store bitmap, or raster image graphics (such as a scanned photo), as a bunch of pixels. "Bitmap graphics" doesn't refer to just files with the Windows bitmap (.bmp) extension; it refers to all images stored in bitmap format, including .gif, .jpg, .tiff, and .png.

The good thing about bitmap graphics is that they let you create superrealistic detail with complex colors, gradients, and subtle shadings. On the downside, bitmaps typically take up a whopping amount of disk space, and they're not particularly scalable. If you scale a photo of a water fountain by 500 percent, it appears blurry. Several bitmap formats (PNG, PSD, TIFF, and TGA) let you import images with transparent areas. This technique is great for creating complex images and special effects.

Why should you care whether a graphics file is a vector or a bitmap? It's important to understand the strengths and weaknesses of both formats when you import and export 2-D images. Bitmaps are better for photorealistic images with lots of colors and shades. Vector graphics are better for line art and images that you're going to scale to different sizes.

- Use the AutoCAD Purge command to remove layers that have content that won't be needed in your SketchUp model. This may be text, dimension marks, hatching, or company logos.

- Since SketchUp may only partially import AutoCAD dynamic blocks, explode the dynamic blocks, or convert them to normal blocks. Normal blocks become SketchUp components.

After you prepare and save the file, follow these steps to bring it into SketchUp:

1. **In your SketchUp document, choose File → Import.**

   A standard file browser window opens.

2. **In the "Files of type" (or Format) menu, choose the type of file you want to import, such as "AutoCAD files (*.dwg, *.dfx)".**

   Initially the Import window is set to SketchUp files, so other types of files are either not visible or they're grayed out. Once you set the menu to the AutoCAD file format, you can select and import .dwg and .dxf files.

Note: If you choose the "All Supported Image Types", SketchUp displays the 2-D file types. AutoCAD files aren't included in this list because they can be either 2-D or 3-D.

---

3. **Navigate to the folder that holds the file you want to import.**

   Both Windows and Mac file browsers let you choose files on your computer or on a local computer network.

4. **Select the file and click Open (Import).**

SketchUp imports the file and displays an Import Results window that provides information about the process, as shown in Figure 13-6. If your SketchUp document already has content, it places the imported AutoCAD entities in a new SketchUp component. If your SketchUp document is empty, the AutoCAD file appears in SketchUp as separate components and entities.

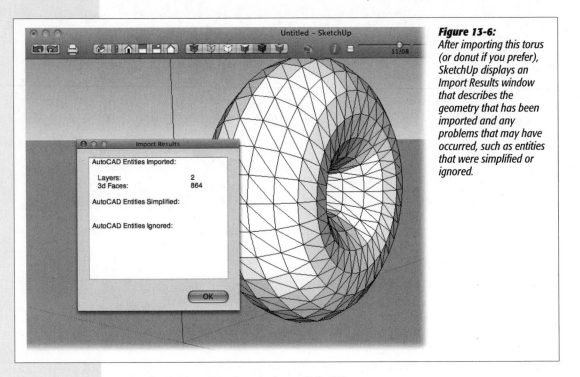

Figure 13-6:
After importing this torus (or donut if you prefer), SketchUp displays an Import Results window that describes the geometry that has been imported and any problems that may have occurred, such as entities that were simplified or ignored.

5. **In the Import Results window, click OK.**

The Import Results box closes, and your graphic appears in the SketchUp window. You can reposition it using the Move (M) tool.

After you've imported an AutoCAD file into SketchUp, you can do a few things to make the new entities in your model cooperate. Your best bet is to organize these new entities by using SketchUp components and layers. If you have 2-D elements that are going to remain 2-D, such as subdivision property lines or parking lot markers, save these entities in a component. Here's a good procedure:

1. **Create a new layer to hold your 2-D elements.**

2. **Select the 2-D element you want to move, and use the Entity Info window (right-click → Entity Info) to move them to the new layer.**

3. **Using the Layers window (Windows → Layers), hide all the layers.**

4. **Use Edit → Select All (Ctrl+A on Windows; ⌘-A on Macs) to select all visible entities.**

5. Choose Edit → Make Component or right-click → Make Component.

6. Name your component and make sure the "Replace Selection with Component" option is turned on.

Tip: AutoCAD defines shapes and objects differently than SketchUp, making it difficult to extrude AutoCAD shapes into 3-D SketchUp objects. You're better off keeping AutoCAD shapes in a component and tracing over them. Then you can extrude those shapes into SketchUp 3-D objects.

Importing Photoshop PSD Files

The way SketchUp handles 2-D images is pretty basic. For example, you don't have many ways to change an image once it's imported. You can scale it, skew it, and position it in the 3-D world, but you can't edit the photo itself. On the other hand, Photoshop (.psd) images can be extremely complex. As with the other 2-D formats, you need to do your image editing in Photoshop before you import the image into SketchUp.

Tip: You can tell SketchUp which program you want to use to edit images. Choose Windows → Preferences → Applications (SketchUp → Preferences → Applications) and click the Choose button. A file browser window opens, where you can navigate to Photoshop or any image editing program you like. Once you select a program in Preferences, you can then right-click (⌘-click) any image and choose Texture → Edit Texture Image to open it in that program.

As mentioned on page 432, unless you make changes in Preferences, SketchUp limits the size of imported images to 1024 pixels. Photoshop does a better job of resizing images than SketchUp, so it's best to resize images before you import them. When you save a Photoshop image in its native .psd format, the last thing you see is the Photoshop Format Options box asking if you want to save the file with "maximum compatibility". Make sure the single checkbox is turned on. If not, you may see an error message similar to the one in Figure 13-7 that says: "This layered Photoshop file was not saved with a composite image".

Figure 13-7:
An identical image was saved with (left) and without (right) Photoshop's compatibility option. The image saved without the compatibility option displays an error message when you try to import it.

Exporting from SketchUp

With the standard SketchUp program, you can export .kmz models for Google Earth, and you can export to a variety of two-dimensional image formats. If you need more options for exporting 3-D models, it's time to step up to SketchUp Pro. See page 442 for all the options available.

Exporting 3-D Images

The standard SketchUp program only exports one type of 3-D model—the .kmz files used in Google Earth. (For the formats exported by SketchUp Pro, see page 442.) The process for exporting .kmz files is simple:

1. **Choose File → Export.**

    A window appears.

2. **From the "Export type" drop-down menu, choose "Google Earth (*.kmz)".**

    This option sets the file format for export.

3. **Type a file name for the model in the "File name" box ("Save as" for Macs).**

    You can navigate to any folder where you want to save the file, including your desktop. You don't have to type the extension (.kmz); SketchUp adds that automatically.

4. **Click Export.**

    SketchUp saves the file in the folder you designated with the name you provided.

Exporting Models to Google Earth

If your goal is to place your model in Google Earth and you don't need to save a .kmz file for other purposes, you can use the Google toolbar (View → Toolbars → Google in Windows; View → Tool Palettes → Google on Mac). As an alternative, you can use the Tools → Google Earth → Place Model command. Before you rush off and populate Google Earth with models, here are a few tips to keep in mind.

• Make sure your model is properly georeferenced as described on page 389. SketchUp uses the longitude and latitude coordinates when it places you model.

• In Google Earth, turn on the 3D Buildings layer. Go to the Sidebar, open the Layers panel and turn on the box next to 3D Buildings.

• After you place your model, it appears in the Google Earth sidebar under Places → Temporary Places with a name like SUPreview2. You can change the name and some of the other properties by Right-clicking the name and choosing Properties from the shortcut menu. At this point, your model appears in Google Earth on your computer, but it isn't visible to the other millions of Google Earth users.

• If you want your model to become a permanent part of Google Earth as seen by everyone, it needs to be approved by a panel of judges. Bonnie Roskes' *Google SketchUp Cookbook* (O'Reilly) offers some great tips on what the judges want from models. They need to be accurate, yet simple. For example, use graphic images to provide details for building features rather than modeling the facades.

Exporting 2-D Images

Think of the 2-D images that SketchUp exports as snapshots of your model, using the modeling window as the camera. Accordingly arrange everything in the image just as you want it, before you take the shot. If you want shadows, make sure you've got Display Shadows turned on in the Shadows window (Windows → Shadows). If you don't want the reference guides you used to build the model to appear in the image, make sure you turn them off (by choosing View → Guides to remove the checkmark).

Once your model is just the way you want it, follow these steps:

1. **Choose File → Export.**

   A file browser box appears, where you can navigate to any folder on your computer.

2. **From the "Export type" drop-down menu, choose the file format you want to use.**

   Your choices are JPEG, PNG, or TIFF.

3. **Click the Options button.**

   A window appears, displaying options for the file format you chose, as shown in Figure 13-8.

4. **Select the options you want and then click OK.**

   Turn on the **Use View Size** checkbox if you want to export an image with the same number of pixels as the view in SketchUp. Otherwise if you turn this box off, you can enter values in the **Width** and **Height** boxes. On a Mac, if you want to make the proportions of the saved file different from the SketchUp image, click the chain link. Once the link is "broken," the width and height values don't have to be proportional.

Note: In the free version of SketchUp, the maximum vertical or horizontal dimensions are limited to the size of the SketchUp window on your computer—in other words, the screen resolution. In SketchUp Pro, the maximum resolution is 8000 pixels. However, on Windows XP, when anti-aliasing is turned on, the maximum resolution is 4000 pixels.

Use the **Resolution** box to set the number of pixels per inch. Your answer to this question depends on how you're going to use the image. If you're putting it up on the Web or emailing it, 72–96 pixels per inch works well. If you want to print the image, use 300 pixels per inch or more. If you're going to print it in a large format like a poster, you may want to use an even higher figure.

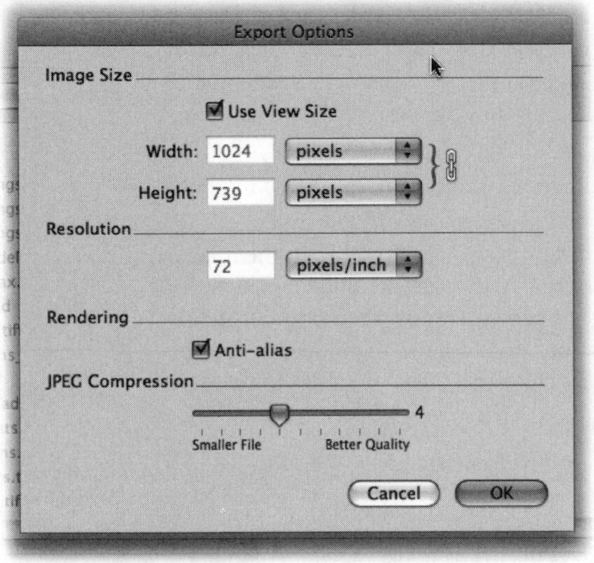

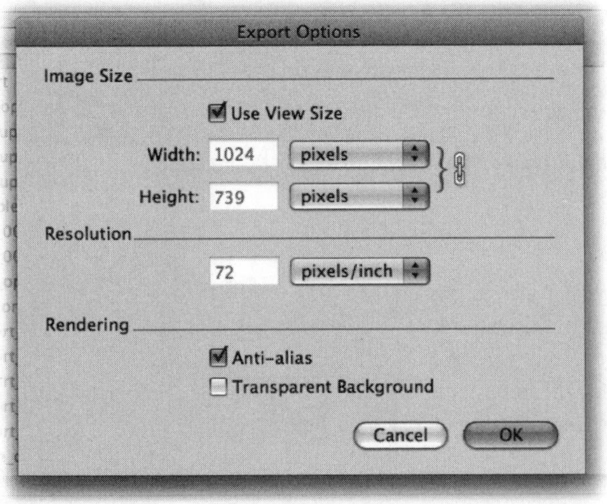

Figure 13-8:
Top: Export options for JPEG images let you choose how much you want to compress the image.

Bottom: On a Mac, the export options for PNG or TIFF images let you choose to make the background of the image transparent.

Leave the **Anti-alias** option turned on, since this minimizes the appearance of saw-tooth edges on diagonal lines.

JPEG only: The **JPEG Compression** slider lets you choose the amount of compression applied to the saved image. Drag the slider to the left for smaller files with more compression. Drag the slider to the right for better quality and larger files.

PNG and TIFF only: The **Transparent Background** option creates an image with a transparent background. It lets you use a cutout of your model in another image or on a Web page.

When you click OK, the Options window closes.

5. **Click Export.**

   SketchUp saves the image using the name you provided in the file format you specified.

Once you save your image in a different file format, you can load it into a program like Photoshop for further enhancement. Take a look at Lewis Wadsworth's Stormhouse in Figure 13-9.

Figure 13-9:
To create this amazing image, Lewis Wadsworth (one of this book's technical reviewers) exported multiple 2-D images from SketchUp that use the same camera view, but different styles and effects. Using Photoshop layers, masks, and transparency controls, he added visual effects that would be impossible using only SketchUp.

Exporting from SketchUp Pro

One of the major differences between the $499 version of SketchUp Pro and the free standard version of SketchUp is the number of file formats that the Pro version exports. Table 13-3 shows the complete list. The most significant difference is that SketchUp Pro exports models that you can open in AutoCAD. You can also export models that can be used in programs such as 3D Studio Max, Lightwave, and other 3-D modeling tools.

The steps for exporting 3-D models from SketchUp Pro are fairly simple:

1. **Choose File → Export.**

   A window appears.

2. **From the "Export type" drop-down menu, choose a file format.**

   You can choose from the file formats listed in Table 13-3.

3. **If you wish, click Options to change settings specific to the file format.**

   For example, AutoCAD options let you choose between different versions of the AutoCAD file format. You can also choose the type of entities you wish to export: Faces, Edges, Construction Geometry, Dimensions, and Text.

The orientation of the X, Y, and Z axes is different for programs that use OBJ, like Blender and Maya, so when you export to OBJ, it's best to turn on the "Swap YZ coordinates (Y is up)" checkbox.

Collada, FBX, OBJ, and XSI options let you limit the entities exported to ones that are selected. In Collada you can also export textures and create "cameras".

VRML options let you export textures and generate cameras.

4. **Type a file name for the model in the "File name" box ("Save as" for Mac).**

You can navigate to any folder where you want to save the file, including your desktop. You don't have to type the extension; SketchUp adds that automatically.

5. **Click Export.**

SketchUp saves the file in the folder you designated with the name you provided.

Tip: SketchUp faces have two sides—an inside and an outside. When exporting 3-D SketchUp models to other file formats, it's important that the faces in the model are properly oriented with all the outside faces facing out. To change the orientation of a face, right-click the face with the Select tool, and then choose Reverse Faces from the shortcut menu.

Table 13-3. Types of 3-D files you can export from SketchUp Pro

File Type	Extension	Note
3D Studio Max	.3ds	Used for film and game development.
AutoCAD	.dwg, .dxf	Used for architectural design projects.
Google Earth	.kmz	Used to place 3-D models in Google Earth.
Collada	.dae	Originally developed by Sony for the PlayStation, the format is often used for interactive 3-D applications.
FBX	.fbx	Originally developed for and used by Filmbox software. Currently part of Autodesk's digital content creation software family.
Lightwave 3D, Maya, Blender	.obj	Used by several 3-D modeling programs to define geometry.
Virtual	.vrml	Stands for Virtual Reality Modeling Language and is used to display 3-D models in web browsers. VRML is an older file format. The replacement format for VRML is X3D.
Softimage	.xsi	Used for film and game development.

Exporting 2-D Images

The standard version of SketchUp only exports three types of two-dimensional graphic images: .jpg, .png, and .tiff. SketchUp Pro exports to several additional file formats, as shown in Table 13-4.

Table 13-4. Types of 2-D files you can export from SketchUp Pro

File Type	Extension	Note
Adobe Reader	.pdf	Exports a PDF document with a single page. The dimensions of the page match the SketchUp modeling window.
AutoCAD	.dwg, .dxf	Creates files that can be imported into AutoCAD.
Encapsulated Post Script	.eps	EPS files can be opened in a variety of programs including Adobe Illustrator and Adobe Photoshop.
JPEG	.jpg	JPG files are relatively small because the format uses a "lossy" compression technique. Some photographic detail may be lost when the file is compressed.
Piranesi	.epx	Piranesi is a program to create high-quality, artistic renderings.
Portable Network Graphic	.png	A newer file format that works well with both photographic images and line art. Compresses images without losing detail.
Tagged Image File	.tif, .tiff	Creates files larger than JPEG images. Compresses images without losing photographic detail.
Windows Bitmap	.bmp	An early raster image file format not used as much in recent years.

Exporting Animations

After you've created a perfect animation using the techniques described in Chapter 12, you can export the result as a video file. If you're making an important presentation, you may find it easier to talk while a video is playing than while controlling a SketchUp walkthrough. Fortunately the steps for exporting SketchUp animation are simple. Windows computers create Video for Windows (.avi) files, and Macs create QuickTime (.mov) files.

The biggest decision is figuring out the optimum video format for what you're doing. If you want to put your video on a DVD, you can go for a large video image and film quality video. If you plan to show a video on a website, you'll want to reduce the size and the quality. If you're thinking of emailing the video to anyone other than an enemy, you need to reduce the file size even more. The following steps include guidelines for determining file sizes:

1. **Prepare your animation using the techniques described in Chapter 12.**

   Your video animation will play just like the animation you see when you use the View → Animation → Play command. However, in SketchUp you can start the animation from any scene. The video file always begins with the first scene that's marked "Include in animation" in the Scenes window and then plays through each of the included scenes.

2. **Choose File → Export → Animation.**

   The Export Animation window opens.

---

3. **Choose the Export type (Format on Mac).**

   Avi File (.avi) is the video format for Windows computers. QuickTime Movie (.mov) is the format for Macs.

Tip: If your audience uses a variety of computers, don't worry. Both Windows and Macintosh computers can play both types of files these days. The worst that can happen is that some members of your audience may need to download the specific software before viewing your animation.

   In addition to saving an animation as a video file, you can save animations as a series of still images in several different formats, including JPG, PNG, and TIFF. Windows can also save in the BMP format.

4. **In the "File name" or "Save as" box, type a file name for the model.**

   You can navigate to any folder where you want to save the file, including your desktop. You don't have to type the extension; SketchUp adds that automatically.

   If you were happy with the technical details of the last video SketchUp produced, here's some good news—you don't have to change anything. SketchUp remembers your last-used image size, frame rate, and codec. If you don't need to make any changes, you can choose the Export button and skip the rest of these steps.

5. **To make changes to the size or quality of the video, click Options.**

   The Animation Export Options window opens (Figure 13-10). (On a Mac, it's just called Export Options.)

Figure 13-10:
You change the size of your video image using the Width and Height settings in the Animation Export Options window. Video files of just about any size and aspect ratio look good on a computer monitor. If you want your video to play well on TV, choose one of the standard formats: 1920×1080, 1280×720, 704×480, or 640×480.

6. **Choose the dimensions.**

   In Windows: In the drop-down menu, choose 16:9 for a widescreen format or 4:3 for a standard format. Then set the width: HD video is 1280 pixels; DVDs use 720 pixels. For CDs and websites, widths from about 640 to 320 pixels work well. If you're going to email a video to someone, you may want to go down to about 120 or 160 pixels. When you set the width, the height automatically changes to fit the format, as long as the chain links next to Width and Height aren't broken.

   On Mac: Use the Format drop-down menu to set the format, dimensions, and frame rate in frames per second (fps). Your choices are Email (160×120, 10 fps), Web and Web streaming (240×180, 12 fps), CD-ROM Medium (320× 240, 15 fps), CD-ROM Large (640×480, 15 fps), and Full Quality DV (720× 480, 29.97 fps). These are pretty good guidelines, but you can override them by typing any value you want in the Width, Height, and Frame Rate boxes.

7. **Choose a frame rate.**

   Choosing a higher frame rate produces smoother video, but keep in mind the tradeoff is a larger file. Standard television uses a video rate of 29.97 frames per second (fps), while motion pictures have always used 24 fps. A SketchUp video can look good at 15 frames per second. If you're emailing the video or have another reason to trade quality for file size, you can use a frame rate as low as 10 fps.

8. **Optionally, choose a Codec. In Windows, click the Codec button. On a Mac, click Expert.**

   Codec is a techie term for compressor-decompressor. Unless someone asks you to use a specific codec for your video, you probably don't need to make changes here.

   Initially Windows computers are set to use the Cinepak Codec. Cinepak is an older codec, but it's not a bad choice, since it's compatible with a wide variety of computer programs and video devices. If you want to upgrade to a higher quality codec, choose 3ivx MPEG-4, a codec capable of producing broadcast quality video.

   Mac computers start out with the H.264 codec. H.264 is a good choice for Macs, since it's the codec that Apple uses for iTunes, iPods, and AppleTV. The H.264 codec is also known as MPEG-4 Part 10. It's a popular codec that produces high quality video in smaller files.

9. **Click OK to close the Video Compression window (Compression Settings on a Mac). Then click Export.**

   SketchUp displays a progress bar as it "renders" your video.

Printing SketchUp Views

In many ways, printing is like exporting a two-dimensional image. The difference is that the output goes to paper instead of to a computer file. As when exporting a 2-D image, you have to set up your view before you export. Make sure that your camera position, angle, and field of view are exactly the way you want. Double-check things like shadows and guides to make sure they're visible or invisible (whichever you want them to be). Remember that perspective views don't provide output to scale. If you want to print a scale plane, make sure you use the parallel projection view before choosing the Print button.

Tip: If you want to change the proportions of the image before you print, change the size of your SketchUp document window. In Windows, if your window fills the screen, click the Restore Down button in the upper-right corner. (It's the middle button of the three in the corner.) Then drag any edge of the window to resize the modeling window. On Mac, drag the lower-right corner to resize the SketchUp window.

Printing from Windows

After you have your view arranged properly, follow these steps to print from Windows:

1. **Choose File → Print Setup.**

   The Print Setup window (Figure 13-11) appears.

2. **Adjust the Print settings to match your job. Then click OK.**

   Windows remembers your printer's usual settings, so you usually don't need to change the choice of printer and paper size. However, you may want to double-check the Orientation options, since SketchUp images usually use Landscape orientation, and most other documents use Portrait. When you click OK, the window closes.

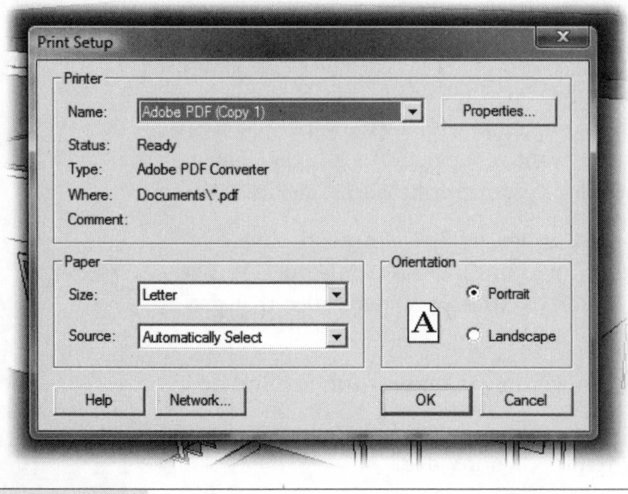

Figure 13-11:
The Windows Print Setup window gives you options to choose a printer, the paper size, and the orientation of the paper. You seldom need to tweak any of the other options.

3. **If you like, choose Print Preview.**

   SketchUp displays the Print Preview window, with the same options you use to print the document. When you click OK, you see a preview of the image on a page, exactly as it will print. If you're happy with the results, choose Print and the image will hit the page.

4. **If you didn't visit the Print Preview window, choose File → Print.**

The Print window (Figure 13-12) opens with options to choose the printer, the number of copies, and the image's dimensions.

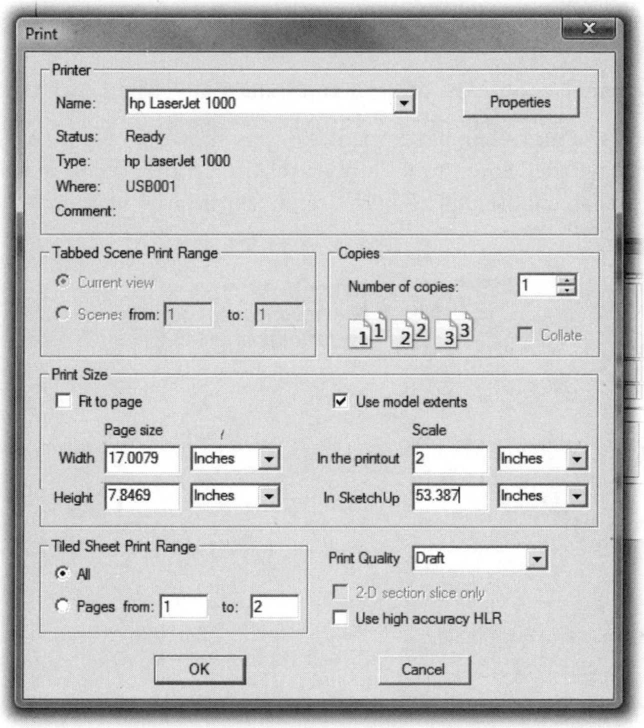

Figure 13-12:
In the Windows Print window, you can choose standard options like printer and number of copies. Turn on the "Fit to page" checkbox to automatically size the image to fit the paper. Turn off the checkbox if you want to print an image to scale.

5. **Choose the options you want to use.**

If you want more than one copy, type a number in the Copies box. If you choose the "Fit to page" option, the image is sized to match the paper. If you want to print to scale, make sure the view of the image is in Parallel Projection (Camera → Parallel Projection). Then turn off the "Fit to page" option. The values under Scale show the current scale of the printout. You can manually change these values, which changes the size of the image. Images too big to fit on a single page will print on multiple pages. The number of pages needed to print your image appears in the Tiled Sheet Print Range box.

Note: Perspective views cannot be used to print plans to scale. Your camera view of the model must be in a Parallel Projection view (Camera → Parallel Projection). When SketchUp can't print a view to scale, the Scale setting is grayed out. For best results choose head-on views: Front, Back, Top, Bottom, Left, and Right.

6. Click OK.

SketchUp prints the image according to your specs.

Printing from a Mac

1. Choose File → Page Setup.

   The Page Setup panel drops down from the top of the window.

2. **On the Page Setup panel, choose the options you want to use. Then click OK.**

   Choose your paper size and your page orientation, as shown in Figure 13-13. Usually it's fine to leave the "Format for" box set to Any Printer. If you're using a special plotter, you can choose that as an option in the drop-down menu.

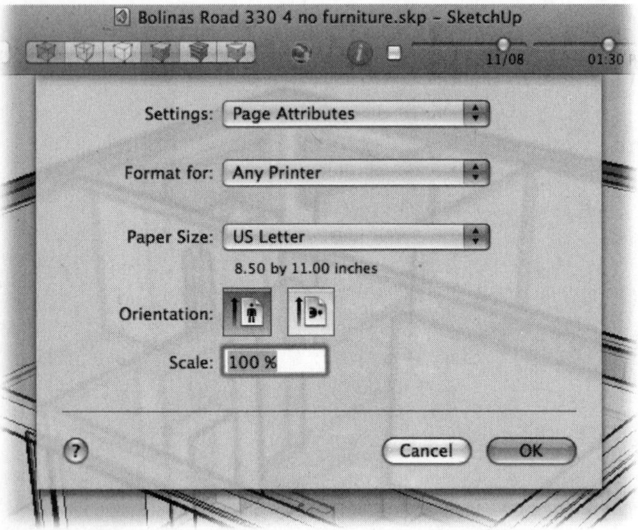

Figure 13-13:
Use the basic setup option that you want to use for the print job.

3. Choose File → Document Setup.

   A panel appears where you can size the image and set the scale (Figure 13-14). Choose "Fit View to Page" to have SketchUp automatically scale the image to fit the paper size. If you want to enter custom dimensions, turn off the "Fit View to Page" option, and type dimensions in the Width and Height boxes. If your model isn't a perspective view, you can enter values in the Print Scale boxes to set the scale.

4. Choose File → Print.

   The Print panel appears, where you can choose a printer and the number of copies to print, as shown in Figure 13-15.

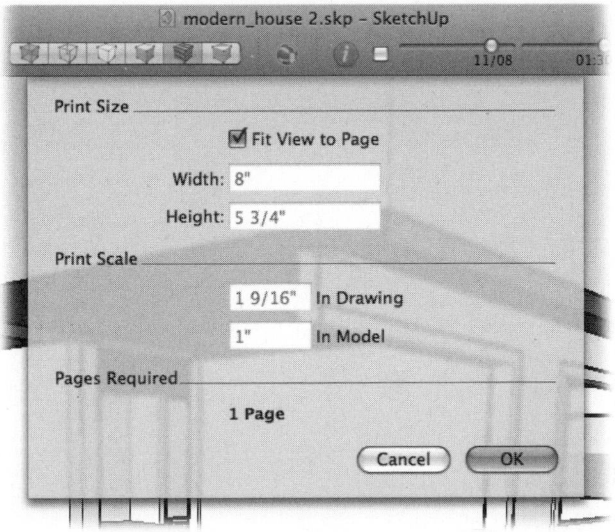

Figure 13-14:
Use the document settings (File → Document Setup) to set the size of the image on the page, and if you're creating a plan view, you can also set the scale.

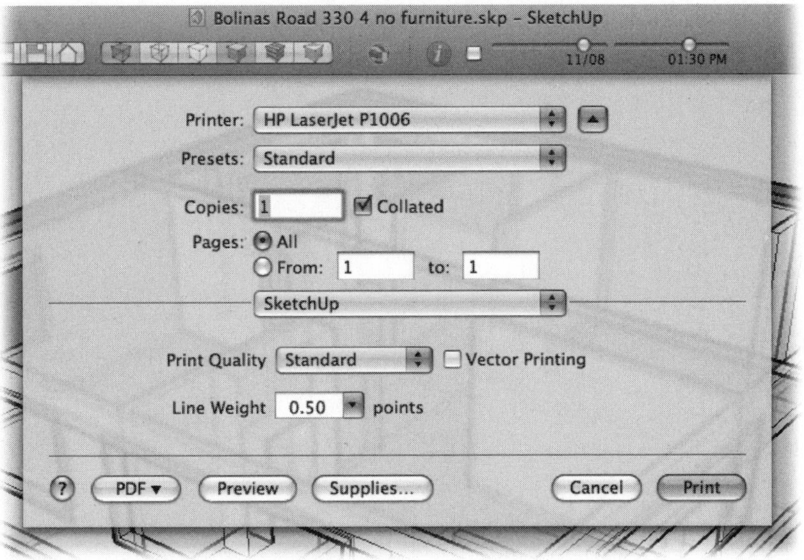

Figure 13-15:
In the Print window, you can choose the printer and the number of copies you want. If you want to double-check the image one last time before you print, click the Preview button.

5. **If you want to double-check, click the Preview button.**

   SketchUp displays the image exactly as it will appear by using the Mac's Preview program. When you're through previewing, press ⌘-Q to close the Preview program and go back to SketchUp.

6. **In the Print window, click the Print button.**

   SketchUp prints the image according to your specs.

CHAPTER 14

Finding, Creating, and Sharing Components

One of the great things about components is that you don't always have to build your own from scratch. Need a garage door? Need a model of a Mayan temple? Want to put a Porsche in your garage? You can find the models you need at the 3D Warehouse. The first part of this chapter gives you the details for finding components. You'll learn how to do quick searches, and then for help with those hard-to-find components, you learn how to use the advanced search tools. Dynamic components are customizable components that any SketchUp user can modify. In previous chapters you saw examples of windows that you could resize and doors that opened and closed.

You can use dynamic components with any version of SketchUp 7, but you need SketchUp 7 Pro to *create* a dynamic component. This chapter introduces the basic steps for creating a dynamic component that changes size and color. Once you create a great component, you may want to share it with others in the SketchUp community. You can do that by uploading your best creations to the 3D Warehouse.

Finding Components in the 3D Warehouse

Using SketchUp without using the 3D Warehouse is like using a computer and never going on the Internet. You needn't build everything from scratch, since chances are, whatever you need is already out there. Suppose you spend days creating a model of a house complete with interiors and exteriors. You want to create a walkthrough video, but you'd really like to have the house furnished. Instead of spending hours designing furniture for every room, take a trip to the 3D Warehouse and download chairs, tables, and sofas. Get appliances for the kitchen, and park a car in that garage. You'll find everything you need prebuilt. Using the ware-house is as simple as, well, a Google search. Check it out:

1. **In a new SketchUp document, choose Window → Components.**

   The Components window opens. The Components window shows details about a selected component at the top. Below that, you see three tabs: Select, Edit, and Statistics.

2. **Click the Select tab and then in the text box that says "Google", type** *Chichen Itza.*

   A progress bar appears briefly, and then the bottom part of the Components window fills with mini Mayan temples (Figure 14-1). At the very bottom of the window, you see a report on the results of your search, as in "Results 1-12 of about 21." That means the current window shows 12 models, and if you want to see more, click the arrow in the lower-right corner.

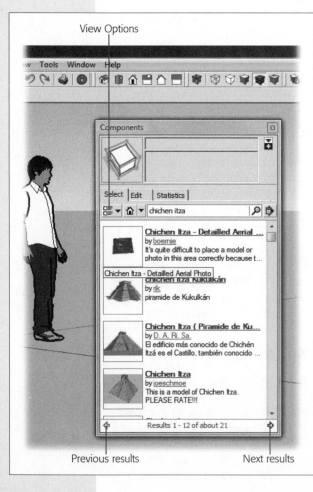

View Options

Previous results

Next results

Figure 14-1:
A search for Chichen Itza—a structure designed without the help of SketchUp—displays more than 20 models and images. When you have more results than fit in the Components window, use the Next and Previous buttons to see them.

Tip: You can download models from the 3D Warehouse without a Google Account. But to *upload* models, you need to sign into a Google Account. If you don't have one, you can create one as described in the box on page 454.

3. **Click a Chichen Itza thumbnail picture, and then click in your modeling window.**

   When you click the picture, the model is automatically downloaded, after which it's attached to your cursor so you can place it in your modeling window with a single click. As shown in Figure 14-2, some of the Chichen Itza models include Google Earth photos for positioning.

Tip: Just because you download a 3D Warehouse model, doesn't mean you have to use it. Check out a few of the models and use the one you like best. There's no extra charge—they're all free.

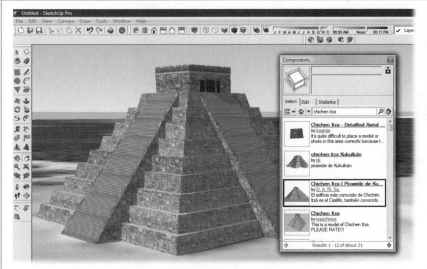

Figure 14-2:
This 3D Warehouse model of Chichen Itza by D. A. Ri Sa included a large Google Earth image. To get a good view of the actual model, you need to zoom way in on the image.

4. **Click the View Options button and then choose Details.**

   You have several views in the Components window: Large Thumbnails, Small Thumbnails, Details, and List. As shown in Figure 14-2, the Details view shows a thumbnail image and also shows the model and designer's names.

5. **Click a model name.**

   Model names are shown in blue with an underline, to indicate that these are actually web links. Clicking the model name opens the 3D Warehouse browser window and displays a web page devoted to the model.

6. **Click a designer's name.**

The designers' names are displayed in green with an underline (Figure 14-3). Click a name and you see a web page showing the models created by that designer.

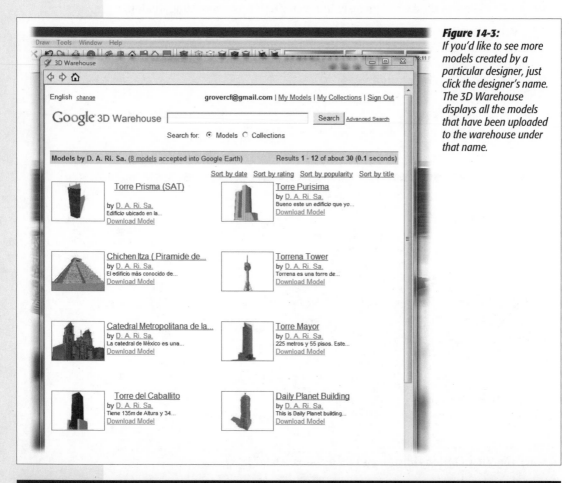

Figure 14-3:
If you'd like to see more models created by a particular designer, just click the designer's name. The 3D Warehouse displays all the models that have been uploaded to the warehouse under that name.

Signing into the 3D Warehouse

SketchUp expects you to sign in when you upload models to the 3D Warehouse. So on your first visit, you need to either provide an existing Google Account name and password or create a new account (Figure 14-4).

It won't cost you any money, just a couple of seconds. Click the "G" icon in the lower-left corner of the SketchUp window (Figure 1-3). When the "Create an Account" page opens,

type your email address and a password. Provide a nickname, which is the name other people see when you use the account. Last but not least, you need to agree to the terms of service. If you plan on using the 3D Warehouse frequently, turn on the "Remember me on this computer" box. If you're using a public computer or sharing a computer with people you don't trust, don't turn on this box.

Figure 14-4:
You need to sign in to use the 3D Warehouse. If you don't already have a Google Account, you need to create one. Click the "Create an account now" button and provide the usual details.

Exploring the Model Browser Window

Conveniently, the 3D Warehouse isn't a big industrial building; it's a website. You can get there in various ways, as explained in the box on page 456. Whether you get there through SketchUp or by using your favorite web browser, the view looks pretty much the same. Pages for individual models look like Figure 14-5.

Often you have several ways to view a model. Sometimes in addition to seeing a simple image, you can see a 3-D view. Drag the 3-D image to see the model from different angles. Below the model, you see a report on the number of times the model has been viewed and downloaded in the past 7 days. If you decide to download the model, click the Download Model link (Figure 14-5). The "Model complexity" section has three categories: Simple, Moderate, and Complex. Complex models may be made up of thousands of polygons, which can really put a strain on SketchUp and your other computer resources. Other models may be made up of just a few polygons and photo texturing. Why is the complexity of a model important? If all you're doing is adding a refrigerator to an already complex kitchen model, a simple model is probably better. If you need a perfectly accurate, detailed model of a Whirlpool side-by-side refrigerator, model number ED5HHAXVQOO, with in-door water and ice, then it's likely you want the more complex model.

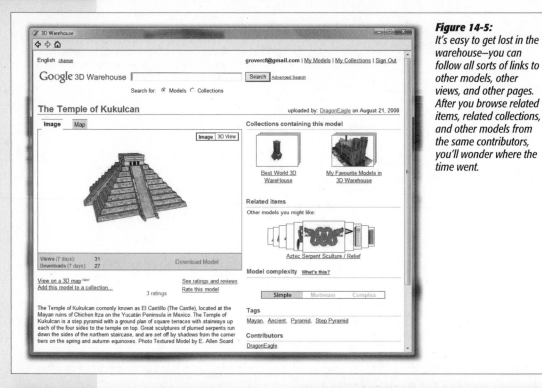

Figure 14-5:
It's easy to get lost in the warehouse—you can follow all sorts of links to other models, other views, and other pages. After you browse related items, related collections, and other models from the same contributors, you'll wonder where the time went.

Many Roads to the Warehouse

You may have noticed more than one road to the 3D Warehouse. From inside of SketchUp, you can use the Components window as described on page 332. If you have the Google toolbar displayed, click the Get Model button, and the 3D Warehouse window opens displaying the 3D Warehouse, as shown in Figure 14-6. It may not look like your usual computer browser, but the window is a web browser dedicated to the 3D Warehouse. If you're outside of SketchUp, you can still find the 3D Warehouse using your everyday web browser. The address is *http://sketchup. google.com/3dwarehouse/*, but it's probably easier just to type *3D warehouse* in the search box on your browser.

Advanced Searching in the 3D Warehouse

It's possible that your warehouse searching may never take you beyond the search box in the Components window. You may find that the models you need always seem to pop up. On the other hand, when your search needs go beyond the ordinary, it's good to know that you can use the advanced search tools shown in Figure 14-7.

The advanced search tools give you a way to hunt down just about any information that appears on a model's information page. (For an example of a model info page see Figure 14-5.) The individual search topics are grouped in a few categories. You certainly don't have to fill out every box and choose every button.

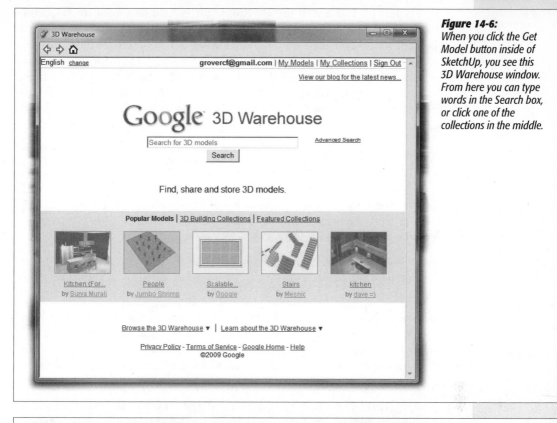

Figure 14-6:
When you click the Get Model button inside of SketchUp, you see this 3D Warehouse window. From here you can type words in the Search box, or click one of the collections in the middle.

Figure 14-7:
When your 3D Warehouse search seems like looking for a needle in a haystack, it's time to call on the advanced search tools. You can search for specific tag words, models created by a certain person, models located in a certain place, or models designed on a specific date.

Just provide the details you think are necessary to hunt down that perfect model. Here are the major search categories:

- **Find results.** Three text boxes let you search on words that appear in the title, words that appear in the description, and words that are used as tags. A drop-down menu lets you specify the order of the results. Choose to have the results sorted by date, sorted by rating, or sorted by popularity. For many searches, you may not need to go past these options.

- **Item type.** You can search the warehouse for individual models or for collections of models. A collection can be just about any grouping of SketchUp models, from windows made by a certain manufacturer to models of trains new and old. If you're searching for models, you can choose to search for three types of models: SketchUp (.skp), Google Earth (.kmz), or Collada (.zip). (Collada is a 3-D model format that's often used to share models between different programs.) You can also limit the search to models of 3-D buildings in Google Earth, downloadable models, or dynamic models.

- **Rating.** The 3D Warehouse uses a simple five-star rating system. Anyone who uses a model can provide a rating. Use the Rating drop-down menu to limit your search to the better-rated models.

- **Author.** You remember this great model of Notre Dame in Paris, but you can't seem to find that exact one you want. If you remember the name of the designer, pop it in the Author text box and see what appears.

- **Date.** Two drop-down menus let you limit the results to a specific time frame. You can base your search on when a model was created or the last time that it was modified.

- **Location.** Some models, such as buildings, are tied to a specific location using Google Earth. Other models, such as a certain type of casement window, aren't. Under Location, you can limit your search based on this criterion. Even better, you can type an address in a text box, and the search is limited to models that are nearby.

- **Grouping.** 3D Warehouse collections are stored on a specific page, so there's a specific web address for each collection. If you want to search inside a specific collection, enter its web address here. It's best to cut and paste the address, because it usually looks something like this: *http://sketchup.google.com/ 3dwarehouse/details?mid=4c1c0aca4c6df7b6b15cd835a6effb08.*

Tip: You can use advanced search features from inside any 3D Warehouse search box, including the one in the Components window. To search on a particular field, type *field name* followed by a colon (:) and the search word. Leave a space, and then type any other search words you want to use. For example, if you wanted to find models of benches created by Grover, type your entry like this: *author:grover bench.*

Creating a Dynamic Component (SketchUp Pro Only)

In Chapter 5 you saw how components give you a great way to create multiple instances of a single object like windows for a building or fence boards. If that's not enough SketchUp magic for you, you can use *dynamic* components, which let anyone using SketchUp change their properties. For example, you can change the dimensions of the window or change the color of those fence boards. In this section you'll learn how to create your own dynamic components. The only caveat is, you have to have SketchUp Pro (page 3) to do it.

In the first part of this exercise, you create a bench dynamic component that lets anyone using the component change its color or material by making a selection from a drop-down menu. In the second part of the exercise, you'll modify the bench component so that anyone who uses your component can change the length of the bench.

Preparing Your Component with Color Swatches

When you want to create a dynamic component that lets other SketchUp designers change colors or materials, you must save those colors or materials *within* the component. That's how folks get access to the materials. An easy way to accomplish that is to create color swatches within the model. The swatches don't have to be anything more than a face with the color or material applied.

Note: This exercise uses a bench similar to the one created in Chapter 1. You can download *bench_dc_begin.skp* from *http://missingmanuals.com/cds*. The finished version of model, *bench_dc_finished.skp,* is also available.

---

1. **Open *bench_dc_begin.skp* and then double-click the bench.**

   You see the simple bench made out of four pieces of lumber: a bench seat, a bench support, and two bench legs. The bench is already a component that contains other subcomponents (seat, legs, support). In the following steps, you'll give it dynamic properties. Double-clicking the bench opens the bench_dc component for editing.

2. **Using the Rectangle (R) tool, begin to draw a rectangle in front of the bench and then type *12,12*.**

   You've created a 12" × 12" face in front of the bench, which will serve as a color/material swatch.

3. **Click the Top view button or choose Camera → Standard Views → Top, and then triple-click the 12" × 12" face.**

   The face (swatch) is selected.

4. **Press M to select the Move tool, and then press the Ctrl key (Option on a Mac).**

   The Move tool in copy mode is ready to use.

5. **Click the swatch; then move the copy to the right and click again.**

   Using the click-move-click method, you've created a second swatch to the right of the first.

6. **Type *3x* and then press Enter (Return).**

   You've created an array of four color/material swatches.

7. **Choose Window → Materials and then choose Colors-Named in the drop-down menu.**

   The Materials window shows the Colors-Named collection. The Materials window looks slightly different in Windows and Mac, but the capabilities are the same. (For more details on the Materials windows, see page 196.)

8. **In the Materials window, scroll through the colors and then click 0035_Tan.**

   Your cursor changes to the Paint Bucket tool, as it always does when you choose a color or material. The Paint Bucket is loaded and ready to apply 0035_Tan to the next face you click.

9. **Click the first swatch.**

   The swatch color changes to tan.

10. **Repeat steps 8 and 9 to color two more of the swatches. Color one swatch with 0022_Maroon, and then color the next with 0072_DarkSeaGreen.**

    You have three swatches with colors applied. The last swatch will use a "wood" material.

11. **Use the drop-down menu to change to the Wood collection of materials. Then click the Wood_Cherry_Original material.**

    The materials in the Wood collection apply both colors and textures.

12. **Click the last swatch.**

    The last swatch changes to display the wood material. Your modeling window should look similar to Figure 14-8.

This completes the setup for your model. The advantage of creating color swatches is you know that the colors won't be purged from your document. Later, when you no longer need the colors, you can hide them from view. Now's a good time to save your SketchUp document under a new name (File → Save As). Next, the fun stuff—actually creating attributes for your dynamic component.

Creating Material Attributes for a Dynamic Component

In the previous section, you created color swatches to store materials with your dynamic component. In the next steps, you'll create dynamic component attributes, like length and position. If your model with the color swatches isn't open, open it now and follow these steps:

1. **Choose Window → Outliner and then next to the component "bench_dc", click the Expand button.**

   Nested inside the bench_dc component are four entities, all of them instances of components: Bench Seat, Bench Support, and two Bench Leg instances.

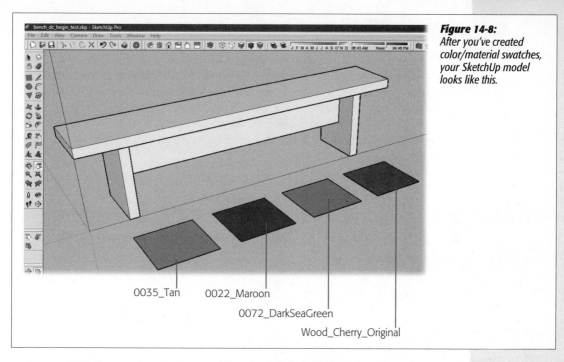

Figure 14-8:
After you've created color/material swatches, your SketchUp model looks like this.

0035_Tan

0022_Maroon

0072_DarkSeaGreen

Wood_Cherry_Original

2. **Choose Window → Component Attributes and then click the bench.**

The Component Attributes window opens. If nothing is selected, Component Attributes appears empty. If the "bench_dc" component is selected, the window looks like Figure 14-9.

Figure 14-9:
Two windows are related to dynamic components. The Component Attributes window, shown here, is used to create dynamic components. You must have SketchUp Pro to access this window. The Component Options window (page 334) lets anyone using SketchUp work with dynamic components.

3. **In the Component Attributes window, next to the bench_dc component name, click the "Add attribute" button. It looks like a plus sign (+) inside of a circle.**

The Component Attributes window changes. On the left, your cursor automatically appears in the "Enter Name" box. That's for naming custom attributes. You're not creating a custom attribute, so don't type in anything. To the right, the Attribute List shows the standard attributes, including LenX, LenY, and LenZ for dimensions, and Material for colors and materials. You may need to expand the Component Attributes window to see all of the attributes, as shown in Figure 14-10.

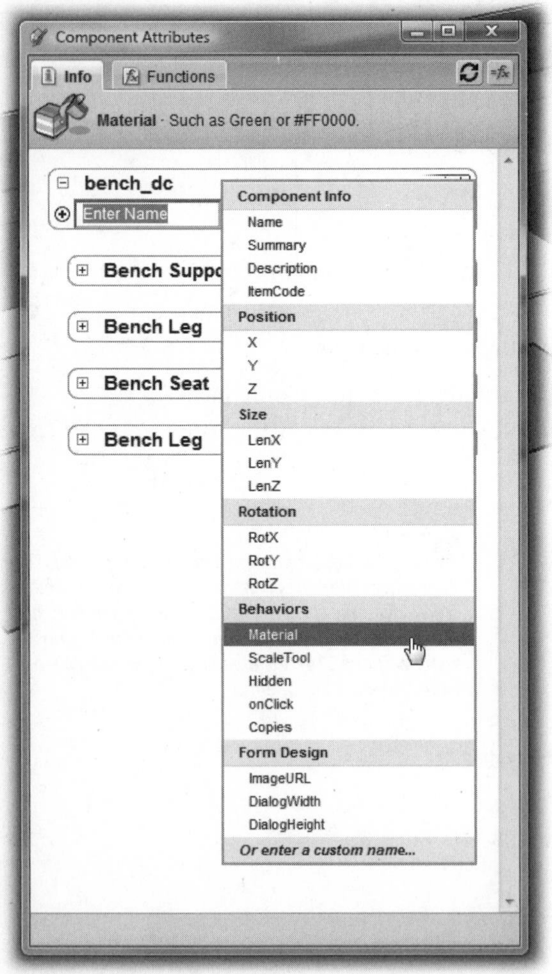

Figure 14-10:
The list on the right displays all the standard attributes that you can apply to a dynamic component. As you gain experience, you can also create your own custom attributes, but that's not covered in this book.

4. **In the Attribute List on the right, click Material.**

   SketchUp displays the dynamic component attribute name, Material, at the top of the Component Attributes window, along with a hint about using it, as in "Such as Green or #FF0000." To the right of the Material attribute, you see the Details button, which looks like an arrow with a menu on top.

5. **Next to the Material attribute, click the Details button.**

   The Component Attributes window changes. At the top is the name "bench_dc!Material" followed by "Such as Green or #FF0000". This cryptic message tells you that if you want to reference this attribute in a formula, the official name of this attribute is "bench_dc!Material". Below the name of the attribute is the "Display rule" drop-down menu. The "Display rule" menu lets you determine how the attribute appears to the designers who use your dynamic component.

Tip: SketchUp dynamic components are created (you could also say "programmed") by using spreadsheet-style language. If you're an Excel jockey, the format of the name bench_dc!Color may look familiar.

---

6. **Click the "Display rule" menu, and then choose "Users can select from a list".**

   The "Display rule" menu gives you four options (Figure 14-11):

   - **Users cannot see this attribute.** You control the attribute through programming, but the component user can't see any of the details.

   - **Users can see this attribute.** Component users see the attribute's settings, but can't change the settings.

   - **Users can edit as a textbox.** Users can type in whatever they want to change the attribute.

   - **Users can select from a list.** Often this option works best. You get to show component users a list of options that they can choose from a drop-down menu. This option works well for choosing colors.

     After you choose "Users can select from a list", the Component Attributes window displays two more drop-down menus: "Display label" and "Display rule". If you want to change the attribute name that's shown to the designers who use your component, type a new name in "Display label"; however, Material works fine for this example.

7. **At the bottom of the Component Attributes window, click the "Add option" button.**

   SketchUp places your cursor in a box that says Enter Option Here—your cue to give a name to the color option. The option list is made up of pairs. Each option has a name and a related value.

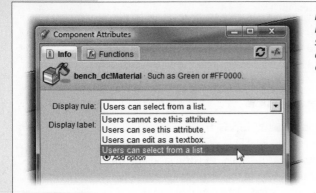

Figure 14-11:
Here the "Display rule" drop-down menu is open,
showing four options: "Users cannot see this
attribute"; "Users can see this attribute"; "Users can
edit as a textbox"; and "Users can select from a list".

8. **Under List Option, type** *Tan* **and then press Tab.**

   After you press Tab, the word "Tan" appears under both List Option and Value. You've named your option, but you still have to put a valid value in the Value box. For colors, the appropriate value is the exact name of the color as shown in the Materials window.

9. **In the Materials window (Window → Materials), click the In Model button (looks like a house).**

   The Materials window displays the colors and materials that are actually in your model.

10. **In the Materials window, click the Tan color chip.**

    The color's official name appears at the top of the Materials window—0035_Tan.

11. **In the Materials window, double-click the name "0035_Tan", and then press Ctrl+C (⌘-C).**

    SketchUp places the color's name on the Clipboard.

12. **In the Component Attributes window, under Value, double-click the word "Tan" and then press Ctrl+V (⌘-V).**

    Double-clicking selects the current value in the Value box. Then with Ctrl+V you paste the official name of the color, replacing the old value.

13. **Repeat steps 7 through 12 to paste in color names for the other two colors (Maroon and Green) and the Wood_Cherry_Original material.**

    You could just type in the name of the color or material, but when you cut and paste, you have less chance of making a typing mistake. When you're done, the Component Attributes window looks like Figure 14-12.

14. **In the Component Attributes window, click Apply.**

    The window shows the model's components and subcomponents.

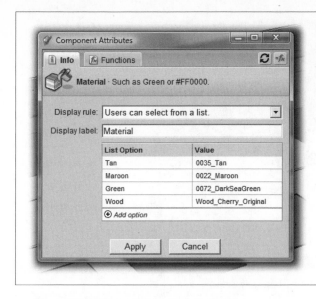

Figure 14-12:
When you create a list using the Display rule "Users can select from a list", you have to specify the list options and the values. Component users see what you type for list options in the Component Options window, and when they make a selection, SketchUp applies the Value to the component.

15. **Choose Window → Component Options.**

    The Component Options window opens, where the designers who use your component can modify it, using the attributes that you defined. Right now the only option is the Material option controlled by a drop-down menu.

16. **In the Component Options window, test all four options: Tan, Maroon, Green, and Wood, by choosing an option and then clicking Apply.**

    As you test your dynamic component, the bench changes color to match your choice.

17. **Choose File → Save or File → Save As.**

    Once you have things working properly, it's always wise to save your work. You may want to use the Save command to overwrite the file, or you can use Save As to save the document under a new name.

Well, computer programmer, treat yourself to a Jolt cola, a pocket protector, and some stock options. You've just created and programmed a dynamic component. Giving SketchUp designers the option to choose colors is handy for all sorts of projects, from furniture and appliances to sports cars and children's toys.

Along the way, you followed the basic steps that SketchUp designers use to access dynamic component attributes. Naturally some of the details change depending on the attribute you're providing. If you scanned the Attribute List, you may have noticed the other types of attributes that you can program such as position, size, rotation, and behaviors. Your dynamic component is fine as is, but if you want to make it even more versatile, work through the next section, where you create a bench that designers can resize.

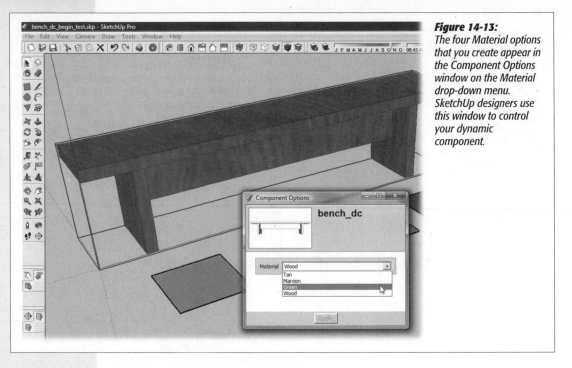

Figure 14-13:
The four Material options that you create appear in the Component Options window on the Material drop-down menu. SketchUp designers use this window to control your dynamic component.

Hiding color and material swatches

The color swatches don't need to be a visible part of your component. If you delete them entirely, the colors will remain in your document, but there's always a possibility that you can erase them by using the "Purge unused" command in the Materials window. A better solution is to make the swatches invisible.

Select them all and then save them in a group (right-click → Make Group). Now you can hide them using a right-click → Hide. If you need to get at them again, open the Outliner (Window → Outliner) to unhide them. Leaving the swatches out in front of the bench makes the component's bounding box appear larger than the component. So use the Move (M) tool to slide them under the bench. You also may want to use the Scale tool to shrink them.

Making a Resizable Dynamic Component

Next to changing colors and materials, one of the most popular options you can provide in a dynamic component is the ability to resize it. Resizing comes in handy for everything from doors and windows to outdoor furniture—like a simple bench that can change colors. Sure, you can resize the bench using the Scale tool, but look what happens. As it is, the bench is 6 feet long. Suppose you want it to be 3 feet long. Go ahead—give it a try with the Scale tool (Figure 14-14). Resize the bench along the red (X) axis, and the bench seat and the support between the two legs do just fine, but the bench legs get squished. Instead of nice sturdy 2-inch legs, your bench has thin, spindly legs, out of proportion with the rest of the model. So when you make a component that designers can resize, you need to pay attention to the proportions. You need to constrain some of the dimensions, while permitting others to change. That's exactly what you learn to do in this next exercise.

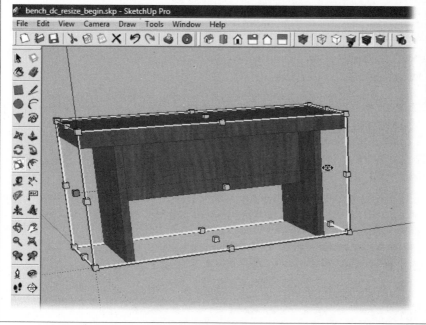

Figure 14-14:
Use the Scale tool to turn a 6-foot bench into a 3-foot bench, and it distorts some of the bench parts. These formerly 2-inch bench legs are now only an inch thick.

In this example, you give designers the option to choose sizes of 3 feet (36 inches), 4 feet (48 inches), 5 feet (60 inches), and 6 feet (72 inches). You constrain the attributes of all the entities that you don't want to change—like the legs. You manage all of this in the Component Attributes window, in much the same way you worked with the color and material attributes in the previous section.

To start the process, follow these steps to change the attributes to resize the bench:

1. **Select the bench_dc component and then choose Window → Component Attributes.**

   The Component Attributes window opens displaying the previous Material attribute you created in the steps starting on page 460. At the top you see the attributes for the bench_dc component. Below you see the four subcomponents that are inside of the bench_dc component: Bench Seat, Bench Support, and two Bench Leg components. In this exercise, you change attributes for the main component and the subcomponents.

2. **In the Component Attributes window, under bench_dc, click the "Add attribute" button.**

The Component Attributes window changes. On the left, your cursor automatically appears in the Enter Name box, which is used for creating custom attributes. You're not creating a custom attribute, so don't type anything. To the right, the Attribute List shows the standard attributes, including the Size attributes: LenX, LenY, and LenZ.

3. **In the Attribute List, click LenX.**

The Component Attributes window changes to accommodate the new attribute LenX, as shown in Figure 14-15.

Tip: Make sure you click the LenX attribute, not the X attribute. The X, Y, and Z options control the position of the component, not the dimensions.

4. **To the right of the word "LenX", click the Details button (it looks like an arrow with a menu pasted on top).**

The Component Attributes window changes to show the settings related to the LenX attribute. At the top of the window, you see the name bench_dc!LenX. Below it are two drop-down menus: Units and "Display rule". The Units is set to inches, so you don't need to change it.

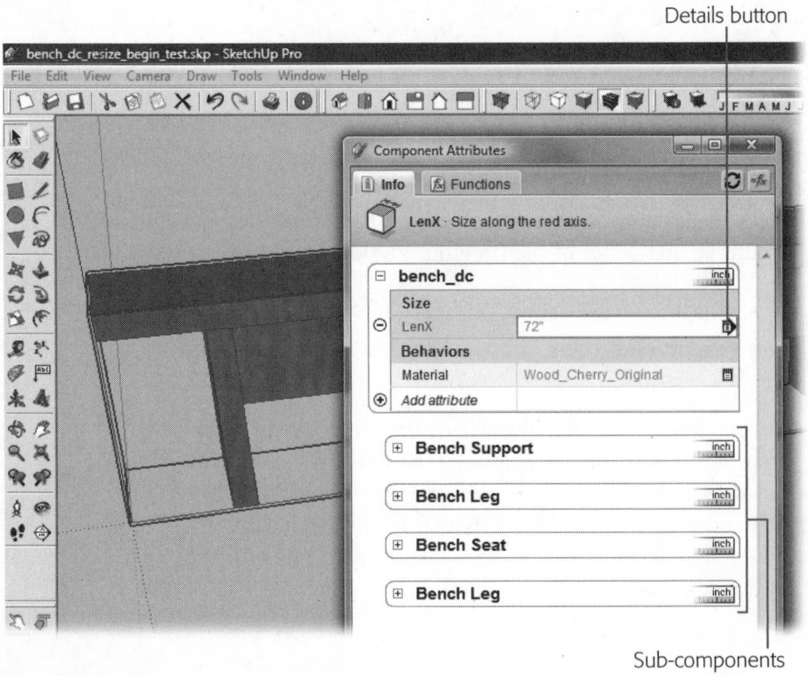

Details button

Sub-components

Figure 14-15:
As you add new user-changeable attributes, the Component Attributes window keeps track of them all. Here the window displays the new LenX attribute. As you see in this project, you can modify attributes for nested components, too.

5. **From the "Display rule" menu, choose "Users can select from a list".**

   The Component Attributes window displays the "Display label" text box and a table where you add option names and values.

6. **In the "Display label" box, type** *Bench Length.*

   SketchUp displays this attribute name to designers who use your component.

7. **In the table, click the "Add option" button.**

   A new row appears in the table, and your cursor is automatically placed in the box under the List Option heading. Here's where you provide the name for the option that designers see. Each option is made up of two parts. The List Option is the name that designers who use your component see on a drop-down menu. The Value is the value that SketchUp applies to some attribute of your dynamic component. In this case it's the LenX attribute, which is the length of the component along the red axis.

8. **Type** *3 feet* **and then press Tab.**

   When you press Tab, the cursor moves to the next box under Value. Here's where you supply the value that's applied to your component.

9. **Type** *36"* **and then press Tab.**

   You just programmed your component so that when designers select the "3 feet" option, the value of LenX (the length of your bench) changes to 36 inches. When you press Tab, a new option row appears, and you can add another option to the list. If you press Enter (Return), SketchUp assumes you're done and doesn't add another option.

10. **Repeat steps 8 and 9 to create options for 4 feet, 5 feet, and 6 feet.**

    When you're done, the Component Attributes window looks like Figure 14-16.

11. **Click the Apply button.**

    SketchUp saves your changes to the LenX attribute. The Component Attributes window changes to show the components in bench_dc.

You're not done with this component, but now's a good time to save and test it. Open the Component Options window, and you see exactly what the designers who use your component see (Figure 14-17). Click the Bench Length menu, and test the different options. You have to click the Apply button for the changes to take place. You haven't constrained the Bench Leg dimensions, so the resize squishes the bench legs as it did when using the Scale tool.

Constraining the Dimensions of Dynamic Components

When you look at this simple bench, you can see that only two dimensions of two components change to make benches of different lengths. The Bench Seat and the Bench Support (between the legs) need to change along the X axis (red axis). On

---

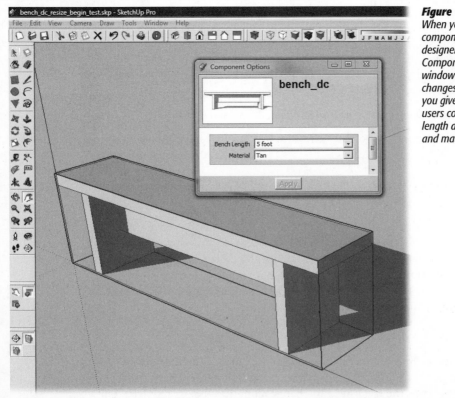

Figure 14-16:
*Use the Component Attributes window to set up the
drop-down menu that designers see when they use
your dynamic component. Here the Bench Length
attribute is designed to display options: 3 feet,
4 feet, 5 feet, and 6 feet.*

Figure 14-17:
*When your dynamic
component is finished,
designers can use the
Component Options
window to make
changes. In this exercise,
you give component
users control over the
length and the color
and materials.*

the other hand, you don't want the two bench legs to get thicker and thinner when the length of the bench changes. The solution is to constrain the LenX attribute for the Bench Leg subcomponent. To make sure the Bench Seat remains 2 inches thick, you use the formula *=2"*. That's simply a way of saying: "This dimension attribute (LenX) equals 2 inches. Leave it that way until another formula comes along with different instructions."

1. **Select the bench_dc component and then choose Window → Component Attributes.**

   The Component Attributes window opens, displaying the attributes you've created so far. At the top, you see the attributes for the bench_dc component. Below, you see the four subcomponents that are inside of the "bench_dc" component: Bench Seat, Bench Support, and two Bench Leg components.

2. **In the Component Attributes window, under Bench Leg, click the "Add attribute" button.**

   The Component Attributes window changes. On the left your cursor automatically appears in the Enter Name box, which lets you create custom attributes. You're not creating a custom attribute, so don't type anything. To the right the Attribute List shows the standard attributes, including the Size attributes: LenX, LenY, and LenZ.

3. **In the Attribute List, click LenX.**

   The LenX attribute appears in the Component Attributes window. In the box to the right of the attribute name, you see the current value—2". That's the thickness of the Bench Leg subcomponent.

4. **Click in the box with the value.**

   Your cursor appears in the box. The value continues to be displayed as 2".

5. **Press the Home key or use the left arrow key to move the cursor to the front of the value and then type =.**

   The box displays the simple formula *=2"*.

6. **Press Enter (Return).**

   The formula box closes, and your cursor is no longer in position to edit the value. The box no longer displays the formula, so you don't see the equal sign. Instead the box shows the current dimension for LenY, which remains 2". This setup makes it a little hard to tell whether the box contains a formula. When you need to see the actual formula, just click in the box, as shown in Figure 14-18.

7. **Under bench_dc, click the "Add attribute" button again, and this time choose the LenZ option.**

   The LenZ attribute is added to the list of attributes, displaying 17", the height of the bench.

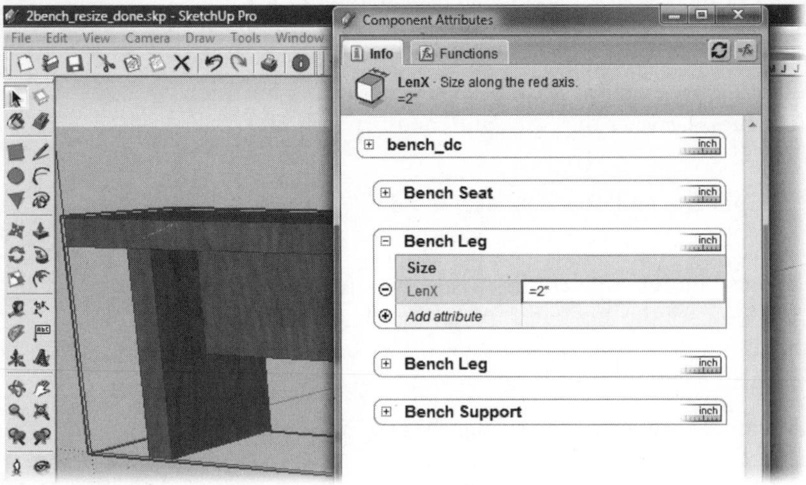

Figure 14-18:
The value box next to an attribute displays the current value in the model. If you need to view or edit an attribute's formula, click in the box to open it for editing. In this example, the LenX box is open for edits.

8. **Click the value box and then type = (equal sign) in front of the 17" value. Press Enter (Return) to close the box.**

   The LenZ attribute is now constrained by the formula to 17 inches.

9. **Under bench_dc, click the "Add attribute" button and choose LenY.**

   You see the LenY value: 12".

10. **Click the value box and then type = (equal sign) in front of 12". Press Enter (Return) to close the box.**

    You've constrained the LenY attribute to 12 inches. The three dimensions—LenX, LenY, and LenZ—for the bench_dc component are defined by formulas. Designers using your component can change its length using the Component Options window without distorting the other dimensions.

11. **Save your component and then choose Window → Component Options.**

    The Component Options window opens, showing two attributes that anyone can change using drop-down menus: Bench Length and Material. Give them a try!

12. **Choose your Bench Length and Material options and then click Apply.**

    The bench dynamic component changes to match your choices.

Preventing Dynamic Components from Scaling

Your work isn't quite done. You've given designers four specific bench lengths, which is similar to what you'd do if you were a bench manufacturer. Designers can drop your bench in their model and choose a length and color. That, hopefully, would result in some bench sales. The problem is, right now nothing stops designers from changing the dimensions of your bench by using the Scale tool. That's not how you want them to use your component, so you need to limit your dynamic component to show only the sizes you manufacture. You could try to do this by constraining the dimensions of all the components and subcomponents in your model, but SketchUp provides an easier way to accomplish the same goal:

1. **Select the bench component bench_dc and then choose Component Attributes.**

   The Component Attributes window opens, showing the changes you made to the bench_dc component and the Bench Leg subcomponent.

2. **Under bench_dc, click the "Add attribute" button, and then choose Scale Tool from the list on the right.**

   When you click "Add attribute", the program displays on the right a list of the changeable attributes. After you select ScaleTool, SketchUp adds it to the bench_dc attributes under LenX and Material, as shown in Figure 14-19.

Figure 14-19:
All the modified attributes you've added to a dynamic component appear in the Component Attributes window. Here the bench_dc component displays the LenX, Material, and ScaleTool attributes. To modify more attributes, click the "Add attribute" button. To program an attribute, click the Details button next to its name.

3. **Click the Details button.**

   As shown in Figure 14-20, the Component Attributes window shows the Scale-Tool attribute's settings, which consist of a group of checkboxes with names like "Scale along red. (X)" and "Scale in green/blue plane. (Y+Z)".

4. **Turn off all of the checkboxes and then click Apply.**

   By turning off all of the checkboxes, you make it so no one can change the bench_dc dynamic component.

Help

Figure 14-20:
Here the Component Attributes window shows the options for the Scale tool. Using these checkboxes, you choose exactly which scaling handles are visible when someone uses the Scale tool with your component.

5. **Press S or choose Tools → Scale, and then move the Scale tool over the bench.**

   A highlight appears around the bench, but you have no handles to grab. You cannot change the size of the component with the Scale tool.

6. **Open the Component Options window (Window → Component Options), and then use the drop-down menus to change the length and material for the bench.**

   The bench changes according to the settings in the Component Options window.

Dynamic components can be as simple or as complicated as you want. This bench project introduced some of the concepts behind creating dynamic components and providing tools for component users to make changes. When you design a dynamic component, you use tools that are similar to those used by spreadsheet programmers. In fact, you can use a whole slew of functions available for use with dynamic components. The topic is a little too deep for this book, but you can find more information about dynamic components on the SketchUp online help page. Go to Help → Help Center and type *dynamic components* in the Search box.

Sharing Components

Once you've create a component (dynamic or otherwise), you may want to share it with the whole wide world. Just think of the glory that will accrue to you as a SketchUp designer. Your path to fame is to upload your model to the 3D Warehouse. When you do so, you're giving Google permission to share the component with everyone and, sadly, you're not going to get paid. Not even a few shares of Google stock. Still your friends and colleagues will admire your skills as a SketchUp artist, and hey, you've used other designers' models from the 3D Warehouse, haven't you?

Purge Before Saving

Before you share your masterpieces with other SketchUp artists, it's best to get all the extra stuff out of the file. So if you're sharing the bench used in the previous exercises, you get rid of all the entities in the model that aren't related to the bench. Perhaps you added some trees or even a few extra lines as you were working. If that's the case, just select them and press Delete. Once the modeling window is cleaned up, here's a checklist of some other steps to make you component document lean and mean:

- Open the **Components window** (Window → Components), and click the In Model button. Then click the Details button and choose Purge Unused. This removes any components such as the model Sang from the document. Make sure to purge components before you purge materials. Otherwise you may end up with unneeded materials in your document.

- Open the **Materials window** (Window → Materials), and click the In Model button (Figure 14-21). Then click the Details button and choose Purged Unused. This command removes any colors and components that are no longer needed in the document. For example, after you purge Sang from your document, you may no longer need the color that was used on his shirt.

- Open the **Styles window** (Window → Styles), and click the In Model button. Then click the Details button and choose Purged Unused. This sequence removes any styles that you may have opened while browsing. SketchUp saves only styles used in the dynamic component with the document.

Tip: Here's a shortcut that purges your model of extra stuff. Open the Model Info window (Window → Model Info). On the left, click Statistics. The window displays details about your model. At the bottom, click Purge Unused. SketchUp performs the purging steps described above. Why wouldn't you always want to use this instead of three separate steps? Sometimes you want to control what's kept and what's purged from your model. For example, you may want to purge unused components, but keep certain styles or materials in your model.

Uploading a Model to the 3D Warehouse

Once your document file is all cleaned up and saved, you can upload it to the 3D Warehouse where other SketchUp artists can use and admire it. To upload, edit, or remove a component to the 3D Warehouse, you need to log in by clicking the "G" button in the lower-right corner. Here are the steps for uploading a model to the 3D Warehouse:

1. **With your model open in SketchUp, choose File → 3D Warehouse → Share Model.**

   If you haven't purged your model completely of components, materials, and styles, you may see an alert box that prompts you to do so. Otherwise a window opens that displays the 3D Warehouse "Terms of Service".

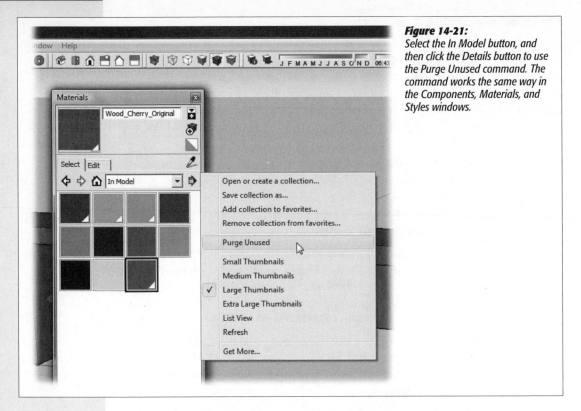

Figure 14-21:
Select the In Model button, and then click the Details button to use the Purge Unused command. The command works the same way in the Components, Materials, and Styles windows.

2. **Read the terms; check with your lawyers and heirs. Then if everyone agrees, click the "I accept Terms of Service" button.**

   In short, the terms want to make sure you're of legal age and that you have the right to share the models you upload. It explains that you're making the material available to other 3D Warehouse users. You can at some time in the future ask Google to discontinue sharing the model; but at that point, Google can't stop the people who may have already downloaded the model from using it. Accept the terms, and the Terms window closes. A 3D Warehouse upload window appears, showing the file name and size of your model at the top. You see several text boxes, where you can enter details about your project.

3. **Enter details about your model in the text boxes (Figure 14-22).**

   The details you enter appear in the 3D Warehouse. Other designers use the information you provide to find your model and decide whether they want to use it.

   - **Filename.** SketchUp automatically provides the file name and size.

   - **Model Title.** Give your model a title that's as descriptive as possible, but keep it relatively short.

- **Model Description.** Provide a complete description of your model. It will help others decide whether they want to download and use it.

- **Tags.** Think of the tags as keywords people might use when they're searching for a particular model. Use single words and short phrases separated by commas.

- **Additional content.** Optionally you can provide other details that help people find you, the model's creator. For example, if you're the manufacturer of outdoor furniture like this bench, then you may want to attract designers to your website where they'll find more details about your products. You can add a URL and logo to the page with your model. You can also choose whether everyone can view your model when they search the 3D Warehouse. Last but not least, turn on the "Allow 3D Warehouse users to contact me about this model" checkbox if you want to hear from admirers.

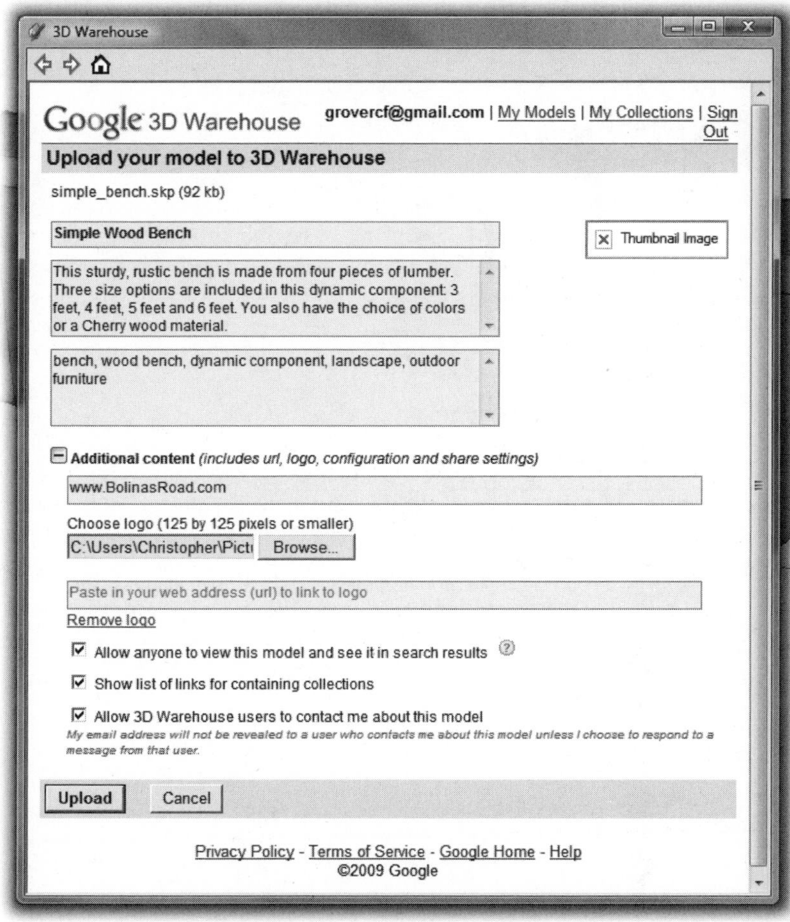

Figure 14-22:
As you fill out the details in the 3D Warehouse, think about the way you search for components. Give your model a good, descriptive name, and be as specific as possible as you fill in the description and tags.

4. Click Upload.

When you click the Upload button, you see a series of progress bars as SketchUp sends your model and the details to the 3D Warehouse.

Within a few minutes of uploading your model, you should be able to find it in the 3D Warehouse, as shown in Figure 14-23. Where do they find the room? Your model also now pops up in the Components window (Figure 14-24).

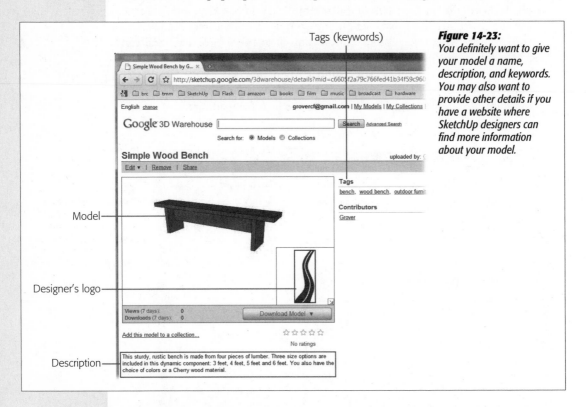

Tags (keywords)

Model

Designer's logo

Description

Figure 14-23:
You definitely want to give your model a name, description, and keywords. You may also want to provide other details if you have a website where SketchUp designers can find more information about your model.

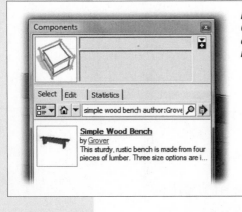

Figure 14-24:
Once your SketchUp document is in the 3D Warehouse, other designers can find it and download it from the Components window in SketchUp.

Sharing Models with a Geographic Location

You need to take a couple of extra steps when you share a model such as a building that's tied to a particular location. (See page 385 for the details about positioning a model on Google Earth.) Models with a specific location and orientation include a "terrain image" from Google Earth. Naturally you need to make sure that your model was positioned correctly in the first place. For example, it's important that Terrain is toggled on when you position your model in Sketchup.

Otherwise your model may be buried inside a mountain when someone else attempts to use it. Test your model in Google Earth before uploading—you'll save yourself and others aggravation. It's also best to save your model using the latest version of SketchUp if you want things such as textures to display well for the widest audience of SketchUp users.

Editing Your Model Details in the 3D Warehouse

After you've uploaded a model to the 3D Warehouse, you may want to update the model or change some of the descriptive details on the model's page. To make such changes, find your model in the 3D Warehouse. When you're viewing the page of a model that you uploaded, you see a few menu items above the image: Edit, Remove, and Share (Figure 14-25). Under Edit are two options: Edit Details and Edit Model. Click Edit Details to change your model's name, description, and keywords. Click Edit Model, and the 3D Warehouse downloads your model to you, so you can make changes and then upload the new, improved version.

Removing Your Model from the 3D Warehouse

You can remove your model from the 3D Warehouse. That stops people from downloading it in the future, but it can't prevent those who've already downloaded it from using the model. To Remove a model from the warehouse, click the Remove button above the model's image (Figure 14-25). An alert box appears and asks if you really want to remove the model. Click OK, and the model is gone.

Changing the Share Options for Your Model in the 3D Warehouse

You have a certain amount of control over the way people use the 3D models that you upload to the warehouse. Click the Share button over your model's image, and you see a page of options grouped according to Privacy Settings, "Invite people", and "Advanced permissions", as shown in Figure 14-26.

Using the two checkboxes under Privacy Settings, you can choose to make your model publicly viewable. When you turn on public viewing, your model will appear when it matches a 3D Warehouse visitor's search criteria. The second checkbox, "Make this model publicly-editable", leaves the model open so other designers can make changes to it. If you want to review and approve any changes people make, choose "Advanced permissions".

Figure 14-25:
To make changes to your model after you've uploaded it to the 3D Warehouse, use the menu above the image. Click the Edit, Move, and Share options to make changes.

Use the "Invite people" settings to send messages to other designers asking them to view or collaborate with you in developing the model. You need to provide their email addresses separated by commas in the text box.

Under the "Advanced permissions" options, you control just how much your collaborators can mess with your model. The options are:

• Collaborators may change who can edit or view this model

• Collaborators may delete the model

• The owner must approve all changes to this model

• Only the owner and collaborators may download the model

Uploading a Dynamic Component

At this writing, dynamic components are a relatively new feature, and they require a few special steps to upload and share via the 3D Warehouse. According to Google, new upload features for dynamic components are in the works. If you're lucky, those new upload tools will be ready to use when you read this. Otherwise you can use the steps below for saving and uploading dynamic components.

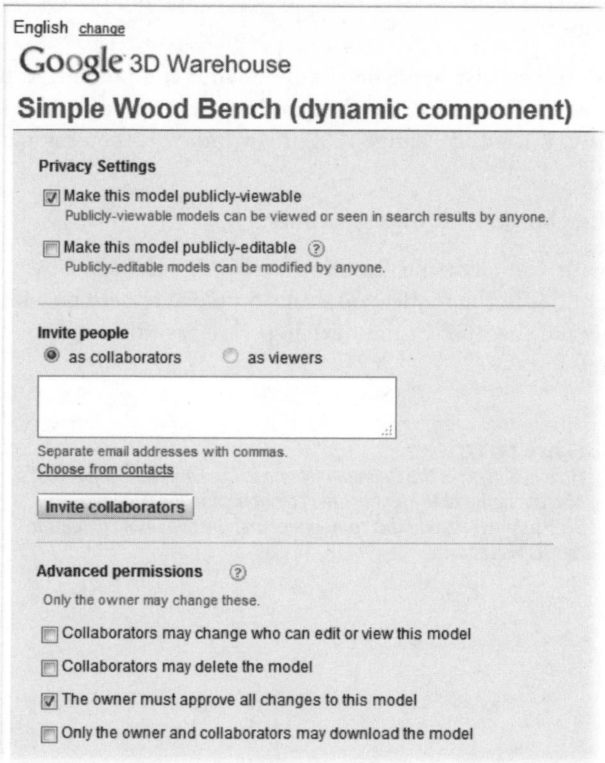

Figure 14-26:
The share options for models uploaded to the 3D Warehouse are organized into three groups: Privacy Settings, "Invite people", and "Advanced permissions".

Here are the steps to take after you've built your dynamic component:

1. **With the component open in SketchUp, choose Window → Model Info.**

   The Model Info window opens.

2. **On the left of the Model Info window, click Statistics.**

   The window changes to show details about all aspects of your model. At the bottom of the window are two buttons: Purge Unused and Fix Problems.

3. **Click Purge Unused.**

   This removes extra components, styles, and materials from your model, as described on page 224. Purging your model of extra elements helps keep the document file as small as possible.

4. **Choose File → Save.**

   Your purged model is saved under its current name.

5. **Use the Select (space bar) tool to select your dynamic component, and then choose Window → Entity Info.**

The Entity Info window opens, displaying details about your component. At the bottom, you see Definition Name. What you type here will be your component's official name. If you want to change that, this window is the only place you can do it.

6. **In the SketchUp menus, choose Window → Outliner.**

The Outliner opens with your dynamic component highlighted, as shown in Figure 14-27. All the entities in the model you want to upload should be within the highlighted component, because in the next step, you save the component under a different name.

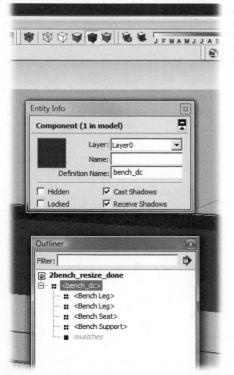

Figure 14-27:
Here bench_dc is the Definition Name in the Entity Info window. It's also the name of the highlighted component in the Outliner. SketchUp will upload this component and the entities it contains to the 3D Warehouse.

7. **In the SketchUp window's lower-right corner, hold your cursor over the G (for Google) button.**

If you're already signed into Google, you see a message that says something like: "Signed in as *yourname@gmail.com*". If the message doesn't say "Signed in", click the button and then sign in. For details about signing into Google, see the box on page 454.

8. **With your dynamic component still selected, right-click the component and choose Save As.**

You must use the shortcut menu for this step, not the standard command on the File menu. A file browser window opens, where you can save your new document. This is your final document file that will be uploaded to the 3D Warehouse. To keep your document files straight, you may want to have a separate folder for all your "final" document files.

9. **Type a name for your model and click the Save button.**

SketchUp saves your dynamic component in a new file.

10. **Open the newly saved document.**

In Windows, you can do this by starting up a new instance of the SketchUp program (Windows → Google SketchUp) or by finding the new document in Windows Explorer and double-clicking its name. On a Mac, you can open the new document using the File → Open command.

11. **With your new document open, choose Window → Outliner.**

In Outliner, your component is the only entity, so it's the parent at the top of the list. There's no shell to hold your component, because the SketchUp document now serves as the shell. You can't select your component and display a bounding box, and you can't see any of the Component Options that you created at this stage.

12. **Choose Window → Model Info and then on the left, select Credits.**

The Model Info window displays the component's credits (Figure 14-28). But wait! Your name's not there!

13. **Click the Claim Credit button.**

After you click Claim Credit, your name appears under the Model Authors.

Figure 14-28:
If the Claim Credit button is grayed out, use the Line tool to create a small line in the model and then delete the line. After you've made a change to the model (even if you immediately deleted it), the Claim Credit button comes to life.

14. In the Model Info window, click File and then type a description for your component.

    This description appears in the Components window when other designers use your model. You also need to provide a description in the 3D Warehouse, as described on page 479.

15. In the Google toolbar, click the Share Model button (Figure 14-29), or choose File → 3D Warehouse → Share Model.

    A 3D Warehouse window opens, where you provide details for your model. See Figure 14-22.

16. Click the Upload button.

    Your dynamic component heads off to the 3D Warehouse, where it will give other SketchUp designers and builders hours of use and pleasure.

Figure 14-29:
Click the Share Model button on the Google toolbar to send your dynamic component to the 3D Warehouse. Or you can use the menu command File → 3D Warehouse → Share Model.

Designing Edge Styles in Style Builder (SketchUp Pro)

As described in Chapter 6, a style tells SketchUp how to draw edges, how to shade faces, and how to display color in the imaginary ground and sky planes. In the free version of SketchUp, you can choose from dozens of predesigned styles that come with the program, and you can modify styles by mixing and matching these elements. You can even load styles created by other SketchUp designers. A style's edges—especially when they look hand-sketched (page 234)—add some of the most distinctive effects. Unfortunately, the one thing you can't do in the free version is create your own edge styles.

Tip: The name "Style Builder" is a little misleading. The program works on only one element of styles—the sketchy edges that give SketchUp its hand-drawn look.

If you have SketchUp Pro, you can create your own styles using the Style Builder tool. Style Builder is a standalone program with a focused purpose. It helps you create sketchy edges and package them in new SketchUp Styles documents. Once you've saved the edges in a .style file, anyone with any version of SketchUp can load them and use them. To perform this feat of SketchUp design, you need SketchUp Pro, Style Builder, and a graphics program like Adobe Photoshop. It also helps to have either a scanner or a graphics tablet.

Style Builder Overview

It's the edge styles that put the "sketch" in SketchUp. Most computer programs create graphics that look machine-made, with perfectly straight lines and uniformly solid colors. SketchUp is unusual in that it lets you create images that look as if they were sketched with all the beautiful imperfection of the human hand. These edges give SketchUp graphics their character (Figure 15-1).

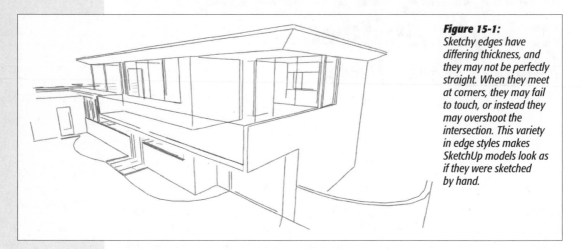

Figure 15-1:
Sketchy edges have differing thickness, and they may not be perfectly straight. When they meet at corners, they may fail to touch, or instead they may overshoot the intersection. This variety in edge styles makes SketchUp models look as if they were sketched by hand.

SketchUp provides two types of edges: *vector* edges and *sketchy* edges. Vector edges are straight lines that look computer generated. Sketchy edges come from graphic images of hand-drawn lines. In a neat feat of computer wizardry, SketchUp takes a few images of hand-drawn lines and applies them to your model in a way that makes the whole image look as if it were drawn by hand. Computers are good at consistency and uniformity, but if there's one thing that's hard for computers, it's displaying the kind of random personality that comes as second nature to us humans. You see lots of examples of sketchy edges in SketchUp's Style window. Choose Window → Styles and then click the Select tab. In the drop-down menu choose Sketchy Edges.

With the help of Style Builder, you can create your own sketchy edge styles. Here's an overview of the process:

- By hand, draw several sample lines—called *strokes* in Style Builder—and store them as graphics files. Most styles use somewhere between a dozen and three dozen stroke images.

- Load the strokes into Style Builder. This process creates sets of strokes. A *set* is a collection of strokes of a certain length, such as 64 pixels or 512 pixels. (If you wish, you can rearrange sets or transfer new strokes to existing sets.)

- Use Style Builder settings to modify the look of the sketchy edges. Settings include Halo and Extensions (page 227).

- Save your project with the new strokes in a .style file and load it into SketchUp.

Tip: When you're done, you can use the Mix tab in SketchUp's Styles window to add your sketchy edges to existing styles.

Creating Images for New Sketchy Edge Styles

So how do you teach a computer to draw lines that express a human, random, hand-drawn look? The trick is to split the workload. You draw some sample lines, and then you let the computer modify and apply your lines to models in a way that seems random.

Style Builder expects you to provide samples in a certain format called a *stroke set*. Each stroke set has a specific length in pixels. Computers like numbers divisible by 8, so typical set lengths are 32, 64, 128, 256, and 512 pixels. You can provide several strokes (line samples) for each of those lengths, so you might end up with a few sets that look like those in Figure 15-2. It's your choice exactly how many strokes you provide for a set. Something between three and five strokes per set is reasonable. The more strokes you provide, the more SketchUp gets to work with to create a random appearance. You need to provide the same number of strokes for each set. So if the 32-pixel set has three strokes, then all the other sets must have 32.

Figure 15-2:
Strokes come in sets of certain pixel lengths. This set has three line samples for each of five different lengths.

To create stroke samples, you can draw them on paper and then scan the images into your computer, or you can create the strokes in a graphics program like Photoshop that provides calligraphic brushes. The use of a pressure-sensitive graphics tablet can be helpful. In any case, your goal is to produce samples with a natural hand-drawn variability in thickness and straightness. Once you load the samples into a SketchUp style, you don't have to worry too much about the details—the program handles that. SketchUp uses your short strokes to display short lines and your long strokes to display longer lines. When the view changes, SketchUp redraws the model and reapplies lines using the same criteria. If your sample strokes don't fit perfectly, SketchUp stretches and shrinks them to fit. This resizing actually adds to the randomness of the look, but no stroke gets stretched or squished to the point that it looks unnatural.

Generating a Template for Strokes

SketchUp stores strokes in three different types of files—template, style, and JPEG. You can load all three file types into Style Builder, but the way you get your strokes into Style Builder is to generate a template like the one shown in Figure 15-3.

• **Template files.** Not to be confused with SketchUp templates, template files that store strokes are special .png files you create specifically for the job.

• **Style files.** The .style files are SketchUp's standard format for saving and transferring strokes and other style details.

• **JPEG files.** These are the same files that display all sorts of images on the Internet. You can store a single stroke in a .jpg file. Using single JPEGs to work with strokes is a little cumbersome, but it's good to know that you can do it if, for example, your drawn lines are already in JPEG files.

Tip: If you want an edge style that's truly unique and artistic, you can even use digital photos of real-world objects—like twigs or bits of string—to create strokes.

Here are the steps for generating a template for strokes:

1. **Start SketchUp's Style Builder program.**

   You usually get a Style Builder icon on your desktop when you install SketchUp Pro. In Windows, you can also start the program from Start → Programs → Google SketchUp 7 → Style Builder. On a Mac, you can use a desktop icon, or press ⌘-Space, and begin to type *style builder*. When you see the name of the program in the Spotlight list, press Return.

2. **In Style Builder, choose File → Generate Template.**

   The Style Template Generator window opens (Figure 15-4), displaying three drop-down menus where you can choose "Stroke lengths", "Stroke per set", and "Stroke width".

3. **Set the "Stroke lengths" menu to *32, 64, 128, 256, 512*. Set "Stroke per set" to *3*. Set "Stroke width" to *32*.**

   You can type values or choose from the menu. Until you get used to the process, it's safest to use the menu. The numbers must be divisible by 4 and separated by commas.

4. **Click Save As (Save on a Mac), and save the file as *stroke_template.png*.**

   A window appears where you can navigate to a folder of your choice and save the file.

The template file you save looks like Figure 15-3. It has empty boxes waiting for your strokes. At the bottom you see some basic template instructions. At the top you see an odd looking barcode. Don't mess with the bar code; Style Builder uses it when it loads your new strokes.

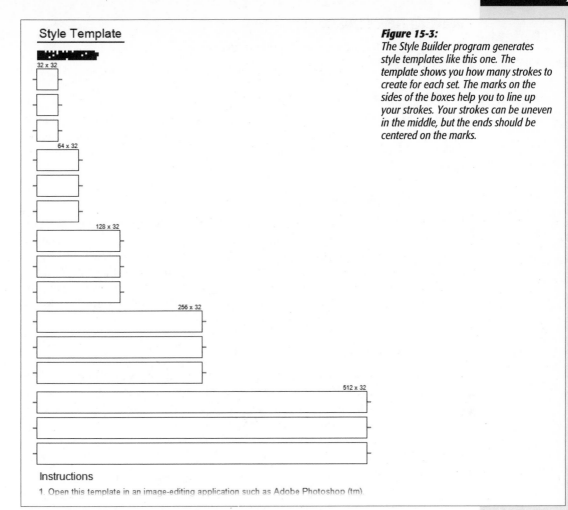

Style Template

32 x 32

64 x 32

128 x 32

256 x 32

512 x 32

Instructions

1. Open this template in an image-editing application such as Adobe Photoshop (tm).

Figure 15-3:
The Style Builder program generates style templates like this one. The template shows you how many strokes to create for each set. The marks on the sides of the boxes help you to line up your strokes. Your strokes can be uneven in the middle, but the ends should be centered on the marks.

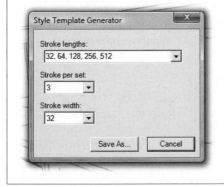

Style Template Generator

Stroke lengths:
32, 64, 128, 256, 512

Stroke per set:
3

Stroke width:
32

Save As...   Cancel

Figure 15-4:
Use the drop-down menus in the Style Template Generator window to create a template for your hand-drawn strokes.

Drawing New Strokes

You can create strokes for Style Builder in two ways:

- Draw strokes using a graphics tab and a program like Photoshop.

- Draw strokes on paper and scan them into your computer.

If you have a graphics tablet, that's the easiest way to get hand-drawn stroke samples into a computer file for Style Builder. On the other hand, you may be able to produce a more natural hand-drawn look by drawing on paper with your favorite pen or marker.

Drawing strokes on a graphics tablet

If you use a graphics table, make sure that it's set up to be pressure sensitive. That way your lines will get thicker or thinner depending on the pen pressure. Open the strokes template in Photoshop or in another graphics program. Open the Layers panel (or the equivalent), and then lock the layer that contains the template. Create a new layer over the template, and draw your strokes in the new layer, using the template as a guide. It's helpful to zoom in as much as 200 percent before you draw. Draw one stroke in every box on the template.

Drawing strokes on paper

Draw your strokes on a clean piece of paper—don't draw directly on the template. Draw stokes that are roughly the correct length for the template, but don't sweat it too much. They don't have to be sized to the pixel at this point; you can stretch or shrink them later. Draw one stroke for every box on the template.

Editing Strokes

No matter how you draw the sample strokes, you need to edit them in a graphics program before they're ready for Style Builder. If you draw strokes using a graphics tablet, they may need only a little editing. If you use the draw-on-paper method, you need a couple of extra steps, as described in this section. First of all, you need to scan the page with strokes into your computer. Once you have your strokes open in your graphics program, you need to open the strokes template and transfer your hand-drawn strokes to the template. It's a pretty typical cut and paste operation.

Importing and editing strokes drawn on paper

Here are the steps for importing and editing the strokes drawn on a piece of paper. You need a graphics editing program to handle these chores that lets you organize your work in separate layers. The steps below explain by using Photoshop as an example, but you could use Adobe Fireworks, Corel Paint Shop Pro, or a free program like the GIMP (*www.gimp.org*) or Paint.NET (*http://paint.net/*).

If you used a graphics tablet to draw strokes, you need to do only the editing part of these steps:

1. **Scan the page with the hand-drawn strokes into your computer, and then open the document in Photoshop.**

   This step varies according to your scanner. If you're using Photoshop, you can scan a document directly into the program by using File → Import. Then choose your scanner from the list of devices. If you scan directly into Photoshop, the scanned file opens in a Photoshop window; otherwise you need to locate and open it.

2. **Choose File → Open, and open the strokes template file *stroke_template.png*.**

   At this point you have two files open in separate windows: *stroke_template.png* and the scanned file with your hand-drawn strokes.

3. **Make the window with the hand-drawn strokes active, and then choose the Rectangular Marquee (M) tool.**

   Your cursor changes to a cross.

4. **Use your mouse scroll wheel or the Zoom (Z) tool to zoom in on one of the strokes.**

   You need to edit your strokes one a time, and it's best to zoom in so you have a clear view of the stroke you're working on.

5. **Drag to place a rectangle around a stroke.**

   Make the marquee so that it just touches the stroke on both ends.

6. **Press Ctrl+C (⌘-C on a Mac).**

   The stroke is copied to the Clipboard.

7. **Switch to the template document, and then press Ctrl+V (⌘-V on a Mac).**

   You've pasted the stroke into the template document. Photoshop automatically creates a new layer for the stroke.

8. **Drag a marquee around the stroke a second time.**

   You need to select the stroke again before you can move and edit it.

9. **Move the cursor over the selected stroke, and then drag it into position over the proper box on the template.**

   The cursor changes to an arrow when it's over the selected stroke.

10. **Press Ctrl+T (⌘-T on a Mac).**

    Handles appear around the stroke showing that it's in free transform mode, as shown in Figure 15-5. You can drag the handles to stretch and shrink the stroke. If you hold the cursor over one of the corner handles, the cursor changes to a curved arrow, and you can rotate the selected stroke.

---

11. **Resize and rotate the stroke so it fits snugly in the template box.**

The ends of the stroke should touch the ends of the box in the template. The ends should also center on the marks on the sides of the box. Make sure the background is white, not gray or speckled. Sometimes scanned images need to be cleaned up a little.

Tip: Change your Photoshop preferences to display pixels. (In Windows, go to Edit → Preferences → Units & Rulers. On a Mac, go to Photoshop → Preferences → Units & Rulers.) Then open the Info window (Window → Info). The "W" value in the Info window shows you the width of the selection in pixels. This width should be the same as the width for the stroke. For example, the W value should be 64 when you've selected a stroke that's 64 pixels long. If it isn't, adjust the length when you're in Free Transform mode.

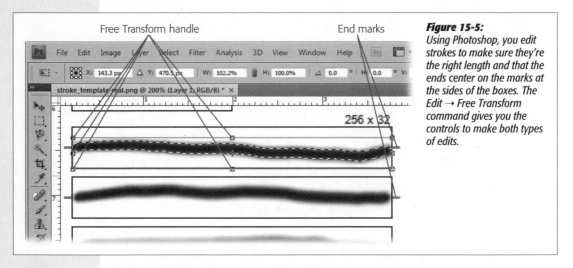

Figure 15-5:
Using Photoshop, you edit strokes to make sure they're the right length and that the ends center on the marks at the sides of the boxes. The Edit → Free Transform command gives you the controls to make both types of edits.

12. **Repeat these steps for each of the strokes.**

It's a little tedious tweaking all the strokes so that they match up with the template, but the payoff is worth it. If you want, after you've pasted in all the strokes, you can select the layers in the Layers window and merge them into one layer by right-clicking the selected layers and choosing Merge from the shortcut menu.

After you finish copying, pasting, and editing, save your strokes template in its .png file. In the next steps, you load this file and all your new strokes into the Style Builder program.

Editing Strokes in Style Builder

With your template document filled out, you're ready to bring it back into the Style Builder program. Now you get to have fun tweaking the appearance of the hand-drawn edges. To load the template file, choose File → Load Template (File → Open Template on a Mac). Navigate to the folder with your template and load it.

Make sure you're on the Strokes tab; the Style Builder window looks like Figure 15-6. When Style Builder loads the template file, it assumes that you want to use these new strokes to create a new style. So it automatically loads the strokes into the sets in the upper-right corner and applies the effect to the preview image at lower-right corner. On the left side, you see the sample strokes at top, with the strokes from your template file underneath.

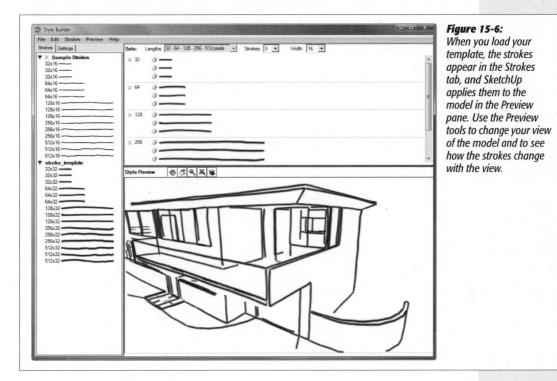

Figure 15-6:
When you load your template, the strokes appear in the Strokes tab, and SketchUp applies them to the model in the Preview pane. Use the Preview tools to change your view of the model and to see how the strokes change with the view.

Changing the Stroke Settings

Click the Settings tab and type a name, such as *Pen and Ink,* in the "Style name" box. This name appears in the Styles window. You also use the Settings tab to modify the look of the strokes. When you change any of the options, you see the effect in the image in the Preview pane. Be a little patient though; sometimes it takes a little while for the effects to show. If nothing seems to happen, try changing the view with one of the preview controls, like the Orbit tool.

Here's a rundown on the various settings (Figure 15-7):

- **Dropout length.** Dropouts create breaks in the edges, as if the pen skipped over a portion of the edge. Larger numbers in the "Dropout length" box create longer skips.

- **Fade factor.** Some lines appear faded while other lines appear bold. The larger the number in the "Fade factor" box, the more pronounced the difference between the faded and bold lines.

- **Halo.** A halo changes the way lines overlap in a drawing by ending the lines before the overlap. A larger value creates a greater gap between two intersecting lines.

- **Extensions.** These emphasize the hand-drawn look by extending lines slightly past their endpoint. Don't worry, this doesn't affect other aspects of SketchUp such as the position of inference lines. Larger numbers produce longer extensions past the intersection.

- **Profiles.** These emphasize the outlines or outer edges of the major shapes in your model. A technique used by traditional artists, this reinforces some of the 3-D visual cues, while giving your model a hand-drawn appearance.

- **Depth cueing.** This enhances the 3-D look of a drawing by making the lines that are nearer the viewer thicker, while the lines farther back in space are thinner.

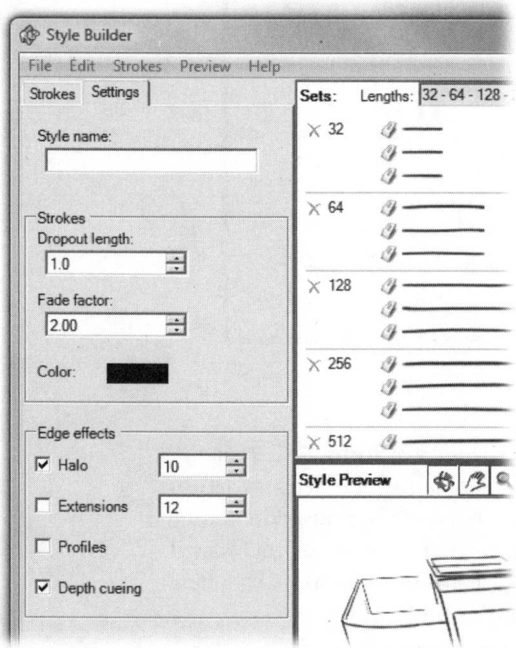

Figure 15-7:
If you've made changes to edges inside of SketchUp, some of the options on Style Builder's Settings tab look familiar. The settings for Halo, Extensions, Profiles, and "Depth cueing" are all accessible in SketchUp, too.

Adding More Strokes

You can add more than one collection of strokes to the Style Builder program. For example, if you followed the steps so far in this chapter, you see the Sample Strokes that were originally in Style Builder and the strokes that you drew and saved in *stroke_template.png*. When you loaded your template, Style Builder automatically applied the strokes to the sets shown on the right. If you're not happy with the results, you can load additional strokes into Style Builder. If you have another template ready with strokes, use the Strokes → Load From Template command. If the strokes are in a .style file, choose Strokes → Load From Style. The newly added strokes appear in the Strokes panel on the left in Style Builder. To make changes, drag a stroke from the Strokes panel to one of the sets on the right (Figure 15-8).

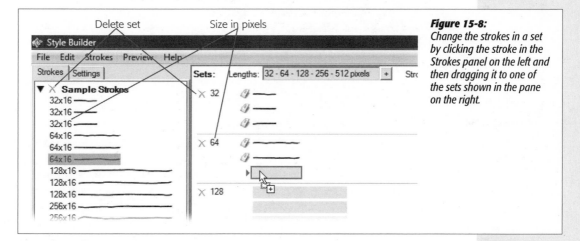

Figure 15-8:
Change the strokes in a set by clicking the stroke in the Strokes panel on the left and then dragging it to one of the sets shown in the pane on the right.

Saving a New Style

When you're happy with your style, choose File → Save. If you want to change the name of the file, choose File → Save As. Style Builder saves a file with the .style extension SketchUp uses. You may have noticed that the only aspect of the style that Style Builder changes is the edge. The .style file also includes basic styles for background colors and faces. If you want to make changes to those, you must do it within SketchUp as described in Chapter 6, page 193.

Opening a New Style in SketchUp

Once you've saved your new style, complete with those custom sketchy edges, open the file in SketchUp. The first step is to find out where SketchUp stores .style files on your computer. You find this tidbit of information in your SketchUp Preferences (Figure 15-9). On a PC, choose Window → Preferences. On a Mac, choose SketchUp → Preferences. When the System Preferences window opens, click Files in the list at left. The window displays a list of the types of files that SketchUp uses. These files store SketchUp documents, components, materials, and styles. The text boxes with the File Folder paths are a little bit short, so you may need to drag in the text boxes to see the entire name. If you want to designate a new folder to hold a particular type of file, click the folder icon at right. A "Browse for folder" window opens. Navigate to the new folder and click OK. That new location appears in the File Folder path.

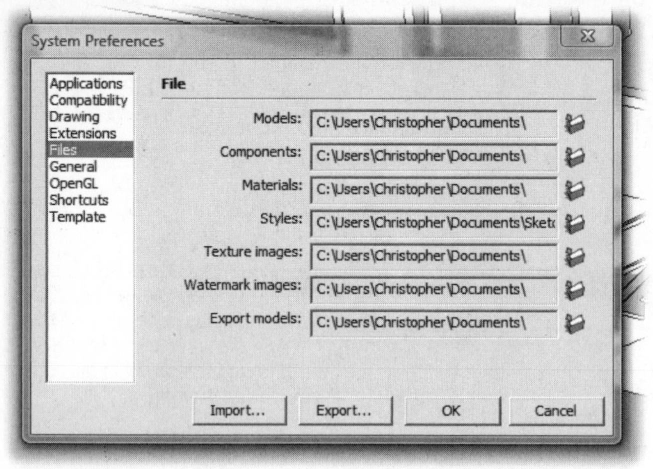

Figure 15-9:
SketchUp expects to find certain types of files in specific folders. Open the System Preferences window, and you see the complete list of file types and the File Folder path to locate them. Want to make changes? Just click the folder icon and designate a new folder.

Tip: Give your style folder a unique name that's not already used in SketchUp styles. Something like *Custom Styles* or even *Phil Brunelleschi's Styles* is good, as long as you remember the name so you can find it in SketchUp's Styles window.

Move the .style document created by Style Builder (*stroke_template.png*) into the Styles folder identified in the System Preferences window (Figure 15-10). Then open the Styles window (Window → Styles). Click the Select tab and then use the drop-down menu to select the name of the styles file folder. At that point, the styles in the Styles folder appear in the Preview pane. Just click the style you want to use.

Tip: In Windows, you can drag .style files from the desktop or a folder directly to a collection in SketchUp's Styles window. The style is automatically saved in the Style Library.

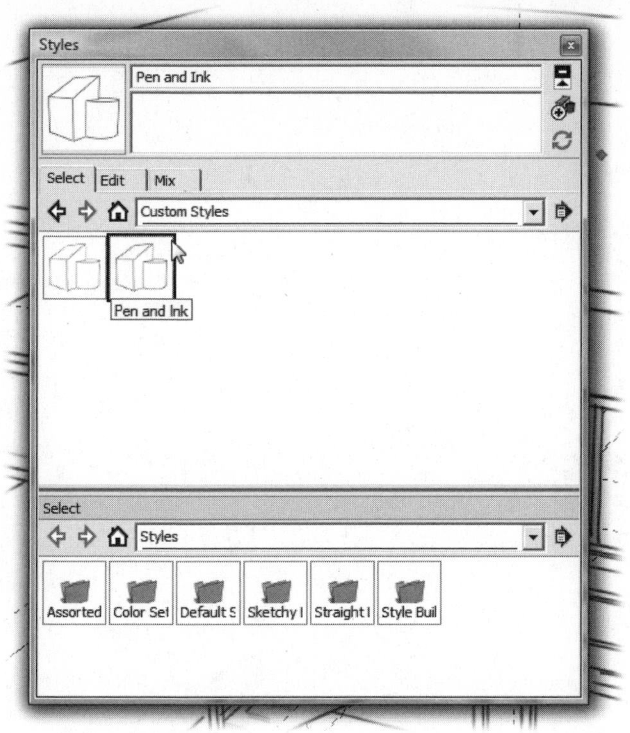

Figure 15-10:
In this example the name of the Styles folder is
Custom Styles, and the name of the new style
with sketchy edges is Pen and Ink.

Presenting Your Model with LayOut (SketchUp Pro)

After you build a spectacular SketchUp model, the next logical step is to show it off. LayOut is your tool for creating professional-quality printed documents and PowerPoint-style presentations. With SketchUp models, the integration between LayOut and SketchUp makes the work go much faster than if you tried to use InDesign or, well, PowerPoint. LayOut understands your 3-D SketchUp model and makes the most of it. For example, suppose you have a model of a college campus and you use SketchUp scenes to create different views of the Science Hall, the Gymnasium, and the Performing Arts Center. You can insert your model into a page in LayOut, and then choose the scene you want to display. Even better, if you want to change the view slightly, you can use the camera tools Orbit, Pan, and Zoom right in LayOut. That's not something you can do with a 2-D graphic.

As a full-featured page layout and presentation program, LayOut is pretty complex. This chapter helps you get started fast. The first few sections give you a quick tour of the LayOut program along with tips for setting up the workspace to suit your needs. If you want to jump right to the techniques for creating LayOut documents and inserting SketchUp models, jump to "Manipulating Your Model in Layout" on page 508.

Workflow for a LayOut Project

LayOut comes with SketchUp Pro, but it's a separate program from SketchUp. Typically you fire up LayOut after you've created a model that you're ready to show the world (or your boss). That doesn't mean your SketchUp model has to be set in stone before you add it to a LayOut project. Perhaps after seeing the pages you printed in Layout, your boss suggests some changes. You can go back to

SketchUp and make those changes. Then when you open your LayOut document, you see the changes, and you're ready to print some new, improved pages.

Here are some of the typical activities that you perform to create a LayOut project:

- **Open a template.** By choosing an appropriate template, you can get a jump start on your project. For example, a template for an architectural project may include a standard titleblock and your company logo. Templates determine the page size for a LayOut document and include text and graphics.

- **Fill in details to appear on multiple pages.** Templates may provide only a portion of the details that should appear on every page. Each LayOut document is likely to have a project and perhaps a designer's name that should appear on every page. Using LayOut layers, you can choose to place text and graphics on a single page or on multiple pages.

- **Add 3-D graphics.** Adding your 3-D SketchUp model is certainly the most entertaining part of your LayOut project. You can show different views of a 3-D model, and you can adjust that view in LayOut as you create pages (Figure 16-1).

- **Add 2-D graphics.** You can import 2-D images like photos or line drawings to your LayOut pages. LayOut also includes 2-D drawing tools that are very similar to SketchUp's drawing tools, so you can produce 2-D graphics without going into a drawing program.

- **Add callouts and captions.** Use LayOut's Text and Label tools to produce callouts and other captions.

- **Add text blocks.** LayOut provides tools for large blocks of text, making it easy to align your text with graphics. You also have the standard control over typefaces, font size, and other typographic details.

- **Print pages.** You can print LayOut pages or export them to PDF files for emailing to clients and colleagues.

- **Show presentation.** You don't have to export your images to PowerPoint; you can present your work in LayOut.

Starting Up LayOut

You start LayOut the same way you start other programs on your computer. Usually the installer places an icon or shortcut to the LayOut program on your desktop. You can start LayOut by double-clicking the shortcut. If you don't immediately see the LayOut icon, one of the easiest ways to start it is to use Windows' search tool or the Mac's Spotlight:

- **Starting LayOut (Windows).** Press the Windows key or click the Start button, and the Search box appears with your cursor inside and ready to go. Type *Lay-Out,* and a list shows all LayOut-related programs and files. At the top of the list under Programs, you see LayOut. If it's highlighted, press Enter; if not, click the program name and LayOut starts up.

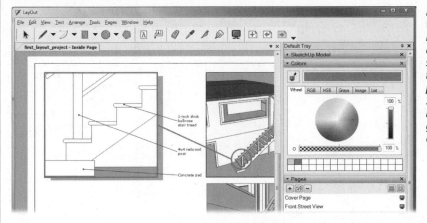

Figure 16-1:
With SketchUp and LayOut you can create dozens of images from a single model. That's not the case when you create pages from traditional 2-D art, where every image is a separate graphic that you must create individually.

(**Mac**). Press ⌘-space bar, and the Spotlight menu opens with your cursor in the search box. Type *layout,* and you see a list of programs and files sorted by applications, documents, folders, and so on. Next to Applications, you see Lay-Out and an icon that looks like a pencil and piece of paper. Click the icon to start LayOut.

• **Reopening a Recent LayOut Project** (**Windows**). Choose Windows → Recent, and a list of recently opened documents appears. Those with names ending with ".layout" are LayOut documents.

(**Mac**). Press ⌘-space bar, type *layout* in the Spotlight box, and then choose your file from the group of Documents. LayOut document names end in .layout.

Tip: When you install SketchUp Pro, you get the LayOut on your computer along with the other SketchUp files. A standard Windows installation usually puts the LayOut in *C:/Program Files/Google/Google SketchUp 7/LayOut.* On a Mac, you can find LayOut in *Macintosh HD/Applications/Google SketchUp 7.*

The first time you start LayOut, you see a couple of windows doing their best to help you. First, there's Tip of the Day, a window that provides basic details in text and animation. The first tip points out how to find online help. Click the Next button, and new tips appear, covering drawing techniques and LayOut features. When you're new to LayOut, the tips can be helpful reminders. When you find them no longer helpful, turn off the "Show tips on startup" checkbox. The second window, Getting Started, is LayOut's launch pad (Figure 16-2). Using the two tabs at the top, choose New to create a new project or Recent to continue working on a project. Of course, you can click Cancel to bypass the whole Getting Started window and to use the standard File → Open command.

Tip: If LayOut crashes while you're working, the next time you start the program, you see the Recovered tab, where you can find the last automatically saved copy of your file.

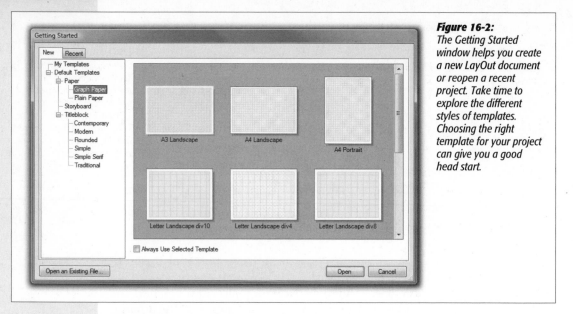

Figure 16-2:
The Getting Started window helps you create a new LayOut document or reopen a recent project. Take time to explore the different styles of templates. Choosing the right template for your project can give you a good head start.

Choosing a Template

Templates are always timesaving devices, and that's exactly how they work in Lay-Out. When you first start SketchUp, you see several predesigned templates (Figure 16-2). The Titleblock templates appeal to architects, while the Storyboard templates are filmmaker favorites. Some templates include more than one page. For example, the Titleblock templates usually start you off with a cover page and an inside page.

Here are some of LayOut's template types:

- **Graph Paper** templates display a customizable grid of major and minor lines. The lines appear on your computer screen and when you use LayOut's Presentation feature.

- **Plain Paper** gives you exactly that—an empty page so you can start from scratch. As with most of the templates, you can choose between several paper sizes.

- **Storyboard** templates give filmmakers a head start (Figure 16-3). Each template provides predesigned boxes for scene images, descriptions, and dialogue. The templates match the dimensions of common film/video formats: 1.33, 1.85, and 2.35.

- **Titleblock** templates are tools for architects, engineers, and designers. Several options are available giving you a choice between traditional or more contemporary styles.

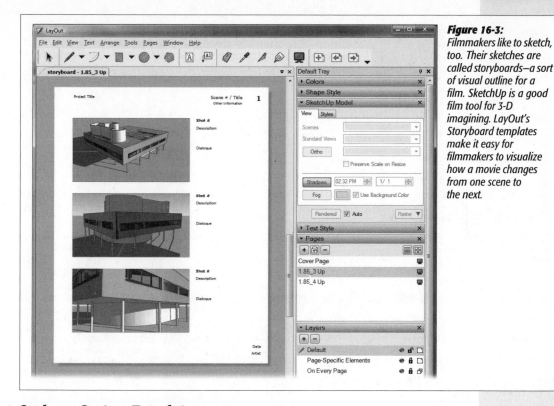

Figure 16-3:
Filmmakers like to sketch, too. Their sketches are called storyboards—a sort of visual outline for a film. SketchUp is a good film tool for 3-D imagining. LayOut's Storyboard templates make it easy for filmmakers to visualize how a movie changes from one scene to the next.

Saving a Custom Template

Even if you don't find the perfect template for your needs, you may want to start off with a close fit, make some changes, and then save your own custom template. After inserting your company logo and any of the other elements you want in a template, choose File → Save As Template (Figure 16-4). Type a name for your template, and choose the folder where you'd like to save it. The next time you see the Getting Started window, your template appears with the others.

LayOut Program: The Quick Tour

Once you get past the getting started windows, you see the LayOut program window (Figure 16-5). If you've used a page layout program like Adobe InDesign or Microsoft Publisher, you'll feel right at home. The main portion of the window shows you a page in your document. Under the menus, you have tools for drawings and text. At right, you see dialog boxes—called *trays* in LayOut—including Colors, Shape Style, Text Style, Pages, and SketchUp Model. At bottom left, a status bar provides hints and displays messages like "Auto Save Complete." Sharing the status bar is the Measurements box, which works like SketchUp's Measurements toolbar.

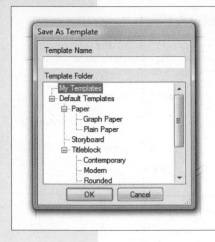

Figure 16-4:
The Save As Template window shows two boxes: Template Name and Template Folder. LayOut automatically selects My Templates as a location for your new template, but you can select any of the other folders in the list.

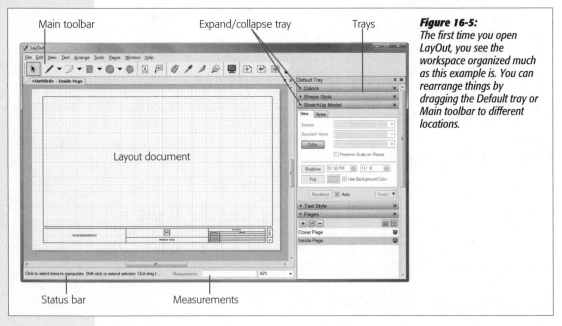

Figure 16-5:
The first time you open LayOut, you see the workspace organized much as this example is. You can rearrange things by dragging the Default tray or Main toolbar to different locations.

Menus

As in SketchUp, LayOut's menus are a sure path to every tool, window, and tray (Figure 16-6). Mostly you use the menu commands to work with files. Besides using them to open and close documents, you use menus to insert models and to export files such as portable document format (PDF) documents. Even though the menus show many other commands, it's often easier to click an icon in the toolbar, right-click an object, or to adjust the settings in the trays.

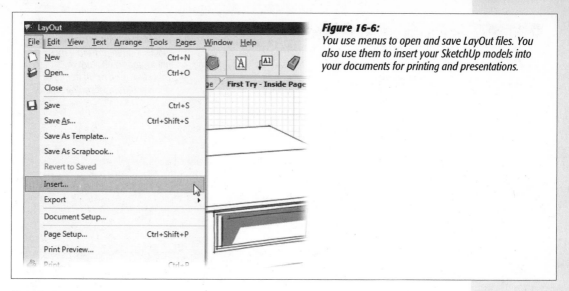

Figure 16-6:
You use menus to open and save LayOut files. You also use them to insert your SketchUp models into your documents for printing and presentations.

Toolbars

When you first start LayOut, you see the Main toolbar (Figure 16-7), which provides quick and easy access to the most frequently used tools. To reposition a toolbar in Windows, drag the little grip lines on its left side. You can dock the toolbar on any edge of the program window, or you can use it undocked. On a Mac, the toolbar is a fixed feature at the top of the document window. As you become familiar with LayOut, you may want to customize the Main toolbar or to create your own specialized toolbars.

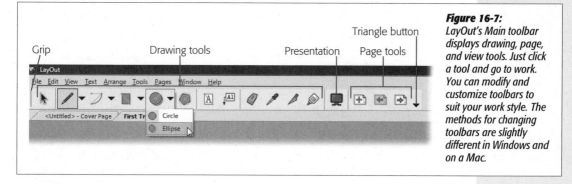

Figure 16-7:
LayOut's Main toolbar displays drawing, page, and view tools. Just click a tool and go to work. You can modify and customize toolbars to suit your work style. The methods for changing toolbars are slightly different in Windows and on a Mac.

Customizing Windows toolbars

To add and remove buttons from the Main toolbar, click the triangle at the right end of the toolbar, and then choose "Add or Remove Buttons". A menu drops down showing a list of Main toolbar buttons (Figure 16-8). Use the checkboxes to customize the toolbar.

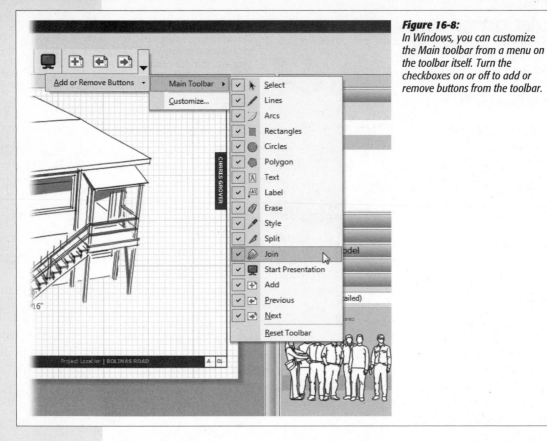

Figure 16-8:
In Windows, you can customize the Main toolbar from a menu on the toolbar itself. Turn the checkboxes on or off to add or remove buttons from the toolbar.

If you want to create a new toolbar, click the Customize option (Figure 16-8). The Customize window (Figure 16-9) opens, where you can create and manage toolbars. Click the New button to create a new toolbar.

Customizing Mac toolbars

Macs have a standard system for customizing toolbars, so the method for customizing the LayOut toolbar is similar to the method used in SketchUp (page 20). Control-click a document window's title bar, and then choose Customize Toolbar from the shortcut menu. The window displays all available buttons. To customize the toolbar, drag buttons from the window onto the toolbar. To remove buttons, drag them off the toolbar.

Trays

LayOut uses lots of little dialog boxes for important tasks related to drawing, working with SketchUp models, and specifying type, colors, and shape styles. Other programs may call these "palettes" or "windows"—LayOut calls them *trays* (Figure 16-10). (A rose by any other name…) When you start LayOut the first time, all trays are docked at the right side. Click the bar at the top of a tray to expand or collapse the view. Drag the same bar to reposition trays. Click the X button in the tray's upper-right corner to hide it. To bring it back, choose Window → Pages or Window → Text Style.

The Default tray serves as a container for all the other trays. You can click the bar at the top of the Default tray and drag the trays to other places on your screen. If you need more workspace, click the pushpin icon in the Default tray bar to put the trays in auto-hide mode. Then, when you need a tray, just move your cursor over the Default tray tab, and the trays you can choose appear.

Status Bar, Measurements, and Zoom View

At the bottom of the LayOut window you find the status bar, the Measurements box, and the Zoom View drop-down menu (Figure 16-11). The status bar gives you hints and tips about what to do next. For example, if a box with a SketchUp model is selected, the status bar may suggest: "Drag selection to move or drag grips to scale or rotate." The status bar's Zoom View drop-down menu, at far right, lets you change your view of the LayOut document. If you've got a mouse with a scroll wheel, it's usually easier just to give it a spin.

LayOut's Measurements box works like the Measurements toolbar in SketchUp. As you're creating graphics, type a measurement to set dimensions or to move entities. You don't need to click in the Measurements box first—LayOut knows what you mean. As long as you haven't selected another tool or command, you can change the values simply by typing new numbers. The Measurements box is an all-purpose tool. Use it to enter dimensions, the distance you want to move an object on the page, the number of degrees you want to rotate an object, or the number of sides for a polygon.

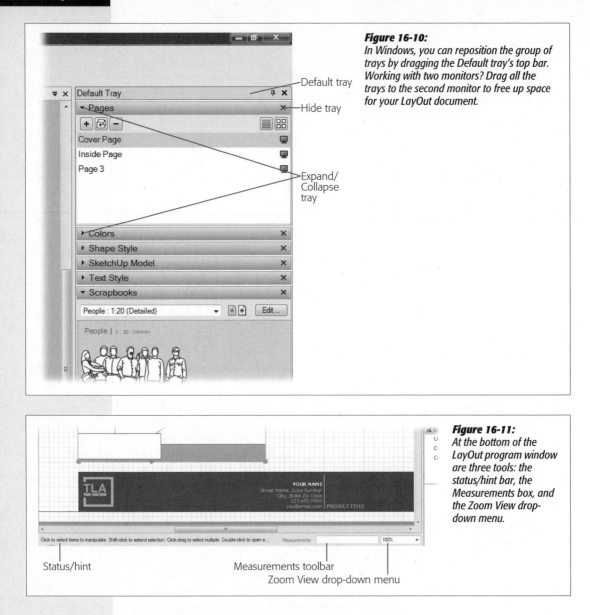

Figure 16-10:
In Windows, you can reposition the group of trays by dragging the Default tray's top bar. Working with two monitors? Drag all the trays to the second monitor to free up space for your LayOut document.

Default tray

Hide tray

Expand/ Collapse tray

Figure 16-11:
At the bottom of the LayOut program window are three tools: the status/hint bar, the Measurements box, and the Zoom View drop-down menu.

Status/hint

Measurements toolbar

Zoom View drop-down menu

Manipulating Your Model in LayOut

As with any page layout program, working inside of LayOut is a matter of adding and arranging words and graphics on pages. The main difference between LayOut and programs like InDesign or Publisher is the ease with which you can work with SketchUp models. After inserting your model, LayOut's text tools give you everything you need to create callouts, captions, and large blocks of text. You can create new 2-D graphics using the drawing tools on the LayOut toolbar. You fine-tune the entities on the pages using the tray settings. The next few sections describe how to work with LayOut's layers and pages and how to add graphics and text to your document. To begin, create a new LayOut document using the following steps:

1. **Start LayOut. In the Getting Started window's New tab, click Titleblock.**

   A list of Titleblock templates appears under the Titleblock item, as shown in Figure 16-12. All the Titleblock templates are displayed in the Getting Started window.

2. **Click Contemporary.**

   The Getting Started window displays only the contemporary-style Titleblock templates.

3. **Use the scroll bars to find the Letter Landscape thumbnail, and then double-click it.**

   The Getting Started window closes, and a copy of the Letter Landscape template opens.

Tip: Below the template thumbnails is a checkbox called "Always Use Selected Template". Turn on this box if you want SketchUp to open the same template every time you start the program.

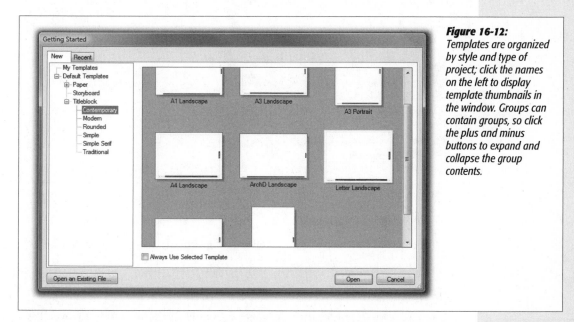

Figure 16-12:
Templates are organized by style and type of project; click the names on the left to display template thumbnails in the window. Groups can contain groups, so click the plus and minus buttons to expand and collapse the group contents.

Several of the templates, including the Titleblock Contemporary template, start off with more than one type of page. Use the toolbar page buttons (Figure 16-13) to move back and forth through the pages in your document. You do other page management tasks using the Pages tray, as explained in the next section.

Managing LayOut Pages

Just like a document in a word processor, LayOut puts words and images on pages. Usually the page size and orientation (portrait or landscape) is determined by the template you choose when you create a new document. Many templates start off with more than one type of page—like a cover page and an inside page. Layout only shows one page at time. You can move from one page to another in a few ways:

- On the toolbar, click the Next page and Previous page buttons.

- Choose Pages → Next and Pages → Previous.

- In the Pages tray, click a page name.

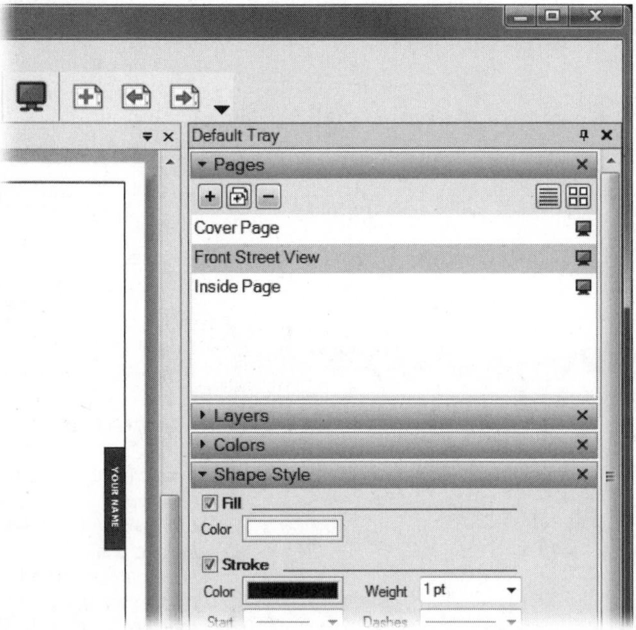

Figure 16-13:
On the Pages tray's right side, use the buttons to show page names or page thumbnails. The video screen button to the right of each page name is a toggle that determines whether the page is included in LayOut's PowerPoint-style presentations.

With the document from page 508 open, follow these steps to display the Pages tray and use some of its settings:

1. **Click the Window menu and make sure a checkmark is next to Pages.**

   When Pages is selected, the Pages tray is displayed.

2. **If the tray is collapsed, click the bar that says Pages to expand the tray.**

   The Pages window lists the two pages currently in the document: Cover Page and Inside Page. See Figure 16-13.

3. **Click the Add Page button.**

   A new page named "Page 3" is added to the list.

4. Double-click "Page 3" and then type *Front Street View.*

The page is renamed Front Street View.

5. Click each of the page names in the Pages tray, and leave the Cover Page selected.

When you click the page name, LayOut displays the page in the main window. The Cover Page has a different titleblock than Inside Page and Front Street View. The bottom of the Cover Page in the titleblock shows a logo and several text fields.

6. With the Select tool, double-click the YOUR NAME field and type your name, or if you prefer to remain anonymous, type *PHIL BRUNELLESCHI.* When you're finished, press Enter (Return).

The name appears in the titleblock. You can't click and move the words or graphics in the Cover Page. They're locked in place, using Layer settings as explained on page 511.

7. In the Pages tray, click Inside Page.

LayOut displays the Inside Page. On the right side is a field that says "YOUR NAME". Changing the text in the Cover Page didn't change the Inside Page.

8. Double-click YOUR NAME and type a name of your choice. Then in the Pages tray, click Front Street View.

The name appears on both the Inside Page and Front Street View pages, since these pages share content. This sharing is also a function of Layers, as explained on page 511.

9. Choose File → Save, give your file the name *first_layout_project,* and then click OK.

Your file is saved under the name *first_layout_project.layout.*

You can reorder your pages using the Pages tray. Just click the page name, and drag it to a new position in the list. If you want to make your document seem complete and official, fill in some of the text fields.

Organizing Elements with Layers

The previous section showed how some entities appear on multiple pages while others appear only on a single page. You also saw that text and graphics can be locked in place. All those LayOut tricks are controlled by the Layers settings. Here are some of the things that Layers can do:

• **Show and hide entities.** Entire layers are displayed or hidden using the visibility toggle, which looks like an eyeball (Figure 16-14). Layers' visibility is unique to each page, so a layer that's hidden on page 1 may be visible on page 2. When the eye is grayed out, the layer is hidden.

- **Prevent content from changing.** Lock or unlock the content for a layer using the lock layer toggle (padlock). Layer locking is unique to each page, so a layer that's locked on page 1 may be unlocked on page 2.

- **Display elements on multiple pages.** Use the shared layer button to control whether a layer's content is shared across multiple pages.

- **Organize the stacking order of entities.** Drag a layer up or down in the Layers list. The entities in higher layers cover the entities in lower layers. A single page icon indicates the content is limited to a single page.

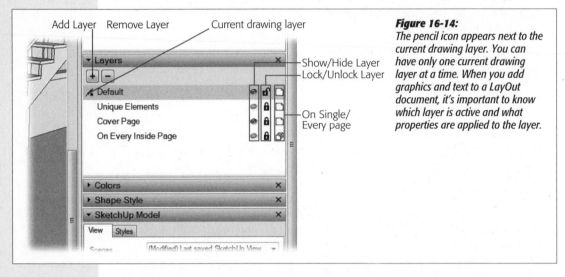

Add Layer   Remove Layer   Current drawing layer

Show/Hide Layer
Lock/Unlock Layer

On Single/
Every page

Figure 16-14:
The pencil icon appears next to the current drawing layer. You can have only one current drawing layer at a time. When you add graphics and text to a LayOut document, it's important to know which layer is active and what properties are applied to the layer.

You can easily move entities to the current layer by right-clicking (⌘-clicking) the entity and choosing "Move to Current Layer" from the shortcut menu.

Creating Content that Appears on Multiple Pages

The LayOut document you started on page 509 has four layers. The layers' purposes are fairly clear from their names: On Every Inside Page, Cover Page, Unique Elements, and Default. When you first use a template to create a document, the layer selected as the current drawing layer is Default. It's also the only unlocked layer.

If you want to add text or a graphic that appears on every page except the cover page, click the padlock icon on the On Every Inside Page line to unlock the layer, and then click the layer. With the layer active and unlocked, you can add the text or graphics. When you're done, you can protect the shared content by clicking the padlock to lock the layer. You can show or hide the On Every Inside Page text or graphic on a page-by-page basis. This lets you show an entity on most pages without showing it on every page.

Tip: Text created with the Text and Label tools is locked in position when it's in locked layers, but you can edit the actual text by double-clicking it. In this way, you can create changeable text fields like the YOUR NAME field in the exercise on page 511.

Inserting a Model into LayOut

If there's a single feature that distinguishes LayOut from every other page layout tool, it's the ability to insert 3-D SketchUp models and then manipulate the view from within the document. It's easier to do than you might think, though sometimes it makes the program crash. So before continuing, if you have something worth saving in your document, save it using the File → Save or File → Save As command. You're then ready to follow these steps:

1. **With *first_layout_project.layout* open, in the Pages tray click Cover Page.**

   The relatively empty cover page is displayed.

2. **Choose File → Insert.**

   A file browser window opens, where you can navigate the folders and files on your computer and network.

3. **Find *modern_house_layout.skp* and then double-click the file name.**

   LayOut loads the model, creates a graphics box on the layout page, and then displays an image of the model in the box (Figure 16-15). The length of time before an image appears depends on your computer's speed and the model's size. Be patient—with complex models the process can take minutes, not seconds. The graphics box remains selected, and when you hold your cursor over the box, you see the Move cursor.

4. **Drag the box with the model to position it on the page. Drag the blue triangle handles to resize the box.**

   The box changes position and dimensions. With 2-D graphics, when you change the proportions of an image, the image gets distorted—stretched or squished. That's not the case with SketchUp models in LayOut. Change the box any way you want, and your model still appears well-proportioned in whatever space you give it.

5. **With the box selected, choose Arrange → Center → Vertically on Page, and then choose Arrange → Center → Horizontally on Page.**

   LayOut centers the model's box vertically and horizontally, which may not be exactly what you want for the cover page. Go ahead and make changes until you're pleased with the page layout.

6. **Choose File → Save.**

   The changes you've made are saved to *first_layout_project.layout*.

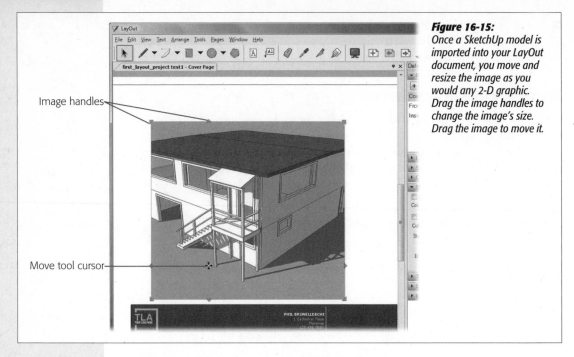

Image handles

Move tool cursor

Figure 16-15:
Once a SketchUp model is imported into your LayOut document, you move and resize the image as you would any 2-D graphic. Drag the image handles to change the image's size. Drag the image to move it.

As shown in the exercise, working with the box that holds a graphic is similar to working with a rectangle shape in SketchUp. You drag to change the box's position and shape. You can also use the Measurements box for moves and dimension changes. Just start to move or change the box, and then type a value.

Changing the View of a 3-D Model in LayOut

Once you've got a copy of your 3-D model pasted into a LayOut document, you don't need to use the File → Insert command to create additional images for your pages. You can copy and paste the model to create new graphics. Follow these steps to show a different view of the model on a different page:

1. With *first_layout_project.layout* open to Cover Page, right-click the model and choose Copy. In the Pages tray, click Inside Page.

   The Inside Page appears in the window. It's empty except for the titleblock entities that appear on every page.

2. Right-click in the center of the page and choose Paste.

   LayOut pastes a copy of the model on the Inside Page. Its size and view are identical to the graphic on the cover page.

3. Use the image handles to make the image fit on about a quarter of the page.

   As the box gets smaller, the view of the model shrinks to fit.

4. Right-click the image and then choose Scenes → "rise and run" from the shortcut menu.

The image changes to a close-up detail of the stairs in parallel line mode. It looks more like a 2-D graphic than a 3-D model.

5. With the Select tool, move the cursor over the model graphic. Press Ctrl (Control), and then drag a new copy of the model to a new location on the page, as shown in Figure 16-16.

When the move is complete, you have two copies of the model on the Inside Page. As you move objects, you see inference guides to help you with alignment. The Move tool also snaps to horizontal and vertical axes on the page.

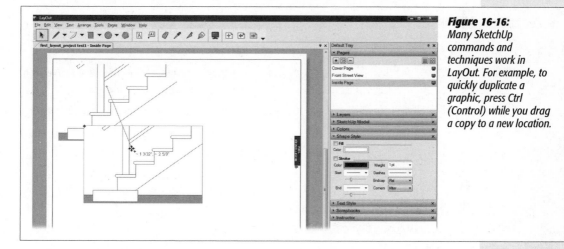

Figure 16-16:
Many SketchUp commands and techniques work in LayOut. For example, to quickly duplicate a graphic, press Ctrl (Control) while you drag a copy to a new location.

6. Double-click the second image and then drag it.

When you double-click a SketchUp model in LayOut, the Orbit cursor appears, making it easy to change the view. Suddenly the image looks like a 3-D model again, and you can change the view using several standard SketchUp view tools.

7. With the 3-D model still selected, right-click it and choose Camera Tools → Pan. Then drag to position a new view of the model in the box.

Right-clicking the model gives you access to many SketchUp commands. The Camera tools include the usual suspects: Orbit, Pan, Zoom, Zoom Window, Look Around, and Walk (page 413). Lower on the menu are the standard views: Front, Back, Left, and Right.

8. Right-click the model and choose Perspective. Then right-click again and choose Shadows.

Checkmarks appear in the menu next to the selected options. The Perspective view and Shadows give the model a better 3-D appearance.

9. **Use the view tools to set up a good 3-D view of the stairs.**

   When you're done, the image may look like Figure 16-17.

10. **Click outside of the model, on the empty white space.**

    Clicking outside of the model takes you out of 3-D mode and back to the page layout mode. Now if you right-click one of the model graphics, you see a different context menu with options like Cut, Copy, and Paste. You also see the blue handles around the image.

11. **Choose File → Save.**

    The changes you've made are saved to *first_layout_project.layout*.

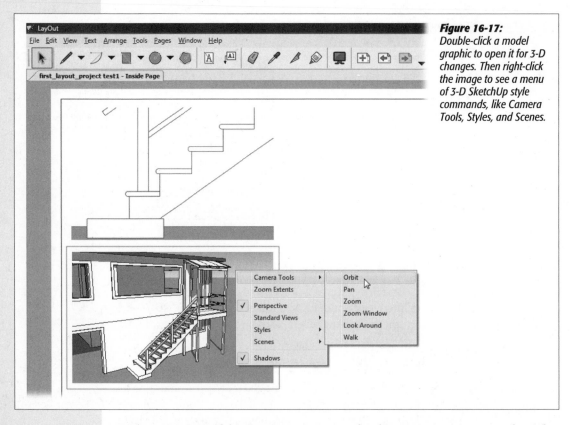

Figure 16-17:
Double-click a model graphic to open it for 3-D changes. Then right-click the image to see a menu of 3-D SketchUp style commands, like Camera Tools, Styles, and Scenes.

With your 3-D model in LayOut, you can make changes to its appearance by right-clicking the model and then choosing from the Styles, Scenes, and Shadows menus. For some changes, like altering the angle of the shadow or its intensity, you must go back and edit your model in SketchUp. You can do that by choosing "Open with SketchUp" from the shortcut menu.

If you spend too much time waiting while LayOut renders each incremental change to the 3-D model, go to the SketchUp Model tray and turn off Rendered Auto. With auto mode turned off, you can make changes and when you're ready, click the Render button.

Updating Links to SketchUp Models

When LayOut inserts a SketchUp model into a page, it doesn't paste a fixed image. Instead, it creates a link from the LayOut document to the SketchUp file stored on your computer or network. That way, if you make changes to that SketchUp file, those changes are shown in the LayOut document, too. If you move or delete or rename the file, LayOut won't be able to link to it. In some cases LayOut may still be able to show an image, but it won't be able to update the model. If the graphics in LayOut become disconnected from the original file, you can use the Document Setup window to fix the problem (Figure 16-18). Go to File → Document Setup, and the Document Setup window opens. At left, click References, and the window displays the references to linked files. These files may be SketchUp models or 2-D graphics from other programs.

Examine the status field to see whether files are Embedded, Current, or Missing. Missing files are listed in red text. If a file is missing, click the Relink button at the bottom. A file browser window opens, where you can hunt down the missing file. Use the Update Reference button to force SketchUp to update the images in the LayOut pages to match the model. SketchUp usually updates images automatically, but sometimes it needs to be prompted. You can also update an image by right-clicking the image in a page and choosing Update from the shortcut menu. Use the Unlink button to break the connection between a SketchUp file and a LayOut image. At that point, the image still appears in LayOut, but it won't show any changes made to the original image outside of LayOut. Click Edit to open the file for editing. If it's a SketchUp model, SketchUp starts up with the file loaded. Use the Purge command to remove unneeded files from the list.

Drawing in LayOut

LayOut comes with a respectable set of drawing tools, most of which you can find on the toolbar. If you're familiar with SketchUp's basic drawing tools for lines and 2-D shapes, you'll be comfortable in LayOut. The tools for lines, arcs, and shapes work as they do in SketchUp. You'll even find inferences to help you find center points and align different objects on the page. The main differences between LayOut and SketchUp are that LayOut has no 3-D drawing tools, and the selection tools work differently. A single click selects objects—no need to double- and triple-click.

You use the Colors and Shape Style trays to specify colors and the thickness of lines (Figure 16-19). Special options are available to choose line styles and to create arrows, endcaps, and mitered corners.

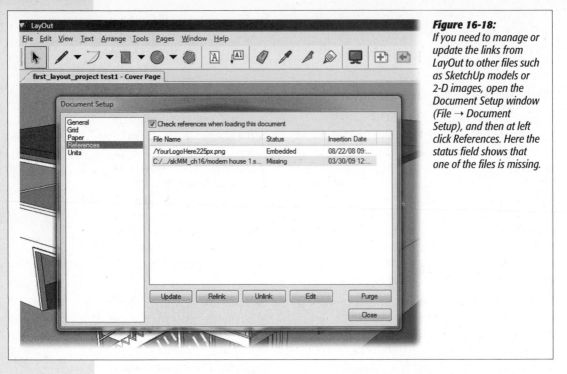

Figure 16-18:
If you need to manage or update the links from LayOut to other files such as SketchUp models or 2-D images, open the Document Setup window (File → Document Setup), and then at left click References. Here the status field shows that one of the files is missing.

In the previous exercise, you created a closeup view of the stairs on Inside Page. The wall color for the model is pale yellow, so the image gets a little lost on the page. In the next few steps, you use LayOut's drawing tools to create a border around the image and to add a drop shadow:

1. With *first_layout_project.layout* open to Cover Page, use the Select tool to click the closeup graphic of the stairs.

   Blue triangular handles appear on the selected graphic.

2. Click the Colors and Shape Style trays to show their contents.

   The two trays look like Figure 16-19.

3. In the Shape Style tray, turn on the Stroke check box.

   A stroke appears around the selected graphic. The color and weight of the stroke match the Color and Weight shown below the Stroke checkbox.

4. In the Colors tray, click the color wheel to select a new color. Then click the color in the Selected Color preview box. Press the mouse button as you drag the color onto the Color box under Stroke.

   You can drag selected colors onto color boxes and faces in LayOut pages (Figure 16-20). Think of it as dragging a color chip onto an object to change its hue.

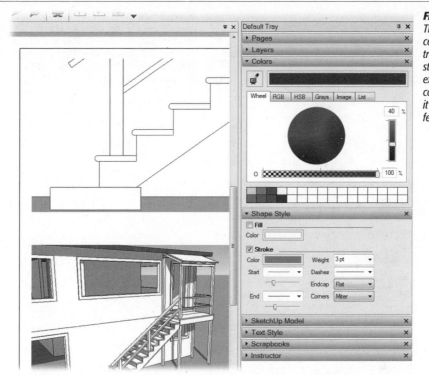

5. **In the toolbar, click the Rectangle tool, and then draw a rectangle over the closeup graphic of the stairs.**

   LayOut draws the new rectangle over the graphic, hiding the image.

6. **With the Select tool, click to select the rectangle.**

   Selection handles appear around the rectangle.

7. **In the Shape Style tray, turn on the Fill box, and turn off the Stroke box.**

   The rectangle has a fill color and no stroke.

8. **In the Colors tray, mix up a solid black, and then drag the transparency slider to 30 percent.**

   The rectangle becomes semitransparent. You can control the transparency of shapes within LayOut, but unfortunately you can't control the transparency of models and images after inserting them in LayOut.

9. **With the Select tool, drag the rectangle down and to the right of the model image.**

   Put it in a good position for a drop shadow effect.

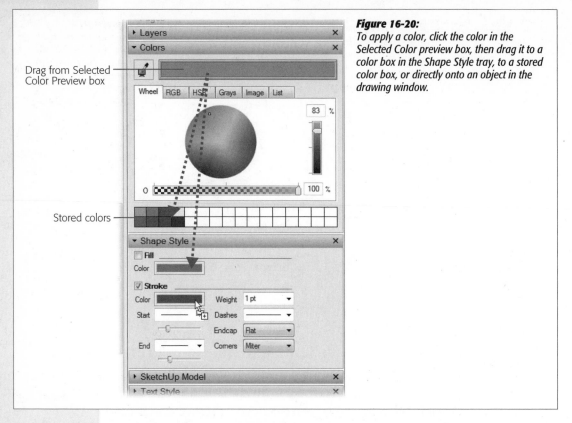

Drag from Selected
Color Preview box

Stored colors

Figure 16-20:
*To apply a color, click the color in the
Selected Color preview box, then drag it to a
color box in the Shape Style tray, to a stored
color box, or directly onto an object in the
drawing window.*

10. **Right-click the rectangle and choose Arrange → Send to Back.**

The rectangle is placed behind the model graphic. The dark semitransparent
box shows on two edges of the image, as shown in Figure 16-21.

Tip: LayOut's Polygon tool is similar to SketchUp's. To set the number of sides for a polygon, select the
Polygon tool and type the number of sides, followed by the letter "s". Then draw the polygon. Also, as in
SketchUp, you can use the same technique to change the number of sides after a polygon is drawn.

Adding Text to Your LayOut

In a couple areas, pages created in LayOut are superior to images printed directly
out of SketchUp. Callouts are one of those areas. A *callout* is a bit of text that draws
attention to a particular part of an image, like the words "Inference line" in
Figure 16-22. LayOut's Label tool is made specifically to create callouts. In the next
few steps, you'll add a few callouts to the closeup image of the stairs:

1. **On the toolbar, click the Label tool.**

The Label tool looks like a box with "A1" inside; an arrow points down from
the box.

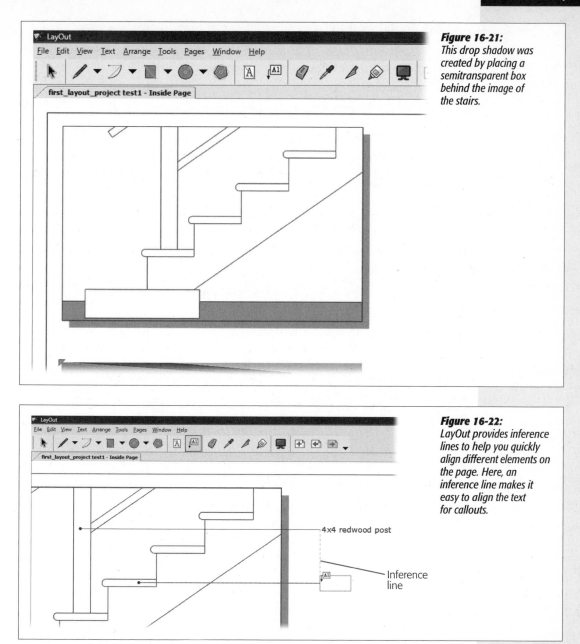

Figure 16-21:
This drop shadow was created by placing a semitransparent box behind the image of the stairs.

Figure 16-22:
LayOut provides inference lines to help you quickly align different elements on the page. Here, an inference line makes it easy to align the text for callouts.

2. In the Shape Style tray, set the Stroke color to black, the line weight to 0.5 pt, and in the Start drop-down menu, select either an arrow or a circle end point.

LayOut will apply the settings in the Shape Style tray to the graphic you created with the Label tool.

3. **Click the stair post and then move the cursor to the right of the image.**

   You can use the same click-move-click method in LayOut that you use in SketchUp. Inference lines show up when you move the cursor along the vertical or horizontal axes.

4. **Click in the page's white space, and then type *4x4 redwood post*.**

   Your callout points to the stair post, and the text identifies it as a redwood 4×4.

5. **With the Label tool, click one of the stair treads, and move the cursor to the right until you see an inference line extending from the first callout, as shown in Figure 16-22.**

   As you work in LayOut, keep looking for inferences that help you align text and graphics. They're tremendous timesavers.

6. **When you see an inference line from the first callout, click; then type *1-inch bullnose tread*.**

   The callout for the stair tread is perfectly aligned with the callout for the redwood post.

The Label tool works well for callouts. Use the Text tool to create blocks of text. Click the Text tool button, and your cursor changes to a pencil. Use the pencil to drag a box on the page. Press Enter (Return), and your cursor is placed in the box so you can type some text. You can move and modify the box containing text just as you would any rectangle.

To format text created by either tool, double-click the text to open it for editing. Then drag to select the text you want to format. Open the Text Style tray, and you find tools to specify a typeface, font size, and alignment options (Figure 16-23).

Storing Favorites in Scrapbooks

The Scrapbooks tray offers pages and pages full of artwork (Figure 16-24). The drop-down menu at the top lists pages devoted to arrows, cars, people, and architects' drawing reference symbols. Want to use any of the graphics in a scrapbook? Just click an image and then click a layout page. If you want to add multiple copies of an item, just keep clicking. The idea behind scrapbooks is to keep the images that you want to use over and over close at hand.

The scrapbooks have a pretty comprehensive set of graphics for architects, but it's easy for you to create your own scrapbook pages. Scrapbooks are really just .layout documents. To create your own scrapbook, just collect the images you want to save on one or more pages in a LayOut document, and then save it using the File → Save As Scrapbook command. A dialog box opens where you can name and save your scrapbook.

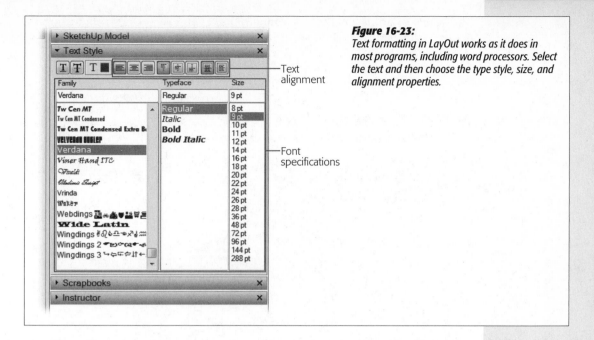

Figure 16-23:
*Text formatting in LayOut works as it does in
most programs, including word processors. Select
the text and then choose the type style, size, and
alignment properties.*

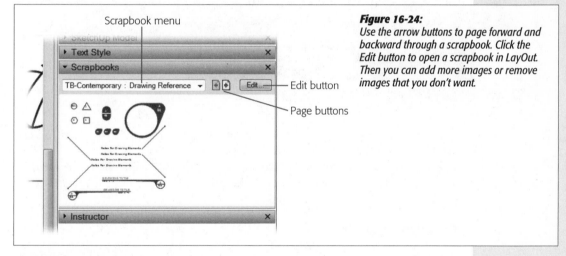

Figure 16-24:
*Use the arrow buttons to page forward and
backward through a scrapbook. Click the
Edit button to open a scrapbook in LayOut.
Then you can add more images or remove
images that you don't want.*

Printing from LayOut

Printing LayOut documents is a straightforward affair, though the process is a little different in Windows and Mac. In Windows, choose File → Print Preview to see
your pages as they will be printed. (Figure 16-25). If you're happy with the way the
pages look, click the Print icon in the upper-left corner. If you don't want to preview your pages, choose File → Print. You see a standard Print dialog box where
you can choose your printer and specify the number of copies to print. To adjust

the quality of prints and exports from LayOut, go to File → Document Settings → Paper → Rendering, and choose from the Output Quality menu between Low, Medium, and High.

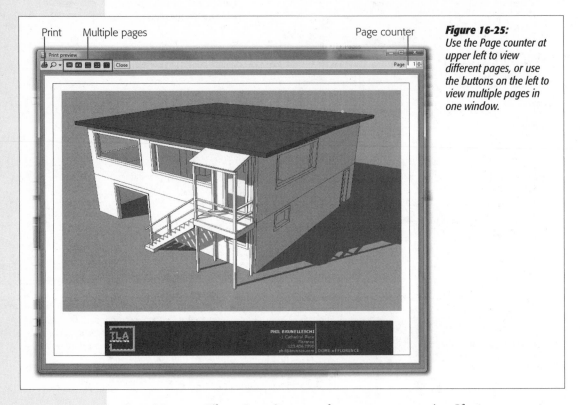

Print   Multiple pages   Page counter

Figure 16-25:
Use the Page counter at upper left to view different pages, or use the buttons on the left to view multiple pages in one window.

On a Mac, use File → Page Setup to choose your paper size. If you want to see a preview of your pages before printing, choose File → Print → Preview. A Preview window opens where you can see the pages as they'll look when they're printed. To print from the Preview window, click the printer icon. To print a LayOut document from the main window, choose File → Print.

Exporting PDF Files

If you, your clients, and colleagues are scattered around the globe, you may prefer to save your LayOut documents as PDF (portable document format) files. Then, provided the files aren't too huge, you can attach them to emails and send them off.

• **Exporting PDF files in Windows.** Choose File → Export → PDF, and the Export Images dialog box appears. In the "File name" box, type a name for your LayOut document. Then click Save.

- **Exporting PDF files on a Mac.** Choose File → Export, and the Export dialog box appears. In the Save As box, type a name for your LayOut document. In the Format drop-down list, choose PDF and then click Save.

LayOut documents don't have to follow the gridlike arrangement suggested by the templates. You're free to go off on creative tangents, as shown in Figure 16-26.

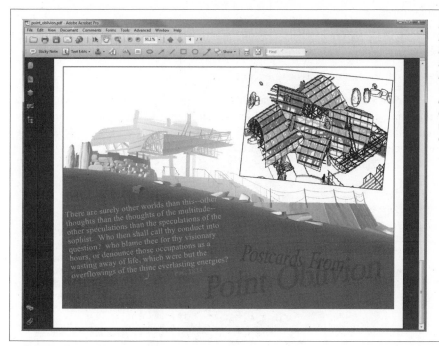

Figure 16-26:
Lewis Wadsworth used LayOut to create this fanciful document titled Post Cards from Point Oblivion. You can download the file point_oblivion.pdf *at* http://missingmanuals.com/cds.

Presenting from LayOut

When you want to deliver a personal presentation, you can use LayOut pages as if they were PowerPoint slides. The features of LayOut's presentation mode are simple but impressive. Unlike with your standard 2-D PowerPoint presentation, you can show off your 3-D models in LayOut by panning and orbiting. You can even run SketchUp animations within LayOut pages. You'll find LayOut presentations work for many situations.

1. **Click the Presentation button or choose View → Start Presentation.**

   All the menus, toolbars, and trays disappear, and you see your LayOut page in full-screen mode, as shown in Figure 16-27.

2. **Click your mouse to go to the next page.**

   LayOut presentations work differently depending on the type of mouse you have. If you have a three-button mouse, a left-click moves forward a page, and a right-click moves back. If you have a single-button mouse, a click moves you forward. You can also use keyboard arrow keys to navigate.

3. **If you want to show a SketchUp model in its 3-D glory, double-click the model.**

   The model opens, giving you access to 3-D tools. The Orbit tool is automatically selected, but you can access other 3-D tools by right-clicking the model.

4. **Right-click the model and choose Play Animation from the shortcut menu.**

   LayOut shows the animation for your SketchUp model. You'll wow them at the client meeting.

   Press Esc to leave the model 3-D mode and to return to the standard presentation page view.

5. **Drag to draw on your Layout pages.**

   The cursor acts as a freehand marker if you want to draw circles and arrows to emphasize a point during your presentation. Press Esc when you're done drawing; a dialog box opens, asking if you want to save your annotations. Click Yes or No; either way, you leave presentation mode and return to LayOut in order to save the changes.

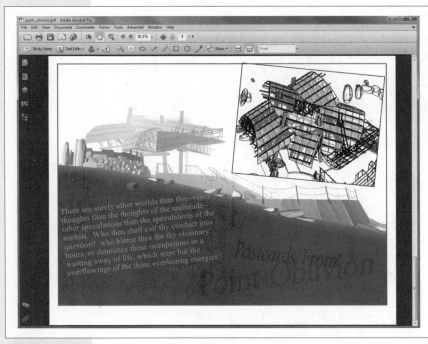

Figure 16-27:
When you're in presentation mode, LayOut pages are shown full screen. The cursor acts as a freehand marker. Double-click on a SketchUp model, and you can manipulate it with Orbit, Pan, and Zoom tools. If that doesn't wow your audience enough, you can run SketchUp animations within LayOut presentations.

6

Part Six: Appendixes

Installing SketchUp and Getting Help

As long as you're connected to the Internet with a Windows or Mac computer, it's easy to get a copy of SketchUp and to install it. This appendix explains how. It also shows you how to find help in SketchUp and from some outside sources.

Installing SketchUp

SketchUp is available in two versions: SketchUp (free) and SketchUp Pro ($495). For the differences between the two versions, see page 3. You can install either version of SketchUp on Windows or on Mac OS X. Installing SketchUp is a two-step process: First, download the program from Google's website. Then run the installation program on your system. Once it's installed, you start SketchUp like any program—from an icon on your desktop, from Windows' Start menu or Quick Launch toolbar, or from the Mac's Dock.

Downloading SketchUp

In your web browser, go to *http://sketchup.google.com/*. On the right side of the page, you see a big blue button that says "Download Google SketchUp". Click that to go to the downloads page. On the right side of the downloads page, you see another big blue button that reads "Download Google SketchUp Pro" (Figure A-1). Below it you see a much less conspicuous link, "Download Google SketchUp 7".

When you download the free version of SketchUp, a web page asks you to provide an email address if you want to receive the Google SketchUp newsletter. When you download the Pro version, SketchUp asks you to provide a mailing address and

Figure A-1:
You'll find two links on the SketchUp download page. Clicking the big, fancy button downloads SketchUp Pro. Clicking the less conspicuous link downloads the free version of SketchUp.

other details. In either case you have to agree to Google's terms before you download and use the software. But before you read all those pages of legalese, rest assured that nothing unusual was in the terms at the time of this writing. Basically, you agree not to modify or reverse engineer the program, and not to sue Google or anyone else involved ("You agree to hold harmless and indemnify Google and its subsidiaries…") over anything to do with the program. Still, if you're concerned about protecting yourself, go ahead and read through the terms. (The terms for the Pro version include limits on installing the software on multiple computers or a network, and so on.)

Before you download, you choose between operating systems: Windows XP/Vista and Mac OS X (10.4 or later). The download goes fairly quickly. The name of the installation file stored on your computer varies depending on the operating system and the version that was downloaded.

Installing SketchUp in Windows

After you download SketchUp for Windows, you've got the SketchUp installer program on your computer. You may see links to the program on your computer desktop, but the program itself is probably stored in your Downloads folder. Your browser may prompt you to open or run the program. These options vary depending on your version of Windows, your settings, and the web browser you use.

Here are the steps for installing SketchUp on a PC:

1. **Run the SketchUp installer program: GoogleSketchUpWEN.exe (or Google-SketchUpProWEN.exe for SketchUp Pro).**

   You may be prompted to open or run the installer from your web browser, or you may see links on your desktop. As a last resort, you can go to Start → Run (in Windows XP) or press the Windows key in Vista, and then begin to type the installer file name. A list appears in the Start window, where you can double-click the file name to run the installer.

   Windows displays a warning to make sure you want to run a program that was downloaded from the Internet. On Windows XP, you see a message box. On Vista, you see the User Account Control box, unless, like a lot of folks, you've turned UAC off.

2. **In the security warning window, click Run (Allow in Vista).**

   A progress bar appears as Windows decompresses the downloaded files. Then the Google SketchUp 7 Setup window appears. At the bottom of the window you see Back, Next, and Cancel buttons that you can use throughout the installation.

3. **Click Next.**

   The End-User License Agreement appears.

4. **Read the terms of the Agreement, turn on the "I accept the terms in the License Agreement" box, and then click Next.**

   The Destination Folder panel appears with a text box displaying the suggested location to store the SketchUp application. Usually this path is *C:\Program Files\Google\Google SketchUp 7*.

5. **Click Next to accept the path.**

   After you click Next, the "Ready to install Google SketchUp 7" panel appears.

   If you want to store the application in a different folder, click the Change button and browse to a new location. Then click OK.

6. **Click Install.**

   A progress bar appears as the program is installed. When the process is complete, you see a message: "Completed the Google SketchUp Setup Wizard".

7. **Click Finish.**

   The installer closes and SketchUp is ready to run. On your desktop, you'll find a shortcut to run the program. You can drag the shortcut to Windows' Quick Launch toolbar, making it easy to start the application in the future.

Tip: If you purchase SketchUp Pro, there's an extra step. After completing the online purchase, you get an email with an authorization code and serial number. You can authorize your copy of SketchUp the first time you use it, or later you can go to Help → License → Authorize. If you don't authorize your copy, the Pro features stop working after the 8-hour trial period.

Installing SketchUp on a Mac

Most of the time, the Google SketchUp Installer runs automatically after it's downloaded (page 529). The Install Google SketchUp Pro 7 window opens. Items displayed on the left side of the window list the steps to install the program, like Introduction, License, and Destination Select. In the lower-right corner are Continue and Go Back buttons that you can use throughout the installation process (Figure A-2).

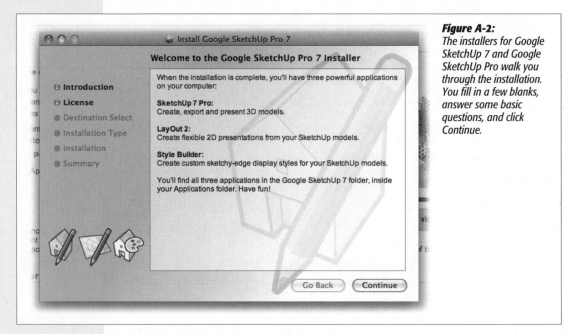

Figure A-2:
The installers for Google SketchUp 7 and Google SketchUp Pro walk you through the installation. You fill in a few blanks, answer some basic questions, and click Continue.

1. **Read the "Welcome to Google SketchUp" details and click Continue.**

   The window changes to show the Software License Agreement.

2. **Read the license and if you agree, click Continue.**

   A banner appears with Disagree and Agree buttons.

3. **If you want to continue to install the software, you must click Agree.**

   When you click Agree, the window displays the next window—"Select a Destination". If you click Disagree, the installation program stops.

4. **Choose your hard drive as the destination, and then click Continue.**

   The "Select a Destination" window shows places where you can install the program. The usual place to install SketchUp is your hard drive, which is usually called Macintosh HD. If you've renamed your hard drive, it will have the name you specified.

   When you click Continue, the Installation Type details are displayed. These details list how much space SketchUp needs.

5. **Click the Install button.**

On most systems, you see a message that says "Installer requires that you type your password." A box shows your account name, and another empty box is labeled "password". Mac OS X is telling you that it needs permission to install a program. If you're in charge of the computer, type in your password. If someone else manages the computer, you probably need their help to install the program.

6. **Type your password and click OK.**

A progress bar appears as the program is installed. When the process is complete, you see a Summary message that says "Install Succeeded".

7. **Click Close.**

The SketchUp application is ready to run. You can find the application in the Applications → Google SketchUp 7 folder. Drag the SketchUp icon to your Dock, and you can start SketchUp anytime with a single click.

If you installed SketchUp Pro, you can use the program for 8 days to see if it meets your needs. After that, you need to license (that is, pay for) the program to keep using it. To license the program, choose SketchUp → License → Purchase. You land at the Google website, where you can make an online purchase. After you pay, Google gives you a license number to enter in the SketchUp → Licenses window.

Getting Help for SketchUp

When it comes to help, SketchUp provides some good in-program help, a lot of web-based help tools, and some not so great help documents in PDF format. In addition a large community of SketchUp fans shares experiences, tips, and techniques. If you've got a question, you can find an answer someplace.

SketchUp Hints

As mentioned throughout this book, one of the first places to turn when you need help with a tool is the lower-left corner of the SketchUp window. Down in the status bar, SketchUp constantly provides tips and hints. When you pick a tool, the hints suggest what you should do next and let you know what modifier keys you can use. For example, if you select the Move tool and then hold it over an object in the drawing window, SketchUp helpfully suggests: "Pick two points to move." In addition you see tips on modifier keys that work with the Move tool: "Ctrl = toggle Copy, Alt = toggle Auto-fold, hold Shift = lock inference." The hints are brief and to the point. They're probably a little more helpful once you've learned some SketchUp basics.

The Instructor Window

The Instructor window (Windows → Instructor) provides quick information about specific techniques. The Instructor window combines brief step-by-step text with simple animations. It's helpful when you're learning a new tool or technique, and it doesn't disrupt the creative flow too much. Like the hints in the status bar, the Instructor window is linked to the tools you select. For example, click the Follow Me tool, and the Instructor window's animation shows a circle extruded along a path to a pipe-like shape (Figure A-3). The text shows seven steps for using Follow Me. Below those instructions, the Instructor window lists the tool's modifier keys. At the very bottom, under Advanced Operations, you see links to related, web-based help files.

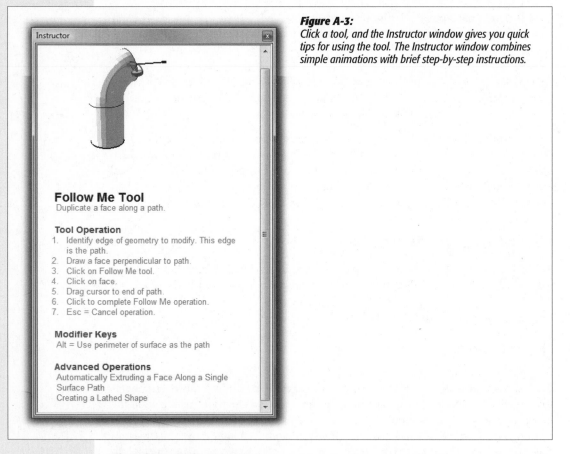

Figure A-3:
Click a tool, and the Instructor window gives you quick tips for using the tool. The Instructor window combines simple animations with brief step-by-step instructions.

SketchUp Help Center

What you see on SketchUp's Help menu is a little different from most programs. Most of the menu items are links to web-based resources. The link that most resembles a typical help tool is Help Center. Choose Help Center, and a page opens in your web browser (Figure A-4). You still need to dig a bit to find the answer to a specific question. The quickest way to get an answer is to type a few words in the Search box and to click the Search SketchUp Help button. The next page you see resembles the results of a Google search. (Not surprised, are you?) Read the descriptions, and click the link that seems best suited to your question. You can always click the Back button on your browser to explore some of the other links. When you finally get to the help pages, you'll find some pretty clear, helpful information.

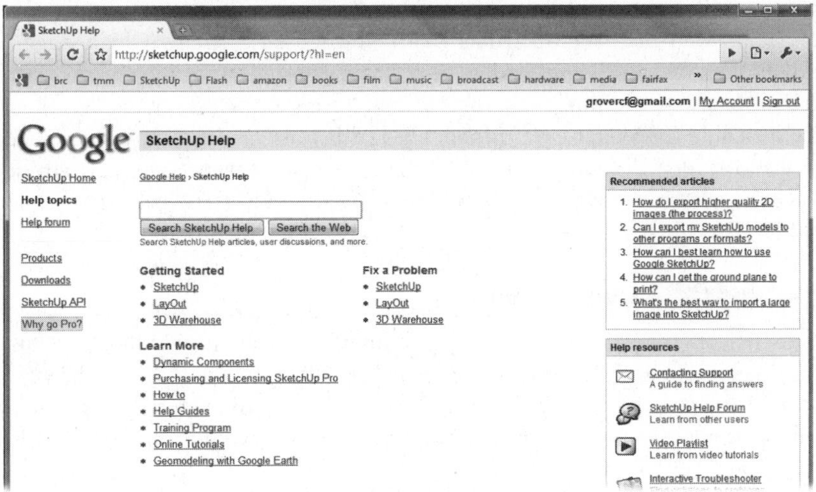

Figure A-4:
In SketchUp, click Help →
Help Center, and this
page opens in your web
browser. Type a question
or some key words in the
Search box, and click
Search SketchUp Help.
The window displays the
results of the search in
true Google fashion.

In addition to the Search tool, the SketchUp Help Center displays links to other help resources. The links lead to a sprawling maze of help pages, contest announcements, and user forums. It's worth browsing around and looking for resources, because you can find some gems hidden there. For example, when you're new to SketchUp or you're researching a new tool, the Online Tutorials can be very helpful. You can use the link to the tutorials that is below the Search box, in the Learn More group. The video tutorials are also great when you're trying to get up to speed on a subject. On the right side of the Help Center, in the "Help resources" box, click Video Playlist.

Note: It's always a little risky pointing book readers to websites. Books last a long time, and aside from coffee spills and getting a little dinged up, they don't change much. Websites, on the other hand, change pretty quickly. These directions may lead to web resources that have changed. If that's the case, a Google search may very well lead you to the pages and tools you need.

Downloading SketchUp Documents

SketchUp is delivered to your computer from Google's website, so it comes as no surprise that you don't get a nice printed book to go along with the program. Few software companies provide printed manuals nowadays no matter how they deliver the application. Like most other companies, SketchUp offers documentation in a PDF file. You can view PDF documents with Adobe Reader (or Preview on the Mac).

At this writing, the SketchUp documents are serviceable but certainly not great. They're organized more as a reference than as a guide for newcomers. You may not want to print the nearly 900 pages, since many of the pages have only a few lines of text. Your best bet is to use the PDF document's search box to find answers.

To download PDF copies of the manual, in SketchUp choose Help → Online Help Center. Your web browser opens its main, web-based SketchUp help page for SketchUp. You see a Google Search box. Type *manual,* and among the search results (probably at the top of the list) you'll see an entry that reads, "Is there a manual available for SketchUp?" Bingo. Click this link, and it takes you to a page with links to several different versions of the SketchUp, LayOut, and Style Builder manuals. Google has versions for both SketchUp 6 and SketchUp 7, and versions for both PCs and Macs.

Google SketchUp Help Group

The Google SketchUp Help Group is an online forum where you can post questions and get answers from other experienced SketchUp users. To visit the group, go to *http://groups.google.com/group/SketchUp.* After you join the group, you'll find answers to frequently asked questions and find forums devoted to SketchUp issues and techniques (Figure A-5).

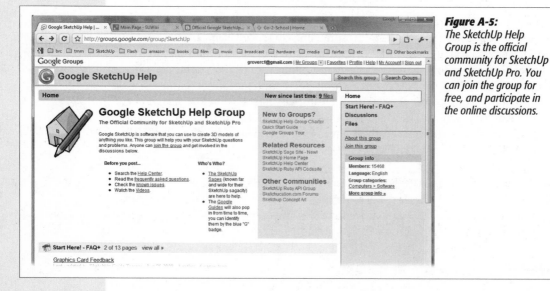

Figure A-5:
The SketchUp Help Group is the official community for SketchUp and SketchUp Pro. You can join the group for free, and participate in the online discussions.

Third-Party Help and Tutorials

A huge community of SketchUp fans has stories to tell and help to offer. Here are just some of the websites where you can find help and tutorials:

- The experts at **Go-2-School** developed many of the exercises that appear in this book (Figure A-6). They provide DVD training videos, private training, web tutorials, and many other paths to SketchUp enlightenment. Check out their website at *www.go-2-school.com*.

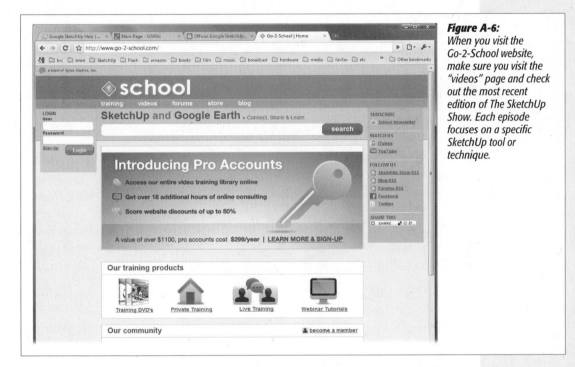

Figure A-6:
When you visit the Go-2-School website, make sure you visit the "videos" page and check out the most recent edition of The SketchUp Show. Each episode focuses on a specific SketchUp tool or technique.

- **SketchUcation** offers a number of resources for the SketchUp artist. On their website (*http://www.sketchucation.com/*) you find tutorials, forums, and news about SketchUp. You need to register to access many of the resources on the SketchUcation site.

- In the "wiki" tradition, **SUWiki** (*www.suwiki.org*) is a site where SketchUp fans build an ever-growing body of information. When you first visit the home page, you see a list of tutorials. Use the Search box to find answers to your questions. If you've used Wikipedia, you'll feel at home here.

- The **Official Google SketchUp Blog** is hosted on Google's own Blogger (*http://sketchupdate.blogspot.com/*). You'll find all sorts of information on topics like the 3D Warehouse, Tips and Tricks, Contests and Competitions, and News (Figure A-7).

Figure A-7:
If you're looking for the admiration of your SketchUp peers, click the "Contests and Competitions" link on the right side of the Google SketchUp Blog. You'll find out how to enter modeling contests, and see lists of winners for some of the many competitions.

SketchUp Menu by Menu

Google SketchUp: The Missing Manual gives you all the details, explanations, and examples you need to create awesome 3-D models in SketchUp. This appendix provides quick thumbnail descriptions of every command in every menu.

Note: Many of the menu commands have multiple keyboard shortcuts. Each command in this list shows the available shortcuts for Windows and Mac systems. When more than one command is available, they're separated by a semicolon (;).

File

The File menu commands work on your SketchUp documents as a whole. Use the File menu for major events like starting a new project, opening a file you created previously, and shutting down SketchUp when you're finished working.

New

Windows: Ctrl+N
Mac: ⌘-N

The New command opens a new SketchUp document, the proverbial clean slate. On Windows computers if you have a document already open, SketchUp prompts you to save the current document before opening a new one. If you need to open more than one SketchUp document in Windows, start SketchUp a second time and then open the second file. Macs let you open more than one document at a time by simply creating new windows.

Open

Windows: Ctrl+O
Mac: ⌘-O

Opens the standard window where you can navigate through your folders and open SketchUp files. Use Open to quickly find and open SketchUp documents. See New for ways to open more than one SketchUp document at a time. The techniques are different for Windows and Mac.

Open Recent (Mac)

Displays a submenu that lists SketchUp files that were recently opened. Click any file to reopen it. (For Windows, see Recent Files.)

Save

Windows: Ctrl+S
Mac: ⌘-S

Saves the changes that you've made to your SketchUp document. In Windows, if you haven't made any changes in the document, the command is dimmed. If you haven't yet saved the document, the command is similar to Save As, next.

Save As

Mac: Shift-⌘-S

Saves the current document with a new name, or in a previous SketchUp file format such as SketchUp 5 or SketchUp 6. After choosing the command, you see a standard window where you can navigate to a different folder and type in a new name. When SketchUp is done saving, the document is still open, but has the new name.

Save a Copy As

Saves the current document with a new name similarly to Save As. When the save finishes, the current document is still open in SketchUp and has the original file name.

Revert

Discards any changes you made to the document since the last save. Revert is handy when you decide you've gone down the wrong path and just want things the way they were when you started.

Send to LayOut (SketchUp Pro Only)

Exports the current SketchUp document to the LayOut program (page 499). Lay-Out is only available in SketchUp Pro and provides features for producing detailed documents from SketchUp models.

3D Warehouse

Gives access to the 3D Warehouse, Google's web-based site where the SketchUp community can share models. Why reinvent the wheel when you can download it from the 3D Warehouse? At the warehouse, you find complete buildings and building components like doors and windows from major manufacturers. Furniture, appliances, and non-architectural models like cars, airplanes, and animals are also available. You may be surprised at what you'll find at the 3D Warehouse. Into Elvis Presley? You can download the Graceland mansion and models of Elvis himself.

Export

Exports your SketchUp model to different 2-D and 3-D file formats. The 2-D formats—like JPG, TIFF, and PDF—create images based on the current view in the modeling window. The free SketchUp program only exports to one 3-D format: the .kmz file format used by Google Earth. SketchUp Pro exports to several other formats, including standard AutoCAD formats such as .dxf and .dwg. You can also use this command to export animations and section slices.

Import

Imports 2-D and 3-D files into SketchUp for modeling, for Photo Match, or to use as raw material for creating a new SketchUp model.

Print Setup (Windows)

Opens the standard Windows Print Setup window, where you choose your printer, paper size, and page orientation.

Print Preview (Windows)

Leads to the Print Preview window, where you can adjust print settings including scale. Click OK to see a preview. From the Print Preview, you can print the image or return to SketchUp.

Page Setup (Mac)

Mac: Shift-⌘-P

Leads to a standard Mac panel where you set printer options including page size, page orientation, and the printing scale in percentage.

Document Setup (Mac)

Leads to a panel where you can adjust the print size and print scale for the document. Perspective view cannot create scalable documents, so you must set the view to Parallel Projection (Camera → Parallel Projection).

Print

Windows: Ctrl+P
Mac: ⌘-P

Displays the standard Print window, where you choose a printer and the number of copies you wish to print.

Generate Report (SketchUp Pro Only)

Creates an attribute report for Dynamic components.

Recent Files (Windows only)

Mac: ⌘-P

Windows computers display a list of recently opened SketchUp documents on the File menu. To open a document, click the name.

Exit

Windows: Alt+F4
Mac: ⌘-Q (found on the SketchUp menu)

Stops the program and then closes the SketchUp window. If documents are open, SketchUp closes them. If documents are unsaved, the program prompts you to save them before quitting.

SketchUp Menu (Mac Only)

Mac programs have a standard menu under the program name. These menus access basic services and preferences.

About SketchUp

Displays a box that lists the version number for SketchUp and web links to help and license details.

License (SketchUp Pro)

Displays license details for SketchUp Pro. This option is grayed out on the free version of SketchUp.

Check Web for Update

Checks the Google SketchUp website to determine if you're running the most recent version of SketchUp. A window displays the search results.

Services

Leads to standard Mac services like Finder, Disk Utility, and Font Book. You can customize the options on this list through the Mac operating system.

Hide SketchUp

⌘-H

Hides the SketchUp menu and window so you can view other objects on your computer desktop.

Hide Others

Option, ⌘-H

Hides all programs *except* SketchUp.

Show All

Displays the windows of all currently running programs.

Quit SketchUp

⌘-Q

Stops the program and then closes the SketchUp window. If documents are open, SketchUp closes them. If documents are unsaved, the program prompts you to save them before quitting.

Edit

This menu holds the standard Cut, Copy, and Paste commands as well as several specific commands that work with SketchUp components and groups.

Undo

Windows: Ctrl+Z
Mac: ⌘-Z

This command undoes the last command you applied. So if you accidentally delete an edge or face in the modeling window, the Undo command brings it back like magic. Remember Undo for those moments when you smack your head and say "Oh no! Why'd I do that?" SketchUp keeps track of your actions sequentially, so you can use multiple Undo commands to backtrack through your recent actions. Most actions can be undone, but a few—like the deletion of a scene—can't be undone.

Redo

Windows: Ctrl+Y
Mac: Shift-⌘-Z

Redo lets you undo an Undo command. If you undo an action or a command and then decide that you preferred it before the Undo, use the Redo command to get back to square one. You can use multiple Undos and Redos to move back and forth through your recent SketchUp activities.

Cut

Windows: Ctrl+X
Mac: ⌘-X

Removes the selected entity (or entities) from the modeling window, and places a copy of it on your computer's Clipboard. Once it's on the Clipboard, you can paste it back into the modeling window.

Note: The term *entity* refers to any selectable object in SketchUp. An entity can be a single edge, a face, or a complex group or component.

Copy

Windows: Ctrl+C
Mac: ⌘-C

Copies a selected entity (or entities) and places the copy on the Clipboard. The original entity stays in place. Using this command, you can copy and paste entities from one SketchUp document into another.

Paste

Windows: Ctrl+V
Mac: ⌘-V

Attaches a copy of an entity (or entities) stored on the Clipboard to the Move tool. Click a location to paste the entity in the modeling window. If you decide not to complete the paste action, press Esc or choose another tool.

Paste In Place

Pastes a copy of entities on the Clipboard back into position using the same XYZ coordinates as the original. This command is particularly useful for moving entities into or out of groups and components.

Delete

Windows: Delete
Mac: Delete

Removes selected entities from the modeling window. Unlike Cut, Delete doesn't put the entity on the Clipboard, and you can't paste it back into the window.

Tip: You can use Undo immediately after Delete to bring back something you deleted.

Delete Guides

Guides are dashed lines used for measurement and alignment. When you're ready to create an animation or to print images from your model, you can use this command to remove the guide lines.

Select All

Windows: Ctrl+A
Mac: ⌘-A

Selects all entities in the modeling window.

Select None

Windows: Ctrl+T
Mac: Shift-⌘-A

Removes the selection from all currently selected objects. SketchUp builders often simply click an empty space in the modeling window to deselect everything. Use Select None to make absolutely sure nothing is selected.

Hide

Mac: ⌘-E

Hides any selected entities from view in the modeling window. This command doesn't erase or delete the entities; you can make them visible with the Unhide command (next).

Unhide

Makes hidden entities visible again. (See the previous command.) So how do you see and select a hidden object? If it's a group or a component, you can use the Outliner to select the hidden object. Otherwise you can use the View → Hidden Geometry command to make entities visible and selectable. They're still considered hidden until you use the Unhide command. The Unhide command has three submenu options:

Unhide → Selected

Unhides entities that are selected using one of the techniques described in the previous paragraph.

Unhide → Last

Unhides the last entity that was hidden. The entity doesn't have to be selected.

Unhide → All

Mac: Shift-⌘-E

Unhides all the hidden entities in the modeling window. The entities don't have to be selected.

Lock

Locks groups and components. You can't move locked groups and components until you unlock them (next).

Unlock

Unlocks groups and components that have been locked using Lock (previous).

Make Component

Windows: G
Mac: Shift-⌘-G

Collects the selected entities and saves them in a SketchUp component. Components appear in the Components window, and you replicate them by creating new instances. All instances created from a single component are identical. (See page 157 for more detail on groups and components.)

Make Group

Mac: ⌘-G

Saves the collected entities in a group. Groups don't appear in the Components window. (See page 157 for more on groups and components.)

Close Group/Component

Mac: Ctrl-Shift-⌘-G

Closes an open group or component. (Groups and components must be opened—by double-clicking, for example—to be edited.)

Intersect

In SketchUp, entities (like a rectangle and a cone) can pass through each other without cutting through any of the other faces. Unlike in the real world, they can occupy the same face. When you want to change that behavior, you create shared edges by using the Intersect commands. The way faces and entities intersect with each other is important in SketchUp: It determines the way the entities behave and the way they can be manipulated. The Intersect command automates the process of creating shared edges. To use the Intersect commands, select an entity and then choose one of the three submenu options:

Intersect With Model

Creates intersections where other entities overlap the current selection.

Intersect With Selected Only

Creates intersections among the entities included in the selection.

Intersect With Context

Creates intersections between two entities within the current context (in the same group or component) and excludes entities outside of the context.

No Selection/Entity/Group/Component

This menu and its submenu options show commands related to the currently selected entities. You can see many of these same options in a shortcut menu by right-clicking selected entities. If a single face or edge is selected, the name on the menu changes to "edge" or "face". If several edges and faces are selected (but aren't in a group or component), you see something like "5 Entities". When a group or component is selected, you see "group" or "component" as the menu name. The options displayed in the submenu change depending on the selection.

Edge → Select

Selects other entities with another submenu showing these options: Connected Faces, All Connected, or "All on Same Layer".

Edge → Soften

Smoothes the angles formed where faces meet at an edge.

Edge → Divide

Divides a single edge into multiple edges. After selecting the command, type a number and press Enter (Return on a Mac).

Edge → Zoom Extents

Changes the view so the selected edge fills the modeling window and is entirely within the window.

Face → Select

Selects other entities with another submenu showing these options: Bounding Edges, Connected Faces, All Connected, "All on Same Layer", and "All with Same Material".

Face → Area

Using submenus, this command calculates the surface area covered by a face, covered by a specific material, or in the current layer. The result appears in the Measurements toolbar.

Face → Intersect

Creates intersections between the face and other entities in the model. For more on intersections see page 112.

Face → Align View

Aligns the SketchUp camera to point toward the currently selected face.

Face → Align Axes

Repositions the axes relative to the selected face.

Face → Reverse Faces

Reverses the inside/outside orientation of the faces. Using the standard face colors, white faces (front faces) become blue, and blue faces (back faces) become white.

Face → Orient Faces

Changes the orientation of several faces to match the selection. SketchUp does a little guessing here to try and decide how you want the faces oriented. Often it works just right. When it doesn't, you can always use Undo and orient the faces one by one using Reverse Faces.

Face → Zoom Extents

Changes the view so the selected face fills the modeling window and is entirely within the window.

Group → Edit Group

Opens a group for editing.

Group → Explode

Changes the entities in the selected group to individual entities no longer grouped.

Group → Make Component

Turns a group into a component, with all the features of a component.

Group → Unglue

Frees a group from being glued to another face in your model.

Group → Reset Scale

Changes a group that you've scaled back to its original proportions.

Group → Reset Skew

Changes a group that you've skewed back to its original proportions.

Group → Intersect

Creates intersections between the group and other entities in the model. For more on intersections see page 112.

Group → Flip Along

Flips a group along a selected axis (red, blue, or green). Flipping doesn't create a mirror image of the group.

Group → Zoom Extents

Changes the view so the selected group fills the modeling window and is entirely within the window.

Component → Edit Component

Opens a component for editing. Any changes made affect all other instances of the component.

Component → Make Unique

Makes a single instance of a component into a new, separate component. The original component otherwise remains unchanged.

Component → Explode

Makes the entities in a component into separate entities, no longer contained in the component. The original component is still in the Components window.

Component → Unglue

Frees a component from being glued to another face in your model.

Component → Reload

Updates the currently selected component with a version saved in your computer's file system.

Component → Save As

Saves a component as a new SketchUp document under a different name. (You can also load any SketchUp document into any other SketchUp document as a component; see page 342.)

Component → Change Axes

Redefines the origin of the axes in the selected component. Other 3-D programs sometimes refer to this as the *local coordinate system*. You can use this command to align the component's bounding box with the component's geometry, which helps prevent entities from skewing awkwardly when scaled.

Component → Reset Scale

Changes back a component that you've scaled to its original proportions.

Component → Reset Skew

Changes back a component that you've skewed to its original proportions.

Component → Scale Definition

If the selected component has been scaled, choosing this option makes that scale the correct scale for all instances of the component. Other instances won't change in size, but they will have the option to Reset Scale. SketchUp uses the newly defined scale definition for the reset.

Component → Intersect

Creates intersections between the component and other entities in the model. For more on intersections see page 112.

Component → Flip Along

Flips a component along a selected axis (red, blue, or green). Flipping isn't the same as creating a mirror image of the group.

Component → Soften/Smooth Edges

Smoothes the edges adjoining two surfaces, making those two surfaces look like a single curved surface. Opens the Soften Edges window, where you can adjust the angle setting.

Component → Zoom Extents

Changes the view so the selected component fills the modeling window and is entirely within the window.

Component → Dynamic Components

Opens the Component Options box for Dynamic Components.

Special Characters (Mac Only)

Mac: Option-⌘-T

Opens a window with special characters like arrow and math symbols, which you can use with SketchUp's 3D text tool.

View

Commands on the View menu mostly let you show and hide different features in the modeling window. (The options that manage the angle and orientation of your view of the modeling window are under the Camera menu.)

Toolbars (Mac: Tool Palettes)

Shows and hides tool palettes. Windows and Mac handle tool palettes differently. In Windows, this menu manages all tool options. Windows toolbars can be docked or floating. To move toolbars, drag the handle on the left side. Use the Large Buttons option to change the size of the button on all the toolbars. PC toolbars include Getting Started, Large Tool Set, Camera, Construction, Drawing, Face Style, Google, Layers, Measurements, Modification, Principal, Sections, Shadows, View, Walkthrough, and Dynamic Components.

On this menu, a Mac has three toolbars that you can show or hide: Large Tool Set, Google, and Dynamic Components.

Note: Mac tools are customized primarily using the Customize Toolbar command (page 20).

Scene Tabs

Shows and hides scene tabs that appear at the top of the modeling window.

Hidden Geometry

Shows and hides entities that you've hidden using the Edit → Hide command. This command also shows additional geometry in some entities like smoothed surfaces.

Section Planes

Shows and hides the section plane used to create section cuts.

Section Cuts

Shows and hides section cuts in the modeling window.

Axes

Shows and hides the red, green, and blue axes.

Guides

Shows and hides the guides you place in your model as references.

Shadows

Shows and hides shadow effects.

Fog

Shows and hides fog effects.

Edge Style

The Edge Style view options show and hide different visual effects applied to edges.

Edge Style → Display Edges

Shows and hides edges in the model.

Edge Style → Profiles

Shows and hides the visual effect that increases the thickness of some edges to enhance the three-dimensional appearance of models.

Edge Style → Depth Cue

Shows and hides a visual effect that changes line thickness depending on the distance from the camera.

Edge Style → Extension

A sketchy (page 227) visual effect that extends lines slightly beyond their endpoints, making the model look hand drawn.

Face Style

Changes the appearance of faces in your model. These options are also available on the Face Style toolbar, which is usually a more convenient way to access them.

Face Style → X-ray

Changes the transparency of faces so you can see through your model. This option toggles on and off and can work in combination with any of the other face styles.

Face Style → Wireframe

Hides faces, leaving only edges visible.

Face Style → Hidden Line

Displays faces in the model without any shading or textures.

Face Style → Shaded

Faces display material but not textures.

Face Style → Shaded With Textures

Faces display both material and textures.

Face Style → Monochrome

Displays faces without material effects using the default material—usually white for front faces and blue for back faces.

Component Edit

Displays and hides model entities relative to the selected component.

Component Edit → Hide Rest of Model

Displays the selected component, but hides the other entities in the modeling window.

Component Edit → Hide Similar Components

Hides other instances of the selected component. This command comes in handy when you're working on an array of components and need a less cluttered view.

Animation

Controls features related to scenes and animations.

Animation → Add Scene

Mac: Option-⌘-+

Adds a new scene to the SketchUp document.

Animation → Update Scene

Mac: Option-⌘-

Updates the scene to match the current view.

Animation → Delete Scene

Deletes the selected scene.

Animation → Previous Scene

Windows: Page Up

Moves to the previous scene.

Animation → Next Scene

Windows: Page Down

Moves to the next scene.

Animation → Play

Plays the animation.

Animation → Settings

Opens the animation settings in the Model Info window.

Hide Toolbar (Mac Only)

Hides the Mac toolbar at the top of the modeling window.

Customize Toolbar (Mac Only)

Used to display and hide specific tools in the Mac toolbar above the modeling window. In Windows, the Tool Palettes command (page 19) performs similar functions.

Camera

In SketchUp, you view through a camera the three-dimensional world where your model lives. Most of the commands on this menu set the position and properties of that camera.

Previous

Changes the camera position and view to the immediately previous setup. You can use Previous multiple times to step back through different views of your model. Keep in mind, this isn't an Undo command, so your model doesn't change as you step back, just your angle of view.

Next

Used after using the Previous tool. Permits you to move forward again through your camera views.

Standard Views

Lets you repostion the camera through which you view your model.

Standard View → Top

Mac: ⌘-1

Changes the camera to view the modeling window from the top.

Standard View → Bottom

Mac: ⌘-2

Changes the camera to view the modeling window from the bottom.

Standard View → Front

Mac: ⌘-3

Changes the camera to view the modeling window from the front.

Standard View → Back

Mac: ⌘-4

Changes the camera to view the modeling window from the back.

Standard View → Left

Mac: ⌘-5

Changes the camera to view the modeling window from the left.

Standard View → Right

Mac: ⌘-6

Changes the camera to view the modeling window from the right.

Standard View → Iso

Mac: ⌘-7

Changes the camera to view the modeling window from an angle.

Parallel Projection

Changes the camera to view the modeling window without the converging lines of the perspective views. This view can help with some alignment chores. In other cases it can be confusing. In general the perspective views provide a better sense of three dimensions and distance.

Perspective

Creates a view where an object in the distance appears smaller than objects close to the camera. SketchUp uses three-point perspective unless you tell it otherwise (next).

Two-Point Perspective

Creates a view using two-point perspective, which has two vanishing points instead of SketchUp's standard three-point perspective. This type of view is similar to view cameras or lenses that correct parallax problems. While in two-point perspective view you can use the Pan tool to change the view; however, if you use the Orbit tool, the view changes back to Perspective.

Match New Photo

Opens a file browser window so you can bring a photo into SketchUp for photo-matching; the Edit Matched Photo tools become available. Photo matching makes it easier to create an accurate model from a photograph. For details, see Chapter 10.

Edit Matched Photo

Puts SketchUp in Photo Matching mode, giving you the tools to adjust the modeling window so you can accurately create a model from a photograph.

Orbit

Windows: O
Mac: O; ⌘-B

Mouse shortcut: Drag while pressing the middle mouse button.

A camera movement tool that lets you move around the 3-D modeling space in any direction. This tool is very useful for readjusting your angle of view.

Pan

Windows: H
Mac: H; ⌘-R

Mouse shortcut: Press Shift as you drag with the middle mouse button.

Displays a hand cursor that lets you drag the view of the modeling window to change your view. Unlike a cinematic pan, where the camera pivots on a tripod, this command actually changes the camera position.

Zoom

Windows: Z
Mac: Z; ⌘-\

Mouse shortcut: Press Ctrl as you drag with the middle mouse button.

Like the zoom lens on a camera, it gives you a closer or more distant view in the modeling window.

Tip: The Zoom metaphor doesn't entirely hold up. The Zoom tools actually move the camera position; they don't change the field of view, which is what a camera's zoom lens does (for that, see the next command). Martin Scorsese would have named this command "dolly."

Field of View

The field of view is an angle measurement in degrees that describes how much or how little of the modeling window the camera sees. You can use degrees (deg), where larger numbers equal a greater view, or millimeters (mm) for camera lens size, where larger numbers produce a narrower view. Choose this command and SketchUp displays the field of view in the Measurements toolbar. You can then type a new measurement—like *30 deg* or *50mm*—to change the field of view.

Zoom Window

Windows: Ctrl+Shift+W
Mac: ⌘-]

After choosing this command, drag a rectangular window on screen. SketchUp changes the modeling window view to fit the area you mark.

Zoom Extents

Windows: Ctrl+Shift+E
Mac: ⌘-[

When chosen from the camera menu, Zoom Extents changes the view to comfortably fit all the entities in the modeling window, which is great for returning to a familiar view when you get lost in your model (page 94). When chosen from a shortcut (right-click) menu, Zoom Extents fills the modeling window with the selected entities, helping you to quickly focus on a specific entity.

Zoom to Photo

If you've applied a photo to a scene's background as part of a Match Photo session, this zooms the view until the photo fits entirely within the view.

Position Camera

After choosing this command, click a surface or the SketchUp ground plane to position the camera in a specific location.

Walk

Mac: ⌘-, (comma)

Lets you manually move the camera through your model (page 413).

Look Around

Mac: ⌘-. (period)

Use this command to pivot the camera horizontally and vertically around a single point; it does the same thing as panning and tilting in motion picture lingo.

Draw

Commands in the Draw menu fire up SketchUp's basic drawing tools. Most of these tools use SketchUp's click-move-click drawing method. They also let you use the Measurements toolbar to draw with great accuracy (page 16).

Line

Windows: L
Mac: L; ⌘-L

Activates the Line tool. To draw lines, click the starting point, and then move the cursor and click the ending point.

Arc

Windows: A
Mac: A; ⌘-J

Activates the Arc tool. To draw arcs, click to create one starting point, then move the cursor, and click to set the ending point for the line. Then click a third time to create the curve of the arc.

Freehand

Mac: ⌘-F

Activates the Freehand tool used for drawing irregular lines. The Freehand tool is one of a few tools you drag. To use the Freehand tool, press the mouse button as you trace a line in the modeling window.

Rectangle

Windows: R
Mac: R; ⌘-K

Activates the Rectangle tool. To draw a rectangle, click to set one corner of the rectangle, and then click again to set the opposite corner.

Circle

Windows: C
Mac: C

Activates the Circle tool. To draw a circle, click to set the center of the circle, and then click to set a point at the edge of the circle.

Polygon

Mac: ⌘-;

Activates the Polygon tool. To create a Polygon, click to set a point for the center, and then click to set a point on the edge of the polygon. To set the number of sides, type the number of sides followed immediately by the letter *s*. For example, *3s* for a triangle; *8s* for an octagon. After selecting the Polygon tool, you can type the number of sides before or immediately after creating the polygon.

Sandbox

Sandbox tools let you model terrain and other organic shapes in SketchUp. The design element used to create these shapes is referred to as a TIN or *triangulated irregular network.*

Note: To activate the sandbox tools, go to Window → Preferences → Extensions (SketchUp → Preferences → Extensions) and turn on the Sandbox Tools checkbox.

Sandbox → From Contours

Use From Contours to create a TIN from the contours formed by SketchUp edges. Most often, these edges are created by using the Freehand tool.

From → Scratch

Creates a flat triangulated TIN that you can sculpt using sandbox tools such as the Smoove tool (Tools → Sandbox → Smoove).

Tools

The Tools menu holds most of the non-drawing tools, including the basic Select, Move, Rotate, and Scale tools. You also find some of the tools that make SketchUp unique, such as the Push/Pull, Follow Me, and Offset tools. Several of these tools use the Measurements toolbar (page 16) to perform their tasks with accuracy.

Select

Windows: Space bar
Mac: Space bar; ⌘-/

Activates the Select tool (and generally ends the operation of other SketchUp tools). Often you must select a SketchUp entity before using other tools or commands. For example, you must select several lines and edges (entities) before making a group or component. Click an entity once to select it. Click twice to select the entity and the other entities immediately touching it. Click three times to select the entity and all the entities that are connected to it by edges and faces.

Note: You can drag to make a selection, but keep in mind that the Select tool behaves differently depending on whether you drag it to the left or to the right (page 171). Drag to the right and the Select tool selects entities that are completely within the selection window. Drag to the left to select every entity that is partially within the selection window.

Eraser

Windows: E
Mac: E

Activates the Eraser tool (page 67). Click entities to erase them, or drag to erase several entities at a time. To hide an edge, press Shift while clicking the edge. To soften an edge (making the angle less acute), press Ctrl (Option on a Mac) while clicking the edge.

Paint Bucket

Windows: B
Mac: B

Activates the Paint Bucket tool (think B for bucket). Choose colors and textures from the Materials window (Windows → Materials); then click a face to paint it (page 196). Press Alt (⌘ on a Mac), and the bucket turns into an eyedropper. Click the eyedropper on faces with color or materials to load the Paint Bucket tool with the color or material.

Move

Windows: M
Mac: M; ⌘-0

Activates the Move tool (page 44). Move edges, faces, groups, or components using the click-move-click method. Click an entity, and it becomes attached to the cursor. Move to a new location, and click to place the entity. You can also use the Move tool to rotate groups and components. Hold the Move tool over a group or component, and red crosses appear at certain locations. Hold the cursor over a cross, and it displays the Rotate cursor. Rotate the object using the techniques described for the Rotate command (next). Toggle the Ctrl key (Option on a Mac) to put the Move tool in copy mode. The original entity remains in place; a copy of the entity is moved to the new location. You can move an entity with precision by clicking the entity with the Move tool and then typing a distance. The distance with a measurement, such as 4', appears in the Measurements toolbar. Press Enter (Return), and the entity moves the specified distance.

Rotate

Windows: Q
Mac: Q; ⌘-8

Activates the Rotate tool (page 42). The cursor looks like a protractor and determines the plane of rotation. To rotate entities, click one point, and the cursor displays a rubber band line; click another point to set a temporary line. Then as you move the cursor, the entity rotates around the first point you clicked. Click a third and final time to complete the rotation. Toggle the Ctrl key (Option on a Mac) to put the Rotate tool in copy mode. The original entity remains in place; you rotate a copy of the entity into position.

Scale

Windows: S
Mac: S; ⌘-9

Activates the Scale tool. Click an entity, and a bounding box with handles appears around the entity. Hold the Scale cursor over one of the handles, and a tooltip appears explaining the effect of dragging that particular handle. For example, a message may say "Blue Scale About Opposite Point", meaning the object will be scaled along the blue axis.

Push/Pull

Windows: P
Mac: P; ⌘-=

Activates the Push/Pull tool, which is used to extrude faces into three-dimensional objects. Click a face and then move the cursor perpendicular to the surface. You can also type a dimension to extrude a face with precision. For example, type *4'* after clicking a face, and the face is extruded 4 feet.

Follow Me

Activates the Follow Me tool, which extrudes a profile along a path. Select the path first, and then click the face or profile to extrude.

Offset

Windows: F
Mac: F; ⌘--(hyphen)

Activates the Offset tool, which is used to offset the edges of a face (page 144). For example, the Offset tool lets you create a perfectly proportioned rectangle inside of another rectangle with just two clicks. Click the edge that you want to offset, and then move the cursor and click again. The original edge remains in place and a duplicate appears at the point of the second click.

Tape Measure

Windows: T
Mac: T

Activates the Tape Measure tool, which is used both for measuring distances and for setting guides in your modeling window (page 281). To measure, click a point, move the cursor, and then click a second point. The distance appears in the Measurements toolbar. To create a guide, click an edge or face in the modeling window, move the cursor to a new location, and click again. A guide appears as a dashed line in the modeling window. Use Ctrl (Option) to toggle Guide mode on and off. Erase individual guide lines using the Eraser tool. Choose Edit → Delete Guides to remove all the guides in your document. To hide guides temporarily, go to View → Guides.

Protractor

Use the Protractor tool to measure angles and create guides based on angles. The process requires three clicks. The first click sets the intersection of the angle, a second click defines one line, and the third click defines the second line. The measurement is shown in degrees in the Measurements toolbar. You can also use the protractor to create guides. The Ctrl (Option) key toggles Guide mode on and off. Erase individual guide lines by using the Eraser tool. Choose Edit → Delete Guides to remove all the guides in your document. To hide guides temporarily, go to View → Guides.

Axes

Use the Axes command to reposition the Origin in the modeling window and to change the alignment of the three axes. The Origin is the point where the red, blue, and green axes meet. After choosing the command, click a location in the modeling window to move the Origin to the new point.

Dimensions

Activates the Dimensions tool, which lets you place dimension marks and labels in your document. To display the dimension of an edge, click the edge (avoiding mid- and endpoints), and then move the cursor perpendicular to the edge. Dimension text and marks appear; click to set their position. To make other measurements, click to set one point, and then click again to set a second point. Move the cursor away from the line created to position the dimension lines and text. You can change typeface, size, and marker styles by choosing Window → Model Info → Text.

Text

Activates the Text tool. Click the Text tool in the modeling window to place a text box. Type the text you want. To edit previously placed text, double-click the text. You can reposition text using the Move tool. Text isn't placed in the 3-D world— it's as if you placed it on the camera lens. For example, text remains in the same position in the modeling window even when you use tools such as Orbit and Pan. To place text in the context of the 3-D world, use the 3D Text tool described next.

3D Text

Opens the Place 3D Text window. Type the text you want, and use the settings to choose a typeface and to format the text. Click Place to close the window when you're done, and then click in your modeling window to place the text. The block of text is a component listed in the Components window (Windows → Component). You can manipulate text in the modeling window using the standard tools such as Move and Rotate.

Section Plane

Mac: ⌘-Y

Used to create cutaway views of your model. Objects on one side of the plane are hidden. Click a point in your model to create a section plane (page 417). You can reposition section planes using the Move and Rotate tools.

Google Earth

The Google Earth commands help you coordinate your SketchUp modeling activities with Google Earth tools.

Get Current View

Moves a Google Earth image into SketchUp. The most common use of this command is to position a model accurately in terms of latitude and longitude. SketchUp imports a black-and-white copy of the Google image and orients it so that the green axis line points north.

Toggle Terrain

Displays an image as terrain and indicates the elevations, after you import a Google Earth image into SketchUp.

Place Model

Sends your model to Google Earth by creating a temporary file of your model and placing it in the proper location in Google Earth. You use this technique primarily while modeling (page 438). You can remove models from Google Earth by right-clicking the model name in the Places (or Temporary Places) folder and then choosing Delete.

Interact

Lets you manipulate dynamic models in SketchUp. For example, a door or window may open and close when you click it with the Interact tool.

Sandbox

Sandbox tools let you model terrain and other organic shapes inside of SketchUp. The design element used to create these shapes is referred to as a TIN or *triangulated irregular network*. TINs are automatically stored in groups, so you must double-click the shape before editing.

Sandbox → Smoove

Sculpts terrain or organic shapes formed by a TIN. The Smoove tool highlights the area to be changed. After activating the Smoove tool, you can adjust the area affected by the Smoove tool by typing a radius like *20'*. The number appears in the Measurements toolbar, and the size of the highlight changes accordingly.

Sandbox → Stamp

Use the Stamp tool to create impressions on the TIN by "pressing" geometry into the surface.

Sandbox → Drape

Lets you project edges (lines) over the irregular surface of a TIN.

Sandbox → Add Detail

Subdivides certain areas of the TIN, made up of lots of small triangles, into even smaller triangles. You can then sculpt finer details. It also adds to the complexity of your SketchUp model.

Sandbox → Flip Edge

Lets you manually make adjustments to the TIN. It's particularly useful when unwanted flat areas appear in terrain developed from contour lines.

Windows

SketchUp's extensive Windows menu is used to open windows where you manage your model and its features like components, styles, layers, and scenes. You do a lot of your SketchUp project management and fine-tuning in some of these windows. The options under the Windows menu are slightly different in Windows and on a Mac.

Minimize (Mac Only)

Mac: ⌘-M

Hides the active SketchUp modeling window. You can show the window again by clicking its icon in the Dock.

Zoom (Mac Only)

Expands (or shrinks) the size of the SketchUp modeling window onscreen.

Model Info

Mac: Shift-⌘-I

Opens the Model Info window, where you can change settings related to your model. General categories for these settings are Animation, Components, Credits, Dimensions, File, Location, Rendering, Statistics, Text, and Units.

Entity Info

Mac: ⌘-I

Opens the Entity Info window, where you can change settings related to the selected entity. (An entity may be a single edge or face, a selection of edges and faces, or a group or complex component.) Use the Entity Info box to manage layers, show and hide entities, and manage shadow behavior. Entity Info is always available from a shortcut menu by right-clicking.

Materials

Mac: Shift-⌘-C

Opens the Materials window, where you manage and edit materials and colors that are applied to faces in your model.

Components

Use the Components window to manage the components in your model. The Search feature gives you direct access to the 3D Warehouse (page 331), where you find thousands of SketchUp components that are ready to use. The Edit tab lets you change the alignment or glue-to settings for your components (page 342). The Statistics tab gives you a running list of the entities and elements inside of a component.

Styles

Opens the Styles window, where you manage the appearance of your SketchUp model. With a click of a button, you can dramatically change the appearance of the edges and faces in your model.

Layers

Layers (page 273) are a way to show and hide portions of your SketchUp model. The Layers window lets you add and remove layers and control their visibility.

Outliner

Opens the Outliner, where you can manage your model's groups and components. The Outliner lets you name and create nested groups and components. It's also a handy way to find groups and components that have been hidden using the Hide command. You can access the shortcut menu for any group or component by right-clicking its name in the Outliner.

Scenes

Use the Scenes window to create, update, and remove scenes from your document. By reordering scenes in the list, you can change their order in animations. You can save or update specific visual properties in your scenes such as camera location, hidden geometry, visible layers, section panes, style and fog, shadow settings, and axes location.

Show Fonts (Mac Only)

Mac: ⌘-T

Opens the standard Mac Fonts window used to specify typeface and font size.

Shadows

Opens the Shadow Settings window used to show or hide shadows. You can use the Time and Date settings to control the angle of shadows. The Light and Dark slider controls let you fine-tune the appearance of shadows.

Fog

Opens the Fog window, where you can show or hide fog in the SketchUp modeling window. Settings in the window let you control the intensity and appearance of the fog effect.

Match Photo

Starts the Match Photo process (page 349), which lets you bring photos in the SketchUp modeling window and then arrange the view so you can accurately create a 3-D model using the photo for reference points.

Soften Edges

Changes the appearance and angle of the selected edges in your model.

Instructor

Displays a few basic, animated tutorials for SketchUp.

Preferences (Windows Only)

In Windows, this option opens the Preferences window, where you can adjust some of the settings for SketchUp including the Template that SketchUp uses when it starts a new document. On the Mac, you find this information under SketchUp → Preferences. Other preferences include:

- Location of files and libraries

- Creation and timing of backups

- Management of shortcut keys

- Resolution of imported textures

- Use of graphics card acceleration

- Management of SketchUp extensions

- Selection of an application to edit 2-D images

Hide Dialogs

Hides some of the open windows and dialog boxes. (Oddly, this doesn't seem to hide all of the open dialog boxes.)

Ruby Console

Opens the Ruby Console, used to create and load add-on programs for SketchUp—a topic not covered in this book.

Component Options

Displays, in the Component Options window, details related to dynamic components. Component developers may make some properties available to designers using the component (page 334). For example, a fence component may let users change the height of the fence and the style of the fence boards.

Component Attributes (SketchUp Pro Only)

Opens the Component Attributes window, which displays spreadsheet-type settings that you use to develop dynamic components.

Bring All to Front (Mac Only)

Brings all open SketchUp windows to the foreground.

Model Windows by Name (Mac Only)

Displays the names of all the open modeling windows at the bottom of the Windows menu. This system lets you jump back and forth between models using menu commands.

Help

All roads on the Help menu lead to Google one way or another. The most helpful option in the bunch is the Online Help Center.

Welcome to SketchUp

Opens the welcome window that you see when you first fire up SketchUp. Turn off the "Always show on startup" checkbox if you don't want to see the "Welcome to SketchUp" window every time you start SketchUp.

Help Center (Mac: Online Help Center)

Takes you to SketchUp's web-based help system (page 534). The advantage of having this system on the Web is that Google can easily upgrade the help services. The disadvantage is that you must have an Internet connection to get to the help system. Online you find tutorials, videos, PDF documents, and user forums.

Contact Us

Opens a window where you can provide feedback to Google and get installation help. If you've purchased SketchUp Pro, you can receive technical support.

License (Windows Only)

Use the License menu options to activate and deactivate your SketchUp license. (On the Mac, you find this information under SketchUp → License.)

Check for Update (Windows Only)

Quickly searches the Web to see if a newer version of SketchUp is available. (On the Mac, you find this link under SketchUp → Check for Web Updates.)

About SketchUp (Windows Only)

The About window displays information about your version of SketchUp and a few links where you can get information, help, and license details. (On the Mac, you find this information under SketchUp → About SketchUp.)

Index

Colophon

Rachel Monaghan and Adam Witwer provided quality control for *Google SketchUp: The Missing Manual*.

The cover of this book is based on a series design originally created by David Freedman and modified by Mike Kohnke, Karen Montgomery, and Fitch (*www.fitch.com*). Back cover design, dog illustration, and color selection by Fitch. David Futato designed the interior layout, based on a series design by Phil Simpson.

This book was converted by Abby Fox to FrameMaker 5.5.6. The text font is Adobe Minion; the heading font is Adobe Formata Condensed; and the code font is LucasFont's TheSansMonoCondensed. The illustrations that appear in the book were produced by Robert Romano using Adobe Photoshop CS3.

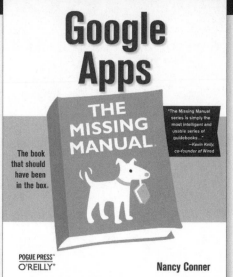

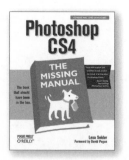